THE NEGRO
ON THE
AMERICAN FRONTIER

Kenneth Wiggins Porter

With a preface by William Loren Katz

ARNO PRESS and THE NEW YORK TIMES
NEW YORK 1971

LC 77-135872
ISBN 0-405-01983-1

The American Negro: His History and Literature
General Editor
WILLIAM LOREN KATZ

Associate Editor for this volume
Nancy Lincoln

Manufactured in the United States of America

A complete list of the titles in the American Negro Collection
is located at the back of this volume.

Contents

Preface

In recent years the reading and television public has finally been introduced to black frontiersmen and cowboys. In many cases they were benefiting directly or indirectly from the research of Kenneth Wiggins Porter.

As a graduate student at Harvard under Arthur Meier Schlesinger during the early years of the Great Depression, Porter first began to examine the black frontier experience. His first paper, documenting the neglected relationship between black and red men, was published in the *Journal of Negro History* several months before Franklin Delano Roosevelt first became President. Despite his prodigious scholarly output over the next generation and more, Professor Porter's work is known only to a few scholars and is unmentioned except in footnotes and an occasional acknowledgment page, yet he has provided the field of black frontier history with many suggestions and much of its basic material. His documentation of slave resistance in Florida preceded Herbert Aptheker's monumental *American Negro Slave Revolts* (1943). When actor Bill Cosby recently told a nationwide television audience about black frontiersmen and cowboys, he was presenting information uncovered by Kenneth Wiggins Porter before the young black actor had entered the first grade. Nearly a decade before Philip Durham's and Everett Jones's *The Negro Cowboys* (1965), and well over a decade before William H. Leckie's *The Buffalo Soldiers* (1967), about black troopers in the West, Professor Porter's research had unearthed much basic information and numerous bibliographical references.

This collection of his most important articles, providing material much of which is still unmatched today, also includes the pertinent and perceptive analyses of a fine historian who has always demanded the best of himself. As an admirer of his pioneering labors and a most grateful beneficiary, it has been a delightful fulfillment of a scholarly debt to have helped in some small way to bring Kenneth Porter's monumental contribution to a wider public.

William Loren Katz

Foreword

My interest in the frontier — and in the Negro on the frontier — goes back to my childhood in a small Central Kansas town, near the intersection of Coronado's route in quest of the "Kingdom of Quivira," the Santa Fe Trail, and the cattle trail from Texas to Ellsworth (Negroes trudged after Coronado, trailed herds to Ellsworth, scouted for Indians along the trail to Santa Fe); thirty five years before my birth the county's population totaled five and the town site was windy prairie. Before I was old enough to go to school, or read, my mother — daughter of a Union veteran, granddaughter of an Abolitionist and "Black Republican" — used on each "ironing day" to entertain me with an oral version of *Uncle Tom's Cabin*, which she always managed to bring to its climax and conclusion as the last garment was finished. As I grew older I began to wonder why so many of the Negroes in the community either gave evidence in their names of American Indian origin or lost no opportunity to claim such ancestry. One of these Negroes, with whom I worked one summer on a construction gang, had named one of his sons Hiawatha and, after spending the summer as a laborer, he would winter in the Rockies, hunting and trapping. Some day, I resolved, I would investigate this intermingling of the American Negro and the American Indian peoples, and in my omnivorous reading of history and literature I kept my eyes open for pertinent material.

Other aspects of American Negro history also came to my attention. My photographer-father, preparing an exhibit of pictures of local Union veterans, commented — no doubt hyperbolically — that when he first came to town about 1889 there were more Union veterans among the Negroes than among the whites. My mother used to tell me about the Negro community of Nicodemus in northwestern Kansas, on the "sodhouse frontier" to which she had come by covered wagon from Iowa as a girl, and about the young people with whom she had attended school. (Much later I learned that some of the older Negroes in my own community had come to Kansas by covered wagon from Illinois.[1])

Not until I was a graduate student at Harvard, in a course in American social history taught by the late Arthur Meier Schlesinger, did I have a real opportunity to investigate the problem that had so long concerned me. When I suggested the relations between Negroes and Indians as a thesis topic, Professor Schlesinger considerately endeavored to dissuade me, doubting the adequacy of available materials, but finally gave his consent. The resultant paper was published in the *Journal of Negro History*,[2] awarded the annual prize of the Association for the Study of Negro Life and History, and reprinted as a separate volume.

Although this article — of which an extended supplement appearing the next year was essentially a part[3] — manifested weaknesses in organization, interpretation, and expression that now cause the author some embarrassment, it is nevertheless a pioneer study of a particular aspect of Negro experience on the American frontier, is in general factually accurate, and brings together information on more aspects of Negro life in various parts of the West over a longer period of time than any other publication known to me. Scholars over the years seem to have found it useful.

These articles inaugurated a continuing historical interest, which, however, led in two directions. They revealed the opportunities for further investigation of relations between Negroes and Indians, particularly within the Seminole tribe, in which such relations were particularly close, extensive, and important. They also suggested that the experiences of the Negro on the frontier went far beyond his relations with the aborigines. My research for a biography of John Jacob Astor[4] had turned up numerous references to Negroes on the fur-trading frontier.[5] A brief study of the Negro in the fur trade,[6] although with some of the same weaknesses as the two pioneer articles, is nevertheless factually accurate and the only available study of the subject.

A hiatus of several years, devoted to completing my Ph.D. and getting started as a teacher, delayed until late 1940 my resumption of major research interest in the Negro on the frontier. The next few years saw the publication of several articles on Negro history, particularly on Seminole Negroes and the Florida War,[7] the most important of which was "Florida Slaves and Free Negroes in the Seminole War, 1835-1842,"[8] which revealed the role of Florida Negroes, other than those already identified with the Seminole, in this greatest of all "Indian wars," and thus brought to light an overlooked and important slave insurrection.

During 1944 I began to develop greater interest in the Negro on the American frontier apart from his role in the Seminole War. Two books were largely responsible for this expansion and partial redirection of my interest. *The American: The Making of a New Man*, by James Truslow Adams, startlingly revealed this Pulitzer-Prize-winning historian's ignorance of the history of the Negro in the United States and his overt, although perhaps unconscious, racism, as indicated in his dictum:

> The very variously assorted Negroes who were brought here had among them many excellent qualities . . . . even temper, affection, great loyalty . . . imitativeness, willingness to follow a leader or master . . . . but, not only were they not the qualities which . . . made good . . . frontiersmen, but the entire institution precluded them from becoming such . . . not only were the Negroes as unfitted by nature from becoming founders of communities on the frontier as, let us say the Scotch-Irish were pre-eminently fitted for it, but they had no chance.[9]

But how, if "they had no chance," could Mr. Adams be sure that Negroes were "unfitted by nature" for frontier life? I remembered the Negroes who fled from bondage to establish communities along the Apalachicola and the Suwanee Rivers; the Seminole Negro community — formerly a military colony — that I had visited in Coahuila, Mexico, in 1942 and 1943; and the "Exodusters," whom my mother had known in the 1880's and 1890's on the sodhouse frontier of northwest Kansas.[10]

Another incentive to a broader approach to the theme of the Negro on the American frontier was a rereading of Julius W. Pratt's *Expansionists of 1812* (New York, 1925), which advanced the thesis that a major cause for the War of 1812 was the northern desire for British Canada and the southern craving for Spanish East Florida. Although Professor Pratt presented the clearest evidence that Negroes were largely responsible for temporarily thwarting the attempt to annex East Florida, he made no point for the significance of their role. Using the Pratt volume as a starting point, I prepared an article, "Negroes and the East Florida Annexation Plot, 1811-1813," which was read at the annual meeting of the Association for the Study of Negro

Life and History, Boston, October 28, 1944.

My discovery that Negroes had been the decisive factor in this international episode suggested that they might have been more significant than hitherto realized in other similar cases. (Their importance in the Second Seminole War, 1835-1842, was already abundantly clear.) An examination of the southern frontier before and after the East Florida annexation plot revealed that runaway slaves and potential or actual slave insurrections were a major factor in delaying the victory of Great Britain in the southeast;[12] and that the invasions of Florida in 1816 and 1818 by United States forces, which soon led to its annexation, were largely motivated by the desire to break up the runaway Negro settlements in Spanish territory that were a menace to slavery on our southern border.[13]

I also discovered — and in some cases later reported — not only that Seminole Negroes, serving as military colonists for the Mexican government[14] and as enlisted scouts for the United States army,[15] had been largely responsible for abating the Indian menace in Coahuila and eliminating it in West Texas, but also that the first Negroes to fight for the Union in the Civil War were Creek and Seminole Negroes in the Indian Territory and runaway Negroes in a Kansas regiment on the Missouri border; that four regiments of Negro troops served constantly on the frontier during the post-Civil War generation and proved among the most effective units of the Indian-fighting army;[16] and that approximately a quarter of the trail drivers during the heroic age of the American cattle industry, including some of the best riders and ropers, were Negroes.[17]

Various commitments to full-time teaching and compensated research, however, prevented me from devoting more than spare-time attention to the general topic of the Negro on the American frontier until 1964, when I received a sabbatical from the University of Oregon and a grant-in-aid from the American Philosophical Society for a year's research and writing on the subject. My plans called, first, for detailed consideration of the Negro on the cattleman's frontier and, next, of the Negro in the Indian-fighting army. However — fortunately for Negro history and unfortunately for my plans — by this time other scholars had developed an interest in the Negro on the frontier. Early in 1965, when I was in an advanced stage of work on a book-length manuscript dealing with the Negro in the cattle country,

The Negro Cowboys, by Philip Durham and Everett L. Jones, was published;[18] and in 1967, when I was ready to begin writing on the Negro in the Indian-fighting army, *The Buffalo Soldiers: A Narrative of the Negro Cavalry in the West*, by William H. Leckie, appeared. My sabbatical period having been exhausted by work on these two topics, I was unable to advance my research significantly in other areas.

The "Negro Revolution" of the 1960's, however, inspired a great interest in all aspects of Negro history and in the teaching of Negro history in the schools and colleges of the United States, with a corresponding need for texts, supplementary reading material, and reference works. Consequently, when William Loren Katz, general editor of the Arno Press series, "The American Negro: His History and Literature," suggested that I collect and edit my own most significant published articles on the Negro on the American frontier, I saw in this suggestion an opportunity to present certain select preliminary historical studies without abandoning my ultimate plans for a thorough and comprehensive study of the subject.

An examination of the articles included in this volume will reveal a strong emphasis on the southeastern frontier — the region bordering on and eventually including Florida — and the southwestern frontier of Texas and northern Mexico. A partial justification for this emphasis is not only that Negroes on the first of these frontiers were particularly numerous, but also that the existence on both these frontiers of international boundaries and powerful Indian tribes gave them a special strategic value. Negroes were consequently an important element in the relations of the British colonies of the South with Spain, France, and the Creek Nation; of the United States with Spain, Great Britain, and the Creek and Seminole Indians; and of Texas and the United States with Mexico and various southwestern Indian tribes.

There is also a special emphasis on the Seminole Negroes — runaway slaves, mostly, who became associated with the Seminole Indians in Florida and shared their destinies in the Indian Territory and Coahuila — for the Seminole Negroes were the Negro frontiersmen *par excellence*: runaways and rebels, settlers, town founders, military colonists, hunters, stockraisers, farmers, scouts, guides, interpreters, and, above all, fighting men. They were thus the living denials of the stereotype of the docile, contented, unaggressive Negro, traditionally thought unfitted for frontier life. They demonstrated that, given the slightest opportunity – such as proximity to a friendly or neutral Spanish, Mexican, or Indian border – Negroes could develop and display all the "frontier" qualities they supposedly did not possess. The Seminole Negroes, and to a considerable extent their racial and cultural kinsmen, the Creek Negroes, for approximately a century – from their participation in the repulse of the "Patriot" invaders of Florida in 1812, through the Red Stick War of 1812-1814, up to the last scattering rifle shots that Creek and Seminole Negroes and full-bloods directed against the "Jim Crow" government of Oklahoma in the so-called Crazy Snake Uprising in 1909 – were quick to recognize and defend their legitimate interests, whether against southern militiamen, United States regulars, Texas filibusters and slavers, Confederate soldiers, or racist possemen.

Because of the concentration on certain subjects, such as the Seminole wars, and because each article was independently published and is complete in itself, there are repetitions in the articles that follow. Moreover, since my research and publications in this field began nearly forty years ago, errors and omissions have come to light; the more important of these are indicated following each article. The page numbers cited in references to these articles are those in this volume.

For ease in identification, the titles of periodicals that are repeatedly cited are abbreviated as follows:

American Philosophical Society Year Book	*APSYB*
Chronicles of Oklahoma	*CO*
Florida Historical Quarterly	*FHQ*
Hispanic American Historical Review	*HAHR*
Journal of Negro History	*JNH*
Journal of Southern History	*JSH*
Kansas Historical Quarterly	*KQH*
Labor History	*LH*
Minnesota History	*MH*
Negro History Bulletin	*NHB*
Southwestern Historical Quarterly	*SWHQ*

Of course, Negroes were present in greater or lesser numbers on frontiers other than those dealt with in the articles reprinted here. I have, therefore, included brief comments on all aspects of Negro frontier history, with suggestions for further reading, and, sometimes, research.

I wish to thank the editors of the publications in which the reprinted articles first appeared, both for their original hospitality and for permission to reprint. It is literally true that a complete listing and acknowledgment of all the institutions and individuals in one way or another assisting me during the nearly forty years I have been involved in these articles, and in research and writing for other studies as yet unpublished, might very possibly require a preface of almost double the present length. Consequently, I must make my acknowledgments general but hope that they will, nevertheless, be recognized and accepted individually and personally. The articles themselves recognize some very special assistance.

Kenneth Wiggins Porter
Eugene, Oregon   July, 1970

NOTES

1. Obituary, Mrs. Nola Jane (Stewart) Nichols, *Sterling* (Kansas) *Bulletin*, January 17, 1963, p. 1.

2. "Relations between Negroes and Indians within the Present Limits of the United States," pp. 8-88.

3. "Notes Supplementary to 'Relations Between Negroes and Indians,' " pp. 96-135.

4. *John Jacob Astor: Business Man*, 2 vols. (Cambridge, Mass., 1931).

5. "Notes on Negroes in Early Hawaii," *JNH*, XIX (April, 1934), pp. 193-97, was also a by-product of my Astor researches.

6. "Negroes and the Fur Trade," pp. 139-51.

7. "Abraham," *Phylon*, II (Second Quarter, 1941), pp. 105-16; "Three Fighters for Freedom ('Maroons' in Massachusetts; John Caesar: A Forgotten Hero of the Seminole War; Louis Pacheco: The Man and the Myth)", *JNH*, XXVIII (January, 1943), pp. 51-72; "Davy Crockett and John Horse: A Possible Origin of the Coonskin Story," *American Literature*, XV (March, 1943), pp. 10-15; "Wild Cat's Death and Burial," *CO*, XXI (March, 1943), pp. 41-43; "A Negro Philhellene, 1827," *NHB*, VII (October, 1943), p. 5; "The Early Life of Luis Pacheco Ne Fatio," *NHB*, VII (December, 1943), pp. 52, 54, 62, 64; "A Black Man, An American, One of the Crew . . .", *NHB*, (February, 1945), pp. 117-18. The articles on Abraham, John Caesar, and Louis Pacheco were subsequently redone in the light of further research.

8. pp. 262-93.

9. James Truslow Adams, *The American: The Making of a New Man* (New York; 1943), p. 131.

10. A critical review of the Adams volume that appeared in the *Journal of Negro History* was awarded the annual prize of the Association for the Study of Negro Life and History. See *JNH*, XXIX (April, 1944), particularly pp. 215-18.

11. pp. 183-203.

12. "Negroes on the Southern Frontier, 1670-1763," pp. 155-80.

13. "Negroes and the Seminole War, 1817-1818," pp. 205-36.

14. "The Seminole in Mexico, 1850-1861," pp. 424-59.

15. "The Seminole Negro-Indian Scouts, 1870-1881," pp. 472-91.

16. *APSYB* 1965 (Philadelphia, 1966), pp. 430-31.

17. "Negro Labor in the Western Cattle Industry, 1866-1900," pp. 494-520.

18. I have since resumed study of and writing on this subject. *Black Riders: The Negro on the Frontier of the Cattle Country* is scheduled for publication by the Quadrangle Press (Chicago).

Introduction

The Westward movement, the frontier experience, is still to most Americans the great American adventure. The frontier produced what is still, despite erosion, our most important historical theory and school of historians.[1] American popular heroes, despite competition from airmen, G-men, spacemen, and World War soldiers, are still principally men of the traditional frontiers—log-cabin builders, "long hunters," prospectors, overlanders, scouts, Indian fighters, sheriffs and trail-town lawmen, and, above all, cowboys—as "Western" books, movies, and television series amply reveal. Mody Boatright declares that the cowboy is "our leading folk hero."[2]

During approximately two centuries of American frontier history the Negro was one of the largest ethnic elements in the population. At the time of the first census (1790) Negroes numbered more than three-quarters of a million, almost a fifth of the total population, and were probably more numerous than either of those famous frontier peoples, the Scots-Irish and the Germans. At the eve of the Civil War, despite the mass immigration of the antebellum generation, Negroes, numbering nearly four millions, were still about a seventh of the population—in the slaveholding states, about a third. But at the end of the century, when the frontier period was almost or quite over, although Negroes had increased to nearly nine millions, large-scale immigration had reduced their proportions to a little over a ninth—still, however, a substantial fraction.[3]

Yet in spite of the considerable numbers of Negroes in North America during its frontier periods, Negroes, until recently, received little or no attention as an element in the frontier population and experience, except from specialized writers in specialized publications.[4]

There are, of course, obvious reasons that could be advanced to explain this disregard of the Negro on the frontiers—that is, if an explanation were considered necessary. Negroes, par-

1

ticularly during slavery, were usually not proportionately as prominent on a frontier as in the total population. Many settlers on the frontier were poor people, seeking cheap land, who could not afford slaves, while those who could afford them were sometimes hesitant about bringing valuable property to dangerous country. Moreover, since the overwhelming number of Negroes were slaves, they were unable to move to the frontier on their own initiative—and only a few were able to do so illegally. Yet, in spite of these obstacles, there were frontiers—such as the South Carolina frontier of the mid-eighteenth century and the Florida frontier on the eve of the Second Seminole War—where Negroes were almost as numerous as, or even more numerous than, the white population.[5] And, few though free Negroes were, in relation to the slave and white populations, they were to be found on every frontier.

After Emancipation, Negroes, in comparison to whites, were still limited in their movements by lack of funds and information; nevertheless, in the postbellum period, freedmen did move to the frontiers. On the Texas cow-country frontier, Negroes were as numerous proportionately among members of trail-herd outfits as they were in the population of the entire state, and far more numerous than their proportions in the counties in which the trail herds originated,[6] and yet, until very recently, one who was not an authority on the Texas cattle industry, with a special interest in the Negro, would have been unlikely to discover this fact. Certainly no one largely dependent on Western movies and television programs could possibly have learned that there were *any* Negro cowhands, still less that they were proportionately so numerous.

If Negroes had been as few on all frontiers as on the frontiers of New England and New York, the Old Northwest, the Old Oregon Country, even Kentucky and Tennessee (although they were present and sometimes even prominent on all these frontiers), the extent to which American historians have disregarded their frontier roles would be understandable, but when South Carolina, Florida and Texas are included in this disregard, then some other explanation must be sought. The explanation, with little doubt, was the necessity, first, to justify Negro slavery, and, after Emancipation, to justify discrimination and segregation. In both cases the justification was the Negro's alleged essential and irretrievable inferiority to the white man. The Negro could not, then, be permitted to manifest those heroic qualities, traditionally associated with the frontier, that would contradict this ascription of inferiority.[7] If the cowboy was, and is, the American folk hero, as Mody Boatright reasonably asserts, Negro cowboys would have had to be included in the pantheon of American heroes. And if the Negro, as cowboy, is a hero, what becomes of Negro inferiority? The only solution was to fail to notice, or to forget, the Negro cowboy and the Negro frontiersman in general. And once this tradition of Negro inferiority, involving the non-existence of the Negro frontiersman, had been established, it was as difficult to upset as any other hallowed American historical tradition—for example, that the Pilgrims landed on Plymouth Rock to establish religious freedom and political democracy. Historians—and other writers utilizing their work— saw no reason not to follow the established tradition of the Negro as non-hero and, therefore, non-frontiersman.

Negroes, particularly in the West, are aware both of the traditional significance of the frontier and of the prevalent belief that they have no part in that tradition. Negroes display particular pride in Indian ancestry, not, usually, because they are ashamed of their Negro blood, and still less because they want to claim to be Indians. At Brackettville, Texas, near Old Fort Clark, longtime headquarters of the Seminole Negro-Indian Scouts,[8] the aged Seminole Negro woman Rosa Fay proudly proclaimed: "We's cullud people. I don't say we don't has no Injun blood, 'cause we has. But we ain't no Injuns. We's cullud people!" The pride of the Negro in Indian ancestry is largely because it is evidence—since the Indian is undeniably associated with the frontier—that the American frontier experience is a part of his heritage.

Historians of the frontier, writing during the first half of the twentieth century, have not probably so much deliberately avoided mentioning the Negro on the frontier as they have suffered from a blind spot, which prevented them from noticing his presence or, if they noticed it, from ascribing to it any significance.[9] The Negro really should not have been on the frontier and therefore, if he was there, there was no need to notice him—in fact, it would have been almost improper to do so.

Historian after historian has in one way or another indicated his belief that the Negro and the frontier were naturally incompatible. James Truslow Adams put his conviction most bluntly when he declared in 1943 that the Negroes' "excellent qualities" were not those that made frontiersmen, that Negroes were, indeed, "unfitted by nature from becoming founders of communities on the frontier."[10] Stanley Vestal, an authority on the Northern Plains Indians, two years later barred the Negro historically from the frontier of his own special interest with the flat statement: "The Negroes came to the east bank of the Missouri and stopped; they knew that was the end of their country."[11] A historian of the Upper Missouri frontier, also writing in the early 1940's, mentioned Negroes exactly once, and then only to say: "While every race and nationality were represented in the mining population, very few Negroes migrated to the camps."[12] Doubtless Negroes *were* comparatively few in that region, but a historian writing from contemporary sources a quarter-century later declared that Negroes were prominent in the Black Hills gold rush and referred to a large Negro picnic at the mining town of Deadwood, Dakota Territory, in the summer of 1879, to celebrate the anniversary of emancipation in the West Indies.[13] The earlier historian saw only that Negroes were "very few," and did not really notice such Negroes as were there, but during the intervening years the Negroes of the Upper Missouri mining camps, however few, had at least become visible.

This volume aims at increasing the visibility of Negroes on a variety of American frontiers. Its thesis is simply: "They were there." It does not intend, in over-reaction to previous disregard or minimization of the frontier Negro, to present Negroes as the most important ethnic element on the American frontier. Negroes, because of their smaller numbers in comparison to white men, because of the legally servile condition of nearly all of them during their first three centuries on the North American continent, and because of the discrimination to which they were subjected even after Emancipation, could not, save by a miracle, have played the same roles in the drama of the expanding frontier as did the dominant whites. What is surprising and significant—and what these studies are intended to demonstrate—is that they were as important on the frontier as they were—in some cases definitely out of proportion to their relative numbers as, for example, in the cases of the Seminole Negro scouts and the Texas trail-drivers.

NOTES

1. Frederick Jackson Turner, "The Significance of the Frontier in American History," *The Frontier in American History* (1920, and various later editions). This essay was first presented before the American Historical Association in 1893 and published the following year.

2. Mody C. Boatright, "The American Myth Rides the Range: Owen Wister's Man on Horseback," *Southwest Review*, XXXVI (Summer, 1951), p. 163.

3. E. Franklin Frazier, *The Negro in the United States* (New York, 1949; rev. ed., 1957), pp. 171, 175.

4. A pioneer in writing about the Negro on the American frontier is Professor W. Sherman Savage, whose "The Negro in the History of the Pacific Northwest," *JNH*, XIII (July, 1928), pp. 255-64, initiated a series of articles about the Negro on other frontiers.

5. "Negroes on the Southern Frontier, 1670-1763," pp. 155-80; "Negroes and the Seminole War, 1835-1842," pp. 238-61.

6. *Report on Population of the United States at the Eleventh Census: 1890*, Part I (Washington, 1895), xcv, pp. 430-32.

7. These traditional frontier qualities of courage, fortitude, enterprise, self-reliance, loyalty, etc., were, of course, in actuality also associated with such less admirable traits as violence, lawlessness, materialism, and anti-intellectualism, but the frontier "myth" treasured the first-mentioned body of qualities.

8. "The Seminole Negro-Indian Scouts, 1870-1881," pp. 472-91.

9. Some writers, indeed, managed to disregard the presence of Negroes even in the South! Hal Steed, for example, in *Georgia: Unfinished State* (New York, 1944), blandly commented that "the Anglo-Saxon . . . race . . . makes up nearly one hundred per cent of the population of the South." When a young European scholar expressed surprise at this figure — "But I saw so many Negroes there" — the Negro poet and scholar Sterling Brown had to explain that Steed meant by population "the people that count." Sterling A. Brown, "Count Us In," *What the Negro Wants*, Rayford W. Logan, editor (Chapel Hill, 1944), pp. 308-309.

10. James Truslow Adams, *The American: The Making of a New Man* (New York, 1943), p. 131. Quoted at length on p. xi.

11. Stanley Vestal, *The Missouri* (New York, 1945), p. 163.

12. Harold E. Briggs, *Frontiers of the Northwest: A History of the Upper Missouri Valley* (New York, 1940), p. 74.

13. Watson Parker, *Gold in the Black Hills* (Norman, Okla., 1966), p. 142.

THE NEGRO
ON THE
AMERICAN FRONTIER

EXPLORATION, 1529-1909

The first "frontier" on which Negroes — or for that matter, whites — appeared was the frontier of exploration, which preceded, sometimes by centuries, the various frontiers of settlement and even, in some cases, the fur-trading frontier, although fur traders on occasion preceded official explorers.

Negroes on this frontier frequently started out as body servants but then took advantage of their opportunities to become experienced, all-round frontiersmen, whether on the plains and mountains of the American West or in the frozen wastes of the Arctic.

Two of the best-known Negro companions to the explorers were Estevanico, who accompanied Panfilo de Narvaez to Florida in 1528, and York, who was the servant of Captain William Clark in the Lewis and Clark expedition across North America from 1803 to 1806. Their stories are told in part in the following article, which originally appeared in the July, 1932 issue (Vol. XVII, No. 3) of the *Journal of Negro History*.

RELATIONS BETWEEN NEGROES AND INDIANS WITHIN THE PRESENT LIMITS OF THE UNITED STATES

INTRODUCTION

Whole libraries have been written concerning the relations of the white settlers of the continent of North America with the native inhabitants whose country they gradually took over and with the Africans whom they imported to assist in the development of the territory thus acquired, but little attention has been paid to the much less important but still significant and perhaps equally interesting question of the relations which developed between these two exploited races, both of which had been deprived of their land by the white man, though in sharply contrasting fashions. The fact that important contacts did take place between the American Indian and the African Negro has long been known, but only recently has it been brought to the attention of the general public. That these relations were intimate and extensive is attested by the most certain of proofs, namely, the presence in this country of a considerable number of persons, classed either as Negroes or Indians, some of whose ancestors are known to have been of the other race.

A recent writer upon the question has pointed out that the American Negro has in his veins not the blood of one race alone, nor of two, but of three.[1] This statement appears as a truism to those who have had any intimate contacts with the Negro race, particularly in the midwest and in the cities of the Atlantic Coast, but it is unlikely that even they were prepared for the statement of the anthropologist Melville J. Herskovits, that of 1,551 Negroes examined by him at Howard University and in Harlem "33 per cent—one-third— . . . claimed partial American Indian ancestry. There are several ways of checking these statements. With regard to the Indian ancestry I tabulated the places of birth of the

[1] Embree, Edwin R., *Brown America* (N.Y., 1931). Weird mixtures of Negro, white, and Indian blood with that of Filipinos, Japanese, and other Orientals are also not infrequently encountered among urban Negroes.

men who claimed to be descended from the Indian in part, and I found that by far the greatest number of them came from those States where, historically, we know there were large Indian populations.'' These figures fully substantiate his statement that Negroes ''have . . . mingled with the American Indians on a scale hitherto unrealized.''[2] That the two races did mingle their blood on a large scale may then be accepted as a fact. The question next arises: ''When, where, and under what circumstances did this intermixture take place?'' To this no complete answer has been given nor is one likely to be forthcoming. It is my purpose, however, to present herewith certain facts which will indicate something of the character of the relations between Negro and Indian within the present limits of the United States.

According to a theory which dates back to the time of the Spanish conquest, and to the support of which Dr. Leo Wiener has recently lent the support of his vast erudition, the New World was known to certain Negroes long before Columbus landed on the shores of Hispaniola. According to Peter Martyr, Balboa found Negroes in Darien in 1513, some of whom were in bondage to the Indians while others had established a colony from which they waged war on the neighboring tribes. It was believed that these Negroes were Ethiopian pirates, shipwrecked on the coast. From such statements as the above in the old Spanish chroniclers, and from a wealth

[2] Herskovits, Melville J., ''The American Negro Evolving a New Physical Type,'' *Current History* (1926) vol. xxiv, pp. 898-903, p. 901; Herskovits, Melville J., *The American Negro* (N.Y., 1928) pp. 3, 9, 16. It is well-known to anyone who is personally acquainted with any considerable number of members of the Negro race in this country that, while the possession of those characteristics which can only come through a proportion of white blood is tacitly admitted to be an advantage, white ancestry is not regarded as a subject for overt pride, but rather a matter to be passed over in discreet silence, like the inheritance of tainted wealth. On the other hand, an Indian ancestor is a distinction to be trumpeted abroad from the housetops. It is possible, then, that some of the subjects examined laid claim to Indian blood which they did not in fact possess, but it is even more likely, Indian blood in a Negro not being so conspicuous as white blood, and for other reasons which we shall later note, that a greater number had Indian ancestors of whom they knew nothing.

of linguistic and archeological evidence which it is impossible for the layman even to follow, much less to criticise, Dr. Wiener has reached the conclusion that, long before Columbus, Negro traders from Guinea had founded a colony in Mexico, perhaps on the site of the City of Mexico, from which they exerted a cultural and commercial influence which extended north to Canada and South to Peru, the Maya, Aztec, and Inca civilizations being directly or indirectly of African origin.[3] This theory has naturally been received with acclamation by most Negro historians.

Whether or not there is an African basis for Indian culture, it is certain that the Negro had little or no personal contact with the Indians of what is now the United States until near the end of the first third of the sixteenth century. The first Negro, known to us by name, to set foot on the soil of this country was "Estevanico, . . . an Arabian black, native of Açamor," who accompanied his master on the expedition of Narvaez to Florida and was one of the four men who survived shipwreck in 1529 and the hardships that followed. For several years the four men wandered about among the Indians of Texas, at first as slaves, later, in 1535 and after, as medicine men. Estevanico particularly distinguished himself by his linguistic ability and was "in constant conversation" with the Indians.[4]

After the four had finally escaped from their hosts or masters and reached the Spanish settlements in Mexico, Estevanico was sent with a couple of friars, in 1539, to discover the fabled Kingdom of Quivira. Estevanico seems to have decided to take ample compensation for his decade of hardships. Consequently he "did not get on well with the friars, because he took the women that were given him and collected turquoises, and got together a stock of everything." Did the chronicler mean to imply that Estevanico declined to share

    [3] Wiener, Leo, *Africa and the Discovery of America*, 3 vols. (Philadelphia, 1920-22) vol. ii, pp. 139-140, vol. iii, p. 365.
    [4] "Cabeza de Vaca, Narrative of," *Spanish Explorers in the Southern United States, 1528-1543* (N.Y., 1907) pp. 55, 65, 71, 73, 78, 80, 102, 107, 112, 113, 126.

his spoils with the padres? Apparently jealousy also entered here. "Besides," the historian continued, "the Indians in those places through which they went got along with the negro better because they had seen him before." Estevanico consequently, was "sent on ahead to open up the way and pacify the Indians."

The further Estevanico penetrated the country the more avid he became for gain and glory. He decided to push on at full speed and thus gain all the credit for anything he might discover. He travelled in "savage magnificence," arrayed in the full regalia of a medicine man and accompanied by a large retinue of Indians who were firm believers in his power, among whom was included a harem of "beautiful women." At the head of this company, who were "loaded with the large quantity of turquoises they had given him," the Negro reached the Zuñi pueblo of Cibola. He informed the inhabitants that they were shortly to be honored by a visit from a body of white men who would give them valuable instructions, but the Zuñi were fully conscious of the color line and concluded that he was lying, since it was unlikely that white men would have a black ambassador. When Estevanico fool-hardily endeavored to enforce his usual tribute of "turquoises and women," they "decided to kill him. They did this." Estevanico was shot to death with arrows while trying to escape. The tradition of the death at the hands of their ancestors of "one of the Black Mexicans, a large man, with chilli lips," that is, with lips swollen as if from eating chili peppers, has been preserved among the Zuñi to the present time.[5] Thus Estevanico's triumphal march upon the gold-paved Kingdom of Quivira came to a bloody end. It was, then, through a Negro representative that the New Mexican Indians first came into contact with the Old World.

The earliest contacts between Africans and Indians, as we have just seen, came through Negro slaves accompanying

[5] Castañeda, Pedro de, "The Narrative of the Expedition of Coronado," *Spanish Explorers in the Southern United States, 1528-1543* (N.Y., 1907) pp. 288-290; Lowery, Woodbury, *The Spanish Settlements within the Present Limits of the United States, 1513-1561* (N.Y. and London, 1901) pp. 278-282.

exploring expeditions. When Coronado in 1541 penetrated as far north and east as central Kansas in search of the mythical golden city which had cost Estevanico his life, he was accompanied by Negroes.[6] The contact was not always a friendly one, as Estevanico's experience showed. Almost exactly 250 years later, on August 16, 1788, the *Lady Washington,* commanded by Robert Gray, was anchored in Tillamook Bay on the North West Coast. While some of the men were on shore "an Indian seized a cutlass which the captain's servant—a native of the Cape Verde Islands named Marcos Lopez—had left sticking in the sand and ran away with it, Lopez following in pursuit." The officers and one man also followed and "found Lopez, who had caught the thief, surrounded by a group of Indians, who at once killed Lopez with their knives and arrows, and then attacked the three" who escaped by hard fighting, all wounded.[7] Thus the first African on the North West Coast of the United States, like the first in the South West, met his death at the hands of the natives.

The progress of York, the "black servant belonging to Captain Clark," who crossed the Continent with the Lewis and Clark expedition of 1803-06, is somewhat reminiscent of that of Estevanico, but unmarred by any tragedy. Nothing had quite such an influence upon the Indians whom the expedition encountered as the promise to show them a man "perfectly black, whose hair was short and curled." York, "a remarkably stout, strong negro," as well as something of a clown, more than fulfilled their expectations. "By way of amusement he told them that he had once been a wild animal, and caught, and tamed by his master; and to convince them showed them feats of strength which, added to his looks, made him more terrible than we wished him to be."[8]

[6] Castañeda, *op. cit.,* p. 333.

[7] Bancroft, Hubert Howe, *The Northwest Coast,* 2 vols. (San Francisco, 1884) vol. i, p. 189.

[8] Coues, Elliott, ed., *The History of the Lewis and Clark Expedition,* 4 vols. (N.Y., 1893) vol i, pp. 2, 100, 159, 243, vol. ii, p. 506; Thwaites, Reuben Gold, ed., *Original Journals of the Lewis and Clark Expedition, 1804-1806,* 7 vols. (N.Y., 1904) vol. i, pp. 185, 186, 209, 243, iii, 161, 162.

Captain Clark commented in his journal: "Those people (the Arikaras) are much pleased with my black Servent. Their womin verry fond of carressing our men &c." Presumably York shared in these attentions. Later on, among the Mandans, Clark noted: "I ordered my black Servent to Dance which amused the crowd verry much, and Somewhat astonished them, that So large a man should be active &c. &c." York similarly entertained the Indians on the Columbia. Among the Gros Ventres he was regarded as great medicine. But a careful perusal of the original journals of the expedition will reveal that, far from being a mere body-servant, who on occasion assumed the role of a circus-exhibit and entertainer, and quite aside from his useful activities in these connections, York was in other respects one of the most valuable men in the party. Along with the other members of the expedition he suffered uncomplainingly from cold, exhaustion, and improper food,[9] but his powerful physique brought him safely through these hardships. He was an expert swimmer and a skillful hunter,[10] and also, strange to relate, sometimes acted as interpreter.

Charles Mackenzie, of the North West Company, thus described York's function in that connection: "A mulatto (York), who spoke bad French and worse English, served as interpreter to the Captains (Lewis and Clark), so that a single word to be understood by the party required to pass from the Natives to the woman (Sacajawea), from the woman to the husband (Charbonneau), from the husband to the mulatto, from the mulatto to the captains."[11] That is to say, the Indians would talk to Sacajawea, Indian wife of the French-Canadian Charbonneau, who would manage, probably in a mixture of Indian dialects and Canadian French, to convey their meaning as she understood it to her husband.

[9] Thwaites, *op. cit.*, vol. i, pp. 53, 235, ii, 214, 215, 154, iii, 280, 287, 293, v, 38.

[10] Thwaites, *op. cit.*, vol. i, pp. 40, 143, ii, 91, iii, 227, 228, v, 278, 290, vii, 105.

[11] Mackenzie, Charles, "The Missouri Indians," L. R. Masson, *Les Bourgeois de la Compagnie du Nord Ouest* (Quebec, 1889) vol. i, p. 336.

He in turn would put the communication into French and repeat it to York who would turn the result into English for the
benefit of his master.

We learn from this not only that York was a mulatto
but also that in all probability he was a St. Louis Negro who
had picked up French in Missouri. Later he probably applied
his linguistic skill to the task of acquiring a smattering of
Indian dialects, for on several occasions, later in the progress
of the expedition, he was assigned the duty of trading with
the Indians for food.[12] It is evident that Clark made no mistake when he selected the Negro York for one of his companions on the famous expedition, and, as we shall later see,
there are indications that York himself was very favorably
impressed by the opportunity he had enjoyed of travelling
among and associating with the various Indian tribes.

These casual contacts during the exploring period are,
however, of much less importance than interest. The subject
of Indian-Negro relations during the period of colonization
and afterwards is of considerably greater significance and is
easily divided, partly according to chronological considerations but principally along geographic lines, into three main
topics which are themselves of widely varying importance.
These are: (1) relations between Negroes and Indians in
New England, the middle colonies or states, and the Upper
South; (2) among the slave-holding Indians in the Deep
South and in the Indian Territory; and (3) in the other parts
of the country, particularly the Old North West, the Rocky
Mountain Region, and the Pacific Coast.

[12] Thwaites, *op. cit.*, vol. v, pp. 67, 72, 75, 98, 101.

CHAPTER I

ASSOCIATION AS FELLOW SLAVES

The first intimate relation of an extensive character to be established between Negro and Indian in the New World was that of fellow slaves. It will be remembered that Negroes were imported into Spanish America to take the place of the Indians, who lacked the physical stamina to endure the labors on plantations and in mines to which they were subjected by their conquerors. Without much doubt the blood of the two races was first mingled in the West Indies.[13] Many of the slaves imported into the English colonies came by way of the West Indies[14] and some of these were doubtless of mixed blood. Indian and Negro slavery had been simultaneously introduced into the Bermudas in 1616;[15] extensive importations of African slaves followed, and after the Pequot and King Philip wars "a large number of redskins" who had been taken prisons were also shipped to the islands, sometimes in exchange for Negroes. "Many of the colored people, "we are told, "show in their physiognomy the influence of the Indian type."[16] Probably some of the descendants of these deported prisoners were later sold into slavery on their native continent.

Indians and Negroes were united in the bounds of a common servitude on the North American continent as well. All the great colonizing nations of the Continent held Indian slaves, and all the English colonies, in which we are particularly interested, at one time or another contained a greater or lesser number of native bondservants.[17] Some of these

---

[13] Herskovits, *op. cit.,* p. 3.

[14] Helps, Sir Arthur, *The Spanish Conquest in America,* 4 vols. (London and N.Y., 1900-1904; first pub. 1855) vol. iii, p. 154.

[15] Butler, Nathaniel, *The History of the Bermudas or Summer Islands,* J. H. Lefroy, ed. (London, 1882) p. 84.

[16] Bolton, H. Carrington, "Gombay, A Festal Rite of Bermuda Negroes," *Journal of American Folk Lore,* vol. iii, p. 222; Williams, George Washington, *History of the Negro Race in America,* 2 vols. (N.Y., 1883) vol. i, pp. 173-174.

[17] Lauber, Almon Wheeler, "Indian Slavery in Colonial Times within the Present Limits of the United States," *Columbia University Studies in History, Economics and Public Law* (1913) vol. liv, no. 3.

had been captured in war, others kidnapped,[18] still others purchased from their Indian captors or brought from the West Indies. Two slaves from that region, John Indian and his wife Tituba, won for themselves an unenviable immortality through the prominent part they played in the Salem witchcraft trials. Though always described as Indians,[19] it is quite possible that they also numbered Negroes among their ancestors. Certainly, if any more exotic source than the Massachusetts of the Mathers is to be sought for the performances which went on at Salem, the West Coast of Africa would seem to offer a most likely field of investigation. But most of the Indian slaves held in the colonies of North America were natives of that continent. In 1730 there were 700 slaves in Connecticut, mostly Negroes but some Indians.[20]

During the eighteenth century there are not infrequent advertisements of runaway slaves who were of mixed Negro and Indian origin. In 1734 a one-eyed fiddler, half-Negro, half-Indian, speaking both English and the local Indian dialect, ran away from a New Jersey master. In 1747 a Negro with some Indian blood ran away from his master, taking with him a boy whose mother was Indian—probably his son, though this is not specifically stated. They had with them a gun, ammunition, and some blankets and, since they could both talk Indian, it was believed that they intended to clothe themselves in garments appropriate to that race and in that disguise escape to the Carolinas, probably to take refuge among the Indians there, though this also in an assumption. In 1778 mention was made of a Negro woman, presumably a slave, who was married to an Indian. This woman, prob-

[18] An unusually late case of the kidnapping of Indians for slaves is that of Diza Mallory, an Indian who is said to have been stolen from her parents at Yorktown and sold in the Norfolk slave market. Her daughter Dianah Mallory, whose father apparently was a Negro and who was born a slave, in 1830 married a man of French descent, which would seem to place her mother's enslavement late in the eighteenth century. ("Letters Largely Personal or Private," *Journal of Negro History* (1926) vol. xi, pp. 63-64.)

[19] Upham, Charles W., *Salem Witchcraft*, 2 vols. (Boston, 1867) vol. ii, pp. 2, 28-30, 95, 240-241, 255.

[20] Williams, *op. cit.*, vol. i, p. 259.

ably with her husband's aid, stole their little daughter from her owner and fled, apparently accompanied by her Indian husband, since a reward was offered for the arrest of all three.[21] All these Negro-Indian halfbreeds, or mustees, mentioned above, chance to have been slaves of New Jersey masters. It is interesting to note that the New Jersey Negroes are said to have been noticeably modified in physical appearance by an unusually extensive intermingling with Indian slaves.[22]

Negro and Indian slaves occasionally united in less innocent relations than those of wedlock. In 1708, for example, "an Indian man Slave and a Negro woman," in Queen's County, New York, killed their master, his wife, and five children. The man was hanged, the woman burned, and two Negro accomplices were likewise put to death.[23] In 1712 a desperate slave insurrection broke out in New York City itself. More than nine whites were killed and five or six wounded. Of the rebels, six committed suicide, and twenty-one were executed by hanging, burning, breaking on the wheel, and hanging in chains. Some were acquitted and others recommended for pardon. In the last category were two Spanish Indians, Husea and John, who had been taken prisoner from a Spanish vessel by a privateer and sold as slaves.[24] Apparently the reason for leniency in their case was that, as free men and Spanish subjects who had been apparently wrongfully enslaved, they were to some extent justified in taking up arms for their liberation. Carried to its logical conclusion his theory might have proved embarrassing.

[21] Cooley, Henry Scofield, ''A Study of Slavery in New Jersey,'' *Johns Hopkins University Studies in History and Political Science* (1896) vol. xiv, p. 422; Johnston, James Hugo, ''Documentary Evidence of the Relations of Negroes and Indians,'' *Journal of Negro History* (1929) vol. xiv, pp. 28, 43.

[22] *Ibid.*, p. 28.

[23] Riddell, William Renwick, ''The Slave in Early New York,'' *Journal of Negro History* (1928) vol. xiii, pp. 53-86, 69; Northrup, Ansel Judd, ''Slavery in New York,'' *New York State Library Bulletin, History* (May, 1900) no. 4, p. 265.

[24] *Ibid.*, p. 268; Lauber, *op. cit.*, p. 318.

Racially, the principal result of the relations of Negroes and Indians as fellow slaves has been thus summed up by Dr. Reuter. "Slavery of the native Indians existed in a number of the English colonies before the coming of the Negroes. Those captured in battle were in some cases sold into slavery in distant colonies. Others were kidnapped along the coast and sold as slaves in the more settled regions. . . . With these enslaved Indians the Negro slaves came into close and intimate contact. The social status was the same and as slaves they met on terms of equality. Intermarriage followed and, as the body of Negro slaves increased and Indian slavery declined, the Indian slaves were gradually absorbed into the larger black population."[25] Another possible effect appears in the assertion that such Negro folk tales as the "Uncle Remus" stories are actually of Indian origin and became known to the Negroes through their association with Indian slaves.[26]

[25] Reuter, Edward Byron, *The American Race Problem* (N.Y., 1927) pp. 122-123.
[26] *Nineteenth Annual Report of the Bureau of American Ethnology, 1897-1898*, pt. i, pp. 233-234.

CHAPTER II

CONTACTS IN WARFARE

Although the white colonists numbered Indians among their slaves, it was not as a slave that the Indian was of greatest significance to the colonist. The white settler knew the Indian best as an active or potential enemy. We have observed the relations of the Negro slave with his Indian companion in bondage; we have even seen them co-operating upon occasion in acts of violence against their white masters. The question then arises: "What was the character of the relations—if any existed—between the Negro slave and the Indian warrior?" The theory has been advanced that, from their first contact, the Negro and Indian felt an instinctive sympathy one for the other; that they were united by the mystical bond of a common darkness of pigmentation as allies against the fair-skinned dominant race. As an evidence of this "consciousness of kind" existing between Negroes and Indians, we are told that "in certain Indian massacres the Indian murdered every white man but saved the Negro."[27] No example is given or authority cited by the historian just quoted, but one of the massacres referred to is doubtless that which took place in Virginia in 1622.[28] It is quite true that there is no mention of any Negro in the "List of those that were massacred . . . the 22nd . . . March," but this is not conclusive proof that none were slain, since this list is specifically stated to have been prepared in order "that their lawfull heyres may take speedy order for the inheritance of their lands and estates." Even had a Negro been killed, it is unlikely that the fact would have been recorded in a list prepared for this particular purpose. However, it is probably quite true that this massacre caused no casualties among the Negro population of Virginia, which had begun in 1619 by the famous introduction of about a

[27] Johnston, *loc. cit.*, p. 26.

[28] Russell, John H., "The Free Negro in Virginia," *Johns Hopkins University Studies in History and Political Science* (1913) ser. xxxi, no. 3, pp. 127-130.

score of blacks by a Dutch vessel, for on February 16, 1623, twenty-two Negroes—sixteen men and six women—were living in Virginia, and another Negro had died since April, 1622. We do not even know whether or not these Negroes were exposed to the massacre, since we are told where they were located in February, 1623, but not where they were a year before. Assuming, however, that all the Negroes after the massacre returned to approximately the same plantations at which they were at the time it took place, we discover that almost exactly half the Negroes in Virginia at that time were at Flowerdieu Hundred and the rest were scattered among half a dozen different plantations. At Flowerdieu Hundred six persons—a comparatively small number—were killed in the massacre; at the other plantations on which Negroes were located in 1623 no casualties are mentioned. The escape of the Negroes from massacre at Flowerdieu Hundred probably had no other reason than did the similar exemption from destruction of the majority of its white inhabitants. In the massacre 347 Virginians perished, but in the months between April, 1622, and February 16, 1623, no less than 371 died, most of them from natural causes; eighteen of these were from Flowerdieu Hundred— three times the number which that plantation had lost by the massacre—and only one of the entire 371 was a Negro.[29] It seems clear that the good fortune of the Negroes so far as the massacre was concerned can be explained as purely a matter of chance, and requires no theory of an inborn sense of solidarity among the darker races.

If any Negro did escape death on this occasion for any reason other than his being in a place of comparative safety or his ability to keep out of the way of his would-be murderers, the explanation is probably to be found rather in superstitious fear than in a feeling of kinship. We are told that in New England when the Indians first saw a Negro they thought he was "Abamacho or the Devill, deeming all Devils

[29] *Colonial Records of Virginia* (Sen. doc., extra, 1874) pp. 37, 40, 42, 45, 46, 48, 49, 51, 55-56, 60, 61, 63, 66.

that are blacker than themselves.''[30] We are similarly informed that when the Indians of Virginia saw the Negroes for the first time, ''they thought they were a true breed of Devils, and therefore they called them *Manitto* for a great while: this word in their language signifies not only God but likewise the Devil.''[31]

It is difficult to believe that the Indian warrior would feel any spontaneous sympathy for the Negro, whom he beheld toiling side by side with the white servant in the tobacco fields which were encroaching more and more upon his hunting grounds, merely because his skin was as much darker than the Indian's as the Indian's was than the white's. Most of the Indian tribes were at constant warfare with one another and had no scruples in allying themselves upon occasion with the white man for this purpose; they could hardly be expected to feel any particular sympathy for those members of an alien race who were to all appearances assisting the conquering whites in their exploitation of the Indians' birthright. Indeed the Indian would be more likely to despise the Negro because he was a slave to the white man than to feel that they were essentially brothers in their common oppression by the conquering race. A century later, indeed, it was said of the Indians of Virginia that ''they hate, and despise the very sight of a *Negroe,* but they seem to like an *East-Indian,* and fear and revere the *Whites.*''[32] This is undoubtedly putting the situation much too strongly, but there was probably some justification for the statement in the attitude of certain tribes.

In some parts of the New World and even of North America a very definite and pronounced sense of solidarity developed between Negroes and Indians, but it had a much more

[30] Wood, William, *New Englands prospect,* E. M. Boynton, ed. (Boston, 1898; first pub. 1634) p. 81. Wood was at the Massachusetts Bay from 1629 to 1633.

[31] Kalm, Peter, *Travels into North America,* 3 vols. (Warrington, 1770) vol. i, pp. 395-396. Kalm's travels took place during the years 1748-1751.

[32] Jones, Hugh, *The Present State of Virginia* (N.Y., 1865; first pub. 1724) p. 4.

substantial basis than pigmentation. In Spanish America during the first half of the sixteenth century there is almost constant mention not only of Negro slaves revolting and leading Indian slaves in insurrections, but also of their stirring up the Caribs to revolt or rising in conjunction with the natves.[33] In Mexico City, for example, in 1537, the Negroes elected a king, communicated with fellow blacks in other towns and mines, and planned to massacre all the Spaniards in the city, after which, joining with the natives, they would take possession of the country. The plot was betrayed, as was usual in such cases, and twenty-four of the conspirators were hanged and quartered.[34] From the very first the Negroes were regarded as a disturbing element, and only their great physical strength—itself a source of danger, but which made them indispensable on the plantations and in the mines— kept them from being barred from the Spanish colonies.[35] Similarly in Louisiana in 1729 the Chickasaws are said to have incited the fierce Banbara Negroes who were among the slaves at New Orleans to conspire to massacre the whites and establish a Banbara colony, but here too the plot was betrayed and ten conspirators executed.[36]

No slave revolt, instigated by Indians, and no Indian attack upon a white settlement encouraged by or in co-operation with Negro slaves, ever took place within the present limits of the United States save perhaps in the Deep South.[37]

[33] Wiener, *op. cit.*, vol. i, pp. 155-158.

[34] Bancroft, Hubert Howe, *Mexico*, vol. ii, *1521-1560* (San Francisco, 1883) pp. 384-385.

[35] Helps, Sir Arthur, *The Spanish Conquest in America*, 4 vols. (London and N.Y., 1900-1904; first pub. 1855) vol. i, pp. 154-155.

[36] Dunbar-Nelson, Alice, ''People of Color in Louisiana, I, *Journal of Negro History* (1916) vol. i, pp. 361-376, p. 368.

[37] The fictional account by Mary Johnston, in *Prisoners of Hope* (Boston and N.Y., 1898), of the revolt, on a Virginia plantation of the 1660's, of the Negro and convict servants, assisted by two allied Indian tribes, has, so far as I can ascertain, no historical foundation in the place and period mentioned. Something of the kind might have occurred on a Spanish American plantation of the previous century, on a Louisiana plantation in the next century, or even on a Georgia or Florida plantation of the early nineteenth century, but hardly in any English colony during the seventeenth century.

The nearest thing we have to such an affair is an alleged conspiracy by slaves in East Jersey in 1734 to rise in revolt, seize horses, and escape "towards the Indians in the French interest."[38] The reason, of course, that the Negroes failed to play the same part in the English colonies that they did among the Spanish in particular was doubtless the comparatively few numbers of both the Indians and the Negroes and the much greater area over which the former were scattered, which prevented the two races from developing the fellow-feeling which otherwise might have resulted.

We have pointed out that in the English colonies of North America the relation between Negro slave and Indian warrior which was of most significance in the Spanish settlements did not develop. What, then, was the character of such relations as did exist? In many ways they were the same as those between the wild Indian and the white man. We have no evidence that the northern Indian made any distinction between Negro and white on the basis of skin color, at least not in the early period and when uninfluenced by white allies. When a band of Indians captured a white settlement or farmhouse they were likely in the first fury of the attack to kill everyone they encountered, man, woman, and child, armed and unarmed, master and servant, black and white. But when resistance had ceased they rarely at that time put anyone to death in cold blood. They would probably tomahawk the wounded and any who, on account of age, extreme youth, or other handicap, seemed likely to become an encumbrance on the march to the raiding party's village, and on the return journey they would put to death those who were unable to keep up. When the warriors reached home they would quite likely torture to death one or more of the male prisoners, but it was also probable that they would adopt the others into the tribe; this was always done with the women and children unless they were held for ransom, as was usually the case when the Indians were allies of the French. The

---

[38] Coffin, Joshua, *Slave Insurrections* (N.Y., 1860) p. 14; Cooley, *op. cit.*, pp. 42-43.

Indians had no compunctions about killing women or children in the heat of an attack or in cold blood when their weakness or weariness made it expedient; and they might treat captives on the homeward march with great brutality, but they never put a woman or a child formally to the torture and such captives were usually well-treated after the Indian village had been reached. It is against the background of these practises that the attitude of the Indian warrior to the Negro slave must be considered.

Should a Negro slave fight in defense of his master's family during a successful Indian attack—and this would be the natural thing for a well-treated household slave, who was a man of courage, to do—[39] he would have to take his chances with his white comrades. Even if he did not resist he was apparently no more likely to receive the treatment theoretically proper to a non-combatant in civilized warfare than if he were white. The mention of casualties among Negro slaves in the course of Indian wars is by no means infrequent. For example, in 1676 the Indians "killed a Negro Servant" belonging to Andrew Harris at Patuxet.[40] Sex was not a much greater safeguard than was color, for the French Indians who stormed the house of the Rev. John Williams at Deerfield in 1704 killed Parthena, a Negro woman-servant who was the Williams children's nurse. This murder was committed at the height of the excitement incident to this affair, but even after resistance had been entirely overcome, the Indians murdered a Negro man-servant belonging to Williams. But this may be explained by the fact that they had been partaking freely of the contents of the ministerial cellar.[41]

Once on the homeward way, however, the able-bodied

[39] Many cases could be accumulated of Negro slaves assisting their masters in fights with the Indians. One which happens to come to hand is an incident which took place in Kentucky in 1782 (McDougle, Ivan E., "Slavery in Kentucky," *Journal of Negro History* (1918) vol. iii, pp. 211-328, p. 295.

[40] N.S., "A Continuation of the State of New-England, 1676," *Narrative of the Indian Wars*, Charles H. Lincoln, ed. (N.Y., 1913) p. 66.

[41] Parkman, Francis, *A Half-Century of Conflict*, 2 vols. (Boston, 1892) vol. i, pp. 58, 68.

male Negro was in considerably better case than the white men who had been taken prisoner, for, so far as the records show, the Indians never put a Negro prisoner to the torture, probably because he, like a woman, was normally a non-combatant, and torture was an honor reserved for the warrior. The fact that both women and Negroes sometimes put up a fight not less formidable than that of the white husband or master apparently did not cause the conservative and sportsmanlike red man to break this rule.[42]

It is hard to say definitely just what was done with Negro prisoners when the Indian captors were not co-operating with the French or British of Canada. Presumably they would be adopted into the tribe, though I have been unable to find satisfactory evidence of any definite case. The question probably came up very rarely and it would not be surprising if such cases of adoption occurred, unknown to white historians.[43] When the Indians were in alliance with French or British the problem of the disposition of captives presented no difficulties. Whites would be held for ransom, Negroes sold in Canada. The Negro's market value gave his Indian captor a very cogent reason for treating him with some tenderness—perhaps even more than he would show toward a white captive—for in the latter case there was often a long and wearisome delay before the prisoner's friends could raise, or persuade the government to supply, the amount of his ransom, and therefore the Indian had to wait for his profit, unless he could persuade some white friend to take a flier in the stock market by purchasing the captor's rights in the

[42] See however *A Narrative of the Life of John Marrant* (Leeds, 1815; first pub. 1786) in which is told of the alleged experiences of a Negro captured by the Cherokees when only 14 years old, in 1769, and sentenced to be tortured to death, but who escaped through prayer which led to the intercession of a Cherokee Pocahontas. Another Negro who left a record of his experiences with Indians as a captive was Briton Hammon, who fell into the hands of the Florida Indians in 1747 (Loggins, Vernon, *The Negro Author*, N.Y., 1931, pp. 30-33).

[43] Mary Johnston's *The Great Valley* (Boston, 1926) contains an imaginative reconstruction of some of the experiences of a Negro slave, captured and adopted by the Indians.

prisoner. The Negro, on the other hand, could be sold for ready cash—an important consideration to such an over-valuer of the present as the Indian. Many instances are recorded of Negroes captured during the Revolutionary War from New York Whigs or the French of Illinois and sold in Canada.[44]

Even in the Spanish colonies, where the relations between Negroes and Indians were particularly close and friendly, in Honduras in 1539 and in Peru in 1554, Negroes had been used as soldiers against the natives, one of the motives, perhaps, in addition to the obvious one, being a desire to alienate the two races from each other.[45] In 1729 the governor of Louisiana used slaves to exterminate "a small tribe of Indians, the Chouchas," living a few miles above New Orleans, by whom the settlement believed itself to be menaced. A little before this the Natchez had taken a number of prisoners from the French, including many slaves. The French recruited all their forces for an attack on the enemy and even armed a number of their Negroes. Those who had been captured by the Natchez were promised freedom if they would fight against their former masters, and so the struggle resolved itself into a contest between the two parties of Negroes, those who remained loyal to their old masters being victorious. In 1735 free Negroes under their own officers served with the French forces in the war with the Choctaws.[46]

Even among the Dutch this device was suggested. In 1641 a native of New Netherland had been killed by a "savage," and the director and council enquired of the commonalty whether it would not be proper to punish the murder and, if so, how, when, and by whom, to which it was replied that it

[44] Smith, Thomas Watson, "The Slave in Canada," *Collections of the Nova Scotia Historical Society*, vol. x, pp. 35-36; "Papers from Canadian Archives," *Wisconsin Historical Collections*, vol. xi, pp. 154, 156; *Jefferson, Thomas, The Works of*, 12 vols., Paul Leicester Ford, ed. (N.Y. and London, 1904) vol. vii, p. 342, letter to Harry Innes, May 23, 1793, in regard to "slaves carried off by the Indians."

[45] Wright R. R., "Negro Companions of the Spanish Explorers," *American Anthropologist* (1902) vol. iv, pp. 217-228, p. 220.

[46] Dunbar-Nelson, *loc. cit.*, p. 368.

would be expedient that an attack should be made on the Indians, for which purpose "The Director shall employ . . . as many of the strongest and most active of the Negroes as he can conveniently spare, and provide [each of] them with a small ax and a half pike."[47] We have no evidence that this suggestion was followed. But we are told that "Charles Craven, colonial governor of South Carolina," in 1715, "at the head of 1200 men, part of whom were negro slaves, met and routed the (Yemassee) Indians in a series of desperate encounters."[48] However, despite these examples and the lack of any evidence of sympathy between Negro slaves and Indians hostile to the colonists, the English settlers, on no other occasion that I can discover, employed Negroes as soldiers against the natives.

[47] Northrup, *loc. cit.*, p. 251.
[48] *National cyclopaedia of American Biography*, vol. xii, p. 155.

CHAPTER III

CONTACTS AS ALLIES

We have observed that there is no evidence of an understanding between Negro slaves in the English colonies and the hostile Indian tribes. The same is not altogether true as to Negro slaves and those tribes which had either been subdued by the whites or which were not actively hostile. From the earliest appearance of Negro slavery in the Spanish possessions, the Negroes, when not engaged in fomenting revolts among the neighboring Indians or starting insurrections on their own account, seem to have contented themselves with running away to take refuge among the natives, whom they were easily able to dominate. As early as 1502—only a decade after Columbus had landed on San Salvador—Ovando, governor of Hispaniola, had "solicited that no negro slaves should be sent to Hispaniola, for they fled amongst the Indians and taught them bad customs, and never could be captured."[49]

Taking refuge among the Indians of the Spanish colonies, however, was a much easier feat than escaping to the natives of the regions bordering upon the more northerly of the English colonies. A Negro fresh from Africa would feel not at all out of place in the tropic jungles of South and Central America, but he would be altogether a stranger in the bleak forests of North America. Yet, by taking advantage of the proper season for such an adventure and perhaps counselling with an Indian comrade in bondage, many Negro slaves from time to time did seek for liberty among the natives.[50] "Runaway slaves," says Dr. Reuter, "frequently made their way by accident or otherwise to the Indian camps. In some cases the Indians returned these escaped slaves to their masters; sometimes they were killed or otherwise maltreated. But in other cases they were protected and kept as slaves to the Indians among whom they

[49] Helps, *op. cit.*, p. 251.
[50] McDougall, Marion Gleason, *Fugitive Slaves: 1619-1865* (Boston, 1891) pp. 7-8.

sought refuge or were taken into the Indian tribes by adoption."[51] In 1676 the Maryland Assembly offered "a Matchcoate . . . or the value thereof" to any Indian or Indians apprehending a runaway servant.[52]

In 1705 some of the Negro slaves in Albany ran away to the French, and were probably assisted on their way by Indians favorable to France. It was found necessary to prescribe the death penalty for any slave apprehended forty miles north of Albany, without a pass from his master; this enactment was repeated in 1745. In 1717 complaint was made that slaves in the colony of New York ran away and "were secreted by the Minisinks," intermarrying with the Indian women.[53] A familiar feature of treaties with the Indians was the provision that they should return the runaway slaves who had found refuge among them. The Indians always denied that any fugitives were among them and cheerfully promised to give up any whom they might encounter in the future, but it is unlikely that the point would be so stressed were the charge altogether baseless. In 1721, for example, the governor of Virginia arranged with the Five Nations for the return of runaway slaves. In 1723 the governor of New York told the Six Nations that he had heard there were runaway Negroes among them, which they denied. In 1733 the governor again requested that runaway slaves should be given up, to which the Indians replied that "to the best of our knowledge we know not that there is one among any of the Six Nations." In 1764 the Hurons promised to give up any runaway slaves among them and in the next year the Delawares made a similar agreement. In the same year the Six Nations again made their perennial promise.[54] We have no record that any of these runaways were actually returned.

It was probably the exceptional slave who succeeded in making good his escape. Those half-Indians whom we have earlier mentioned would have the advantage over the aver-

[51] Reuter, *The American Race Problem*, pp. 122-124.
[52] *Maryland Archives*, vol. ii, pp. 523, 524-525.
[53] Northrup, *loc. cit.*, pp. 262, 279.
[54] *Ibid.*, p. 275; Riddell, *loc. cit.*, p.

age slave, as would the Pennsylvania mulatto slave, experienced in the backwoods, who in 1746 was believed to be making his way north to join the French and Indians, as he had previously threatened to do.[55] An interesting proof of the existence of runaway Negroes among the Indians appears in a vocabulary of the dialect of the Nanticokes, a tribe inhabiting the eastern shore of Maryland, compiled about 1750 by J. C. Pyrlaeus, a Moravian missionary. Many years later, upon examination by a linguist, this alleged Indian dialect turned out to be pure Mandingo. Evidently the missionary had stumbled upon some runaway Mandingo slave who had not yet forgotten his native language and, perhaps endeavoring to take advantage of the little English known by the runaway, had only succeeded in listing some words from the fugitive's own native dialect rather than from that of the tribe among whom he was living.[56]

It might also be mentioned in passing that Josiah Henson, the original of Uncle Tom, on his way to Canada was given shelter in an Indian camp in Ohio.[57] Inasmuch as the Indians among whom the Negroes sought refuge were not ordinarily those actively hostile to the settlers—though doubtless glad to give them what annoyance they conveniently could, through secreting their slaves or by any other means—I have found no record of any runaway Negro later participating in a raid on a white settlement in company with a war party of his adoptive people. This, of course, applies only to New England, the middle colonies and states, and the Upper South. The descendants of the comparatively few runaway Negroes who did succeed in establishing a per-

[55] "Eighteenth Century Slave Advertisements," *Journal of Negro History* (1916) vol. i, p. 201.

[56] Brinton, D. G., "On Certain Supposed Nanticoke Words Shown to be African," *American Antiquarian and Oriental Journal* (1887) vol. ix, pp. 350-354.

[57] Hartgrove, W. B., "The Story of Josiah Henson," *Journal of Negro History* (1918) vol. iii, pp. 1-21, p. 9. "The Ottawa Indians of the village of Chief Kinjeino, were among the earliest friends of fugitives in the [north] western part of Ohio." Siebert, William Henry, *The Underground Railroad from Slavery to Freedom* (N.Y., 1898) pp. 37-38, 92.

manent residence among the Indians in time disappeared into the tribe, just as Indian slaves were swallowed up by the
greater numbers of the Negroes. However, on the reservations of the Six Nations in Ontario, the mixture of Negro and
Indian remained perceptible because of the number of fugitive Negroes who were attracted to that region by reason of
Joseph Brant's reputation for hospitality to runaway
slaves.[58]

We have observed that intermarriage took place between
Negro and Indian slaves and have even noticed an instance
in which a Negro woman, apparently a slave, was married to
an Indian, presumably free. There was doubtless a perceptible amount of racial intermixture between Negro slaves and
peaceful Indians of the vicinity. A traveler of the early nineteenth century remarked that ''while slavery was supposed
to be maintainable by law in Massachusetts, there was a particular temptation for taking Indian wives, the children of
Indian women being acknowledged to be free.''[59] It is not
probable, however, that alliances between Negro slaves and
free Indians were ever of great importance.

The great factor in amalgamation of Negroes and Indians was intermarriage between freed Negroes and reservation Indians. This intermixture began under slavery and
was greatly speeded up by emancipation. Consequently it
was most conspicuous in the North, where slavery was most
early abolished, and the position of the Negro highest in the
social scale. In Duke's County, Massachusetts, intermarriage between Negroes and Indians is said to have begun
about 1764, ''in consequence of which the mixed race has increased in numbers, and improved in temperance and indus-

[58] Hamilton, J. C., ''The African in Canada,'' *Proceedings of the American Association for the Advancement of Science* (1889 vol. xxxviii, pp. 364-370;
Hamilton, J. C., ''Slavery in Canada,'' *Transactions of the Canadian Institute* (1889-90) vol. i, pp. 102-108, p. 107; Chamberlain, A. F., ''African
and American: The Contact of Negro and Indian,'' *Science* (1891) vol. xvii,
pp. 85-90; Siebert, *op. cit.*, p. 203.
[59] Kendall, Edward Augustus, *Travels through the Northern Parts of the
United States in the Year 1807 and 1808*, 3 vols. (N.Y., 1809) vol. ii, p. 179;
Williams, *op. cit.*, p. 180.

try.''[60] About 1767 there were in the Indian reservation of Mashpee on Cape Cod ''twenty-one shingled houses and fifty-two wigwams . . . belonging to and inhabited by Indians and mulattoes.''[61] It is possible, however, that in this case ''mulatto'' was meant to apply to any half-breed. In 1790 there were supposed to be in Massachusetts 4000 Negroes and 2000 persons of Indian descent, many of whom were of Negro blood as well.[62] In 1792 there were 441 persons of Indian blood in Duke's County, of whom less than one-third were pure.[63] In the same year of the 280 Indians at Mashpee at least two-thirds were mixed.[64]

In 1795 it was said of Massachusetts: ''They [the Negroes] have generally . . . left the country and resorted to the maritime towns. Some are incorporated, and their breed is mixed with the Indians of Cape-Cod and Martha's Vineyard; and the Indians are said to be meliorated by the mixture.''[65] By 1802 the inhabitants of Mashpee had increased to 380, or a gain of a hundred in the last decade. Very few, however, of the pure race were left. ''[Some] of the women,'' it was said, ''lead a vagabond life in the country, where at last they find Negro husbands, whom they bring home to enjoy all the privileges and immunities of Mashpee.''[66]

In 1807 it was said that the sixty-five Indians on Chappaquiddick were ''much intermixed with white and negro blood, . . . and they have been much improved in their industry and general habits by the intermixture.'' In the same

[60] Gookin, Daniel, ''Historical Collections of the Indians in New England,'' *Massachusetts Historical Collections* (1792) ser. i, vol. i, pp. 141-227, p. 206, note.

[61] ''Report of a Committee on the State of the Indians in Mashpee and Parts Adjacent,'' *Mass. Hist. Colls.* (1815) ser. ii, vol. iii, pp. 14-17.

[62] Rantoul, Robert, Sr., ''Negro Slavery in Massachusetts,'' *Historical Collections of the Essex Institute* (1887) vol. xxiv, pp. 81-108, p. 101.

[63] Gookin, *loc. cit.* p. 206, note.

[64] *Mass. Hist. Colls.* (1792) ser. i, vol. i, p. 230, letter from Nathaniel Freeman, Sandwich, September 23, 1792.

[65] ''Judge Tucker's Queries respecting Slavery, with Doctor Belknap's Answers,'' *Mass. Hist. Colls.* (1795) ser. i, vol. iv, pp. 191-211, p. 206.

[66] ''A Description of Mashpee in the County of Barnstable. September 16th, 1802,'' *Mass. Hist. Colls.* (1815) ser. ii, vol. iii, pp. 4-5.

year there were one hundred and forty-two at Gayhead, of whom only nine men and a somewhat larger number of women were of the pure Indian blood. "The rest," it was reported, "are intermixed, chiefly with negroes: the mixed race is better than the pure Indians."[67]

Two years later it was said that of the 400 Indians at Mashpee twenty or less were pure, the rest being mixed with Negroes, or with Hessians from Burgoyne's army, who had settled in the community. This observer also repeated the almost unanimous verdict that the mixed race was an improvement.[68] There was probably some error in his estimate of the extent of intermixture, however, for in 1820, when the population of Mashpee had declined to 320, the local missionary thought that fifty or sixty of that number were *"pure-blooded* Indians." In his opinion, "the mixture of blood arises far more frequently from connexion with *negroes,* than with *whites."*

In 1820 there were twenty-two Negroes among the 429 Narragansetts of Rhode Island: "the rest are of Indian extraction, but are nearly all, if not every individual, of mixed blood and color, in various degrees and shades."[69] In 1832 the Groton Pequots of Connecticut were considerably mixed with Negro and white blood and by 1849 the Paugussets or Weponaugs of the same state also had a large proportion of Negro blood. The remnants of both these tribes were in a degraded state,[70] in contrast with the favorable opinion expressed earlier in the century concerning the Negro-Indians of Massachusetts. In 1890 the Gay Head Indians were still described as being of a high type, despite or because of their "admixture of negro and white blood,"[71] whereas it is

[67] "A Description of Duke's Country, Aug. 13th, 1807," *Mass. Hist. Colls.* (1815) ser. ii, vol. iii, pp. 93-94.

[68] Kendall, *op. cit.,* vol. ii, pp. 179, 193-194.

[69] Morse, Jedidiah, *A Report to the Secretary of War on Indian Affairs* (New Haven, 1822) rep. 24, app. 69-70, 73.

[70] De Forest, John William, *History of the Indians of Connecticut* (Hartford, 1853) pp. 356-357, 443, 445.

[71] Clark, William B., "The Geological Features of Gay Head, Mass." *Johns Hopkins University Circulars* (1890) no. 84, p. 28.

claimed that in Mashpee there had been a steady process of deterioration, intensified about 1870 by the addition to the community of *bravas,* or black Portuguese from the Cape Verde Islands, brought to New Bedford on whaling vessels.[72]

In 1890 N. S. Shaler expressed the opinion that "any descendants of the blacks who were there [in New England] in the last century . . . have become co-mingled with the remnants of the Indians of Gay Head and Mashpee."[73] Of course, persons of Negro-Indian descent, while they might be classed as Indians so long as they remained a part of what was technically an Indian community, became Negroes as soon as that contact was lost. Thus the result of Negro-Indian intermixture in New England has been to Africanize those few descendants of the aboriginal inhabitants who still cling at least to the tradition of Indian blood and at the same time to divert a stream of Indian blood into the veins of the Negro population of that region.

In other states the result was similar. In 1889 the 150 Shinnacook Indians living on the southern shore of Long Island were "nearly all mixed with Negro blood, dating back from the times of slavery in the northern states."[74] In the same year the Montauk Indians, also of Long Island, represented a similar mixture.[75] In 1872 it was said that "there are no full-blooded aborigines on the Eastern Shore [of Maryland], although many of the free-born negroes show Indian traces."[76] In 1724, Hugh Jones, speaking of the Virginia Indians, declared: "They hate, and despise the very sight of a *Negroe,*" but a little later nevertheless found it

[72] Kittredge, Henry C., *Cape Cod* (Boston and N.Y., 1930) pp. 49-51.

[73] Shaler, N. S., "The African Element in America," *The Arena* (1890) vol. ii, pp. 660-673, p. 666; Shaler, N. S., "Science and the African Problem," *Atlantic Monthly* (1890) vol. lxvi, pp. 36-45, p. 40.

[74] Gatschet, Albert S., "Linguistic and Ethnographic Notes," *Am. Antiq. and Orient. Journ.* (1889) vol. xi, p. 390.

[75] Tooker, William Wallace, "Indian Place-Names in East-Hampton Town, with their Probable Significations," *Records of the Town of East-Hampton,* 5 vols. (Sag Harbor, 1889) vol. iv, pp. i-ix, p.iv.

[76] Townsend, G. A., *Scribner's Monthly* (1872) vol. iii, pp. 513-524, pp. 518-519.

necessary to add, without further explanation: "Such as are born of an *Indian* and *Negroe* are called *Mustees*."[77] About 1750 Peter Kalm, after mentioning that at first the Virginia Indians thought the Negroes were devils, went on to say that "since that time, they have entertained less disagreeable notions of the Negroes, for at present many live among them, and they even sometimes intermarry, as I myself have seen."[78]

The Negroes referred to were doubtless freed slaves. In Virginia the results of this intercourse were similar to those which ensued under similar conditions in Massachusetts. Thomas Jefferson noted that the remnants of the Mattaponies had "more Negro than Indian blood in them."[79] Free Negroes resorted to the Indian reservations in such numbers that by 1787 the population of the Gingaskin reservation was asserted to be nearly all black. The same was said in 1821 of the reservation of the Nottaways and in 1843 concerning that of the Pamunkeys. Other mustees mingled with the general population as free people of color.[80] A recent writer on the Negro casually mentions a number of modern instances of Negroes from Virginia who were of Cherokee blood.[81] "As the coast tribes dwindled they were compelled to associate and intermarry with Negroes until they finally lost their identity and were classified with that race, so that a considerable proportion of the blood of the southern Negroes is unquestionably Indian."[82]

Another result of the relations between Negroes and Indians was the establishment of communities, populated by people of mingled Negro, Indian, and white blood, who neither classed themselves nor were classed by their neigh-

[77] Jones, *op. cit.*, pp. 4, 37.

[78] Kalm, *op. cit.*, vol. i, pp. 395-396.

[79] *Jefferson, Thomas, The Works of*, Paul Leicester Ford, ed., 12 vols. (N.Y. and London, 1904) "Notes on Virginia," vol. iii, pp. 497-498.

[80] Russell, *op. cit.*, pp. 127-130.

[81] Embree, E. R., "A Few Portraits in Sepia," *Atlantic Monthly*, October, 1931.

[82] *Nineteenth Annual Report of the Bureau of American Ethnology, 1897-98*, pt. i, p. 233.

bors as belonging to either of these three races; who mingled freely with none of them, and who consequently were forced to lead rather isolated lives, with a natural resultant tendency toward stagnation if not actual degeneration. These communities are found principally in the South, because here the caste and racial lines were most strictly drawn. A half-breed of mingled Indian, Negro, and white blood, who had no tribal affiliations to give him prestige, was nevertheless inclined to regard himself as superior to the Negro, but at the same time realized that he would not be welcomed by the whites. The Negroes, on the other hand, especially if the slaves of a prominent planter, looked down in their turn on the man with no master and no definite race.

The natural result was to force these mixed-bloods into the mountains, where they established communities populated by their own kind and by such vagabond whites, runaway slaves, and freed Negroes as were not too fastidious to resort thereto and were acceptable to the original inhabitants. An interesting sociological study of such a group, located in the foothills of the Blue Ridge, was recently made. This community was apparently founded by wandering Indians who settled in that region just after the Revolutionary war and intermarried with the lower class of whites. Some of their descendants mated illegitimately both with Negro slaves and with free Negroes. Later they married principally within their own group. As a result of this inbreeding among persons not originally of a high type, the members of the community are inclined to be of low mentality, uneducated and sexually loose, but in many cases not unindustrious and usually neither diseased nor alcoholic. Other similar groups are to be found in New Jersey,[83] Delaware, Maryland, Virginia, North Carolina, South Carolina, and Tennessee.[84]

[83] *Boston Herald,* March 8, 1932, p. 10, col. 5, near bottom.

[84] Estabrook, Arthur H., and McDougle, Ivan E., *Mongrel Virginians: The Win Tribe* (Baltimore, 1926) pp. 18-19, 182-197. *Po'buckra,* by Mrs. Gertrude Mathews Shelby and Samuel Gaillard Stoney, published in 1930, has as its central figure a member of one of these Indian-white-Negro communities of the South.

One of the best known of these groups is the "Melungeons," inhabiting the upper counties of Eastern Tennessee, particularly Hancock County. The founders of this group came from North Carolina near the end of the eighteenth century, claiming to be Portuguese or, sometimes, Portuguese and Cherokee. They were popularly regarded as a mixture of white, Indian, and Negro, based upon an original foundation of Cherokees who had mingled with runaway slaves. Those who looked with a sympathetic eye upon their claim to Portuguese origin thought that Portuguese pirates might have been wrecked or marooned upon the North Carolina coast and there mixed with Negroes and natives. One investigator claims that the community was founded by two North Carolina Indians (who some think were of the Croatan tribe) and was later joined at various times by an English fur trader, a Negro, and a Portuguese, the last, some believe, being actually a West Indian maroon who, with others, had been set ashore from a Portuguese pirate vessel for insubordination. From these four lines, which intermarried with one another, the "Melungeon" (melangés) community descended, and a tradition developed of non-intercourse with outsiders. In 1834 the Melungeons were disfranchised as "free persons of color," but it is said that some of them succeeded in proving their right to vote by demonstrating that their feet possessed a non-negroid arch. As "free persons of color," emancipation put them upon a level with the newly-freed slaves and after the Civil War intermarriage both with Negroes and whites began upon a considerable scale, though strongly disapproved by the older generation.[35]

A group much larger in numbers and of a correspondingly superior type is the so-called Croatan Indians of North Carolina, numbering about 10,000; 3000 living in South Carolina were formerly known as "Redbones." The members of this community were in 1835 declared "free persons of

[35] Burnett, Swan M., "A Note on the Melungeons," *American Anthropologist* (1889) vol. ii, pp. 347-349; Dromgoole, Will Allen, "The Malungeons" and "The Malungeon Tree and Its Four Branches," *The Arena* (1891) vol. iii, pp. 470-479, 745-751.

color," which procedure doubtless speeded up the intermixture with Negroes which apparently had already begun. But nearly half a century later Hamilton McMillan became convinced, upon what would seem to be at least very tempting evidence, that the lineal descendants of Sir Walter Raleigh's lost colony of Roanoke were to be found among the Croatan Indians, with whose ancestors of the late sixteenth century he believed the colonists had sought refuge. Accordingly, in 1885, though "found of all colors from black to white," they were recognized as "Croatan Indians" by an act of the legislature, given separate schools, and forbidden to intermarry with Negroes,[86] that the blood of the Elizabethan settlers might be no further contaminated!—a remarkable example of changing race by legislative enactment.[87]

It will thus be observed that through the contacts in the northern colonies and states and those of the Upper South between the natives and the Negroes, as fellow slaves, through the escape of Negroes to the Indians, but most conspicuously through the resort of free Negroes to Indian reservations which became literally melting pots for racial fusion, the remnants of the coast tribes disappeared into or were strongly affected by the Negro population, which in turn received a significant infusion of Indian blood. Less important was the formation of mixed-blood communities, unconnected with any tribal reservation, and isolated to a greater or lesser degree from all three of the races whose blood mingled in the veins of the inhabitants.[88]

[86] Estabrook and McDougle, *op. cit.*, p. 192; Weeks, Stephen B., "The Lost Colony of Roanoke," *Papers of the American Historical Association* (1891) vol. v, pp. 441-480.

[87] For a dramatic treatment of the Croatan Indians about the year 1873, see Paul Green's "The Last of the Lowries," *Carolina Folk-Plays*, F. H. Koch, ed. (N.Y., 1922). "A Play of the Croatan Outlaws of Robeson County, North Carolina."

[88] For a careful study of the intermixture of Negroes and Indians in a single state, see Carter G. Woodson's "The Relations of Negroes and Indians in Massachusetts," *Journal of Negro History* (1920) vol. v, pp. 45-57; for a more general and very suggestive survey of the same problem consult James Hugo Johnston's "Documentary Evidence of the Relations of Negroes and Indians," *Journal of Negro History* (1929) vol. xiv, pp. 21-43. Edward Byron

Those persons of African descent more or less mingled with the blood of the whites, who, now amounting to some 12,000,000 in the United States, regard themselves and are regarded by others as Negroes, Afro-Americans, colored people, or whatever term you find preferable, have, during the last century and a half and particularly since the Civil War, produced a significant array of distinguished orators, musicians, artists, scientists, literary men, educators, and publicists. During a somewhat longer period the American Indian has produced comparatively few men of distinction, the full-bloods usually being known only as warriors while the half-breeds sometimes find a place in political activities as well.

What has been the contribution of the Negro-Indian mixture to the roll of men who have found a place, large or small, in American history? Considering their small numbers, their record is not one of which to be ashamed. Probably the first of the group to attain fame or notoriety was the "first martyr to American liberty," Crispus Attucks, the mob leader who was killed in the Boston massacre. He is usually described as a mulatto, but it seems probable that he was a Natick Indian from Framingham who was also of Negro blood.[89] The circumstances of his death thus take on a peculiar quality of poetic irony.

Of perhaps more real distinction was Paul Cuffe, ship owner and navigator, born in 1759 on Cuttyhunk, his father being a native of Africa while his mother, Ruth Moses, was an Indian. Paul Cuffe was a leader in the movement which resulted in Negroes receiving in 1783 legal rights and privileges in Massachusetts. In the same year he married "a young Indian woman, Alice Pequit." Others in the Cuffe

---

Reuter's *Race Mixture*, pp. 48-49, and *The American Race Problem*, pp. 122-124, neatly sum up the ways in which the two races became intermingled, and are particularly effective in synopsizing the part which the Indian reservations and the "wasted Indian tribes" played in the process.

[89] Fisher, J. B., "Who Was Crispus Attucks?" *American Historical Record* (1872) vol. i, pp. 531-533; Kidder, Frederick, *History of the Boston Massacre* (Albany, 1870) p. 29, note 3.

family also married Indians. Cuffe became a Quaker in 1808 and was an advocate of Negro emigration to Africa in the midst of his activities for which cause he died in 1817.[90]

Probably the most distinguished man of Negro and Indian blood which this country has yet produced was Frederick Douglass, who "was born at Tuckahoe near Easton, Talbot County, Md. (February, 1817), the son of an unknown white father and Harriet Bailey, a slave who had also some Indian blood."[91] Some other Negroes of Indian blood have won distinction more purely in the literary field. Ann Plato, who published in 1841 at Hartford, Connecticut, a slim volume of essays and poetry which was exceedingly depressing, both from the literary point of view and from the character of the subject matter, may be regarded as a fore-runner of this group, but can hardly lay claim to a place in their number. Though classed as a Negro, her poem "The Natives of America" seems to indicate that her father was of Indian blood.[92] Of an entirely different character was the work of the poets Joseph Seamon Cotter, Sr., and James David Corrothers, born respectively in Kentucky in 1861 and in Michigan in 1869. Both were complicated mixtures of Negro, Indian, and Scotch-Irish blood, to which Cotter added a strain of English and Corrothers one of French. Cotter's son and namesake before his premature death likewise gave evidence of poetic gifts.[93]

[90] Ricketson, Daniel, *History of New Bedford* (New Bedford, 1858) pp. 253-262; Sherwood, Henry Noble, "Paul Cuffe," *Journal of Negro History* (1923); Brawley, Benjamin, "Paul Cuffe," *Dictionary of American Biography*, vol. v., p. 583. For a very romantic account of Paul Cuffe and his father Sam Cuffe (Said Kafu), see *The Pedro Gorino* (Boston and N.Y., 1929), written by Captain Harry Dean, who claims to be Paul Cuffe's great-grandson, with the assistance of Sterling North. Captain Dean has nothing to say of any Indian element in his ancestry, and asserts that Paul Cuffe's program for African colonization included raids on sea-board plantations, from which those slaves desiring freedom were to be conveyed to Africa.

[91] DuBois, W. E. B., "Frederick Douglass," *Dict of Am. Biog.*, vol. v, pp. 406-407.

[92] Loggins, Vernon, *The Negro Author* (N.Y., 1931) p. 248; Plato, Ann, *Essays* (Hartford, 1841) p. 110.

[93] White, Newman Ivy, and Jackson, Walter Clinton, *An Anthology of*

Other Negroes with Indian blood, of lesser note, might be mentioned, known only among their own race, while still others made significant contributions within their own communities to the progress of their people: Cyrus Bustill, the Philadelphia baker, born in 1732 at Burlington, N.J., married a Delaware Indian and had a son who, like Paul Cuffe, was a Quaker, and who took a prominent part in anti-slavery agitation; the Sampsons and Gallees, property owners and school teachers, though predominantly of Indian blood were leaders among the free Negroes of Petersburg, Virginia, in 1860.[94] Two from the community of the so-called Croatan Indians attained to secure historical niches of varying prominence. Lewis Sheridan Leary, who was killed in John Brown's raid on Harper's Ferry, was a Croatan Indian who also possessed Irish and Negro blood. Hiram R. Revels, the first man of African race to sit in the United States Senate, and usually spoken of as a quadroon, was a Croatan Indian who had moved to Mississippi.[95] These few examples possibly indicate that the Negro-Indian mixture has not altogether failed to justify the favorable expressions of those who observed it soon after emancipation in Massachusetts.

Verse by American Negroes (Durham, N.C., 1924) pp. 146, 163; "James David Corrothers," *Dictionary of American Biography*, vol. iv, p. 452.

[94] "Hershaw," *The Crisis*, November, 1931, p. 375; Jackson, L. P., "Free Negroes of Petersburg, Virginia," *Journal of Negro History* (1927) vol. xii, pp. 365-388, 380-381; Smith, Anna Bustill, "The Bustill Family," *Journal of Negro History* (1925) vol. x, pp. 638-644; Boris, Joseph J., ed., *Who's Who in Colored America, 1928-29* (N.Y., 1929) pp. 265, 310, 386.

[95] Weeks, *loc. cit.*

Chapter IV

RELATIONS IN THE SOUTH

The various native peoples whom the white settlers encountered in North America were by no means all on the same cultural level. Among the most advanced were certain tribes to the south and west of the southern colonies, the Cherokees, Chickasaws, Choctaws, and Creeks, from which last tribe the Seminoles were a secession. All these tribes, as well as others of less note, leavened by intermarriage with white traders, mostly Scotch, took with enthusiasm to many institutions of civilized life, and particularly to Negro slavery. Slavery among the Indians was known in South Carolina at least as early as 1748.[96] The Five Civilized Tribes, as they came to be called, became large slaveholders for the same reason as their white neighbors, while the more northerly tribes abstained for the same sort of reason. Slavery took various forms among the different tribes and with individual members of the same tribe. A careful observer traced the variation as follows: "The full-blood Indian rarely works for himself and but few of them make their slaves work. A slave among wild Indians is almost as free as his owner, who scarcely exercises the authority of a master beyond requiring something like a tax paid in corn or other product of labor. Proceeding from this condition, more service is required from the slave until among the half-breeds and the whites who have married natives, they become slaves indeed in all manner of work." Even some full-bloods were finally inspired to follow the example of the whites in this respect.[97]

The Cherokees are usually regarded as the most advanced of the Five Tribes. In 1809 there were 12,395 Cherokees with 583 slaves;[98] in 1824 the citizens of the Cherokee Nation num-

[96] Furman, McDonald, "Negro Slavery among the South Carolina Indians," *Am. Antiq. and Orient. Journ.* (1890) vol. xii, p. 177.

[97] Hitchcock, Ethan Allen, *A Traveler in Indian Territory*, Grant Foreman, ed. (Cedar Rapids, Ia., 1930). This journey was made in 1841-42 by an army officer who had also been acquainted with the Indians before their removal across the Mississippi.

[98] Morse, *op. cit.*, app. 152.

bered 15,560 and were the owners of 1277 Negroes.[99] A traveler of 1820 among those Cherokees who had already removed to the Arkansas observed: "The Cherokees are said to treat their slaves with much lenity."[100] However, when the Cherokees adopted the institution of slavery they took it over as a whole, and consequently there was little or no intermixture of Negro blood to be found among the members of the tribe, though doubtless there were illicit relations between masters and slaves as among white slaveholders.

The Chickasaws and Choctaws possessed a cultural standing only inferior to that of the Cherokees. About 1820 it was said: "Some of the [Chickasaw] Chiefs are half-breed, men of sense, possess numerous negro slaves, and annually sell several hundred cattle and hogs."[101] In 1861 these two tribes together numbered 25,000 with 5000 slaves.[102] Unfortunately, in regard to their treatment of their slaves, the Chickasaws at least suffered in comparison with the Cherokees. Most of the instances which we encounter of cruelty to Negroes by Indians seem to have been committed by Chickasaws. For example, in 1816 the Chickasaws are noted as having murdered several Negroes, in some cases because they did not like the owners; in others the master put his own slave to death by whipping and burning.[103] The Choctaws and Chickasaws were both, even more than the Cherokees, great sticklers for racial purity.[104]

[99] Hitchcock, *op. cit.*, p. 57.

[100] Long, Major S. H., *Account of an Expedition from Pittsburgh to the Rocky Mountains*, 2 vols. (Philadelphia, 1823) vol. ii, p. 267.

[101] Morse, *op. cit.*, app. 201.

[102] *Smithsonian Report* (1885) pt. ii, p. 214.

[103] *American State Papers, Indian Affairs*, vol. ii, p. 107. It is of some significance in this connection that the two narratives of contact between Indian and Negro among the slave-holding Indians, included in William Faulkner's *These Thirteen* (N.Y., 1931), the ghastly "Red Leaves," and the grimly humorous "A Justice," are supposed to have taken place among the Choctaws. They should, however, be considered in relation to the other stories in the volume, in order that due allowance may be made for the apparent abnormality of nearly all Faulkner's leading characters.

[104] Frederick Law Olmsted found Choctaw Indians in Louisiana working side by side with Negro slaves, "hired for farm labour at three bits (37½

The Creeks, who because of their lack of race prejudice, are usually regarded as somewhat lower in the scale of civilization than the three tribes previously mentioned, had an entirely different attitude toward their Negroes. Their idea of slavery was patriarchal, and like Abraham and Jacob they took slave women for their handmaids and brought up the children they had by them on a practical equality with their full-blooded offspring. One of the leading Creek chiefs, Tustennuggee Emarthla or Jim Boy, was "a colored mixed."[105] Nevertheless, some of the Creeks engaged in agriculture on a large scale and George Catlin said: "It is no uncommon thing to see a Creek with twenty or thirty slaves at work on his plantation" on the south side of the Arkansas.[106]

In no other tribe was the Negro's position higher than among the Seminoles. As early as 1738 slaves had made a practice of escaping from South Carolina and taking refuge among the Creeks of Georgia and the Spanish of Florida.[107] They always received a welcome, and the Spanish in particular were glad to have buffer settlements of friendly Negroes and Indians along their northern border. In 1739, for example, Colonel Palmer of Oglethorpe's forces was defeated near St. Augustine by a Spanish company of 500 men, among whom were many Negroes and Indians.[108] About 1750, internal dissensions in the Creek tribe led a part of its members to secede and move into Spanish territory, from which action they received the title of Seminoles or "runaways." They settled in close proximity to other "runaways" of the

---

cents) a day." He also encountered a Choctaw boy who worked at a corn mill, "getting no wages, but 'living there with the niggers.' They seldom consort;" Olmsted was informed, "our host knew but one case in which a negro had an Indian wife." Nothing was said about the number of Indian men who "consorted" with Negro women. (Olmsted, Frederick Law, *The Cotton Kingdom*, 2 vols. (N.Y., 1862) vol. ii, p. 38.)

[105] Hitchcock, *op. cit.*, pp. 151-152.

[106] *Smithsonian* Report (1885) pt. ii, p. 211.

[107] Giddings, Joshua Reed, *The exiles of Florida* (Columbus, 1858) p. 2; Wilson, Henry, *History of the Rise and Fall of the Slave Power in America*, 3 vols. (Boston, 1872) vol. i, p. 124.

[108] *Journal of Negro History* (1927) vol. xii, p. 664.

Negro race, with whom these Creek seceders were not slow in striking up friendly relations.[109]

It is difficult, almost impossible, to arrive at any very definite idea of the number of slaves among the Seminoles, this uncertainty being the result of the number of vaguely defined categories into which the Negroes living among them could be separated. Roughly, these Negroes could be divided into legal slaves of the Seminoles, acquired by purchase or capture from the English or Spanish; and their allies, runaway slaves or their descendants, who were sometimes called maroons from the Spanish term for a runaway slave who has made good his freedom, though this title was also applied, improperly, to the slaves of the Indians. In 1820, for example, mention was made of "fifty or sixty negroes, or mulattoes, who are maroons, or half-slaves to the Indians," but later on there was a reference to the "maroon negroes, who live among the Indians" and who were said to number "upwards of three hundred." This probably referred only to one such community of Negroes, since another estimate made at the same time spoke of "five or six hundred maroon negroes, or mulattoes, who live wild in the woods or in a state of half slavery among the Indians."[110] In 1822 another estimate fixed the number of Seminoles at 3899, to which were added 800 slaves, of whom 150 were men.[111] It is probable that the "slaves" contained in this estimate included a great many of the maroons.

The "maroons" among the Seminoles fell into two classifications, those who had escaped but recently and who were consequently almost certain to be reclaimed by their masters should they come within reach of the white authorities, and those who had been born among the Seminoles and who thus, though legally the slaves of those from whom their parents had fled, or of their heirs, were not in such great danger of having a claim made to their persons. Other maroons, whose freedom was of such long standing that it would

[109] Giddings, *op. cit.*, p. 3.
[110] Morse, *op. cit.*, app. 149-150, 311.
[111] Sprague, John T., *The Florida War* (N.Y., 1848) p. 19.

have been difficult for their erstwhile masters to identify them with any certainty, might be classed with this last group. To state that there were only fifty or sixty slaves among the Seminoles in 1820 was probably a grave underestimate. In 1817 it was said that there were 600 Negroes under arms in the Seminole towns, but this, though it doubtless referred both to slaves and maroons, was probably an equally great exaggeration.[112] The estimate that in 1836 there were 1400 Negroes among the Seminoles, of whom 200 were slaves, is probably somewhere near the truth.[113]

The difficulty of distinguishing a maroon from a slave can be explained by the extraordinarily liberal form which slavery took among the Seminoles, which caused every observer who came into contact with it to regard its peculiar characteristic as worthy of being recorded. "These [Seminole] Indians," it was said in 1820, "have negro slaves, who live in separate families; of from five to ten in a family. They raise corn for their subsistence; if they have a surplus it goes to the families of their masters."[114] But a later report considerably modified the last statement. In 1834 it was said "[The slaves of the Seminoles] live in villages separate, and, in many cases, remote from their owners, and enjoying equal liberty with their owners, with the single exception that the slave supplies his owner annually, from the product of his little field, with corn, in proportion to the amount of the crop; and in no case that has come to my knowledge, exceeding ten bushels; the residue is considered the property of the slave. Many of these slaves have stocks of horses, cows, and hogs, with which the Indian owner never assumes the right to intermeddle."[115] Other observers still more strongly emphasized the idyllic character of slavery among the Seminoles.[116]

Not all Seminole slaves, however, led such an unrestricted

---

[112] *American State Papers, Indian Affairs*, vol. ii, p. 155.

[113] Giddings, *op. cit.*, p. 97.

[114] Morse, *op. cit.*, app. 309.

[115] *American State Papers, Military Affairs*, vol. vi, pp. 533-534.

[116] Williams, John Lee, *The Territory of Florida* (N.Y., 1837) p. 240; Kennedy, William, *Texas, Its Rise, Progress, and Prospects*, 2 vols. (London, 1841) vol. i, p. 350.

life. In 1836 the head chief Micanopy "owned one hundred negroes . . . and was raising large and valuable crops of corn and cotton," though since he was noted for his kindness to his slaves it is unlikely that even their life was an onerous one.[117] It is easy to see how it would be difficult to distinguish between a settlement of runaway slaves or maroons, raising a crop entirely for their own benefit, and a settlement of slaves, raising a crop from which an almost nominal payment was due to their owner. Indeed, in many ways the slaves were more advantageously situated than the maroons, for the former had masters who would act as their patrons in case any attempt was made to return them to the rigorous servitude of plantation life, whereas the latter were left much more to their own resources.

But this was not all. Not only were the Seminole slaves not slaves in the usual sense of the word; they might even lay claim to being the true rulers of the nation. Some had been purchased from the Spanish; others had originally belonged to the English. They thus had a better knowledge of the white man and of his customs than did their masters, and were indispensable as go-betweens and interpreters whenever an occasion arose for negotiations between their old masters and their new. The greater freedom they were given among the Seminoles stimulated their intelligence so that it was noted as being distinctly superior to that of the slaves among the whites, and they lost no opportunity to advance the interests of their masters, which they rightly recognized as being identical with their own. Their agricultural skill gave them an economic advantage over the Seminoles, and as a consequence of their importance in all these relations they were accepted as the equals of their masters both in war and in council, and the most prominent persons of the nation did not think it beneath their dignity to form matrimonial alliances with these black Mamelukes. One runaway slave, who had later become a slave to the Seminoles but had been freed, married the widow of the principal chief of the

[117] Williams, *op. cit.*, p. 214; *Smithsonian Report* (1885) pt. ii, p. 214.

nation; of the two wives of the head chief of Micanopy, one was a half-breed Negro woman. The maroons and runaways, who, through a process of natural selection, had come to represent a high degree of intelligence and courage, likewise had great influence, both directly and through the slaves, over their protectors the Seminoles.[118]

Before the Civil War opinions differed as to the benefits or disadvantages conferred upon the Indians through the possession of slaves. One author, just before the outbreak of war, ascribed all progress among the Indians to the beneficent influence of slavery;[119] another, nearly a score of years earlier, had said: "The possession of Negroes, by rendering the Indians idle and dependent on slave-labour, has confirmed the defects of their character."[120] Probably the immediate effect was an improvement in the condition of the Indian, which was later checked by the feeling of dependence noted above. But whatever the effect upon the Indian, one can hardly doubt that among the Seminoles at least, slavery was a distinct advantage to the Negro.

It was natural that the presence on contiguous but foreign territory of a tribe of Indians in which the slaves and runaway Negroes exerted such a peculiar influence should rouse the jealousy and enmity of the slave-holding whites within the borders of the United States. The inevitable clash, however, was complicated with matters unconnected with slavery. It seems rather a far cry from Tecumseh's plan for a confederation of Indian tribes to resist the white encroachments to a war over runaway slaves on the borders of Florida, but such a connection, nevertheless, can be traced. Although Tecumseh was a member of the Shawnee tribe, one of his parents was a Creek, and to this tribe he made an ap-

[118] *American State Papers, Military Affairs,* vol. vi, pp. 454, 458, 464; Morse, *op. cit.,* app. 149-150, 310, 311; *Williams, op. cit.,* p. 214; *Smithsonian Report* (1885) pt. ii, p. 214; Cohen, M. M., *Notice of Florida* (Charleston, 1836) p. 238; *Executive Documents,* 25th Cong., 2nd sess., 1837-38, vol. iii, no. 78, p. 118.

[119] "Slavery Among the Indians," *Southern Literary Messenger* (1859) vol. xxviii, pp. 333-335.

[120] Kennedy, *op. cit.,* vol. i, p. 350.

peal for assistance which at first seemed to have no effect. But the outbreak of the War of 1812 gave encouragement to that party among the Creeks who were most hostile to the whites, and these, sometimes led on by half-breeds, took the war path under the name of the Red Sticks.

There were many slaves among the Creeks, some sixty or seventy of whom had been captured or had deserted from citizens of Georgia from the end of the Revolution to 1790, in which year a treaty had been made in which the Creeks promised to return all prisoners, including Negroes. However, late in 1794, this had not yet been done and the Creek agent asserted that it could not be done and that the United States should no longer insist on the fulfillment of this provision but should instead compensate the owners of the captured slaves.[121] There were thus among the Creeks a number of Negroes who were legally the slaves of white planters, and who, in view of the comparatively mild character of slavery among this tribe, were probably anxious to continue in their present situation. Negroes played a part in the Red Stick war which, though small, was nevertheless significant for the future. In the first clash of the Creek War, the Battle of Burnt Corn, the Red Sticks were led by the half-breed Peter McQueen. Of the Red Stick forces five Indians and one Negro were killed. The Negro was doubtless one of McQueen's slaves, a detachment of whom he had probably armed and brought along as "household troops," but the presence of a Negro among the Red Stick casualties is nonetheless significant as indicating the *rapprochement* which was taking place between the two races.

Fort Mimms in Alabama near the northwest corner of Florida had become a haven of refuge for hundreds of refugees, white and half-breed planters with their families and slaves who had flocked in from the surrounding country. Late in August a couple of Negroes hunting cattle had returned to the fort to report that Red Sticks were in the vicinity, but a scouting party of whites failed to confirm their statement

[121] *American State Papers, Indian Affairs,* vol. i, pp. 81-82, 546.

and one of the slaves was actually whipped for attempting to
cause a false alarm. Other Negroes similarly engaged were
captured by the hostiles and, perhaps, under compulsion,
gave their captors valuable information concerning the situation at the fort. On August 30, 1813, a surprise attack on the
fort was almost immediately successful. We are told that
"Siras, a negro man, cut down the pickets," but whether this
partisan of the Red Sticks was a Creek slave or a treacherous
Negro in the fort is not revealed. Nearly five hundred half-
breeds and whites—of whom the former were hated with
peculiar bitterness by the hostiles—were killed in the massacre that followed the capture of the fort, the only occupants of which to escape were a few whites who fled into the
swamp, and the Negro slaves.

These bondmen may have been preserved purely for an
economic reason, but the account of a Negro who was in
Mimms's house at the time seems to indicate that there may
have been something more behind this policy. "Come out,"
was the command addressed to him by a Red Stick, "the Master of Breath has ordered us not to kill any but white people
and half-breeds." This was at least placing the exemption of
the Negroes from the general slaughter upon a high plane of
authority. The Negro who gave this information had been
captured by friendly Creeks. It was reported from another
source that the Creek war party had later killed several of
their Negro captives, but this may have been an error, or
perhaps some of the prisoners, to whom a life among the hostiles did not appeal, had unwisely endeavored to escape. At
any rate the danger of such a fate did not seem to disconcert
the Negro from whom the story of the massacre at Fort
Mimms had been obtained, for he, who had the advantage
of being able to speak the Creek tongue, soon contrived to
escape and presumably returned to the hostiles.[122]

[122] *Ibid.*, pp. 851, 853, 855. After the Battle of Burnt Corn, McQueen is
said to have called at the home of a white enemy and, on finding the owner
absent, to have beaten one of his Negroes "almost to death." Robert W.
Chambers has given a graphic fictional account of the massacre at Fort
Mimms, but he largely disregards the racial aspects of this episode. Speaking

Andrew Jackson crushed the Red Stick power in March, 1814, at the battle of Horseshoe Bend, but two or three months later a statement was made which revealed that the Negroes were taking their place beside the Indians as a menace to the settlers of the Deep South. This report was to the effect that the British obviously intended to "revive the Creek war . . . and to place arms into the hands of the blacks."[123] The war, however, was not renewed immediately, although a faction of the Creeks declined to accept the treaty which concluded the war and fled to their kinsmen in Florida. These presented a constant menace to the frontier, but it was the episode of the Negro Fort which really brought on and colored the entire character of what is known as the First Seminole War. During the War of 1812 the British had built a fort on the eastern side of the Appalachicola River for the use of themselves and their Indian allies. When the war ended the fort was deserted but not dismantled, and in it was left a complete assortment of arms and ammunition, including a battery of half-a-dozen cannon. The runaway Negroes promptly took advantage of this gift of the gods by moving in and making the fort their headquarters; by the summer of 1816 "their fields extended fifty miles up the river" and they are also alleged to have used the place as a basis of operations for plundering expeditions into the territory of the United States. It is certain that the fort became a beacon light to restless slaves of the Georgia and Alabama planters, who flocked to the protection of its sturdy ramparts until its garrison consisted of 300 Negroes under their leader Garçon, with whom were allied a score of "renegade Choctaws." Since this center of disaffection was on Spanish territory the United States authorities could do nothing directly, but it seems clear that the military and naval officers of that region awaited only a reasonable excuse to put an end to the

---

through the mouth of his principal character, he refers loosely to "quadroons" and "maroons," apparently without any very clear idea of what meaning he intends to convey by these terms. (Chambers, Robert W., *The Rake and the Hussy*, N.Y. and London, 1930, pp. 194, 205-234, esp. 230 and 232.)

[123] *American State Papers, Indian Affairs*, vol. i, p. 859.

menace. The Negroes and their Indian allies, on the other
hand, seem to have had an altogether too elevated idea of
their own importance and were apparently spoiling for a
fight. Thus the inevitable clash came somewhat earlier than
might have been the case had it not been for this mutual desire for a trial of strength.

In order to supply the forts on United States soil on the
Appalachicola it was necessary for the vessels to pass beneath the guns of the Negro Fort. The temptation was too
great for the runaways to resist. On July 17, 1816, a boat's
crew from a gunboat was ambushed by about forty Indians
and Negroes and all but one killed or captured. The officer in
charge sent out a reconnoitering party which fell in with a
band of friendly Creeks, who claimed that they themselves
had as their intention the capture of the fort and the return
of the Negroes to their rightful owners. Since their force was
in no way adequate for this purpose their statement may be
doubted. However, the Americans accepted them as allies
and, pushing on, they captured a Negro with a white man's
scalp at his belt. Convinced that the inhabitants of the Negro
Fort were the guilty parties, the gun boat was sent for. When
it had been brought into position the friendly Indians called
on the garrison to deliver over the fort. The Negroes and
their allies contemptuously refused and hoisting "the English jack, accompanied with the red or bloody flag"—an item
which should certainly have been included in the Lusk Report
—opened a hot artillery fire upon the gun boat. The guns of
the latter were too light, it soon appeared, to make any impression upon the formidable bulwarks, so, after firing about
eight shots to get the range, some cannon balls were heated
red-hot in the galley with the intention of seeing what fire
could accomplish. By some freak of good or evil fortune the
very first of these new missiles entered the fort's magazine
and nearly the entire garrison were killed or mortally injured in the succeeding tremendous explosion. Garçon and
the Choctaw leader, on its being learned that one of the
prisoners from the boat's crew had been tarred and burned,

were delivered to the friendly Indians for execution and the few surviving Negroes were returned to their masters.[124]

Although at one stroke a large contingent of the fugitive Negroes had been eliminated from the situation, the rage which this catastrophe aroused in the breasts of the survivors may be imagined, and of it the Red Stick refugees took advantage. Early in 1817 it was reported that a British agent was stirring up the Seminoles and Negroes at the mouth of the Appalachicola and that there were 600 Negroes under arms in the Seminole towns with officers of their own choosing, drilling and parading under strict military discipline, accompanied by an equal number of Indians and being daily joined by others of both races.[125] Their boast was that if they encountered the whites "they would let them know they had something more to do than they had at Appalachicola." The peculiar character of slavery among the Creeks and Seminoles came out clearly in their military arrangements. Indians and Negroes apparently regarded one another as allies rather than members of a single community. They did not "act together in the performance of military duty . . . but they always said they would fight together." To an enquiry addressed to one well-acquainted with conditions among the hostile Negroes and Indians, "Did not Nero command the blacks, and did not Bowlegs [the Seminole war chief] own Nero; and was not the latter under the immediate command of Bowlegs?" the answer was given that "Nero commanded the blacks, and was owned and commanded by Bowlegs; but there were some negro captains who obeyed none but Nero."

It is not my intention to give a history of the First Seminole War but merely to indicate something of the relative parts played in it by the Indians and by the Negroes. Throughout the summer of 1817 the Negroes and Indians

[124] *American State Papers, Foreign Relations,* vol. iv, pp. 559-560; *State Papers,* 15th Cong., 2nd sess., vol. vi, nos. 119-122; Williams, *op. cit.,* pp. 202-203; McMaster, John Bach, *A History of the People of the United States,* 8 vols. (N.Y. and London, 1890-1913) vol. iv, pp. 430-434.

[125] *American State Papers, Indian Affairs,* vol. ii, p. 155.

were engaged in raiding and recruiting. The United States military authorities on the ground determined that the menace presented by an alliance between Indians and runaway slaves, established in such close proximity to slave-holding communities of the United States, must be abated, even though an invasion of the territory of a friendly power were thereby necessitated. General Gaines consequently wrote to the Seminole chiefs: "You harbor a great many of my black people among you at Sahwahnee. If you give me leave to go by you against them I shall not hurt any thing belonging to you."[126] The Indians, however, would not desert their black allies.

In November, 1817, the Red Sticks and Seminoles were said to amount to "more than two thousand, besides the blacks, amounting to near four hundred men, and increased by runaways from Georgia." Another more moderate estimate, made in the following month, reduced the number of hostiles to "between eight hundred and twelve hundred Indians and negroes, and increasing daily." Raids on white settlements, characterized by murder and the carrying off of Negroes, continued. Early in April, 1818, the Negroes and Indians appeared before the Spanish fort of St. Marks and bullied its commander into giving them arms and ammunition.

After a number of minor actions, however, on April 16, 1818, Andrew Jackson captured Bowleg's Town on the Suwanee River; nine Indians and seven Negroes were captured and nine Negroes and two Indians found dead after the action—a hint as to the relative numbers of the allied races engaged as well as to the determination with which they fought. It it claimed, indeed, that in the pursuit a number of the Negroes took advantage of the darkness to rally and make a stand. "They fought desperately, and did not give way until eighty out of three hundred and forty, were killed." The survivors retreated into the swamps whither the United States troops did not care to follow and "this savage and

[126] *American State Papers, Military Affairs,* vol. i, pp. 723, 727.

negro war," as Jackson called it, came to an actual if informal conclusion.[127] It seems clear that the war was almost entirely due to the position held by Negroes among the Seminoles, and that the invasion of Florida was almost as much a slave-hunting as it was a punitive expedition.

When in 1819 the sovereignty of Florida passed from Spain to the United States, the latter power acquired therewith the responsibility for solving the problem of the Seminoles and their Negro slaves and allies. The presence of the maroon Negroes was a matter requiring particular attention. In 1821 the Indian agent in Florida stated: "It will be difficult to form a prudent determination, with respect to the maroon negroes, who live among the Indians, on the other side of the little mountains of Latchioua. Their number is said to be upwards of three hundred. They fear being again made slaves, under the American government; and will omit nothing to increase or keep alive mistrust among the Indians, whom they in fact govern. If it should become necessary to use force with them, it is to be feared the Indians would take their part. It will, however, be necessary to remove from the Floridas this group of lawless freebooters, among whom runaway negroes will always find refuge. It would, perhaps, be possible to have them received at St. Domingo, or furnish them with the means of withdrawing from the United States."

It will be observed that this agent did not seem even to consider the possibility of re-enslaving these fugitives or descendants of fugitives, and indeed any Georgia or Florida planter who could sleep well of nights, knowing that among his slaves were one or more of these wild maroons, might well be regarded as brave even to fool-hardiness. This agent and others emphasized again and again the great influence exerted by both slaves and maroons "over the weak minds of the Indians."[128]

In 1823 the Seminoles signed a treaty at Fort Moultrie,

[127] *Ibid.*, vol. i, pp. 686, 689, 690-691, 700-701, 702; Williams, *op. cit.*, p. 206; McMaster, *op. cit.*, vol. iv, pp. 437-444.

[128] Morse, *op. cit.*, app. 149-150, 311.

promising to return all runaway slaves and other fugitives entering their territory. Early in 1826 they returned many runaways—who had perhaps been received too recently to have acquired standing in the tribe—but complained that in the meantime some of their own slaves had been seized by the whites while other attempts had with difficulty been thwarted. John Hicks, a leading Seminole chief, asserted that the whites would sell Negroes to the Indians and then claim them again.[129] The United States authorities were relieved when in 1832 some of the chiefs signed the treaty of Payne's Landing, in which the Seminoles agreed to move across the Mississippi and settle in the Indian Territory among their kinsmen the Creeks.[130] But this treaty was not the end but the beginning of real trouble with the Seminoles and the Negroes who dominated their councils. The other civilized tribes of the south were to remove at the same time, as some had done several years before. All withdrew reluctantly—the Cherokees in particular—but only the Seminoles put up a violent resistance. Indeed the seven years war which was necessary before their removal could be accomplished is usually ranked as the most serious Indian War in which the United States has ever engaged.

The presence and peculiar social position of Negroes among the Seminoles was the principal factor in their refusal to emigrate, as it was one of the reasons for the protracted character of the struggle, the other being the defensible nature of their country. The Seminoles naturally objected to leaving their own country and removing to a strange and far land, entirely unlike that to which they were accustomed; it is probable that in any case some would have refused to go. But it is unlikely that their resistance would have been so general, desperate, and prolonged had it not been for considerations connected with the Negroes among them. The treaty of Payne's Landing—which most of the Seminoles repudiated and which lead to the death of its

---

[129] *American State Papers, Indian Affairs*, vol. ii, pp. 429, 603; Wilson, *op. cit.*, vol. i, pp. 514-515; Sprague, *op. cit.*, pp. 34, 65-67.

[130] McMaster, *op. cit.*, vol. vi, p. 330.

principal signer—provided that the Seminoles should be settled among the Creeks. Added to their reluctance to submit themselves to the authority from which their fathers had fled in the previous century was their fear that the Creeks would deprive them of some of their Negroes. It will be remembered that in 1790 a treaty had been made between the United States and the Creeks in which the latter promised to return captured Negroes. As late as 1820 the Georgia commissioners were still insisting on the fulfillment of this provision.[131] The Creeks, despite their insistence that the missing Negroes were among the Seminoles, were mulcted of part of their treaty money to be used as compensation to the owners. Once under the dominance of the Creeks the Seminoles felt sure that their property—which in many cases was also a part of their families—would not be safe from seizure.

An even stronger reason for the refusal of the Seminoles to remove was the opposition of the Negroes. For the purpose of emigration it would, of course, be necessary for the Seminoles to assemble at some government post and make the journey under military supervision and control. The Negroes who had escaped from their owners in comparatively recent years had, of course, no intention of presenting themselves at any place where they might be recognized by their former masters, and therefore they could not accompany the Indians to their new home; and although they probably could have continued in their fastnesses for some time without disturbance, they did not wish to be deprived of the protection represented by the presence of the Seminoles. Their influence, however, was probably not of great significance. The maroons—some of them runaways of long standing but a larger proportion probably descendants of runaways—were but little less reluctant to come within reach of the official arm. Legally, they knew, they were the property of the men from whom they or their ancestors had fled, or of their heirs, and they knew that the burden of proof would rest upon them

[131] *American State Papers, Indian Affairs,* vol. ii, p. 253.

to demonstrate their right to freedom, failing in which they might quite likely become the property of anyone who urged a plausible claim to their ownership.

Even the Negroes whom the Indians claimed as slaves were unwilling to run the risk of enslavement by the whites. They knew that during the past years other Seminole slaves had been seized, legally or illegally, and an exchange of their present easy life for one of plantation slavery was a calamity too great to be risked. Even could they have been positively insured against a change of masters their attitude to resistance would probably have been but little modified. They were agriculturists rather than hunters, and as such were attached to the soil by even stronger ties than were their masters. They understood the methods of farming in Florida and had no desire to be compelled to learn agricultural processes all over again, especially in a country in which, they understood, the climate was much colder than that of Florida. In short, they felt that while a removal could not in the least better their condition, it might result in a change immeasurably for the worse; against such a possibility they determined to resist with all the means in their power, not the least of which was their influence over their masters, with whom some of them were bound by family ties as well as by a personal and property relationship.

An officer in the Seminole War summed up their attitude as follows: "The negroes exercised a wonderful control. They openly refused to follow their masters, if they removed to Arkansas. Many of them would have been reclaimed by the Creeks, to whom some belonged. Others would have been taken possession of by the whites, who for years had been urging their claims through the government and its agents. In Arkansas, hard labor was necessary for the means of support, while Florida assured them of every means to indulge in idleness, and enjoy an independence corresponding with their masters. In preparing for hostilities they were active, and in the prosecution blood-thirsty and cruel. It was not until the negroes capitulated, that the Seminoles ever thought of emigrating.'"[132]

The immediate cause of the war, it is said, can be traced directly to the problem of Negroes among the Seminoles. Most prominent of the younger leaders was Osceola, or Powell, as he was frequently called, after his foster-father (often spoken of as his actual father), an English trader among the Seminoles. Osceola himself has been described as a full-blooded Muskogee but it seems probable that he had a Scotch grandfather.[133] One of his wives was the daughter of a runaway Negro woman and a Seminole chief, and was therefore legally a slave. It is said that on a visit to the Indian agency she was seized and carried into slavery and that Osceola's violent protests resulted in a brief period of incarceration.[134]

When released Osceola bided his time. An opportunity soon presented itself. It was decided to send a body of about one hundred soldiers under Major Dade to re-inforce the garrison of Fort King. The major, on looking about for a guide, was advised to employ Louis Pacheco, the slave of a Spanish family, who was not only an excellent guide but who also spoke, read, and wrote Spanish, French, and English as well as speaking and understanding the local Indian dialect. Louis immediately notified the Seminoles of the route by which he intended to lead Major Dade's party. Osceola took a party of men and hurried off to assassinate the Indian agent whom he blamed for his wife's seizure and his own imprisonment, and when that deed of vengeance had been accomplished hastened to the place where it had been planned to ambush the soldiers, but discovered that he had arrived too late.

Caught in a country in which they themselves had no cover while at the same time they were exposed to the fire of the enemy concealed in the high grass, most of Dade's command fell at the first volley. Among them was the treacherous

[132] Sprague, *op. cit.*, p. 81; *American State Papers, Military Affairs.* vol. vi, p. 454.

[133] *Smithsonian Report* (1885) pt. ii, p. 218.

[134] Wilson, *op. cit.*, p. 516.

guide, who, however, merely simulated death till he had the opportunity to join his friends, after which he participated in the attack on those whom he had led into this death-trap. The rest of the soldiers retreated to a position where they could throw up some slight breastworks from which they kept up a futile resistance for some time, but one by one they were put out of action. All the wounded save one, who escaped by playing dead, were finished off by the knives and axes of forty or fifty Negroes in the party, who rode up on horseback for the work of vengeance. The bodies were later found lying in remarkably regular order, untouched save for the removal of the scalp in most cases, and undespoiled except for their arms and accoutrements. Louis Pacheco took especial care to remove all papers from the bodies, and imparted their contents to his new allies.[135]

The annihilation of Dade's command was achieved on December 28, 1835. The alarm it aroused may well be imagined. It was realized that this was not an ordinary Indian war, and the great fear was that "the whole frontier may be laid waste by a combination of the Indians, Indian negroes, and the negroes on the plantations." "Some of the most respectable planters," it was said, "fear that there is already a secret and improper communication carried on between the refractory Indians, Indian negroes, and some of the plantation negroes."[136] Once the latter began to be generally affected there was, of course, a possibility that slave uprisings would take place all through the Deep South. The forces arrayed against the United States at the beginning of the war were estimated as totalling about 1,800 or 2,000 warriors, including Negroes; a separate estimate put the number of the latter at about 250.[137] Their titular leader was Micanopy, who was, however, quite incapable of taking the actual command. His spirit is illustrated by the fact that two of the younger

[135] Wilson, *op. cit.*, p. 516; Giddings, *op. cit.*, pp. 101-105; Cohen, *op. cit.*, pp. 72, 75; Williams, *op. cit.*, pp. 218-219.

[136] *Executive Documents*, 25th Cong., 2nd sess., 1837-38, vol. iii, no. 78, pp. 499-500.

[137] *Ibid.*, p. 657; Sprague, *op. cit.*, p. 97.

warriors literally had to carry him to the scene of the attack on Dade's company. The day after the massacre of Dade's command a force of 250 warriors, twenty of whom were blacks, clashed with white troops on the Withlacoochee. When Micanopy learned that among the dead were two of his slaves, his displeasure was extreme and he ordered that members of his household should not in the future so expose themselves.[138] Consequently the actual leadership was divided among the various other hostile leaders. Osceola, however, was undoubtedly *primus inter pares.*

The principal Negro partisans were probably John Caesar, Inos, and Abraham, and of these the greatest was undoubtedly Abraham, who made a deep impression upon all the whites with whom he came into contact and must have been one of the most remarkable men that his race had produced in North America up to that time. Abraham or Abram, otherwise known as Yobly, was about forty-five or fifty at the outbreak of the war. He had fled from Pensacola as a boy and had become the slave of Micanopy, whom he had once accompanied to Washington as an interpreter, receiving his freedom for his services on that occasion. Being, according to the unanimous testimony of all who met him, "a sensible shrewd negro," "the most cunning and intelligent negro we have seen," he had become "a principal counsellor of his master" and had "married . . . the widow of the former chief of the nation." He was said, probably with considerable exaggeration, to have been in command of 500 Negroes, and was spoken of as "a good soldier and an intrepid leader"; he also frequently acted as interpreter in parleys between the Seminoles and the white officers.

Abraham's personal appearance apparently had in it nothing remarkable; he was of large figure, with a broad square face and thick lips, but he is said to have combined in his manner all the cunning and courtesy proper to a member of the old French *noblesse.* "Plausible, pliant and deceitful," deceptively meek, "with an appearance of great mod-

[138] *Ibid.,* p. 92.

esty, he is ambitious, avaricious and withal very intelligent''
—these characterizations from his foes reveal his quality
and explain why he had ''as much influence in the nation as
any other man.'' A familiar portrait of him, if authentic, reveals him as a fine-looking Negro, wearing the characteristic
Seminole turban, and resting on a rifle, with a slight inclination of the head which we are informed was a habitual gesture. His importance is well-expressed by an officer in the
forces opposed to him: ''Abraham was the most noted, and
for a time an influential man in the nation. He dictated to
those of his own color, who to a great degree controlled their
masters. They were a most cruel and malignant enemy. For
them to surrender would be servitude to the whites; but to
retain an open warfare, secured to them plunder, liberty,
and importance.''[139]

It is not my purpose to give a skirmish by skirmish or
even a campaign by campaign account of the seven years war
against the Seminoles and their Negro allies, but merely to
indicate something of the part the latter played at various
stages of the conflict. The proportionate number of Negroes
engaged and of the casualties among them is of significance.
On November 21, 1836, 420 Seminoles and 200 Negroes beat
back the government troops at the ford of the Withlacoochee.[140] In the next month it was noted that four of the most
prominent Seminole chiefs, ''Powell, . . . Micanopy, Philip,
and Cooper, . . . are about a day's march from each other,
each with from one hundred and twenty to two hundred Indian and negro warriors—the latter, perhaps, the more numerous. . . . This, you may be assured,'' was General Jesup's
conclusion, ''is a negro, not an Indian war; and if it be not
speedily put down, the South will feel the effects of it on their
slave population before the end of the next season.''[141]

During the month of January, 1837, matters went badly

[139] Cohen, *op. cit.*, p. 239; *Executive Documents*, 25th Cong., 2nd sess., 1837-
38, vol. iii, no. 78, pp. 113-118; Williams, *op. cit.*, pp. 214, 272-273; Sprague,
op. cit., p. 100.

[140] Sprague, *op. cit.*, p. 166.

[141] *Executive Documents*, 25th Cong., 2nd sess., 1837-38, vol. iii, no. 78, p. 52.

with the hostile Indians and Negroes. After a fight on the 27th one Indian and two Negroes were found dead and twenty-two Negroes were captured. In another encounter with "a party of hostile Indians and negroes" two warriors were killed, eleven Indians and nine Negroes captured. Late in the month the main body of the army moved "to attack the Indians and negroes in the strongholds which they were said to occupy on the headwaters of the Ocklawaha." The chief Osuchee and three warriors were killed, while nine Indians and eight Negroes fell into the hands of the victors. Most important of all, Osceola's personal following was surprised and the chief escaped with only three warriors, leaving behind him fifty-two Negroes and three Indians as prisoners.[142] It will be observed that the band of this leading chief was made up almost entirely of Negroes. It is probable, however, that the comparatively large numbers of Negroes reported captured owed something to the fact that the troops were much more eager to make prisoners of Negro women and children than of those of the Indians.

The apparent importance of these results was, however, minimized by the statement soon after that: "in all the numerous battles and skirmishes that have taken place, not a single first-rate warrior has been captured, and only two Indian men have surrendered. The warriors have fought as long as they had life, and such seems to me to be the determination of those who influence their councils—I mean the leading negroes." Nevertheless it was not long after this, on March 6, 1837, that some of the chiefs capitulated by the treaty of Fort Dade, which provided for the removal of the Seminoles and their Negroes. General Jesup was anxious that everything should be done to keep the latter in a mood favorable to peace. "The negroes rule the Indians," he said, "and it is important that they should feel themselves secure: if they should become alarmed and hold out, the war will be renewed."[143] However, Jesup was not to be allowed to forget

[142] *Ibid.*, p. 70; *American State Papers, Military Affairs*, vol. vii, pp. 825-826, 827-828, 993-994.

[143] *Ibid.*, vol. vii, p. 832, 835; McMaster, *op. cit.*, vol. vi, p. 463.

that he was engaged in a slave-hunt as well as in an Indian war. Slave-hunters began to appear in camp to lay claim to some of the Negroes who had surrendered. Some of the latter became alarmed and fled; Jesup rushed the others off to a more secure place of detention—and the war was on once more. Thus, either actively or passively, the Negroes were responsible for the continuance of the conflict.

In May, 1837, it was estimated that there were in East Florida 2,500 warriors, "not including ... negroes, who fight as well as the best of them." In June, 1837, the general was almost ready to make terms with the Seminoles for their continuance in Florida. His reasons were as follows: "The two races, the negro and the Indian, are rapidly approximating; they are identified in interests and feelings; and I have ascertained that at the battle of the Wahoo, a negro, the property of a Florida planter, was one of the most distinguished leaders; and I have learned that the depredations committed on the plantations east of the St. John's were perpetrated by the plantation negroes, headed by an Indian negro, John Caesar, since killed, and aided by some six or seven vagabond Indians, who had no character among their people as warriors. Should the Indians remain in this Territory, the negroes among them will form a rallying point for runaway negroes from the adjacent states; and if they remove, the fastnesses of the country would be immediately occupied by negroes. I am very sure they could be confined to a small district near Florida Point, and would accept peace and the small district referred to as the condition for the surrender of all runaway negroes."[144] From the above it would seem that though at the beginning of the war most of the slaves had remained faithful to their masters, despite the attempts of Abraham to stir them to rebellion,[145] that loyalty, it was feared, was wavering.

However, the capitulation of Fort Dade, though it had failed to bring the war to an end, had greatly weakened the

[144] *Ibid., American State Papers, Military Affairs,* vol. vii, pp. 835, 871, 876.
[145] Cohen, *op. cit.,* p. 81.

most important element of the resistance. Over a hundred
Seminole Negroes who had come in under that treaty had
been hurried off to Tampa for safe-keeping and nearly as
many more runaways had been returned to their masters;
it was the latter fact, indeed, which had caused the stampede
of some of the other Negroes and the renewal of the war.
But among the Seminole Negroes who had failed to escape
were nearly all the Negro leaders, so that it could be said in
July that "the negro portion of the hostile force of the Seminole nation not taken is entirely without a head."[146] Among
the Negro leaders under custody as a result of the capitulation at Fort Dade was "Ben, 40, One of the most important
and influential characters among the Indian negroes," "Inos,
45, . . . The commander of the negro forces on the Withlacoochee, the chief counsellor among the negroes, and the
most important character," and—greatest loss of all—
"Abram, . . . The principal negro chief."[147] John Caesar, as
we have just seen, had been killed.

In August, 1837, the locations of the various bands of
Negroes, who seem in their leaderless condition to have
rather drifted away from the Indians, were thus described:
"The captured and runaway negroes are between St. John's
and the Indian rivers, and the Indian negroes on the Kissimmee, Caloosahatchee, and Pease creek." The Indians, save
for "small roving bands," were "south of Fort Mellon, on
the St. John's and Kissimmee."[148] "Captured Negroes" was
a euphemism employed to describe Negroes who had become
runaways during the course of the present war and at the
personal inducement of some of the hostiles; "Indian negroes" referred to the Seminoles' nominal slaves. The
treacherous capture of Osceola and other chiefs in the fall
of 1837 still further weakened the Seminole power, but led
on by the other chiefs, especially by Cooacoochee, or Wild

[146] *American State Papers, Military Affairs*, vol. vii, p. 842.

[147] Executive Documents, 25th Cong., 2nd sess., 1837-38, vol. iii, no. 78, pp. 113-118.

[148] *American State Papers, Military Affairs*, vol. vii, pp. 876-878.

Cat, who made his escape from St. Mark's, they continued the war.

There were, of course, some Negroes and Indians who were government partisans. Most of the slaves, with commendable discretion, decided that it would be wise to remain quiet. Some actually fought for their masters when their plantations were attacked by hostile Negroes and Indians.[149] General Jesup's proclamation of freedom to all Seminole Negroes who would desert their masters and join the government forces or induce the Indians to make peace had been of no great effect,[150] but this inducement or others had caused certain Negroes to attach themselves to the troops as guides and interpreters. Among these were Morris, Sampson, Sandy, Gopher John with his "unerring rifle," and Ben Wiggins, who distinguished himself in one encounter by killing three Indians, he himself being severely wounded. Jim Boy, a Creek chief of Negro blood, joined the government forces with 700 warriors, who, inspired by the promise of plunder, were of great service in tracking down and capturing the fugitive Negroes. The friendly Indians and the Negro guides were naturally regarded with the most bitter enmity by their hostile kinsmen. Sampson and Sandy once fell into the hands of a band of hostiles when a small force for which they were acting as guides and interpreters was annihilated in July, 1839, and the latter was put to death by torture. In the last important battle of the war, which took place in April, 1842, it was noticed that "the fire of the enemy was concentrated principally upon the Indian guides and negro interpreters."[151]

Long as the war continued, it is believed that only the adoption of a wiser policy in regard to the Negro allies of the Seminoles kept it from being still further prolonged. It

[149] Williams, *op. cit.*, pp. 248-249, 250.

[150] Abel, Annie Heloise, *The Slaveholding Indians*, 3 vols. (Cleveland, 1915-25) vol. i, *As Slaveholder and Secessionist*, pp. 164-165, note.

[151] Cohen, *op. cit.*, p. 95; Sprague, *op. cit.*, pp. 233, 459; Hitchcock, *op. cit.*, pp. 151-152.

was realized that hostilities would never cease so long as any of the Negroes or Indians survived, unless the slave-hunting aspects of the campaign were eliminated or minimized. Originally, captured Negroes had been turned over to their former owners, as was done with about a hundred after the treaty of Fort Dade, but the authorities came more and more to doubt not only that this policy would help to terminate the war but also that its effects upon the institution of slavery would be particularly favorable. This doubt appeared in September, 1837, after the Creek friendlies had captured eighty Negroes, who were regarded as part of their plunder. But General Jesup had become so skeptical of the further value of these captives as slaves that he paid the Creeks a nominal sum for their claims and wrote to Washington: "It is highly important to the slaveholding States that these Negroes be sent out of the country, and I would strongly recommend that they be sent to one of our colonies in Africa."[152]

General Zachary Taylor has been given credit for hastening the end of the war by announcing that he would treat both Negroes and Indians as prisoners of war, thus causing many to come in.[153] Whenever a Negro, claimed by a white man, was also claimed by an Indian, the latter's claim would be recognized as superior by a board of officers and the white claimant given compensation. Doubtless many runaways, taking advantage of this act of military necessity, left Florida as the nominal slaves of their Indian comrades. It was in this way that Louis Pacheco escaped, as the slave of Cooacoochee, to whom he had attached himself after the Dade massacre.

The subterfuge mentioned above was employed both to end the war and get the runaway Negroes safely out of the country. Why the latter seemed desirable will become abundantly clear on reading the notes attached to the names of some of the prisoners: "Ben, 22, Jacob, 24, Muredy, 20, Most intrepid and hostile warriors," "Prince, 35, Toney, 25, Toby,

[152] *American State Papers, Indian Affairs,* vol. vii, p. 882.
[153] Wilson, *op. cit.,* p. 524.

32, Hostile, either qualified to take the lead in an insurrection," etc.[154] It is easy to see why the distribution of Jacob, Tony, Toby et al. among the plantations of Georgia and Florida would probably be the equivalent of becoming accessory before the fact to murder and arson on a large scale, since they would probably either start a revolt or run away again, to seek out their old haunts in a doubly dangerous mood. An officer in the Seminole War commented, "The Negroes, from the commencement of the Florida war, have, for their numbers, been the most formidable foe, more bloodthirsty, active, and revengeful, than the Indian. . . . Ten resolute negroes, with a knowledge of the country, are sufficient to desolate the frontier, from one extent to the other.' "[155]

Yet despite the new policy toward the Negro prisoners, it is alleged that from January 1, 1835, to August 14, 1843, more than 500 Negroes were enslaved,[156] to say nothing of the hundreds of Negroes and Indians killed. Against this may be set an expenditure of $32,000,000 and the lives of 600 soldiers and twenty-eight or thirty officers lost in the course of the war.[157] Such were some of the costs of what is usually spoken of as the most serious Indian war in the history of the United States but which perhaps should rather be described as a Negro insurrection with Indian support.[158]

It was found to be impossible to compel all the Seminoles to leave Florida, and peace was finally made with the recalcitrant remnant. Half a century after the removal of the main body of the Seminole nation, Kirk Munroe, the well-known writer of juvenile fiction, made an investigation of the Seminoles who were still in Florida. He declared that of 400 Seminoles only one family had Negro blood, the father having married a Negro woman "captured in the Seminole

[154] *Executive Documents*, 25th Cong., 2nd sess., vol. iii, no. 78, pp. 113-118.
[155] Sprague, *op. cit.*, p. 309.
[156] Giddings, *op. cit.*, p. 315.
[157] *Smithsonian Report* (1885) pt. ii, p. 215.
[158] For a concise discussion of the Negro aspect of the Second Seminole War, see Benjamin Brawley's *A Social History of the American Negro* (N.Y., 1921) pp. 91-115.

War." Their children, he asserted, were not regarded as the equal of other Seminoles, who in general regarded the Negro as occupying a rank somewhat below that of a dog.[159] This, if true, would have been a remarkable reversal of attitude and, as a matter of fact, Munroe was probably in error, for only ten years earlier the ethnologist Clay McCauley also made a study of the 280 Seminoles in five settlements and found among them three Negro women, adopted into the tribe, and seven Negro-Indian children, who were "on terms of perfect equality" with the other members of the tribe. McCauley considered the Seminoles to be the finest in appearance of any Indians he had ever met, but stated that the most intelligent and progressive Seminole he encountered was of Negro blood.[160] It is probable that more credence should be given to the report of an ethnologist than to that of a writer of fiction.

The epic of the emigrating Seminoles did not end when their last band reached the Indian Territory. Their suspicion of the Creeks had been intensified by the part warriors from that tribe had played in putting down the Seminole insurrection, and they therefore declined to settle in Creek territory, instead locating themselves temporarily among the hospitable and friendly Cherokees, who admired them for the resistance to removal which their hosts had not ventured to make. They were finally induced to settle on a part of the Creek territory, set aside for them, but soon discovered that their doubts of the neighborliness of their kinsmen had been only too well-founded. The civilized tribes in the Indian Territory were anxious to build up their slave property, the Creeks particularly so. A government investigator in 1841 and 1842 reported: "Comanches steal negroes sometimes from Texas and sell them to Cherokees and Creeks. The latter have been known to pay $400 and $500 for a negro."[161]

[159] Munroe, Kirk, "A Forgotten Remnant," *Scribner's Magazine* (1890) vol. vii, pp. 303-317, pp. 306-307.

[160] McCauley, Clay, "The Seminole Indians of Florida," *Fifth Annual Report of the Bureau of Ethnology, 1883-84* (Washington, 1887).

[161] Hitchcock, *op. cit.*, p. 28.

It was natural that they should endeavor to revive their old claim to the slaves of the Seminoles, and in the years after 1845 they began to make raids on the Seminoles for the purpose of seizing Negroes, when successful carrying them over into Arkansas where they were sold and sent down the river to New Orleans.

Such outrages were unendurable. The leaders of the party among the Seminoles which was most favorable to the Negroes of the tribe—the Negro Abraham and the young chief Cooacoochee, with whom Louis Pacheco had great influence —resolved upon another exodus. In 1850 about 300 Seminoles and Negroes left the Indian Territory and made their way across Texas toward the Republic of Mexico, where slavery was illegal. They were pursued in true Biblical fashion by a slave-hunting party of Creeks, whom they beat back in a sharp skirmish, and succeeded in reaching Mexico, where they received several grants of land in return for services in guarding the border—a function for which these intrepid warriors, red and black, were admirably qualified. They were followed by others, some of them probably from the ranks of those alleged Seminole slaves who, "after the immigration west was determined or consummated," claimed their freedom under General Jesup's promise to all Negroes who would come in or induce their masters to emigrate.

These slaves were taken to the Indian Territory and protected by the government until about 1848 or 1850; when this protection was withdrawn "said slaves in great numbers escaped, some of whom reached Mexico, some were killed by the wild Indians, and the remainder were only captured at great and ruinous expense." In the claim for compensation made by the Seminole chiefs in 1856 on account of the damages suffered because of Jesup's "illegal proclamation," these fugitives were numbered at 234. The fate of some of these runaways was discovered by a United States exploring party in the early '50's. "Within the past few years the Comanches have (for what reason I could not learn) taken an inveterate dislike to the negroes, and have massacred several small parties of those who attempted to escape from the Seminoles and cross the plains for the purpose of joining Wild Cat upon the Rio Grande. Upon inquiring of them the cause of their hostility to the blacks," the Comaches, putting their conduct upon the highest ethical grounds, "replied that it was because they were slaves to the whites" and "they were sorry for them."

The explorers, however, were not altogether convinced of the purely altruistic character of the Comaches' motives, but shrewdly suspected that they wished to prevent Wild Cat's band from increasing to such a size that it would seriously interfere with their marauding along the Rio Grande. Their enmity to the Negroes was apparently not based on color-prejudice, for they had also massacred Delawares and Shawnees who were suspected of intending to join Cooacoochee. In 1857 Wild Cat died of small-pox, and later a delegation from the Seminoles of the Indian Territory persuaded his followers to break up their settlement and return to the United States, much to the regret of the Mexican government.[162]

[162] Giddings, *op. cit.*, pp. 114, 330-336; Wilson, *op. cit.*, vol. i, p. 526; Abel, *op. cit.*, vol. i, pp. 164-165, note; Coe Charles H., *Red Patriots* (Cincinnati, 1898) pp. 167-169; Marcy, Randolph Barnes, and McClellan, George B., *Exploration of the Red River of Louisiana* (Washington, 1853) p. 101.

Chapter V

AFTER THE REMOVAL TO THE WEST

No particular development in the relations between Negroes and Indians can be observed as taking place in the Indian Territory until the time of the Civil War, although many references to slave-holding among the Indians can be found in the accounts of travelers in that area.[163] Henry Bibb, one of the leaders in the African colonization movement, was sold to an Indian by a Red River planter in the early 1840's.[164] The slave-holding Indians had some of the same difficulties in regard to his human possessions as did the white planter, to which he added some peculiar to his race. "Slaves belonging to the Indians were often enticed away by the abolitionists and still oftener were seized by Southern men under pretense of their being fugitives. In cases of the latter sort, the Indian owners had little or no redress in the federal courts of law."[165] There were a number of free Negro settlements in the Creek country and strays from these communities sometimes gave the Indians trouble. Early in 1852 the chief of the Pushmataha district of the Choctaw Nation complained to the agent "about those free negroes upon the head waters of Boggy . . . the negroes and some Indians are banded together and have built a little Fort." He requested the agent to send the military to remove those Indians and Negroes thus "Forted up," which the agent promised to do.[166] Apparently Florida traditions died hard among some of the Negroes.

All the Five Civilized Tribes suffered severely from the

[163] Nuttall, Thomas, *Journal of Travels into the Arkansa Territory during the Year 1819*, Reuben Gold Thwaites, ed. (Cleveland, 1905) p. 129, for example.

[164] Landon, Fred, "Henry Bibb, A Colonizer," *Journal of Negro History* (1920) vol. v, pp. 437-447, 440.

[165] Abel, *op. cit.*, vol. i, pp. 22-23. "Early in March, 1860, two citizens of Tabor, Iowa, were captured while conducting four runaways from the Indian Territory to a station of the Underground Railroad." They were acquitted. (Siebert, *op. cit.*, p. 284.)

[166] *Ibid.*, vol. i, pp. 24, 23-25, note.

Civil War. Sentiment in each tribe toward the Confederate cause was largely determined by its citizens' attitude toward the Negro.[167] The Choctaws and Chickasaws "had a decided aversion" to intermixture with Negroes.[168] "In that respect they differed very considerably from the Creeks" and from the Seminoles, among whom "the status of the free negro was exceptionally high, partly due with respect to the latter, to conditions growing out of the Second Seminole War. As already intimated, the Creeks had no aversion whatsoever to race mixtures and intermarriage between negroes and Indians was rather common. The half-breeds resulting from such unions were accepted as bona fide members of the tribe by the Indians in the distribution of annuities, but not by the United States courts."[169]

On the outbreak of the war, the great majority of the Choctaws and Chickasaws became enthusiastic supporters of the Confederacy. The Cherokee Nation was pretty evenly divided, the half-breeds inclining to the Southern position, while the full-bloods tended to sympathize with the North and advocated neutrality, though the great leader of the anti-secession party, John Ross, had very little Indian blood. The Creeks and Seminoles in general were opposed to the Confederacy, but in these tribes, as in all the others, some chiefs were found who could be inveigled into making treaties with the secessionists, which were later used as an excuse for treating all members of the civilized tribes, innocent as well as guilty, in a peculiarly unjust and disgraceful fashion. Some Indians, particularly Cherokees, entered the Confed-

[167] The following estimate has been made of the number of slaves held by the Five Civilized Tribes at the outbreak of the Civil War. "When war broke out, the Seminoles had a thousand slaves; the Cherokees and Chickasaws had each about fifteen hundred slaves; the Creeks and Choctaws had each about three thousand slaves. In these Red nations there were less than fourteen thousand fullblooded Indians to ten thousand Negro slaves." (Dixon, William Hepwourth, *White Conquest*, 2 vols., London, 1876, j. 284.)

[168] J. H. Johnston, however, presents (*loc. cit.*) evidence indicating that among the Choctaws, at least, this antipathy to Negro intermixture has been greatly exaggerated.

[169] Abel, *op. cit.*, vol. i, pp. 20, note, 23, note.

erate service at first but later deserted to the Unionists; hundreds of loyal Indians, Seminoles in particular, fled north into Kansas, suffering great hardships on the Way, and there joined the Federal forces.

In the general disorder the Negroes living among the Indians were in many cases left largely to their own resources. In 1862 freed blacks in the Cherokee country pillaged indiscriminately among Unionists as well as Confederates. The Negroes in the Indian Territory seem to have had a keener interest in the character of their future status than did those among the whites. In 1864 "loyal Africans from the Creek Nation" petitioned for "equal rights with the Indians," advancing as a claim to consideration the fact that most of their "boys" were in the Union army.

As the war drew to a close and it became evident that the cause of the South and of slavery was doomed, a feeling of bitterness against Negroes in general appeared among some of the Indians, particularly, as might have been expected, among the Chickasaws and Choctaws. A curious theory was formulated, not that the Negroes had been the cause of the war but that they had been responsible for the failure of the South to bring it to a satisfactory conclusion. As a result, "a reign of terror is reported to have set in," directed by Choctaws and Chickasaws who were devotees of this interesting opinion in regard to the influence of the Negro upon the course of the war. On one occasion, it was said, the bodies of five blacks were seen "in one place piled together, killed by the Indians."[170]

The comparative helplessness of the Indians caused the reconstruction policy applied to them to be of a particularly severe character; the most serious aspect of their punishment was the confiscation of the western half of their ranges. The relations between the Indians and the Negroes of the Indian Territory also came into consideration. At the peace council of Fort Smith in 1865 the government demanded abolition of slavery, "the unconditional emancipation of all

[170] *Ibid.*, vol. iii, pp. 74-75, notes 117, 518.

persons held in bondage, and . . . their incorporation into the tribes on an equal footing with the original members, or suitably provided for.''

Some of the more radical of the white reconstructionists wanted to open the Indian Territory to general Negro colonization. In the Senate of the United States, Jim Lane, a former free-state partisan leader in the warfare of the Kansas-Missouri border, indulged in a rhapsody which would cause a eugenist of the Grant-Stoddard School to scream and foam at the mouth. ''The finest specimens of manhood I have ever gazed upon in my life,'' the senator proclaimed, ''are half-breed Indians crossed with negroes. It is a fact . . . that while amalgamation with the white man deteriorates both races, the amalgamation of the Indian and the black man advances both races. . . . I should like to see these eighty thousand square miles . . . opened up to the Indian and to the black man, and let them amalgamate and build up a race that will be an improvement upon both.''[171]

Not even those tribes most sympathetic with the Negro looked with favor upon the proposal to have their country turned into a sort of Negro cuckoo's nest. All tribes agreed to emancipation, but Osages,[172] Choctaws, Chickasaws, Cherokees, Creeks, and Seminoles alike objected to colonization. On other matters connected with the Negro their reactions were determined by their past history. The Seminoles were willing to provide for the adoption of their own slaves and Negro free men living among them before the rebellion, though they would not agree to Negro colonization, and their Negroes were accordingly adopted and put on an equality, despite the protests of the Southern Seminoles against their incorporation into the tribe on equal terms.[173] The attitude of the Creeks was similar. The loyal Creeks were willing to accept Negro incorporation, and the protests of the seces-

---

[171] *Ibid.*, vol. iii, pp. 189, 253-254.

[172] Edna Ferber in *Cimarron*, N.Y., 1930, pp. ix, 238-246, vouches for a story illustrating the almost unbelievable antipathy which the Osages are alleged to have had for the Negro.

[173] Abel, *op. cit.*, vol. iii, pp. 192-193, 323, footnote, 435.

sionists were unavailing to prevent the adoption of their
freedmen, who received thereby an equality of interest in
land and national funds.[174] The Southern Cherokees would
not consent to "the general colonization of Negroes" nor to
"tribal incorporation of negroes," and their influence was
sufficiently great that it was agreed to provide for, but not to
incorporate, the Cherokee freedmen.[175]

As might have been anticipated, the Choctaws and Chickasaws put up the stiffest resistance to the concession of equal
rights to their Negroes. The Choctaws, in direct opposition
to the Creek practise, had "ever insisted that legally the
offspring of Indian men and negro women are negroes, un-
alterably and forever." Both tribes objected to "opening
their territory indiscriminatingly to the negroes. . . . Suitable provisions for their own blacks, something short of actual incorporation into the body politic of the tribe, they were
willing to concede." They were consequently required to give
their freedmen land and certain civil and political rights,
including the electoral franchise, but were not forced to adopt
their Negroes or to allow them a share in the tribal lands,
annuities, etc. Neither nation, however, passed the requisite
laws, and in 1876 the Choctaws protested against the pressure exerted against them to force them to admit freedmen
to full citizenship rights.[176]

The provisions in regard to the welfare of the freedmen
in the Civilized Tribes were carried out with varying degrees of success. These measures worked out with less friction among the Seminoles than with any other tribe. In 1869
it was said: "Accepting fully the results of the war, and
granting to the freedmen unconditional citizenship, the Seminoles are living in a state of more perfect peace than any

[174] *Ibid.*, vol. iii, pp. 210, 340-341, notes 443, 608.

[175] *Ibid.*, vol. iii, pp. 287, 361.

[176] *Ibid.*, vol. iii, pp. 190-191, 298, 331, note 600. About this time a British
traveller published a book giving a sensational and probably considerably over-
drawn account of the deplorable condition of Negroes in the Indian Territory,
both under slavery and during reconstruction (Dixon, William Hepwourth, *White
Conquest*, 2 vols., London, 1876, pp. 272-317).

other tribe within the superintendency." The Seminoles "adopted their former slaves, and made them citizens of their country, with equal rights in the soil and annuities. Their negroes hold office and sit in their councils." Among the Creeks the path of the freedmen had not been quite so smooth. The Negroes, adopted as citizens, had only after difficulty finally received a share of the $200,000 granted to the Creeks "to restore their farms," etc., after it had at first been decided that they were not entitled to any part of this grant. According to the superintendent, the Negroes were playing an obstructive role in the politics of the Creek Nation, having been won over to the faction opposed to white men, mixed blood, and progress, by the plea that this opposition was the loyal party, which, indeed, was the case.[177] In 1888 it was said: "The . . . Creek Negroes have the rights of suffrage and all the rights of Indian citizens."[178]

In 1869 the Negroes were described as being oppressed among the Choctaws, Chickasaws, and Cherokees. The treaty of July 19, 1866, with the last nation, provided that all freedmen, as well as all free colored people resident in the nation at the time of the rebellion, should be given all the rights of native Cherokees, but no agreement could be reached in the nation on legislation for carrying out this provision. Consequently in 1883 it was said that political and social prejudice was still depriving some of the former slaves of their rights, but at the same time it was believed that time was correcting the situation. This belief was soon to be justified, for in 1885 it was reported that among the Cherokees were included descendants of Cherokees and Negroes and also adopted citizens, some of whom were full-blooded Negroes. In 1888 there were in the nation 23,300 Cherokees and about 2,400 Negroes, adopted citizens, who possessed "the rights of suffrage and all the rights of Indian citizens, except participation in public annuities. . . . They are given their full quota of school privileges, however, and are doing well in a ma-

[177] *Report of Commissioner of Indian Affairs* (1869) pp. 398, 400, 417.
[178] *Ibid.*, (1888) vol. ii, p. 132.

terial way. One peculiar difference exists between negro and
Indian in the Five Nations, *i.e.* intermarriage with Indian
gives a U. S. citizen, male or female, rights, but intermarriage with a negro does not.'' In 1895 there were fourteen
primary schools and one high school, kept up at the expense
of the Cherokee government for the use of the Negro citizens
of the nation; in 1898 there were more than 34,000 citizens
of the Cherokee Nation, of whom 4,000 were Negroes.[179]

In 1869 it was noted, as we have seen, that the Negroes
were being oppressed by the Cherokees, Choctaws, and
Chickasaws; the last two tribes had failed to adopt their Negroes and the United States was urged to make provisions
for their removal, using for that purpose certain funds which
had been granted to the tribes on the condition that they
should adopt their freedmen. But by 1888 it could be said:
''The Negroes of the Choctaw Nation . . . have been adopted
by the Choctaws, given a pro rata of schools, right of suffrage, and citizenship as provided by treaty.'' But at the
same time it was also reported: ''The negroes of the Chickasaw Nation are still in the forlorn status as stated in my
last report. The Chickasaws are firmly resolved never to receive them.'' And these unreconstructed Indians never did.
In 1888 the Chickasaw National Party opposed ''the adoption of the negro in any way, shape, or form,'' and less than
ten years ago a history of the Chickasaws written by a Southern white gave them high praise for the insistence on racial
integrity manifested by their steadfast refusal to adopt their
freedmen.[180] The Chickasaws even refused to grant land to
their ex-slaves, but here the United States government
stepped in and gave each freedman forty acres regardless.

[179] *Ibid.*, (1869) pp. 398-399; Royce, Charles C., ''The Cherokee Nation
of Indians,'' *Fifth Annual Report of the Bureau of Ethnology* (1883-84) pp.
121-378, pp. 336, 344, 369, 377; *Smithsonian Report* (1885) pt. ii, p. 225;
Report of Commissioner of Indian Affairs (1888) vol. ii, p. 132; *Nineteenth
Annual Report of the Bureau of American Ethnology* (1897-98) pt. i, pp. 155,
157.

[180] *Report of Commissioner of Indian Affairs* (1869) pp. 398-399; *ibid.*,
(1888) pt. ii, pp. 116, 132; Malone, James H., *The Chickasaw Nation* (Louisville, 1922) pp. 412-419.

They were thus left in a better condition than their brethren in the South, even though they did not receive in addition the traditional mule.

Racially, slavery among the civilized tribes of the Indian Territory, followed by emancipation and, in most cases, by adoption, had curious effects. In 1907 it was said that there was then not a Seminole family entirely free from Negro blood and only two or three Creek families. One supposed Creek Indian, who was nearly white, upon looking up his family tree for some purpose discovered that he had not one drop of Indian blood and was one-sixteenth Negro; his position in the white society among which he had hitherto been moving was completely destroyed. But "the Cherokees, Choctaws and Chickasaws . . . seldom . . . mixt their blood with the Negro." [181]

[181] Abel, *op. cit.*, vol. i, p. 20, note; Abbott, L. J., "The Race Question in the Forty-sixth State," *Independent* (1907) vol. lxiii, pp. 206-211. As late as 1888, however, it was reported that although "among the Creeks is some negro miscegenation," its extent had been "much exaggerated in reports on that subject." (*Report of Commissioner of Indian Affairs*, 1888, vol. ii, p. 131.)

CHAPTER VI

CONTACTS IN OTHER PARTS

We have considered the relations between Negroes and Indians during the period of exploration, on the Atlantic Coast between North Carolina and Massachusetts inclusive, and among the slave-holding Indians, both in the Deep South and in the Indian Territory. It remains for us to examine the relations between these two races in the remainder of the vast territory of the United States, distinguished for our purpose from the other two areas by the fact that in it slavery was never an important social institution and by the more nomadic character of the native inhabitants. For these reasons relations between Negroes and Indians were of distinctly minor·importance.

Almost the first mention we encounter is one of hostility. During the year 1790 the Moravian missionary David Zeisberger entered in his diary: "From Sandusky we learned that two Negroes who went through from Detroit, had killed five Wyandots in the bush, where they met." We are not told the motive for this slaughter. It may be that the two Negroes—and I should have demanded that they produce the five scalps before giving full credence to their story—were some of Joseph Brant's Negroes, so-called, that is, runaway slaves to whom that Mohawk chief had given refuge, and that they had imbibed hostility for the Wyandots from their Mohawk comrades. It is known that "some Mohawk Indians and a negro of Brant's" had been "on the Miami" about that time.[182] It is more pleasant to relate an example of another nature concerning the relations between a representative of the Negro race and the Wyandots settled along the southern shore of Lake Erie to Sandusky something over a quarter of a century later. "For three years past, the Wyandots have had a Methodist preacher, a man of color, among them. His name is Stewart. His preaching has

[182] *Zeisberger, David, Diary of,* 2 vols. (Cincinnati, 1885) vol. ii, pp. 117, 316.

wrought a great change among them;" specifically about fifty Wyandots had laid aside their rosaries and crucifixes and become Protestants.[183] As we have already seen, the Ottawas of northwestern Ohio early showed friendship for fugitive slaves.

A family of Negro blood became prominent as fur traders among the Ojibways and Chippewas. The founder of this family was a Negro named Joas (Jean) Bonga or Bongas. He had been the slave of Captain Daniel Robertson, the British officer in command at Mackinac from 1782 to May 17, 1787, and is said to have been brought from the West Indies, but one of his grandsons in 1872 expressed the opinion that he had been captured from one of the French settlements in Missouri during the Revolutionary War and sold to Indian traders at Mackinac, which could easily have happened. Among the members of the Robertson household was a Negro woman named Marie Jeanne, and in 1780 and 1786 we know that she bore to Bonga two daughters, Rosalie and Charlotte, the latter being described at her baptism in 1794 as "a free negress." After Robertson's death in 1787 the Negroes stayed on, probably having been freed. In 1794 Bonga's children were legitimatized by his marriage to Marie Jeanne, and early in the next year died "Jean Bongas, a free negro."

Jean and Marie Jeanne probably had other children in addition to Rosalie and Charlotte. It is probable that Pierre Bonga, the Negro who was with Alexander Henry, Jr., of the North West Company in the valley of the Red River of the North in 1802, was one of Jean Bonga's children. George Bonga said in 1872 that his father, who was employed by the North West Company and spoke nothing but French, had come to Lake Superior with a Chippewa trader more than a century before, and this is doubtless a reference to Pierre Bonga; the lapse of time could easily have been exaggerated. Pierre Bonga probably married into the Ojibway tribe, for in 1819 "among the residents [of an Ojibway village] were

[183] Morse, *op. cit.*, app. 91.

the children of an African by the name of Bungo, the servant of a British officer who once commanded at Mackinac. Their hair was curled and skin glossy, and their features altogether African.'' George Bonga, who was born about 1802 near Duluth, was thus probably half-Negro and half-Ojibway.

In 1819 one of the principal traders among the Ojibways was a Bonga, probably Pierre; in 1820 his son George, who had been educated at Montreal and who, unlike his father, knew English, acted as an interpreter for Governor Lewis Cass in a council at Fond du Lac. George in 1833-34 was a licensed trader at Lac Platte and it was probably he who was ''an interpreter at the treaty with the Chippeways in 1837, at Fort Snelling.'' Presumably George too married among the Indians—one account says into Chippewa tribe. From being in the employ of the American Fur Company as a *voyageur* he ''became quite a prominent trader and a man of wealth and consequence. . . . He was a thorough gentleman in both feeling and deportment.'' Many stories are told of his hospitality. He was, as noted above, purely African in appearance but ''never having heard of any distinction between the people but that of Indians and white men, he would frequently paralyze his hearers when reminiscing by saying, ''Gentlemen, I assure you that John Banfil and myself were the first two white men that ever came into this country.'' George had a son named Stephen who died in 1884. George himself was alive at least as late as 1872; many of his letters are in the collection of the Minnesota Historical Society.

The Bongas all seem to have been distinguished for physical strength. Of George Bonga it was said that ''when he came into the country from Lake Superior, [he] packed 700 pounds for a quarter of a mile over the portage at the Dalles of the St. Louis river. He was half negro, . . . a giant in strength, over six feet high, over 200 pounds weight, as straight as an Indian, with sinews and cords in his limbs like a horse.'' His nephew Jack Bonga, probably a son of George's brother Jack, was packer for a surveyor in 1875.

He was "one-quarter negro and three-quarters Indian. He would pack two sacks of flour of a hundred pounds each every day rather than make two trips for the same baggage. Two hundred pounds is a regular pack for a horse in the mountains." A quarter of a century later the Bonga breed had apparently not degenerated, for it was recorded: "About Leech lake there are perhaps a hundred descendants of the negro Bungo; nearly all these are very muscular, and some have been of unusually fine physique."

The "numerous descendants" of Jean Bonga were probably the only Negroes the Indians of Minnesota saw for many years. We are told that "among the few slaves brought within the limits of Minnesota, several belonged to Major Taliaferro. The Indians at that time had no prejudice against those of African descent, and welcomed them to their lodges with the same courtesy as white persons. The wooly head they looked upon as 'wakan,' [strange or mysterious] and designated them as 'black Frenchmen.' Some would put their hands upon the coarse curly hair of the negro, and then laugh."[184] It seems rather clear that the English-speaking

[184] "The Mackinac Register, 1695-1821," *Wisconsin Historical Collections*, vol. xiv, pp. 83, 97, 157; "The Mackinac Register, 1725-1821," *Wisconsin Historical Collections*, vol. xviii, p. 497; "Letters of George Bonga," *Journal of Negro History* (1927) vol. xii, pp. 41-54, pp. 53-54; Neill, Edward D., "History of the Ojibways," *Minnesota Historical Collections* (1885) vol. v, pp. 395-510, p. 381; Neill, E. D., *History of Minnesota* (Philadelphia, 1858) pp. 322-415-416; *ibid.*, (1883 ed.) pp. 873, 874, 912; Flandrau, Charles E., "Reminiscences of Minnesota during the Territorial Period," pp. 197-222, *Minnesota Historical Collections* (1901) vol. ix, p. 199; Butler, Nathan, "Boundaries and public Land Surveys of Minnesota," pp. 649-670, *Minnesota Historical Collections* (1908) vol. xii, p. 670; Gilfillan, The Rev. Joseph A., "The Ojibways in Minnesota," pp. 55-128, *Minnesota Historical Collections* (1901) vol. ix, p. 56. There is probably no basis for the story told by Flandrau that George Bonga and his brother Jack were "two black servants" of "an officer of the army from the South . . . stationed at Mackinac" " at quite an early period," or for the tradition recounted by Butler that George was "the son of a fugitive slave." All the most trustworthy evidence indicates that Jean and Marie Jeanne Bonga, slaves of the British captain Daniel Robertson, commanding at Mackinac Island from 1782 to 1787, were the progenitors of this Negro-Indian clan.

slaves of the Indian agent were given the curious appellation of "black Frenchmen" because the only Negroes whom these Indians had previously known were the French-speaking Bonga brood, to whom the title must have originally been given.

The few persons of Negro descent who came into contact with Indians in the Old Northwest, the Rocky Mountain region, or on the Pacific Coast, during the period before the Civil War, must have been, almost to a man, either scattered slaves of Indian agents, army officers—the historic Dred Scott was one of the "black Frenchmen"—or fur traders, or else free persons of Negro ancestry who, like the Bongas, decided for some reason to settle among the Indians. It is a curious fact that two men "of mixed Negro blood," namely, Edward Rose and James P. Beckwourth, were "recognized Crow leaders for many years." "Edward Rose was the son of a white man, a trader among the Cherokee Indians, and of a half-breed Cherokee and negro woman." He came up the Missouri in 1807 or 1809 and joined the Crows, remaining with them till 1834 and later, distinguishing himself by his shrewdness and bravery in encounters with the Blackfeet, at whose hands he finally met his death.

The immortal liar James P. Beckwourth, originally plain Jim Beckwith, was born in Fredericksburg, Virginia, April 26, 1798, and was a "mulatto or some other combination of White and African blood"—a matter on which his so-called autobiography preserves a stony silence. He was sometimes said to have been "born . . . of a negro slave mother and an Irish overseer" but another account has it that he was the "offspring . . . of a *quadroon* and a planter," which is more probable, in view of the fact that he is said to have had much of an Indian look about him. Beckwourth was brought to St. Louis at the age of seven or eight and in 1824 enlisted in General Ashley's fur-trading expedition to the Rockies. He was adopted by the Crows and lived among them for several years, during which period his lodge was successively occupied by a number of Indian wives.[185]

It is said that Captain Clark's servant, York, whom we have already met in another connection, after returning to Missouri and receiving his freedom, later "accompanied a trader up the Missouri," about 1820, and he settled down with the Indians. In 1832-34 he was "residing in the Crow village at the junction of Bighorn and Stinking rivers . . . had . . . four Indian wives, and possessed much reputation and influence among the Crows, from whom he secured the return of some horses which they had stolen" from the party of Zenas Leonard, who told the story.[186] The reason for the friendliness of the Crows to Negroes, and indeed to white men as well, is an interesting subject for speculation.

Relations were not always friendly between the Indians and the few Negroes who found their way into the Far West. In 1843, for example, at Fort McKenzie, "through one of those chance misunderstandings which now and then occurred, the Blackfeet . . . killed a negro servant" belonging to Francis A. Chardon. This misadventure so irritated his master that, with the assistance of a cannon loaded with grape shot, he made an earnest attempt to wipe out the next band of Blackfeet who called at the post to trade, and though he did not fully succeed in his project, he made a very satisfactory beginning.[187]

Few Negroes who might wish to escape from slavery in Missouri possessed so little discretion and so much foolhardiness as to endeavor to flee west to the Indians instead of north and east into the free states and Canada. We know, however, of at least one who made the attempt. In 1846, near Fort Laramie, Francis Parkman encountered a Negro who had been picked up by Indians in a starving condition after

[185] Chittenden, Hiram Martin, *The American Fur Trade of the Far West*, 3 vols. (N.Y., 1902) vol. ii, pp. 684-685; Bonner, T. D., *The Life and Adventures of James P. Beckwourth*, Charles G. Leland, ed. (London, 1892) pp. 7, 9.

[186] *Leonard, Zenas, Adventures of* (Clearfield, Pa., 1839) quoted in Thwaites, *op. cit.*, vol. i, p. 185 n.

[187] Chittenden, *op. cit.*, vol. ii, p. 694.

having wandered on the prairies for thirty-three days. He had run away from his master in Missouri and joined a party of trappers, from whom he had become separated in a storm while hunting for some stray horses.[188]

There were a few Negroes in the Pacific Northwest during this period. In 1844, a Negro, Saul, in the Tualatin district, married to an Indian, threatened to stir up the natives against the whites. There is also mention of a quarrel in 1847 between a couple of free Negro settlers and an Indian employee.[189] The very slight character of the relations between Negroes and Indians in the general area which we have been discussing is indicated by the fact that we have had to deal almost entirely with individual Negroes.

After the Civil War Negro troops were used to some extent against the hostile Indians of the West. The Indians called them "buffalo soldiers," in allusion to their wooly hair, which was thought to resemble that of the bison. The Tenth United States Cavalry was a Negro regiment, and a detachment from it under Colonel L. H. Carpenter was the force which in 1868 relieved the party of Kansas scouts besieged by the Cheyennes on Beecher's Island near the eastern boundary of Colorado. I do not know of any instance of desertion to the enemy by any Negro soldier engaged against the Indians. It is a curious fact that a prominent Cheyenne warrior bore an Indian name signifying "Negro" [literally, "Black White Man"], the reason for which strange christening it is hard to surmise.[190]

Isaiah, a Negro, Sioux interpreter for the Seventh Cavalry, was killed with Custer at the Battle of the Little Big Horn in 1876. A Cheyenne who took part in the battle said: "I saw by the river, on the west side, a dead black man. He was a big man. All his clothing was gone when I saw him,

[188] Parkman, Francis, *The Oregon Trail* (Boston, 1895; first pub. 1847) p. 151.

[189] Savage, W. Sherman, "The Negro in the History of the Pacific Northwest," *Journal of Negro History* (1928) vol. xiii, pp. 255-264, pp. 258, 261-262.

[190] Grinnell, George Bird, *The Fighting Cheyennes* (N.Y., 1915) pp. 213, 250, 280-282.

but he had not been scalped nor cut up like the white men had been. Some Sioux told me he belonged to their people but was with the soldiers." Evidently it was Isaiah's adoptive membership in the Sioux tribe which, though it did not preserve his life, kept his body from mutilation, since Crow and Shoshone scouts killed with Custer were not exempted from the operations of the scalping-knife.[191] It is interesting to observe that at least one Negro was a member of the ordinarily hostile Sioux tribe.

To my personal knowledge there is a good deal of Indian blood among the Kansas Negroes, many of whom are descendants of Union soldiers who came to Kansas soon after the Civil War, when there were still many Indians in the state. This combination is probably one of the factors which assists to give the Negroes of that state considerable independence of character. Proximity to Oklahoma with its Negro-Indian mixtures has also been an influence in bringing about this intermingling of races. Negroes are to be encountered bearing as surnames the tribal designations of the Indians from whom they derive part of their blood, e.g. "Kiowa." It is hard to decide whether the Kansas Indians have undergone a similar intermixture to any significant extent. Dr. Dubois, perhaps maliciously, hinted as much in relation to a certain personage of Kaw Indian blood who is high in the political life of the country. The Georgia boxer "Young" Stribling was once matched for a bout in Kansas with the "Indian" fighter Chief John Metoquah. The Georgian took one look at his opponent and then walked out of the ring, refusing to fight a "nigger." He was finally induced to go on with the contest, by the plea that from earliest times the Kaw Indians have been distinguished for the unusual darkness of their coloration.

In comparatively recent times another Indian element has been brought into contact with the Negroes of Kansas. The need for common labor on sugar-beet plantations, in the

[191] Marquis, Thomas B., *A Warrior Who Fought Custer* (Minneapolis, 1931) p. 261.

salt-mines, and on the railroad, has brought a large immigration of Mexican peons, usually unaccompanied by their women. The only important social contacts possible to them are with the Negroes, and intermarriage is not uncommon. It is doubtful whether anything else could do so much to Americanize Mexican residents as such marriages; they certainly have an encouraging effect upon the membership of "La Iglesia Metodista Mejicana."

This hasty survey of the relations between Negroes and Indians within the present bounds of the United States reveals that the contact between these two races has had as its main results, historically, the bringing about of two so-called Indian wars, one of great importance; and racially, the Africanizing of two of the principal Indian tribes, as well as of a number of Indian peoples of lesser importance, and the infusing into the blood of the American Negro of a perceptible and significant Indian element. It has also tended to indicate that under favorable circumstances the descendants of Negroes and Indians are probably at least the equals of members of either race. But aside from any question of historical importance, the subject is of absorbing interest in its own right.

Corrections and Additions

p. 14, l. 4-6: "York was . . . in all probability . . . a St. Louis Negro who had picked up French in Missouri." According to a nephew of Captain William Clark, York was a Virginia-born Negro, of a family that had long belonged to the Clarks, and had lived since 1785 in Kentucky. Probably he had picked up a smattering of French from French-speaking local Negroes during the months the expedition had spent in Missouri, December, 1803-May, 1804. William Clark Kennerly, as told to Elizabeth Russell, *Persimmon Hill: A Narrative of Old St. Louis and the Far West* (Norman, Okla., 1948), pp. 12, 14-15, 19-20, 25, 31, 52.

p. 14, l. 13-15: "York . . . was very favorably impressed by the opportunity . . . of . . . associating with the various Indian tribes." A reference to the incorrect belief that about 1820 York settled among the Crows.

p. 17, last line: "his theory" should be "this theory."

p. 22, bottom of page: "No slave revolt, instigated by Indians, . . . ever took place . . . save perhaps in the Deep South." Strike out "perhaps".

p. 25, l. 10-14: "Negro prisoners, . . . Presumably . . . would be adopted into the tribe, though I have been unable to find satisfactory evidence of any definite case." I have since encountered several such cases.

p. 30, l. 24-28: ". . . no record of any runaway Negro . . . participating in a raid on a white settlement in company with a war party of his adoptive people. This, of course, applies only to New England, the middle colonies and states, and the Upper South." I have since found cases of runaway or captured Negroes accompanying Indians on their raids in Kentucky.

pp. 35-38: Indian-Negro-white communities — Melungeons, Croatans, *et al.* For a comprehensive scholarly study of these communities, see Brewton Berry, *Almost White* (New York, 1963).

p. 39, l. 25: "Of perhaps more real distinction was Paul Cuffe . . . ." Strike out "perhaps."

p. 44, l. 23 - p. 45, l. 2: "About 1750, internal dissensions in the Creek tribe led a part of its members to . . . move into Spanish territory. . . . They settled in close proximity to other 'runaways' of the Negro race, with whom these Creek seceders were not slow in striking up friendly relations." It is doubtful that friendly relations between the Creek seceders (Seminole) and runaway Negroes were established before the Revolutionary War, at the earliest. The authority for the original statement is Joshua R. Giddings (*The Exiles of Florida* [1858]), whom I have come to regard as extremely untrustworthy.

pp. 45-46: The number of Negroes among the Seminole — legal slaves, legally free, captured Negroes, runaways or "maroons" — is impossible to estimate with any pretense to great accuracy. I have done the best I could with this problem in "Negroes and the Seminole War, 1835-1842" (pp. 238-61). I should now regard as a great exaggeration Giddings's estimate that in 1836 there were 1,400 Negroes among the Seminole.

p. 47, l. 34-36 "One runaway slave, who had . . . been freed, married the widow of the principal chief. . . ." The reference is to Abraham; however, that he married the widow of the principal chief is an error. See specific reference to Abraham, p. 61, and correction below.

p. 48, top line: "head chief of Micanopy." Strike out "of.'

pp. 51-55: The Negro Fort and the First Seminole War. See "Negroes and the Seminole War, 1817-1818," (pp 205-36) for detailed accounts of these episodes.

p. 56, l. 18: ". . . only the Seminoles put up a violent resistance." Insert "and protracted" after "violent." A comparatively small Creek faction also resisted, in 1836, but were speedily put down.

p. 57, l. 14: ". . . which in many cases was also a part of their families;" "in some cases" would probably be more accurate.

pp. 59 ff: The Second Seminole War, 1835-1842. The most complete and concise account of this war as it involved Negroes is "Negroes and the Seminole War, 1835-1842." See pp. 238-61 and also pp. 262-356, which deal with particular aspects of this war.

p. 59, l. 10: The statement that Osceola had a part-Negro wife who was seized and carried into slavery is of more than doubtful authenticity. See Porter, "The Episode of Osceola's Wife: Fact or Fiction?", *FHQ*, XXVI (July, 1947), pp. 92-98.

p. 59, last line - p. 60, l. 3: ". . . the treacherous guide . . . participated in the attack on those whom he had led into this death-trap." That Louis Pacheco participated actively in the destruction of Dade's command is at least questionable, although his own denial, under the circumstances, cannot be accepted as conclusive. See Porter, "The Early Life of Luis Pacheco ne Fatio," *NHB* (December, 1943), pp. 62-64, for his own account of the affair.

p. 61, l. 11: The little that is known about John Caesar is told in "John Caesar: Seminole Negro Partisan," pp. 339-56.

p. 61, l. 12: "Inos" is a misreading of a manuscript entry: "Jno" (John). John, however, was such a common name among the Seminole Negroes that this leader cannot be further identified.

pp. 61-62: For a detailed account of Abraham, see "The Negro Abraham," pp. 295-337. However, the Seminole Negro referred to as "a good soldier and intrepid leader . . . the most cunning and intelligent negro we have here . . . married to the widow of the former chief of the nation" was not Abraham but Toney Barnett.   See "Negroes, &c, Captured from Indians in Florida, &c," *25th cong., 3d sess., H. of R., War Dep't., Doc. No. 225*, p. 69.

p. 65, l. 13: "Inos". See note for p. 61, l. 12 above.

p. 66, top line: "St. Mark's" is an English form of the name of the old St. Augustine fortification, el Castillo de San Marcos, also known as Fort Marion.

p. 66, l. 14: Gopher John, with his "unerring rifle," here described as a government partisan, was earlier in the war, under the name of John Cavallo (Ca-Wy-Ya, etc.), a prominent and hostile Negro subchief. See "Negroes and the Seminole War, 1835-1842," pp. 238-61.

p. 66, l. 14: The remarkable guide, interpreter, and fighting man, Ben Wiggins, was not a Seminole Negro but a free colored man.   See Porter, "Negro Guides and Interpreters in the Early Stages of the Seminole War, Dec. 28, 1835-Mar. 6, 1837," *JNH,*

XXXV (April, 1950), pp. 179-80.

p. 67, l. 27; p. 70, l. 9-10: Louis Pacheco was sent to the Indian Territory not as the slave of Coacoochee but as Jumper's slave; Coacoochee was not involved in the "Dade massacre." Abraham and Louis Pacheco were not involved in Coacoochee's migration to Mexico, which got under way in 1849 rather than in 1850. It is unlikely, too, that the Seminole Negroes on their way to Mexico defeated a pursuing party of Creeks; the only such encounter on record ended with the defeat of the fleeing Negroes and the capture of most of the party. See "The Negro Abraham," pp. 295-96; "The Seminole in Mexico, 1850-1861," pp. 424-59; Porter, "Louis Pacheco: The Man and the Myth," *JNH*, XXVIII (January, 1943), pp. 65-72. Errors in regard to Louis Pacheco, Abraham, Coacoochee (Wild Cat), and the Seminole migration to Mexico are principally the work of Joshua R. Giddings (*The Exiles of Florida* [1858]), who frequently wrote as a novelist rather than as a historian.

p. 74, top of page: ". . . hundreds of loyal Indians, Seminoles in particular, fled north into Kansas . . ." Should be: "Creeks, Seminole and Cherokee in particular, fled north . . ." See Porter, "Billy Bowlegs (Holata Micco) in the Civil War," *FHQ*, XLV (April, 1967), pp. 391-401.

p. 74, l. 3: For "on the Way," read "on the way."

p. 79, l. 6-15; p. 88, l. 13-22: The references to "the Africanizing of two . . . principal Indian tribes" (p. 88), and the earlier similar statement (p. 79), are ridiculous exaggerations, based principally on a single sensational authority. These statements probably constitute the major error in this article.

p. 81, l. 6-7: "fur traders among the Ojibways and Chippewas."

"Ojibway" and "Chippewa" are synonymous.

p. 84, l. 6-14: Not all Negroes who "came into contact with Indians in the Old Northwest, the Rocky Mountain region, or on the Pacific Coast . . . before the Civil War" were slaves, or free persons who "decided . . . to settle among the Indians." Some were free Negroes who encountered Indians on the same basis as did white settlers. George Bush and George Washington, for example, were free mulattoes who were among the early settlers of the Pacific Northwest. See comment for p. 86, l. 5-13, below.

p. 86, l. 5-13: The paragraph on the "few Negroes in the Pacific Northwest" omits the two most important Negroes of the early period — George Bush, one of the earliest American settlers in what is now Washington, and George Washington, the founder of Centralia, Washington. Something over sixty Negroes and mulattoes were listed in the first Oregon census (1850).

p. 86, l. 14: The statement that "Negro troops were used to some extent against the hostile Indians of the West" implicitly minimizes the fact that not only the Tenth United States Cavalry but also the Ninth Cavalry and the Twenty-fourth and Twenty-fifth Infantry were Negro regiments that were continuously employed on the Indian-fighting frontier until as late as 1890. See: *APSYB 1965* (Philadelphia, 1966), pp. 430-31; William H. Leckie, *The Buffalo Soldiers: A Narrative of the Negro Cavalry in the West* (Norman, Okla., 1967).

p. 86, l. 22: Since writing that I did not know of any instance of a Negro soldier's deserting to the Indians, I have learned of at least one probable case — a Negro bugler of the Tenth Cavalry who joined the Comanches and was killed at the battle of Adobe Walls, 1874. See "Relations between Negroes and Indians on the Texas Frontier, 1831-1876" (p. 420).

p. 86, l. 25-28: The reason for a Cheyenne warrior calling himself Black White Man (Negro) was as a compliment to Andrew Green, a servant at Bent's Fort in Colorado, who, because of his color, was nicknamed "Black White Man." See "Notes Supplementary to 'Relations between Negroes and Indians,' " pp. 129-30.

p. 87, l. 27: The Kansas Indian boxer, Chief John Metoquah, was probably not a Kaw but a Potawatomi or Kickapoo.

The year after the foregoing article appeared, supplementary notes were published in the *Journal of Negro History* (Vol. XVIII, No. 3 – July, 1933), and are reprinted here.

NOTES SUPPLEMENTARY TO "RELATIONS BETWEEN NEGROES AND INDIANS"

The publication of an article frequently seems to act as a lodestone to bring together scattered pieces of pertinent information hitherto unknown or disregarded. Since the publication in the July, 1932, issue of the JOURNAL OF NEGRO HISTORY of my article, "Relations between Negroes and Indians within the Present Limits of the United States," a sufficient quantity of new material has come, or been brought, to my attention to justify its arrangement and publication. The information which follows is to be regarded not as complete in itself but as supplementary to the article above mentioned, in connection with which it should be used. In arranging this new material I have as near as possible followed the outline furnished by the earlier article.

I am able to add some details of interest, and even of some significance, to the account of Estevanico given in the earlier article. As to his personal appearance we learn that he was "a blacke man which had a beard," a "Negro which wore about his legs & armes certain things which did ring," or, as elsewhere expressed, "was wont to weare bels, & feathers on his armes & legs." A variety of reasons for his death at the hands of the Indians, in addition to the usual one of his attempt to enforce a tribute of turquoises and women, have been preserved. One account is that he sent "his great Mace made of a gourd . . . which gourd had a string of bells upon it, and two feathers, one white and another red" to the headman of the pueblo of Cibola, who was angered at its appearance, the implication being that he recognized it as of the type employed by the medicine-men of a hostile tribe. Coronado was told that the Negro not only made too free with the women of the people he encountered, but that he even "killed women," which, despite Estevanico's alleged foolhardiness, appears so improbable that it may quite likely be an "atrocity story." Another account has it that the Negro claimed to have many brothers not far off, and that he was killed lest he encourage his kinsmen to conquer the people to whom he made this boast. Among the plunder acquired by the Negro's murderers was a dog of European breed, which the Indians finally killed after keeping it a long time, and four green dinner-plates, which caused a great stir of envy among the other chiefs of the region. Estevanico's body was cut up and distributed among the pueblos as a curiosity.[1]

All the early Spanish explorers were accompanied by Negroes, who, like Estevanico in the earlier part of his career, usually got along well with the natives. De Soto, in aid of his exploration of the Mississippi region, was given by royal grant the privilege of taking with him fifty Negro slaves.[2] One of these slaves, it is said, distinguished himself by eloping with the "queen" of the Yuchi.[3] The story is told by the "Gentleman of Elvas," one of the chroniclers of the expedition. This "cacica of Cutipachi," described as a very personable young woman, in return for her kindness to the explorers was made a captive, but managed to escape, "going to Xualla, with three slaves who had fled from the camp. A horseman, named Alimamos, who remained behind, sick of a fever, wandering out of the way, got lost; and he laboured with the slaves to make them leave their evil design. Two of them did so, and came on with him to the camp ... the Cacica remained in Xualla, with a slave of Andre de Vasconcelos, who would not come with him, and ... it was very sure they

---

[1] Hakluyt, Richard, *Voyages*, 12 vols. (Glasgow, 1905), vol. ix, Fernando Alarcon's account, pp. 300, 304; Friar Marco's account, p. 139; Coronado's account, p. 112.

[2] Smith, Buckingham, ed., *Narratives of the Career of Hernando de Soto* (New York, 1866), p. 269.

[3] Chamberlain, A. F., "Negro and Indian," *Handbook of American Indians*, Frederick Webb Hodge, ed. (Washington, D. C., 1910), pp. 51-53.

lived together as man and wife, and were to go together to Cutifachiqui.''[4]

The question might arise: ''How can we be sure, in view of the number of Indians enslaved on this expedition, that the 'queen's' paramour was not one of her own race, rather than an African?'' Aside from the fact that all commentators agree that the fortunate slave was a Negro, there are in the story itself definite indications to that effect. No one who has read the chronicles of the De Soto expedition can fail to remember that the salient characteristic of the natives they encountered and tried to subdue was a murderous ferocity which almost approached the stage of lunacy. Had a lone lost Spaniard, ill, too, be it remembered, encountered three runaways from the ranks of these recently enslaved Indians and ''laboured'' to make them ''leave their evil design'' the first and only result of his efforts would have been to have his brains beaten out. Runaway Negroes, in a strange land and with no recent memories of liberty, would be more likely to be amenable to reason. We also know from another source—the diary of de Soto's secretary—that about this time three slaves and even one or two Spaniards became either deserters or stragglers. Of the slaves one was an Indian boy from Cuba, one a ''Berber,''—perhaps a ''Barbary Moor'' like Estevanico—and the third a Negro named Gomez. A little later a Negro named Johan Biscayan likewise deserted.[5] True, none of these deserters is stated to have belonged to Vasconcelos, the owner of the cacica's companion, but a confusion in the identity of that lucky individual's master would be easy: Later explorers learned that two deserters, a soldier and a Negro, lived among the Coosa Indians for a

[4] Smith, *op. cit.*, p. 68.

[5] Bourne, Edward Gaylord, ed., *Narratives of the Career of Hernando de Soto*, 2 vols. (New York, 1904), pp. 105-106, 114.

number of years.[6] It would be of interest to know how
the black consort of the Yuchi "queen" was received by
her people and what was the future history of the happy
couple.

John Spencer Bassett makes the specific statement that
Indian slaves in North Carolina intermarried with and
were finally completely absorbed by the Negroes.[7] Evidence of this intermixture in a number of states appears
in the not infrequent claims to freedom made by slaves
who asserted descent on the maternal side from Indians
who had been reduced to servitude, and who advanced in
support of their claims various gubernatorial proclamations or acts of assembly which declared Indians to be not
subject to perpetual and hereditary servitude. For example, in 1827, in Virginia, a man laid claim to freedom
on the ground that he was the grandson of a woman who
was Indian and Negro, asserting that the Negro blood
came from her father, and that her mother—and therefore her descendants—were legally Indian, and consequently free.[8] An interesting case appeared in the Missouri courts about the same time. Marguerite, born in
1778, was the daughter of Marie Jeanne, sometimes
called Marie Scipion, who was herself said to be the
daughter of an Indian woman, captured by the French
near Natchez and brought to Fort Chartres, and of "a
negro man named Scipion." Marie Scipion died June,
1802, aged about 60 years. Her mother had belonged to
the strange Natchez tribe, exterminated or enslaved by
the French early in the 18th century, 300 of whom had
been sent to the West Indies to join the Pequots, the In-

[6] Lowery, Woodbury, *The Spanish Settlements within the Present Limits
of the United States*, 1513-1561 (New York and London, 1901), p. 365.

[7] *Slavery and Servitude in the Colony of North Carolina* (Johns Hopkins University Studies: Baltimore, 1896), pp. 240-242.

[8] Catterall, Helen Tunnicliff, *Judicial Cases concerning American Slavery
and the Negro*, 2 vols. (Washington, D. C., 1926), vol. i, p. 147, and see
index under "Indians."

dians enslaved after King Philip's War, and the Yemassees from South Carolina. The grand-daughter of this Natchez slave-girl claimed her freedom on the grounds of Governor O'Reilly's proclamation in regard to Indian slaves, made in 1769. Marguerite failed in her action in 1828 but six years later the earlier decision was reversed and she was declared to be entitled to her freedom.[9] Undoubtedly for every slave of Negro-Indian blood who attempted to obtain his freedom because of an Indian ancestress there were a number who did not venture to make the claim, or who did not know of its possibility or even of their own Indian blood.

In the earlier article I pointed out that the character of the relations between Negroes and Indians depended upon circumstances and were not determined solely or even principally by any feeling that as members of the darker races they were natural allies. It is well known that Indians visiting white settlements were not infrequently abused or even killed by members of the rougher element among the whites. It is equally true, though not so well known, that Negroes were not guiltless of ill-treating Indians who were visiting in the settlements. In 1702 a Pennacook Indian, a member of a delegation to the governor of New York, was killed in a brawl with four Negroes. But, strange to relate, before succumbing to his injuries, he requested that the lives of his assailants be spared, inasmuch as they knew no better. The other members of the delegation urged his request upon the governor, who insisted upon executing the ringleader but agreed to reprieve the others. Another case of the murder of Indians by Negroes occurred later in the century, when a Negro killed two Indian women at Detroit in 1766. The English authorities promised to inflict suitable punishment.[10]

[9] *Missouri Reports*, vol. ii (1828), pp. 50-63; vol. iii (1834), pp 285-303.
[10] *New York Colonial Documents*, vol. iv, pp. 997-998, 1001; vol. vii, p. 856.

In the earlier article I also mentioned that casualties among Negroes in Indian warfare were by no means unusual. A few more instances might be added to make the assortment of typical cases more complete. For example, about the middle of the eighteenth century the Piankeshaws are reported to have killed slaves near Fort Vincennes.[11] In 1789 Indians killed a small Negro girl in Virginia after taking her prisoner, and also made a prisoner of her mother, threatening her with death if she complained of the murder of her child.[12] In 1792 the Cherokees attacked a station near Frankfort, Kentucky, killed three white men, "as many negroes, and made the rest prisoners."[13]

As mentioned in the earlier article, Negroes not only sometimes became the unoffending victims of the savages in Indian warfare but also occasionally acted effectively as the partisans of their masters and of the whites in general. In 1756 a Negro teamster, after having been made prisoner by French and Indians in an attack on a wagon-train, escaped and carried the news to Fort Williams.[14] Quite likely he was a free Negro. In the Battle of Lake George, when the English and their Indian allies met the French and their native partisans, Negroes served with the British and it was said that "Our Blacks behaved better than the Whites."[15] It is recorded that "John Har-

[11] *New York Colonial Documents*, vol. x, p. 248.

[12] Ellett, Mrs. Elizabeth F., *The Pioneer Women of the West* (Philadelphia, n.d.), p. 118; De Hass, Wills, *History of the Indian Wars of Western Virginia* (Wheeling and Philadelphia, 1851), pp. 306-307.

[13] Frost, John, *Pioneer Mothers of the West* (Boston, 1859), pp. 59-60, quoting from Butler, *History of Kentucky*.

[14] *New York Colonial Documents*, vol. x, pp. 403-405, 529. Early in June, 1778, in an attack by Indians on the Greenbriar settlements, Dick, the black servant of Col. Donnally, together with a white borderer for some time held the door against the enemy, who had actually cut through the planking in several places (De Hass, *op. cit.*, p. 242).

[15] *Ibid.*, vol. vi, p. 1005; at the Battle of Fallen Timbers a runaway Negro who had attached himself to Wayne's army distinguished himself by killing three Indians (Pritts, Joseph, *Incidents of Border Life*, Lancaster, Pa., 1841, p. 453).

ris, the founder of Harrisburg, set free the faithful negro Hercules, who had saved his life from the Indians.''[16]   A thrilling episode took place in 1784 when Indians attacked the cabin of the Woods family in Lincoln County, Kentucky, at a time when none of the men were at home, and one forced his way in before the door could be shut.   A Negro slave, although lame, immediately grappled with him and brought him to the floor. Although the Negro fell undermost he succeeded in holding the warrior and keeping him from drawing his knife until Mrs. Woods, at the slave's request, could kill the Indian with two blows of an axe.   The Negro then proposed that they should let the Indians enter the cabin one by one and dispose of them singly, but the arrival of help made it unnecessary to put this daring and hazardous plan into effect.[17]

As I explained in the earlier article, though Negroes were sometimes killed by hostile Indians or fought by the side of their masters against the savages, the Negro was regarded by the Indian as being on a different basis from the white man, being treated in much the same way as the white woman, who, though she might kill or be killed in the height of action, was not ordinarily tortured, so far as we have trustworthy record, and was usually held as a prisoner for adoption or ransom.   The fact that the Negro had a ready cash value in Canada was a factor in aiding him to good treatment by his Indian captors and in leading them to capture rather than kill him in the first place. We see an example of this in the following record from Montreal for July 16, 1748, ''Sieur de Niverville Montizambert is arrived . . . with his party; he brings 3 scalps and one Negro prisoner.''[18]

[16] Turner, Edward Raymond, *The Negro in Pennsylvania* (Washington and London, 1911), p. 57, quoting from George H. Morgan, *Annals . . . of Harrisburg* (Harrisburg, 1858), p. 11.

[17] Frost, *op. cit.*, pp. 120-121; Pritts, *op. cit.*, pp. 386-387.

[18] *New York Colonial Documents,* vol. x, p. 172. In May, 1782, Wyandots killed a white man and captured a Negro south of the Kentucky River (Butler, Mann, *A History of Kentucky,* Cincinnati and Louisville, 1836, p. 120).

It was quite natural that, just as slaves who were discontented for some reason should try to escape to the French in Canada,[19] as we saw in the earlier article, just so slaves who had been well-treated by their original owners should not take kindly to the change of masters incident to being captured and carried into Canada. Late in October, 1747, four such captive Negroes, assisted by a Pani slave, escaped from Montreal. "Some of the Saut Indians have been sent in pursuit of them, who returned without having been able to overtake them; they are suspected of having favored the escape of these negroes." But, however this may have been, others were not so sympathetic and the fugitives were soon overtaken and brought back to Montreal, where it was intended to put them, as dangerous characters, "on board a small vessel bound to Martinico."[20]

Of course, among the more "civilized" Southern Indians, Negro captives would be neither adopted nor sold, but instead would merely exchange a white for an Indian master. In 1788 Cherokees massacred a party of whites on the Tennessee River and captured several Negroes, who, with their descendants, were not recovered till 1813.[21]

The Negro slaves of the Spaniards seem usually to have gotten on quite well with the Indians among whom they found themselves. Such close sympathy between the two races does not seem to have appeared in any of the English colonies, or in the United States, save among the Seminoles. However, there seems to be no doubt that runaway slaves not infrequently found a refuge among the Indians of certain tribes in the more northerly part of

[19] For example, just before the beginning of the French and Indian War, a French agent to the Indians mentioned having encountered a very fine Negro, of about twenty-two years of age, a fugitive from Virginia, on the nothern shore of Lake Ontario (Parkman, Francis, *Montcalm and Wolfe*, Boston, 1897, vol. i, p. 73).

[20] *New York Colonial Documents*, vol. x, p. 138.

[21] Frost, *op. cit.*, pp. 128, 132, 137, 158, 161.

what is now the United States. A series of treaties between the various governors of New York and the Iroquois
confederacy, the Hurons, and the Delawares, between 1721
and 1764, uniformly provided, in some formula or other,
for the return of "Negroes, Panis, or other Slaves . . .
who are British property" and who had taken refuge with
the Indians, to employ the phraseology used by William
Johnson in the treaty negotiated with the Hurons in 1764.
True it is that the Indians usually denied "that there is
one among any of the Six Nations," but there are, nevertheless, indications that some of the Indians did know of
runaways sheltering themselves in the Indian country.
For example, in 1722 the Indians of the Six Nations, while
professing willingness to return fugitives, said that the
ones who had fled from Virginia were too much out of
their way and should be reclaimed through more conveniently located tribes. In 1765 it was specifically provided
that the Delawares were to bring runaway Negroes to a
conference at Johnson Hall, and their failure to do so was
noted.[22] It seems quite clear that a significant number of
Negroes were known to have escaped to the above-mentioned Indians and that their willingness to return the
fugitives was almost exclusively verbal. In 1829 a Negro
ran away from Kentucky and took "refuge among the
Indians," but was found "on the northwestern frontier"
and brought back.[23]

In only one source have I found any statement claiming marked activity on the part of Indians in the return
of runaway slaves. An early writer on North Carolina
says: "When they [the Negro slaves] have been guilty of
these barbarous and disobedient Proceedings [mutiny or
insurrection], they generally fly to the Woods, but as soon
as the *Indians* have Notice from the *Christians* of their

---

[22] *New York Colonial Documents*, vol. v, pp. 637, 639, 674, 676, 965,
968; vol. vii, pp. 650, 718, 732-733, 739.

[23] Catterall, *op. cit.*, vol. i, p. 313.

being there, they disperse them; killing some, others flying for Mercy to the *Christians* (whom they have injured)
rather than fall into the others Hands, who have a natural aversion to the Blacks, and put them to death with
the most exquisite Tortures, they can invent, whenever
they catch them.''[24] The North Carolina Indians' treatment of runaway Negroes, if of the character here alleged,
was probably rather the result of their desire to oblige
and be rewarded by the whites than the ''natural aversion'' asserted by this writer.

In the earlier article I made reference to the fact that,
in spite of the probable presence of Negro runaways
among the Indians of the northern part of the Thirteen
Colonies, I had ''found no record of any runaway Negro
later participating in a raid on a white settlement in
company with a war party of his adoptive people.'' However, the idea of an Indian raid, accompanied and supported by a slave insurrection, was not unfamiliar or
absurd to the minds of the slave-holders of the eighteenth
century. A letter written from Staunton, July 26, 1763,
during the panic caused by Pontiac's insurrection, contains the statement that ''the Indians are saving and
caressing all the negroes they take; should it produce an
insurrection, it may be attended with the most serious
consequences.''[25]

In 1780, when the Gilbert family of Northampton
County, Pennsylvania, were captured by Indians in the
British interest, the war-party on its return journey was
joined by four runaway Negroes whom the Indians had

[24] Brickell, John, *The Natural History of North Carolina* (Dublin, 1737),
pp. 263, 272, 357.

[25] Parkman, Francis, *The Conspiracy of Pontiac*, 3 vols. (Boston, 1898),
vol. ii, p. 221, note. A few years earlier than this, in 1755, just after
Braddock's defeat, Governor Dinwiddie of Virginia spoke of the excitement
this disaster had caused among the blacks, who had become ''very auda-
cious;'' he was inclined to wonder whether it might not be a good idea to
nip their potential wickedness in the bud by making an example of one or
two (Parkman, *Montcalm and Wolfe*, vol. i, p. 237).

encountered in the wilderness while the Negroes were on
their way to Niagara and whom they had left with a supply of corn while the raiding party proceeded against the
settlements. These Negroes treated the captives with
more severity than did the Indians themselves, insulting
and whipping them.[26] But this is the only actual example
of co-operation between runaway Negroes and a raiding
party of Indians in the northern part of the English colonies or of the United States that I have been able to discover. During the siege of Fort Henry in 1782 a Negro
escaped from the Indians to the fort, being severely
wounded before the sentry realized that he was not an
Indian. He was, however, regarded as a spy and, for the
duration of the siege, was kept in fetters and under close
guard.[27] The poor fellow was probably merely a runaway
slave who had taken refuge with the Indians and found
the "wild, free life of the forest" not quite as enjoyable
as he had anticipated.

To the little information concerning relations between
Negro slaves and peaceful Indians of the neighborhood
which I was able to present in my earlier article, I can
now add a single detail of some interest. We are told
that among a number of slaves mentioned in a discussion
of slavery in eighteenth century Pennsylvania, "one negro
says that he has been a preacher among the Indians."[28]

Passing on to relations between reservation Indians
and free Negroes in the northern part of the United States
we encounter new information about the Shinnacook Indians of Long Island, mentioned in the earlier article. An
observer in 1903 wrote, "Although an Indian reservation
in name . . . it seems to be a negro settlement pure and
simple. But a closer examination shows that many of the
people have Indian blood." The inhabitants of this res-

[26] Pritts, *op. cit.*, pp. 217-218, 220.
[27] De Hass, *op. cit.*, p. 268.
[28] Turner, *op. cit.*, p. 51.

ervation were noted to have a mixture of racial characteristics, ranging from persons who were apparently pure
Indians, or nearly so, to others who were in appearance
almost purely Negro, and including almost every possible
combination of racial traits. The flower of the tribe, of
which most of the adult males were sailors, perished in
1876 in the wreck of the *Circassian*.[29]

Recognition of the fact that "it is probable that many
of the negroes of the whole lower Atlantic and Gulf region
have much of Indian blood"[30] has recently begun to appear in works of fiction. To the novels mentioned in the
earlier article others may now be added. Du Bose Hey-
ward, in his novel of life among the Negroes of Charleston, South Carolina, and vicinity, recognizes the Indian
element among the Southern Negroes by making his principal character, Mamba, and her "daughters," Hagar and
Lissa, the possessors of a strain of Indian blood.[31] In Roy
Flanagan's *Amber Satyr* (Garden City, New York, 1932)
the central figure is a Virginia swamp Negro of Indian
blood, one of a group calling themselves "Indians of the
Hehonee tribe," who with the members of the "Tohan-
nock tribe" are endeavoring to preserve their status as
Indians and to avoid being classed as Negroes by legislative enactment.[32]

The list of persons of mixed Negro and Indian blood

[29] Harrington, M. R., "Shinnecock Notes," *Journal of American Folklore*, vol. xvi, (1903), pp. 37-39.

[30] Chamberlain, *loc. cit.*, pp. 51-53.

[31] *Mamba's Daughters* (New York, 1929), pp. 6-7, 207.

[32] A similar recognition of the Indian strain in the Negro has also appeared in fiction of a quite unsociological nature. In Mark Twain's *Pud-
din'head Wilson*, Roxana, the 15/16ths white Negro slave who is the *dea ex
machina* of the novel, claims descent from "Pocahontas, de Injun queen"
as well as from "a nigger king outen Africa," and this may have been
intended by the author to represent a confused tradition of an Indian
strain in her ancestry. In J. P. Marquand's romantic novel, *The Unspeakable Gentleman*, stress is laid upon the Indian blood of Brutus, the formida-
able body-servant who plays a conspicuous part in the action.

who have attained distinction could probably be indefinitely extended by dint of further investigation. A case which comes readily to hand is that of Elizabeth Prophet, "a descendant of Negroes and Narragansett Indians, born in Rhode Island and still in her young womanhood," who is making a name for herself as a sculptor.[33]

Turning to the South, we discover new evidence that as early as 1721 Fort Augustine was garrisoned by three or four hundred whites and about 200 Indians, who made a practice of sheltering runaway slaves from the English colonies.[34]

In the portion of my earlier article which dealt with the Red Stick War I mentioned that among the Creek casualties in the Battle of Burnt Corn was the death of one Negro. I suggested that though the dead man was doubtless a slave to Peter McQueen, the half-breed leader of the hostile Creeks, nevertheless this was "significant as indicating the *rapprochement* which was taking place between the two races." The significance of the appearance of this Negro among the Red Stick dead is, however, somewhat decreased by the information that he was a noncombatant, who was killed while "engaged in cooking." But Negroes were prominent on both sides in the massacre of Fort Mimms. It was said that " 'a large and powerful negro man,' wielding an axe, 'killed more Indians than any other man in the fort,' but he fell at last, covered with wounds 'from knife, and club, and tomahawk.' " On the other hand, Creek slaves took a conspicuous part in the attack on the fort. The buildings were set on fire with blazing arrows discharged by "The Shawnee Siekaloo . . . and some of the McGillivray Negroes."

Although in the confusion of the massacre some Negroes, in addition to those who fought in defense of their

[33] "Can I Become a Sculptor: The Story of Elizabeth Prophet," *The Crisis*, October, 1932, p. 315.

[34] *New York Colonial Documents*, vol. v, p. 612.

masters' families, fell at the hands of the hostile Creeks, still the latter did not treat Negroes and white prisoners the same, doubtless hoping to win over the former to the Indian cause. Later in the war the Creeks armed their slaves extensively and in the Battle of the Holy Ground, December 25, 1813, twenty-one Creeks and twelve Negroes were killed. During the subsequent destruction of the hostile village a runaway mulatto was found hiding in one of the houses and was shot as he tried to escape. The Choctaw allies of the whites in this battle, though they scalped the dead Negroes, contemptuously threw the trophies away immediately after, and even one of the Creek chiefs, Kinnie Hadjo, later censured his fellow-tribesmen for their lack of pride in using Negro slaves to fight their battles.[35]

Readers of my earlier article will remember that the First Seminole War began in 1816 with the destruction of the Negro Fort on the Appalachicola. It is of interest to note that one of the United States officers concerned in this affair wrote contemptuously of the conduct of his Creek allies but in a tone of admiration concerning the spirited attitude of the defenders of the fort. "Many circumstances convinced us that most of them determined never to be taken alive." The garrison, he went on, observed that "they wished to fight and had gone into the fort for no other purpose."[36]

Going forward nearly two decades in time to the period of Indian removal, we discover some interesting new statistical information in regard to the relative number of Indians and Negroes among some of the slave-holding tribes. In 1833 there were 14,142 Creeks in the upper towns, including 445 Negro slaves; in the lower towns were 8,552, of whom 457 were Negro slaves. Of the Creek

[35] Halbert, H. S., and Ball, T. H., *The Creek War* (Chicago and Montgomery, 1895), pp. 135, 155-156, 158n., 208, 258, 259.

[36] *Army and Navy Chronicle*, vol. ii (1836), pp. 114-116.

population 6,557 were heads of families.[37]   In 1835 there were 16,542 Cherokees, exclusive of 1,592 Negro slaves and 201 intermarried whites.[38]   The greater proportion of slaves among the Cherokees was a circumstance befitting this acknowledgedly more advanced tribe.

In the earlier article we noted that only the Seminoles made serious resistance to their removal across the Mississippi.   However, certain small bands among the Creeks did engage in acts of violence at this time.   Late in 1836 hostile Creeks killed a white man and two Negroes on an Alabama plantation and similar acts of violence took place early in the succeeding year.[39]   The Creeks were never so friendly to Negroes as were the Seminoles, though distinctly more so than the Choctaws and Chickasaws, in particular.   These Creeks were probably inspired by no particular dislike of the slain Negroes, whose murder they probably regarded principally as an injury to the white masters—similar to the houghing of a cow or the burning of a barn.   At about the time of the Creek removal, members of this tribe were made the victims of encroachments by slave-hunting whites, similar to those of which we have seen the Seminoles made the object.   In February, 1837, for example, we are told that some whites stole free Negroes living with friendly Creeks.[40]

[37] Something of the character of slavery among the Creeks is indicated by the fact that the commissioners for Indian removal had to apply to the government for definition of the status of Creek Indians married to Negro slaves, and free "mestizos" (meaning in this case persons of mixed Indian and Negro blood) with Negro slaves for wives. Moreover, among the heads of families in the Creek nation were listed such persons as "Meter, (wife of Nero, a free black)," "Molly (or Mary, a half negro)," "Hannah, (widow of Eupolika, a free black woman)," and, perhaps most curious of all, "Polly (half negro and having a negro slave 'for a husband,' named John)," ("Indian Removal," *United States Senate Document No. 512*, 23rd Congress, 1st sess., 5 vols., vol. iii, p. 444; vol. iv, pp. 380, 385, 350, 381).

[38] Foreman, Grant, *Indian Removal* (Norman, Okla., 1932), pp. 111, 250. This book is the most valuable for the purposes of this study of any single publication of recent years.

[39] *Ibid.*, p. 180.

[40] *Ibid.*

Turning again to the status of Negroes among the Seminoles at about the time the question of removal to the west began to be agitated we find that one of their principal chiefs, noted for his hostility to the Americans, was of Negro blood. A characterization of him was given in 1832 by an Indian agent: "Mulatto King, or Vacapu-hassee, the cowdriver, was made head chief of Choconicla, by *Colonel Arbuckle.* Mulatto is a half negro and Indian, was always a bitter enemy of the Americans, is bad tempered, insubordinate and mischievous, and would be more so but that he is totally without courage." Apparently Colonel Arbuckle, commanding along the Florida frontier in the first Seminole War, was exceedingly ill-advised to use his influence toward the appointment of such an unsuitable person to the headship even of one Seminole village.[41] One gathers from the above description not only the opinion had of its subject by the author but also that Mulatto King must have arisen to his lofty title from a rather low original position, quite aside from his mixed blood.

But not only were there chiefs of mixed Indian and Negro blood among the Seminoles, and free Negroes acting as principal counsellors and war-captains, but, as we saw in the earlier article, the position of the very slaves was so influential that the Seminole nation might present to students of political science an interesting and perhaps almost unique example of a very close approach to a doulocracy, or government by slaves—if such a term possesses more than a theoretical significance.

I am able to add from sources to which I was guided by information contained in Grant Foreman's recently published *Indian Removal* some new details of the part played by Negroes in the Great Seminole War of 1835-1842. In the earlier article an official estimate placed the

[41] *United States Senate Documents,* No. 512, 23rd Congress, 1st sess., vol. iv, p. 695.

number of Seminole warriors arrayed against the United States as from 1,800 to 2,000, including Negroes, while a separate and unofficial estimate placed the number of the latter at about 250. An estimate for February 20, 1836, in the *Army and Navy Chronicle* agrees quite closely with the preceding, enumerating the Seminole force as 1,500 "warriors" (probably meaning Indians alone) and from 200 to 300 Negroes (probably referring only to adult males), bringing the whole Seminole fighting force to from 1,700 to 1,800 or not much below the number previously given.[42]

It was thought worthwhile in June, 1836, to announce to the world the capture of a Negro heavily armed with a musket, twenty balls, and plenty of powder. The destruction late in 1836 of a Negro village on the lake at the head of Oklawaha and the capturing of forty-one of its inhabitants was undoubtedly an event of major importance.[43]

As has been noted, the second year of the war began badly for the Seminoles and their black allies. Early in January friendly Creeks surprised and captured sixty Negroes; among them was Primus, who had originally been a slave to Erastus Rogers, a sutler, one of the men who had been killed with General Wiley Thompson when Osceola began the war by wreaking vengeance on the Indian agent who had imprisoned him. He had been sent as a messenger to the Seminoles twice and on the second occasion had joined them. The unfortunate man, torn between two allegiances, was given the choice of furnishing information about his recent allies or being hanged.[44] It would be difficult to condemn his decision, whatever it was.

Also in January, 1837, a scout of mounted men and Indians killed the Seminole chief, Cooper, his son, and an Indian doctor, and captured sixteen, the families of the

[42] *Army and Navy Chronicle*, vol. ii (1836), p. 151.
[43] *Ibid.*, vol. iii, p. 27; vol. iv., p. 12.
[44] *Ibid.*, vol. iv, p. 79.

slain men and some Negroes. The interest in this episode
for our purpose lies in the fact that "Cooper was brother-
in-law to Mikanopy and the immediate commander of the
negroes, and conspicuous for his cruelties and courage."
He was killed and scalped by a Creek.[45] When these misfortunes are added to those recorded in the earlier article,
it is easy to see why the hostile Seminoles and their allies
might have become disheartened.

On January 7, 1837, a report from Tampa, printed in
the *New Orleans Bulletin,* stated that "the Indians themselves are determined to hold out, and are encouraged and
sustained by the gang of sable banditti nominally their
slaves, but who are really their chief counsellors, and in
effect their masters. It is a negro, not an Indian war."[46]
But the misfortunes mentioned above, it was believed, had
modified the attitude of the hostile Indians and Negroes,
and accordingly the whites decided to attempt negotiations. "They had captured a negro named Ben, a slave of
Mikanopy, who told the officers that Jumper and Abraham
were in the neighborhood and would come in if they were
sure of their lives. Accordingly, on January 31, Ben was
sent to Jumper with offers of a liberal treaty. Three days
later Abraham came in with pacific messages from Jumper
and Alligator, whom he brought in on February 3 . . . .
Accordingly, largely through the negotiations of the negro,
Abraham, on March 6, 1837, at Camp Dade, a treaty was
concluded between Jesup and the Seminole chiefs Jumper
and Holantochee claiming to represent Mikanopy . . . .
By the terms of this treaty the Indians agreed to cease
their hostilities, come to Tampa Bay by April 10, and
board the transports for the West. The chief Mikanopy
was to be surrendered as a hostage for the performance
of their promises. However, to induce them to accept these
terms, General Jesup was obliged to agree to the one con-

[45] Foreman, *op. cit.,* p. 343.
[46] *Army and Navy Chronicle,* vol. iv, p. 80.

dition that the Indians had insisted on from the beginning; and that was that their allies, the free negroes, should also be secure in their persons and property; and 'that their negroes, their *bona fide property,* shall accompany them to the West.' ''[47]   It is obvious that this provision in regard to the Negroes was to the ultimate advantage of both parties, to the Indians for an obvious reason, to the white army-officers because, even were the Seminoles willing to come in without protection for their slaves and allies among the Negroes, they could not force the latter to accompany them, and it was the opinion of the army-officers that a mere handful of "resolute Negroes, with a knowledge of the country," would be "sufficient to desolate the frontier, from one extent to the other," inasmuch as the "negroes . . . fight as well as any in the country."[48]

However, as I showed in the previous article, the Treaty of Fort Dade was never really carried out because the appearance of slave-hunters in the camp caused a stampede among the Negroes and the revival of the war with redoubled fury. To the alarm of planters and army-officers, some of the hostiles began to give evidence of an intention of "carrying the war into Africa," to use a phrase later made famous by John Brown, by bursting from their swamp refuges to make raids upon the more settled country and trying to instigate revolt among the plantation slaves. In May, 1837, for example, a runaway Negro—could it have been the "Indian negro, John Caesar"?—led a party of Indians in an attack on the plantations of Camden County, Florida, the section from which he had earlier fled as a fugitive slave.[49]

But although the Treaty of Fort Dade did not bring the war at once to an end, it did, as we earlier saw, greatly weaken the Seminole powers of resistance, through de-

[47] Foreman, *op. cit.,* p. 344.

[48] *Army and Navy Chronicle,* vol. iv, p. 329.

[49] *Ibid.,* vol. iv, p. 378.

priving the Seminole Negro contingent of nearly all of its leaders. A considerable number of the rank-and-file Negroes had also been eliminated from the hostile ranks, and the 700 friendly Creeks under their Negro-Indian chief were very efficient in tracking down and killing or capturing their rebellious Seminole kinsmen. By June, 1837, "the Creek and white troops had captured and brought in 125 negro slaves, thirty-five of whom were returned to their owners and the remaining ninety, General Jesup sent to Fort Pike near New Orleans, pending further orders for their disposition." Said General Jesup: " 'The Seminole negro prisoners are now the property of the public . . . The Creek Indians were entitled to all the Indian property they captured. I compromised with them by purchasing the negroes from them on account of the Government, for which I agreed to pay them eight thousand dollars . . . I was also compelled to pay the Indians a reward of twenty dollars each for the negroes captured by them, the property of citizens.' "

It was General Jesup's intention, in purchasing the Seminole Negroes from their Creek captors, to prevent the dissemination among plantations in the Deep South of Negroes, accustomed to freedom and trained in the use of arms, who might take the lead in slave-insurrections. But General Jesup's laudable intention was in the way of being thwarted by the greed of the Creeks and the unscrupulousness of the slave-dealers who haunted the camp. The Creeks decided that, after all, they had not formally accepted the offer of $8,000 for their ninety Negro captives, and sold them to a Georgia slave-trader for from $14,000 to $15,000. General Gaines tried to keep the Negroes from being carried into bondage, but with little help from the courts of New Orleans. However, most of the Negroes succeeded in embarking with the party of 1,160 captives who left New Orleans in May, 1838. "Nearly one third," it was said, "were Negroes who had been reared among the Indians." Also in the party were "about 150 Spanish Indians or Spaniards who have intermarried with the Seminoles." The Negroes, something less than ninety in number whose status was under dispute, were pursued up the Mississippi River by the slave-trader with an order from the commissioner of Indian affairs to deliver them. The Indians objected to giving up their comrades and the governor of Arkansas, on being appealed to by the slave-trader, would not force their surrender. General Arbuckle, at Fort Gibson, also declined. The loyalty of the Seminoles conquered and the Negroes who had been left at New Orleans were finally brought up the river also.[50]

New information which has recently come to my notice enables me considerably to fill out the picture of the leading Seminole Negro partisan, Abraham, the outline of whose figure was drawn, with a few patches of light and shade, in my earlier article. In that article I gave a few of the high points in Abraham's life from his flight, as a boy, from servitude in Pensacola to the Seminole country, up to his part in the exodus of the "Negro party" among the Seminoles from the Indian Territory into Mexico, in 1850. I also quoted the verdicts upon his character pronounced by various army-officers who became personally acquainted with him at Fort Dade. Another of them also said: "Micanope (nominally the principal Seminole chief) is a fat, lubberly . . . kind of man, and is ever a stupid fool, when not replenished by his 'sense bearer,' (as he calls him) Abraham." At the conference in March, 1836, between United States officers and Seminole chiefs, which resulted in a truce of several days, were present "Abraham, and Caesar, negro advisers." Again the question arises: Is the reference to John Caesar, previously noted as having later been killed while "carrying the war into

[50] Foreman, *op. cit.*, pp. 347, 365-366.

Africa''? As already mentioned in the present article, the treaty was concluded ''largely through the negotiations of the negro, Abraham.'' An interesting description is given of Abraham's appearance and manner upon his arrival for the treaty-negotiations. '' 'Abraham who is sometimes dignified with the title of ''Prophet'' . . . is the prime minister and privy counsellor of Micanopy; and has through his master, who is somewhat imbecile, ruled all the councils and actions of the Indians in this region. Abraham is a non-committal man, with a countenance which none can read, a person erect and active and in stature over six feet. He was a principal agent in bringing about the peace, having been a commander of the negroes during the war, and an enemy by no means to be despised.' When sent for by General Jesup 'Abraham made his appearance bearing a white flag on a small stick which he had cut in the woods, and walked up to the tent of General Jesup with perfect dignity and composure. He stuck the staff of his flag in the ground, made a salute or bow with his hand, without bending his body, and then waited for the advance of the General with the most complete self-possession. He has since stated that he expected to be hung, but concluded to die, if he must, like a man, but that he would make one more effort to save his people.' '' Other comments of a less friendly nature are: ''Abraham is a cunning negro, of good consideration with the Seminoles, and who can do more than any other,'' and ''Abraham, well known as an interpreter and a wily and treacherous rascal,''[51] yet even these evidence a vivid consciousness of his ability. Another officer in a letter of May 22, 1837, remarked: ''We have a perfect Talleyrand of the Savage Court in Florida in the person of a Seminole negro, called Abraham.''[52]

[51] Foreman, *op. cit.*, pp. 328, 330, 344, note 5 (quoted from *Army and Navy Chronicle*, vol. iv, p. 378), 370.

[52] *Army and Navy Chronicle*, vol. iv, p. 378.

General Jesup, in announcing that the "Seminole negro prisoners are now the property of the public," added: "I have promised Abraham the freedom of his family if he be faithful to us, and I shall certainly hang him if he will not be faithful."[53] Just what was involved in Abraham's required "faithfulness" we are not specifically informed. We know that Abraham was employed by General Jesup in negotiating peace treaties with the various hostile chiefs, and that on March 24, 1838, he was sent with a Seminole chief as a messenger to General Taylor.[54] Abraham was among the Seminoles and Negroes who embarked at Tampa for the western country on February 25, 1839.[55]

It is regrettable that one cannot properly leave this discussion of the Negro Abraham without dealing with a rather serious charge against him of disloyalty to the interests of the Seminole people in return for a bribe from the United States government. This accusation is implied in a letter from Major Ethan Allen Hitchcock, dated from Tampa Bay, Florida, October 22, 1840, and now in the possession of Mrs. W. A. Croffut, Washington, D. C. Major Hitchcock upon arrival in Florida to serve in the Seminole War had speedily become convinced of the unjust character of the conflict on the government's side. He wrote: "When negotiations were opened with them in 1832 to induce their emigration, the Indians at once answered 'let the 20 years [for which term the Treaty of Fort Moultrie had been concluded] pass and we will talk with you.' This was the language to the Govt. Commissioner for several days in succession, when the articles in the treaty proposed for their acceptance were altered by introducing one article giving the interpreter $100 and another by which the Indians were to send a delegation of 6 Indians to examine the new country west of the Arkansas.

[53] Foreman, *op. cit.*, p. 349.
[54] *Ibid.*, pp. 361, 362.
[55] *Ibid.*, p. 370.

"Now the interpreter was a runaway slave from Pensacola on whom the $100 in prospect operated as a *bribe* and it was so spoken of by the Comr. in an interview with Gen. Jackson in the presence of Capt. Thruston, who stated the fact to me. Col. Gadsden, Commr., remarked to President Jackson, that he 'never could have done anything with the Indians if he had not bribed the interpreter with $100.' " Major Hitchcock went on to state that after the deputation had inspected the country to which the United States government wished them to remove they were forced, far from their own land and people, by methods of intimidation to express satisfaction with "the country designed for them in the Treaty." This paper was presented to the United States Senate as a completing treaty and ratified by the Senate as such, though it was not of the character alleged nor had the deputation the power to confirm the treaty.[56]

There is no doubt that Abraham was the interpreter referred to in Major Hitchcock's letter as having been bribed by the United States Commissioner. We know from another source that Abraham had fled from slavery in Pensacola, and also that he had accompanied the Seminole delegation to the Indian Territory, 1832-33, as interpreter.[57] The knowledge that Abraham was induced for a monetary consideration, even though given openly and in the form of compensation for his services as interpreter, to use his influence toward inducing his Seminole friends to take a step which he might not have advocated purely from the viewpoint of advantage to the tribe, certainly would not advance him in our estimation. But in seems hardly fair to condemn as a traitor, on the authority of a letter containing a second-hand account of a chance-heard conversation, a man the other known facts in whose life are quite inconsistent with the charge. It must be

[56] Foreman, *op. cit.*, pp. 376-378, note 17.
[57] *Ibid.*, p. 322.

remembered that in addition to the article providing $100
for the services of the interpreter there was another new
provision, namely that a delegation of Indians should be
sent to examine the new country and report to the tribe on
its suitability, before a decision should be made as to the
completion of the removal-treaty through its ratification
or rejection by the tribe in general. The promised compensation may have made Abraham more favorable to the
ratification of the treaty, but one may well question
whether without the provision for a delegation to inspect
the land Abraham's influence in favor of the treaty would
have been forthcoming or, assuming for the sake of argu-
ment that the $100 was the sole consideration motivating
him, whether even his advocacy would have prevailed upon
the 15 chiefs who signed the document. Abraham, as well
as the signing chiefs, may have reasoned that, with their
approval of the land set aside for them established as a
condition of the treaty, they might as well as not—indeed
much better—go for a junket in the Indian Territory, all
expenses paid and no obligations necessarily involved, believing that if dissatisfied with the land, sincerely or not,
the treaty would remain of no effect. Neither Abraham
nor the chiefs were suspicious enough to anticipate the
tactics of mingled force and fraud which were brought to
bear on them while they were in the Indian Territory; no
implication is made that Abraham lent himself in any way
to obtaining the signature of the chiefs to their forced approval of the country. It may even be questioned whether
Abraham ever realized that he was being "bribed." It is
quite clear that the Seminoles never lost faith in him.

Abraham, through his approval of the Treaty of
Payne's Landing, for whatever reason, did have a part in
putting the delegation in a situation where such methods
could most successfully be applied, but his co-operation
was probably quite unintentional and there is no doubt

that some other pretext would easily have been found for obtaining some paper, which could be called a treaty, had the Treaty of Payne's Landing never been signed and had no Seminole delegation ever gone near the Indian Territory. Whatever Abraham's error was in this connection, there is little doubt that he amply redeemed himself in the Seminole War, first by his intelligent and intrepid leadership of the Negro forces in the armed conflict and by his shrewd counsel to the Seminole leaders, and secondly by his able negotiation of the Treaty of Fort Dade, which, had it been loyally kept by the whites, would have brought the war much earlier to its inevitable conclusion and spared much effusion of blood and suffering on both sides.

Moving forward two decades at a bound to the time of the Civil War and the part played by the Five Civilized Tribes of the Indian Territory in this great struggle over slavery, we discover that those characteristics of Negro servitude, among those tribes, which had most impresed observers when they were still east of the Mississippi, had survived transplanting to the western country and the years which had intervened. The Negro slave among the Indians enjoyed a life which in its freedom and absence of severe labor stood in exceedingly favorable contrast to that of the plantation-slave of the Deep South. The natural result was that the slaves of the Indians were regarded as badly spoiled. "Owners and dealers in slaves in Missouri and Arkansas did not hesitate to acknowledge that Indian negroes were undesirable because of the difficulty of controlling them."[58] Imagine a Seminole Negro, who in his youth had taken part in the Florida war and had then spent a number of years as a member on terms of virtual equality of an Indian family in the Territory, being finally sold by some trick of fate to a white plantation owner in Arkansas! In some such cases there might

[58] Britton, Wiley, *The Civil War on the Border* (New York and London, 1904), vol. ii, p. 25.

be reason for the master to thank a merciful providence
that his new acquisition escaped before he had enjoyed
the opportunity of splitting the overseer's head with a hoe.

Florida and Alabama precedent was also followed during the Civil War in the regiments formed in Kansas of
refugee Indians loyal to the Union. "Most of the colored
men," we are told, "who had belonged to Indian masters
had enlisted in the Indian regiments . . . . There was no
recognized difference of social status between the Indians
and negroes, so they mingled together on terms of perfect
equality," as in the two Seminole wars and to a certain
extent in the Red Stick war. These Indian Negroes did
good service in the border-warfare. "An intelligent negro
man of the Indian brigade," we are told, "was captured
by the Southern forces," and, apparently terror-stricken,
gave them a variety of misleading and damaging information, later escaping to his own regiment.[59]

We now, following the precedent of the earlier article,
move geographically into a part of the United States in
which Negroes were never a large element of the population and where slavery never became an important institution, the Old Northwest. Because of these factors, relations between Negroes and Indians were much less extensive and also of a somewhat different character from
what they were in the sections previously considered. In
1790, for example, a Wyandot and his partner, a runaway
from Kentucky, were trading from Detroit among the Indians of Ohio. We learn this fact from a captive among the
Indians who encountered the pair and mentioned the courtesy with which he was treated by the runaway Negro.[60]

But an interesting evidence of the slight character of
relations between Indians and Negroes in Ohio is found
in the account given by Josiah Henson of his flight in 1830,

[59] Britton, *The Union Indian Brigade in the Civil War* (Kansas City,
Missouri, 1922), p. 17.
[60] Pritts, *op. cit.*, pp. 414-415.

with his wife and family, through Ohio into Canada. The fugitives were kindly received and entertained in an Indian camp but Henson commented on the almost fearful curiosity with which they were regarded by the generality of their hosts.[61]

Moving farther west into Illinois we encounter an exceedingly interesting example of a Negro in close association with Indians. Mrs. John Kinzie writes: "In giving the early history of Chicago the Indians say, with great simplicity, 'the first white man who settled here was a negro.' This was Jean Baptiste Point-au-Sable, a native of San Domingo, who, about the year 1796, found his way to this remote region, and commenced a life among the Indians. There is usually a strong affection between these two races, and Jean Baptiste imposed upon his new friends by making them believe he had been a 'great chief' among the whites." Dr. Quaife, who edited Mrs. Kinzie's narrative, believes that Jean Baptiste was not a West Indian. He writes: "Although his parentage is not known, there is considerable reason for believing that he belonged, on his father's side, to the family of Dandonneau *dit* du Sablé, one of the most noted in the annals of New France . . . Point Sable had an Indian wife and at least two children . . . He died about the year 1815." Miss Stella M. Drumm likewise adds to our knowledge of Jean Baptiste. From her we learn that he was a mulatto who had a trading-house on the site of Chicago as early as 1779. Suzanne, his natural daughter by an Indian woman, on October 4, 1790, married Jean Baptiste Pelletier at Chicago and on October 7, 1799, a child of this union was baptized at St. Louis. Jean Baptiste Point du Sable also had a son, Baptiste Point du Sable, Jr., who died sometime before February 17, 1814. His father was still alive in September of that same year but is believed to have

[61] (Henson, Josiah), *Father Henson's Story* (Boston and Cleveland, 1858), pp. 117-120.

died soon thereafter. Either father or son, probably the latter, was with Manuel Lisa on his famous fur-trading expedition to the Upper Missouri in 1812-13.[62]

In times of Indian warfare the relations between Indian and Negro in the Old Northwest followed much the same pattern as those in the New England and Middle Atlantic States or colonies. The domestic Negro servant usually took an active part as an ally of the household to which he belonged. At the time of the Chicago massacre, for example, Black Jim, a Negro servant, was put in charge of a boat in which a wounded white woman was concealed. When an Indian, pistol in hand, approached and began to search the vessel the Negro seized an axe and threatened to cleave the Indian's skull unless he desisted. The Indian retired.[63]

I am able to add some details to the story of the Bonga family, with some members of which I dealt in my earlier article. "Pierre Bonza or Bonga: a negro" was with Alexander Henry, Jr., who was in charge of the Red River brigade which left August 21, 1800, as Henry's personal servant. Henry recorded in his journal: "Mar. 12th (1801). Pierre's wife was delivered of a daughter—the first fruit at this fort, and a very black one." The mother

[62] Kinzie, Mrs. John H., *Wau-Bun*, Milo M. Quaife, ed. (Chicago, 1932), pp. 219-220; Luttig, John C., *Journal of a Fur-Trading Expedition on the Upper Missouri, 1812, 1813*, Stella M. Drumm, ed. (St. Louis, 1920), p. 155. Quite a different account of Jean Baptiste is given in another source, which states that he was a slave near Lexington, Kentucky, who had once been a captive among the Indians and had acquired a taste for their way of living. About 1790 he stole a rifle, a knife, and other useful articles, and ran away, marrying among the Indians, and settling in 1796 on the present site of Chicago. He wanted to become chief and to that end he turned Catholic, in order to obtain the influence of the missionary, Father Bonner, but despite this assistance was unable to obtain the coveted honor. Despite the fact that the narrator claims to have obtained his information from a grandson of Jean Baptiste, living on the bank of Cahokia Creek, St. Clair County, I regard it as largely or entirely fictitious (Matson, N., *Pioneers of Illinois*, Chicago, 1882, pp. 213-214).

[63] Kinzie, *op. cit.*, (ed. 1901), p. 180.

was without much doubt an Indian woman. During one
of Henry's absences Pierre was one of two men left in
charge of the fort. On returning Henry wrote: "J. Des-
ford had threatened to kill my servant in my absence, but
did not escape without a sound beating." We are not specifically informed who inflicted this chastisement but from
the giant size and strength which was typical of Pierre's
descendants we can easily believe that he was himself
quite capable of inflicting the appropriate punishment. Dr.
Coues notes that "Pierre Bonza appears as an interpreter
N. W. Co., Lower Red r., 1804" and also that he was at
the capture of Fort William, August 13, 1816.[64]

In the party which went overland from St. Louis to
Astoria, 1810-1812, were at least two men of Negro blood,
the interpreter Rose, son of a white trader among the
Cherokees and a woman who was half-Cherokee and half-
Negro, and whom we noted in the earlier article, and
François Duchouquette, who made the complete journey,
while Rose was only with the party for a couple of months,
from the Aricara Village to the Crow country. Of Duchouquette's ancestry we read: "One of the early inhabitants
of Prairie du Chien was a Mrs. Menard, in whom French
blood was mixed with African. She came from one of the
French villages farther south. By her first husband, Du
Chouquette, she had two sons, one of whom joined Astor's
expedition to the mouth of the Columbia River. After the
death of her second husband, one Gagnier, by whom she
had three sons and three daughters, she married Charles
Menard. Three sons and two daughters were born to
them. Aunt Mary Ann, as she was generally called, was
midwife, nurse, and healer, and enjoyed more or less practice even after Fort Crawford had been erected and a
surgeon had been provided for the post. In fact, the

[64] Coues, Elliott, ed., *New Light on the Early History of the Greater
Northwest*, 3 vols. (N. Y., 1897), vol. i, pp. 50, 194, 231, and index under
"Bonza or Bonga, Pierre."

army surgeons employed her, and to her good nursing
they attributed the recovery of not a few of their pa-
tients.'' François Duchouquette was thus of French blood
on both sides of his line of descent and of Negro blood on
his mother's. He may have inherited Indian blood from
his father but this is purely an assumption. He probably
joined the Astorians at St. Louis, though he first appears
in the journals of the expedition at the Aricara Village,
where on June 15, 1811, he purchased blue beads to the
value of $1.50—an article for which in that particular
quantity nearly all the members of the expedition seem to
have suddenly experienced a peculiar passion, inexplicable
only to those who have never read first-hand accounts of
the fur-trade. Duchouquette arrived safely at Astoria and
probably entered the service of the North West Company,
after the break up of the Pacific Fur Company. On May
1, 1814, he was one of those who went with the express to
Fort William.[65] One may well wonder how much Negro
blood has filtered into the veins of the white race through
the medium of French-Canadians who, habituated to the
idea of racial intermixture through long-continued familiarity with intermarriage between French and Indians,
have mingled their blood with such families of Negro blood
as the Point du Sables and that from which came Mrs.
Duchouquette-Gagnier-Menard, whose members, unlike the
Bongas, chose to intermarry with French instead of with
Indians.

It is quite evident that the fur-trade made Indians to a
considerable degree familiar with persons of Negro blood.
When Manuel Lisa's expedition to the Upper Missouri
started up the river in 1812 among the company was not
only the half-Indian, quarter-French, quarter-Negro en-

[65] *Wisconsin in Three Centuries*, 4 vols. (New York, 1906), vol. ii, p.
225; *Astor Papers*, Baker Library, Soldiers Field, Boston, journal of overland expedition No. 2, June 15, 1811.

gagé, "Baptiste Pointsable," but also "George, *negre.*"[66]
S. H. Long writes of his expedition to the Rockies, 1819-
1820: "A negro belonging to the Fur Company coming in
on an errand, they [the Omahas] spoke of him as the *black
white man,* and one of them jokingly said he was a Wassabajinga, or a little black bear."[67] Prince Maximilian
wrote of "a negro slave belonging to Mr. McKenzie" at
Fort Union in 1833, and of an incident at Fort Clarke in
the same year, "Our cook, a negro, had a violent dispute
with an Indian . . . who had taken a piece of meat out of
his pot." This same "cook of the fort, a negro from St.
Louis," later gave medical advice to which Maximilian
credited his recovery from a very nearly fatal attack of
scurvy.[68]

Larpenteur mentions an episode which is also noted in
my previous article, that the Blackfeet in the winter of
1842-43 killed a "negro by the name of Reese. Mr. Chardon, it appears, set great store by that negro and swore
vengeance." One wonders whether the favor uniformly
shown to Negroes, such as Beckwith, Rose, and York, by
the Crows, the Blackfeet's deadliest enemies, may have
been a factor in the death of Reese, even though he himself, so far as we know, had no connection with the Absa-
rokas. Larpenteur also mentions John Brazeau (or Brazo), whom an editorial note describes as a "full-blooded
Aethiopian, apparently, of small stature and intelligent,
though not handsome, face. He must have been 70 or over
when he died. He enunciated his English well . . . spoke
French better than most Canadians, also Sioux and other
Indian languages. He was hardy, courageous." According to this account he died in 1868 or thereabouts, having

[66] Luttig, *op. cit.,* pp. 157, 158.

[67] Long, S. H., *Account of an Expedition . . . to the Rocky Mountains
. . . 1819, 1820,* in *Early Western Travels,* Reuben Gold Thwaites, ed., vol.
xiv, p. 287.

[68] Maximilian, *Travels in the Interior of North America,* in Thwaites,
Early Western Travels, vol. xxiii, p. 192; vol. xxiv, pp. 47, 87.

worked many years for the American Fur Company and its successors. Larpenteur himself in 1836 wrote of him as "a mulatto named John Brazo—a man of strong nerves and a brave fellow." Larpenteur mentions him in a number of connections and what he tells us of Brazeau's character is not particularly prepossessing though doubtless it was well-matched to his surroundings. Larpenteur speaks of the composure and even apparent pleasure with which he disposed of the Indian dead in a great small-pox epidemic. He was also always at the service of his bourgeois for any job of flogging or assassination that might be needed; the first he ably performed with evident enjoyment, the latter he was ready to attempt with willing efficiency. But cold-blooded murder, even on a wholesale scale, was not a particularly serious matter in the fur-trade days during which Brazeau served his apprenticeship.[69]

It has been said that dislike of Negroes is to be found among "some of the Indian tribes of the plains and the far W." Nevertheless, "the Caddo, former residents of Louisiana and E. Texas," it has been said, "appear to have much negro blood," and though the existence of prejudice against the Negro was found true "in 1891 . . . to a certain extent of the Kutenai of S. E. British Columbia. Nevertheless a few cases of intermarriage are reported from this region." Although the number of Negroes in the Pacific Northwest is comparatively few, "according to Swanton the richest man among the Skidegate Haida is

[69] Larpenteur, Charles, *Forty Years a Fur Trader on the Upper Missouri*, 2. vols. (New York, 1898), Elliott Coues, ed., vol. i, pp. 217, 121. A very curious and interesting reason for the familiar presence of Negroes on fur-trading expeditions was given by "Col. Stevenson of the Bureau of Ethology, who has spent thirty years among Indians for study of them, [and who] remarked upon . . . the fact that the old fur-traders always got a Negro if possible to negotiate for them with the Indians, because of their 'pacifying effect.' They could manage them better than white men, with less friction" (*Ten Years' Work for Indians at Hampton Institute, Va.*, 1878-1888, pp. 13-14).

a negro." "Grinnell reports a few persons of evident negro blood among the Piegan and Kainah [Blackfeet]."[70] Of the Plains Indians Prof. Walter Stanley Campbell (Stanley Vestal) of the University of Oklahoma writes: "So far as I know the Cheyennes and Sioux seldom intermarried with Negroes. I know of one Arapaho family here which did."[71] However, as we shall see, there were instances, though few, of intermarriage between Negroes and members of these Plains tribes.

In my earlier article I mentioned the use of Negro troops, "buffalo soldiers," against the hostile Indians of the West in the period immediately following the Civil War. Mrs. Custer writes of the reckless bravery displayed in a fight with Roman Nose's Cheyennes near Fort Wallace, in June, 1867, by a dozen Negro infantrymen who dashed out to the battle-line in a four-mule-team wagon, standing up in it and firing at the Indians until they arrived at the forefront of the action, when they leaped out, formed a skirmish line, and fought until the enemy had been driven off. One Negro, indeed, ran far out ahead of his companions toward the Indians and was seen to throw up his hands and fall. Everyone believed he had been killed, but, after the enemy had retreated, he was observed to rise and walk back toward his friends. When asked the reason for his curious tactics he replied: "Well, you see, I thought that when the Indians saw me fall some of them would come up to take my scalp and I'd be able to get one of them!"[72]

In the earlier article I mentioned the curious fact that a prominent Cheyenne warrior bore a name signifying

[70] Chamberlain, *loc. cit.*

[71] Letter of January 2, 1933, to the author. Two brothers, Frank and Peter Black Hawk, attending Hampton Institute in the 1880's, were "half Negro and half Sioux" (*Twenty-two Years' Work of the Hampton Normal and Agricultural Institute* [Hampton, 1893], pp. 382, 467).

[72] Custer, Mrs. Elizabeth B., *Tenting on the Plains* (New York, 1895), pp. 387-388.

"Black Whiteman" or "Negro." At the time I was unable to explain why a Cheyenne should be so named. The explanation is this: Two Negroes, Andrew and Dick Green, were residents of the famous fur-trading post, Bents Fort on the Arkansas River in Colorado. They were servants to the Bent brothers, Andrew to William and Dick to Charles. Andrew was very black and for that reason received from the Indians the name of "Black Whiteman," or "Negro," *par excellence.* Andrew could talk Cheyenne and was quite a favorite with the members of that tribe, who gave him the additional, more personal, name of "Turtle Shell." A young Cheyenne, out of compliment to Andrew, assumed his name of "Black Whiteman" and it later became a common Cheyenne name. Dick Green, his brother, after his master, Governor Charles Bent, had been killed by the Indians at Taos, accompanied Colonel St. Vrain's company of trappers and traders when they marched to avenge his master's death. He took a leading part in the storming of the Taos pueblo in 1847 and killed several Indians in the affray.[73]

At present I know a good deal more about the Negro Isaiah, Sioux interpreter to the Seventh United States Cavalry, killed in the Battle of the Little Big Horn, than I did when I wrote my earlier article. Isaiah Dorman, according to Ben Arnold Connor, was among the woodcutters for Durfee & Peck, working near Fort Sully on the Missouri in 1868. Connor described him as "a negro named Isaiah, who could talk Sioux." He was married to a Santee Sioux woman, but they had no children. Isaiah had been on the river for some years. In the winter of 1868 he carried mail from Fort Rice to Fort Wadsworth, 200 miles in all kinds of weather. He was "a good worker, faithful and reliable in every trust." He is said to have acted in 1876 as Custer's personal servant, as well as

[73] Grinnell, Dr. George Bird, "Bent's Old Fort and Its Builders," *Kansas Historical Collections,* vol. xv, p. 61.

Sioux interpreter, and was killed on the west side of the Little Big Horn, before the command retreated to the east side. Isaiah had fed Sitting Bull during the winter of 1868 and the latter did not forget his kindness.[74] Isaiah's death is thus described: "As he [Sitting Bull] approached the end of the brush near the prairie-dog town, he came upon the Negro, 'Teat' Isaiah.[75] Two Bull, Shots-Walking, and several others rode up at the same time. 'Teat' was badly wounded, but still able to talk. He spoke Sioux, and was well liked by the Indians. He had joined the troops as scout because, he said, he wanted to see that western country once more before he died. And now, when he saw the Sioux all around him, he pleaded with them, 'My friends, you have already killed me; don't count coup on me.' He had been shot early in the fight. Sitting Bull arrived just then, recognized 'Teat' and said, 'Don't kill that man; he is a friend of mine.' The Negro asked for water, and Sitting Bull took his cup of polished black buffalo horn, got some water, and gave him to drink. Immediately after, Isaiah died." (He had probably been shot through the stomach.) "The warriors rode away. Afterward, some spiteful woman found the Negro's body and mutilated it with her butcher-knife."[76] The Cheyenne quoted in my earlier article saw Isaiah's body after it had been stripped but before it had been mutilated.

No study of Negro-Indian relations with any pretension to completeness may fail to include some mention of the bold experiment introduced into Hampton Normal and

[74] Crawford, Lewis F., *Rekindling Camp Fires* (Bismarck, N. D., 1926)

[75] "He was called Teat by the Indians, because the Sioux word for teat resembles Isaiah in sound" (letter from Professor W. S. Campbell, January 21, 1933).

[76] Campbell, Walter Stanley (Stanley Vestal) *Sitting Bull* (Boston and New York, 1932), p. 170. All my new information about Isaiah, and practically all my additional material concerning relations between Negroes and Plains Indians, comes from sources either directly furnished to me, or to which my attention was called, by Professor Campbell.

Agricultural Institute in 1878, when to this co-educational institution, founded a decade before in the interests of the freedmen, were admitted a number of Indians. While this innovation was bold it was carefully safeguarded from any charge of recklessness and, partly because of necessary dietary considerations as well as in concession to exterior prejudice, there was considerable racial segregation. In the words of an Indian graduate of the school, writing in praise of the influence of the Negro students upon their Indian comrades, "Indians do not come in contact with the Negroes as most people suppose, as they live in different buildings, have different dining-rooms and class-rooms, except the few who are in the Normal Classes." An official report of the school stated: "General social intercourse between the races of opposite sexes is limited and guarded. Trouble might come of it. None ever has." And yet it was inevitable that some of the contacts between the two races should be of quite an intimate character. It is well-known that Booker T. Washington was for a time in charge of the Indian boys' "Wigwam" or dormitory and Negroes frequently acted as teachers of classes made up of Indians. The official report cautiously stated the situation thus: "While there is not intimacy, there is the best of good feeling. The Indian students at Hampton are frequently under the charge of our colored graduates. They always get on well." We are told, nevertheless, that there was at first some prejudice against Negroes by Indians from the Indian Territory, where slavery had recently been an institution. It is noteworthy, however, that the Indians from the Indian Territory in attendance at the Institute were practically all members of non-slaveholding tribes, Sacs and Foxes, etc. A few of the Negroes were members of the Seminole and Creek nations. In contrast to the attitude of these few Indians from the Territory was that of the Sioux, who

petitioned a month after arrival for "colored room-mates
in order to get on faster in English and civilized customs."[77] Owing to the withdrawal of government appro-
priations for the support of Indians at Hampton it has
now been some years since any have been in attendance
there.

In concluding this investigation, the results of which
are embodied in both the original article and the present
supplement, of relations between Negroes and Indians
within the present limits of the United States, one may
venture a few tentative generalizations, being careful in
each case to remember that the immediate situation was
always the most potent factor in the determination of
these relationships. In the absence of the white man and
the white man's racial attitudes, the relations between the
two races under discussion were usually friendly, as was
also the case when individuals of these races found themselves united by the bonds of a common servitude. Indians were usually ready also to offer refuge to Negroes
who fled to them from servitude among the whites. On
the other hand, hostile Indians, particularly in the northern colonies or states, where the natives did not understand the relationship between black and white as well as
they did in the plantation regions of the south, were
quite ready to kill Negroes found in the company of their
white enemies, and Negro slaves, on the other hand, were
frequently prompt to fight in defense of their master's
families against the savage foe. But when the Indian was
allied with the French or British of Canada, the Negro's
cash-value was something of an insurance against unnecessary violence from the hostile warrior.

Among the slave-holding Indians of the South another
set of attitudes was to be found. On the one hand there
was the Chickasaw who regarded his Negro slave much

[77] *Ten Years' Work for Indians at Hampton Institute, Va.*, 1878-1888,
pp. 9, 13-14, 58.

as would the white slave-owner, while at the opposite extreme was the Seminole whose slave was, at the worst, a member of the household on a practical equality with those of his master's own blood and at the best the counsellor and almost the real ruler of his master, particularly in relation to dealings with the whites. Relations between Seminoles and Negroes resulted in two of the most important "Indian" wars ever fought by the United States.

In that part of the United States where slavery was never an important institution the relation between Negro and Indian was much the same as that between Indian and white in the same area, save that, in general, the relations were probably more friendly in the former case, because of the Negro's lesser desire or ability to exploit the Indian. In the Old Northwest and the Far West the Negro traded with the Indian, intermarried with him, sometimes became a member or even a chieftain of the tribe, fought against him when hostile, and in general conducted himself in practically the same way as might a French-Canadian voyageur in the same region.

Racially, these relationships have affected both Negro and Indian. Through intermarriage with runaway slaves before emancipation and, later, with free Negroes drifting to their reservations, many small, peaceful tribes on the Atlantic coast have been "swamped" by Negro blood and are now more negroid than Indian in blood and appearance. Through intermarriage with slaves, runaway Negroes, and freedmen adopted into the tribe, Negro blood has been thoroughly disseminated through two of the Five Civilized Indian Tribes, while others of the tribes have been similarly affected, though to a lesser degree. The presence of Negroes in large numbers in the Indian Territory has also infused an African element into certain of the tribes residing there which had not previously come into intimate or extensive relations with the Negro. Contact with fugitive Negroes, and with Negro scouts and traders, has also resulted in the presence of individuals of mixed blood among the members of tribes which have not been in a large way affected by Negro intermixture.

On the other hand, through intermarriage between Negro and Indian slaves before emancipation, and later between free Negroes and Indians who had lost tribal connections, and also through recruits of mixed blood who have left the reservations with which they were formerly associated and "gone Negro," Indian blood has been diffused through a large proportion of the Aframerican population.

A less healthy result of Negro-Indian relationships has been the development of isolated communities of Negro, Indian, and white blood in various secluded parts of the United States.

A sufficient number of persons of Negro-Indian blood have attained to such positions of usefulness and even distinction as to set at rest any idea that this racial mixture is necessarily a bad one, biologically speaking.

Thus we observe that relations between Negroes and Indians have been of significance historically, through influencing on occasion the Indian relations of the United States government, and to a much larger extent biologically, through modifying the racial make-up of both the races and even, as some believe, creating a new race which might, perhaps, for want of a better term, be called "Aframerindian."

Corrections and Additions

p. 114, l. 26: The "runaway Negro" who, in May, 1837, led Indians in an attack on Camden County (Georgia, not Florida), could not have been John Caesar, who had been killed in January.

p. 116, l. 14-19: As already noted in a comment on "Relations Between Negroes and Indians," p. 70, l. 9-10 (see p. 93 above), Abraham was not involved in the Seminole exodus from the Indian Territory.

p. 116, l. 23: Delete "1850." Insert "1849."

p. 116, bottom of page: Caesar, mentioned as present at a conference in March, 1836, was indeed the John Caesar who was killed in January, the following year.

p. 134, l. 29-30: That "Negro blood has been thoroughly disseminated through two of the Five Civilized Tribes" is probably an exaggeration. See comment (p. 93) on "Relations Between Negroes and Indians," p. 79, l. 6-15; p. 88, l. 13-22.

p. 135, l. 22-27: That "relations between Negroes and Indians have been of significance . . . biologically, through modifying the racial make-up of both the races" is also at best half-true. While Melville Herskovits, *The American Negro* (New York, 1928), has revealed that perhaps a third of the American Negro population then "claimed partial American Indian ancestry," and although some small "broken" Indian tribes have been "swamped" by Negro blood, American Indians in general have not had their physical character materially influenced by Negro ancestry. One reason for this, of course, is that in the United States a person of Indian ancestry who also displays Negroid characteristics is likely to be regarded as a Negro rather than as an Indian.

Further Reading

Works dealing with Negroes who accompanied the early explorers are: Richard R. Wright, "Negro Companion of the Spanish Explorers," *American Anthropologist*, new series, IV (April-June, 1902), pp. 217-28, a pioneer article reprinted in *Phylon*, II (1941), pp. 325-36 edited by Rayford W. Logan; and J. Fred Rippy, "The Negro and the Spanish Pioneers in the New World," *JNH*, VII (April, 1921), pp. 183-89.

Less well known than Estevanico and York was Jacob Dodson, John Charles Fremont's companion on his second and third exploring expeditions, to Oregon and California in 1843-1844 and to California in 1845-1846, whom a contemporary writer described as "expert as a Mexican with the lasso, sure as a mountaineer with the rifle, equal to either on horse or foot." See John Charles Fremont, *Memoirs of My Life* (New York, 1887), I, 165-66, 188, 229, 275, 337, 342-43, 424, 497; Walter Colton, *Three Years in California* (New York, 1859), pp. 377-84; Frederick S. Dellenbaugh, *Fremont and '49* (New York, 1914), pp. 112, 375.

Matthew Alexander Henson, Robert E. Peary's long-time assistant in Arctic exploration and his companion in the dash to the North Pole on April 7, 1909, was the ablest and, according to Donald B. MacMillan, "easily the most popular man" on the expedition. Henson was an expert dog-driver, a mighty hunter, a master carpenter and mechanic, a fluent speaker of the Eskimo language, whom Peary selected as his companion because he was "easily the most efficient" of all his assistants. Matthew Henson has told his own story in *A Negro Explorer at the North Pole* (New York, 1912; reprinted by Arno Press, 1969). His story has also been told in semi-fictional form and without documentation in Bradley Robinson's *Dark Companion* (New York, 1947), which, however, was written with Henson's cooperation and the manuscript read and corrected by Arctic explorers Donald B. MacMillan and Vihljalmur Stefansson. See also Robert E. Peary, *The North Pole: Its Discovery in 1909 under the Auspices of the Peary Arctic Club* (New York 2d ed., 1910), pp. 73, 81, 109, 172, 179, 184, 191, 231, 246, 287, 296, 301, 311-12, and especially pp. 20, 272-73, 318; Henson appears in the frontispiece and in a photograph facing p. 294.

FUR-TRADING, ca. 1725-1867

Fur traders sometimes closely followed the explorers, sometimes preceded them. In the fur trade Negroes occupied all positions from servant, packhorseman, voyageur, and cook, through trusted and responsible employee to independent trader. Besides the article that follows, which originally appeared in the December, 1934 issue of *Minnesota History* (Vol. XV), see "Relations Between Negroes and Indians," pp. 81-86, and "Notes Supplementary to 'Relations Between Negroes and Indians,'" pp. 123-30, for material on Negroes in the fur trade. For references to Negroes as members of fur-trading outfits in the early Carolinas, see "Negroes on the Southern Frontier, 1670-1763," p. 176.

NEGROES AND THE FUR TRADE

Even a casual study of the North American fur trade is likely to suggest the possibility that, in various parts of the continent, certain races or national groups correspond closely to certain economic and functional categories into which the persons connected with this great industry may be divided. The fur trade as carried on in the regions about the Great Lakes, with Montreal as headquarters, was characterized by the fact that the entrepreneurs, the *bourgeois,* were nearly all Highland Scots — McTavishes, McGillivrays, Forsyths, and the like — though as time went on Canadians of French stock, such as Pierre de Rocheblave, assumed an increasingly prominent rôle. The dominance of the Highland Scots appeared even in fur companies chartered in the United States. The conspicuous example is the Pacific Fur Company, which, though chartered by the state of New York, included seven Highland Scots from Canada among its eleven partners.

The dominant racial stock in the fur trade as conducted from St. Louis, however, was French — Louisiana French rather than French-Canadian. Berthold, Chouteau, Pratte, Cabanné were some of the conspicuous names in the St. Louis fur trade, the Spaniard Manuel Lisa being one of the earlier discordant racial notes. Soon after the Louisiana purchase, traders from the former thirteen colonies entered the trade, and only a little later the inevitable Highland Scots — Ramsay Crooks for one — began to come down from Canada. Still, the *bourgeois* of the St. Louis fur trade remained dominantly French, as that of Canada remained Highland Scotch. In Wisconsin, in the region of Green Bay and Prairie du Chien, were many small fur traders chiefly of French-Canadian origin — Rolette, Porlier, Grignon. Farther east, in the portion of the fur country which early in the nineteenth century was already menaced

by the advancing frontier line, the fur traders were naturally
to a large extent American citizens of British colonial stock.
Since clerks in the fur trade were regarded rather as ap-
prentices than as employees and were interested more in
prospective advancement than in immediate wages, it was
to be expected that racially they would be of the same stock
as the members of the class they aspired to enter.

The outstanding example of racial solidarity in the fur
trade is to be found in the class of general laborers, the
voyageurs, who almost to a man were French-Canadians.
Such solidarity also was characteristic of the hunters, who
constituted a small but interesting class, particularly in the
fur trade of the United States.   Typically, the hunter was
of Kentucky or, what is the same thing, of Virginia backwoods stock.   The Canadian fur traders depended to a
large extent on the aborigines for the services performed
south of the border by hired hunters, and they sometimes
made use of the Christianized Iroquois.   In the United
States, next to the Kentuckian among the hunters, was the
French-Indian half-breed.

The persons connected with the Astoria expedition may
be considered fairly typical of a group active in the fur trade
of the United States.[1]   Of the partners, two, Ramsay
Crooks and Donald McKenzie, were Highland Scots from
Canada; Wilson P. Hunt, Robert McClellan, and Joseph
Miller were United States citizens.   The one clerk, John
Reed, seems to have been an American citizen, though of
Irish birth.   The voyageurs bore French names, to a man.
Of the fifteen hunters more or less prominently connected
with the expedition, ten bore typical Anglo-Saxon surnames.
The names of the other five indicate French origin, but it is
noteworthy that no less than three of them are known to
have been of mixed French and Indian blood, as was at least
one of the group of ten.

[1] See Kenneth W. Porter, " Roll of Overland Astorians, 1810–12," in
Oregon Historical Quarterly, 34: 105–112 (June, 1933).

Some of the racial aspects of the fur trade have been indicated — entrepreneurs and clerks: Highland Scots, French, and British Americans; voyageurs: French-Canadians; hunters: Kentucky backwoodsmen and French-Indian half-breeds. Yet this analysis is inadequate, for it neglects to mention one of the largest racial elements in the United States of the early nineteenth century. Any picture of the racial aspects of the fur trade of that period which omits the Negro is so incomplete as to give a false impression, for representatives of that race were to be found in all three groups connected with the trade.[2] Among the overland Astorians, at least two, a voyageur and a hunter, were of Negro origin.

It is rather surprising to note that the earliest Negroes known to be connected with the fur trade were among those who occupied the highest functional category, that of independent entrepreneurs. "In giving the early history of Chicago," wrote Mrs. John H. Kinzie, "the Indians say, with great simplicity, 'the first white man who settled here was a negro.' This was Jean Baptiste Point-au-Sable," or Point Sable, or Point du Sable, who is referred to variously as a "French-West-Indian mulatto" and doubtless apocryphally, as a runaway slave from Kentucky. Dr. Milo M. Quaife finds "considerable reason for believing that he belonged, on his father's side, to the family of Dandonneau *dit* du Sablé, one of the most noted in the annals of New France." He had a trading house on the site of Chicago as early as 1779 and had at least two natural children by an Indian woman. In 1790 his daughter Suzanne married Jean Baptiste Pelletier at Chicago and in 1799 a child of

[2] Some of the material included in this paper has been employed in another connection in the writer's articles entitled "Relations between Negroes and Indians within the Present Limits of the United States" and "Notes Supplementary to 'Relations between Negroes and Indians,'" which appear in the *Journal of Negro History,* 17: 287–367, 18: 282–321 (July, 1932; July, 1933). The author wishes to thank the editor of the *Journal,* Dr. Carter G. Woodson, for permission to draw upon these articles in preparing the present narrative.

this union was baptized at St. Louis. A son, Baptiste Point du Sable, Jr., died sometime before February 17, 1814, and the elder Point du Sable probably died sometime in the following year.[3] A less important but perhaps even more interesting example of an early entrepreneur of Negro blood is furnished by a runaway slave from Kentucky, who in 1790, in partnership with a Wyandotte Indian, was trading from Detroit into Ohio.[4]

But the most usual and typical rôle of the Negro in the fur trade was the same as that which he played in contemporary American economic life, namely, that of a servant or slave. His entrance into the fur trade in the capacity of a personal servant, however, sometimes opened to him the opportunity for participation in its activities in higher and more responsible capacities. Typical of such progress is the experience of York, the Negro slave who accompanied the Lewis and Clark expedition. Though trading in furs was not one of the purposes of this expedition, its story nevertheless belongs to the history of the fur trade. York's nominal function in the expedition was that of personal service to Captain Clark, but before the expedition was far advanced he was acting as hunter, trader, and interpreter, as well as vaudeville performer before appreciative audiences of Indians, to say nothing of the eugenic function he was induced occasionally to fill.[5]

With Alexander Henry when he was in charge of the Northwest Company's Red River brigade in August, 1800,

[3] Mrs. John H. Kinzie, *Wau-Bun: The " Early Day " in the North-West*, 219, 220 (Quaife edition, Chicago, 1932); John C. Luttig, *Journal of a Fur-trading Expedition on the Upper Missouri, 1812–1813*, 155 (St. Louis, 1920).

[4] Joseph Pritts, *Incidents of Border Life*, 414 (Lancaster, Pennsylvania, 1841).

[5] *History of the Expedition of Captains Lewis and Clark*, 1: 113 (Hosmer edition, Chicago, 1902). See also the entries under " York, Clark's negro servant," in volume 7 of Reuben G. Thwaites's edition of the *Original Journals of the Lewis and Clark Expedition, 1804–1806* (New York, 1904).

was a Negro, Pierre Bonza or Bonga, Henry's servant.
Pierre was the son of a Negro named Joas or Jean Bonga
and of Marie Jeanne, both slaves of Daniel Robertson,
British commandant at Michilimackinac from 1782 to 1787.
The two Negroes were married in 1794, thus legitimatiz-
ing their children. Pierre married a Chippewa woman, and
his wife was delivered of a daughter on March 12, 1801.
Henry reposed such confidence in his servant that in the
trader's absence in January, 1803, Pierre was one of two
men left in charge of the fort at the mouth of the Pembina
River. A certain J. Duford threatened to kill Bonga during his master's absence, "but did not escape without a
sound beating." After having acted satisfactorily as personal servant and as joint castellan of a fur-trading fort,
Pierre appeared in 1804 as an interpreter for the Northwest
Company on the lower Red River.[6] In 1819 a Bonga,
probably Pierre, was one of the principal traders among the
Chippewa.

Among Pierre's children was one George, who also entered the Indian trade, at first as a voyageur for the American Fur Company. He, like his father, married into the
Chippewa tribe, and in 1820 he acted as an interpreter for
Governor Lewis Cass at Fond du Lac. He later became a
prominent independent trader and a man of wealth and consequence, noted alike for his gentlemanly manner and for
his tremendous size and strength. As a voyageur he packed
seven hundred pounds for a quarter of a mile over the portage around the dalles of the St. Louis River. Although
half Indian, Bonga was purely African in appearance.
Never having heard of any racial distinction other than that

[6] Elliott Coues, ed., *New Light on the Early History of the Greater
Northwest: The Manuscript Journals of Alexander Henry and of David
Thompson,* 1: 50, 194, 231 (New York, 1897); William W. Warren,
"History of the Ojibways, Based upon Traditions and Oral Statements,"
in *Minnesota Historical Collections,* 5: 381; "The Mackinac Register,"
in *Wisconsin Historical Collections,* 18: 497; 19: 83, 97.

of white and Indian, Bonga, who was a popular and princely host, would amuse his guests by remarking reminiscently, "Gentlemen, I assure you that John Banfil and myself were the first two white men that ever came into this country." In 1833–34 George Bonga was listed as a licensed trader at Lac Platte; he was probably the Bonga who acted as interpreter at the treaty with the Chippewa at Fort Snelling in 1837. George and his brother Jack had many descendants, most of whom were noted for their powerful physiques.[7] The Bongas are an example of a fur-trading family of Negro blood the members of which advanced from positions as personal servants or voyageurs to stations as interpreters, and who finally became independent entrepreneurs.

Few Negroes who entered the fur trade in menial capacities ever became independent entrepreneurs. The position of interpreter or subordinate trader on a salary was about as high a station as they could expect to reach. The famous, or notorious, Edward Rose was the son of a white trader among the Cherokee and a woman who was half Cherokee and half Negro. He went to St. Louis about 1807 after a career of alleged brigandage and piracy along the lower Mississippi, and for a quarter of a century or more he alternated between life among the Crows and the Arikara. Among the former he attained the rank of chief, and he served as interpreter, guide, and hunter with various fur-trading and government expeditions. He was probably with Manuel Lisa in 1807 or with the Missouri Fur Company in 1809; he was certainly with the Astorians during part of the summer of 1811, with Lisa in 1812, with General William H. Ashley of the Rocky Mountain Fur

[7] Warren, in *Minnesota Historical Collections,* 5:381; Edward D. Neill, *History of Minnesota,* 322, 416, 873, 874 (Minneapolis, 1882); Joseph A. Gilfillan, "The Ojibways in Minnesota," Charles E. Flandrau, "Reminiscences of Minnesota during the Territorial Period," Nathan Butler, "Boundaries and Public Land Surveys of Minnesota," in *Minnesota Historical Collections,* 9: 56, 199; 12: 670.

Company in 1823, and with General Henry Atkinson on a treaty-making expedition in 1825.[8]

Somewhat similar was the career of the interpreter, *raconteur*, squaw man, and Crow chief, James P. Beckwourth or Beckwith, who was born in Virginia in 1798. According to one account he was the son of a Negro slave woman and an Irish overseer; according to another, the offspring of an octoroon and a planter. At any rate, he was some kind of a mulatto and he bore a strong resemblance to an Indian in features and physique. He was taken to St. Louis at the age of seven or eight and was enlisted as a horse wrangler in Ashley's fur-trading expedition of 1824. Although he gave exaggerated accounts of his own exploits, there seems to be no question that he was a man of great courage, and this quality, with his appearance, led to his adoption into the Crow tribe and his attainment of the rank of chief. His prestige with the Indians caused him to be employed for some time at a good salary as a trader for the American Fur Company.[9]

There were other persons of Negro blood who, coming into contact with the Indians through the medium of the fur trade, entered upon a vagabond life as members of various tribes, but without gaining the prestige among their new friends attained by such heroes as Rose and Beckwourth. Late in June, 1814, the well-known fur trader Ezekiel Williams was captured by the Kansa. "I gave," he wrote, "my gun, etc., to a mulatto man to be my friend and speak for me." Finally, "four Indians and the mulattoe brought me in. On the first day of September I arrived at Boons Lick."

[8] Hiram M. Chittenden, *The American Fur Trade of the Far West*, 1: 189; 2: 590, 597, 609, 685, 688 (New York, 1902). A sketch of Rose by the present writer will appear in a future volume of the *Dictionary of American Biography*.

[9] Harrison C. Dale, "James P. Beckwourth," in *Dictionary of American Biography*, 2: 122 (New York, 1929); Chittenden, *American Fur Trade*, 2: 684; Charles G. Leland's introduction to T. D. Bonner, *Life and Adventures of James P. Beckwourth* (London, 1892).

It is possible that this mulatto was the famous Rose, of
whose movements at this time it is known only that he was
in the section where Williams was captured.   Beckwourth
tells of a mulatto who " could speak the Crow language tol-
erably well " and who stirred up Indians and renegade whites
to rob a trader.[10]

The great majority of Negroes who entered the fur trade
as personal servants or common employees were no better
able than the ordinary French-Canadian voyageur to make
their way out of the menial classification.   Some were
estopped from advancement by the fact that legally they
were slaves.   Racial discrimination, however, does not seem
to have been very significant in retarding the advancement
of free Negroes connected with the fur trade, as is evidenced
by the examples given above.   This was probably because
on the frontier the racial division lay between Indian and
white rather than between white and Negro.

A casual exploration of fur-trade literature, in manuscript
or in print, will reveal many mentions of Negroes, named
or anonymous, who acted as cooks, voyageurs, or in some
unspecified capacity.   On September 17, 1806, the Lewis
and Clark expedition on its return from the West encountered "a large keel-boat commanded by a Captain McClan-
en, loaded with merchandise and bound to the Spanish
country by the way of the river Platte. . . . He had fifteen
hands, an interpreter and a black." [11]   With the overland
Astorians were at least two persons of Negro blood, the
interpreter Rose and a voyageur.   The latter was François
Duchouquette, whose mother, Aunt Mary Ann Menard —
to employ the name by which she was known at Prairie du
Chien, where for many years she acted as midwife, nurse,

---

[10] " Ezekiel Williams' Adventures in Colorado," in *Missouri Historical Collections*, 4: 202–208; Bonner, *Life of Beckwourth*, 208–210.

[11] Patrick Gass, *Journal of the Voyages and Travels of a Corps of
Discovery, under the Command of Capt. Lewis and Capt. Clarke*, 261
(Philadelphia, 1810).

and healer—was of mingled French and African blood. During the course of her life she bore thirteen children to three husbands.[12]   Stephen H. Long, writing of his expedition to the Rocky Mountains in 1819 and 1820, mentions a Negro belonging to one of the fur companies to whom the Omaha Indians referred as "the black white man" or, jokingly, as a *wassabajinga* or "little black bear." Willis or Thillis, a "black man," was on Ashley's expedition to the Rocky Mountains in 1823 and he was among those wounded in a fight with the Arikara on June 2.   Rose was interpreter for the expedition.[13]

Four white men and a Negro who had been killed and plundered by Osage between the Arkansas and Red rivers in 1823, and "William (a black)" who was robbed of his horse by Osage near Santa Fé in 1825 are included in a list of persons engaged in the fur trade who had been plundered or murdered by Indians between 1815 and 1831 which was compiled for the government in the latter year.   In 1833 some Kiowa killed a white man and a Negro engaged in the fur trade in what is now Oklahoma.[14]   In 1833 Maxmilian of Wied encountered at Fort Union "a negro slave belonging to Mr. McKenzie."   The prince mentions also the cook at Fort Clarke, "a negro from St. Louis," who was involved in a serious quarrel with an Indian, and who gave medical advice that enabled the prince to cure an attack of scurvy.[15]

A conspicuous figure in the journal of Charles Larpenteur

[12] *Wisconsin in Three Centuries,* 2: 225 (New York, 1906).

[13] Edwin James, *Account of an Expedition from Pittsburgh to the Rocky Mountains . . . Compiled from the Notes of Major Long, Mr. T. Say, and Other Gentlemen of the Party,* 1: 287 (Reuben G. Thwaites, *Early Western Travels,* vol. 14 — Cleveland, 1905) ; 18 Congress, 1 session, *Senate Documents,* no. 1, p. 80 (serial 89).

[14] 22 Congress, 1 session, *Senate Documents,* no. 90, p. 82, 83 (serial 213) ; Grant Foreman, *Pioneer Days in the Early Southwest,* 121 (Cleveland, 1926).

[15] Maxmilian, Prince of Wied, *Travels in the Interior of North America,* 2: 192, 3: 47, 87 (Thwaites, *Early Western Travels,* vols. 23, 24 — Cleveland, 1906).

is John Brazeau or Brazo, according to one account a "full-blooded Aethiopian," according to another, a mulatto.   He went to the fur country as the servant or slave of a man from whom he took his name.   "He was hardy, courageous," spoke good English and French, and knew the Indian languages.   His character, according to contemporary accounts, was not particularly attractive, though it doubtless was well suited to the exigencies of the Indian country. Larpenteur mentions the coolness and apparent enjoyment with which he disposed of the Blackfeet dead in a terrible smallpox epidemic.   He also seems to have been something of a bravo, and in 1836 he did his *bourgeois* a good service by shooting and seriously wounding a hunter who was giving trouble.   He was employed for a number of years by the American Fur Company, but he was cast off in his old age and he died in 1868, when over seventy years old, an object of charity.[16]

In the winter of 1842–43 the Blackfeet killed a "negro by the name of Reese," by whom that notorious ruffian and fur trader Francis Chardon "set great store."   By means of a cannon loaded with grapeshot, Chardon tried to massacre the next band of Blackfeet who arrived at his fort, and he succeeded in killing several Indians.[17]   At Bent's Fort on the Arkansas River in Colorado were two Negroes, Andrew and Dick Green, servants respectively of William and Charles Bent.   Andrew was very black, could speak the Cheyenne language, and was popular with the members of the tribe, who called him "Black Whiteman" and, sometimes, "Turtle Shell."   A young Cheyenne, out of compliment to Andrew, adopted the name "Black Whiteman," and in time it became a common name in that tribe.   Dick was with Colonel St. Vrain's trappers and traders when they

[16] Charles Larpenteur, *Forty Years a Fur Trader on the Upper Missouri*, 1: 121 (Coues edition, New York, 1898).
[17] Larpenteur, *Forty Years a Fur Trader*, 1: 217; Chittenden, *American Fur Trade*, 2: 694.

stormed the Taos pueblo in 1847 to take vengeance for the murder of his master, and in the affray he killed several Indians.[18]

Near Fort Laramie in 1846 Francis Parkman encountered a Negro who had been picked up by Indians in a starving condition. He ran away from his master in Missouri and joined a party of trappers from whom he became separated in a storm while hunting for some stray horses.[19] This is probably the only case in which a runaway Negro became associated with the fur trade of the Far West. The others mentioned were all apparently Negro slaves accompanying their masters, or free persons of color who were usually, it would seem, free-born.

St. Louis, for a variety of reasons, was the distributing center for most of the Negroes connected with the fur trade. The fur trade of the West had its headquarters in that city, which was located on the Missouri, the principal avenue of access to the Indian country of the Great Plains and the Rocky Mountains. The area of which St. Louis was the metropolis was an enclave of early settled, slave-holding territory jutting out into the Indian country; and it thus contained a large number of fur traders to whom the use of Negro slaves for personal service and other menial labor in the fur trade would seem natural. St. Louis was a city dominated by French traditions and closely connected by the Mississippi with New Orleans, a city with a similar background. In both cities free persons of color occupied a more conspicuous and respectable position than in slave-holding communities where Anglo-Saxon ideas of race prevailed. It was thus natural that both Negro slaves and free *gens du couleur* should constitute a not insignificant racial element in the fur trade as conducted from St. Louis.

A list of the *engagés* employed by Manuel Lisa on an ex-

[18] George Bird Grinnell, "Bent's Old Fort and Its Builders," in *Kansas Historical Collections*, 15: 61.
[19] Francis Parkman, *The Oregon Trail*, 151 (Boston, 1895).

pedition to the upper Missouri which left St. Louis in May,
1812, gives an excellent idea of the part played by Negroes
in the fur trade. "George, *negre*," who was probably a
slave acting as cook or personal servant, is listed in a conspicuous position at the very end of the muster roll. At
first glance he seems to be the only representative of the
African race with the expedition, but further investigation
reveals one "Edouard Rose," none other than the notorious
guide, interpreter, hunter, and Crow chief. Another familiar name is that of Baptiste Pointsable, the half-Indian,
one-fourth French, one-fourth Negro son of the "first white
settler in Chicago." Still more careful examination brings
to light at least one more person of Negro blood—Cadet
Chevalier, a free mulatto who engaged in the fur trade
from about 1802 until his death during this expedition on
January 4, 1813.[20]

Colonel James Stevenson of the Bureau of American Ethnology, who "spent thirty years among Indians for study
of them," is quoted as having "remarked upon . . . the
fact that the old fur traders always got a Negro if possible
to negotiate for them with the Indians, because of their
'pacifying effect.' They could manage them better than
white men, with less friction."[21] Stevenson's opinion of
the affinity of the Indian for the Negro is upheld by such
independent and well-qualified observers as John H. Kinzie,
the Reverend Edward D. Neill, and the journalists of the
Lewis and Clark expedition. But whether or not this rather
extreme statement of the relation of the Negro to the Indian trade is accepted, the facts presented herein give some
idea of the varied parts played by Negro slaves and free
persons of color in the drama of the American fur trade—
rôles which included the entire range of cast, from cooks,
personal servants, voyageurs, hunters, guides, and interpre-

[20] Luttig, *Journal of a Fur-trading Expedition*, 101, 157, 158. ,
[21] *Ten Years' Work for Indians at Hampton Institute, Va.*, 1878-
1888, 9, 13 (Hampton, Virginia, 1888).

ters to salaried traders and independent entrepreneurs. The Negroes have not dominated any one rôle, as have the Highland Scots, the French-Canadians, or the Kentuckians, but it is probably fair to say that they have been more versatile in their fur-trading activities than any of the latter. Any survey of the racial aspects of the American fur trade, to be complete, must include the people whose African blood is sometimes mingled with that of the Caucasian or the Indian or both, who are colloquially known as the American Negroes.

Further Reading

Additional information about the mulatto fur-trader Jean Baptiste Point-au-Sable, "the first white man" at what is now Chicago, can be found in Romeo B. Garrett, "The Negro in Peoria, 1773-1905," *NHB*, (April, 1954), pp. 147-50; and Thomas A. Meehan, "Jean Baptiste Point du Sable: The First Chicagoan," *Mid-America: An Historical Review*, XIX (April, 1937), pp. 83-92.

The mulatto mountain-men, Edward Rose and James P. Beckwourth, both of whom are said to have become Crow chiefs, deserve further scholarly and comparative study; some of their feats have probably been confused. Since Beckwourth's "autobiography," *The Life and Adventures of James P. Beckwourth* (New York: 1856; reprinted by Arno Press, 1969), prepared by the early "ghost writer," T. D. Bonner, has had its authenticity questioned, it might be worthwhile to prepare a biography of Beckwourth based entirely on the contemporary records and the accounts of others.

"Negroes and the Fur Trade" could also be supplemented by material from many histories of fur-trading expeditions and biographies of important fur-traders, which frequently contain references to Negroes, usually, however, in subordinate positions. See, for example, Frances Fuller Victor, *Eleven Years in the Rocky Mountains* (Hartford, Conn., 1879), pp. 77, 197-98; J. Cecil Alter, *Jim Bridger* (Norman, Okla., 1962; 1st ed., 1925), pp. 167-68; Dale L. Morgan, *Jedediah Smith and the Opening of the West* (Indianapolis and New York, 1953), pp. 194-95, 413, 204, 259, 267-68, 341, 345; Kenneth L. Holmes, *Ewing Young: Master Trapper* (Portland, Oregon, 1967), pp. 97, 117, 164.

NEW ENGLAND, THE MIDDLE REGION, THE UPPER SOUTH AND THE OLD NORTHWEST
ca. 1676-1800

Negroes, usually slaves, were comparatively few on these frontiers but were nevertheless found on all of them — their numbers increasing from north to south. Their frontier roles were much the same as those of white employees and indentured servants. They felled the trees, plowed the soil, tilled and harvested the crops, did the usual chores, aided in resisting the attacks of hostile Indians, and, in the case of the women, worked in the fields, as well as helping with the housework. They were frequently skilled in various crafts, and some were experienced woodsmen. For the most part they identified their own interests with those of their masters. However, because of their race and consequent legal position, they could not be completely identified with those interests and some discontented Negroes escaped, or tried to escape, to the French and — during the Revolution — to the British enemy, or to the hostile Indians.

A good deal of information about Negroes on these frontiers is brought together on pp. 16-21, 24-26, 29-31, 80, 101-106 of this book. J. Reuben Sheeler, "The Negro on the Virginia Frontier," JNH, XLIII (October, 1958), pp. 279-97, deals with the period from 1716 to 1800. Much more scholarly work on the Negro on these various frontiers remains to be done. Scattered references can be found in almost any history of these regions in the frontier period, particularly in histories of slavery. Particularly useful are J. Winston Coleman, *Slavery Times in Kentucky* (Chapel Hill, N.C., 1940), pp. 7-8, 10-11; John Edwin Bakeless, *Daniel Boone: Master of the Wilderness* (New York, 1939), pp. 161, 163, 165-66, 198, 204, 216, 218, 222; Harriet Simpson Arnow, *The Flowering of the Cumberland* (New York, 1963), pp. 92-96, 403, note 5.

THE COLONIAL SOUTH, 1670-1763:
THE CAROLINAS AND GEORGIA

The activities of the Negroes on the southern colonial frontier — which was both a frontier of settlement and a military frontier, bordering on territories claimed by Spain and France as well as by powerful Indian nations — were considerably different from, and more important than those of the Negroes on the more northerly and westerly frontiers, where the comparatively few Negroes for the most part identified their own interests with those of their white masters and associates. On the southern frontier, Negroes — because of their large numbers and their proximity to hostile or potentially hostile borders — operated as allies of their English masters only temporarily and exceptionally, principally during the early episode of the Yemassee War. Their principal role — apart from their accepted and assigned function as laborers — was as actual or potential enemies: runaways to, and military colonists for, the Spaniards; plotters and insurrectionists; and French and Spanish secret agents among the Indians.

The following article, which originally appeared in the *Journal of Negro History* (Vol. XXXIII, No. 1 — January, 1948), adequately deals with this topic.

NEGROES ON THE SOUTHERN FRONTIER, 1670-1763[1]

NUMBERS

"Charles Town," settled April 1670, "was the beginning of the colony which later became South Carolina."[2] From the beginning slaves were an important element in the population and continued to be increasingly so. The total number of Negroes was almost never estimated as less than twice that of the whites and by the end of the period the whites were estimated at 30-40,000, the Negroes at 70-90,000.[3]

[1] This paper, it will be noted, employs no manuscripts, although such source material as records, narratives, and journals in printed form, as well as reprints of contemporary pamphlets, have been utilized, and it makes large use of secondary works, such as those of Crane, Meriwether, and Alden, referred to in note 3, which are themselves almost exclusively based on manuscript sources. A more extensive study, making primary and direct use of manuscript material, might prove profitable.

[2] Jernegan, Marcus Wilson, *The American Colonies, 1492-1750*, New York, 1929, p. 75.

[3] "A short description of ... South Carolina ... 1763," London, 1770, *South Carolina historical collections*, iii, 478; Hewit [sic], Dr., "An historical account of ... South Carolina and Georgia," London, 1779, *S. C. hist. colls.*, i, 231-232. For other estimates of the slave population of South Carolina, 1699-1761, see: Salley, Alexander S., ed., *Narratives of early Carolina, 1650-1708*, N. Y., 1911, p. 204; McCrady, Edward, *The history of South Carolina under the proprietary government, 1670-1719*, N. Y., 1897, p. 477; Crane, Verner W., *The southern frontier, 1670-1732*, Philadelphia, 1929, pp. 112-113; Meriwether, Robert L., *The expansion of South Carolina, 1729-1765*, Kingsport, Tenn., pp. 3, 5 n. 4, 6, 10; Aptheker, Herbert, *American Negro slave revolts*, N. Y., 1943, pp. 174 n. 39, 185; "A description of South Carolina," London, 1761, *S. C. hist. colls.*, ii, 218, 261; *The colonial records of the state of Georgia* (GCR), edited by Allen D. Candler, iii, Atlanta, 1905, pp. 396-418; GCR, v. 475; "An impartial enquiry into the state and utility of the province of Georgia," London, 1741, *Collections of the Georgia historical society*, i, Savannah, 1840, p. 167; Alden, John Richard, *John Stuart and the southern colonial frontier, 1754-1775*, Ann Arbor, 1942, p. 125 n. 6; "A description of South Carolina," *loc. cit.*, 218.

"About 1750 there were approximately 12,000 Indian warriors in the southern nations, divided among some twenty tribes. .... Johnson estimated one warrior to every five Indians. On this basis there were about 60,000 southern Indians in the third quarter of the eighteenth century."[4] The Negroes in South Carolina *alone* were, then, superior in number to *all the Indians throughout the entire southern region,* from the Ohio and Potomac to the Gulf, from the Mississippi to the Atlantic, divided among over a score of tribes.

During most of the period, also, the British frontier of South Carolina and, subsequently, Georgia, was a region of international tension, one of the arenas in which the struggle among European powers for the control of the fur-trade, for dominant influence over the Indians, and, eventually, for the possession of the entire eastern half of North America, was being carried on. The struggle in this region was a particularly complicated one, involving three great European powers (the British, the Spaniards, and after 1699, the French) and several particularly powerful Indian nations, such as the Creeks, Cherokee, Chickasaw, and Choctaw.

Here, it is evident, the Negroes, despite their legally servile condition and the strict supervision employed to keep them in such a condition, had an opportunity, by virtue of their great numbers, and the complicated balance and tension among European colonists and Indian tribes, to play a role of greater importance than would have been possible in any other British colonial region or at any other time. It is the object of this paper to ascertain to what extent they did play a distinctive and significant part, aside from their accepted and assigned function as field-laborers, in the life of these times and that region, and particularly in the arena of international conflict.

[4] Alden, 7.

MILITARY SERVICE

It is ironical that a principal role of Negroes on the southern frontier was as allies of their masters against hostile Indians; so far as I can discover, in no other part of the British colonies in North America were slaves so employed. Their use for this purpose, however, had good classical precedent in the proud Spartiates' employment of helots and Perioeci as light-armed troops, and many a South Carolina planter doubtless remembered his Plutarch well enough to be reminded of this, were reminder or justification required aside from the exigencies of the immediate situation. Outnumbered by their slaves, on a frontier constantly exposed to attack by enemies both European and Indian, it was a sound if daring policy for the British colonists to endeavor to attach a part of the slave population to them by the conferring of special responsibilities and privileges. Accordingly, a law of 1708 required each militia captain " 'to enlist traine up and bring into the field for each white, one able Slave armed with gun or lance.' "[5] Probably the latter weapon was the more usual.

The Negro militiamen were no doubt carefully selected from the most trustworthy of the slave population. In anticipation of an attack on Charleston in the year of the above law, "The provincial militia was strengthened by a force of negro cattle-hunters" as well as by a large body of friendly Indians.[6] "Cattle-hunters" — in other words, cowboys—would be chosen from the most responsible of the slaves, who had justified by previous good conduct their assignment to duties which, because of their independent nature, were no doubt highly prized.

It was probably not difficult to recruit Negroes for the service. The exemption from heavy labor while engaged in drill, the sense of importance derived from military ac-

[5] Crane, 187 n. 1.
[6] Crane, 91.

tivities, the prospect of excitement and adventure, possibly a tot of rum on muster-days, were doubtless sufficient to bring into the ranks as many as were desired. The sort of inducement which was thought capable of stimulating the Negro militiaman to good conduct is revealed in a Georgia law. If a slave, impressed for military service, showed courage in battle, he was to receive every year "a livery coat and ... Breeches ... of Good Red Cloth turned up with Blue," a hat, stockings, shirt, and shoes, and should be exempt from service "that day in every year ... on which such action shall have been performed."[7] Should such a uniform have been furnished to the slave on induction, instead of only as a reward, it would no doubt have greatly assisted in recruiting.

As a matter of fact, however, the British seem to have employed Negro troops on the southern frontier to a significant extent on only one occasion—the desperate struggle in 1715, against the Indians roused by Emperor Brims of the Lower Creeks, which is usually, though inadequately, called the Yemassee War, after the tribe which spearheaded the attack. It would not have been surprising had the Negro slaves of South Carolina been not merely willing but even glad to have an opportunity of fighting the Yemassee, who had been, up to the very eve of the rising, allies of the English against the Spaniards and mission Indians of Florida, and consequently always ready to apprehend and return slaves who had taken refuge in the woods or were trying to make their way to Spanish territory. There was consequently no love lost between the two peoples, and no reason for the Negroes to feel any sympathy for the Yemassee when, driven to madness by exactions of greedy traders and encroachments on their lands, and instigated by the crafty Brims, they turned without warning on their erstwhile allies, the English. Here was a serious flaw in the Emperor's calculations. Had he gone on from uniting

[7] Flanders, Ralph Betts, *Plantation slavery in Georgia*, Chapel Hill, 1933, p. 33.

the Indians of the southern frontier against the English, to the organizing of the potential enemy within their gates— the slaves—his blow might have been decisive and have swept the English from the South Carolina coast into the sea, drastically changing the course of southern history. But he overlooked the potentialities of the slaves and, failing to make them allies, found them dangerous enemies instead.

Negroes did good service in the so-called Yemassee War. In the initial outbreak they fell fighting side by side with their comrades-in-arms, the white militiamen. A "garrison consisting of 70 white people and 40 blacks" was "surprised and cut to pieces."[8] But when the first attack failed to be decisive, the South Carolina authorities rallied, drafted Negroes as well as whites into the army, threw the enemy back, and then invaded his country in turn. Gov. Craven in July "crossed the Santee with about a hundred whites . . . and another hundred negroes and Indians" while among the troops under Maurice Moore marching into the Cherokee country later in the year to overawe that tribe was "Captain John Pight with his negro company." It is interesting to note that when a part of this force was withdrawn, "Captain Pight's negroes" remained, at the request of the Cherokee themselves,[9] who had presumably discovered the Negro soldiers to be particularly friendly and helpful, as other peoples in more recent times have also found them.

But though Negroes continued to appear on South Carolina militia lists to the end of this period, and though among a force of nearly 2,800 in Grant's expedition against the Cherokee in 1760 were over 200 "wagoners and negro pioneers"[10]—probably some, though not all, of the wagoners

[8] "An account of missionaries, sent to South Carolina," *S. C. hist. colls.*, ii, 550.

[9] Crane, 171, 173, 181, 183.

[10] Meriwether, 94, 105, 146, 156 n. 29, presents mixed white and slave militia lists for the South Carolina backcountry in 1757. See also: *ibid.*, 237.

as well were also Negroes—they do not seem, after the Yemassee War, to have been used as fighting-men. In 1760 "a motion to equip 500 Negroes to serve against the [Cherokee] savages, was lost [in the South Carolina assembly] only by the casting vote of the speaker."[11] but it *was* lost, and its nearness to passing is a measure of the desperate straits the colony was in at this point.

Between the Yemassee War and the 1760 motion the situation had changed—to such an extent that some of the Negroes who served in 1715 may a few years later have been assisting these same Yemassee in attacks on the South Carolina frontier from Spanish Florida, where the Yemassee had taken refuge after their defeat and where they were eventually joined by numerous runaway slaves.

FLIGHT AND INSURRECTION

The more alert and enterprising of the South Carolina slaves early learned that Spanish Florida was a refuge. In the autumn of 1687, eight Negro men and two women, one with a child at the breast, arrived at St. Augustine by boat from South Carolina. They expressed, doubtless after some preliminary coaching, a desire for "the waters of baptism," asserting that their former masters were not Catholics and would not permit them to learn the doctrines of the true religion. They were claimed by an emissary from South Carolina, but it "not appearing to be the proper thing to return them after becoming Christians," since they would not have the benefits of the Catholic religion in South Carolina and to do so might endanger their souls. Gov. Quiroga paid their former owners 160 ps. for each Negro. The men were put to work on the fort then under construction and the women were employed at house-work.[12]

11 Alden, 113-114.

12 "Dispatches of Spanish officials bearing on the free Negro settlement of Gracia Real de Santa Teresa de Mosé, Florida," *Journal of Negro history*, ix (Apr., 1924), 145-146, 150-153; Chatelain, Verne E., *The defense of Spanish Florida, 1565 to 1763*, Washington, D. C., 1941, pp. 160-161 n. 4.

Runaways probably continued to make their way to St. Augustine, though the way was long and Indians friendly to the English were on the watch to intercept them and return them to their masters. They were encouraged by a royal decree of Oct. 10, 1699, promising protection "to all Negro deserters from the English who fled to St. Augustine and became Catholics" and which was "repeated from time to time." We learn no details about such escapes, however, for a generation. Early in 1725 seven Negroes arrived at St. Augustine from Carolina. The Spaniards were, of course, themselves slave-owners, and in 1730—so slowly moved the official wheels—it was decided to sell such Negroes in Florida and give the proceeds to their former masters; the Negroes would thus receive the benefits of baptism and residence in a Catholic community but his Majesty's Exchequer would be spared. The Council of the Indies, however, decided the following year that these Negroes should neither be returned nor paid for, nor should any who might take refuge in Florida in the future. In 1733 and again in 1736 the decree of 1699, promising protection to Negro deserters, was repeated.[13]

The Yemassee, settled near St. Augustine, were a factor in inducing Negroes to leave Carolina for Florida. They had been allied with the English long enough, up to a decade or so before, that some of them probably spoke English and could communicate with Negroes who had also acquired such knowledge. "Their skill in border forays, developed under English tutelage, was still in requisition, but now for scalping and negro-stealing raids against the plantations of Port Royal and Pon Pon.... They were frequently joined by recalcitrant Lower Creeks ... and by negroes, the runaways whose retention in Florida had been a constant article of complaint against the Spaniards." These

[13] "Dispatches ...," 145-146; Chatelain, 160-161 n. 24; Corry, John Pitts, *Indian affairs in Georgia, 1732-1756*, Philadelphia, 1936, pp. 119-120; "Statements made in the introduction to the report on General Oglethorpe's expedition," *Collections of the South Carolina historical society*, ii, 356-357.

Yemassee raiders and their runaway Negro allies "took every opportunity to carry to the border plantations" the word that Florida was a land of freedom. Slaves carried off by the Yemassee, such as those of David Ferguson in 1727,[14] or who deserted of their own accord but probably under their direct or indirect instigation, swelled the number of runaways at St. Augustine who could be drawn on for subsequent raiding parties.

By 1738 war between England and Spain was rapidly approaching and this situation was reflected in the increasingly active hospitality extended by the governor of Florida to the Negro slaves of South Carolina. In March 1738, various Negroes appeared and claimed their freedom, which was granted. The governor promised them a place to be called Gracia Real where they could cultivate the soil. He further published a proclamation that all who came in the future should be free, as he was about to go against the English and wished to encourage the slaves "to unite themselves to our arms." The grateful Negroes accordingly promised, June 10, 1738, that "they would always be the most cruel enemies of the English." The grapevine telegraph rapidly spread the governor's word throughout the border settlements. "Several negroes ... employed in Pettiaugers, and other like Craft" took "the Benefit of the Spaniards' Proclamation" and went to St. Augustine. Capt. Davis was quoted on Dec. 18, 1738, as saying "that no less than nineteen Negro Slaves which he had in Carolina, run away from him lately all at once, under that strong Temptation of the Spaniards ... which he said he found verified; for he saw all his said Negroes now at St. Augustine, who

[14] Crane, 255, 247-248; Corse, Carita Doggett, *The key to the golden islands*, Chapel Hill, 1931, pp. 83-84; "Statements ... on General Oglethorpe's expedition," 1741, *S. C. hist. colls.*, ii, pp. 354-359. Raids by Spaniards, Negroes, and Indians on South Carolina had occurred as early as 1686 when Edisto was raided and money, plate, and 13 slaves carried off to St. Augustine. Salley, 205.

laughed at him. ...." Twenty three Negro men, women, and
children arrived at St. Augustine, Nov. 21, 1738—possibly
the same as the 24 who were reported escaped from Port
Royal about this time. The governor stated Feb. 6, 1739,
that he would establish the runaways at a place called Mosé,
where 38 men, mostly married, and provided with a chap-
lain, were already settled. Mosé, also Mosa, and Mousa,
variously translated as "moss" and "maize," was "situated at the head of Mosa Creek, a tributary of the North
River which could be navigated by small vessels, and being
directly in the path of the route of travel between St.
Augustine and the mouth of the St. Johns River, this position was one of great strategic value." The settlement was
defended by a barricade of "sod, stakes, and thorns," with
a ditch; "it is likely that some of the Yemassee Indians
also lived here."[15]

The Yemassee, of course, did not always return un-
scathed from their raids on the Georgia and South Carolina
frontiers, and it is probable that of the married Negro men
at Fort Mosé, a number had taken to themselves wives from
among the surplus Yemassee women, since the men among
the runaway Negroes usually far outnumbered the women;
some, of course, may have married free Negro women who
were natives of Florida, but their close association with the
Yemassee and the undoubted superfluity of women among
these Indians suggest the former solution. A century later
an interpreter who knew the Yemassee well described them
as having "dark skins, coarse hair, thick lips, and flat
feet. ...,"[16] presumably from intermarriage with runaway
Negroes.

[15] "Dispatches ...," 145-146; Chatelain, 92-93, 167 n. 87; GCR, iii, 396,
iv, 247-248; v, 139, 164, 315, 293; Meriwether, 26. "Letters of Montiano,"
Collections of the Georgia historical society, vii, pt. 1, pp. 29-30.

[16] Woodward, Thomas S., *Woodward's reminiscences of the Creek or Muscogee Indians*, Montgomery, Ala., 1859, p. 130. Near the end of this period
the Yemassee had dwindled to only 20 warriors. "A description of South
Carolina," *loc. cit.*, ii, 218.

"There were above forty thousand negroes in the
province [of South Carolina], a fierce, hardy, and strong
race," wrote a former resident, "whose constitutions were
adapted to the warm climate, whose nerves were braced
with constant labour, and who could scarcely be supposed
to be contented with that oppressive yoke under which they
groaned. ... Two Spaniards were caught in Georgia, and
committed to jail, for enticing slaves to leave Carolina and
join this regiment"—the force of Negroes at St. Augustine
which was said to be on the same pay and rations as regular
Spanish soldiers, and to have officers appointed from among
themselves. Accordingly, as a result of the proclamation of
1738, "Numbers of Slaves did, from Time to Time, by Land
and Water, desert to *St. Augustine.* And, the better to
facilitate their Escape, carried off their Master's *Horses,
Boats,* &c. some of them first commiting Murder; and were
accordingly received and declared free." Negroes who fled
and headed rebellions included "Overseers ... , and Masters
of Pettiaguas." Among those who escaped after acts of
violence were "Five negroes who were cattle hunters at
Indian land, some of whom belonged to Captain M'Pherson,
[who] after wounding his son and killing another man,
made their escape. Several more attempting to get away
were taken, tried, and hanged at Charlestown." It is not
surprising that about this time, indeed even a year earlier,
Lieut. Gov. Broughton should have declared: "our Negroes
are very numerous and more dreadful to our Safety, than
any Spanish Invaders."[17]

When groups of slaves committed murder in seizing
boats and horses by which to escape to St. Augustine, it
was, of course, not far from insurrection, and insurrection
beyond question it soon came to be.   Conspiracy among

[17] "Statements ...," *loc. cit.*, ii, 354-359; Hewit [Hewat], 331-332;
Jones, Charles C., *The history of Georgia*, 2 vols., Boston, 1883, i, 298-300;
Meriwether, 27 n. 28, 188; GCR, v. 476.

slaves was by no means a new thing in the province.   In 1702 a Negro was put in irons "for threatening that he with other negroes would Rise and Cutt off the Inhabitants of this Province." In the spring of 1711, the white South Carolinians were kept "in great terror and fear" by "several Negroes [who] keep out armed, and robbing and plundering houses and plantations." Two years later a plot "in Goose Creek quarters" was betrayed by a slave. The most serious plot up to that time, and the first evidencing a connection with St. Augustine, was in 1720 — "A very wicked and barbarous plott of ... the negroes rising with a designe to destroy all the white people in the country and then to take the towne in full body but it pleased God it was discovered and many of them taken prisoners and some burnt, some hang'd and some banish'd." Fourteen of the conspirators tried to get to St. Augustine, but the Creek Indians would not guide them and they were captured by the garrison at Savannah Town (now Augusta, Ga.) "half starved," and, it was reported, "will be executed as soon as they come down."

This severe punishment may have quelled the menace for a decade, but in 1730 an uprising in "Charles Town" was planned for Aug. 15. Disagreement developed as to whether the Negroes on each plantation should destroy their own masters or whether they should all rise in a body. The supporters of the latter view, it would seem, "soon made a great Body at the back of the Town, and had a great Dance, and expected the Country Negroes to come & join them; and had not an over-ruling Providence discovered their Intrigues, we had been all in blood. ... The Chief of them, with some others, is apprehended and in Irons, in order to a Tryal...." It is not surprising that, according to a historian of South Carolina in this period, "What visions of expansion and greater wealth the planters had were clouded by the danger of insurrection by the new and half-savage slaves. Formerly the problem of defense had been largely external, represented by the Spaniard and the Indian, but by 1729 there had come about a fundamental change. Letters and papers of the time are full of allusions to the peril, and for forty years it remained perhaps the strongest influence in the province on public policy.''

During the 1730's conspiracies thickened. In 1733 large meetings among the slaves were reported and 12 Negroes were ordered arrested and questioned; runaway slaves ''near the Congerees'' engaged in robbery, and rewards were offered for their capture dead or alive; slaves fled to St. Augustine. Three Negroes were arrested for conspiracy in 1737. Flights to St. Augustine greatly increased the next year, as already noted, and in the following year the situation reached a climax with several conspiracies, having as their objective the organization of the slaves to rise *en masse* and fight their way to Florida.[18]

The year 1739 was inaugurated by ''a Conspiracy ... formed by the Negroes in Carolina to rise, and forcibly make their Way out of the Province, to put themselves under the Protection of the Spaniards, who had promised Freedom to all who should run to them from their Owners.'' Its center was ''at Winyaw, the most Northern Part of that Province,'' so the assumption was that it involved all the territory south of that point as well. On its being discovered, the Negroes who were involved mostly went off by boat, presumably for St. Augustine.

A distorted version of this affair may have been the basis of a report which had reached St. Augustine by Aug. 19, 1739, that ''the English had set out with more than 100 negroes to build a fort; that the negroes rose, slew all the English ... hamstrung all the horses, [and] scattered. ...''[19]

[18] *Conspiracies, 1702-1738:* Aptheker, 168, 171, 173-176, 180-191; Crane, 232; Meriwether, 6.

[19] GCR, iii, 396, iv, 275, 277; ''Montiano,'' 32.

The numerous conspiracies in which the slave-popula-
tion of South Carolina had expressed its discontent had
never yet developed into actual insurrection; plots had always been discovered in time to be suppressed before an
outbreak occurred. Violence by recalcitrant Negroes had
been confined to robberies by outlying Maroons and an occasional rather casual and unpremeditated killing incident to
the seizure of horses or boats in order to escape to Florida.
But while Gen. Oglethorpe was preparing for his invasion
of Florida, word reached him of the most formidable slave-
insurrection ever to occur in a British colony of North
America—the bloodiest to take place in North America for
nearly a century. This uprising was ascribed, of course, to
Spanish instigation and certainly it would not have taken
the form it did had the rebels not been fully conscious of
the haven offered by Florida. A Spanish officer, it was said,
had come to Charleston the previous July with a Negro in
his company "that spoke *English* very well;" presumably
this Negro had achieved communication with discontented
blacks in South Carolina.

The uprising broke out at Stono, 20 miles below Charleston, Sept. 9, 1739, on a Sunday, that day being selected because the slaves were free from field-labor and the white
people were away from the plantations, at church. About
50 Negroes gathered with such weapons as they could im-
provise, broke into a public storehouse, killed the two men
in charge, cut off their heads and set them up on the stairs,
seized arms, ammunition, and, unfortunately, liquor, and
set out for Florida, banners displayed, two drums beating,
and calling out "Freedom!" Their numbers were swelled
as they marched and they killed, plundered, and burned all
before them till the country seemed full of flames. In those
days, however, for fear of just such occurrences, all able-
bodied men customarily brought their arms to church, and
the lieutenant-governor, encountering the rebels on their
march and riding around them, alarmed a congregation,

the men of which immediately constituted themselves a
militia company and set out in pursuit, the word being
spread meanwhile to other whites.

About a hundred armed planters caught up with the
main body of the rebels in an open field, celebrating their
success by drinking and dancing and probably expecting
to be joined by others before proceeding. The planters fired
on them and an engagement ensued in which the Negroes
are said to have "behaved boldly," but they were probably
ill-armed and must have been wearied from marching and
fighting. Fourteen Negroes were killed and the rest fled
into the woods with the exception of "One Negroe fellow"
who, seeing his master among the militiamen, singled him
out and advanced upon him; "his Master asked him if he
wanted to kill him the Negroe answered he did at the same
time snapping a Pistoll at him but it mist fire and his
Master shot him thro' the Head about fifty of these Villains
attempted to go home but were taken by the Planters who
Cutt off their heads and set them up at every Mile Post they
came to." According to another account, which may be
merely a version of this same episode, 20 militia encountered 90 Negroes, killed 10, and took four prisoners.
Twenty-odd more Negroes, in addition to the 14 first killed,
were killed in the next few days and about 40 taken, "who
were immediately some shot, some hang'd, and some Gib-
beted alive." Twenty-one whites and 44 Negroes—the last
probably an underestimate—are said to have lost their
lives.[20]

The failure of the Stono rising did not, however, prevent
another attempt the following June. One hundred and fifty
Negroes assembled near Charleston, but the gathering was

[20] *Contemporary sources for the Stono uprising:* "A ranger's report ...,"
222-223; "Statements ... on General Oglethorpe's expedition," 354-359; GCR,
iv, 412-413; "An impartial inquiry ...," 172-173; Hewitt, 331-332. *Secondary authorities:* Aptheker, 184-191 (Aptheker bases his account entirely on
original sources); Meriwether, 26; Jones, i, 298-300; McCrady, *1719-1776,*
185-187.

evidently premature and without effective leadership as we are told that they had no arms and that "there was no Corn on the Ground ripe for their Subsistence." Fifty were captured, 10 of whom, it was said, were being hanged each day.[21]

These events, of course, produced the utmost alarm. "The greater number of blacks which a frontier has," it was commented, "and the greater the disproportion is between them and her white people, the more danger she is liable to; for those are all secret enemies, and ready to join with her open ones upon the first occasion." Gen. Oglethorpe himself put it more pithily, June 29, 1741, in extended paraphrase of the Roman epigram: "As many slaves ... so many Enemys to the Government and consequently Friends to the Spaniard." These expressions were implemented by a law of 1740 placing a prohibitive duty of £14 on the importation of slaves, not, however, to begin until after 16 months, and to last only three years.[22]

Negroes, Indians, and Spaniards all cooperated in the resistance to Oglethorpe's invasion of 1740. Of the 965 troops in St. Augustine, not counting militia and Indians, 200 were "Armed Negroes." Gov. Montiano extensively employed "free Negroes (of those who are fugitives from the English Colonies)" as scouts. Negroes, including runaways from Carolina, were reported killed and captured in actions before St. Augustine. Gen. Oglethorpe found on approach that the Spaniards were engaged in "building a new one [fort] of Stone called Moosa to protect the Plantations they had granted to run away Negroes who were armed and officered in order to garrison the same. ... On my first Inroad the Spaniards quitted Moosa and drew off the Negroes." This withdrawal was probably strategic,

21 GCR, iv, 592; Aptheker, 191.

22 "An impartial inquiry ...," 167; "Letters from General Oglethorpe," 105-109; Meriwether, 27. Capt. Thompson, of Georgia, commented, May 4, 1740: "Had we permitted the use of negroes, both S. Carolina and Georgia might have been undone by this time," GCR, v. 342.

however, for on June 15, 1740, a force of Spaniards, Indians, and Negroes, the last doubtless including the former garrison of the fort, surprised and almost annihilated its British garrison, commanded by Col. Palmer.[23]

When the Spaniards counter-attacked against Georgia in June 1742, their force included "a regiment of negroes. The negro commanders were clothed in lace, bore the same rank as the white officers, and with equal freedom and familiarity walked and conversed with their comrades and chief. Such an example might justly have alarmed Carolina," as Gen. Oglethorpe indicated when, informing Gov. Bull of the invasion, he stated that he asked no aid of South Carolina, "since you can spare none but think myself obliged to give you this notice that you may prepare to prevent any Revolt among the Negroes." Fortunately for the English, the Spaniards were repulsed from Georgia and did not proceed to attack South Carolina. Dr. Hewat believes that had they directed their attack rather against South Carolina it might have been successful, "For should the enemy penetrate into that province, where there were such numbers of negroes, they would soon have acquired such a force, as must have rendered all opposition fruitless and ineffectual." The Spaniards, indeed, were under orders, after they should take Port Royal, to proclaim liberty to "the slaves of the English" through "slaves of all languages," and offer them lands in Florida.[24]

The Spanish power in Florida had, however, exhausted itself in this unsuccessful attempt at retaliation, and Span-

[23] "A ranger's report of travels with General Oglethorpe, 1739-1742," *Travels in the American colonies*, edited by Newton D. Mereness, N. Y., 1916, pp. 224-225, 227; "Letters from General Oglethorpe," *Georgia historical collections*, iii, 105-109; Corse, 98; Hurston, Zora Neale, letter from, JNH, xii (Oct., 1927), 664-667; McCrady, *History of South Carolina under the royal government, 1719-1776*, N. Y., 1899, pp. 203-205, 208-209; "*Montiano*," 35, 36, 48, 49, 61.

[24] Hewit, 365; Williams, John Lee, *The territory of Florida*, N. Y., 1837, p. 185; Meriwether, 189; *Ga. hist. colls.*, vii, pt. iii, 33-34.

ish encouragement, which had raised conspiracy and insurrection to such a crescendo, 1738-1740, being now withdrawn,
such activities thereafter dwindled. Discontent and rumored
conspiracy continued, to be sure, but found no violent expression on a large scale. In 1744 the friendly Indians were
asked to help round up Negroes who were out in the woods,
armed, and in 1747 intended insurrections were rumored.
Dissatisfaction was reported, 1759-1761, and in 1760 "Bull
... defended the province [South Carolina]" for its lack of
activity in the war then being waged against the Cherokee
"on the ground that it contained only 6,000 able-bodied
white men and 57,000 potential 'intestine' black enemies."
The *South Carolina Gazette* stated, May 31, 1760: "Good
reasons have been suggested to us, for not inserting in this
Paper any Account of Insurrections, especially at this
Time," because of the danger that such reports would im-
pede recruiting, particularly in the plantation area. Rumors
of insurrection plots, 1765-1766, followed the importation
of 8,000 slaves during the former year. On Jan. 14, 1766,
"107 slaves were reported ... to have left masters and ...
fled to join runaways already in Colleton County swamps."
By this time, however, the Spanish power in Florida, mori-
bund for a score of years, had been extinguished. The
Pueblo de Gracia Real de Mosé, which had been placed under a captain and lieutenant in 1752 and equipped with four
small cannon in 1756, had been broken up, and its former
garrison, along with most of the Spanish residents of Florida, had been evacuated to Cuba.[25] The British were at last
in control and runaway Negroes from South Carolina and
Georgia could no longer find refuge under the walls of St.
Augustine.

[25] Aptheker, 195-198; Meriwether, 226 n. 37, 243; Alden, 125 n. 6;
"Dispatches ...," 145-146, 164; Siebert, W. H., "Slavery and white servitude in East Florida, 1726 to 1776," *Florida historical quarterly*, x (July,
1931), 5; Southall, Eugene P., "Negroes in Florida prior to the Civil War,"
JNH, xix (Jan., 1934), 76-86.

RELATIONS WITH INDIANS

The authorities of South Carolina and Georgia were fully aware of the danger that their slaves might become allies of some powerful and potentially hostile Indian tribe bordering on their territories. Emperor Brims, as we have seen, failed to recognize the value of such an alliance, with resultant failure to his plan for sweeping away the English through an alliance of the southern tribes, but there was always a possibility that some more astute Creek or Cherokee chieftain might successfully attempt it. The English had no concern as to the small tribes of "tame Indians" nearby. These broken tribes in the tidewater region "were quite inoffensive, and were valued for their services in hunting runaway negroes. In the Stono insurrection of 1739 they killed three of the rebellious slaves and aided in the capture of others . . . the Catawbas . . . served the colony by coming down from time to time to hunt negroes out of the swamps. . . ."[26]

It was another matter as to the more remote and independent Indian nations. The use of slaves in the Indian country was generally forbidden. Col. Chicken, on a mission to the Cherokee in 1725, commented disapprovingly: "Sharp and Hatton have brought up their Slaves altho' by Law they are to fforfiet one hundred pounds for so doing . . . it's my Opinion that the Law ought to be punctually Complyed with . . . because the Slaves that are now come up talk good English as well as the Cherokee Language and . . . too often tell falcities to the Indians which they are very apt to beleive. . . ." "Bull . . . as a slave owner . . . feared [1760] that the Overhill [Cherokee] country, like the mountains of Jamaica, might become a refuge for fugitive Negroes."[27]

This particular fear, of course—that the hill-country of the Cherokee might become a stronghold of runaway slaves

26 Meriwether, 12-13.

27 Alden, 19; "Colonel Chicken's journal to the Cherokees, 1725," Mereness, *Travels*, 138-139; Corry, 45.

—was not justified by events. The swamps and hammocks
of Florida, rather than the hills of North Carolina and
Tennessee, were to be the region ultimately corresponding
to the Cockpit region of Jamaica, but not within the period
of this study. Nor did Negro slaves, in this period, ally
themselves on a large scale with any hostile Indian tribe;
that, again, was to be delayed until the next century and
Florida rather than the Carolinas was to be the scene of
this alliance. It was, however, true that association between
Negroes and Indians was potentially dangerous, as it might
encourage the former to run away and would make them
particularly formidable should the Indians with whom they
had become acquainted be courted by a foreign power. A
Negro from a British colony, for example, who learned the
Creek tongue, escaped to Florida, and became associated
with the Spanish, would be a key man in negotiations involving the Spanish government and Indians whose friendship was being sought by both the Spanish and the English.

Such Negroes were very active in the back-country,
though it was but rarely that the English were so situated
as to be able to observe and record their activities.   An
Englishman who did have such an opportunity, though
hardly to his satisfaction, was Capt. Tobias Fitch, on a mission to the Lower Creeks at the same time that Col. Chicken
was visiting the Cherokee. He noted in his journal: "Arrived at the Pallachocola Town. Two Spaniards, on(e)
Negro, and four Commantle Indians. ... The Spanyard
was Shye of Comeing into the Square for Some Time but
the Negro Sat in the Square in a Bould Maner." Fitch did
not venture to interfere with the "Bould" Negro at the
time, but at the "Cussetaw Town," the chief and people of
which were friendly, he claimed the Negro as "a Slave Belonging to our Country," and said he intended to take him,
to which the Indians agreed. Fitch proceeded to the Coweta
Town, capital of the Lower Creek confederacy, to which he
had been preceded by the Spaniards and Negro and their

cortège, where he again announced that he intended to take
the Negro since "tho he has Been Taken by the Yemassees
and Lived among the Spanyards Yet that dis not make him
free." Emperor Brims agreed, and the Negro was accordingly seized by some of Fitch's Cussetaw followers. The
Spaniards "appeared in Behalf of the Negro Assuring me
that he was a Good Christian" and offering to ransom him
with two Indian slaves—a testimony to his usefulness
which, of course, simply confirmed Fitch in his determination to deprive the Spaniards of such a valuable aide and
thereby further cause them to lose face before the Indians.

The Spanish Negro was not the only one of that race
operating among the Lower Creeks. One of Fitch's purposes was to induce the Lower Creeks to make war against
the Yemassee allies of the Spanish and he succeeded in
getting Emperor Brims's heir to lead a war-party against
them. But a Negro in the French interest followed after
the party and "Turned back 70 Warriours." Fitch, consequently, "came down to the lower Tallapoopes and there . . .
did take" that Negro. The French captain at Fort Toulouse
protested and offered to buy him if Fitch had a good claim
— another example of the importance of these Negro
"linksters" (interpreters) and diplomats.

These two Negroes still did not account for all among
the Lower Creeks, and one of Fitch's principal intentions
seems to have been to capture all such. He wrote: "There
being a Negro then in the Pallachocole town Belonging to
Andrew Partoson of Port-Royal, I sent five White men to
take him and bring him to me. They Accordingly Took the
Negro and had him, but the King of the Town"—notorious-
ly hostile to the English—"Cutt the Rope and threw it into
the fire and the King of sd Town told the White men that
they had as Good Guns as they, and Could make as good use
of them; upon which the white man Returned unto me."

This was just the first of Fitch's disappointments in his
role of slave-catcher, for "The Negro Which I Took from

the Spanyard ... did make his Escape from the White man
that were Carring him Down and Returned to Squire
Mickeo [a chief hostile to the English] who Imediatly assisted him with Cunnue [canoe] and provissions sufficient to
Carry him to Saint Mallagoes [San Marcos].'' Remained
only the Negro in the French interest, and he is probably
the one referred to as follows: ''I left the Cowweetaus
December the 2d and Brought with me a Negro ... and
being Within 20 miles of the Savana Town left the sd negro
In Charge of two white men well arm'd and the negro
Prisoned. Notwithstanding he got the white men's armes
and Shot on[e] John Sergant through the Brest and made
his Escape.''[28] Fitch thus returned Negro-less. The opposition of some of the Lower Creek chiefs, well supplemented
by the decision and daring of some of the Negroes themselves, had proved too much for him. When one considers
that this is the account of but one half-year's delegation to
the Lower Creeks, and when one regards the prominence of
Negroes in the annoying and thwarting of this English
representative during that period, the part they must have
played as French and Spanish agents in that region over a
longer period takes on a new and significant character.

[28] ''Captain Fitch's journal to the Creeks, 1725,'' Mereness, *Travels*, 184-
187, 199-201, 205-206, 210-212. The identity of the ''Commantle Indians''
who accompanied the Spaniards and their Negro ''mouth'' is of some interest.
The word is sometimes spelled ''Tommantle,'' which suggests that they may
be identified with the Tamali, sometimes spelled Tamatlé and Tum-mault-lau,
who lived at this time ''on the west bank of the Chattahoochee River below all
the other Creek towns on that stream,'' and thus close to Spanish territory. It
might also be noted that there was a Yemassee town called Tolemato. The late
Howard Sharp interestingly reports that Jamaican plantation-laborers at
Canal Point, Florida, some of whom were Maroons, said that they knew the
word ''Commantle'' and that it signified ''woolly or wooly haired.'' This
derivation would suggest that ''Commantle Indians'' might signify Yemassee
who, because of mixture with Negroes, had wooly hair. It seems more probable,
however, that they were Lower Creek Indians in the Spanish interest from
the Lower Chattahoochee. Swanton, John R., *Early history of the Creek
Indians and their neighbors*, Washington, D. C., 1922, pp. 183, 400, 409, 427,
104, 105, 340.

FREE NEGROES

A study of Negroes on the southern frontier would not be complete without at least a word—more would hardly be profitable—on the few free Negroes who ventured into that region. A large part of these, like a large part of the population of whatever color on any frontier, were of a reckless and even lawless character. In 1739 inhabitants of the Welsh Tract complained "That several Out Laws and Fugitives from the Colonies of Virginia and North Carolina most of whom are Mullatoes or of a mixed Blood" had encroached upon them, paying no taxes or quit rents, and were a "Pest & Nuisance." A trader with the Cherokee and Choctaw named John Vann—probably the ancestor of the large and important Cherokee family of that surname—in 1751 had an establishment near 96 Creek which included three Negroes and a mulatto, probably free. He dispatched one of his Negroes to kill a rival trader, who escaped much wounded.[29]

Other Negro settlers were, however, of an entirely respectable character. "In 1752 Matthew Chavous applied for a warrant for three hundred acres, explaining that he was a free negro, and had been in the province twelve years." The council was uncertain as to the propriety of "giving away lands to Negroes ... and their Posterity," and apparently nothing was done. But a year earlier "John Chevis, a free negro carpenter from Virginia ... asked for land on the rights of himself, wife, nine children and a foundling infant, saying that he had begun improvements on Stevens Creek. This warrant the governor and council granted with the condition that he prove that he was free," which apparently he was able to do. The names of these free Negro applicants—Chavous, Chavis—are so similar that it seems probable they were related; perhaps both were

[29] Meriwether, 95, 121-122.

derived from Chavez and indicate a West Indian origin.[30]

Free Negroes also produced their small quota of daring frontiersmen. A Negro slave named Abraham, on promise of freedom slipped out of Fort Loudoun, besieged by the Cherokee, early in 1760, and bore the word of its situation to Charleston, where presumably he received his promised reward—and also suffered an attack of smallpox. Now a free man, he returned to Fort Loudoun, and back to Charleston again. Charles McLamore, referred to for some reason as "a renegade mulatto," also got through the enemy lines to report the capitulation of Fort Loudoun and returned as the emissary of Gov. Bull to propose an exchange of prisoners.[31]

It is significant that these free Negroes were found on the western frontier, and for the most part after the Spanish power in Florida had declined to the point of extinction. They would otherwise probably have not been allowed on the frontier.

CONCLUSION

Although Negroes did good service to South Carolina in the Yemassee War and one or two Negro frontiersmen played useful roles in the war against the Cherokee, it is obvious that, apart from their normal functioning as

[30] Meriwether, 128, 133. Could John Chavis, ca. 1763-1838, a free Negro who was privately educated at Princeton under the tutelage of President Witherspoon, and subsequently was ordained to the Presbyterian ministry and became master of a classical school in which sons of some of the best families in North Carolina were prepared for college, have been some kin, perhaps a later-born son, of John Chevis, the free Negro carpenter? His birthplace is unknown, though it is usually said to have been either the West Indies or Granville Co., N. C. "John Chavis," DAB. Chavis, Cheves, Chavers, etc., was one of the commonest surnames among North Carolina free Negroes. Franklin, John Hope, *The free Negro in North Carolina, 1790-1860*, Chapel Hill, 1943, see index.

[31] Meriwether, 223, 224; Alden, 114, 119.

manual laborers, the principal importance of the Negroes on the southern frontier was as a source of annoyance and danger to the British colonies of that region, and thus rather negative in character. Their importance was, indeed, to a considerable extent rather potential than actual. *If* Emperor Brims had recognized the value of an alliance with the South Carolina slaves. ... *If* the Spaniards, who did recognize its value, had utilized its possibilities more effectively in the invasion of 1742. ... The South Carolina Negroes were under the double disadvantage, historically speaking, not only of being slaves, and thus almost hopelessly handicapped in representing their own interests effectively, but also of having those interests identified with a declining international cause. Their interests lay with the Spanish in Florida, with the French of the Mississippi Valley—not because these peoples were not slave-owners, with their quota of the brutal, the sadistic, and the merely insensitive—but because, at the worst, their slave-codes, both in principle and practice, were more lenient than those of the English, and because among them, lacking the virulent racism of the Anglo-Saxon, the position of the free Negro was incomparably superior to what it was among the English.[32] It is notable that there is no record of a Negro slave fleeing *from* the French or the Spanish *to* the English, while the movement in the other direction was considerable. But the rising commercial and industrial capitalism of the British controlled the future, and before it the colonial powers of France and Spain in eastern North America, with their Indian and Negro allies, were to go down.

And yet it is clear that, as the Indian allies of the French in the northern arena of the struggle, helped delay that perhaps inevitable result, so the Negro allies, actual or potential, of the Spanish in the southern arena, were also a

[32] See Frank Tannenbaum's *Slave and citizen: The Negro in the Americas*, N. Y., 1947, for a discussion of this matter.

factor of delay.[33] Those Negroes who made good their escape to Florida and there served as military colonists, assisted, through their border-raids in association with Yemassee and recalcitrant Lower Creeks, in weakening South Carolina, and the large Negro element in the garrison of St. Augustine, drawn to a conspicuous extent from South Carolina refugees, certainly contributed to the discomfiture of Gen. Oglethorpe's invasion and siege of 1740. Runaway slaves operated to an unknown extent, but evidently with considerable effectiveness, as French and Spanish agents among Indian tribes bordering on the English settlements.

Probably even more important, however, were the Negroes who did *not* escape to Florida but remained a permanent part of the South Carolina population—and a permanent source of potential and actual danger. From the 1720s, at least, the South Carolina slaves were recognized, in the words of a lieutenant governor in the following decade, as "more dreadful to our Safety, than any Spanish Invaders." Or, as Gov. Oglethorpe of Georgia expressed it: "As many slaves ... so many Enemys to the Government and consequently Friends to the Spaniard." These opinions the slaves had justified by frequent flights to Florida, sometimes at the cost of the lives of those who tried to stop them, by numerous conspiracies and one bloody uprising, and by the activities of outlying Maroons. It was their presence— and the evidences of their persistent hostility—which weakened South Carolina militarily for the invasion of Florida

[33] I have pointed out in my article, "Negroes and the East Florida annexation plot, 1811-1813," *JNH*, xxx (Jan., 1945), that the Florida Negroes were the principal factor in *delaying* for nearly a decade the annexation of East Florida to the United States, which was in any case achieved by 1821 but would probably have been accomplished by 1812 had it not been for the intelligent and effective resistance put up by the Negro population, particularly by those living among the Seminole Indians. The South Carolina slaves, in, of course, a less direct fashion, played a somewhat similar role in postponing the triumph of the British in the southeast during the second generation of the 18th century.

and prevented her from adequately contributing to resistance to the Spanish counter-invasion of Georgia—which a qualified observer believed would have been successful had it been directed against South Carolina so that it could have been assisted by the slaves—and which a score of years later similarly hampered South Carolina in her war with the Cherokee and must have contributed to the Fort Loudoun disaster.

It is noteworthy, finally, that in all the reports by British officials and other observers on the Negroes of the southern frontier in this period, there is not the slightest hint of "docility ... submissiveness ... contentment." The assumption is always that the slave population is made up of " 'intestine' black enemies" chafing under their "oppressive yoke," "a fierce, hardy, and strong race," who constantly keep the province "in great terror and fear" lest some "wicked and barbarous plott" of theirs should put "all in blood." The South Carolina planters and officials evidently believed that when in 1738 the runaway Negroes in Florida promised that "they would always be the most cruel enemies of the English" they not only meant exactly what they said but were well qualified to make their words good. The "danger of insurrection by the new and half-savage [sic] slaves," writes a recent historian of the South Carolina frontier, "... for forty years ... remained perhaps the strongest influence in the province on public policy."[34]

[34] Meriwether, 6. The other quoted phrases in the concluding paragraphs also appear in a more extended context at various points in the third section of the paper.

Further Reading

Although no errors of moment appear in this article, students particularly interested in the subject might profitably supplement it with information from such authorities as Chapman J. Milling, *Red Carolinians* (Chapel Hill, N.C., 1940), pp. 121, 153-54, 157, 159-60, 183 note 29; Lawrence H. Gipson, *The British Empire before the American Revolution*, II, *The Southern Plantations* (Caldwell, Idaho, 1936), pp. 169-70; Gipson, *Zones of International Friction: North America South of the Great Lakes Region, 1748-1754* (New York, 1939), pp. 19-21, also note 25; John Jay TePaske, *The Governorship of Spanish Florida, 1710-1763* (Durham, N.C., 1964), p. 141; David H. Corkran, *The Cherokee Frontier: Conflict and Survival, 1740-1762* (Norman, Okla., 1962), pp. 140, 156; Richard Maxwell Brown, *The South Carolina Regulators* (Cambridge, Mass., 1963), *passim*.

THE SOUTHEAST, 1783-1842:
FLORIDA AND THE SEMINOLE WARS

The southeastern frontier was essentially Spanish Florida and, after 1821, the Territory of Florida, together with adjacent areas of Georgia and Alabama. A virtual hiatus of at least twenty years in the history of the Negroes on the southern frontier followed the British annexation of Spanish Florida in 1763. Such slave conspiracies as were reported were rarely more than rumors. Slaves continued to escape into the woods where they lived as maroons, but discontented Negroes no longer had a friendly region to the South in which their freedom was secure and from which came encouragement for insurrection.

During the "English time," however, which lasted until the retrocession of Florida to Spain in 1783 — and particularly during the confusion of the Revolutionary War, Negroes — both legal slaves and, particularly, runaway and "captured" Negroes — became an important element among the Lower Creeks and their Florida kinsmen, the Seminole. These Negroes were treated, particularly by the Seminole, more as vassals and allies than as slaves. From 1812 to 1842 they played significant — sometimes even dominant — roles in five important border wars:

1. the so-called "Patriot" invasion of East Florida, 1812-1814
2. the Red Stick War in Alabama, 1813-1814
3. the United States invasion of Florida in 1816, culminating in the destruction of the "Negro Fort"
4. Andrew Jackson's slavehunting invasion of Florida in 1818 (the so-called First Seminole War)
5. the Second Seminole War, 1835-1842, generally recognized as the most protracted and expensive Indian war in the history of the United States, but which the general in command at its most crucial stage described as "a negro, not an Indian war."

The half-dozen articles following are devoted to events on this frontier, and supersede the information on pp. 45-68 and 108-21.

NEGROES AND THE EAST FLORIDA ANNEXATION PLOT, 1811-1813* †

South of the United States borders, in the territory still precariously held by the Most Catholic King of Spain, the Negroes and Indians of East Florida were, in 1812 and '13, being entangled in a net of international intrigue.[1] "The persistent desire of the United States to possess the Floridas," which K. C. Babcock declares "between 1801 and 1819, amounted almost to a disease, corrupting the moral sense of each succeeding administration," had resulted, after a local insurrection, in a proclamation of Oct. 27, 1810, annexing to the United States the "territory from the Mississippi to Perdido."[2] Congressional confirmation of this presidential action was followed, Jan. 15, 1811, by a secret act of Congress authorizing the President to take possession of all or any part of Florida in case of agreement with the *local* authorities or in the event of any attempt by a foreign government to occupy any part of that territory. Gen. George Mathews, formerly governor of Georgia, was accordingly dispatched to East Florida to obtain the transfer of that region to the United States.

"Local authorities" was a term capable of being liberally construed, and Gen. Mathews therefore devoted himself to nurturing the ambitions of American settlers in the Spanish territory of East Florida, who might be encouraged to set themselves up as a "local government" favor-

---

*In the absence of Dr. Porter on account of illness, this paper was read by Dr. Merze Tate of Howard University at the annual meeting of the Association for the Study of Negro Life and History in Boston, Massachusetts, on October 28, 1944.

[1] Unless some other source is specified, statements concerning the Patriot and annexationist movement in Florida are based on Julius W. Pratt, *Expansionists of 1812*, N. Y., 1925, pp. 61-127, 189-237, esp. 104, 117, 193, 194, 201-202, 207-209.

[2] Babcock, Kendric Charles, *Rise of American Nationality* (American Nation, xiii), N. Y., 1906, pp. 22-25; Adams, Henry, *History of the United States During the First Administration of James Madison*, i, N. Y., 1891, pp. 306-312; Channing, Edward, *History of the United States*, iv, N. Y., 1917, p. 417.

†This article originally appeared in the January, 1945 issue of *JNH* (Vol. XXX, No. 1).

able to annexation by the United States. United States troops on the border were expected to assist in any such movement. On Mar. 14, 1812, the so-called "Patriots"—consisting mostly of citizens of Georgia—hoisted their flag at Rose's Bluff and, with the threatened assistance of American gun-boats, forced the surrender, Mar. 18, of Amelia Island, which was thereupon turned over to the United States, represented by Gen. Mathews. St. Augustine, the capital of East Florida, was the next objective, and was invested by the Patriot forces; Picolata, their headquarters, was in due course turned over to Lieut. Col. Smith, USA, on April 12.

The fall of St. Augustine, and with it the whole province of East Florida, seemed at this point inevitable. The entire garrison of the province consisted of only about 400 men, mostly untrained city militia. In this emergency, however, the Spanish authority still possessed two potential sources of military strength: the Indians and the Negroes. Gov. Estrada had gotten into communication with the Seminole Indians of the Alachua towns immediately upon the insurrection of the Patriots and the invasion by American troops, but in his despair felt that the Indians might even side with the Americans. There was actually little danger of this, for the Patriots were contemptuously obvious in their attitude toward the Indians, coolly apportioning their land as bounties to volunteers, regardless of Aesop's fable concerning the man who sold the lion's skin while it was still on the beast's back. The Spanish authorities indeed asserted that the Patriots had not even been content to allow their actions to speak for them, but had put their intentions into unmistakable words. Gen. Mathews, it was said, had told King Payne, the principal Seminole chief, that "he intended to drive him from his land," while John H. McIntosh, a leading Patriot, had notified another prominent chief, Boleck or Bowlegs, Payne's brother, that "he intended to make him as a waiting man." But, cut off from St. Augustine and munitions by the blockading force at Picolata, the Indian for a time took no overt action.

The Indians of Florida were threatened with the loss of their homes to the land-grabbing Patriots and the flood of colonists to whom Florida would be opened by annexation to the United States, but the Negroes were confronted with a more serious menace. Even the slaves dreaded the stricter slave-code of the southern United States, but the numerous free Negroes, many of them runaways from the United States, or their descendants, saw themselves and their families deprived of hard-won freedom should Florida come under United States rule. It had long been a policy of the Spanish government, dating back at least as far as 1688, to encourage Negroes from the British settlements to take refuge in Florida. The Spaniards, of course, had slaves of their own, but they were far-seeing enough to realize that the flight of Negroes from the British colonies weakened the traditional enemy and strengthened the Spanish colony, and that this unofficial migration would continue only so long as the fugitives were assured that they would not be merely exchanging one slavery for another. A colony of runaway Negroes was consequently established in 1739 near St. Augustine, and a fort constructed for their protection and garrisoning; the settlement was known as Gracia Real de Santa Teresa de Mosé, the fort, in brief, as Fort Mosé or Moussa.

Negro sergeants, with secret *rendezvous* in Carolina, were sent into that colony to instigate desertions from the plantations and, if possible, insurrection. The slaves were informed that the governor of Florida had formed a regiment of runaway slaves, "appointing officers from among them, and placing both officers and enlisted men upon the pay and rations allowed to the regular Spanish soldiers." This propaganda contributed to a constant leakage of runaways from the Carolina plantations to strengthen the manpower and military strength of the Spanish settlements, and it was a factor in at least one large-scale, though unsuccessful, uprising. The participants in this affair revealed their inspiration, after a preliminary slaughter of twenty whites, by marching toward Florida, banners displayed and drums beating, crying out "Freedom!", but were eventually cut to pieces and dispersed. Among the troops at St. Augustine reported at one point in the early 1740's were: "One regiment of Negroes, regularly officered by Negroes, One ditto of Mulattos, Ninety Indians, and 15 Negroes who ran away from South Carolina"—these last, presumably, recent arrivals. When, by the Treaty of Paris in 1763, Florida was ceded by Spain to Great Britain, the colony at Fort Mosé was transferred to Cuba.[3]

With Florida under British rule it was, of course, no longer such a tempting haven of refuge to discontented slaves on Georgia and South Carolina plantations; certainly it no longer offered any official welcome, overt or covert. But about the middle of the eighteenth century a body of discontented Lower Creeks from Georgia, under the leadership of a chief named Secoffee, perhaps the same as the one known to the English as The Cowkeeper, began to move into northern Florida and establish settlements,[4] where runaway slaves could find refuge. In welcoming and giving protection to such fugitives, the Seminole, no more than the Spanish authorities, were inspired by philanthropic motives, nor were they moved by a similarity of their own condition—"Seminole" means separatist—to that of the Negro "seceders" from plantation-society.

The Seminole had observed that prestige was attached by the Florida settlers to the presence of Negroes, and some

[3] "Dispatches of Spanish officials bearing on the free Negro settlement of Gracia Real de Santa Teresa de Mose, Florida," *Journal of Negro History*, ix (1924), 144-195; Southall, Eugene P., "Negroes in Florida Prior to the Civil War," JNH, xix (1934), 76-86; Jones, Charles C., Jr., *The History of Georgia*, 2 vols., Boston, 1883, i, 298-300, 344.

[4] Swanton, John R., *Early History of the Creek Indians and Their Neighbors*, Washington, D. C., 1922, pp. 398-400.

of the chiefs were sufficiently impressed to purchase a few black people in exchange for the half-wild cattle which, along with horses and hogs, they had acquired in their earlier home and had driven with them on their migration. Forty cattle are said to have been the standard price for a Negro slave. Once in possession of Negroes, however, the Seminole were rather at a loss to know what benefit they were supposed to derive from them, since they had no intention of devoting their lives to the management of slaves. They soon solved the problem, however, in much the same manner as the barbarians invading the Roman Empire had dealt with a similar situation when they found themselves in possession of Roman slaves whom it was beneath a warrior's dignity personally to supervise. The Seminole simply supplied their Negroes with axes and hoes, and told them to cut down trees, build houses for themselves, and raise corn. When the crop was harvested, the master was satisfied with a reasonable proportion of it—one observer said that it was never more than ten bushels annually—and the remainder served as sustenance and compensation for the so-called slaves, who soon also acquired cattle, horses, and swine, with which the master never presumed to meddle so long as he was supplied with a fat hog or side of beef at slaughtering time.

It was a mutually advantageous arrangement, in which the master furnished protection and the slave paid a moderate rent in kind, rather than anything even approaching the familiar system of plantation slavery.

The grapevine telegraph soon informed slaves in Georgia and South Carolina of the advantageous position enjoyed by the "slaves" of the Seminole, and fugitives from plantations of the Deep South began to find their way through woods and swamps to the Seminole villages. These fugitives put themselves under the protection of prominent Seminole chiefs and in turn supplied an annual tribute in corn and other such products. The implication was that each Negro's patron would assert ownership over his *protegé* should the latter be claimed by his former master or any other white man. White men in general, however, not well acquainted with this arrangement, understood this relationship to be the only one familiar to him as existing between Negro on the one hand and Indian or white on the other—that of slave and master; actually, it seems, the Indians did not so regard it. The Negroes lived apart from the Indians, in their own villages—an evidence of independence which they greatly prized, were under no supervision by their masters or patrons, dipped their spoons into the sofky pot along with their lord and his family whenever they happened to be at his home, habitually carried arms, frequently possessed large herds of livestock, and, save for their annual tribute, were under no greater subordination to the chiefs than were the Seminole tribesmen themselves. The relationship might be described as one of primitive democratic feudalism, involving no essential personal inequality between lord and vassal. Gen. Gaines, a generation later, spoke with approximate accuracy of "the Seminole Indians with their black vassals and allies."[5]

The Indians eventually found the Negroes useful in ways other than that of relieving their patrons of a part of their agricultural responsibilities, and allowing them greater opportunity for the more congenial activity of the chase. The Negroes all spoke some European language—English, or, in case of fugitives from Florida and Louisiana plantations, Spanish or French; they soon learned the Muskhogean tongue of the Seminole. They were thus almost the only interpreters available for intercourse between the Indians and the whites—and the only interpreters in whom the Indians could put any confidence, since their opinion of the Creek half-breeds who sometimes fulfilled that function was usually not high. The Negroes who had fled to the Seminole as adults were also acquainted with the white man's ways—

[5] *American State Papers, Military Affairs*, vii, 427.

at the least much better acquainted than the Indians—and were capable of giving advice as to his probable intentions in any particular situation. In a time of actual or threatened hostility a runaway Negro could wander into a white man's town or camp and gather information unobserved, when an Indian would immediately be apprehended. From interpreters and spies it was an easy transition for the Negroes to become unofficial advisers, and then to be recognized, in some cases, as tribal counsellors. A relationship which had originally been merely one of mutual material advantage eventually became cemented by reciprocal respect and affection. Intermarriage inevitably took place, though probaby not to such an extent as would have been the case had the Negroes lived less independently and separately.

The contrast of the Seminole Negro's existence with that of their kinsmen on the plantations was so striking as to call forth comment from all observers. His everyday life was universally described as positively idyllic. He lived in a Negro village, separate from that of the Indians with whom he was associated, in a house built after the Indian style of palmetto planks lashed to upright posts and thatched with palmetto leaves, but usually of better construction, in the midst of well-cultivated fields of corn, rice, sweet potatoes, melons, beans, peppers, and cotton. Horses, cattle, and swine belonging to him grazed in the woods and on the savannas. He dressed after the Indian fashion, on occasions of particuar festivity wearing moccasins, leggins, a long full smock, or hunting shirt, of gaudy hue, belted at the waist, and a turban composed of bright-colored bandannas, or a similarly brilliant shawl, ingeniously twisted about his head and topped with plumes; a series of brightly-polished metal crescents hung about his neck and descended upon his chest. A more sober and less elaborate variation of this costume sufficed for everyday wear. The younger boys, of course, ran about nude or, as they approached adolescence,

were invested with a long homespun shirt. The Seminole
Negro was not a slave of the hoe, but spent a part of his
time hunting and fishing. In time of war the men and
grown boys of the Negro villages assembled, equipped with
rifle or musket, axe, and knife, under their own captains,
who were in turn responsive to the orders of the Seminole
chief to whom they owed allegiance. Under this regime
they throve amazingly. An observer a decade later, when
the Seminole Indians and Negroes were in a considerably
less prosperous condition, nevertheless declared: "The Negroes ... both men and women [are] stout and even gigantic
in their proportions ... the finest looking people I have ever
seen. ... They are much more intelligent [sic] than their
masters, most of them speaking the Spanish, English, and
Indian languages. Though stouter than the aborigines ...
they resemble the Indians in figure, being longer limbed,
and more symmetrically formed than the Negroes of the
plantations. ..."[6]

There was consequently no group of people in Florida
with a greater stake in resistance to invasion and annexation by the United States than the Seminole Negroes; the
Spaniards would lose thereby their independence, the Indians their land, but the Negroes would lose at once their
independence, their homes, and the very freedom of themselves and their families. By no means all the free Negroes
in Florida in 1812 were among the Indians. There were
many who owed their freedom to the lenient Spanish emancipation laws; there were others who had escaped to the
British during the turmoil of the Revolution, or to the Spanish, again, after the retrocession of Florida; but the Seminole Negroes were the boldest, the best trained to arms, and

[6] The best of the numerous accounts describing the idyllic relations between the Seminole Indians and their Negroes, and the enviable situation of
the latter, are: (Simmons, William Hayne), *Notices of East Florida*, Charleston, 1822, pp. 41, 50, 76; ASP, MA, vi, 533-534; Williams, John Lee, *The
Territory of Florida*, N. Y., 1837, p. 240; Kennedy, William, *Texas, the Rise,
Progress, and Prospects*, London, 1841, i, 350.

the most strategically located for bringing into the struggle not only themselves but their Indian masters or patrons as well.

Such were the only allies to whom in this dark hour the Spanish authorities at St. Augustine could turn with any hope for relief. But at the darkest hour, a thin ray of light penetrated. The United States Government, under Federalist and Northern pressure, belatedly decided that its agent, Gen. Mathews, had proceeded too openly in his relations with the Patriots and early in April, 1812, he was dismissed. This by no means meant, however, an immediate withdrawal of United States troops and was, indeed, in large measure a subterfuge, for a few days later the Secretary of State requested Gov. D. B. Mitchell of Georgia to assume control of affairs in East Florida and to arrange with the governor of the province for the restoration of the original situation—but only on condition that the governor would agree to extend amnesty to the Patriots who, under the encouragement of the United States, had hoisted the banner of rebellion. This left the agent with an excuse to retain United States troops in Florida—and, since the United States agent was also the governor of Georgia, he could even draw on the militia of that state for additional military support. A part of the latter, indeed, was immediately mobilized, its commander expressing the hope that the Florida Indians would "take up the cudgels" in behalf of the Spanish government, since this would "afford a desireable pretext for the Georgians to penetrate their country, and Break up a Negroe Town: an important Evil growing under their patronage."

Still, the withdrawal of Mathews sufficiently discouraged the Patriots that the Spanish authorities enjoyed a brief breathing-spell. This they utilized in recruiting and obtaining reinforcements. The forces in St. Augustine were presently said to consist of 400 white and 500 black troops.[7]

---

[7] *Niles Register*, iii (Jan. 23, 1813), 330.

"They have armed," Mitchell indignantly announced, "every able-bodied negro within their power, and they have also received from the Havana a reinforcement of nearly two companies of black troops. . . ."—some of them, perhaps, descendants of the colonists evacuated from Fort Mosé half a century before. "It is my settled opinion," Mitchell continued, "that if they are suffered to remain in the province, our southern country will soon be in a state of insurrection." Mitchell consequently protested to Gov. Kindelan: "Your certain knowledge of the peculiar situation of the southern section of the Union in regard to that description of people [Negroes] one might have supposed, would have induced you to abstain from introducing them into the province, or from organizing such as were already in it."

The wrath which the Spanish governor must have experienced on being read this self-righteous lecture, by the agent of a government which had instigated a rebellion in his province, and was even then in occupation of a part of it, on the impropriety of his use of the only troops available for resisting this uprising and invasion, may be more easily imagined than described; it is best expressed in his own words in a letter of Dec. 12, 1812, in which he points out that the colored population served in the militia of all Spanish provinces on an equality with the whites, and sarcastically compares Mitchell's protest to that of a burglar who complains that a householder is provided with a blunderbuss whereas the burglar possesses only pistols![8]

Matters must soon come to a head. The Spanish garrison at St. Augustine, although reinforced from Havana, were closely besieged from the land-side and cut off from provisions. Some diversion was necessary or St. Augustine must fall from starvation if not by military force. This diversion must be supported by the Indians to be effective, but, to bring it about, Negro agency was required. Before

8 *N. R.*, iii (Jan. 16, 1813), 311-312.

leaving Florida, Gen. Mathews had summoned the Indian chiefs to a talk, and warned them against intervention; they had since sat peacefully if sullenly in their villages. But in July a Negro from St. Augustine, speaking the Indian language, arrived at Payne's town of Alachua to warn its inhabitants and those of the town of Alligator Hole, and of the Negro villages in the region, against the designs of the Americans. "The Americans are playing with you," he said. "They are going to take your country beyond the St. John's; your young men, then, will be forced to work for them, the young females will be put to spin and weave for them, while the old people will sweep the yards of the white men." This incitement, which coincided so well with what Payne's people had so long feared and observed, tipped the balance in favor of war and against the Americans, so far as the 200 Indian "gun men" of Alachua and Alligator Hole, and the 40 "negro gun men" of the neighborhood were concerned.[9]

On July 25, accordingly, the Seminole Indians and Negroes fell upon the plantations along the St. John's belonging to Americans who were cooperating with the Patriots, killed eight or nine settlers, and "carried off" a large number of probably not altogether unwilling slaves. Patriots began to desert their camp to look to the safety of their families and property. Negroes of the St. Augustine region seem to have joined with the Seminole Indians and Negroes on these raids. Lt. Col. Smith reported, Aug. 21, 1812: "The blacks assisted by the Indians have become very daring & from the want of a proper knowledge of the country the parties which I have sent out have always been unsuccessful."[10] Despite the arrival on Aug. 15 of Maj. Daniel

9 *State Papers and Publick Documents of the United States*, ser. 1, vol. ix, pp. 181-187, "Talk of Tuskegee Tustumugee (sic), Creek Agency, Sept. 18, 1812, to Col. Benj. Hawkins."

10 Davis, T. Frederick, ed., "United States Troops in Spanish East Florida, 1812-13 (letters of Lieut. Col. T. A. Smith)," *Florida Historical Quarterly*, ix (July, Oct., 1930, Jan., Apr., 1931), 3-23, 96-116, 135-155, 259-278, x (July, 1931), 24-34: ix, 111.

Newnan of the Georgia militia with 250 volunteers, the position of the United States troops and Patriots before St. Augustine was rapidly becoming untenable, not only because of the strengthening of the Spanish garrison and the Negro-Indian raids upon the besiegers' rear, but also because the invasion, which, from the beginning, had been supported by Georgia volunteers, was now being resisted by other volunteers from Georgia—Negro slaves who, taking advantage of the confusion, were deserting the plantations and making their way to the allied Spanish, Indian, and Negro forces. Gov. Mitchell, Sept. 9, declared that the Spanish "governor has proclaimed freedom to every negro who will join his standard, and has sent a party of them to unite with, and who are actually at this time united with the Indians in their murderous excursions. Indeed the principal strength of the garrison of St. Augustine consists of negroes . . . the most of our male negroes on the seaboard are restless and make many attempts to get off to Augustine, and many have succeeded."[11]

The siege of St. Augustine ended suddenly and disastrously. On Sept. 12, a train of wagons, escorted by 20 United States Marines and Georgia volunteers, under the command of Capt. Williams, USMC, and Capt. Fort of the militia, was proceeding from Davis Creek to the besieging camp. At Twelve Mile Swamp—so-called from its distance from the St. John's—lay ambushed a company of about 50 Negroes, or Negroes and a few Indians, warned by scouts of the wagon-train's approach, and under the command of "a free Black named Prince"—a free man who intended to remain so. His orders to his troop were to immobilize the wagons and pick off the officers. Out of the darkness crackled a volley, mortally wounding the Marine captain in eight places, wounding the militia officer, killing the sergeant, wounding six privates, laying several of the horses dead in their harness. Out of the shadows Negroes and

[11] *S. P. & P. D.*, ix, 168-172.

Indians leaped in for the kill, axe and knife in hand, but the dozen Marines and militiamen still on their feet, responding to the commands of their wounded officers, returned the fire and followed it up with a charge so unexpectedly fierce that the enemy melted away into the darkness, enabling the survivors to make their escape, carrying their wounded and abandoning the horseless wagons and their contents.

But though the little company had escaped absolute annihilation, this action of only twenty-five minutes had nevertheless been decisive. Lt. Col. Smith frantically summoned the Georgia militia to his aid with men and horses, and with their assistance retreated from before St. Augustine to the supply depot on Davis Creek, where he could be protected by United States gunboats. "Thus ingloriously ended the siege of St. Augustine," is Julius W. Pratt's comment—raised, be it noted, by a Negro-instigated diversion in the rear by Seminole Indians and Negroes, followed up by a cutting of the supply lines by a force of Negroes and Indians under Negro leadership.[12]

Although the siege of St. Augustine was at least temporarily lifted, it might be resumed were the enemy in the rear crushed. Maj. Daniel Newnan, adjutant-general of Georgia and commander of the Georgia volunteers in Florida, had on Aug. 21, a few days after his arrival, been ordered to proceed against the hostile Indians and destroy their towns and supplies. Difficulty in obtaining horses and provisions, and the ravages of malaria, had delayed his departure until after the catastrophe of Twelve Mile Swamp, at which time his volunteers had less than a week to serve. He was resolved, however, to carry out his orders if at all possible, so asked for volunteers to serve as long as the expedition required. Only 84—about a third—of his own force vounteered, but enough Patriots and militiamen from other

[12] *S. P. & P. D.*, ix, 175-177; Williams, John Lee, *The Territory of Florida*, N. Y., 1837, p. 197; McClellan, Maj. Edwin N., *Indian Fights* (Hist. U.S.M.C., 1st ed., 1st rev., i, ch. 19: mimeographed).

detachments were added to bring the total to 116. With this force, twelve horses, and four days' provisions, on Sept. 24 he marched jauntily but determinedly off to destroy the Alachua towns.

The morning of the fourth day when, it was thought, they were only six or seven miles from the Alachua settlements, they suddenly encountered a force of 75 to 100 Indians on the march, some mounted, most on foot, either moving on the St. John's for a final blow at the American forces or warned by scouts of the approach of an invading army. They were led by the aged head-chief Payne, mounted on a white horse, and by his brother, the war-leader, Bowlegs. At sight of the enemy the Seminole promptly threw down their packs, "trimmed their guns," formed a line of battle, and opened fire. The octogenarian King Payne rode to and fro, encouraging his men, but as the Seminole closed in the border rifles crackled and the white horse ran riderless.

The Seminole, infuriated by the death of their chief, fought desperately and, although somewhat outnumbered by the Georgians and though the muskets with which most were armed were outranged by the frontier rifles, they kept up the action for two and a half hours, constantly endeavoring to outflank the enemy. The Georgians, however, eventually drove them back, taking with them the body of their chief, into a swamp where the whites dared not follow. After scalping the bodies left on the field, Newnan's forces took advantage of the enemy's withdrawal to erect log-barricades and dig fox-holes. The Georgians were left undisturbed—save for the sight of Indians in the distance, on the edge of the swamp, painting themselves and consulting —until half an hour before sunset.

The next attack was heralded by a furious yelling, in which for the first time the deep-chested shouts of Negroes mingled with the shrill outcries of the Indians. Word of King Payne's death had reached the Negro villages, and their.warriors, resolved to avenge their protector, were arriving on the battlefield. Crouching low, led by their chiefs, the Indians and Negroes, now perhaps 200 in number, closed in rapidly and, at about 200 yards, opened fire on the entrenched borderers who replied with their usual accuracy. The attack continued until eight o'clock, the Negroes in particular displaying conspicuous bravery, which led Maj. Newnan to comment, "Negroes . . . are their best soldiers," but finally the Seminole again retired.

Then began the severest test of the expedition. For two days no attack ensued, but the Georgians knew themselves constantly under observation. A messenger had been sent back for reinforcements, but it was four days to the St. John's and another four to return, and their provisions had been exhausted on their march. They had been depending on the beef and corn of the Alachua towns, still six or seven miles distant, but now horse-meat was their only resource. It must have been almost a relief when after two days the attack re-commenced, but in a form harder to endure than the previous frontal actions. The enemy had learned respect for the deadly accuracy of the Georgia rifles and henceforth were determined to play by their own rules. Riflemen, carefully concealed, began a desultory and nerve-wracking sniping which continued for five or six days, while more and more of the invaders succumbed to wounds, disease, and starvation until over half were *hors de combat.*

After a week of siege, Newnan, in desperation, determined on a night-retreat and, carrying the sick and wounded on stretchers, set out for the St. John's. The enemy, who could hardly have been ignorant of this move, let them go; the Indian and Negroes had suffered perhaps as many as 50 casualties, and were unwilling to incur further loss in the extermination of an enemy now desirous only of escape. Perhaps they were far-seeing enough to consider the moral effect of this battered half-starved band upon other would-be invaders. Newnan's party struggled on through the wilderness for several days. They lived on "gophers, alligators, and palmetto stocks," missed one relief party, were briefly attacked by about 50 Indians, finally encountered another relief expedition, were escorted to the St. John's, and conveyed by gunboat to Col. Smith's camp. "The punitive expedition," says Pratt, "had degenerated into a desperate retreat. Newnan ... had not come within sight of an Indian town or supply depot."[13]

The Georgians and Patriots for the time being could only rend the air with dire prophecies of slave insurrection; the danger was really too great for them to do more than remain passive and hope for relief. Their only forces were inadequate, in the face of the growing enemy strength, for any aggressive action. A letter of Jan. 3, 1813, declared: "A number of slaves have lately deserted their masters & gone to Augustine from the St. John's."[14] The Patriot leader, McIntosh, on Jan. 24, complained to James Monroe: "Our slaves are excited to rebel, and we have an army of negroes raked up in this country, and brought from Cuba to contend with. ... St. Augustine, the whole province will be the refuge of fugitive slaves; and from thence emissaries ... will be detached to bring about a revolt of the black popuation in the United States." These appeals were not without effect upon a government in which the slavery interests were so powerfully represented, and the general government prepared to reinforce its troops in Florida for the suppression of the Indians and Negroes and the ultimate seizure of the province.

The citizens of East Tennessee, however, were so situated as to be more immediately concerned and capable of taking action. Observing their brothers in the western part of the state preparing for a march against Mobile and Pensacola under Gen. Jackson, they had been organizing a regiment of volunteer cavalry. East Tennessee was not a

---

[13] *N. R.*, iii (Nov. 14, 1812), 171; *ibid.*, iii (Dec. 12, 1812), 235-237; Williams, *Territory of Fla.*, 198.

[14] *Davis*, loc. cit., ix, 269.

plantation area, and its citizens were probably chiefly concerned with the Indian menace, but other Tennesseans were conscious of the danger to slavery in the Florida situation and one of them, Willie Blount, wrote from Nashville, Dec. 12, 1812, to William Eustis, complaining of "disaffection among the blacks" and incitement "to commit murder and depredations."[15]

Upon learning of Newnan's defeat the Tennesseans acted immediately. Under John Williams of Knoxville over 200 mounted volunteers set out for the south early in December, 1812, and arrived at Colerain on the St. Mary's River, Jan. 7, 1813, when they put themselves under the command of Brig. Gen. Flournoy. The Indians, alarmed at these preparations, had sued through the Creek agent, Benjamin Hawkins, for peace; Maj. Gen. Pinckney, nevertheless, decided to order the expedition to proceed and to unite with it 200 regulars under Col. Smith. The Georgians were determined to proceed independently to oust the Indians from the coveted Alachua lands if the Federal Government refused to take action and the East Tennesseans would probably have put themselves under the command of Georgia state authorities had United States officers refused to coperate. It seemed wise, therefore, to take advantage of the presence of so large and determined a body of volunteers and to give them all the assistance available; otherwise they might proceed on their own responsibility, and should they be defeated, this, added to the Newnan debacle, would greatly reduce the prestige of the United States.

The East Tennesseans, accordingly, joined by a few Georgians, started out early in February for the "Aulotcheewaus." They intended to drive the Indians from their fertile lands and, in many cases no doubt, themselves ultimately assume occupancy. For those who had no such intentions the lure of adventure and plunder sufficed. They were informed of the rich stores of deerskins and beeswax

[15] *S. P. & P. D.*, ix, 155-160.

accumulated in the villages, the horses grazing on the savannas which could be used for the transport of the loot
and which, together with the large herds of cattle, could be
driven north to a market; probably most important of all
was the possibility of capturing some of the women and
children of the Negro villages who, roped together, could be
driven off with the other livestock and restored at a good
price to the slavery from which they or their parents had
escaped.   Col. Smith was to unite with this company of adventurers near the first Seminole town.

The plan proceeded according to schedule.   The two
forces united on Feb. 7 and moved upon the Alachua towns.
The Indians and Negroes, who had mustered at the most
200 warriors against the early Georgian invasion, knew
themselves incapable of resisting a force nearly four times
as large as Newnan's and over twice their own.   They had
hurried their women and children deep into the swamps,
and the warriors, lurking on the borders of their fastnesses,
watched for an opportunity to harry the foe.   The expeditionary force reached Payne's town on the 9th and found
it deserted.   The next objective was Bowlegs' town, ten or
twelve miles southwest, and a body of volunteers under
Williams set out for it on the 10th.   This division of the
enemy gave the Indians and Negroes an opportunity, and
on the first day of the march 200 warriors attacked the Tennessee column but were repelled with heavy casualties.   The
resistance, however, held up the invaders long enough so
that they did not reach Bowlegs' town until the 12th.   The
expeditionary force, the enemy driven from the field, turned
with enthusiasm to the work of plunder and destruction,
burning 386 houses, together with several thousand bushels
of corn, in the two large towns and in the smaller villages,
including a Negro town, appropriating 2,000 deerskins, and
rounding up 400 horses and as many cattle. Driven to desperation by the sight of smoke from their homes and store-
houses, the Indians and Negroes again and again took ad-

vantage of the invaders' preoccupation with plunder, to emerge from their fastnesses and strike at the ravagers. They were always beaten off, but the resistance was sufficient to convince the invaders that it would be unwise to proceed against a third more distant Indian town. They decided to be satisfied with the destruction of the two principal towns, and with the fact that "the balance of the Seminole Nation is completely in waste." Perhaps a desire to convey their plunder to safety was also a factor. Fifty or sixty Indians, it was declared, had been killed at the cost of only one white man dead and seven wounded. The Alachua region was open to white settlers. Almost the entire Seminole food supply was destroyed and by spring the survivors were "literally starving." It had indeed been "a famous victory."[16]

One victory, however, does not necessarily win a campaign. The Indian and Negro resistance to American occupation had held it up until Northern and Federalist opposition in Congress had forced a suspension of the attempt. By May 15, 1813, United States troops had been withdrawn from Florida, leaving the Patriots, scornful of an offer of amnesty, to cope with the Spanish government for themselves. Some of them removed to the United States and those who remained justified the reference to them by the leading authority on the movement, as "a band of unscrupulous adventurers," by confiscating the property of their recreant erstwhile comrades and selling such free Negroes as were unlucky enough to fall into their hands.[17] They had the impudence to suggest to the Spanish governor an armistice on condition of the removal of Negro troops, a grant of the Alachua lands, and complete amnesty—a proposal which was ignored. The Patriots then moved into the

[16] *N. E.*, iv (Mar. 13, 1813), 29; (Mar. 20, 1813), 48; (Mar. 27, 1813), 67; (Apr. 17, 1813), 116; Davis, *loc. cit.*, ix, 271-274; McClellan, 15-16.

[17] For plundering activities of the Patriots, see "United States vs. Ferreira," 36th cong., 1st sess., sen. misc. doc. no. 55.

Alachua lands, cleared of Indians a year earlier, built a fort, and requested annexation to the United States, which on Apr. 19, 1814, was finally and conclusively refused.[18] Thus ended, for that time, the attempt to annex East Florida to the United States.

That it ended in failure rather than in success was in large part due to Negro resistance. That the majority of the Spanish garrison in St. Augustine were black troops is a matter of no great significance in this connection; they were merely acting under orders, as were their white comrades. It is important, however, to note that the initial action in raising the siege of St. Augustine was a diversion in the rear by Seminole Indians and Negroes acting at Negro instigation, that local Negroes, joined by runaway slaves from Georgia and Florida plantations, harried the besieging force in co-operation with the Indians, and that the besiegers' supply-lines were cut and the siege finally raised by a force consisting almost entirely of Negroes under Negro leadership. Maj. Newnan's final desperate attempt to strike at the center of Indian and Negro resistance was thwarted by a force in which, as the major himself testified, the gun-men of the Negro towns were the best soldiers.

To be sure, had not Congressional action resulted in the recall of United States troops from East Florida, the Negro-Indian resistance would have proved ultimately ineffective, but, on the other hand, a Congress confronted by a *fait accompli,* which was prevented only by the Negro-Indian opposition, would probably not have withdrawn its army of occupation.

It might, indeed, be said with truth that, from the long-range viewpoint, the Negro and Indian resistance to the East Florida annexation plot was of little effect. Five years

18 The Patriots accepted peace terms from the Florida government in 1816. Wyllys, Rufus Kay, ''The East Florida Revolution of 1812-1814,'' *The Hispanic American Historical Review,* ix (Nov., 1929), pp. 415-445, esp. 445, quoting from Brevard, Caroline. *A History of Florida,* 2 vols., Deland, Fla., 1924, i, 31.

after the Tennesseans' vengeful destruction of the Alachua towns, Andrew Jackson marched at the head of another Tennessee force through East Florida, defeated the hopelessly outnumbered Negroes on the Suwanee, broke up the Indian and Negro settlements, and sent their inhabitants flying southward, thus making inevitable that annexation of East Florida which was agreed upon the following year, in 1819, and which went into effect two years later. Negro-Indian resistance thus delayed annexation less than a decade.

What is, then, the ultimate significance of Negro resistance to the East Florida annexation plot? Simply that it demonstrates a fact which would hardly seem to require demonstration had it not been so generally disregarded, perhaps even concealed, by many writers in the field of American history: namely, that Negroes, as well as Indians or whites, have, in an international situation, displayed a capacity for recognizing their own interests and taking action to safeguard them. In the face of the East Florida annexation plot the Negroes potentially affected—free Negroes, Seminole Negroes, Florida and Georgia plantation-slaves—readily discerned that the maintenance of Spanish rule in East Florida was essential to their well-being; the action they took in its defense was courageous, skilful, and effective.

Corrections and Additions

p. 186, l. 15-16: The discontented Lower Creeks who entered Florida about the middle of the eighteenth century were led by The Cowkeeper (Ahaya), not by Secoffee (various spellings), who was an entirely different person. See Porter, "The 'Founder' of the 'Seminole Nation' — Secoffee or Cowkeeper?", FHQ, XXVII (April, 1949), pp. 362-84. These Lower Creeks, or Seminole, were allies of the British, and it is unlikely that they gave protection to runaway slaves from South Carolina and Georgia until the outbreak of the Revolutionary War turned the Georgians and South Carolinians into enemies of the British and, consequently, of the Seminole. The Seminole, however, were traditionally enemies of the Spaniards and may have protected runaway slaves from the Spanish in Florida.

p. 196, l. 11-18: King Payne, although wounded on September 27, 1812, was not killed. However, he was probably weakened by his wound and died sometime the following year. Rembert W. Patrick, *Florida Fiasco: Rampant Rebels on the Georgia-Florida Frontier, 1810-1815* (Athens, Georgia, 1954), pp. 202, 207, 209-10.

p. 201, last line - p. 202, l. 5: See the following article for additional information on the last stage of the "annexation plot."

This article originally appeared in the July, 1951 issue of *JNH* (Vol. XXXVI, No. 3).

NEGROES AND THE SEMINOLE WAR, 1817-1818

INTRODUCTION

Florida and the territory adjacent thereto were the region of North America in which the Negro population, because of its numbers, the complicated balance and tension among nations and tribes, the existence of an international border and the character of the terrain, was best able for approximately a century and a half to act aggressively and to some extent even effectively and independently in behalf of its own interests. An important episode in this long struggle was the so-called Seminole War, 1817-1818, but for an understanding of its significance a brief survey of its remote background and a more detailed examination of the events more immediately leading up to it are required.

Negroes on the Southern Frontier, *1670-1812*

THE SPANISH PERIOD, 1670-1763

During the period of warfare, open or covert, between Spain and Great Britain, from the settlement of South Carolina in 1670 to the cession of Florida to Great Britain in 1763, the South Carolina slaves, outnumbering their masters two or three to one, were a source not only of labor to the colony but also of difficulty and danger. A South Carolina lieutenant governor in 1738 went so far as to describe them as "more dreadful to our Safety, than any Spanish Invaders." They persistently ran off to St. Augustine, where the Spaniards received them hospitably, employed them in association with Indian allies in raids on the South Carolina and Georgia frontiers, enlisted them in Negro regiments, and garrisoned with them a strategically located Negro fort. Other runaways operated with considerable effectiveness among the Indian tribes of the frontier as Spanish—and French—agents. The plots and conspiracies among slaves who did *not* run away to Florida and who in 1739 broke out in open and bloody insurrection, as well as the depredations of the Maroon Negroes who hid out armed in the woods and swamps, also notably weakened the colony for warfare both against the Spaniards and against hostile Indians and helped to delay indefinitely the almost inevitable British triumph in southeastern North America.[1]

The British Period, 1763-1783

The British annexation of Florida for the time being virtually eliminated the Negroes on the southern frontier from consideration as a factor of importance except to the labor supply. The Negro garrison of Fort Moussa had been evacuated to Cuba, along with most of the other Spanish and Negro population. Florida was no more a land of freedom to fugitives from South Carolina and Georgia. Spain no longer tacitly or openly encouraged slave revolts and conspiracy consequently declined to mere rumor, though the more restless slaves continued to transform themselves into Maroons by escaping into the woods and swamps. The Florida Indians offered no refuge to the fugitive, for the

[1] For a documentation of the above thesis, see: Kenneth Wiggins Porter, "Negroes on the Southern Frontier, 1670-1763," *Journal of Negro History* (hereafter referred to as *JNH*), XXXIII (January, 1948), 53-78; especially 53-54, 58-73, 75-78.

principal tribe, King Cowkeeper's Alachua—the "original" Seminole—had entered Florida as the enemies of the Spanish and the staunch allies of the British, and British allies they remained.[2]

It was probably during "the English time," the twenty years from the annexation of Florida by the British to its return to the Spanish, and particularly during the confusion of the Revolutionary War, however, that Negroes became an important element among the Creek Indians and their Florida kinsmen, the Seminole. Seminole and Creek chiefs, observing the prestige which the whites attached to the ownership of Negroes, were sufficiently impressed to purchase a few blacks, usually in exchange for cattle; forty head is said to have been the standard price.[3] British agents gave Negroes to Creek chiefs in return for their services during the Revolution, such Negroes being known as "King's gifts." Other Negroes were captured during the Revolution[4] or subsequently in isolated raids on planta-

[2] In my article, "Negroes and the East Florida Annexation Plot, 1811-1813," *JNH*, XXX (January, 1945), 12, I mistakenly accept the usual identification of Cowkeeper with the Creek chief and Spanish supporter, Seacoffee or Sacafaca, and in consequence I incorrectly describe the Seminole, during the period of British rule and prior to the Revolution, as giving refuge to runaway slaves from South Carolina and Georgia. In my article, "The Founder of the Seminole Nation," *Florida Historical Quarterly (FHQ)*, XXVII (April, 1949, 362-384—"Founder" and "Nation" should really be enclosed in a special set of quotes—I endeavor to clear up the confusion between the French and Spanish partisan, Seacoffee, and Cowkeeper, the consistent supporter of the British. I assign to the latter the title of first chief of the "original" Seminole.

The Seminole under Cowkeeper as late as 1774 seem not to have had Negroes among them, either as slaves or allies. Bartram (William Bartram, *Travels* (Philadelphia, 1791), pp. 168, 182, 183) mentions that Cowkeeper possessed slaves but they are never identified as Negroes and from the context seem almost certainly to have been Yemassee Indians—Spanish allies—captured in war.

[3] 25th Cong., 3rd sess., H. of R., War Dep't., Doc. 225, pp. 119-120.

[4] John R. Swanton, *Early History of the Creek Indians and Their Neighbors* (Washington, 1922), pp. 262-263, quoting from Benjamin Hawkins, *A Sketch of the Creek Country in 1798 and 99*, Georgia Historical Society Collections (Savannah, 1848), III, 66.

tions. Others probably joined the British and their Indian allies on the promise of freedom.

The extent to which the British utilized runaway Negroes in their Southern campaigns has been given insufficient attention. It is known, however, that thousands of Negroes joined the British during the siege of Savannah and took ship with them on the evacuation of the city. Others preferred to endeavor to maintain themselves in a country with which they were familiar. As late as 1786 "a corps of runaway negroes, the leaders of which, having been trained to arms by the British during the siege of Savannah, still called themselves the King of England's soldiers, . . . ranged both sides of the Savannah River," terrorizing the countryside. The Georgia militia, assisted by South Carolina troops, had to be called out to break up their fortified camp in a swamp on Bear Creek.[5]

THE SEMINOLE INDIANS AND THE NEGROES

Slaves who fled from Georgia plantations to Florida during the Revolution probably often preferred at the departure of the British to take refuge among their Seminole allies. The Creeks, and more particularly the Seminole, rarely attempted to control or direct the Negroes who lived among them, whether acquired by gift, purchase, capture or flight. The Seminole seem to have contented themselves with supplying them with axes and hoes, leaving them to fell trees, build houses and raise corn. The master or patron contented himself with a reasonable proportion of the crop—one observer said never over ten bushels annually. The rest served as sustenance and compensation for the so-called slaves, who also soon acquired cattle, horses and swine with which the master never presumed to meddle so

[5] Rev. William Bacon Stevens, *A History of Georgia* (Philadelphia, 1859), II, 376-378.

long as he was supplied with a fat hog or a quarter of beef at slaughtering-time.

The grapevine-telegraph informed slaves in the border regions of the United States of the advantageous position enjoyed by the "slaves" of the Seminole and, in time of peace as in time of war, runaways began to steal through woods and swamps to the Seminole villages. These fugitives put themselves under the protection of the chiefs, tendering them in return tribute and service. The service included acting as interpreters between the whites and the Indians, and their knowledge of the white man's ways as well as of his language often resulted in the interpreter developing into the advisor and counsellor. By 1812 and probably earlier, the existence among the Seminole of Negro towns occupied by "several hundred fugitive [sic] slaves from the Carolinas & Georgia" was a source of general irritation to the slave-owners of the Deep South.[6]

Under this regime of freedom and responsibility the Seminole Negroes throve amazingly, developing a way of life usually described as positively idyllic. We have little direct or detailed knowledge of the Seminole Negroes prior to the annexation of Florida in 1821 and virtually none at all before the abortive annexation attempt of 1812. But even in 1822, after the American invasions of 1813 and 1818 had destroyed many Seminole villages, dislocated the population and considerably impaired their prosperity, an American surveyor described the Seminole Negroes as "stout and even gigantic in their proportions . . . the finest looking people I have ever seen," living in separate villages of well-constructed houses and possessing carefully cultivated fields and large herds of livestock. They wore the Indian garb and were hunters and fishermen as well as tillers of the soil and stock raisers; the men all carried

[6] T. Frederick Davis, ed., "United States Troops in Spanish East Florida, 1812-1813 (Letters of Lieut. Col. T. A. Smith)," *FHQ*, IX (July, 1930), 106-107.

arms, went into battle under their own captains, and were on terms of familiar intimacy with their so-called masters.[7]

Background of the Seminole War, 1812-1817

The most important phase of the Seminole War, 1817-1818, was Andrew Jackson's invasion of Florida and its most important result was the annexation of Florida by the United States—an inevitable consequence of the Spanish government's inability to resist the armed invasions by American forces of which Jackson's was merely the last and most successful. The original impulse behind these invasions was general American expansionism, inspired by the same frontier land-hunger as was also directed in the same general period against Canada; but another objective, which became increasingly important and eventually developed into a primary purpose, was to safeguard the slave system in adjacent states by breaking up the runaway Negro settlements in Florida. An understanding of these invasions will, however, also involve consideration of Tecumseh's plan for an Indian confederacy, the resultant Creek Red Stick War and the War of 1812.

NEGROES AND THE EAST FLORIDA ANNEXATION PLOT, 1812-1814

Early in 1812 the so-called Patriots—mostly Georgians who had been secretly instigated to seize control in Florida and bring about its annexation to the United States—were closely investing St. Augustine with the support of American troops and gun-boats. The fall of the Florida capital seemed almost inevitable and with it the loss of the entire province, but at this critical moment the Negro population of Florida—the people most seriously menaced by annexation—intervened decisively. To the Spanish, annexation would mean American domination; to the Indians, the even-

---

[7] For a more detailed description of the relations between Seminole Negroes and Seminole Indians in the early 19th century, with references, see: Kenneth Wiggins Porter, ''Negroes and the East Florida Annexation Plot, 1811-1813,'' *JNH*, XXX (January, 1945), 12-16, especially note 6, p. 16.

tual loss of their lands; but to the numerous free Negroes and the runaways living among the Indians it meant the loss of hard-won freedom, while even the slaves dreaded the stricter slave-code of the southern United States. The Seminole Negroes were of all Florida Negroes the boldest, the best trained to arms and the most strategically situated for bringing into the struggle not only themselves but the Indians as well.

A Negro from St. Augustine, who spoke the Indian language and was probably therefore a Seminole Negro, convinced the Indians that the Americans intended to seize their lands and make them their servants. The Indians and Negroes late in July, 1812, fell upon the plantations of American settlers who were cooperating with the Patriots, thus causing the owners to leave the camp of the besiegers and look to the safety of their homes. Negroes of the St. Augustine region joined in these raids and harried foraging parties sent out by the invaders. Negro slaves in both Florida and Georgia took advantage of the confusion to desert the plantations and join the Indians and Spaniards.[8] The siege of St. Augustine ended suddenly and disastrously when a company of St. Augustine Negroes ambushed a wagon train escorted by Patriots and Marines, thereby cutting the besiegers' supply-lines and forcing them to withdraw.

A part of the Georgia militia had been mobilized in support of the invasion, in the expressed hope that the Indians would "take up the cudgels" in behalf of the Spanish government, since this would "afford a desireable pretext for the Georgians to penetrate their country, and Break up a Negro Town: an important Evil growing under their patronage." The Indians and Negroes had now definitely "taken up the cudgels" much more effectively than the Georgians desired. Major Daniel Newnan, commander of

[8] "East Florida Documents," *Georgia Historical Quarterly*, XIII (June, 1929), 154-158.

the Georgia volunteers, marched off late in September to strike at the Alachua towns of the Seminole and by crushing the enemy in the rear make possible the resumption of the siege. A party of Indians under head-chief Payne and his brother Bowlegs, the war-chief, met the invaders six or seven miles from their towns. Payne fell early in the action but Newnan's force was unable to proceed further. They dug in and were besieged for a week, the warriors from the Negro towns displaying such conspicuous bravery in the attacks on Newnan's position that the Georgia major declared them to be the Seminole's "best soldiers." The invaders finally beat a retreat under cover of darkness, reaching the St. John's River in a starving condition.

Early in 1813, however, Tennessee militia and United States troops invaded the Alachua territory, this time in overwhelming numbers. A principal incentive of the invasion is indicated by Brigadier General Flournoy's announcement: "Every negro taken in arms will be put to death without mercy."[9] The invaders destroyed two principal towns and several smaller villages, including a Negro town, laid the region waste, and forced the Seminole Indians and Negroes to retreat westwardly to the Suwanee. This "glorious victory," however, came too late for the annexation cause. Indian and Negro resistance had held up annexation until Northern and Federalist opposition in Congress could force suspension of the attempt. The Patriots found themselves abandoned and their request for annexation was, on April 19, 1814, conclusively refused. Colonel Benjamin Hawkins, United States Agent to the Creek Indians, even announced on June 16 that the United States had no objection to the Seminole "going to war against the people [i.e., the Patriots] who are trespassing on their rights at Aulotchewau [Alachua]."[10] This blow

[9] Rowland H. Rerick, *Memoirs of Florida*, Francis P. Fleming, ed. (Atlanta, 1902), I, 121.

[10] *American State Papers, Indian Affairs* (hereafter referred to as *ASP, IA*), I, 844, 845.

coincided with the death of the principal Patriot leader, General Buckner Harris, who is said to have been "waylaid and killed" by "a party of negroes."[11]

Thus ended for the time the attempt to annex East Florida to the United States. That it ended in failure was obviously due primarily to Negro and Negro-instigated resistance.[12] Negroes were also to play a significant, though a considerably less effective role, in subsequent events culminating in the eventual annexation of Florida in 1821.

THE RED STICK WAR, 1813-1814

The Shawnee chief Tecumseh, with his vision of an Indian Confederacy uniting all tribes from the Great Lakes to the Gulf, in October, 1811, visited the annual council of the Creeks, his mother's people, at Tuckabatchee on the Tallapoosa. Choctaw and Cherokee delegates were also present. The old chiefs received him courteously and noncommittally; they wanted peace. But when he returned north he left behind him medicine-men prophesying of the day when the white men should be driven into the sea and warriors dancing "the dance of the Indians of the Northern Lakes." During his absence the approach of Harrison's troops to his village of Tippecanoe had acted as a handful of gunpowder sprinkled on glowing coals; the early morning of November 7, 1811, had flared with gun-fire which a generation later was briefly to provide a president of the United States, though its immediate effect was temporarily and partially to wither Tecumseh's hopes. His sun finally set in defeat and death at the Battle of the Thames two years later, but the fire he had lit still flickered in the south;

[11] Rerick, *op. cit.*, I, 122; Letter, Mrs. Howard McCall, Atlanta, Ga., January 28, 1945, to the author. (Mrs. McCall is the compiler of *Roster of Revolutionary Soldiers in Georgia*, Georgia Society, Daughters of the American Revolution, 1941).

[12] Porter, "Negroes and the East Florida Annexation Plot," *JNH*, XXX, 9-29. Additional references are to sources not used in the article.

fanned by varying winds and uniting with other flames it burst eventually into a conflagration.[13]

The Upper Creeks, dwelling in the heart of Alabama and less exposed to white and half-breed influence than the Lower Creeks on the Chattahoochee, were correspondingly susceptible to the propaganda of Tecumseh and his prophets. The outbreak of war between Great Britain and the United States and the American invasions of the Seminole country excited those whom Tecumseh's persuasive oratory had already moved. Civil war broke out between the chiefs who stood for peace and the Red Sticks, as the hostiles were called. Two thousand warriors were soon in arms against the whites. Their principal leader, the half-breed Peter McQueen, obtained arms in Pensacola and in July, 1813, defeated the Americans and their half-breed allies at Burnt Corn. At noon on August 30 the Red Sticks rushed Fort Mimms where several hundred whites and half-breeds had taken refuge and massacred nearly the entire garrison. Negroes, whose position among the Upper Creeks was somewhat similar to that of those among the Seminole, were conspicuous in the war-party. "'Siras, a negro man, cut down the pickets" in the rear of the fort, enabling the hostiles to take the defenders from behind, and the buildings within the palisade were fired with blazing arrows shot by "the Shawnee Siekaloo . . . and some of the McGillivray Negroes." The Red Sticks even in the frenzy of victory spared the Negroes in the fort, explaining: "The Master of Breath has ordered us not to kill any but white people and half-breeds." One such Negro, later captured by Creeks friendly to the whites, lost no time in escaping again to the Red Sticks.

For a time the hostiles had everything their own way but by October 12 Andrew Jackson with 3,500 Tennessee militia entered Alabama while on November 24 nearly a thousand

[13] John Bach McMaster, *A History of the People of the United States* (New York, 1892), III, 529-536.

Georgia militia crossed the Chattahoochee. The Red Sticks, inflamed by religious fanaticism and patriotism, fought desperately. Their Negroes, who feared that defeat would mean a transfer to plantation slavery, fought side by side with their masters, sometimes in company with recent runaway slaves. At the Battle of the Holy Ground on December 23, 21 Creek Indians and 12 Negroes were left dead on the field. But Jackson received several thousand reinforcements and on March 6, 1814, in the Battle of Horseshoe Bend, nearly annihilated a force of about 900 Red Sticks. This broke the back of Red Stick resistance and nearly all of those chiefs whose absence from the battle had saved them from destruction fled into Florida with their Indian and Negro followers. The tide of war was rolling closer to the already once-harried Seminole.[14]

The Negro Fort, 1814-1816

In May, 1814, the British war-vessel *Orpheus* anchored at the mouth of the Apalachicola and Captain George Woodbine went ashore with a commission to recruit the fugitive Creeks for the British service. The commander of the expedition, Major Edward Nicholls, sent into the Mobile district "printed proclamations for circulation among the Negroes" who "were offered free lands in the British West Indies at the end of the war and assured that . . . they would not be delivered to their former masters." Major Nicholls then proceeded to Pensacola, where late in July he hoisted the British flag beside the Spanish, issued a threatening and consoling proclamation to the people of Louisiana and Kentucky, and began to recruit and arm the fugitive Red Sticks and runaway Negroes.

Jackson arrived at Mobile on August 15 but had to await reinforcements and orders. He beat off a British attack on

---

[14] *ASP, IA*, I, 851-855; McMaster, *op. cit.*, IV, 158-172; H. S. Halbert and T. H. Ball, *The Creek War* (Chicago, 1895), pp. 135, 155-156, 158, 208, 258-259.

September 15 and when he received reinforcements on November 3 he left Mobile Bay, forced the British to evacuate Fort Barrancas at Pensacola, and was back at Mobile on the 11th. The British sailed again for the Apalachicola where they deposited their Indian and Negro allies, including about a hundred Negro slaves who had enlisted at Pensacola under the promise of freedom. Here on the eastern bank about 15 miles from the mouth, at a place called Prospect Bluff, Major Nicholls built a fort which he called British Post and used as headquarters for his negotiations with Seminole and Red Stick Indians and with the runaway Negroes in whom the region abounded.[15]

Nicholls succeeded in negotiating a treaty with the Seminole chief Bowlegs, on whose behalf he frequently wrote to the Creek Agent, Colonel Benjamin Hawkins. He remained at the fort for some time after the Treaty of Ghent, but early in the summer of 1815 he sailed with his troops for London. He took with him the prophet Francis and other Creek chiefs but left behind most of the Red Sticks, all the Negroes and the arms, including four pieces of heavy artillery, six lighter pieces, thousands of small arms and vast quantities of ammunition.

The Indians soon moved off to the eastward under their various chiefs to establish villages of their own, but the Negroes remained. There were, it was reported, about a thousand runaways in Florida and at the invitation of those at the fort they settled under the protection of its ramparts until their fields and grazing lands extended 50 miles up and down the Apalachicola. Something over 300 Negroes, including women and children, together with about 20 renegade Choctaw and a few Seminole warriors from Bowlegs's town, served as its garrison, under the strict disci-

15 J. Fred Rippy, *Rivalry of the United States and Great Britain over Latin America, 1808-1830* (Baltimore, 1929), pp. 45-48, 55; McMaster, *op. cit.*, IV, 173-174, 179-181, 431; *ASP, IA*, I, 858-860; Richard L. Campbell, *Historical Sketches of Colonial Florida* (Cleveland, 1892), p. 236.

pline of a Negro chief named Garçon. We know nothing about him save his name and two or three episodes of his brief career, but from these we may be entitled to envisage him as a lean, tense man, hot-eyed and tight-lipped, cunning, courageous and cruel.

The Negro Fort was a beacon light to restless slaves for miles around and to it flocked recruits from every quarter. The colonists were in their turn exposed to raids by slave-hunting Indians and half-breeds, friendly to the whites, and by posses of planters seeking their own runaways. Every man's hand was against them and their hand was against every man; it was dubiously reported that they harried the border, drove off cattle, fired on boats and created a veritable reign of terror for the slave-holders of the region. However doubtful or exaggerated the accounts of their depredations, there is no question that the existence of the Negro Fort settlement was an unceasing threat to the property rights of the slave-owners along the border and as such its abatement was demanded.

The Spanish governor, on receipt of protests from Andrew Jackson, commanding the Southern Division, professed entire willingness to suppress these "banditti," coupled with utter inability to do so. Jackson thereupon ordered General E. P. Gaines to destroy the fort "regardless of the ground it stands on . . . and restore the stolen [*sic*] negroes and property to their rightful owners." General Gaines accordingly built Fort Scott at the junction of the Flint and Chattahoochee, close to the Florida border, "in order to overawe the negroes;" and to supply this post two transports with ordnance and provisions, escorted by two gunboats, were dispatched from New Orleans. The little fleet arrived at the mouth of the Apalachicola on July 10, 1816, and was met by an express from General Gaines stating that he had sent Colonel Clinch down the river with troops "to take his station near the fort, and, if the fleet was fired on, raze the post to the ground." The fleet was accordingly ordered not to enter the river until Clinch had taken up his position.

The obvious intent was to provoke an attack from the fort which would justify its destruction and the Negroes were only too ready to furnish the desired provocation; they were apparently spoiling for a fight. They could hardly in any case permit United States troops and vessels, under orders to destroy their stronghold and enslave themselves and their families, to invest their position unmolested.

On July 17 a boat's crew from one of the gunboats, in search of fresh water, saw a Negro on the riverbank near one of the little "plantations" cultivated by the runaways. The midshipman in charge ordered the crew to pull in that direction—under the assumption, no doubt, that he was a fugitive slave who should be captured and whose appearance where he could be seen possibly indicated a willingness to give himself up. The boat touched the bank, the officer shouted to the Negro—and 40 muskets in the hands of ambushed blacks were discharged into the boat. Three sailors, including the officer, crumpled up dead in the bottom; one suddenly finding himself in the water, hurled overboard by the body of a mortally wounded shipmate, swam to safety on the opposite bank; the other survivor dazedly raised his hands under the menace of a dozen gaping muzzles. He was dragged over the bow to the bank, his hands were tied, and he was prodded at the end of a cocked and loaded musket down a narrow, muddy, circuitous path toward the fort. The rest of the party busied themselves with stripping and scalping the bodies in the boat. The Negro had been a decoy—the most cunningly effective that could have been devised.

Clinch, the day before, had started down the river toward the Negro Fort. He was joined by a party of slave-hunting Lower Creeks who had captured near the fort a Negro messenger from Garçon with a white man's scalp in his belt, on his way to summon the Seminole to his aid;

from him they learned of the boat-party's fate. Clinch pushed on, invested the fort, and called on the garrison to surrender. The Negro chief replied by heaping abuse upon the Americans, declaring that he would sink any American vessel that attempted to pass the fort and that if he found he could no longer defend the fort he would blow it up. His followers then raised a yell of defiance, shouting that they wanted to fight and had "gone into the Fort for no other purpose." They hoisted the English Jack, accompanied by "the red or bloody flag" signifying an intention to fight to the death, and loosed a discharge of cannon. The balls crashed through the trees uncomfortably close to the allied force and caused the Creek contingent to show signs of declining enthusiasm. "We were pleased with their spirited opposition," chivalrously commented Surgeon Marcus C. Buck of the Fourth Infantry, "though they were Indians, negroes, and our enemies. Many circumstances convinced us that most of them determined never to be taken alive." Clinch thereupon settled down for a siege and ordered up the gunboats. The Negro Fort seems to have been garrisoned largely by the Negroes from Pensacola, and the American runaways settled along the river left their villages and fields at the approach of the besieging force and took refuge in the forest.

Early in the morning of July 27 the gunboats came within range of the fort and received its fire, which they returned. On the ramparts was great running to and fro and confusion as the inexperienced artillerists plied rammer, lintstock and wiper. But the shots from the light guns of the boats sank harmlessly into the fort's substantial walls and the balls from its heavy pieces, trained by unskilled gunners, whistled harmlessly overhead or splashed into the muddy Apalachicola. Eight balls from the gunboats had crashed ineffectually into the walls of the fort when the sailing-master ordered a ninth to be heated red-hot in the cook's galley. The gun so loaded was elevated slightly, aimed carefully, discharged, and the red-hot ball went screaming over the wall and into the magazine, which had probably been left open for the careless convenience of the artillerists. There was a tremendous roaring, flaming explosion as hundreds of barrels of gunpower sent logs, cannon, human bodies and miscellaneous debris spinning catastrophically through the air. Clinch's force and the Creeks rushed in, as soon as they had recovered from the shock and indistinguishable fragments had ceased to rain down; they found the wreckage strewn with 270 dead bodies, horribly scorched and mutilated, and took 64 prisoners, only three unhurt and most burned and maimed beyond hope of recovery. Two of the three uninjured survivors, if properly identified, were by some freak of fate the Negro and Choctaw chiefs; perhaps they had been outside the fort skirmishing with the Creeks. On hearing that the sailor captured 10 days before had been "tarred and burned alive," his comrades turned their captives over to the Creeks, who after scalping the Choctaw chief alive, stabbed him to death; they executed Garçon by shooting.[16]

[16] 15th Cong., 2nd sess., House Documents 119 and 122, VI; *American State Papers, Foreign Relations* (hereafter referred to as *ASP, FR*), IV, 499-500, 555-561; *Army and Navy Chronicle* (hereafter referred to as *A. & N.C.*), II (February 25, 1836), 114-116; James Grant Forbes, *Sketches of the Floridas* (New York, 1821), pp. 200-205; John Lee Williams, *A View of West Florida* (Philadelphia, 1827), pp. 96-102; John Lee Williams, *The Territory of Florida* (New York, 1837), pp. 201-203; Mark F. Boyd, "Events at Prospect Bluff on the Apalachicola River, 1808-1818," *FHQ*, XVI (October, 1937), 55-96.

Parton's fascinating style has caused his dramatic version of the Negro Fort episode, in his *Life of Andrew Jackson* (New York, 1861), vol. II, chap. 31, to be accepted generally as the standard account. In the main, it is accurate, but his description of the relations between the garrison of the Negro Fort and the Seminole Indians absolutely reverses the actualities. Specifically, he describes the two groups as violently hostile to one another and in support of this view asserts that the Negroes dispossessed the Seminole of the fort and depredated upon them and that Colonel Clinch in his investiture of the fort was joined by "a large body of Seminoles . . . on a negro hunting expedition." McMaster (*op. cit.*, IV, 430-433) and John Spencer Bassett (*The Life*

The Negroes and the Indians on the Suwanee, 1817

With the Negro Fort destroyed, the Negro power on the Apalachicola was broken, and the settlers on the river fled east to the Suwanee, where Bowlegs and his people, Indian and Negro, had established their villages after having been dislodged from the Alachua savanna by the Tennessee invasion of early 1813. Stunned by the catastrophe which had befallen them on the Apalachicola, they remained quiet for several months, and the Indians with them, but as the Negroes found refuge on the Suwanee, built villages which extended down along the sea coast as far as Tampa Bay, and began to get themselves re-organized; and as the Indians saw the white settlers pressing nearer and nearer their borders, their spirits began to revive and their hostility to rise. Within six months they were thinking of revenge for past injuries and resistance to future aggressions.

A British agent was said to be operating among the Indians and Negroes near the mouth of the Apalachicola early

---

of Andrew Jackson, New York, 1916, I, 237-239), for example, without specifically citing Parton, follow him very closely.

To cite in detail all the evidence against Parton's view of Negro-Seminole relations would be repetitious. A careful examination of the contemporary sources used in this article for the destruction of the Negro Fort and the activities of the Negroes and Indians on the Suwanee the following year will reveal that the Negro garrison and the Seminole were not enemies but allies, that some of the warrors of the Seminole king Bowlegs perished in the destruction of the fort, and that the survivors of the Negro Fort settlement took refuge with the Seminole on the Suwanee.. See, in particular: *ASP, FR,* IV, 492-493, 499-500; *Niles Register* (hereafter cited as *NR*) XIII (November 15, 1817), 189-194, quoting from the *National Intelligencer;* and *Narrative of a Voyage to the Spanish Main* (London, 1819). Parton even contradicts himself when, quoting Ambrister, he refers (p. 420) to ''a few of our Bluff people,'' *i.e.,* from the Negro Fort settlement, being among the Seminole at Suwanee.

Parton's difficulty is that he regards any Indian encountered in Florida as a Seminole. He therefore simply confuses General MacIntosh's half-breed dominated, slave-hunting, Lower Creek allies of the United States with the pro-British, bitterly anti-American Seminole, who were allied with the runaway Negroes.

in 1817, but the greatest activity was observed in February in the Seminole Negro and Indian towns of the Suwanee, since their establishment the refuge of runaway slaves. Six hundred Negroes—probably a considerable exaggeration— were said to be in arms, drilling and parading to the beat of drums, with officers of their own choosing and under strict military discipline. They were accompanied by the same number of Indians and constantly increased by new recruits, Negro and Indian. Tom Woodward, entering Florida in November, 1816 and March, 1817 in pursuit of runaway slaves, penetrated on the latter occasion as far as Bowlegs's Town, but, as he wryly remarked, "found times a little too warm," and returned without attempting their capture. "They have," it was significantly reported of the Negroes on the Suwanee, "a number of the likeliest American horses."

The Negroes had chosen Bowlegs as their king and his chief "slave," Nero, as their commander. They said they would fight along with the Seminole Indian warriors but in their own companies and under their own officers. They were swearing vengeance for the Negro Fort and declared that they were "in complete fix for fighting" and wanted nothing better than an engagement with the Americans or with the half-breed McIntosh's Lower Creeks — "they would let them know they had something more to do than they had at Apalachicola!"[17]

Early in 1817 Alexander Arbuthnot, a Scottish trader from Nassau in the Bahamas, arrived at Suwanee in his schooner *Chance* loaded with powder, lead, knives, paints, beads, blankets, rum and Indian goods of all kinds to open a trading-house. Arbuthnot was an elderly man who had found that fair dealing with the Indians was a paying proposition and who took an interest in their welfare which

[17] *NR*, XIII (November 15, 1817), 189-194; Thomas S. Woodward, *Woodward's Reminiscences of the Creek or Muscogee Indians* (Montgomery, 1859), p. 153; *ASP, FR*, IV, 596; *ASP, IA*, II, 155; *American State Papers, Military Affairs* (hereafter referred to as *ASP, MA*), I, 727.

was to prove fatal to himself. He frequently wrote on King Bowlegs's behalf to American officers and officials—letters which were later remembered and held against him. In the autumn of 1817 when Arbuthnot's schooner arrived at the Suwanee from Nassau, two white men were on board. The older, Captain George Woodbine, was well known to many of the inhabitants of Suwanee since he had recruited Negroes and Indians in Florida for the British service during the War of 1812 and is said to have been given a land grant by the Indians which would probably be valueless should the United States take possession of Florida. His companion, Robert C. Ambrister, a British ex-lieutenant of Marines, was a dashing figure, a young man of good family, who out of patriotism, love of adventure, sympathy for the oppressed Negroes and Indians, and possibly less laudable motives as well—perhaps a share in Woodbine's land grant?—was like Arbuthnot to become fatally involved in the affairs of the folk on the Suwanee. Woodbine soon went away again but Ambrister remained. He "stated that he had come to the country on Woodbine's business" to look after the Negroes whom Woodbine had left at Tampa and "to see the negroes righted." He encouraged the Negroes not to retreat before the advancing Americans for "if they ran farther, they would be driven into the sea," and he took over from Nero the drilling of the Negro warriors and from Arbuthnot the position of counsellor to King Bowlegs.[18]

In August, 1817, General Gaines addressed to "Kenhagee" or "King Hatchy" (to use only two of the 22 known variants of his name), chief of the Mikasuki, dwelling at the town and near the lake of that name, a fantastically ungrammatical and confused letter, the illiteracy and obscurity of which he probably thought would make it good "Indian talk." But whatever the childishness of the in-

[18] Parton, *op. cit.*, II, 407-421, 471-479; Woodward, *op. cit.*, p. 153; *ASP, MA*, I, 732; William Hayne Simmons, *Notices of East Florida* (Charleston, 1822), pp. 44-45.

troduction, the concluding sentences were as plain and hard as a gun-barrel: "You harbor a great many of my black people among you at Suwanee. If you give me leave to go by you against them, I shall not hurt anything belonging to you." The reply of "Kenhagee" (also known in the confusing Seminole fashion as Cappichimicco or Lyewater King) was a model of clarity and brevity: "I harbor no negroes. .When the Englishmen were at war with America, some took shelter among them; . . . it is for you white people to settle these things among yourselves. . . . I shall use force to stop any armed Americans from passing my towns or on my lands." A United States general had demanded of an Indian chief the right to go slave-hunting on Spanish territory, and had been refused. The Mikasuki chief, hitherto inclined to hold aloof from the hostiles, was henceforth an enemy.[19]

The first clash between United States troops and Negroes or Indians since the affair of the Negro fort was, however, on the surface merely a typical episode in the advancing of the frontier. A settlement of about 45 warriors, known as Fowl Town, 15 miles east of Fort Scott and near the Florida line, was so exasperated by the building of forts and the appearance of settlers that the red pole was erected and war-dances held; horses, cattle and swine from the Georgia settlement were collected as informal rent, and the chief, Inihamathla, sent a warning to Major Twiggs at Fort Scott "not to cross or cut a stick of timber on the east side of the Flint." In response to this challenge, detachments from Fort Scott attacked Fowl Town late in October and again on November 21, drove the inhabitants into the swamps after killing 10 or 12 and wounding many, plundered the village, and finally burned it.

The vengeance for Fowl Town was swift and terrible. The hostile-minded Negroes and Indians had been preparing for about a year. The Red Sticks and Seminole were estimated as "more than two thousand, besides the blacks, amounting to near four hundred men, and increasing by

[19] *ASP, FR,* IV, 585-586; *ASP, MA,* I, 723.

runaways from Georgia." A more moderate but still formidable estimate put the hostiles at "between eight hundred and twelve hundred Indians and negroes, and increasing daily." The United States troops had hardly finished sacking Inihamathla's village when a large open boat proceeded slowly up the Apalachicola with 40 United States troops, 7 women, and 4 children. On November 30 an attack from an ambush in a dense swamp killed every soul on board save 4 men who escaped by swimming and a woman taken prisoner. A fleet of five boats was besieged in midstream by Indians and Negroes for four days, suffering heavy casualties, until relieved by troops from Fort Scott.

William Hambly and Edward Doyle, agents of Forbes & Co., a Scottish firm which was regarded as having "gone over" to the Americans, had established a trading-house on Prospect Bluff. They were seized on December 13 by Fowl Town Indians and taken first to Mikasuki and then to the Negro towns on the Suwanee, where they were tried for alleged complicity in the destruction of the Negro Fort. It was suggested that they should be turned over for punishment to five or six Choctaw survivors, but the Negro chief Nero good-naturedly intervened and got them off to St. Mark's, where they were kept in "protective custody" by the Spanish commandant, who was helpless or unwilling to prevent the Negroes and Indians from using his fort as an arsenal, prison and headquarters at their convenience.

The border war which had begun at Fowl Town continued, with the Indians raiding plantations, killing settlers, and carrying off horses, cattle and Negroes. General Gaines in the meantime had been ordered transferred and when word of the outbreak reached Washington, Andrew Jackson, scourge of the Red Sticks, was ordered to replace him at Fort Scott.[20]

[20] *ASP, FR,* IV, 586-597, 577-578; *ASP, MA,* I, 686, 690-691, 695; *Narrative of a Voyage to the Spanish Main* (London, 1819), p. 241; McMaster, *op. cit.,* IV, 437-439; Caroline May Brevard, *A History of Florida* (DeLand, Fla., 1924), I, p. 51.

Invasion of Florida, 1818

Jackson received his orders at the Hermitage on January 11, 1818, mustered two regiments of mounted volunteers, and set off post-haste for Fort Scott. He arrived on March 9 and then set off down the east bank of the Apalachicola to Prospect Bluff where he was gladdened by the arrival of provision ships under convoy and where he built a new fortification—Fort Gadsden. He had heard that the old Red Stick leaders, Peter McQueen of Burnt Corn and the prophet Francis, with the British adventurer Woodbine and the Scottish merchant Arbuthnot—whom he regarded as of the same stripe—were at St. Mark's with a "motley crew" of hostiles, mostly runaway slaves. He now learned that the Indians and Negroes had extorted arms and ammunitions from the commandant and feared that they might seize it as a stronghold. He consequently ordered the fleet to proceed down the Apalachicola and blockade St. Mark's while he marched overland.

On April 1 Jackson was joined by a Tennessee regiment which proceeded in association with McIntosh's friendly Creeks to waste Mikasuki and the other Indian towns of the region; they killed a Negro, captured three Indians, and burned 300 houses—all with little opposition—while Jackson marched on to St. Mark's. He arrived there on April 6 and seized the fort without resistance. He found no Indians or Negroes there, but he did find and arrest the Scottish merchant Arbuthnot. He also found on an American vessel in the harbor two Red Stick chiefs, Imala Micco and the prophet Francis or Hillis Hajo, who had been lured aboard by the display of a British flag. Jackson had the chiefs summarily hanged and Arbuthnot imprisoned to await court-martial.

After 48 hours at St. Mark's the army pushed on toward Bowlegs's town of Suwanee and the Negro villages of which it was the capital. Word of their movement, however, preceded them. Arbuthnot had learned at St. Mark's of the expedition and on April 2 rushed off a letter by Indian runner to his son, who was commanding a schooner lying in the Suwanee just below Bowlegs's town. "The main drift of the Americans," he wrote, "is to destroy the black population of Suwany. Tell my friend, Boleck, that it is throwing away his people to attempt to resist such a powerful force." Arbuthnot was not being overly pessimistic. He knew that despite all exaggerations the Seminole force which could be mustered against Jackson amounted at most to about a thousand warriors, including Negroes, while Jackson's army consisted of 3,300, including 1500 friendly Indians, who were looked on with far greater respect and hatred by the Seminole than an even larger number of whites.

Suwanee had already received some warning of its intended fate and made preparations to resist it. Ambrister, who had now been operating on the Suwanee for about half a year, was not satisfied with the amount of ammunition obtained from Arbuthnot by purchase and on March 20 at the head of 24 armed Negroes had seized his schooner and taken from it nine kegs of powder and 500 pounds of lead; three days later he had plundered Arbuthnot's store, passing out the powder, lead, paint and other articles to the Negroes and Indians. About April 5 or 6, a Negro woman, fleeing from devastated Mikasuki, reached Suwanee. Ambrister donned his uniform, belted on his sword, and sent out a party of Negroes against the Americans, but on their way they encountered such numbers of fleeing Mikasuki that the full measure of the disaster dawned upon them and they returned to Suwanee for further council. In the meantime a Negro had brought in Arbuthnot's warning letter, which he said he had received from an Indian, and Ambrister had read it publicly. The Negroes were at first inclined to regard the messenger as an emissary of the enemy sent to sow alarm and confusion in their ranks, but eventually became convinced of his good faith. They accordingly prepared to send their families and effects across the river—the Negro villages were on the western bank and the Indian on the eastern—and themselves began to get ready to meet the enemy.

Ambrister, as Jackson drew nearer and nearer, began to lose his enthusiasm. He was, after all, a former British officer, a gentleman and a white man. It was one thing to command Indians and Negroes under His Majesty's commission; it was another—as he was soon to discover—for a private citizen to arm, direct and encourage Indians and Negroes against the United States; but it was altogether another matter still for a private citizen personally to command and participate in Negro and Indian resistance to United States troops. Ambrister withdrew to his headquarters on Arbuthnot's schooner and left Nero to resume the command over the Negroes which Ambrister, as a former British officer and an associate of Woodbine, had temporarily usurped.

We know even less of Nero than of the commander of the Negro Fort. According to one authority he was a mulatto. Courageous and masterful he must have been to exercise chieftaincy over a restless horde of runaway slaves even assisted by his prestige as King Bowlegs's chief Negro. He was obviously of a different temperament from the ruthless commander of the Negro Fort, since the most definitely known episode in his career was his intervention to *save* two captives from death by torture. My imagination pictures him as a big man, smiling and resolute, his shoulders straining at a British officer's uniform-coat.

Unaware that word of their coming had preceded them, Jackson's army struggled on through a swampy wilderness. On the morning of April 12, near the Econfina, McIntosh's 1500 friendly Creeks encountered about 200 of Peter McQueen's old Red Sticks who, despite the disproportion in numbers, fought with their customary desperation until

37 warriors had fallen; the "friendlies" were able to round up 97 women and children and 600 head of cattle but only six men. On April 16 about three o'clock in the afternoon Jackson reached a large pond which the Indian guide said was only six miles from Suwanee. He had hoped to strike the village at midday and have the whole afternoon for their destruction. He thought of camping for the night, but mounted Indians were seen in the distance, so the only thing to do was to push on. He divided his force into three divisions and moved forward as rapidly as possible, exultantly sniffing the possibility of crushing at a blow the hostile Negroes and Indians.

The Battle of Suwanee

As rapidly as Jackson's army moved, the half dozen Indian scouts who had glimpsed it near the pond moved faster and galloped into the Negro village, which extended three miles along the river, shouting that Jackson was coming with soldiers on foot and soldiers on horseback—and with Creek scouts in the vanguard! Bowlegs had recognized the wisdom of Arbuthnot's advice and having the river between himself and the enemy lost no time in disappearing into the swamp. The Negroes set about ferrying across the river the women and children not already evacuated and as much of the remaining property as possible, but they were hardly out of the village when Jackson's army appeared as if out of the sunset.

The Negro warriors had remained on the west side of the river to cover the retreat and were joined by a few Indians. They had said they would give the Americans something more to do than they had had on the Apalachicola. Well, here the Americans were, but they had not expected them in such force, and their king with most of the Indian warriors were across the river and in flight. Nevertheless they would do what they could for the women and children—try to hold the white men and Creeks until all

their families could get across the river and lose themselves
under the cover of night in the woods and swamps. So,
their eyes dazzled by the sunset, their British smoothbore
muskets outranged by the American rifles, outnumbered
three or four to one by the Tennessee regiment and Creeks
of Jackson's left wing, the two or three hundred of the
rear guard clung to their ground for those few desperate,
possibly necessary, minutes. Then it was time to look to
themselves. Two Negroes, retreat cut off by the rapidly
advancing enemy, dropped their muskets and sullenly lifted
their hands in surrender; nine Negroes and two Indians
lay dead on the field. The rest ran for the river, plunged
in, and struck out for the eastern shore. How many made
it is uncertain. The Creek and Tennessee rifles soon lined
and fitfully lightened the bank, but a head briefly rising
and quickly ducking again among the ripples of a twilight
river is a test for any marksman and although a figure
crawling out on the opposite shore is a larger mark, it is
still at 300 yards not a target to be despised. On the other
hand, a man weary from wounds and fighting does not make
a strong swimmer. Thirteen of Jackson's army—mostly
Creeks, who had borne the brunt of the action—had wounds
which needed attention.

Such at least was the official account—that, in a brief
skirmish on the west bank of the Suwanee, the Seminole
had lost a dozen or so killed and captured, mostly Negroes.
An anonymous officer neatly summarized the official version: "A small party of negroes were surprised, busily
securing their moveable property . . . and all would have
been captured, but for the bad execution of the movement
of the left column. The [Creek] Indians, instead of getting above, had thrown themselves between the towns and
the centre, thus leaving open the retreat to the river which
the enemy readily embraced, after a slight resistance in
which they lost 8 or 9 killed, and some prisoners."

Louisiana newspapers, however, made much more of the

encounter. The *Louisiana Gazette* wrote: "General Jackson ... discovered an encampment defended by 340 negroes; they were attacked immediately, forced, and about 80 killed or wounded." The *New Orleans Gazette,* after sneering at the alacrity with which Bowlegs's warriors disappeared into the swamp on Jackson's approach, added: "The Indians only are liable to this imputation of pusillanimity; their sable allies displayed greater resolution. A detachment of these latter, having been attacked in the night, defended themselves with the courage of men who are conscious of guilt and hopeless of pardon; and fought till near one half of them were killed." Possibly the encounter on the west bank of the Suwanee was blown up into these much more impressive newspaper stories—or possibly Jackson's men, crossing the river to pursue the fugitives, became involved in a rear guard action which, for reasons which can only be surmised, did not become a part of the official record.

Whatever the character and proportions of the Seminole resistance, it fulfilled its principal purpose: Jackson made no prisoners at the Suwanee except the two Negro warriors taken in arms—the women and children got safely away. One other thing is certain—that whether their loss was nine or eighty or more, it was the Negroes who did the fighting at the Suwanee; as Governor D. B. Mitchell of Georgia put it: "The next enemy . . . engaged were the negroes at Sauwannee." To that extent Nero's fighting-men had fulfilled the boast so proudly flaunted a year earlier when they proclaimed Bowlegs their king and swore alliance with his warriors.

MOPPING-UP OPERATIONS

Jackson found himself in possession of a deserted town, a few stray horses and cattle and 2700 bushels of corn. The sacking and destruction would take a day or two and the men needed rest, so the army encamped on the riverbank and occupied itself with scouring the region for fugitives left behind in the general flight. On the 18th, Creek Indians, scouring the swamp for six miles beyond the river, flushed and killed three warriors and also captured five Negroes and nine Indian women and children. No further pursuit was attempted, the fugitives having broken up into small parties which could never be hunted down. By far the greater prize was the white man who, accompanied by another white man and two Negroes, blundered into the camp at midnight on their way back to Suwanee, not having heard of its capture. This man was Robert C. Ambrister.

The Negro and Indian settlements having been broken up, 300 houses burned, and their former residents killed, captured or driven into hiding in the wilderness, Jackson returned to St. Mark's, where he had Arbuthnot and Ambrister tried by court-marital. On the morning of April 29, the white-haired Arbuthnot hung at the mast-head of his own schooner; a few minutes later the handsome young Ambrister fell before the bullets of a firing-squad. Jackson then returned to Fort Gadsden where, near the end of May, he heard that 550 Indians had gathered at Pensacola, where they were fed by the governor and, using that place as headquarters, had made murderous forays into the United States. Jackson marched on Pensacola, entering it on May 24, and after some resistance forced the fort to surrender. Five days later, leaving behind a small' occupying force, he started homeward, more than ever the idol of the army and the people of the Southwest.[21]

21 15th Cong., 2d sess., House Document 14, vol. I; *ASP, FR*, IV, 599-600; *ASP, MA*, I, 689, 700-704, 722, 727-728, 731-732, 741, 749; *NR*, XIV (June 6, 1818), 247; Captain Hugh Young, ''A Topographical Memoir on East and West Florida, with Itineraries of General Jackson's Army, 1818,'' *FHQ*, XIII (October, 1934), 84; An Officer Attached to the Expedition, *A Concise Narrative of the Seminole Campaign* (Nashville, 1819), pp. 30-31; ''Rt. Rev. Michael Portier, A Journey of, From Pensacola to St. Augustine in 1827,'' *FHQ*, XXVI (October, 1947), 158-159; Williams, *Territory of Florida*, pp. 204-206; Williams, *West Florida*, pp. 96-102; Woodward, *op. cit.*, p. 168; Parton, *op. cit.*, II, 448-449; McMaster, *op. cit.*, IV, 438-446.

IMMEDIATE EFFECTS OF JACKSON'S INVASION

For months after Jackson had returned to Nashville the Indian and Negro population of Florida was in motion, like a muddy pool which someone has stirred violently with a stick. The old Red Stick Creeks who had been fighting and fleeing for five years, the Fowl Town Indians, the Mikasuki and the Alachua, all with their Negroes, as well as the runaway Negroes who had as yet no connection with an Indian tribe, were all seeking new homes. The Fowl Town Indians moved down into Florida to the west bank of the Apalachicola; some of the Mikasuki moved to a location about 30 miles west of the upper Suwanee which they called New Mikasuki, while others went east and south to the Alachua savanna where the people of King Payne and King Bowlegs had lived before being dislodged in 1813. The distance the Red Sticks removed was indicative of the disfavor with which they knew the Americans regarded them; most of the villages around Tampa Bay were soon said to be occupied by Upper Creek Red Sticks. The Alachua settled about 120 miles south of their old location, with their principal town, Okihamki, just west of Lake Harris. The Negroes belonging to these tribes resided as before in villages near to but separate from those of the Indians; the chief village of the Alachua Negroes was Pilaklikaha. Other Negro villages were farther west. A report of 1818 states: "The Negroes of Sahwanne fled with the Indians of Bowleg's town toward Chuckachatte"—a town north of Tampa Bay and 60 or 70 miles southeast from the Suwanee towns.

The unattached Negroes "followed upon the steps of the Indians, and formed considerable settlements on the waters of Tampa Bay," where Woodbine had earlier settled some of their former comrades. Hundreds of fugitives, however, both Seminole Negroes and more recent runaways, "made their way down to Cape Florida and the reef," whence "vast numbers" were "carried off by the Bahama wreckers" and "smuggled into the remoter islands." Others, however, unwilling to trust themselves to the wrecking-captains, put to sea in great dugout canoes, taking with them the seeds of corn, peas and pumpkins, and to the number of perhaps 200 made the perilous passage to Andros — an epic story, this — where their descendants, mostly named Bowlegs, still live.[22]

Jackson's exploit in marching virtually unopposed so far as the Spaniards were concerned over the northwestern part of East Florida, attacking and destroying Indian and Negro villages, court-martialing and executing British subjects, capturing Spanish forts and deposing their commandants, had revealed the impossibility of Spain's resisting any serious demand by the United States for the annexation of Florida. In February, 1819, about a year after Jackson's invasion, a treaty providing for its cession was signed, though the formal transfer did not take place until July, 1821.

The Indians and Negroes this time attempted no resistance. They were finally convinced that Spain could not and Great Britain would not assist them further. They had been used as long as it served the purposes of both nations and were now cast aside. Jackson's rough handling had convinced them, at least temporarily, that they could not resist the United States. Their behavior for some years was so quiet and submissive that many were wishfully convinced that the spirit had entirely gone out of them.

[22] Swanton, *op. cit.*, pp. 400, 401, 404, 406, 407, 408, 411; F. W. Hodge, *Handbook of American Indians North of Mexico*, (Washington, 1907), see various towns; Young, *op. cit.*, p. 97; Charles Vignoles, *The History of the Floridas* (Brooklyn, 1824), p. 134; Forbes, *op. cit.*, p. 39; Charles H. Coe, *Red Patriots* (Cincinnati, 1898), pp. 22-23, quoting from the *Bahama Advertiser*, Oct. 2, 1819; John M. Goggin, "An Anthropological Reconnaissance of Andros Island, Bahamas," *American Antiquities*, V (July, 1939), 21-26; Goggin, "The Seminole Negroes of Andros Island, Bahamas," *FHQ*, XXIV (January, 1946), 201-206; Kenneth W. Porter, "Notes on Seminole Negroes in the Bahamas," *FHQ*, XXIV (July, 1945), 56-60.

Conclusion

The so-called First Seminole War—the title might more properly be conferred on the invasions of the Alachua country in 1812-1813—which brought about the annexation of Florida, was thus a culmination of three closely-related early-nineteenth-century American expansionist trends: expansion at the expense of the Indians; expansion at the expense of Spain; and the extension and safeguarding of slavery. The earliest fighting in the Seminole War proper was by Fowl Town and Mikasuki Indians who resented the encroachment of American settlers; the next people to become involved were the refugees from the Red Stick War— the southern manifestation of Tecumseh's plan for a general Indian alliance against the advancing whites. The Seminole War was also the last and most extensive of a series of invasions of Florida, which included the invasion of 1812 in support of the Patriot annexation attempt, the invasion of 1813 which destroyed the Alachua towns, the seizure of Pensacola in 1814—in response to an earlier British occupation—and the invasion of 1816 which had the objective and result of destroying the Negro Fort; Jackson's invasion of 1818 combined most of the elements of the foregoing and presented some special features of its own.

These aspects of the Seminole War have been generally recognized. That United States expansion into territory bordering on slave states naturally involved and was in large measure motivated by a desire for the extension of slavery is also self-evident. But it has not been adequately recognized that Jackson's invasion of 1818 was not primarily aimed at the extinction of Spanish authority or the occupation of Indian lands. It was in its main purpose an extension of the invasion Jackson had ordered in 1816, which was aimed at destroying the Negro Fort on the Apalachicola and the Negro settlements which had sprung up under its protection. The outbreak of the Fowl Town Indians and the Mikasuki was merely a convenient pretext. Jackson's principal objective was to break up the free Negro frontier settlements which were becoming increasingly a menace to the slave systems of adjacent states. His invasion was directed particularly against the Suwanee settlements, inhabited by warriors who had helped to raise the siege of St. Augustine and to beat off Newnan's attack, former soldiers under Nicholls and Woodbine, and refugees from the Negro Fort colony, as well as by recent fugitives who had been encouraged to run away by knowledge of these settlements and their formidable defenders. General Gaines had tipped his hand, which was also Jackson's, months before the Fowl Town outbreak, when he demanded that the Mikasuki chief permit him to go by him against the "black people" at Suwanee.

Bowlegs's people had apparently not been directly involved in the recent actions on the Flint and Apalachicola. Hambly and Doyle, it is true, had been brought as prisoners to the Suwanee settlements, but their captors were Fowl Town Indians and the Suwanee people's participation in the episode took the form of Nero's saving the captives from death by torture. And yet Jackson, having already thoroughly harried the Fowl Town and Mikasuki villages and captured St. Mark's, nevertheless thought it essential to march his army through the wilderness for a week in order to destroy Bowlegs's villages. His reason was correctly stated by Arbuthnot in the letter which proved the writer's death warrant: "The main drift of the Americans is to destroy the black population at Suwany." The Seminole War, which even Jackson referred to as "this savage and negro war," was the culmination of a series of invasions with the primary or secondary objectives of depriving the slaves of neighboring states of a refuge by destroying the Negro towns of Florida and eventually bringing the province under United States rule.

Corrections and Additions

p. 210, l. 17-20: "An understanding of these invasions will, however, also involve consideration of Tecumseh's plan for an Indian confederacy . . ." Insert before "Tecumseh's plan": "the East Florida annexation plot,".

The following article was originally published in *The Journal of Southern History,* November, 1964 (Vol. XXX, No. 4).

Negroes and the Seminole War, 1835-1842

THE SECOND SEMINOLE WAR LASTED FROM DECEMBER 1835 TO
August 1842 and cost over $40,000,000 and the lives of approxi-
mately 1,500 members of the armed forces of the United States,[1]
in addition to those of white settlers and militiamen. It is usually
referred to as the country's most protracted and expensive Indian
war,[2] but Major General Thomas Sidney Jesup, who was in command in Florida during its most crucial period, announced
emphatically late in 1836, "This . . . is a negro, not an Indian war."
The General, of course, was employing hyperbole to emphasize
his belief that if the war were "not speedily put down, the south
will feel the effects of it on their slave population before the end
of the next season"[3]—in other words, that a general slave insurrection might ensue. Actually the war, which was undoubtedly an
Indian war, was just as certainly a Negro war during its most
critical years. There is abundant evidence that Negroes were
more important than Indians in bringing it about and keeping it
up, as well as largely influential in bringing it to a conclusion.

Of the Negroes in the Florida Indian country the most important group were those with a recognized position in the Seminole
tribe. A few of these were admittedly the lawful slaves of the
Indians and an even smaller number were legally free; the great
majority, perhaps four-fifths, were runaway or "captured" Negroes and their descendants, all of whom were thus legally the
property of white citizens.[4] White observers, however, were in-

---

[1] George Catlin, *Letters and Notes on the Manners, Customs, and Condition of
the North American Indians* (2 vols., New York, 1841), II, 219n; John T. Sprague,
The Origin, Progress, and Conclusion of the Florida War . . . (New York, 1848),
526-50; Joshua R. Giddings, *The Exiles of Florida* (Columbus, O., 1858), 315.

[2] See, for example, Ethan Allen Hitchcock, *Fifty Years in Camp and Field* (New
York, 1909), 81.

[3] *Court of Inquiry—Operations in Florida, &c.: Letter from the Secretary of
War* . . . , House Docs., 25 Cong., 2 Sess., No. 78 (Serial 323), 52; *American State
Papers, Military Affairs* (7 vols., Washington, 1832-1861), VII, 820-21.

[4] *Negroes, &c., Captured from Indians in Florida, &c.: Letter from the Secretary
of War* . . . , House Docs., 25 Cong., 3 Sess., No. 225 (Serial 348), 119-20, 57-65;
American State Papers, Military Affairs, VI, 461, 465.

clined to regard all these Negroes—except for very recent runaways or captives—as in some sense the Indians' slaves. Nearly all, regardless of legal status, received almost identical treatment from the Indians, which differed so much from the treatment of slaves by whites that it was a difference of kind rather than of degree. Indian agent Gad Humphreys in 1827 declared, "The negroes of the Seminole Indians are wholly independent . . . and are Slaves but in name; they work only when it suits their inclination"; while brevet Major General Edmund P. Gaines, a decade or so later, referred to them not as the Indians' slaves but as "their black vassals and allies."[5]

Although the Seminole Indians were of all the so-called Civilized Tribes the least influenced by European-American civilization, some of their chiefs, for reasons of prestige, had purchased Negro slaves; and as traditional allies of the British the Seminole also had no scruples about capturing slaves or receiving fugitive Negroes from the rebellious Americans or the Spaniards. The Indians, however, had no intention of spending their lives in supervising Negroes; so, save for a very few employed in personal service, the Negroes were furnished with axes, hoes, and seed corn and left to take care of themselves.

A system of relationships between the Seminole Indians and their Negroes developed which was the admiration or horror of all beholders. The Negroes lived in separate villages of well-built houses, raised crops of corn, sweet potatoes, other vegetables, and even cotton, and possessed herds of livestock; their masters, or rather protectors, never presumed to meddle with any of this property so long as they received a reasonable "tribute" at harvest and butchering time.[6] The Negroes also had plenty of time for hunting and fishing, and under this almost idyllic regime they throve amazingly. Dressed in the easy Indian costume, they were, according to one observer, "stout and even gigantic in their persons . . . the finest looking people I have. ever seen." They were known, moreover, as well-armed and brave warriors; a major of

[5] Clarence Edwin Carter (ed.), *The Territorial Papers of the United States* (Washington, 1934-   ), XXIII, 911, XXIV, 669; *American State Papers, Military Affairs*, VI, 470-71, 533-34, VII, 427.

[6] Sources cited in note 5, and [Woodburne Potter] *The War in Florida* (Baltimore, 1836), 45-46; John Lee Williams, *The Territory of Florida* . . . (New York, 1837), 240; William Kennedy, *Texas: The Rise, Progress, and Prospects of the Republic of Texas* (2 vols., London, 1841), I, 350. See also, however, George A. McCall, *Letters from the Frontiers* . . . (Philadelphia, 1868), 160; and Jedidiah Morse, *A Report to the Secretary of War of the United States on Indian Affairs* . . . (New Haven, 1822), 309-11.

Georgia militia in 1812 declared of the Seminole that the Negroes were "their best soldiers."[7]

The Seminole Negroes' prestige and influence among the Indians were what impressed observers most forcibly. The Negroes speedily acquired the Muskogee or Hitchiti tongue of their protectors without forgetting the English or Spanish they had learned among the whites, which made them valuable interpreters. From interpreting it was an easy step to advising and counseling. Some observers believed they governed the Indians, and one with a taste for classical comparisons said that the Seminole nation approached a doulocracy.[8] A few groups of fugitive Negroes established villages which were not under Seminole control, and the Indians sometimes found it convenient to assert that all Negro settlements in their country were of this character.[9]

For obvious reasons it is impossible to determine how many Seminole Negroes there were on the eve of the Seminole War. Estimates ranged from 300 or 400 to as many as 1,100; the estimate of "more than five hundred" made in 1834 is perhaps the best.[10] The Negro population in Florida, however, consisted mostly of plantation slaves. In East Florida, the principal arena of the Seminole War, about half the population was colored; there were 4,095 slaves, 343 free colored, and 4,515 whites. In the counties bordering on the Indian country the Negroes considerably outnumbered the whites.[11] The slaves in East Florida were looked upon as potentially more dangerous than those in other slaveholding regions. According to an old settler, most of the male slaves in the Mosquito region near the St. Johns River owned guns for hunting to save their masters the expense of supplying them with the usual salt-pork ration. Both slaves and free

[7] See the author's "Negroes and the East Florida Annexation Plot, 1811-1813," *Journal of Negro History*, XXX (January 1945), esp. 22-23, and "Negroes and the Seminole War, 1817-1818," *ibid.*, XXXVI (July 1951), esp. 255-56, 273-75.

[8] For additional sources on the generally idyllic situation of the Seminole Negroes see: [William Hayne Simmons] *Notices of East Florida* (Charleston, S. C., 1822), 44-45, 50, 76; Mark F. Boyd, "Horatio S. Dexter and Events Leading to the Treaty of Moultrie Creek with the Seminole Indians," *Florida Anthropologist*, XI (September 1958), 84; [W. W. Smith] *Sketch of the Seminole War and Sketches During a Campaign* (Charleston, S. C., 1836), 21-22.

[9] Boyd, "Horatio S. Dexter," 91-92; David Y. Thomas, "Report on the Public Archives of Florida," American Historical Association, *Annual Report*, 1906 (2 vols., Washington, 1908), II, 152.

[10] Carter (ed.), *Territorial Papers*, XXIV, 668, 643-45; *American State Papers, Military Affairs*, VI, 465.

[11] *Memorial of the People of the Territory of Florida for Admission into the Union, House Docs.*, 25 Cong., 3 Sess., No. 208 (Serial 347), 25; Carter (ed.), *Territorial Papers*, XXIV, 505-506, 643-45.

Negroes were well acquainted with the Seminole Indians and Negroes, their way of life, and their language. Many of the slaves had "wives among the Indian negroes, and the Indian negroes had wives among them."[12] Ownership of firearms and acquaintance with the Indians were doubtless most extensive among those Negroes owned by whites whose traditions went back to "Spanish days"; but Governor William P. DuVal is quoted as saying in 1828 that "many of the slaves taken to Florida are the very worst in the Union,"[13] and the need for labor on a newly opened frontier may indeed have resulted in an unusually large proportion of slaves who had been "sold down the river" for bad conduct.

Although the attempt to remove the Seminole from Florida— the spark which set off the seven-year war—was ostensibly part of the general program for Indian removal, the presence and peculiar position of the Negroes among them was a decisive factor. The Seminole, who did not lie directly in the path of white settlement, might have been permitted to remain on the peninsula had it not been for the Negroes; in fact, the hardier and more obdurate of the Florida Seminole were in the end allowed to stay.

Sentiment for the removal of the Seminole Negroes preceded that for Indian removal. As early as 1821 the Florida Indian agent said of "the maroon negroes, who live among the Indians" that it would "be necessary to remove from the Floridas this group of lawless freebooters, among whom runaway negroes will always find a refuge," although he admitted that if force were employed the Indians would probably take the Negroes' part.[14] It was soon recognized that it was impossible to persuade the Indians to rid Florida of a "Serious nusance" [sic] by selling their Negroes, because of the Indians' attachment to them. The bodily removal of the Indians themselves was increasingly regarded as the only solution to the Negro problem.[15]

The citizens of Florida, however, would not have been content with the removal of the Seminole Indians if it meant that the Indians would take their Negroes west with them. Planters who had lost slaves through flight to the Indian country were deter-

---

[12] *Reminiscences of James Ormond Concerning the Early Days of the Halifax Country* (n.p.: Ormond Village Improvement Association, 1941), 5-6; Thomas Douglas, *Autobiography of Thomas Douglas, Late Judge of the Supreme Court of Florida* (New York, 1856), 120-23.

[13] Carter (ed.), *Territorial Papers*, XXIII, 1059.

[14] Morse, *Report to the Secretary of War*, 149-50.

[15] Carter (ed.), *Territorial Papers*, XXIII, 434, 454, XXIV, 668, 679.

mined to repossess them. Official circles in Florida argued strongly that the baneful influence which the alleged indolence of the Negroes exerted on the Indians made their separation necessary,[16] but earlier attempts through pressure and fraud to gain possession of the Indians' Negroes[17] suggest that the desire of white men for cheap slaves was a more important motive for the proposed separation of the Negroes from the Indians.

The program for Seminole removal reached a climax on March 28, 1833, when a Seminole delegation inspecting the Indian Territory was wheedled and bullied into expressing satisfaction with the region of Creek country set aside for the Seminole and with the plan of uniting them with the powerful Creeks as one people. The government then asserted that this so-called treaty of Fort Gibson committed the entire tribe to move west within three years. The Seminole, insisting that the delegation was without power to bind the Nation, strongly objected to removal in general and in particular to the prospect that they would become a despised minority in the powerful half-breed-dominated Creek confederacy. One of their objections was that the Creeks claimed the Negro "property" of the Seminole because of slaves who had escaped to the Seminole when the latter were still considered Lower Creeks and for whom the Creek Nation had been forced to pay; they feared that the Creeks would attempt to seize their Negroes, either in satisfaction of the claim or merely by *force majeure*. For the Seminole Negroes, seizure by the Creeks would mean at best substitution of a stricter control in place of slavery in name only; at worst, sale into real servitude among the whites.

The Seminole Negroes' greatest dread was that they would never reach the Creek country. All, regardless of legal status, belonged to a race the members of which normally occupied the position of chattels; the Negro without a recognized owner or without the clearest evidence of freedom was liable to seizure, no matter how long he had been in effect his own master or how dubious the claimant's title might be. Since the Seminole were to be assembled at a central point for transportation west under military supervision, this would give opportunity both for the white owners of fugitive Seminole Negroes to present their legal claims and for the unscrupulous to urge illegitimate claims or even simply to kidnap likely Negroes. Whites, indeed, had already seized or fraudulently acquired numerous Negroes

16 *Ibid.*, XXIII, 414, 1003, XXIV, 668.
17 *Ibid.*, XXIII, 472-75, 483-84; Sprague, *Origin of the Florida War*, 34, 65-67.

claimed by Indians. John Hicks, onetime principal Seminole chief who was friendly to the whites, complained in 1829, "A white man sells us a Negro, and then turns around and claims him again, and our big father orders us to give him up."[18] If this could happen when the Seminole were more or less secure in their own country, what would be their fate when surrounded by white men and in their power? An outrage committed shortly after the outbreak of the Seminole War demonstrates that their fears were not groundless. A band of whites raided the village of the friendly old chief Econchattemicco, rounded up the Negroes, including the chief's half-Negro granddaughter, and carried them off to slavery in Georgia.[19]

The Negroes, described in April 1835 by the officer commanding in East Florida as "bold, active, and armed," were determined not to submit to removal and to do all in their power to persuade their Indian protectors not to remove.[20] They possessed able leaders in Abraham, head chief Micanopy's principal Negro, a middle-aged runaway slave of fluent speech and polished manners from Pensacola, and John Caesar, a shrewd, fierce old man who had been brought up among the Indians and was the "chief Negro" of King Philip (Emathla) of the St. Johns Indians, the second chief in the Nation.[21] During the three years of grace Abraham and Caesar, Osceola and Yaha Hajo, and other Negro and Indian militants were busy preparing for resistance. The plantation slaves, well aware of the idyllic existence of even the "slaves" of the Seminole, were in many cases receptive to urgings that, when war broke out, they should rise with axe and torch, wreak havoc on the plantations, and then, laden with plunder, escape into the swamps and hammocks to a life of freedom and plenty.[22]

[18] Carter (ed.), *Territorial Papers*, XXIII, 472-75, 483-84, 549-50; Potter, *War in Florida*, 24-26; Sprague, *Origin of the Florida War*, 51, 57, 66.

[19] R. H. Stewart to Richard K. Call, May 25, 1836, in Caroline M. Brevard, *A History of Florida from the Treaty of 1763 to Our Own Times* (2 vols., Deland, Fla., 1924), I, 278-79; Potter, *War in Florida*, 15-16.

[20] Carter (ed.), *Territorial Papers*, XXV, 133; Sprague, *Origin of the Florida War*, 100, 81; *American State Papers, Military Affairs*, VI, 454, 458.

[21] See the author's "The Negro Abraham," *Florida Historical Quarterly*, XXV (July 1946), 1-43, and "John Caesar: Seminole Negro Partisan," *Journal of Negro History*, XXXI (April 1946), 190-207.

[22] Charleston, S. C., *Courier*, April 30, 1836; Douglas, *Autobiography*, 120-23; Myer M. Cohen, *Notices of Florida and the Campaigns* (Charleston, S. C., 1836), 81, 86-89; John C. Casey to Lt. F. Searle, August 25, 1837, in Thomas Sidney Jesup Papers (War Department Files, National Archives), No. 2; and the author's "Florida Slaves and Free Negroes in the Seminole War, 1835-1842," *Journal of Negro History*, XXVIII (October 1943), 393.

Abraham, Caesar, and their associates did not neglect the three or four hundred free colored people of East Florida, nearly half of whom were residents of St. Augustine and vicinity. These free blacks had much more to lose and less to gain by supporting Seminole resistance than did the plantation slaves, but they were disgruntled at having recently been deprived of the privileges they had enjoyed under Spanish law and at being put under a territorial code so severe that it had inspired protests even from prominent white citizens.[23] Abraham and the others did not call on those comparatively few free Negroes to rise in arms but rather to furnish supplies and information. With their help, and with that of the Spanish, Indian, and Negro fishermen, lumbermen, and smugglers of the Southern coast, Abraham proceeded to build up a reserve of ammunition. After the war had been going on for a year he reportedly was still receiving consignments of powder, disguised as barrels of flour, from a free St. Augustine Negro.[24]

Near the end of December 1835 the long-smoldering conflict broke out. The Seminole did not wait for brevet Brigadier General Duncan L. Clinch to attempt to carry out his threat that if they were not at Tampa Bay by January 8, 1836, he would remove them forcibly. Instead they took the initiative. On December 26-27 King Philip's Indians and Indian Negroes, with the assistance of many cane-field slaves, fell on the sugar plantations of the St. Johns valley. On December 28 Micanopy's Indian and Negro warriors ambushed and annihilated brevet Major Francis L. Dade's command of over a hundred men near the Wahoo Swamp; an intelligent and literate slave named Luis Pacheco, who had been hired as guide and interpreter to Dade's command, is said to have assisted the hostiles in laying their fatal ambush.[25] Two days later Micanopy's band—numbering from 200 to 250 warriors, of whom from 30 to 50 were Negroes—repulsed 600 regulars and militiamen from the Withlacoochee. Of the three Seminole killed and five wounded in this action, two of the slain and three of the wounded were Negroes.[26]

[23] Carter (ed.), *Territorial Papers*, XXIV, 800-802.

[24] Thomas Sidney Jesup to Brig. Gen. J. M. Hernandez, January 21, 1837, in Jesup Papers, box 14.

[25] *Niles' Weekly Register*, XLIX (January 30, 1836), 365-70; Smith, *Sketch of the Seminole War*, 36-37; Cohen, *Notices of Florida*, 72; Sprague, *Origin of the Florida War*, 91. See also the author's "Louis Pacheco: The Man and the Myth," *Journal of Negro History*, XXVIII (January 1943), 65-72, and "The Early Life of Luis Pacheco né Fatio," *Negro History Bulletin*, VII (December 1943), 52, 54, 62, 64.

[26] Sprague, *Origin of the Florida War*, 92-93.

For many of the whites on the St. Johns, the destruction of Dade's command was less horrifying than the enthusiasm with which plantation slaves rallied to the hostiles. Although the young South Carolina volunteer and writer W. W. Smith insisted that with very few exceptions the slaves preferred to remain in their "happy and secure state of servitude," Florida planters and militia officers in closer contact with the situation were under no such illusions. Nearly 400 Negroes, it was reported, "have joined the Indians and are more desperate than the Indians." That most of them were not captives but volunteers was evidenced by the numbers seen under arms and in war paint. With their support the Seminole swept through the region east of the St. Johns and south of St. Augustine with torch and tomahawk, driving the population to take refuge in St. Augustine and other places of comparative safety.[27] Slave recruitment did not end with the early weeks of the uprising but continued into the spring and summer.

The slave uprising on the St. Johns spread alarm, indeed almost hysteria, throughout Florida and even into adjacent states.[28] The situation in St. Augustine, where displaced planters had taken refuge with such of their Negroes as had not "moved off" with the Seminole, was particularly critical. With several hundred Negroes who were well acquainted with the Indians and their language concentrated within the city walls, "strong apprehensions were felt . . . that they would fire the town, and that, during the confusion," the Indians, "influenced by revenge, cupidity, and the advice of their black counsellors," might attempt to rush the city itself. The St. Augustine whites also had to guard against attempts by Seminole emissaries to enter the town in order to stir up the Negroes and to obtain information, and at the same time forestall attempts by local Negroes to escape to the hostiles with information and supplies. Despite the vigilance of all the available dismounted force, Negroes did escape, meet with the hostiles, and return. Florida passed a bill providing that free Negroes

[27] For the participation of plantation slaves in depredations during the early days of the war, see Porter, "Florida Slaves and Free Negroes," 393-95. See also Mrs. Jane Murray Sheldon, "Seminole Attacks near New Smyrna, 1835-1856 [sic]," *Florida Historical Quarterly*, VIII (April 1930), 188-96; Earl C. Tanner (ed.), "The Early Career of Edwin T. Jenckes: A Florida Pioneer of the 1830's," *Florida Historical Quarterly*, XXX (January 1952), 270-75; *American State Papers, Military Affairs*, VII, 259; Sprague, *Origin of the Florida War*, 106; Smith, *Sketch of the Seminole War*, 20-23.

[28] Porter, "Florida Slaves and Free Negroes," 395-98; Carter (ed.), *Territorial Papers*, XXV, 283.

aiding the Seminole should be sold into slavery, and Major Benjamin A. Putnam of the Florida militia urged Governor Richard K. Call on July 26, 1836, to see to the strict enforcement of this law, suggesting a standing court-martial to deal summarily with captured Negroes. A few days later the Major wrote to Secretary of War Lewis Cass that "if strong measures were not taken to restrain our slaves, there is but little doubt that we should soon be assailed with a servile as well as Indian war."[29] The Major was still unwilling to admit that the war was already what he said he feared it would become.

Sporadic but frequently heavy fighting meanwhile continued in the Withlacoochee region. The Negroes, their ranks swelled by recent runaways, bore at least their full share of the "burden and heat of the day." Two authorities agreed on an estimated total of 250 Negro fighting men (a figure which one divided into 100 "Indian slaves" and 150 runaways) as compared to 1,450-1,650 Indian warriors; but when General Edmund P. Gaines was besieged on the Withlacoochee early in March by a force estimated at about 1,500 warriors, one observer said "there might have been four or five hundred negroes among them." Of three Seminole killed during the siege one was a Negro.[30] The principal action of an October expedition was an attack on a Negro town protected by a stream, but the Negro warriors, posted in and behind trees and assisted by Indian comrades, gave the troops such a warm reception that they were unable to cross.[31] An expedition of the following month drove a body of hostiles into the Wahoo Swamp, where—outnumbered more than three to one—they turned at bay. The force consisted of an estimated 420 Indian warriors and 200 Negro fighting men, "one of the most distinguished leaders" of whom was "a negro, the property of a Florida planter." The whites claimed a victory but on November 21 withdrew.[32]

The first year of the war had ended in complete failure to repress Seminole resistance. Early in December 1836, however, Major General Thomas Sidney Jesup assumed command in Flor-

[29] Porter, "Florida Slaves and Free Negroes," 396-98; Carter (ed.), *Territorial Papers*, XXV, 265, 327-28.

[30] Sprague, *Origin of the Florida War*, 97, 112-13; *Army and Navy Chronicle*, VIII (March 7, 1839), 154; II (1836), 151; *American State Papers, Military Affairs*, VII, 369.

[31] *American State Papers, Military Affairs*, VI, 998; *Niles' Weekly Register*, LI (November 5, 1836), 148-49.

[32] Sprague, *Origin of the Florida War*, 162-66; *Court of Inquiry—Operations in Florida*, 52.

ida. Jesup, recognizing the importance of the Negroes, immediately set about ascertaining their number and location. "Micanopy, Philip, and Cooper [Osoochee] . . . each with from one hundred and twenty to two hundred Indian and Negro warriors—the latter, perhaps, the more numerous"—were reported not far from Jesup's encampment. Osceola, Jumper, and Little Alligator also had numerous Negro followers. It was at this point that the General delivered his famous judgment that this was a Negro and not an Indian war.[33]

Shifting from the attempt to crush Seminole resistance in the field, Jesup instituted a policy of hunting down and capturing the Seminole in their camps, particularly the women and children, who could be used to exert powerful pressure for surrender upon the hostiles. He put special emphasis on raiding Negro villages, a device not original with him[34] but which under his command was made effective for the first time. Jesup was greatly assisted in his program by a regiment of Creek scouts who had been promised "such plunder as they may take from the Seminoles"—"plunder" being understood to mean primarily captured Negroes. From early December 1836 to late January 1837 Jesup's troops were engaged in combing the swamps, destroying villages, and driving to the east such Indians and Negroes as they failed to kill or capture. Their captives numbered 131, nearly all Negroes and mostly women and children. Their greatest triumph was breaking up Osceola's headquarters, a Negro village in the Panosufkee swamp, and capturing fifty-two of his Negro followers and three Indians.[35]

The "principal Indian and negro force . . . retired from the Ocklawaha . . . towards the head of the Caloosahatchee," and on January 27 the army was close on its heels. A captured Negro said "a large number of negroes were in advance, and from forty to fifty Indians, with Abraham . . . in our rear." A sudden dash resulted in the seizure of the Negro baggage train of over 100 ponies and in the capture of something over twenty prisoners, mostly Negro women and children. The main body of the Seminole plunged into the Great Cypress Swamp and in a running fight

[33] Porter, "Florida Slaves and Free Negroes," 400.

[34] *Niles' Weekly Register,* L (May 14, 1836), 188, and LII (April 1, 1837), 71; *American State Papers, Military Affairs,* VII, 277.

[35] *American State Papers, Military Affairs,* VII, 820, 825-28; *Army and Navy Chronicle,* IV (January 5, 1837), 12, and (February 2, 1837), 79, 111; "Major Childs, U.S.A.: Extracts from His Correspondence with His Family," *Historical Magazine,* s. 3, II (December 1873), 371-72; Sprague, *Origin of the Florida War,* 167, 170-71.

killed two Marines and wounded four others. The bodies of two Negroes and an Indian were found on the field, and several more Negroes were captured.[36]

Jesup then conceived the idea of using a Negro captive named Ben, one of Micanopy's principal "slaves," to negotiate with Abraham and through him with the head chief and his circle. The Seminole had been roughly handled and might therefore be in a receptive mood, but no important warrior had surrendered or been captured. "The warriors," Jesup commented, "have fought as long as they had life, and such seems to me to be the determination of those who influence their councils—I mean the leading negroes."[37] Conciliation of the Negroes was seen as essential to successful negotiations.

Recent developments near St. Augustine had made Jesup particularly anxious to terminate the war. His campaign had driven Osceola's and Micanopy's people toward King Philip's territory. Philip himself, old and weary, hesitated to act, but his chief Negro, John Caesar, recognized the necessity of a diversion and organized a guerrilla campaign, employing principally runaway slaves. His campaign, however, was brief. Interrupted on January 17, 1837, in a horse-stealing raid on a plantation only two miles west of St. Augustine, his band was trailed to their camp; Caesar and two others, including a young free Negro named Joe Merritt, were killed and the rest fled in confusion. One would have expected such a coup to produce general satisfaction among the white population of St. Augustine, but actually it caused more alarm than relief. That a band composed almost entirely of Negroes—and plantation slaves at that—should have dared a raid so close to the city, and that their abandoned packs should have contained articles recently purchased in local shops, revived something of the panic of a year before. The city council, declaring that "we know not how soon firebrands may be thrown amongst us," demanded that the militia company responsible for the disruption of Caesar's band be kept near home and "employed to scour the country in the neighborhood."[38]

The most important and far-reaching effect of Caesar's abortive

[36] "Major Childs," 372-73; *American State Papers, Military Affairs,* VII, 828-30; *Court of Inquiry—Operations in Florida,* 69-70; *Niles' Weekly Register,* LII (March 11, 1837), 30-31; Sprague, *Origin of the Florida War,* 170-72.

[37] *American State Papers, Military Affairs,* VII, 828-30, 832; "Major Childs," 373; *Army and Navy Chronicle,* IV (February 2, 1837), 80, and VIII (March 7, 1839), 154-55.

[38] Porter, "John Caesar," 197-201, and "Florida Slaves and Free Negroes," 401-404.

raid, however, was on Jesup. This raid was doubtless in his mind when on January 21 he wrote to General J. M. Hernandez of the Florida militia—one of whose slaves had been in Caesar's band—denouncing the father of the slain Joe Merritt as an agent of Abraham and reiterating, "This war . . . is a negro, not an Indian war."[39] Doubtless, too, it was in his mind a few days later when he sent out the Indian Negro Ben to arrange for a meeting with Abraham.

On January 31 the Seminole Negroes, and Abraham in particular, undertook a new and important role. An army officer has described them as "a most cruel and malignant enemy . . . active . . . blood-thirsty and cruel"; but the Seminole Negro leaders, even fierce old John Caesar, although opposed to a surrender which would expose them to servitude had never been averse to negotiations.[40] Abraham now had the responsibility both of interpreting the talks between the General and the chiefs and of seeing to it that any peace terms should be acceptable to the Negroes.

Jesup's *sine qua non* for peace was immediate emigration. "There would be no difficulty in making peace . . . were it not for that condition . . . . The negroes . . . who rule the Indians, are all averse to removing to so cold a climate."[41] The Negro Abraham, however, an intelligent and widely-traveled man who had been on a mission to Washington, D. C., and another to the Indian Territory, recognized the impossibility of achieving a decent life in Florida in the face of the government's determined attitude. His objective had been to put up a strong resistance until the Negroes were given satisfactory assurances. Now he felt that the time was ripe for negotiations.

The negotiations went on for over a month. On March 6, 1837, representatives of Micanopy and of Alligator—among the latter the subsequently famous Indian-Negro subchief John Ca-Wy-Ya (Cavallo)—signed an agreement to suspend hostilities and for the entire Nation to move to the west, for the performance of which the Indians gave hostages. The provisions affecting the Negroes were necessarily in cryptic language: "Major General Jesup, in behalf of the United States, agrees that the Seminoles and their allies who come in, and emigrate to the West, shall be secure in their lives and property; that their negroes, their *bona fide* property, shall accompany them to the West . . . ." By "their

[39] Jesup Papers, box 14.
[40] Sprague, *Origin of the Florida War*, 100, 81; Porter, "John Caesar," 194-96.
[41] *American State Papers, Military Affairs*, VII, 827.

allies" the Seminole understood the Negroes living among them, and since before the war an estimated four-fifths of the Seminole Negroes, including Abraham, were runaway slaves—and during the war the Seminole had been joined by several hundred more runaways—the Seminole "allies" numbered far more Negroes than the Seminole "slaves." But at this point no United States army officer could explicitly provide for the transportation west of Negroes on whom United States citizens might have a claim; brevet Major General Winfield Scott, one of Jesup's predecessors, had been specifically directed to "allow no pacification with the Indians while a living slave, belonging to a white man, remained in their possession."[42]

Jesup, nevertheless, at first intended to carry out his agreement in good faith. "The negroes," he wrote on March 26, "rule the Indians, and it is important that they should feel themselves secure; if they should become alarmed and hold out, the war will be renewed." But by the end of the month so many Seminole had assembled at Tampa Bay that the General became overconfident and, under pressure from Florida planters, decided to change his interpretation of the agreement. On April 8 he entered into a clandestine arrangement with Coi Hajo and other chiefs "to surrender the Negroes taken during the war." It was easier, however, to make such an agreement than carry it out. Some of the "captured Negroes," to be sure, had been taken against their will and were glad to be returned to their masters, but others, when they heard of the new arrangement, banded together for defense whether against white men or Indians. They were supported by more militant Indians like Osceola, who, when Coi Hajo announced in council that the runaways were to be returned, rose in a rage, declaring that so long as he was in the Nation it should never be done.[43]

Apparently Jesup had not sufficiently considered that legally most of the influential Seminole Negroes were as much the slaves of white men as were the recent runaways. When several Floridians arrived in the emigration camp to search for slaves the Negroes and many Indians fled.[44] On June 2 the young militants, Osceola, Philip's son Wild Cat, and John Cavallo, seized and carried away the Seminole hostages given under the terms of the

---

[42] Porter, "Florida Slaves and Free Negroes," 404-405; *American State Papers, Military Affairs,* VII, 834; *Message from the President . . . Relative to Indian Hostilities in Florida,* Senate Docs., 24 Cong., 1 Sess., No. 152 (Serial 281), 5.
[43] Porter, "Florida Slaves and Free Negroes," 404-407.
[44] *Ibid.,* 408-409.

truce. "All is lost," Jesup despairingly announced, "and principally . . . by the influence of the Negroes."[45] The Seminole force was still largely intact, although an estimate that the warriors in East Florida numbered 2,500, not including Negroes, "who fight as well as the best of them,"[46] was probably an exaggeration.

Jesup was reduced to drafting plans for the future—the confusion of which indicated his own confused state of mind—and putting the best face possible on an admittedly bad situation. He was principally concerned with preventing the war from developing any further slave unrest. "The two races, the negro and the Indian," he declared, "are rapidly approximating; they are identified in interests and feelings." Plantation slaves had been prominent in depredations and one had occupied a position of leadership. "Should the Indians remain in this territory," Jesup continued, "the negroes among them will form a rallying point for runaway negroes from the adjacent states; and if they remove, the fastnesses of the country will be immediately occupied by negroes." But, somewhat inconsistently, he believed that the Indians would agree to "surrender all runaway slaves" if permitted to remain in "a small district near Florida Point."[47]

He also pointed out that he had been able to turn over about ninety captured Negroes to their legal owners and, much more important, had seized over a hundred Indian Negroes, among them a score of warriors including Abraham and three other chiefs. "The negro portion of the hostile force of the Seminole nation not taken," the General optimistically declared, "is entirely without a head."[48] More significantly, the capitulation had committed to emigration, on conditions, the most powerful East Florida group, the Alachua, or "original" Seminole, under Micanopy. And with Micanopy's chief Negro, Abraham, still in his hands, Jesup was well equipped to reopen negotiations with the Micanopy group and, through them, with other groups.[49]

[45] Jesup to Brig. Gen. R. Jones, October 21, 1837, in War Department, AGO Files (National Archives), 207; *Seminole Indians—Prisoners of War: Letter from the Secretary of War . . .* , House Docs., 25 Cong., 2 Sess., No. 327 (Serial 329), 10-11; *Negroes, &c., Captured from Indians*, 18; *Niles' Weekly Register*, LIII (December 23, 1837), 263.

[46] Lt. Col. W. S. Harney to Jesup, May 4, 1837 (photostat, Florida Historical Society); *American State Papers, Military Affairs*, VII, 871; *Army and Navy Chronicle*, IV (1837), 329.

[47] Porter, "Florida Slaves and Free Negroes," 409-11.

[48] *American State Papers, Military Affairs*, VII, 842, 851-52; *Negroes, &c., Captured from Indians*, 18, 65-69.

[49] Grant Foreman, *Indian Removal: The Emigration of the Five Civilized Tribes*

The 1837 summer season was, as usual, uneventful, but early in September a serious break appeared within the Seminole ranks. It involved the Seminole Negroes, previously regarded as the strongest element of the hostiles. It came at a point where the Negroes in the Indian country had been quantitatively strengthened but qualitatively weakened by the mass recruitment of plantation slaves. Twenty months of fighting and hardship since the revolt of the St. Johns plantation slaves had operated to separate the strong, determined, freedom-loving Negroes from those who had been merely caught up in the enthusiasm of the December days and were now ready to exchange freedom to go hungry in the swamps for the regular rations of servitude. Early in September plantation Negroes, half-naked, "haggard and emaciated," began to straggle into forts and camps with pitiable tales of ill-treatment by the Indians. By mid-November over fifty had surrendered. Far more important, John Philip, a "slave" of King Philip and a former member of Caesar's daring guerrilla band, was persuaded by his wife, a plantation Negro, to "come in" and surrender.

The surrender on September 8 of John Philip, whom Jesup now enthusiastically identified as "the only negro chief who had not been previously seized," was comparable to pushing over the first of a line of upright dominoes. The Indian Negro volunteered to guide a detachment to the camp of King Philip, who was captured with his entire party.[50] When King Philip's son Wild Cat learned of this, he rode to St. Augustine and offered, in exchange for his father's release, to bring in Philip's subordinate chiefs for a "talk" and to return all captured Negroes. Seventy-nine Negroes were shortly on their way, although probably under no compulsion since they were unescorted and said to be "in a starving condition." Later, however, the theory was advanced that Wild

of Indians (Norman, Okla., 1932), 349; "Letters of Samuel Forry, Surgeon, U. S. Army, 1837-1838," *Florida Historical Quarterly,* VI (January 1928), 214.

[50] Jacob Rhett Motte, *Journey into Wilderness: An Army Surgeon's Account of Life in Camp and Field During the Creek and Seminole Wars, 1836-1838,* James F. Sunderman, ed. (Gainesville, Fla., 1953), 116-23, 132-33; *American State Papers, Military Affairs,* VII, 849-50, 882; *Army and Navy Chronicle,* V (September 28, 1837), 200, 203; Capt. Harvey Brown to Lt. J. A. Chambers, October 8, 1837, in Interior Department, Indian Office (Emigration) Files (National Archives), 1837 (196/447); *Court of Inquiry—Operations in Florida,* 181, 109-12; Capt. Nathan S. Jarvis, "An Army Surgeon's Notes of Frontier Service, 1833-1848," *Journal of the Military Service Institution of the United States,* XL (January-February 1908), 277-78; *Niles' Weekly Register,* LIII (September 30, 1837), 66.

Cat and his followers had intended to rescue King Philip and that the Negroes had been sent to be on hand for the attack.[51]

Micanopy and his associates in the meantime had sent the young Negro-Indian subchief John Cavallo to confer with King Philip, Wild Cat, Osceola, and their associates and, if necessary, to interpret between them and white officers. A conference at the Indians' camp near St. Augustine between these chiefs and Hernandez, who represented Jesup, was arranged, but Cavallo's part in carrying away the hostages in June caused Jesup, who had come to expect "foul play" wherever Cavallo was involved, to order Hernandez to have him and the other Seminole seized at once if they did not reply satisfactorily to a specified set of questions in regard to surrendering "captured Negroes." While the chiefs were discussing these and other questions they were surrounded and captured.[52]

Wild Cat and Cavallo remained prisoners less than six weeks. On the night of November 29-30 they with eighteen others escaped from Fort Marion—with the help, Jesup was convinced, of local Negroes.[53] Their escape, however, had come too late to prevent a series of important surrenders. On November 30, Osceola's family and about forty plantation slaves surrendered,[54] and a few days later all chiefs belonging to Micanopy's group except Alligator agreed to give themselves up.

By December 1837 two opposing movements had set in among the Seminole Indians and Negroes still at large. One was toward the emigration camp. About fifty Indian Negroes proceeded to Tampa Bay, in response either to the orders of Micanopy and his group or to new appeals from Jesup promising them "something . . . GOOD" if they would "get away from the Indians."[55] The

[51] Motte, *Journey into Wilderness*, 135-38; *Army and Navy Chronicle*, V (October 12, 1837), 236, and (October 26, 1837), 269-70; *Niles' Weekly Register*, LIII (October 14, 1837), 98, and (November 18, 1837), 178; "Letters of Samuel Forry," 88-105 *passim.*

[52] Motte, *Journey into Wilderness*, 138; Jarvis, "Army Surgeon's Notes," 278; *Army and Navy Chronicle*, V (November 2, 1837), 284-85, and (December 14, 1837), 377-78, and VII (July 26, 1838), 50; *Niles' Weekly Register*, LIII (November 4, 1837), 146, and (November 11, 1837), 165-66, and (December 23, 1837), 262-63; *Seminole Indians—Prisoners of War*, 2-8, 11; Hernandez to Jesup, October 22, 1837, and Jesup to Jones, October 21, 1837, both in War Department, AGO Files.

[53] See the author's "Seminole Flight from Fort Marion," *Florida Historical Quarterly*, XXII (January 1944), 112-33, esp. 121.

[54] Jarvis, "Army Surgeon's Notes," 285; Frank L. White (ed.), "The Journals of Lieutenant John Pickell, 1836-1837," *Florida Historical Quarterly*, XXXVIII (October 1959), 159-60.

[55] Brig. Gen. W. K. Armistead to Lt. J. A. Chambers, December 20, 25, 1837,

other current was toward the lower Kissimmee and Lake Okee-chobee where Wild Cat, Sam Jones, Alligator, and Cavallo were mustering die-hard Indians and Negroes for a last-ditch stand. Most of the Seminole Negroes still at large moved toward the camps of these stalwarts. In fact, some Negroes who had started out toward Tampa Bay turned back to join the resistance forces.[56]

During a period of about a month these die-hards fought three of the most savage battles of the seven-year war. On Christmas 1837, 380 Indians and Negroes, with Lake Okeechobee behind them and a swamp in front, met an attack by Colonel Zachary Taylor's thousand regulars and militia. Before the Indian-Negro force retreated they had killed twenty-six men and wounded over a hundred others. The bodies of eleven Indians and only one or two Negroes were found on the field, which suggests that Okee-chobee was principally an Indian battle; probably most of the Negroes who had separated from Tampa-bound masters had not yet reached the camp of the holdouts. On January 15, 1838, how-ever, a landing party of sailors and regulars near Jupiter Inlet was furiously attacked and badly routed, and nine days later Jesup himself encountered at the Locha Hatchee a force estimated at from two to three hundred Indian warriors and "probably as many negroes." This was believed to be the same force which had defeated the whites at Jupiter Inlet. In both encounters the whites suffered heavy losses.[57]

After these costly engagements Jesup built a stockade called Fort Jupiter and considered his next move. His officers urged ending the war by a treaty which would permit the Seminole to remain in the southern part of the peninsula, a plan in accord with the General's own views and one which, when finally carried out over four years later, terminated the war. Negroes who had sur-rendered reported that if permitted to remain in Florida the Indians "would . . . sell and deliver up the plantation negroes." Jesup communicated his plan to Washington and sent out a Semi-nole Negro to invite the chiefs to a conference. By the end of Feb-ruary about 400 Indians and perhaps 150 Indian Negroes were

---

in Jesup Papers, box 5; Lt. R. W. Kirkham to Jesup, August 1, 1846, with state-ment by Tony Barnett, May 14, 1846, in War Department, QMGO Consolidated Files (National Archives).

[56] See, for example, White (ed.), "Journals of Lt. Pickell," 167.

[57] Sprague, *Origin of the Florida War*, 203-14, esp. 214; "The Battle of Okee Chobee," *United States Magazine* (February 1857); *Niles' Weekly Register*, LIII (February 17, 1838), 388, and (February 10, 1838), 369-71; *Army and Navy Chronicle*, VII (July 26, 1838), 49-54; Motte, *Journey into Wilderness*, 195.

encamped near the fort. The Negroes, according to a fascinated and repelled Southern officer, were "the most diabolical looking wretches I ever saw. . . . They had none of the servility of our northern blacks, but were constantly offering their dirty paws with as much hauteur and nonchalance as if they were conferring a vast deal of honor."

Jesup, however, was even more pleased with the presence of these Negroes, whatever their appearance, than he was with that of the larger number of Indians. Convinced that the Negroes would be a source of difficulty so long as they remained in Florida, that the Indians would not surrender so long as the Negroes held out, and that the Negroes would not give in until assured of their freedom, he appealed through Seminole Negro emissaries to "the negro chiefs August & John Cavallo" and to another named July, "to whom, and to their people, I promised freedom and protection on their separating from the Indians and surrendering." This was the vague "something . . . GOOD" hinted at the previous December.

The attraction of the offer was not, of course, "freedom" from Seminole "masters" but rather the "protection" of a United States general and United States troops against claims or kidnapping by whites. As Indian Negroes in Florida would be a constant encouragement to runaways, "it was stipulated that they should be sent to the west, as a part of the Seminole nation" which had already migrated; Abraham, however, assured them that it was a fine country, though a bit chilly, and certainly preferable to the Everglades. During February and March the Negro chiefs August and July, reassured by these promises, voluntarily came in with about 150 Indian Negroes and five slaves of white citizens. Most of the Indian Negroes were promptly sent off "to join their masters," as an officer put it, "in their new homes west of the Mississippi."[58]

But how could Jesup justify granting freedom to Negroes four-fifths of whom were either runaways or their descendants and thus legally slaves? The answer is, of course, wartime necessity. In the first place, the Negroes were regarded as more dangerous

[58] Jesup to Wm. L. Marcy, April 5, 1848, in Jesup Papers, box 15; Kirkham to Jesup, August 1, 1846, with statement by Barnett, May 14, 1846, in War Department, QMGO Consolidated Files; Jesup to Wm. L. Marcy, July 1, 1848, in Interior Department, Indian Office, Seminole Files (National Archives), W-244, and M. Arbuckle to Brig. Gen. R. Jones, January 8, 1849, *ibid.*, J-143; *American State Papers, Military Affairs,* VII, 825-26; *Official Opinions of the Attorneys General of the United States* . . . (Washington, 1852-   ), IV, 720-29; *Army and Navy Chronicle,* VI (March 22, 1838), 177, 190; Motte, *Journey into Wilderness,* 207, 210-11; Sprague, *Origin of the Florida War,* 193-95.

than the Indians; persuading the Negroes to surrender would weaken the Indians "more than they would be weakened by the loss of the same number of their own people."[59] In the second place, it was imperative to remove from the slaveholding South all Negroes who had tasted freedom and knew the fortress of Florida. A well-informed officer commented,

The negroes, from the commencement of the Florida war, have, for their numbers, been the most formidable foe, more bloodthirsty, active, and revengeful, than the Indians. . . . The negro, returned to his original owner, might have remained a few days, when he again would have fled to the swamps, more vindictive than ever. . . . Ten resolute negroes, with a knowledge of the country, are sufficient to desolate the frontier, from one extent to the other.[60]

The sort of thing Jesup feared was illustrated by a communication of February 10, 1839, from an officer at Fort Heileman, stating that the recalcitrant Creek Indians had "all left the Okefenokee & gone South," presumably to join the hostile Seminole. "There were seven runaway negroes from Georgia among them," the officer continued, "well armed & plenty of ammunition . . . the negroes have done most of the mischief in that quarter; the negroes also have left and on their way south burned the houses in the vicinity."[61]

Jesup had adopted the policy of shipping all Indian Negroes west as early as the preceding September, when he had revoked his promise to his Creek allies that they should have all the enemy property they could capture and offered instead to purchase their claims to ninety captured Indian Negroes for $8,000, since, as he wrote, "it is highly important to the slave-holding States that these negroes be sent out of the country." The Creeks declined this less than generous offer, but the army hung on to the Negroes claimed by the Creeks and succeeded in delivering them in the Indian Territory.[62]

To give his policy legal justification Jesup resorted to the fiction that *all* Indian Negroes, instead of a·small minority, were legitimate Indian property. One statement of his order was that "all the property [*sic*] of the Seminole Indians . . . who separated

[59] Jesup to Brig. Gen. R. Jones, February 28, 1838, in Seminole Files, W-244.

[60] Sprague, *Origin of the Florida War*, 309.

[61] Col. D. E. Twiggs to Gen. A. Macomb, February 10, 1839, in War Department, AGO Files, 66.

[62] *American State Papers, Military Affairs*, VII, 882; *Negroes, &c., Captured from Indians*, 20-22, 70-71; Foreman, *Indian Removal*, 347, 349, 365-66.

themselves [*sic*] from the Indians, and delivered themselves up to the Commanding officer of the troops, should be free."[63] Technically, this order would apply only to that small minority to whom Indians had valid title and to only those in that small group who actually "separated themselves" from the Indians. As a practical matter, however, all Indian Negroes who came in were promptly marched to the emigration camp and embarked for the West.

Later, in 1841, the War Department decided that the 1832 treaty of Payne's Landing had canceled all claims against the Indians for any Negroes run away or captured prior to that treaty. "No demand can therefore be recognized for any negroes except those lost since the date of the treaty, unless the Indians are willing to give them up voluntarily. All except these must positively be removed with the Indians to the West . . . ." Still another legal fiction was developed in regard to those Negroes whose status as "Indian slaves" was most doubtful—who were, indeed, with little question the legal slaves of white citizens, captured or run away since the Payne's Landing treaty. The War Department order that these Negroes "should be surrendered" contained the all-important proviso, "unless the effect of this would be to prevent the Indians from coming in and removing." If so, "it will be better, rather than incur this danger that even the negroes to which the whites have a valid claim should also be removed."[64] On August 19, 1841, accordingly, Lieutenant Colonel W. J. Worth announced, "Indians have been solemnly guaranteed retention of slaves indifferently . . . to the mode or time . . . they obtained possession. . . ." That is, if an Indian claimed a Negro, his claim would be recognized without necessity of legal proof, while the citizen claiming such a Negro was, "upon identifying and proving property, paid a fair equivalent, determined upon by a board of officers." In defense of his policy Worth pointed out that "if . . . the swamps of Florida become . . . the resort of runaways, their intelligence, so superior to the Indian, might impose upon the general government a contest quadruplicate in time and treasure than that now being waged."[65]

Although the policy of ignoring the legal status of even recent runaways was not publicly and explicitly announced until 1841,

[63] Certificate from Bvt. Brig. Gen. Z. Taylor, April 30, 1840, in Interior Department, Indian Office Files.

[64] Carter (ed.), *Territorial Papers*, XXVI, 282-83.

[65] Sprague, *Origin of the Florida War*, 309-310; Porter, "Florida Slaves and Free Negroes," 419.

it had been applied several times by 1838. The classic example was that of the famous Luis Pacheco, who, despite his well-known status as slave to Mrs. Antonio Pacheco, had been shipped out of the country as a slave of Chief Jumper, because Jesup thought he was too dangerous to be left in Florida.[66]

Most of the slaves who during the war escaped from plantations or were captured by the Seminole probably were recovered by their owners, principally by voluntary surrender, but those recent runaways who were unwilling to return to plantation slavery and could induce Indians to claim them—no difficult task—could go west with the more legitimate "Indian slaves."

So far as the formidable Seminole Negroes were concerned, the war was practically over by the end of March 1838. During the campaign of September 1837-March 1838, about 250 Seminole Negroes had surrendered or been captured; Operation Fort Jupiter alone had accounted for the taking of 167 Negroes (including fifteen slaves of whites), over forty of whom were warriors, "nearly all armed with rifles." Over 500 Indians, too, had been made prisoners, for when the Secretary of War refused to approve Jesup's peace terms, the General on March 21 simply surrounded their camps near Fort Jupiter and scouring the country that night and the next two days succeeded in rounding up that number.[67]

Jesup was still confronted with the problem of the Negroes and Indians who, justifiably suspicious of all promises, had stayed away from Fort Jupiter. A large part of the Negroes still out were with Alligator and Cavallo, the last Negro chief still in the field. To them the General dispatched the Negro counselor Abraham and Holatoochee, said to have been Cavallo's brother-in-law. Their mission resulted in the surrender of Alligator, "with 88 of his people, among whom was John Cowaya and 27 blacks," and Alligator's capitulation led to the surrender during April of about 360 more Indians and Negroes, including 100 warriors.[68]

These captures and surrenders reduced any future actions to mere raids and skirmishes. They also marked the disappearance of Negroes as a major element in Seminole resistance. A few hos-

[66] *Negroes, &c., Captured from Indians,* 93-94; *Report . . . [on] the Petition of Joseph Elzaudi, House Reports,* 30 Cong., 1 Sess., No. 187 (Serial 524), 1-6; Edwin C. McReynolds, *The Seminoles* (Norman, Okla., 1957), 240.

[67] *Negroes, &c., Captured from Indians,* 25, 81-89; *Army and Navy Chronicle,* VI (April 19, 1838), 248, and (April 26, 1838), 269; Jarvis, "Army Surgeon's Notes," 453-54.

[68] Sprague, *Origin of the Florida War,* 195; *Niles' Weekly Register,* LIV (May 5, 1838), 145; Abraham to Jesup, April 25, 1838, in *Florida Historical Quarterly,* XXV (July 1946), 38-39.

tile Negroes, both "Indian Negroes" and recent runaways, continued as interpreters, counselors, and fighting men, and their influence with the hostile Indians was recognized in the government's decision of 1841 to abandon the idea of restoring "to their rightful owners" any slaves still among the Indians and instead remove them all to the west.[69] But we usually glimpse these Negroes fleetingly and singly[70]—in sharp contrast to the days when Negro warriors were numbered in the hundreds and on some occasions were reportedly as numerous as the Indians. Wild Cat's sadly shrunken band probably included the greatest number of remaining Negroes, some of whom he skillfully employed as spies, but when he was seized in May 1841 his immediate following consisted of fifteen Indians and three Negroes. The company of 229 in which he was shipped west the following October included eighteen Negroes.[71]

The Seminole Negroes, having lost their importance as a factor in resistance, assumed the comparatively new role of government agents whose task it was to induce hostile Indians to surrender. Negro guides, interpreters, and negotiators—often in co-operation with Indian chiefs who had surrendered—were indispensable in establishing contact and communicating with the remaining hostile Indian leaders and, if they remained obdurate, in assisting the troops to locate their camps.

Several Negro guides and interpreters performed outstanding service. Sandy Perryman distinguished himself by locating and bringing in a number of chiefs to Fort King on May 17, 1839, for negotiations which resulted in an agreement that, in return for peace, the Indians should be permitted at least temporarily to remain in Southern Florida. Two months later, however, a band of Indians not parties to this agreement massacred on the Caloosahatchee a party for which Sandy was serving as interpreter and put him to death by torture.[72] Negro John, a "captured" slave of Dr. H. B. Crews, served as guide to the aggressive Lieutenant Colonel W. S. Harney on an expedition of December 1840

[69] Carter (ed.), *Territorial Papers*, XXVI, 276-77, 374-75.

[70] *Army and Navy Chronicle*, IX (August 8, 1839), 93, and XI (October 22, 1840), 268-69; *Niles' Weekly Register*, LIV (August 18, 1838), 386, and LVIII (May 23, 1840), 179-80, and (June 27, 1840), 260, and LX (April 10, 1841), 90; Hester Perrine Walker, "Massacre at Indian Key, Aug. 7, 1840, and the Death of Dr. Henry Perrine," *Florida Historical Quarterly*, V (July 1926), 26-27.

[71] Sprague, *Origin of the Florida War*, 277, 280, 322.

[72] *Army and Navy Chronicle*, VIII (June 13, 1839), 379, and X (January 16, 1840), 39-40; *Niles' Weekly Register*, LVI (July 20, 1839), 321, and LVII (September 14, 1839), 44; Sprague, *Origin of the Florida War*, 233, 316.

which resulted in the killing of the Spanish Indian chief Chekika, a leader in the Caloosahatchee and Indian Key massacres, and eight of his warriors. John himself was wounded in the encounter.[73] Sampson, who had been wounded and taken prisoner in the Caloosahatchee massacre, escaped after two years and in December 1841 served with distinction as guide on an expedition into the Big Cypress which drove the hostiles out of their fastnesses and so softened them up that in the following summer the chiefs in Southern Florida accepted the peace agreement which they had flouted three years earlier, thus bringing the long war to an end.[74]

Most important of these Negro agents was John Cavallo, or Gopher John as he was called by the officers. He had been the last Negro chief to surrender, and it was he who was responsible for the suggestion that delegations of prominent chiefs should be brought from the Indian Territory as proof positive to the hostiles that those who had surrendered had not been put to death but had been both spared and well treated. This move, which utilized Cavallo's old commander Alligator and his brother-in-law Hola-toochee, proved highly effective. Cavallo was declared to have personally participated in bringing in 535 Indians and during the last two years of the war was very nearly the "indispensable man" in the army's relations both with the Indians who were still "out" and those who had finally consented to "come in."[75]

The decision to remove the Seminole from Florida was strongly influenced by the presence and position of the Negroes, and the Seminole Negroes also strongly influenced the general decision to resist removal. These Negroes were shrewd and farsighted in their plans for resistance and active and aggressive in carrying them out. Once convinced, however, that the government was inflexibly determined on Seminole removal, and persuaded, too, that if

[73] Logan Uriah Reavis, *The Life and Military Services of General William Selby Harney* (St. Louis, 1878), 144-45; *Niles' Weekly Register*, LX (April 3, 1841), 71-72; Lt. Col. W. S. Harney to Capt. W. W. Bliss, December 24, 1840, in War Department, AGO Files, A354, and "Old Book 3, Dept. of Florida, Bound as 1, Dept. of New Mexico, Feb. 1, 1842-Aug. 17, 1842," *ibid.*, 30.

[74] Sprague, *Origin of the Florida War*, 315-16, 357, 362, 364, 368, 370; White (ed.), "Journals of Lt. Pickell," 160.

[75] Kenneth W. Porter, "Davy Crockett and John Horse: A Possible Origin of the Coonskin Story," *American Literature*, XV (March 1943), 10-15; Brig. Gen. W. K. Armistead to the Adjutant General, June 15, 1840, in War Department, AGO Files, 1840-146. See also Letter Book of Officer Commanding 8th Infantry (1840-1842), 95, 100-101, 103, 113-14, and "Head Quarters 9th M Department: Letters, from June 2d. 1841 to February 1st. 1842," I, 95-96, 223, both in War Department, AGO Files.

they and the Indians surrendered, their own freedom and the lives of both would be respected, they were almost as influential in persuading the more recalcitrant Indians to surrender as they had previously been in rallying Seminole resistance. Prolonged as the war was, the promise of freedom to the Negroes "tended very materially towards affecting the main object": the emigration of the great majority of the tribe.[76] It also made possible the termination in August 1842 of a struggle which, having already lasted seven years, might otherwise have dragged on for another decade or more with the loss of millions of dollars to the government and hundreds of lives to both whites and Seminole.

[76] Capt. J. T. Sprague to Jesup, July 25, 184?, in War Department, QMGO Consolidated Files, "Seminoles."

Corrections and Additions

p. 249, l. 30-33: Although at least by early 1838, and probably earlier, John Cavallo was closely associated with Alligator, it is not altogether clear that he signed the agreement of March 6, 1837, as Alligator's representative.

FLORIDA SLAVES AND FREE NEGROES IN THE SEMINOLE WAR, 1835-1842

[Originally appeared in *JNH*, October, 1943 (Vol. XXVIII).]

At the outbreak of the Seminole War, the Negroes of Florida were divided into three categories: slaves to the whites, principally on the sugar plantations of the St. John's valley; free Negroes, the result of the lenity of the Spanish law which required the emancipation of any slave offering his master $300, principally in St. Augustine and vicinity; and "Indian Negroes," living among the Seminole, either as legal slaves, through purchases from Spaniards, English, or Americans, or, in a greater number of cases, runaways and their descendants, but all thoroughly identified in customs and interests with the Indians, at the worst as their favored dependents, at the best as advisers to the chief men of the tribe, and in no case treated as chattels.

The Seminole War, ostensibly caused by the insistence of the United States government on the removal of the Seminole to the Indian Territory, along with most of the other Indian tribes east of the Mississippi, in order to make room for white settlers and prevent border difficulties, was in large measure also urged on by the desire of slave traders and slave owners to gain possession of the Negroes living among the Seminole; on the other hand, the unwillingness of the Indians to leave the country in which they had established themselves was reinforced by the fear of the Seminole Negroes lest, emerging from their fastnesses for transportation to the west, they should be seized and enslaved.

All the parties to the controversy were well acquainted with one another. There had been peace between the whites and the Seminole ever since the annexation of Florida to the United States. The Indians and their Negroes had been accustomed to come frequently into St. Augustine and other towns to trade, and were familiar with the city and its inhabitants. Racial ties made the relations among the various categories of Florida Negroes particularly close. Many of the slave-men "had wives among the Indian negroes, and the Indian negroes had wives among them."[1] The Negro slave Louis Fatio, known, as Louis Pacheo, for having reputedly helped betray the first company of United States troops to encounter the hostiles, had both a brother and a sister among the Seminole; his wife was a free Negro woman.[2] Through the Indian Negroes, the plantation slaves and free Negroes became well acquainted with the Indians and even learned their language.[3] The contrast between the free and easy life of the Seminole Indians and their Negro associates and labor in bondage on the sugar plantations is believed to have aroused discontent among the Negro slaves. This is said to have caused Louis, on several occasions during his youth, to run away and spend some time among the Indians.

As 1835 drew to a close it became evident that arrival at a state of open hostilities was only a matter of time. Military preparations for the forcible removal of the Indians were countered by sporadic raids and murders on the part of the Seminole. The white people of Florida did not, in general, however, regard the future very seriously. They considered the Seminole an essentially peaceful, even rather cowardly people, whose resistance could be abated in a few weeks; the war actually lasted for nearly seven years and proved to be the most protracted and expensive "Indian war," both in lives and money, which the United States has ever undergone. The Floridians, and the people of the United States in general, had overlooked or underestimated the Negroes—Indian Negroes, plantation slaves, free Negroes—as a factor of resistance. They were to be speedily disillusioned and enlightened.

It has now long been well-known, to anyone familiar with even such old and well established works as J. B. McMaster's *History of the People of the United States,* that the

[1] *Douglas, Thomas, Autobiography of,* N. Y., 1856, pp. 120-123.
[2] *The Florida Times-Union* (Jacksonville), Oct. 30, 1892, Jan. 8, 1895.
[3] Douglas, *loc. cit.*

Florida War was not merely an "Indian war," but one in which the Negro element among the Seminole played an important and perhaps a dominating role. On this there was general agreement among the officers participating. "The negroes," it was said, "exercised a wonderful control. They openly refused to follow their masters, if they removed to Arkansas. Many of them would have been reclaimed by the Creeks, to whom some belonged. Others would have been taken possession of by the whites, who for years had been urging their claims through the government and its agents. In Arkansas, hard labor was necessary for the means of support, while Florida assured them of every means to indulge in idleness, and enjoy an independence corresponding with their masters. In preparing for hostilities they were active, and in the prosecution blood-thirsty and cruel. It was not until the negroes capitulated, that the Seminoles ever thought of emigrating." The Negroes, we are again informed, "to a great degree controlled their masters. They were a most cruel and malignant enemy. For them to surrender would be servitude to the whites; but to retain an open warfare secured to them plunder, liberty, and importance." The situation was later summed up: "The negroes, from the commencement of the Florida war, have, for their numbers, been the most formidable foe, more bloodthirsty, active, and revengeful, than the Indian."[4]

The importance of the Indian Negroes is confirmed, and reinforced, by the frequent references to battles in which the Negro warriors equalled or exceeded the Indians in numbers and courage, attacks on Negro villages, the death or capture of Negro fighters, the activities and exploits of Negro chiefs. The extent to which the plantation slave and free Negro population of Florida participated in the war, as allies, overt or covert, of the Indians and Indian Negroes, has, however, received little or no attention from the historian.

[4] Sprague, John T., *The Florida War*, N. Y., 1848, pp. 81, 100, 309.

Some of the more far-seeing observers of the time were aware of the danger, and early in 1835, even before the outbreak of open war, Gen. Clinch expressed the fear that "if a sufficient military force . . . is not sent . . . the whole frontier may be laid waste by a combination of the Indians, Indian negroes, and the negroes on the plantations." Early in October he reported that "some of the most respectable planters fear that there is already a secret and improper communication carried on between the refractory Indians, Indian negroes, and some of the plantation negroes."[5] These fears were fully justified by events.

When, late in December, 1835, hostilities broke out on a large scale, it was evident that they had been carefully prepared and coordinated by the savage enemy. The St. John's River Indians, under their chief Emathla, or King Philip as the whites called him, ably seconded by his Negro associate and subordinate John Caesar, fell upon the plantations of that region on the night of Dec. 26-27, plundering and burning,[6] while on the morning of Dec. 28, Maj. Dade's company of over one hundred men was annihilated on the march from Ft. Brooke (Tampa) to Ft. King (Ocala) by the Seminole of the Tampa and Withlacoochee region, led by head chief Micanopy, his war leader and nephew Alligator, his chief counsellor and brother in law Jumper, and his Negro adviser Abraham; Louis Pacheco *ne* Fatio, the slave who had been hired as guide for the expedition, is generally said to have been in communication with the hostiles and to have assisted in the destruction of the troops, although in his old age, fifty-seven years later, he stoutly denied the charge.

The horror caused by the almost complete destruction of an entire command, including many well-known and popular officers, paled beside that inspired by the enthusiasm with which the plantation slaves rallied to the insurgent Semi-

---

[5] *25th cong., 2nd sess., 1837-38, h. doc.,* vol. 3, no. 78, pp. 499-500.

[6] *Niles Register,* vol. xlix, p. 369; A Lieutenant of the Left Wing, *Sketch of the Seminole War,* Charleston, 1836, pp. 19-20.

nole. From plantation after plantation came the menacing word. "Depeyster's negroes were traitors, and must have been in league with the Indians; they assisted them with a boat to cross over to Dummett's . . . the whole of Major Heriot's and Depeyster's negroes . . . moved off with the Indians." "Upwards of two hundred and fifty negroes . . . have joined the Indians and are more desperate than the Indians." Some of the Depeyster Negroes had painted their faces in symbol of their new allegiance. It was cold comfort even to learn that "Anderson's negroes behaved with the utmost prudence and fidelity," concealing as much as possible of their master's property before fleeing, for the reporter went on to announce gloomily that even this loyalty would be of little ultimate value, since the Negroes of neighboring plantations would, of course, readily discover this *cache* and reveal it to the foe. That the plantation Negroes were joining the Indians, Gen. Hernandez understandably declared, "is the very worst feature of the whole of this war."[7]

This co-operation of the plantation slaves with the Seminole Indians and Negroes had not been left to chance. Yaha Hajo, a Seminole war chief, in company with head chief Micanopy's Negro adviser Abraham, had "visited St. Augustine and the sugar plantations in East Florida . . . and it is believed, was at that time engaged in effecting a junction with the negroes now under arms." These were not the only Seminole emissaries to the slaves. "Just before the war broke out, a very intelligent and influential Indian negro, named [John] Caesar, had visited the plantations generally on the St. John's River, and it was supposed that he had been commissioned by the chiefs to hold out inducements to

[7] *The Charleston Courier*, Jan. 12, 21, 22, 1836; National Archives, War Department, Adjutant General's Office, Maj. Benjamin A. Putnam, Cantonment Rosetta, Dec. 29, 1835, to Brig. Gen. J. M. Hernandez, St. Augustine (316), Putnam, Bulowville, Jan. 4, 1836, to Hernandez (25), Hernandez, Dec. 30, 1835, to Lewis Cass (H129/316).

the negroes to join them."[8] These inducements could, no doubt, be summed up in the single word: Freedom—the rights and privileges enjoyed by the Seminole Negroes themselves, including possession of their own homes, families, fields, flocks, and herds.

The situation appeared serious enough to the St. Augustinians, into whose city were crowding the frightened or sullen refugees, white and black, from the devastated plantations to the south. But westwardly, where more than one serious action had already been fought by the beginning of 1836, and where the United States posts were closely invested, it was really critical. The commander at Ft. Brooke, from which the Dade command had marched so confidently, announced, a week after its wiping out: "This place is invested by all the Florida Indians in the field, with a large accession of Negroes, particularly from the plantations of Tomoka & Smyrna, as appears from the examination of a prisoner just taken."[9] Matters were not improving late in the spring. The commander at Ft. Defiance, Micanopy, reported the loss to the enemy of a number of Negroes belonging to a former Indian agent, Col. Gad Humphreys. A Negro woman belonging to a Mr. Wanton had individually absconded to the Seminole, and another woman belonging to the same master thereafter stated that "two nights before the attack, a Negro house . . . was visited by a slave of Judge Sanchez (the husband of the woman who fled with the Indians) accompanied by Toney Barnett and David Bowlegs (Indian Negroes) who informed her of the intention of the Indians to capture Humphreys Negroes on the night they were actually taken." To "capture," when used in regard to Negroes, was a frequently employed euphemism for inducing, persuading, or assisting them to run away. The informant did not explain her strange tardiness in communi-

---

[8] *The Charleston Courier,* Apr. 30, 1836; Douglas, *loc. cit.;* Cohen, M. M., *Notices of Florida,* Charleston, 1836, p. 81.

[9] National Archives, War Department, AGO, Capt. F. S. Belton, Ft. Brooke, Jan. 5, 1836, to the Adjt. Gen. (23).

cating this intelligence. One may be pardoned for wondering what methods of persuasion may have laid behind some of the communications so freely—nay, even eagerly—offered by Negro slaves and prisoners under examination by overseers and army officers. At the time, the woman went on, "two hundred and fifty Indians, headed by Jumper" were "in the hammock."[10] Here the Indian-Indian Negro-Negro slave Axis was in full operation.

Even more serious was the situation described three weeks later at Ft. Drane, which was merely a plantation house belonging to Gen. Clinch, surrounded by pickets. Observing a group of persons in a field at a distance from the fort, a squad of dragoons dashed out and succeeded in capturing one of them, the rest escaping into the woods. The prisoner, a Negro, "proved to be one of General Clinch's gang," i.e., one of his field hands, and his captors were convinced that he was "holding communications" with the enemy. Suspicions and eyes sharpened by this occurrence, Clinch's overseers and the officers of the garrison began investigations and discovered that several of the Negroes "had been all day employed in selling off their little articles of property, and some of them had actually made up their packs," the plan being that eleven of them, at least, were to escape to the Indians that night, simultaneously with an attack on the fort. An investigation of the Negro huts further revealed a rifle, stolen from the commanding officer, hidden under one of the floors. Warned in time, though barely so, "all the male negroes were secured, and . . . under guard employed in completing the defences."[11]

In St. Augustine, where the planters, together with such of their Negroes as had not the desire or ability to "move off" with the Seminole, had taken refuge, they, and their fellows in the immediate vicinity, were still exposed to the

[10] National Archives, War Department, AGO, R. B. Lee, Ft. Defiance, Micanopy, May 22, 1836, to Lt. Col. Bankhead (147).

[11] National Archives, War Department, AGO, Capt. L. Gates, Ft. Drane, June 12, 1836, to Maj. G. T. Heileman (166G).

dangers presented by the Negro-Indian alliance, actual or potential. With several hundred Negroes concentrated within the walls of the city, most of whom "had ... for years lived on the frontier in the neighborhood of the Indians" and "spoke their language," "strong apprehensions were felt ... that they would fire the town, and that, during the confusion resulting ...; the Indians might rush in." Patrols were organized to cope with this menace, but arms of any sort were almost non-existent and it was discovered that during the few weeks preceding the outbreak the Indians had purchased nearly all the powder and lead available in the local shops.[12]

In addition to an actual attack by the Seminole, in co-operation with Negro sympathizers in the town, the whites of St. Augustine had to guard against communications be-tween the hostile Indians and Negroes without and poten-tial allies among the Negroes within. Emissaries of the enemy endeavored to enter the town to induce Negroes to join them and to obtain information, and Negroes within the town endeavored to escape through the lines to join the Seminole, carrying with them knowledge of the plans of the whites, and sometimes supplies. In recognition of this Negro-Indian alliance the Territory of Florida passed an act, "respecting hostile negroes & mulattoes in the seminole nation," providing that any free persons belonging to those categories who should be captured should be sold into slav-ery as a punishment. Maj. Benjamin A. Putnam, command-ing the 2nd Battalion of the 1st Regiment of Florida Militia, wrote to Gov. R. K. Call, July 26, 1836, urging the enforce-ment of this act and describing the danger. Indians and runaway slaves were trying to entice the Negro slaves to join them. All the dismounted force available was required merely for the purpose of preventing such communications. Some days ago a patrol party "came up with three of these negroes ... just come down from the Indians ... who had

[12] Douglas, *loc. cit.*

sent one of their number into the town to opperate with the
negroes in the place to get them off—He has been secured—
two of three were taken . . . the third named Andrew Gay
escaped.'' Andrew was a runaway of the previous month.
Maj. Putnam suggested a standing court martial to deal
summarily with such offenders.[13]

A few days later, the 31st, he wrote directly to Lewis
Cass, secretary of War: "Many [slaves] have escaped to
and joined the Indians, and furnished them with much important information and if strong measures were not taken
to restrain our slaves, there is but little doubt that we should
soon be assailed with a servile as well as Indian war.''[14] It
was probably only a mental shrinking from the recognition
of the fact which prevented Maj. Putnam from discovering
that the war was already that which he feared it might become. Gen. Jesup, to whom, not being a Floridian, a more
objective attitude was possible, declared, later in the same
year, "This . . . is a negro, not an Indian war.''[15]

Among the "strong measures" taken to restrain the
slaves was, of course, the arrest of suspects, among them
"a negro wench of Mr. [John] Rodman against whom there
seems to be the clearest as well as the strongest evidence"
—[16] whatever the distinction between the two types of evidence may have been. But here the custodians of the public
safety ran into an aspect of the slave system which sometimes, as in this case, threatened to impair the efficiency of
the means employed to insure its stability—the unwillingness of a master to believe that any of *his* slaves could possibly be so discontented as to desire, and plot for, freedom.
This was reinforced by the even more natural unwillingness
of a master to be deprived of the services of any of his
slaves on a charge of conspiracy, unless the culprit were

13 "Letter Book of Benjamin A. Putnam," St. Augustine, Historical
Society.

14 *Ibid.*

15 *25th cong., 2nd sess., 1837-38, h. ex. doc.,* vol. iii, no. 78, p. 52.

16 Putnam letter book, July 31, 1836.

caught with hands not only red but dripping. John Rodman accordingly obtained writ after writ against Frederick Weedon, the mayor, at whose order the Negro woman Rebecca, worth $350, had been arrested, and against William G. Davis, the jailer, until finally, after 51 days, she was freed, whereupon Rodman took action, Oct. 8, for false imprisonment. The Rebecca case had given Rodman such experience in the technique of recovering imprisoned slaves that when Tom, a servant of Mary Gay (and probably, therefore, in some way connected with the notorious runaway Andrew Gay), was arrested on Sept. 21, John Rodman, a co-executor with Mary Gay for her late husband's estate, succeeded in getting him out by Sept. 26.[17]

It cannot, of course, be claimed that all the plantation slaves, even those who had the opportunity, aligned themselves with the Seminole. A considerable number of the Indians themselves were, from the first, supporters of the United States government rather than of the cause of their own people. The same cannot be said of the Seminole Negroes, who, apparently to a man, maintained the cause of liberty until the background of resistance was broken and the principal chiefs had begun to surrender. The Negroes who were living among the whites had no such freedom of decision, and reacted according to circumstances and individual differences. The Charleston volunteer Cohen asserts that most slaves remained "faithful" to their masters, that is, did not run away and join the enemy, and a Floridian states that some Negroes fought for their masters when the plantations were attacked. Aside from this passive and defensive "loyalty" of certain slaves, Negro co-operation with the forces of slavery seems to have been chiefly embodied

---

[17] *Inventory of the Miscellaneous File of Court Papers, St. Johns County, Florida*, 2 vols., Florida Historical Records Survey, Jacksonville, Fla., 1940 (mimeographed), nos. 164, 166, 167, 168; court records, St. Johns Co., Fla., court house, John Rodman vs. William G. Davis, Superior, R-3; John Rodman vs. Frederick Weedon, Superior, R-4; John Rodman and Mary Gay, adms. of Anthelm Gay, vs. David Levy, deputy of the U. S. district attorney, Superior, R-6; John Rodman vs. Frederick Weedon, mayor, Superior, R-6.

in the famous "old Ben Wiggins, a mulatto, with probably
a dash of Indian in his composition," who had been reared
both among Indians and among whites and "was at home
with either." This free colored man served effectively as
a guide from the beginning and in one encounter is alleged
to have killed three Indians, himself being severely
wounded.[18]

In the meantime, while the citizens of St. Augustine were
endeavoring to deal with the "enemy within their gates,"
the first year of the Seminole War was drawing to a close,
a year during which neither party had won a decisive advantage but in which, nevertheless, the Negro-Indian allies
had at least held their own and perhaps maintained a slight
superiority. It was a year, too, in which the Negroes, particularly, of course, the Indian Negroes but not neglecting
the recent runaways, had borne their full share of the burden and heat of the day. "Micanopy, Philip, and Cooper ...
are about a day's march from each other, each with from
one hundred and twenty to two hundred Indian and negro
warriors—the latter perhaps the more numerous," wrote
on Dec. 9, 1836, Gen. Thomas Sidney Jesup, the newly appointed commander. "This, you may be assured," he continued, "is a negro, not an Indian war; and if it be not
speedily put down, the south will feel the effects of it on
their slave population before the end of the next season."
Perhaps Gen. Jesup was too recent an arrival to realize
that the St. John's Valley had been feeling these effects for
about a year already, or ever since the war started; if so,
he soon repaired this gap in his awareness, for later on he
commented that "at the battle of the Wahoo [Nov. 21, 1836],
a negro, the property of a Florida planter, was one of the
most distinguished leaders.'"[19]

---

[18] Cohen, *op. cit.*, 81, 95; Williams, John Lee, *The territory of Florida*,
N. Y., 1837, pp. 248-249, 250; Carolinian, *Scenes in the Florida War*, Charleston, 1858, p. 1, reprinted from *Russell's Magazine*.

[19] *American State Papers, Military Affairs*, vol. vii, pp. 820-821; *25th
cong., 2nd sess., 1837-38, h. ex. doc.*, vol. iii, no. 78, p. 52.

But early in 1837, under Gen. Jesup's vigorous leadership, the United States troops and state militia struck a series of staggering blows at the Indian-Negro enemy, Osceola's force, in particular, being completely disrupted. It was at this time that John Caesar, the Indian Negro partisan leader, operating in the St. John's region, began a diversion which might well have been important—a series of guerrilla raids on plantations which extended almost up to the very gates of St. Augustine.

On a Sunday night, about the middle of January, 1837, the hostiles attempted a raid on John M. Hanson's plantation, two miles west of St. Augustine, for the purpose of getting horses. They had pried a plank off the stable and carried out a saddle, but before they could enlarge the opening sufficiently to bring out the animals, they were discovered by a sentinel, who fired on them. Two of them returned the fire, the shots being clearly heard by the night watch in St. Augustine. The raiders then withdrew. Capt. Hanson took up the trail and followed it for a while, but, becoming aware that their number was too large for the force at his disposal, he returned, raised a larger company, trailed them all day, and at about 10 p.m. discovered their camp, which was on the Williams plantation about thirty miles from St. Augustine. The St. Augustine troop crept up close to the camp fire—the raiders must have been extraordinarily bold or careless—discovered eight or twelve sitting around it, and poured in such a well-aimed volley at close range that they killed three, badly wounding at least one other. The rest fled, in such confusion that they left not only their packs and blankets, but also two rifles and six muskets.

One would have expected that such a *coup* would have resulted in general congratulations and unmixed satisfaction, but it seems to have produced at least as much alarm as relief, for no more than two of the gang were Indians, the rest being Negroes, and although two of the slain were Indian Negroes, who had perhaps been singled out by their costumes as more formidable than the others, the third was a free Negro, Joe Merritt, who had gone off with them six weeks before. The packs contained calico, needles, thread, buckshot, tobacco, and such articles, which could be identified as having been purchased in St. Augustine shops only a few days earlier, and the conclusion was that the raiders had been supplied by and were in constant communication with the St. Augustine Negroes, particularly, it was believed, with the free Negroes living on Anastasia Island.[20] That a band composed almost entirely of Negroes should have the temerity to attempt a raid in the immediate vicinity of St. Augustine, even with results so lamentable to themselves, and that the hostile Negroes should be so conclusively demonstrated to be in such close and constant communication with the Negro population of the city, revived something of the panic of the early days of the war.

The city council, Jan. 23, 1837, accordingly passed "An ordinance to prevent the selling of ammunition to Slaves, free Negroes & molattos," which it is rather surprising to learn had not already long since been forbidden.[21] Stephen Merritt *alias* Wright, father of the slain Joe Merritt, and Randall Irving, free persons of color, were indicted at the Superior Court "for treason against the United States, in supplying the Seminole Indians with provisions and ammunition. They were arraigned and pleaded not guilty."[22] The fears of the citizenry were not perceptibly diminished by the capture, in March, of one of the principal malefactors.

Andrew Gue [Gay] . . . belonging to Col. Gue of this city, who ran away from his master in June last, was captured on Thursday morning at 4 A. M. by a detachment of six men under Lieut. John Ferreira, of Capt. Hudson's company of Mounted Volunteers. An-

[20] *The Charleston Courier*, Jan. 21, 1837, letter from St. Augustine, Jan. 20.
[21] "Minutes of the City of St. Augustine, Nov. 18, 1836-Nov. 15, 1854," City Building, St. Augustine, Fla., p. 8.
[22] *The Daily National Intelligencer* (Washington, D. C.), Apr. 17, 1837. There is no record of either of these cases in the above-mentioned *Inventory*.

drew is a young negro not exceeding 21 years of age, and active and enterprising. He went off, joined the Indians, and after being with them for some weeks, he returned clandestinely to town, and held a meeting with some of his friends and enticed some of them off. At this meeting he stated that he had become high in the confidence of the Indians and he only wanted a white man's scalp to make him a great man. On several occasions since he has made his appearance in the vicinity, and was with the gang of negroes when Capt. Hopson [Hanson?] killed John Caesar,[23] at which time he received three wounds. He says he bled considerable, and since that time he has not seen or spoken to any person whatever. He has remained in the neighborhood of the place where he was wounded, subsisting on roots, &c., until he was induced from hunger to come to our neighborhood for provisions, and which led to his capture.[24]

Andrew was duly commited to prison, but even the knowledge that this dangerous character was behind bars and that the formidable John Caesar would no longer trouble the country, seems to have been of little comfort, compared with the uneasiness produced by the knowledge that there were at large other runaway slaves,[25] who, like Andrew Gay, might be longing for a white man's scalp, and with the ability to penetrate into the midst of the town to plot insurrection with their fellows, and imbue them with a desire for similar trophies. The city council on May 2 passed a resolution that Capt. Hanson's company, which

[23] This must refer to the episode of January, and John Caesar must have been one of the two Indian Negroes killed; Andrew doubtless identified him after his own capture. No other encounter corresponding to this description is known to have taken place. For a description of John Caesar's career prior to the final episode in his life, see the author's "John Caesar: A Forgotten Hero of the Seminole War," *The Journal of Negro History*, vol. xxviii (Jan., 1943), pp. 53-65. At the time of writing this article, the author was unaware of the circumstances of John Caesar's death, though, of the three possibilities advanced, one comes pretty close to the facts as now known.

[24] *The Charleston Courier*, Mar. 21, 1837. I have been unable to find any record of this case elsewhere, or any information as to Andrew's fate; his case is not listed in the *Inventory*.

[25] *Ibid.* One such runaway was named Smart, and belonged to the late Pablo Salvate, having gone off the previous summer. He was detected lurking in the vicinity and may have been a member of the disrupted John Caesar band.

had done such good service in hunting down and breaking up John Caesar's band, should be recalled and "employed to scour the country in the neighborhood"—"from within our own community," a resolution of a month later declared, "we know not how soon firebrands may be thrown amongst us," and the necessity for all to join in the defense of the city was stressed.[26] Thus the *fear* of a slave insurrection operated to keep the militia companies near home, deprived Gen. Jesup of their assistance, and relieved the pressure on the Negroes and Indians actually in the field. To that extent John Caesar, Joe Merritt, Andrew Gue or Gay, and their fellows had not shed their blood in vain.

From the last of January to the first of June, 1837, it had seemed probable that hostilities might be speedily and permanently terminated. The war had been going badly for the Seminole and to Gen. Jesup the time seemed ripe for peace negotiations. But he recognized that the terms could not be too onerous, since "in all the numerous battles and skirmishes that have taken place, not a single first-rate warrior has been captured, and only two Indian men have surrendered. The warriors have fought as long as they had life, and such seems to be the determination of those who influence their councils—I mean the leading negroes." Accordingly he communicated through a captured Indian Negro, Ben, with the principal Negro leader, Abraham, and through him got in touch with other principal chiefs, Indian and Negro. On March 6, 1837, an agreement was signed providing that "the Seminoles and their allies, who come in and emigrate West, shall be secure in their lives and property; [and] that their negroes, their bona fide property, shall also accompany them West."[27] This was understood by the Seminole as protecting not only the Negroes to whom some of the Indians might have a more or less valid title, but also "their allies," the other Negroes who were then living

[26] St. Augustine minutes, pp. 11, 13.
[27] ASP, MA, vii, 825-828; *Army and Navy Chronicle*, iv, 80.

among them and fighting with them, and at first Gen. Jesup
had insisted on that interpretation. "The negroes," that
is, the Indian Negroes, "rule the Indians," he wrote on
March 26, 1837, "and it is important that they should feel
themselves secure; if they should become alarmed and hold
out, the war will be renewed."[28] Obviously, any attempt
to meddle with any of the Negroes who had been fighting
in the Seminole ranks for over a year would arouse apprehension among the others. But Gen. Jesup's decision that
the runaway Negroes among the Seminole were "their allies" and protected by the terms of the capitulation, was
inevitably greeted with violent protest by planters who had
lost slaves during the war, and finally, yielding to their
pressure, he was induced to make a clandestine arrangement on April 8 with certain Indian chiefs, notably Coi
Hajo, second chief of the St. John's River Seminole, "to
surrender the negroes taken during the war,"[29] thus endeavoring to introduce a division, based on the time of their
escape, into the ranks of the Negroes among the Seminole.

Bringing in the "captured" Negroes, as those who had
joined the Seminole during the course of the war were officially and euphemistically styled, and delivering them to
the authorities for return to their owners, was a matter
requiring considerable *finesse*. It was necessary to round
them up and bring them by easy stages to some central
location, so that all or most of them could be seized for
delivery simultaneously, since if they were to be taken and

---

[28] ASP, MA, vii, 835.

[29] *Niles Register*, Apr. 29, 1837, p. 133. See: Giddings, Joshua, *The exiles
of Florida*, Columbus, O., 1858, ch. xi, for a detailed discussion of this agreement. Although Coi Hajo had participated in the Seminole resistance to removal, he had been looked on, prior to the outbreak of the war, as weak-
kneed in his opposition—so much so that it is said that it had been intended
to put him to death along with Chalo (Charley) Emathla, leader of the emigration party. National Archives, AGO, Bvt. Lieut. Col. A. C. W. Fanning,
Ft. King, Nov. 28, 1835, to Brig. Gen. D. L. Clinch, St. Augustine (478). It
is possible that jealousy of Philip, head chief of the St. John's River Seminole, may partially account for some of the divagations of the second chief.

turned over by driblets it would attract the attention and
arouse the apprehension of those still at large. "The
chiefs," it was reported, ". . . do not wish to turn over the
negroes . . . till they are about to set off for Tampa"—
where all the Seminole, Indians and Negroes, were, according to the terms of the treaty, to be assembled for emigration—"as many of them would run away."[30] Army officers
with detachments of troops were sent into the recently paci-
fied country to observe and encourage the process, and take
note of any evidence of unwillingness to fulfill the terms of
either the open or the secret agreement.

What was in the wind could not be long kept from the
nostrils of those principally concerned. Not all the Negroes
with the Indians had, of course, joined them entirely of
their own free will, and many of those who had been eager
enough at first had by this time no doubt become tired of
the bargain. The Indians themselves had suffered severely
from lack of food and clothing, and the less-experienced
plantation Negroes had not, of course, been any better off,
probably a good deal worse. Those who had not displayed
any particular enthusiasm for defending their newly acquired liberty with arms in their hands had been sent off,
with the women, old men, and children, to secluded islands
and hammocks, and put to raising corn; they may well have
felt that they had merely exchanged one slavery for another, almost as arduous and even less rewarding in physical comforts. Those who felt thus did not need to be
"brought in;" they eagerly surrendered themselves whenever the approach of a body of troops gave them the opportunity, hoping that the excuse of having been "captured"
would save them from punishment. A dozen Negroes who
surrendered in May were clad only in ragged muddy breech
cloths and complained that they had been forced to live
entirely on koonti-roots, from which the Indians made a
sort of bread, and on alligator tails, and that when things

[30] ASP, MA, vii, 871.

were going badly for the Indians they had sometimes vented their ill-temper on the Negroes by beating them.[31]

Other Negroes prized their freedom higher than considerations of immediate comfort. Lt. Col. W. S. Harney wrote on May 16 that "there was a party [of Negroes] on Cedar Creek who were all runaways and [when they learned that they were to be returned to their masters] resisted telling the Indians that they [the Indians] had not taken them & that they [the Negroes] would not give up."[32] Negroes of this mind and spirit received support from the more militant Indians, such as Osceola. Some of the Negroes who surrendered reported that Coi Hajo had announced in council that the runaway Negroes were to be returned, whereupon Osceola, rising in a rage, declared that so long as he was in the nation it should never be done.[33]

It will be remembered that, before the outbreak of hostilities, one of Osceola's wives had been seized and sent into servitude on the ground that her mother was a runaway slave. But Osceola was not moved primarily by sentimental considerations; he had never accepted the capitulation of Ft. Dade and naturally, therefore, opposed any action which would weaken the tribe's military strength. He had a particular and personal reason for objecting to any decrease in the tribe's Negro population, for, as is apparently entirely unknown to the romanticists who dote on this picturesque and appealing personality, his own band had been largely drawn from that element. This was natural enough. Osceola was not a Seminole by birth, but a Creek from Georgia, and had no hereditary claims to be a chief. Those who followed him at the outbreak of the war were those who were without close ties to hereditary leaders and who were attracted by his militancy, courage, and intelligence;

[31] Motte, Capt. J. Rhett, "Life in Camp and Field," St. Augustine Historical Society (ms.), p. 161.

[32] Florida Historical Society (photostat).

[33] 1st Lieut. R. H. Peyton, May 24, 1837, to Harney, Florida Historical Society (photostat).

Negroes, the element most strongly opposed to removal and
with the loosest allegiance to the recognized chiefs, were
naturally the group most susceptible to his appeal—and the
most recent of the runaways were the most available. Osceola's band was, therefore, recruited principally from Negroes and some of the hot-headed Mikasuki, the most recalcitrant of the Indian bands. When Osceola was surprised
and his band disrupted early in January, 1837, his headquarters were in a Negro village in the Panosufkee Swamp
and of his followers made prisoners in that disastrous action
52 were Negroes and only three, Indians, Osceola himself
escaping with only three warriors.[34] It was necessary for
him to recruit his band, and Negroes like the recalcitrant
runaways on Cedar Creek were the most promising material.

By October—to get a few months ahead of events—
Osceola seems to have built up his band to somewhere near
its former proportions. The spokesman of seventeen Negroes who surrendered about that time, fifteen of whom
belonged to Maj. Heriot, said that he was from "Powell's
[Osceola's] town, . . . on a large lake above Lake Monroe
. . . where Philip lived." He had been permitted to leave
for the purpose of making salt. He said that there were
"about fifty negros with Powell— . . . they all want to get
away as the Indians half starve them— . . . they . . . live
almost exclusively on the pounded root of the Palmetto."[35]
It is of course possible that this informant was putting his
own sentiments into the hearts of "Powell's" Negroes, as
well as giving his white masters the news they most desired
to hear.

The determined opposition of Osceola and other militant
chiefs, and the resistance of freedom-loving Negroes who
had gotten wind of Coi Hajo's plot with Gen. Jesup, natu-

[34] ASP, MA, vii, 825-826.
[35] National Archives, AGO, Capt. Harvey Brown, Ft. Marion, Oct. 8, 1837,
to Lieut. J. A. Chambers (196/447).

rally checked or diminished the movement toward Tampa Bay, particularly of Negroes, whether "Indian" Negroes or "captured." Even the Indian Negroes already assembled at Tampa Bay became uneasy as persons owning, or claiming to own, slaves who had taken refuge among the Indians, began to appear at the emigration camp. Many of the Indian Negroes were themselves runaways, though of long standing, or the children of runaways, and thus legally slaves, whatever the terms or interpretation of Gen. Jesup's already once-broken agreement. Finally, early in June, under the instigation and leadership of Osceola, Wild Cat, and the young Indian Negro chief John Cavallo, most of the Indian Negroes and many Indians fled the camp, taking with them, for good measure, the principal hostages they had given for the fulfillment of the Ft. Dade capitulation.[36]

Too late Gen. Jesup recognized his error. Most of the Indians and Negroes would probably have eventually surrendered to be sent out of the country had he not spoiled everything by trying to force the surrender of recent runaways. He had secured by this policy about a hundred each of Indian Negroes and runaways, but now the war was revived, with a greater danger than ever, in the general's opinion, of spreading to the plantations. "The two races," he wrote in June, "the negro and the Indians, are rapidly approximating; they are identified in interests and feelings"—and it is evident that Gen. Jesup is here speaking of the slave Negro, not the Indian Negro, whose "identity" with the Indian was too self evident to require comment. This is made abundantly clear by the comment which followed. "I have learned that the depredations committed on the plantations east of the St. John's were perpetrated by the plantation negroes, headed by an Indian Negro, John Caesar, since killed, and aided by some six or seven vagabond Indians"—an indication of the significance which

[36] ASP, MA, vii, 871.

Jesup, in sizing up the situation, ascribed to John Caesar's raids. Jesup at this time almost despaired of being able to induce the Indians to remove, but was still hoping to recover the runaways among them. "Should the Indians remain in this territory, the negroes among them will form a rallying point for runaway negroes from the adjacent states; and if they remove, the fastnesses of the country would be immediately occupied by negroes."

The sort of thing Jesup was fearing is illustrated in a letter of May, 1837, from Jefferson, Camden Co., Ga., just across the Florida border. "Indians were conducted to this neighborhood by a runaway negro from this section. The negro is well known to me, and a great villain he is— he is fled to the Oakafanoke, or in that direction, and fears are entertained that he may conduct, the next time, a much greater number."[37] It was not until nearly two years later that trouble caused in that region by refugee Creek Indians, trying, like their kinsmen in Florida, to escape being sent west, and by runaway slaves from the Georgia plantations, was beginning to abate, and that only by reason of a transfer to a new locality. Then it was reported that "the Creek Indians have all left the Okefenokee & gone South, there were seven runaway negroes from Georgia among them, well armed & plenty of ammunition, . . . the negroes have done most of the mischief in that quarter; the negros also have left & on their way south burned the houses in the vicinity."[38]

Gen. Jesup's anxiety to induce the Indians, by almost any means, to give up the runaways among them, is thus easily understandable. "I am very sure," he wrote, "they [the Indians] could be confined to a small district near Florida Point, and would accept peace and the small district referred to as the condition for the surrender of all run-

[37] *A. & N. C.*, iv, 379.

[38] National Archives, War Department, AGO, Col. D. E.. Twiggs, Ft. Heileman, Feb. 10, 1839, to Gen. A. Macomb (66).

away negroes.''[39] In other words, Jesup hoped to make another agreement with the Indian chiefs, a more favorable
one, for them, than that of March 6 and the supplementary
one of April 8—not, ''Come in for emigration, bringing all
the recent runaways for surrender to their masters, and
we will protect your lives and property, including your
bona fide slaves,'' but, ''Bring in and surrender all the runaway slaves, promise not to receive any more in the future,
and you and your Negroes can *remain.*'' It might have been
successful, or partially so; it was a better *quid pro quo* so
far as the Indians were concerned than the earlier offer.
A. runaway Negro who surrendered that fall said that if
the Indians were permitted to stay in Florida ''they would
. . . sell and deliver up the plantation negros,''[40] and certainly some of the chiefs, such as those who were parties to
the secret agreement of April 8, would have been more than
willing, but the government for some time to come was to
insist on a continuance of the Indian removal policy.

Only a sense of humiliation, resulting from the failure
of his carefully worked out plans of early 1837, and driving
him nearly to desperation, can explain—it cannot justify—
several of Gen. Jesup's actions in the autumn of that year
and early in the following. The fortunate capture in September of Philip (Emathla), the St. John's River head chief,
made it possible to use him as a bait to attract, for conversation with his father, his favorite son Wild Cat, who was
then employed as an emissary to draw in about a hundred
Negroes and Indians, including several chiefs and sub-
chiefs, among them those irreconcilables Osceola and John
Cavallo, supposedly for a conference. Instead they were
surrounded and captured. About twenty, including Wild
Cat and John Cavallo, escaped the next month, but it was
nonetheless a serious blow. Over a hundred others, including the head chief Micanopy, were seized by a similar de-

[39] ASP, MA, vol. vii, p. 876.
[40] See note 34.

vice early in December and, discouraged by this, still others
surrendered. But there were still enough hostiles in the
field, under Wild Cat, Alligator, Sam Jones, and John
Cavallo, to fight the most seriously contested action of the
war, on Christmas Day, at Lake Okeechobee, against Col.
Zachary Taylor. Gen. Jesup himself took the field next
month and fought an action on the Laxahatchie west of
Okeechobee—a battle in which an officer said there were as
many Negroes as Indians among the Seminole warriors.[41]

Jesup now considered the time ripe to re-open peace
negotiations. He had learned wisdom in the months since
the previous June. He suggested to the Indians that they
might be allowed to remain on a reservation in southern
Florida, but said nothing about returning runaway slaves.
He was becoming more and more convinced of the inadvis-
ability of returning captured Negroes to servitude. He had
hired a considerable number of Creek mercenaries, promising them as plunder all the Negroes they could capture, but
when, in September, 1837, they succeeded in capturing
eighty, he wrote: "It is highly important to the slaveholding States that these negroes be sent out of the country,
and I would strongly recommend that they be sent to one
of our colonies in Africa," i.e., Liberia. These Negroes were
accordingly taken from the Creeks, and a "reward" of $20
per head substituted, much to the latter's dissatisfaction.[42]
The Negroes were eventually sent not to Liberia but to
the Indian Territory; in either case their freedom was assured.

Jesup also addressed himself directly to the Seminole
Negroes, endeavoring to drive a wedge between them and
the Indians, as he had previously striven to separate the
Seminole, both Indian and Negro, from the recently escaped
slaves. He issued an order "that all the property of the
Seminole Indians in Florida at war with the United States

41 Motte, *op. cit.*, p. 255.
42 ASP, MA, vii, 882.

who separated themselves from the Indians, and delivered themselves up to the Commanding officer of the troops, should be free"—an early and oddly-placed Emancipation Proclamation. Gen. Jesup's idea was now to send the Seminole Negroes to the Indian Territory with those who had already been transported, and put the Indians on a reservation in a remote part of the peninsula, trusting that its inaccessibility to the plantation region, and the absence of Negroes therein, would prevent its becoming a haven for runaways. He explained that "Separating the negros from the Indians weaken[s] the latter more than they would be weakened by the loss of the same number of their own people"[43]—evidence that Jesup still held to his original opinion that the Seminole Indian War might more appropriately be entitled the Negro War. Slavery among the Seminole was not so onerous that this offer in itself was probably of much effect; its importance lay in the suggestion that Jesup was now willing to make a special effort to conciliate the Negro element among the Seminole. In response to Jesup's invitation nearly 700 Seminole, about a fourth Negroes, assembled at Ft. Jupiter for a conference, but in the meantime the Secretary of War had refused to consider any peace except on the basis of emigration, so the general, probably against his real inclinations, accomplished another master-piece of treachery by arresting the entire lot. This discouraged the others so that 450 more, one-third of them Negroes, surrendered shortly after. On March 13 Jesup announced that "nearly all the blacks have left the field, by capture or surrender."[44] The only Negro chief who had not surrendered or been captured was John Cavallo, and he, with Alligator, the Indian chief with whom he was most closely associated, came in early in

[43] National Archives, Department of the Interior, Indian Bureau, Florida (Emigration) File A1282-1842, Statement of Brig. Gen. Zachary Taylor, Ft. Brooke, Apr. 30, 1840; *ibid.*, Seminole File W244-1848, T. S. Jesup, near Ft. Jupiter, Feb. 28, 1838, to Brig. Gen. R. Jones, Washington.

[44] *A. & N. C.*, vi, 190.

April, at the general's special invitation and promise of freedom.[45] Again it seemed that the war was over, and in May, Gen. Jesup was retired and was replaced by Zachary Taylor.

But, though nearly all the principal chiefs were dead or prisoners, several minor chiefs, now, if only for want of competition, become of major importance, were left to carry on the fight—including one, who, for over a year, had been steadily increasing in stature until he could be recognized without qualification as of the first rank—Wild Cat or Coacoochee. After the Battle of Lake Okeechobee he had moved north to his old stamping-ground on the St. John's. Included in his band were a number of recent runaways from that region, and his expert utilization of their services as spies was known and commented upon by his adversaries.[46] He also, as before, found willing allies among the Negro population, slave or free, within the lines of the forces of slavery.

A year had passed since the free Negroes Randall Irving and Stephen Merritt had been indicted at St. Augustine for treason in having, as was alleged, supplied the hostile Seminole with ammunition. The citizenry of St. Augustine, it is only fair to say, appear to have kept their heads very well during these trying times. It is evident, at any rate, that there was nothing of lynch law in the treatment of the accused, even though an official record of the case is lacking, for they must have been either discharged for want of evidence or formally acquitted; otherwise there would have been no need for the petition of sundry citizens of St. Augustine, March 30, 1838: "His Honor the Mayor is Respectfully Requested to look and attend to the Removal from this City [of] the persons of Randal Irvin and Stephen Merrit and families." This was followed by a fuller statement, of

45 *N. E.*, May 5, 1838; *A. & N. C.*, vi, 300, 315.

46 Van Ness, Maj. W. P., "An incident of the Seminole War," *Journal of the Military Service Institute of the United States*, vol. 1 (1912), pp. 267-271.

Sept. 15, over five months later, a "petition . . . setting forth that Randal Irvin and Stephen Merritt heretofore indited by the Grand Jury of the County for the offence and fully convicted, in the opinion of the community, of having had a Traitorous intercourse with the hostile Indians, have with reckless depravity again engaged in their daring communication with our savage enemies." It was therefore urged that they be put in custody until they could be sent out of the county, in order to avoid violence from a right-eously indignant citizenry. The city council resolved that the petition should be granted, and presumably the Irvings and Merritts were duly confined and eventually banished from St. John's County. But so far as we know they were not lynched.

Stephen Merritt and Randall Irving pass out of the story, enigmatic figures. Were they actually peaceful, re-spectable, law-abiding citizens of dark complexion, ground-lessly, perhaps maliciously, accused of traffic with the hos-tiles? That they were not convicted suggests that the evi-dence against them was slight indeed. But popular opinion, over a year after the original accusation, held them guilty not only of the earlier offense but of a recent repetition. If actually guilty of both charges, escaping condemnation the first time through unusual cleverness or luck, then their repetition of the offense makes their accusers' characteriza-tion of them as "reckless" and "daring" seem mild in the extreme. If guilty, what were their motives? And what the motives of Stephen Merritt's young son Joe, another free Negro, who was caught red-handed and paid with his life? A feeling of solidarity with their fellows, runaway slaves and Seminole Negroes, fighting to achieve or to main-tain freedom? Or a mere desire to share in the plunder? The latter hardly seems adequate, considering the danger involved. So they pass on into obscurity, sullen defiant conspirators or bewildered pawns of prejudice and suspi-cion. But their departure did not operate to quiet the nerves of the Augustinians entirely, for a complaint, the following year, concerning the late hours kept by the colored population, resulted in an order of the city council, May 28, 1839, that the patrol ordinance of June 23, 1836, should be put into full force.[47]

One commander followed another as the Seminole War dragged uneventfully on. There was little fighting for a year after Zachary Taylor took over from Jesup. The Seminole avoided combat and endeavored only to keep out of the way of the troops, in which they were highly successful —so much so that on May 18, 1839, Gen. McComb was finally allowed to negotiate an agreement providing that they should be allowed to remain in Florida, on a reservation below Pease Creek. But two months later a band of recalcitrants who were not parties to the agreement annihilated a party of soldiers and sutlers on the Caloosahatchie—perhaps tempted beyond endurance by the criminal carelessness of the whites. The war thereafter, save for a couple of actions which attained the proportions of skirmishes and were dignified by being styled battles, degenerated into surprise attacks by, or upon, small parties of Seminole, usually involving ten warriors or fewer. Most of the hostiles went as far south as possible, and would have been perfectly content had the whites left them alone to cultivate corn and dig koonti; instead they were chased wearisomely about from hammock to island and back, with occasionally the death of a warrior or capture of a squaw to lend zest to the pursuit. Only Wild Cat and Halleck Tustenuggee remained in the vicinity of the settlements and occasionally alternated attacking with being attacked.

Wild Cat, at least, still continued to receive support from the Negro "fifth column of freedom" within the soldier-planter lines. In the early summer of 1840, for example, several slaves belonging to John M. Hanson of near St. Augustine—as a result of a raid on whose plantation

[47] St. Augustine minutes, pp. 27, 37, 54.

John Caesar had met his death three years before—were arrested by the military authorities on the charge of supplying the enemy with powder and information. The witnesses were stated to be "the mother of Wild Cat and Sam the negro lately taken," and it was declared that articles found on captured members of Wild Cat's band could be demonstrated to have been purchased in St. Augustine by the accused. Mr. Hanson protested against the arrest of his slaves as John Rodman and Mary Gay had four years earlier, but the official records do not reveal the disposition of the cases.[48]

During William J. Worth's command the war was finally, in August, 1842, brought to an official and, this time, permanent conclusion—if thirteen years, the time elapsing between the end of the Second Seminole War and the outbreak of the Third, suffice for permanency. This was accomplished partly by the capture—sometimes through methods strongly reminiscent of Gen. Jesup—of the more militant chiefs still at large—Wild Cat, Hospitaka, Halleck Tustenuggee—and writing off the problem of corraling the patriarchal Apiaca, or Sam Jones, and the more youthful Holata Micco, or Billy Bowlegs, as the rather futile job it had long been demonstrated to be. The Seminole now living in Florida are descended from the members of these two bands, mostly of the former, since a part of Billy Bowlegs' band, including Billy himself, were rounded up and shipped west as a result of the Third Seminole War, 1855-1858.

But another contribution to the liquidation of the war was a definitely changed policy toward the Negro element, including not only the Negroes of long standing in the tribe but the recent runaways, or "captured" Negroes, as well, foreshadowed by Jesup's prevention of the sale of captured Negroes by their Creek captors. Jesup's successors

[48] National Archives, War Department, AGO, Letter Book, "1. Dept. of Florida. AGO," May 6, 1840-June 27, 1841, pp. 59-60, 78-79.

devoted themselves exclusively to getting the Indians and Negroes out of the everglades, out of the peninsula, and safely west of the Mississippi, and would on the whole rather ship a Negro west than return him to his legal owner, with the latter process involving the danger of alarming other Negroes who would not only refuse to surrender themselves, but also influence the Negroes in general, and Indians as well, to stay out. The sensible theory developed among army officers that if a Negro didn't really want to be returned to his master—if he did, they would, of course, be glad to be of service—the quicker he was put on a steamboat for New Orleans and the Indian Territory, the better. And they felt that any Negro who was really "longin' for de Ole Plantation" could probably have achieved his desire during the first couple of years of the war, considering the amount of time the Seminole had spent in the vicinity of United States camps during that period in the process of various peace-negotiations. Even officers who were themselves slave-holders, or supporters of the institution, but who had no financial interest in the particular Negroes with whom they had to deal, felt that the public interest and the welfare of the Peculiar Institution could best be served by shipping away, with all the promptitude possible, any Negro who had experienced a taste of freedom, leaving the Indians out in the Territory to worry about him for the future. A few Andrew Gays, with a knowledge of the Okefenokee Swamp or the Big Cypress, would be no Christmas package for a Georgia or Florida plantation owner. The general belief was that such Negroes would run away again, seek refuge in the swamps with which they had become familiar, and then, as one officer commented, "Ten resolute negroes, with a knowledge of the country, are sufficient to desolate the frontier, from one extent to the other."[49]

A conventional technique developed in dealing with Negroes, captured or surrendered along with the Indians. It

[49] Sprague, *op. cit.*, 309.

was to assume that all such were claimed as slaves of some Indian, ship them west, and let their legal white owners, if any, take the matter up with the government. The case of Louis Pacheco was classic. It was perfectly well known that his legal owner was Mrs. Antonio Pacheco, but he was claimed by the Indian chief Jumper, and rushed west, Gen. Jesup later commenting that, had time permitted, he would have hanged him; sending him to the Indian Territory at least got him out of Florida. The officers in charge of Louis on his journey west took Jumper's claim with so little seriousness that Louis was listed as free—which he was, for all practical purposes.

This policy, in its full formulation, found expression in a letter from Col. Worth, Aug. 19, 1841: "Indians have been solemnly guaranteed retention of slaves *indifferently ... to the mode or time ... they obtained possession* [italics mine] ... If ... the swamps of Florida ... become the resort of runaways"—and this, it is evident, is what the colonel thought would result if the runaways already there were not given every encouragement to come in—"their intelligence, so superior to the Indian, might impose upon the general government a contest, quadruplicate in time and treasure than that now being waged."[50] Considering that the present war had already lasted nearly six years and would, within another year's time, attain the cost of twenty million dollars, this was strong language.

The success of this policy is revealed in the minutes of the St. Augustine city council, previously used as a barometer of public emotion, by an entry for June 15, 1841, a resolution providing that, because of the general unwillingness of the citizens, the night patrol should be in the future discontinued.[51] The terror of slave insurrection—the torch in

[50] National Archives, War Department, AGO, Letter Book, "Head Quarters 9th M Department. Letters. From June 2d. 1841 to February 1st. 1842. Vol. 1," pp. 192-194, Col. W. J. Worth, Ft. Brooke, Aug. 19, 1841, to Maj. Gen. Scott.

[51] pp. 101-102.

the night, the axe-blow crashing against the lonely door—which had hung over the city and vicinity for five long years, had finally been dissipated. Wild Cat was in custody. No more would slaves and free Negroes make their way through the lines to his camp, bringing him powder and lead and information. Hostile Negroes who still survived were on their way to, or in, the Indian Territory, or at the emigration camp at Tampa Bay, save for a few far south in the everglades with Billy Bowlegs.

But the long struggle of the Negroes had not been entirely in vain. The Indian Negroes had again conclusively maintained the freedom which they or their ancestors had won first by flight and had then defended by force of arms against raids by Georgia borderers and in the First Seminole War; had they not thus demonstrated their mettle, but come passively in for transportation to the west, there is little doubt that many of them would have been enslaved. The slave raids against Negroes living among the Indians in West Florida, shortly before the outbreak of the Seminole War, are an indication of what the others might have expected, once they were made accessible to white aggression. Many, probably most, of the slaves who joined the Seminole at the outbreak of the war had been captured, through the double-dealing and treachery of Gen. Jesup and the perfidy of a few of the Indian chiefs, but those Negroes with both the initiative to join the Seminole in the first place and the courage, intelligence, tenacity, and good fortune to hold out until the third year of the war, i.e., to about the middle of 1838, won their freedom, through being classified as "slaves" of the Indians, and were shipped to the Indian Territory along with the refugees of longer standing.

The participation of the Florida slaves in the Seminole War cannot, therefore, properly be disregarded. Hundreds, it is now known, seized the opportunity presented by the outbreak of the war to join the hostile Seminole Indians and Negroes. Those properly qualified by age and sex, strength and spirit, fought bravely and desperately at the side of Indian and Indian Negro, sometimes rising to positions of leadership. Others did good service behind the lines, collecting information and obtaining supplies for transmission to the hostiles. Free Negroes, with less to gain and more to lose than any others, nevertheless participated, both in the field and behind the lines. Particularly noteworthy were those Indian Negroes and runaways who operated as spies and secret agents, stealthily passing from Seminole camp to plantation or city slave-quarters and back again, to obtain recruits, information, and supplies. The general atmosphere of discontent and brooding hostility produced by all these operations and prevailing behind the lines held by the supporters of the slave system was such that it kept a large part of the militia at home, to guard against any sudden outbreak, thus relieving the pressure against the Indians and Negroes actually in the field and contributing to the prevention of their utter defeat.

Thus a close tie of common resistance to exploitation and oppression united the Indian chief, Wild Cat, the Indian Negro, John Caesar, the runaway slave, Andrew Gay, and the free Negro, Joe Merritt, who may stand as representatives of many other less known or entirely unknown figures in a fight for freedom of a century ago.

Corrections and Additions

p. 265, l. 22-23: ". . . head chief Micanopy, his war leader and nephew Alligator. . . ." There is no conclusive evidence that Alligator was Micanopy's nephew.

p. 271, l. 19-21: ". . . the Seminole Negroes, . . . apparently to a man, maintained the cause of liberty until the background [sic: backbone] of resistance was broken. . . ." It would be more accurate to write "apparently almost to a man," since a few Seminole Negroes, notably "King" Cudjo and Nero, supported the whites. See Porter, "Negro Guides and Interpreters in the Early Stages of the Seminole War, Dec. 28, 1835-Mar. 6, 1837," *JNH*, XXXV (April, 1950), pp. 174-79.

pp. 273-75: A more detailed account of John Caesar's raid can be found in "John Caesar: Seminole Negro Partisan," pp. 346-49.

p. 279, l. 17-19: ". . . one of Osceola's wives had been seized and sent into servitude on the ground that her mother was a runaway slave." There is no valid evidence for this widely repeated statement. See comment on p. 91 referring to "Relations between Negroes and Indians," p. 59, l. 10.

"The Negro Abraham," which follows, originally appeared in the *Florida Historical Quarterly*, July, 1946 (Vol. XXV).

THE NEGRO ABRAHAM*

One of the most remarkable personalities produced by the African race in this country before general emancipation was an illiterate runaway slave who spent almost all his mature life among Seminole Indians. This judgment is, perhaps, either too cautious to be meaningful or too bold to be convincing, according to the direction from which one chooses to approach it. *"One* of the most remarkable?" Yes, perhaps; but one out of how many? Half a dozen? A dozen? Or perhaps a hundred? ' If one of the smaller numbers is selected, the question arises: Where does this "remarkable personality" rank with such a writer as Phyllis Wheatley? such a scientist as Benjamin Banneker? such a minister and theologian as Lemuel Haynes? such insurrectionists as Gabriel, Denmark Vesey, and Nat Turner? such propagandists, orators, and abolitionists as David Walker, William Wells Brown, Samuel Ringgold Ward, Jermain W. Loguen, Lewis Hayden, not to mention Frederick Douglass? Obviously this illiterate runaway slave could have played no significant part in the same arena with any of these, save, perhaps, the insur-

* A brief article by the author, entitled "Abraham," appeared in *Phylon,* ii (second quarter, 1941), pp. 107-116. It was based entirely on printed sources, which, however, included government documents, contemporary accounts, and compilations of newspaper extracts. During the four years elapsing since this preliminary study, I have utilized the manuscript material in the Indian Office and War Department records, used newspaper material more extensively, and done field-work in the region of Abraham's later residence. I have also been furnished by the P. K. Yonge Library of Florida History, University of Florida, with material from the archives of Hillsborough Co., Fla., and from Gen. Jesup's private papers. This new material justifies this much fuller account. It is proper at this time and place, however, to acknowledge the hospitality to this subject, in an earlier form, extended by Dr. W. E. B. DuBois, then editor of *Phylon.*

rectionists; but none of these, on the other hand, could claim to have been so directly and importantly influential in first bringing about and, ultimately, terminating a serious, protracted, and expensive war. It could, I think, be said, at any rate, that our subject received at one important period in his life more general and, at the same time, more generally respectful attention, South and North, than any of the others mentioned for comparison, for though he was greatly admired by some and strongly disliked by others, his great ability and influence were recognized by all.

Abraham, or Abram, was of middle age when, in the early years of the Seminole War, he first became a figure of national importance, having been born, probably, between 1787 and 1791.[1] Our knowledge of his ancestry, entirely, and of his early life, almost as much so, is derived from inference. He was a full-blooded Negro,[2] who in his youth, had been a slave in Pensacola to Dr. Sierra;[3] but who, despite his residence on Spanish soil and his servitude to a gentleman of Spanish surname, seems to have been himself "English raised," or the son

1. An official statement (*American State Papers, Military Affairs,* vii, 851) issued in 1837 gives his age as 50; a Charleston volunteer (Cohen, M. M., *Notice of Florida,* Charleston, 1836, p. 239) who had never set eyes on Abraham himself but undoubtedly had talked to those who did know him, estimated his age early in the previous year as 45.
2. Cohen, *loc. cit.;* Coe, Charles H., *Red patriots,* Cincinnati, 1898, pp. 45, 46, quoting a letter from Capt. John C. Casey, Ft. Brooke, Fla., Feb. 25, 1837, to his brother.
3. McCall, Maj. Gen. George A., *Letters from the frontiers,* Philadelphia, 1868, p. 302. Cohen, 239; Foreman, Grant, *Indian removal,* Norman, Okla., 1932, p. 377 n. 17, quoting a letter from Maj. Ethan Allen Hitchcock, Tampa Bay, Fla., Oct. 22, 1840, to Samuel Hitchcock, St. Louis. Casey, on the contrary, says that he had "been all his life among the Indians" (Coe, 45-46), and Joshua R. Giddings (*The exiles of Florida,* Columbus, 1858, p. 83) says he was born among the Indians to parents who were fugitives from Georgia; the latter, however, frequently draws on his imagination, and McCall knew Abraham earlier, and probably more intimately, than Casey.

of parents who were, since there is no evidence that he was ever acquainted with Spanish, or with any language except English and the Muskhogean tongue of the Seminole.

Since he was a city Negro, the presumption is that he was a domestic servant of some sort, and this probability is strengthened by the characteristics universally ascribed to him not merely of intelligence, but also of fluency, courtesy, and even courtliness. "He always smiles, and his words flow like oil. His conversation is soft and low, but very distinct, with a most genteel emphasis," commented a careful observer,[4] while another officer, well acquainted with him, referred to "his gentle, insinuating manner,"[5] and still another, speaking from hearsay, probably meant the same when he called him "plausible, pliant and deceitful" and spoke of his "exterior of profound meekness." His carriage was also in conformity with an earlier *rôle* as butler or valet, and it is remarkable that observers independently found something decidedly "French" in his manner. "He walks like a courtier of the reign of Louis XVI," was one comment,[7] while another officer described his "slight inclination forward like a Frenchman of the old school."[8] It is obvious, at least, that here was no heavy-footed field-hand or thick-tongued stevedore, but a Negro who was possessed of manner and "manners."

Abraham's manner was apparently more distinguished than his physique and, perhaps for that reason, the latter was variously and even somewhat contradictorily described. "Abraham is a non-

4. Coe, 45-46.
5. McCall, 302.
6. Cohen, 239.
7. *Niles' register*, lll (Mar. 25, 1837), 49.
8. Coe, 45-46.

committal man," wrote one officer, "with a countenance which none can read, a person erect and active
and in stature over six feet."[9]   Another wrote that
"his figure is large, his face broad and square,
having the thick lips of a full-blooded negro."[10]
Still another, however, found him to be "of ordinary
stature, rather thin, with a slight inclination forward. . . . His countenance is one of great cunning
and penetration;"[11] perhaps it was this characteristic courteous stoop which made his height sometimes appear only ordinary. His physiognomy also
impressed observers somewhat variously. "He had
a remarkably high and broad forehead; but an awful
cast in his right eye, which gave to his gentle, insinuating manner a very sinister effect," commented
one officer.[12]   Another, more briefly but to the
same purpose: "Abraham is an intelligent negro,
cross-eyed, with a bad countenance."[13]   Still another, more favorably though less vividly: "Abraham's countenance combines a vast degree of cunning and shrewdness, and he is altogether a remarkable looking negro."[14]   An alleged portrait,
frequently reproduced, represents him as a rather
fine-looking Negro with a slight mustache and the
characteristic inclination of his head, wearing the
typical Seminole turban and resting on a rifle.[15]
Perhaps these varying descriptions may be recon-
ciled to describe Abraham as a full-blooded Negro,
of somewhat more than average height, sparely but

9. Foreman, Grant, *Indian removal*, 344, quoting *Army and navy
   chronicle*, iv, 378.
10. Cohen, 239.
11. Coe, 45-46.
12. McCall, 302.
13. "Maj. Childs' Diary," *Historical magazine*, 3rd ser., ii (1873),
   374.
14. *N. R.*, lii (Mar. 25, 1837), 49.
15. Sprague, John T., *The Florida War*, N. Y., 1848, facing p.
   100; Giddings, facing p. 33. The Giddings portrait seems to
   have been "improved" from the one in Sprague.

strongly built, with an intelligent face, a distorted right eye, and conspicuously polished manners.

How did it happen that one who, as "a lad," meaning, no doubt, a young man, had been a slave, probably a domestic servant, in the city of Pensacola, should, when we next encounter trustworthy notice of him, several years later, be a confidential "slave" of Mikonopi, head-chief of the Seminoles, far to the south and east, near the headwaters of the Withlacoochee? What circumstances caused him to flee civilization and seek refuge among a comparatively barbarous people? We cannot answer positively; we can only draw inferences from the known events of the time and place.

In 1812 war had broken out between the United States and Great Britain, and in 1814 the conflict approached the shores of supposedly neutral Spanish Florida. Late in July, seeking bases and support for an attack on New Orleans, a British force of something over a hundred men under Maj. Edward Nicholls, with two sloops of war, occupied Pensacola, hoisted the British flag beside the Spanish, issued a threatening and consoling proclamation to the people of Louisiana and Kentucky, and began to recruit and arm both the Red Stick Creek refugees from Gen. Jackson, and the runaway slaves from the United States, many of whom were in the vicinity. He also swelled his scanty force by enlisting and drilling a number of slaves belonging to residents of Pensacola, to whom he offered freedom and free lands in the British West Indies. Among these recruits, very probably, was young Abraham, and when Gen. Jackson stormed Pensacola on November 7, and the British, who had withdrawn to Ft. Barrancas with their Indian and Negro allies, blew up and evacuated the fortifications on the following day and sailed for the Apalachicola, he was probably one of the "about one hundred negro slaves" who were landed on the eastern bank of that river, about fifteen miles from the mouth, at a place called Prospect Bluff, and employed in building a fort which was called British Post and used by Nicholls as a headquarters for his negotiations with Seminole and Red Stick Indians and with the runaway Negroes from the United States in whom the region already abounded.[16]

Nicholls remained at the fort even after the Treaty of Ghent, negotiating with the Seminole chief Dowlegs and frequently writing letters on his behalf to the United States Indian agent, but early in the summer of 1815 finally set sail for London, taking with him his troops and a few Red Stick chiefs, but leaving behind him most of the Red Sticks, all the Negroes, and great quantities of arms and ammunition, including ten pieces of artillery. The Red Sticks soon moved off to the eastward, but 300 Negroes, including women and children, established themselves in the fort under the strict discipline of a Negro chief named Garçon or Garcia, and were joined by about twenty renegade Choctaw and a few Seminoles from Bowlegs' town on the Suwanee. They summoned the thousand or more runaway Negroes then estimated to be in Florida to settle under the protection offered by the guns of the fort, and soon their settlements were extending fifty miles up and down the river, causing such alarm to Georgia planters that Gen. Jackson ordered that the fort be destroyed, regardless of its location on Spanish territory, and the Negroes

16. McMaster, John Bach, *History of the people of the United States*, iv, 173-174, 179-181, 431; *American State Papers, Indian Affairs*, i, 858-860; Campbell, Richard L., *Historical sketches of colonial Florida*, Cleveland, 1892, p. 236; Rippy, J. Fred, *Rivalry of the United States and Great Britain over Latin America, 1808-1830*, Baltimore, 1929, pp. 45-48, 55.

"restored to their rightful owners." By July, 1816, the Negro Fort was invested from the river by a little fleet of two gunboats and two transports and on land by United States troops assisted by slave-hunting Creeks. On the 17th a boat's crew from one of the gun-boats was nearly annihilated by ambushed Negroes, but on the 27th, after a brisk exchange of artillery fire, one of the gun-boats succeeded in planting a red-hot shot in the fort's magazine, which was blown into the air, killing 270 of the garrison and mortally injuring nearly all the others. The Negro chief Garçon and the Choctaw chief, who were among the few survivors, were turned over to the Creeks, who shot Garçon, scalped the Choctaw chief alive, and subsequently stabbed him to death. The Negro prisoners were returned to slavery.

This destruction, however, extended only to the garrison, who seem to have been almost entirely Spanish-speaking Negroes from Pensacola. The American Negroes, refugees from Georgia plantations, who were settled along the river, escaped into the forest at the approach of the blockading force, and were able to reach King Bowlegs' villages on the Suwanee, already a resort for fugitive Negroes. If we are right in our assumption that Abraham was among the Negroes who left Pensacola with the British and settled on Prospect Bluff, we can account for his escape from the general destruction which befell the garrison by imagining that he had earlier left the fort and settled among the possibly more congenial English-speaking runaways.[17]

17. 15th cong., 2d sess., state papers, vol. vi, nos. 119-122; *American State Papers, Foreign Relations*, iv, 499-500, 555-561; Forbes, James Grant, *Sketches . . . of the Floridas*, N. Y., 1821, pp. 200-205; Williams, John Lee, *The territory of Florida*, N. Y., 1837, pp. 201-203; Williams, J. L., *A view of West Florida*, Philadelphia, 1827, pp. 96-102; *Army and navy chronicle*, ii(1836), 114-116; McMaster, iv, 430-433; Boyd, Mark F., "Events at Prospect Bluff on the Apalachicola River, 1808-1818," *Fla. Hist. Quart.*, xvi(Oct., 1937), 55-96.

Abraham, whenever and however he reached Bowlegs' town on the Suwanee, became, on his arrival, the "slave" either of Bowlegs himself or of the heir-apparent, his nephew, Mikonopi. He did not thereby merely exchange one form of servitude for another of a less onerous nature, for so-called slavery among the Seminoles was so utterly unlike that among the whites that the difference was one of kind rather than merely of degree. The Seminoles, observing that prestige was attached among the powerful whites to the presence of black people were glad to have Negroes associated with them, but had no idea of exploiting them, day by day, either as plantation laborers or domestic servants. The so-called slaves, whether legally purchased from Spanish or British owners, or, as was more frequently the case, runaways or the descendants of runaways who had put themselves under the protection of a Seminole chief, lived, according to a contemporary account, "in villages separate, and, in many cases, remote from their owners, and enjoying equal liberty with their owners, with the single exception that the slave supplied his owner annually, from the product of his little field, with corn, in proportion to the amount of the crop; and in no instance, that has come to my knowledge, exceeding ten bushels; the residue is considered the property of the slave. Many of these slaves have stocks of horses, cows, and hogs, with which the Indian master never assumes the right to intermeddle. . . . An Indian would almost as soon sell his child as his slave."[18]

The Negroes were thus in the position of dependents, or *protegés,* of the Indians, rather than that of slaves, the understanding being that in re-

18. ASP, MA, vi, 534. McCall (160) says the Negroes gave one-third of their produce to their masters.

turn for a tribute of corn and other agricultural products from the Negro, the Indian master would protect him against being claimed as a slave by any white man. The Negroes not merely lived apart from their masters, in their own villages—an evidence of independence which they greatly prized —frequently possessed large herds, and were under no supervision by their masters or patrons, but also dipped their spoons into the sofky pot with their lord and his family whenever they happened to be at his home, habitually carried arms, went into battle along with the Seminole warriors, under their own captains, and, save for the slight annual tribute, were under no greater subjection to the chiefs than were the Seminole tribesmen themselves. The relationship might be described as one of primitive democratic feudalism, involving no essential personal inequality. General Gaines spoke with approximate accuracy, when, avoiding the more common term of "slaves," he referred to "the Seminole Indians with their black vassals and allies."[19]

The Indians found the Negroes useful not merely as tributary agriculturists and auxiliaries in battle, but also as interpreters and counsellors. Their knowledge of European languages, their better acquaintance with the mysterious ways of the white men, gave them an advantage over the less sophisticated Indians, who came to depend on them for advice to such an extent that white observers began to say that the Indians were ruled by the Negroes and that the Seminole government was actually a doulocracy, a government by slaves. It was in this situation that Abraham became an element, and to its development an important contributor.

His early life among the Indians is obscure. If our assumption that he was one of the Pensacola

19. ASP, MA, vii, 427.

Negroes who left that city with the British, and
subsequently fled to the Suwanee from the destruction of the Negro Fort, is correct, he must have
been at Bowlegs' Town at the time of the Battle
of the Suwanee, in April, 1818, when the Negroes,
after most of the Indians had fled, though hopelessly outnumbered put up to the inexorable advance of Andrew Jackson's army a brief but desperate resistance which won them the admiration
of some of their enemies. Perhaps it was on this
occasion that he won the war-title of "Souanaffe
Tustenukke" which he was using twenty years later,
and which, although interpreted as "Shawnee Warrior," might perhaps signify "Suwanee Warrior."[20]

Perhaps he was the "Indian Negro, named
Abraham," whom Harmon H. Holliman "employed
. . . to go into the nation for the purpose of bringing in . . . a Negro woman and her child," who had
been plundered by the Seminoles from Georgia. On
his return to "Hope Hill on the St. John's river,
about three miles south of Volutia," in March,
1822, he announced his arrival by a "loud whoop."[21]
He was probably by this time living at the Negro
town of Pilaklikaha, occupied chiefly by "runaway
slaves from Georgia who have put themselves under
the protection of Micanopy, or some other chiefs,"
and who possessed fine fields and good houses. An
officer who visited it in September, 1826, remarked
that the "three principal men . . . bear the distinguished names of July, August, and Abraham
. . . shrewd, intelligent fellows, and to the highest
degree obsequious."[22]

20. National Archives, War Department, General Jesup's Papers,
     No. 2, "Abram," Tampa Bay, Sept. 11, 1837, to "Cäe Hajo,"
     signed "Souanaffe Tustenukke." This letter is included in
     the appendix to this article.
21. ASP, MA, vi, 498.
22. McCall, 160.

The first unmistakable episode of importance in his career was his accompanying as interpreter to Washington in 1825-1826 a delegation of Seminoles headed by his master Mikonopi, who had been principal chief at least since 1823 and probably for two or three years earlier. On his return he was liberated "in consequence of his many and faithful services and great merits,"[23] though his emancipation was not formally recorded until June 18, 1835.[24]

He had already been rewarded by being given for a wife "the widow of the former chief of the nation,"[25] presumably a woman of Negro, or part-Negro blood, and a slave, who had been the wife or mistress of King Bowlegs. She was probably the woman by the name of Hagar whose son by Abraham, named Renty, was freed by his father in 1839; Abraham had at least one or two other sons, one named Washington, and at least one daughter, probably all by this same woman.[26]

The United States government had determined to make room for white settlers and prevent Indian wars by removing the tribes east of the Mississippi to the Indian Territory, a region including much of the area now occupied by the states of Oklahoma and Kansas. The Seminole, alone of the Five Civilized Tribes of the south, put up a violent and protracted resistance to removal. It was natural that they should object to leaving the forests and swamps of their fatherland for the unfamiliar

---

23. Coe, 45-46.
24. Hillsborough Co., Fla., Record Book Historical Records Survey Copy, p. 124.
25. 25th cong., 3d sess., H. of R., No. 225, p. 69.
26. Hillsborough Co. Record Book, 124; National Archives, Department of the Interior, Indian Office, Seminole File 1841; Nat'l Archs., War Dep't, AGO, 1838 Jesup 72, Jesup, Camp Jupiter, Mar. 6, 1838, to Brig. Gen. W. K. Armistead, Charles Ferry, "young Juan, Abraham's son in law."

prairies and more severe climate of the Indian Territory—a land, too, which bordered on the territory of wild and potentially hostile Indians. The reluctance of the Negroes to depart was intensified by the fact that as the agriculturists of the nation they had a special attachment for the fields they had cleared and tilled. The unwillingness of the Seminole Indians to be domiciled, as was the plan, with and under the control of their kinsmen the Creeks, from whom they had seceded nearly a century before, was an important consideration. But the decisive factor was the presence and peculiar position of the Negroes. Some of the Seminole Negroes, such as Abraham himself, were comparatively recent runaways from servitude among the whites, and when Indians and Negroes should be assembled at a central point, under military supervision, for transportation to the west, white slaveowners would not lose this opportunity to reclaim their human property. Even legally-purchased Seminole slaves were not immune from this danger, for it was an old trick for white men to lay claim to Seminole Negroes—sometimes after having themselves just sold them!—and their demands were usually accepted by white authorities. Negroes among the Seminoles, furthermore, were frequently the wives, husbands, children, of Indians.

The Seminole Indians, strongly influenced by the Negroes, among whom Abraham was the leading figure, determined to place every obstacle possible in the way of their removal. On May 9, 1832, however, their principal men were induced to sign the treaty of Payne's Landing, which provided that a delegation of Seminoles should visit the Indian Territory and report on its suitability as a new home. This treaty further provided that "their faithful interpreters Abraham and Cudjo" in case

of removal "shall receive two hundred dollars each,
. . . in full remuneration for the improvements to
be abandoned on the lands now cultivated by them."
"Abraham, Interpreter, his X mark" appears as
a witness.[27] Maj. Ethan Allen Hitchcock, in a letter
of Oct. 22, 1840, asserts that Abraham was bribed,
by the insertion in the treaty of a sum of $100 for
his services as interpreter, to exert his influence
toward its acceptance, which otherwise could not
have been achieved.[28] But the amount provided for
the interpreters was merely a proportion of the sum
to be divided among the entire nation *only* in case
of removal, of which Abraham was actually a leading opponent, though Cudjo seems to have been
early won over to the emigration policy. Abraham
no doubt felt it would do no harm to send a delegation to the Indian Territory to inspect the land set
aside for the Seminoles, and could hardly have anticipated that, once in the west, the delegation which
he accompanied would be bullied, as it was, into
signing, March 28, 1833, the Treaty of Ft. Gibson,
in which the members agreed, for the nation, to
removal from Florida—an agreement completely
outside their authority. "Abraham Seminole Interpreter" witnessed this treaty.[29]

Those officials best acquainted with the situation
recognized the importance of winning over Abraham to the emigration policy, for, whatever disagreement there was about his appearance or his
character, there was none whatsoever concerning
his intelligence, ability, and, particularly, his influence with his former master, head-chief Mikonopi. "The negro Abraham is obviously a great

27. Kappler, Charles J., comp. and ed., *Indian affairs laws and treaties*, vol. ii, Washington, 1904, pp. 344-345.
28. Foreman, *Indian removal*, 376-378 n. 17.
29. Sprague, 78.

man;" wrote an officer, "though a black he has long been appointed 'sense-bearer' to the King (Micke-nopah). . . ."[30] "Abra'm, or Yobly, as the Indians call him," commented another, "is the chief Interpreter, and latterly succeeded Jumper as 'sense carrier' to Miconope. This high chancellor and keeper of the king's conscience, also heads about five hundred negroes of whom he is legislator, judge, and executioner through his influence with the Governor . . . under an exterior of profound meekness, [he] cloaks deep, dark, and bloody purposes. He has at once the crouch and spring of the panther, and certain traits of his character liken him to the Cardinal De Retz."[31]   Again, in this rather romantic description, the "French" qualities of Abraham's character are emphasized.   "Abraham," we read again, "who is sometimes dignified with the title of 'Prophet', . . . is the prime minister and privy counsellor of Micanopy; and has through his master, who is somewhat imbecile, ruled all the councils and actions of the Indians in this region."[32]

"Micanopy owned many negroes," begins one of the most careful analyses of the situation, "who partook of the feeling exhibited around them. His principal slave Abraham, was the most noted, and for a time an influential man in the nation. He dictated to those of his own color, who to a great degree controlled their masters. They were a most cruel and malignant enemy. For them to surrender would be servitude to the whites; but to retain an open warfare secured to them plunder, liberty, and importance."[33]   The briefer characterizations were

---

30. Coe, 45-46.
31. Cohen, 239.   The meaning of Yobly is unknown.   It cannot be translated by authorities either in African or Muskhogean linguistics.
32. Foreman, *Indian removal*, 344 n. 5.
33. Sprague, 100.

in agreement. "Abraham is a cunning negro, of good consideration with the Seminoles, and who can do more than any other." "Micanope is a fat, lubberly . . . kind of man, and is ever a stupid fool, when not replenished by his 'sense bearer', (as he calls him) Abraham."[34] "Abraham . . . his interpreter . . . exercised a wonderful influence over his master."[35] "Abraham . . . has as much influence in the nation as any other man," "he is a sensible shrewd negro, and has ever been the principal counsellor of his master," "with an appearance of great modesty, he is ambitious, avaricious, and withal very intelligent."[36] One officer, however, makes Abraham more of a behind-the-scenes operator than the others: "Abram, a free negro, who, like all the 'Indian negroes', spoke English, was always present at the councils, and frequently interpreted what was said, but seemed publicly to have no voice or influence. In point of fact, however, though not a chief, he had much influence."[37] Abraham's "influence is unlimited"[38] was the view of another, while still another sweepingly stated that Mikonopi was never known to do anything against his advice.[39] "We have a perfect Talleyrand of the Savage Court in the person of a Seminole negro, called Abraham,"[40] was the summation of one of the commentators with a fondness for comparisons drawn from French history.

The principal and indeed the only method advocated for winning Abraham over, was, however,

34. Foreman, *Indian removal*, 344 n. 5.
35. McCall, 302.
36. Williams, 214, 272-273.
37. Churchill, Franklin Hunter, *Sketch of the life of Vvt. Brig. Gen. Sylvester Churchill*, N. Y., 1888, p. 111.
38. Childs, ii, 374.
39. Hitchcock, Ethan Allen, *Fifty years in camp and field*, W. A. Croffut, ed., N. Y., 1909, p. 78.
40. *A. & N.C.*, iv 378.

the sort of covert bribery which, it is alleged, was intended by the insertion of a provision for payment to the interpreters in the treaty of Payne's Landing. Abraham had been cheated out of $280, which he had expended on the trip to the Indian Territory, by Maj. John Phagan, the Indian agent who had accompanied the delegation, by the agent's telling him that it was necessary for Abraham, in order to be paid, to give Phagan a receipt for the money, to be sent to Washington; the agent then submitted the receipt, himself received payment, and the interpreter was left holding an empty sack, it seems permanently. At some point in the transaction, the agent, evidently a thorough scoundrel who, it is interesting to note, was the instrument through which the delegation were induced, or forced, to sign the Ft. Gibson treaty, had refused to pay Abraham unless he would buy the agent's gun at double its price. Abraham was still complaining about this as late as 1852. Abraham's persistent attempts to obtain payment seem to have inspired in the mind of Phagan's successor as agent the not particularly startling conclusion that a Negro, as well as a white man, might be interested in gaining and saving money. Abraham, he announced with an air of discovery, "loves money, I believe, as well as any person I ever saw . . . a few hundred dollars," he continued, "would make him zealous and active" in the cause of emigration. Promises of this character were probably extended to Abraham and, if so, it is evident that he pretended to fall in with them. Actually he was determined to encourage his sluggish master to resist a removal which, he believed, as projected would be fatal to his people.[41]

---

41. ASP, MA, vi, 546; [Potter, Woodburne], *The War in Florida*, Baltimore, 1836, p. 26; National Archives, Department of the Interior, Indian Office, Seminole File 1852-J121, T. S. Jesup. Washington, Oct. 5, 1852, to Luke Lea, Commissioner of Indian Affairs.

Publicly, Abraham, during the two or three years of controversy which elapsed between the signing of the Treaty of Ft. Gibson and the outbreak of open hostilities, confined himself to interpreting at the various councils held between the Seminole agent and the chiefs, in which the agent insisted that they must prepare to depart for the West, while most of the chiefs refused, asserting the earlier treaty of 1823 guaranteed for 20 years their possession of the reservation assigned to them at that time. Secretly, however, he was instigating the head-chief Mikonopi to resistance, and strengthening him in that resolve whenever the indolent old man wavered in his determination. He was also, through free Negroes and Spanish fishermen, building up a reserve of ammunition and making arrangements for a continued supply of powder and lead during the hostilities, whenever they should break out. When the war had been going on for over a year, he was reported as still receiving consignments of powder, disguised as barrels of flour, from a free Negro in St. Augustine.[42]

Abraham recognized that the Seminole Indians and Negroes possessed valuable potential allies in the slaves on the sugar-plantations of the St. Johns river, and he and another Negro leader, John Caesar, accompanied by such Indian chiefs as Yaha Hajo (Mad Wolf), visited all the plantations and encouraged the Negroes, by promises of freedom and plunder, to be prepared to revolt simultaneously with the inevitable outbreak of hostilities.[43] Since it was not uncommon for Indian Negroes to have

42. National Archives, War Department, General Jesup's Papers, Box 14, Maj. Gen. Thos. S. Jesup, Ft. Armstrong, Jan. 21, 1837, to Brig. Gen. J. M. Hernandez, St. Augustine.
43. Cohen, 81.

wives and other relatives on the plantations, and
since, for a number of years, the prevalence of peace
had encouraged intercourse between Negro slaves
and Seminole Indians, it was easy to convince the
slaves, well aware of the advantageous position of
the Seminole Negroes, that their interests and those
of the Indians were the same. At the same time,
however, Abraham gave the whites the impression
that he was working in their interests and in favor
of emigration. Up to the day of his death, Maj.
Dade, who was the first to fall in the heavy fighting
which marked the outbreak of the Seminole War,
was convinced of the "salutary influence" of
Abraham on Mikonopi.[44]

Near the end of 1835, when it had been announced that the Seminoles must assemble for
emigration by the first of the next year or be deported forcibly, Abraham was preparing to throw
off his mask. Some chiefs, reluctantly convinced
that resistance was hopeless, prepared to yield, and
began to sell off their livestock preparatory to departure. The principal man in the emigration party
was Charley, or Chalo, Emathla (Trout Leader),
an able and public-spirited chief whose example was
likely to be influential. Some of the leaders of the
faction militantly opposed to emigration, Osceola, a
young Red Stick Creek who, though not a chief, exerted great influence particularly upon the young
warriors, Holata Micco (Billy Bowlegs), a nephew
of Mikonopi, and Abraham, determined that he
must be made an example, and on Nov. 26, 1835,
"a party of about four hundred warriors . . . proceeded to the residence" of the doomed man. Abraham, at the last moment, perhaps not having
previously realized that more than a warning was
intended at this time, endeavored to induce Osceola

44. *N.R.*, xlix (Jan. 30, 1836), 367.

to spare his life, and succeeded in getting the leaders to delay and hold a council, but his intervention was ultimately futile and Osceola and others proceeded to waylay and shoot down the chief as he was returning from selling his cattle.[45]

Abraham, who was also sometimes known as The Prophet, and seems to have been imbued with the religious enthusiasm of the time, stirred up excitement among the Indians and Negroes, particularly the latter, by assuring them that "God was in their favor." He prophesied concerning General Wiley Thompson, the Seminole agent, that "he would be killed by Indians while walking about his place." The general was actually put to death at the beginning of the war by Osceola and some of his followers while enjoying a stroll and a cigar after dinner.[46]

When the war finally began with the ambushing and annihilation of Major Dade's command of more than a hundred men, Dec. 28, 1835, Abraham was for over a year one of the leading war-spirits. He was said to be in personal command of eighty warriors,[46a] and "no action was complete unless Abraham was reported to be in it, with his *big gun.*"[47] He was undoubtedly a leader in most of the principal actions of the first year or so, particularly Dade's defeat and the various battles on the Withlacoochee. A prisoner, to be sure, reported that "Abraham was . . . at [the first battle of the] Withlacoochee but made off on the first fire,"[48] but he may have been saying what he thought would please his captors, as this is the only report on record ad-

45. Potter, 96-97; Cohen, 56.
46. *A. & N.C.*, iii(Nov. 3, 1836), 285.
46a. *N.R.*, 1 (Apr. 23, 1836), 141.
47. Childs, iii, 282.
48. National Archives, War Department, AGO, Capt. F. S. Belton, Ft. Brooke, Jan. 14, 1836, to the Adjutant General (12).

verse to the Negro chief's courage, the prevalent opinion being that he was "a good soldier and an intrepid leader," "an enemy by no means to be despised."[49]

Abraham, as regards emigration, belonged before the war to the left-wing militant element of the Seminole tribe; afterwards, however, when the emigration party had seceded and taken refuge with the whites, his position among the hostiles became somewhat to the right of center so far as intransigency was concerned. This was partly, on doubt, because of his association with Mikonopi. His position in the tribe depended largely on his influence over the head-chief, and even Abraham was able to move the sluggish Mikonopi only so far. It was primarily, however, in all probability, a matter of temperament and information. Abraham had been to Washington and knew the white man's power. He was consequently aware that the Seminole could not hope actually to defeat the United States government. He did hope, however, that they could put up such a fight that the government would permit the Indians and Negroes to remain in Florida, even on a more restricted reservation, particularly since there was actually as yet no pressure of settlers on the land occupied by the Seminole. Abraham had also been to the Indian Territory and knew that, with all its disadvantages, it was not a bad country; he was consequently also prepared, as an alternative, to accept emigration, provided that satisfactory assurances were given that transportation to the West would not be employed as a device to enslave the Seminole Negroes. He was therefore always willing to negotiate with the whites, in the hope that

---

49. 25th cong., 2d sess., ex. doc. 78, vol. iii, pp. 113-118; 25th cong., 3d sess., H. of R., no. 225, p. 69; Foreman, *Indian removal*, 344 n. 5.

one or the other of the above arrangements could be attained without further fighting, but to that end his plan was to resist so fiercely in the meantime that the whites would be discouraged into granting satisfactory terms.

Abraham, accordingly, on March 6, 1836, during the siege of Camp Izard on the banks of the Withlacoochee, was instrumental in negotiating a truce with General Gaines which might have resulted in a permanent arrangement had not the Seminoles been fired on, through a misunderstanding, by members of another officer's force which arrived during a parley. John Caesar, chief Negro of King Philip, Mikonopi's brother-in-law, chief of the St. Johns river Seminoles, and second in authority only to Mikonopi himself, was also concerned in the negotiations and, indeed, probably initiated them, though this may have been after consultation with Abraham.[50]

After nearly a year of hostilities the Seminoles were still more than holding their own. The whites had been repulsed time and time again, from the Withlacoochee crossing, in the Big Wahoo swamp; one large detachment had been wiped out. The "celebrated negro Abraham and many others had been prophesying . . . that God was in their favor; . . . they had lost only twenty warriors during the

---

50. Potter, 154-160; A. & N.C., ii (April 7, 1836), 214; Sprague, 107-113; Foreman, *Indian removal*, 330. Potter says that Abraham proposed the conference, but admits that this is mere supposition: "Presuming that the voice was Abraham's, his name will be used." A Negro, apparently in authority, representing the Seminole, and seen and heard only from a distance, was likely to be assumed to be the most important and best known of the Seminole Negro chiefs, namely Abraham, unless his actual identity were positively known. Consequently those who said that the initiator of the conference was John Caesar, probably had good reason for their opinion. See the author's "John Caesar: a forgotten hero of the Seminole War," *Journal of Negro History*, xxviii (Jan., 1945), 59-60.

whole war," whereas the whites had lost five times
that number in the single action which began the
war.[51] A new commander-in-chief, General T. S.
Jesup, took over in December, however, and under
his leadership a vigorous campaign was initiated
which drove the Indians and Negroes out of their
former lurking-places along the Withlacoochee and
in the Wahoo swamp and sent them south and east
toward the Everglades.   Abraham, among other
principal chiefs, was reported as being resolved on
Fabian tactics, intending "to fly before the army
and avoid a battle," taking refuge "in the dense
swamps and hammocks of the Everglades." The
army, however, moved too rapidly for him to be able
to carry out these tactics of avoidance, and on Jan.
27, 1837, according to a prisoner, Abraham, with
"from forty to fifty Indians," was in the Big Cypress swamp, hovering on the rear of Colonel Henderson's detachment, preparing to co-operate with
"a large number of negroes" who "were in advance." In the sharp fight which followed, the
Seminoles suffered heavily, not so much in dead and
wounded as in prisoners and *materiel,* for the whites
captured their baggage-train with their provisions
and munitions and a large number of women and
children, particularly Negroes. Abraham later said
that he lost most of his property. "at the Cypress.
. . . I lose most every ting—all my powder and
blankets; a hundred dollars in silver; pots; kettles
—every ting"—including, in addition, his freedom-
papers and his little boy's favorite pony.[52]

General Jesup felt that the Seminoles now might
be ready to treat and, having captured one of
Mikonopi's principal Negroes, named Ben, along

51. *A. & N.C.,* iii(Nov. 3, 1836), 285.
52. 25th cong., 2d sess., ex. doc. no. 78, vol. iii, pp. 55, 69; Childs,
    iii, 283.

with his wife and all his children, sent him out to the
hostiles with the offer of a liberal treaty, and on
Jan. 31 "Abraham made his appearance bearing a
white flag on a small stick which he had cut in the
woods, and walked up to the tent of General Jesup
with perfect dignity and composure. He stuck the
staff of his flag in the ground, made a salute or
bow with his hand, without bending his body, and
then waited for the advance of the General with the
most complete self-possession. He . . . since stated
that he expected to be hung, but concluded to die,
if he must, like a man, but that he would make one
more effort to save his people." General Jesup,
however, convinced him of the government's good
faith and, with great difficulty, Abraham succeeded
on February 3 and 18 in bringing in Jumper, Alligator, and other Indian and Negro chiefs, for peace-
negotiations.[53]

Eventually, "largely through the negotiations of
the negro, Abraham, on March 6, 1837 at Camp
Dade, a treaty was concluded between Jesup and the
Seminole chiefs Jumper and Holatoochee claiming
to represent Mikanopy. . . . By the terms of this
treaty the Indians agreed to cease their hostilities,
come to Tampa Bay by April 10, and board the
transports for the West. The chief Mikanopy was
to be surrendered as a hostage for the performance
of their promises. However, to induce them to accept these terms, General Jesup was obliged to agree
to the one condition that the Indians had insisted on
from the beginning; and that was that their allies,
the free negroes, should also be secure in their persons and property; and 'that their negroes, their
bona fide property shall accompany them to the
West.' "[54]

---

53. Foreman, *Indian removal*, 344; Childs, ii, 374, iii, 283, 169-
170; *A. & N.O.*, iv, 378; viii (Mar. 7, 1839), 154-155; ASP,
MA, vii, 828, 833.
54. Foreman, *Indian removal*, 344; *N.R.*, lii(Mar. 25, 1837), 49.

Abraham was active for the next month as interpreter in various subsequent councils, in using his influence to get other Indians and Negroes to come in, and, always with an eye to the main chance, in supplying the officers with such game as wild turkeys, one noted as weighing seventeen pounds, and in rounding up his cattle and bringing them in for sale to the United States. He was also able to reclaim for his "little boy about six years of age; and a beautiful boy he is," who, according to the officer-commentator, "had hardly ever seen a white person before," the pony which had been captured at the Tohopkaliga during the Battle of Hatchee Lustee or the Big Cypress.

Abraham probably suffered a loss during this period in the death of his father-in-law, whoever he was. He explained his delay in arriving at Ft. Armstrong, where he was expected by the morning of April 1, by stating: "I waited for Wann and Wann's father; and my father-in-law was sick; and had to be carried, two miles, on the black people's shoulders. I 'fraid he won't live to get to Tampa." No aged Negro who can be identified as Abraham's father-in-law appears on any of the lists, so probably his fears were justified. It is possible that "Wann's father" and "my father-in-law" refer to the same person. "Wann" or "Juan", whose name on the printed lists appears incorrectly as "Inos," was one of Mikonopi's principal Negroes and commanded the Negro forces on the Withlacoochee earlier in the war, possibly being field-commander under Abraham.[55]

Unfortunately, however, General Jesup, influenced by the success of the negotiations and under severe pressure from slave-holders, entered into clandestine arrangements with Coi Hajo, second

55. Childs, iii, 280-282.

chief of the St. Johns river Seminoles, for the return to their owners of Negroes who had joined the
Seminoles during the war, and the appearance of
slave-owners, seeking to reclaim their human property, in the emigration-camp at Tampa bay,
caused, first, the gradual disappearance into the
swamps of many of the Indians and Negroes who
had assembled there and, eventually, late in May
or early in June, resulted in a mass-stampede of
most of the remainder, accompanied by the kidnapping by the militant young chiefs Osceola and Coacoochee (Wild Cat) and the Negro-Indian subchief
John Cavallo, of the hostages who had been yielded
by the Seminoles for the carrying out of the Camp
Dade treaty. Abraham, however, and other principal Negro chiefs, remained in the hands of the
troops and General Jesup, angered by the renewal
of a war which he had thought safely ended, announced: "The Seminole negro prisoners are now
the property of the public. I have promised Abraham the freedom of his family if he be faithful to us,
and I shall certainly hang him if he will not be
faithful. . ." The Seminoles gave no evidence at this
time of intending to renew hostilities, and the sickly
summer season was on, which prevented the troops
from then taking overt action.

Abraham could hardly have remained uninfluenced by General Jesup's promise of freedom to
himself and family, particularly when coupled with
a threat of hanging, but he had already committed
himself, and won over most of the principal chiefs,
particularly head-chief Mikonopi and his brother-
in-law and counsellor Jumper, to a policy of emigration under the terms of the Ft. Dade treaty. He
may have regretted its later modification in a sense
hostile to the runaway plantation-slaves, but the in-

---

56. Foreman, *Indian removal*, 349.

terests of the Seminole Negroes of long standing were, of course, pre-eminent in his mind. His influence with Mikonopi remained strong, even when they had been compulsorily separated through the kidnapping of the head-chief, and Mikonopi occasionally succeeded, though a semi-prisoner of the hostiles, in communicating to the whites his strong desire for a consultation with Abraham.[57]

When the season was again propitious, the forces of the United States launched a joint campaign of military operations and peace-propaganda, in which latter Abraham was conspicuous. On September 11, 1837, he wrote "Cäe Hajo," second chief of the St. Johns river Seminoles, urging him to surrender, and signing with his war-name, "Souanaffe Tustenukke."[58] Coi Hajo had from the first been weak-kneed in his opposition to emigration, so much so that he had nearly met the fate of Chalo Emathla, and had been particularly cooperative after the Treaty of Ft. Dade; the capture of his superior, King Philip, though perhaps not known at the time of the letter, increased his importance as a key-man.

"Abraham," it was announced Nov. 6, 1837, "has volunteered to act as guide to our troops, and his services will be accepted. He says he knows the spot where his master, Micanopy, is concealed, and that the Indians are nearly out of ammunition." It

57. ASP, MA, vii. 840-841.
58. National Archives, War Department, General Jesup's Papers, No. 2, "Abram," Tampa Bay, Sept. 11, 1837, to "Cäe Hajo." This letter is included in appendix, *post*. Abraham was probably not the Seminole Negro guide of that name who assisted government forces, Sept. 9 and 10, to surprise and capture King Philip, principal chief of the St. Johns River Seminoles and second chief in the nation, and his vassal and ally Euchee Jack, and their parties, near St. Augustine (25th cong., 2d sess., ex. doc., no. 78, vol. iii, 109-111). Abraham was a not uncommon name among Negroes, and "the Negro Abraham" could hardly have been operating in the vicinity of St. Augustine on Sept. 10 and dictating a letter at Tampa bay the following day.

was probably in large part through the urgings of Abraham, conveyed to Mikonopi, that the head-chief and most of his followers were induced to surrender again the following month.[59] Abraham did not, so far as the record runs, ever take up arms against his former allies, but confined himself to acting as envoy in urging them to surrender. His approaches were, apparently, always received with respect, and no threats against his life by recalcitrant hostiles are recorded. He inspected the battle-ground after the battle of Lake Okeechobee, December, 25, 1837, the hardest-fought action of the entire war, and "From signs made in the sand, supposed to be by Alligator," Mikonopi's nephew and the principal war-chief, gave it "as his opinion that the Indians intend to war to the death."[60] Yet when he was sent with other Seminole chiefs to Colonel Zachary Taylor, March 24, 1838, to negotiate for peace with the hostiles still in the field, he did not hesitate to enter Alligator's camp and was so successful in his mission that on April 4 it was reported that "Abraham & Echoconee came in with Alligator & two negroes, they found Alligator . . . in a hammock with 88 of his people & 27 blacks to the SW of Okee Chobee. . . . John Co-hi-a [the Indian Negro perhaps better known as John Cavallo, who had been a ringleader in the kidnapping of the hostages and a commander at Okeechobee] is with Alligators people & will come in with him. Alligator will send for Coacoochee [another ringleader and commander, King Philip's son and the most important hostile still out], who, he states is . . . between here & the head of the St. Johns."[61]

59. *A. & N.C.*, v(Dec. 14, 1837), 381.
60. *N.R.*, liii(Jan. 13, 1838), 305.
61. Sprague, 195; National Archives, War Department, AGO, Col. Z. Taylor, Ft. Basinger(sic), Apr. 4, 1838, to Maj. Gen. T. S. Jesup (82J).

Abraham wrote to General Jesup, April 25, 1838, in part as follows: "We wish to get in writing from the General the agreement made with us. We will go with the Indians to our new home, and wish to know how we are to be protected, and who is to have the care of us on the road. We do not live for our selves only, but for our wives & children who are as dear to us as those of any other men. When we reach our home we hope we shall be permitted to remain while the woods remain green, and the water runs. I have charge of all the red people coming on to Pease's Creek, and all are satisfied to go to Arkansas. . . . Whoever is to be chief Interpreter we would wish to know. I cannot do any more than I have. I have done all I can, my heart has been true since I came in at Tohopo Kilika. . . . All the black people are contented I hope."[62]

Abraham had finally, he believed, accomplished his objective of bringing about the end of the war through the surrender of nearly all the Seminoles acknowledging allegiance to head-chief Mikonopi, on terms which guaranteed to the Indians their property and to the Negroes their exemption from seizure by whites. He had not, however, fulfilled all the duties demanded of him by General Jesup, and on May 14 it was ordered that he, together with Cudjo and August, the former a partisan of the whites from the beginning, should be retained as interpreters at $2.50 per diem—other interpreters, however, receiving only one dollar.[63] He continued as interpreter, without particular event, for nearly another year, but on February 25, 1839, was finally shipped

---

62. Original in P. K. Yonge Library of Florida History, University of Florida, Abram, Ft. Deynaud, Apr. 25, 1838, to Gen. Jesup, Tampa. This letter is included in appendix *post*.

63. Order Book, Army of the South, Jan. 29-May 22, 1838, in P. K. Yonge Library of Florida History, University of Florida, (Order 118, Tampa Bay, May 14, 1838).

west. He was noted in the local press *en route* as
"Abraham, well known as an interpreter and a wily
and treacherous rascal."[64] The company of which
he was the leading member was turned over to the
Seminole agent at Ft. Gibson, Indian Territory,
April 13, 1839; the muster-roll included two unnamed male slaves belonging to Abraham, who may,
however, have been his children.[65]

• • •

Abraham's life in the Indian Territory, which
was to extend over another generation, was considerably of an anti-climax to a man who had been
a principal agent first in bringing about a serious
war and second in bringing it to a conclusion. It
was not, however, devoid of usefulness. We lose
sight of him for a couple of years after his arrival.
Presumably he reassumed his position as interpreter
to Mikonopi, and no doubt contributed to the notably better adjustment of his band to their new life,
settling down, as they did, on Deep Fork, to raise
corn, beans, pumpkins, melons, and even a little
rice, whereas more recalcitrant bands, such as those
of Wild Cat and Alligator, refused to enter the
Creek country and squatted on Cherokee territory,
where they remained for several years in a miser-
able state of poverty and uncertainty.[66]

During and after 1841 we begin again to get
occasional glimpses of Abraham in his new environment. On April 17, 1841, at Ft. Gibson, Mikonopi
sold to Abraham for $300 a 16-year-old Negro boy
named Washington, whom, on September 14, Abraham emancipated, out of the love and affection he
bore the boy, his son—the second of his children

---

64. Foreman, Indian removal, 370; *A. & N.C.*, viii, 205.
65. 27th cong., 2d sess., H. of R., ex. doc. no. 55, "Seminole War—
    Slaves Captured," p. 5.
66. Foreman, *The Five Civilized Tribes*, Norman, Okla., 1934,
    223-278, *passim.*

whose emancipation is on record.[67] At a conference between Captain Ethan Allen Hitchcock and Coacoochee, at Ft. Gibson, Nov. 28, 1841, Abraham interpreted.[68]

During 1843 and 1844 the reports of the Seminole sub-agent listed "Abraham (colored man), interpreter" at a stipend of "$300 per annum," and on January 24, 1845, at the Creek agency, "Abraham, U. S. Interpreter for Seminoles," was a witness to a treaty intended to adjust the unhappy relations between the Creeks and the Seminoles by giving the latter local autonomy, subject, however, to the general control of the Creek council, and providing that controversies between the two tribes over property rights, which the Seminoles understood as referring to their Negroes, should be decided by the president of the United States.[69]

Abraham did not subsequently appear in the *rôle* of government interpreter at the Seminole sub-agency, as later in the year he was removed from his position by the sub-agent on the charge of unfitness. "The conduct of Abraham," he wrote, "was such that I was compelled to procure the services of young Mr. Brinton . . . Abraham is very much addicted to the use of ardent spirits; so much so that he is entirely incompetent for a Government Interpreter. He was unable to render me any assistance upon the day of issue, being upon the ground intoxicated, and engaged in broils and dissensions with the Indians themselves. Besides, Abraham has by no means the confidence of the

67. National Archives, Department of the Interior, Indian Office, Seminole File 1841.
68. Hitchcock, *Fifty Years in Camp and Field*, 138.
69. *Annual report of the Commissioner of Indian Affairs*, 1842-1843, p. 161, 1843-1844, p. 176; *Indian laws and treaties*, ii, 552.

Seminoles.'"⁷⁰ It should be noted that, during this general period, no one connected with the Seminole sub-agency, from interpreter and blacksmith up to and including the sub-agent himself, long escaped accusations of drunkenness, venality, inattention to duty, and general worthlessness, from persons coveting these positions for themselves or their friends. No other accusation of this character against Abraham is on record, and one need not imagine him as a teetotaller in order to feel that there is probably considerable exaggeration in this portrayal of him as a complete sot.

That Abraham lacked the confidence of some, at least, of the Seminoles, is, however, doubtless true. He himself complained a few days after this accusation was lodged against him, and while it was probably still unknown to him, that "his conduct in Florida in favour of the whites has procured him many enemies, and that he leads an uncertain and unhappy life—knowing 'Abram,'" the writer continued, "you [Gen. Jesup] will be able to judge how much of this is true."⁷¹ Evidently Abraham's amanuensis had no high personal regard for the interpreter's veracity. Abraham had probably been drawn into the feud which was racking the Seminole tribe at the time, between the militants, led by Wild Cat and Alligator, who were opposed to Creek domination, even of a qualified character, and those who were inclined to accept it, at least passively. Both factions, however, were accustomed to use the accusation of having assisted the whites

---

70. National Archives, Department of the Interior, Indian Office, Seminole File 1845. A1852-1865, Gideon C. Matlock, Seminole sub-agent, Little River, July 18, 1845, to Maj. William Armstrong, Acting Superintendent of Indian Affairs for the Western Territory.
71. Charles O. Collins, Ft. Gibson, July 27, 1845, to Maj. Gen. Jesup, Ft. Smith, Ark. in P. K. Yonge Library of Florida History, University of Florida.

in Florida, to arouse sentiment against their
opponents.

Abraham had taken no part in the activities of
the militants—even of the Negroes who, seriously
concerned with the menace of kidnapping by
whites and half-breeds, were under the leadership
of John Cavallo, allied with the Wild Cat-Alligator
faction among the Indians. He had been, from his
first arrival in the Indian Territory, prepared to
accept the plans for the Seminoles drawn up by
the United States government, which included residence among the Creeks as a part of the Creek
tribe. Shunning anti-Creek agitation, he had probably devoted himself to improving the material welfare of the Seminole, Indians and Negroes, directly
under Mikonopi's command, through encouraging
agriculture. He was too important a figure, his
right to freedom too well established, to be seriously menaced by kidnapping, and it is by no means
creditable to his public spirit at this point that we
do not find him associated with any of the protests
against kidnapping made by John Cavallo, Tony
Barnett, and other Seminole Negro leaders. When
a delegation headed by Wild Cat and Alligator,
with John Cavallo as interpreter, went to Washington in April, 1844, to demand relief for the Seminole,
and Mikonopi, jealous of the challenge to his authority involved in Wild Cat's assumption of leadership, was induced through some influence to head
a list of chiefs disclaiming and protesting against
the delegation, Abraham signed the document as a
witness, indicating where his associations lay.[72]

It is unfortunate that the principal and, indeed,
the only authority in print on Abraham subsequent
to the Seminole War, Congressman Joshua R.

72. National Archives, Department of the Interior, Indian Office,
    Seminole File 1844, M1941, Apr. 20, 1844.

Giddings, treated him rather as a character in a work of fiction than historically, asserting, on the alleged basis of hearsay evidence and unnamed newspaper accounts, that he was actually the most prominent leader in the Seminole Negro resistance to domination by the Creeks and that, with Wild Cat, he led a migration of Seminole Indians and Negroes to Mexico in 1850. No positive evidence for this assertion is extant, and all available information counts against it. The rather full manuscript material on the Wild Cat migration never so much as mentions Abraham, and all indications are that he was at the time living quietly on Little river and avoiding involvement in the daring plans of the Seminole militants. The Negro leader in the migration was unquestionably the Indian Negro John Cavallo, better known among army officers by his nickname of Gopher John.[73]

Abraham was, in 1852, called from the obscurity in which he had been plunged by his dismissal from the position of government interpreter seven years earlier, in order to serve as interpreter to one of the delegations which were sent to Florida with the design of inducing Billy Bowlegs, Mikonopi's nephew, and chief of the largest band of Seminoles still at large, to come in and surrender with his people for transportation to the West. The delegation landed at Tampa and proceeded to Caloosa-

---

73. Giddings, 332-337. Giddings writes that, in 1852, eight of the men in the party guarding the United States commissioners who were establishing the Mexican border were seized by Seminoles and taken to their village, where "Abraham was yet living . . . regarded as a ruling prince by his people." After satisfying himself that the prisoners had no evil intentions, he ordered them dismissed. As a matter of fact, Abraham was at this time in Washington, New York, or Florida, on, or returning from, a junket with Billy Bowlegs, mentioned below. Giddings also treats the famous Louis Pacheco's career with similar disregard for the evidence.

hatchee, "confident of being able to induce Billy
Bowlegs and Sam Jones to emigrate." They succeeded in establishing contact with Billy Bowlegs
and persuaded him to go, with certain of his chiefs,
on an excursion to some of the principal cities of
the eastern seaboard, in the hope that he might
be sufficiently impressed by the grandeur and power
of the whites as to give up the struggle and yield
himself and his people to the emigration agents.
They left Ft. Myers, August 31, 1852, and proceeded
first to Washington, where they had an interview
with the president. They arrived in New York on
September 11 and put up at the American Hotel.

Abraham attracted a great deal of attention
from the press. He was described as "an intelligent
old negro, . . . quite a venerable, dignified looking
personage, a sort of Indianized major domo, with
his face set off with a wooly moustache. . . ." "Time
and trial, and anxiety," a fuller account reads,
"have made a wreck of Abraham. Yet he is
straight, and active, and looks more intelligence out
of his one eye than many people look out of two.
He is in the full costume of the Seminoles. Turban,
a la Turk, and hunting shirt, leggins, etc. Abraham
must be 70 or 80 years old." He was actually, it
is probable, in his early or middle sixties. Sometime during the delegation's stay in New York, they,
including Abraham, became the subjects of the accompanying group-photograph.

It was reported in Jacksonville News (Oct. 2,
1852) that "King Billy and cabinet, including the
old negro interpreter Abraham, are gone home to
the court of the Everglades. They passed up on
. . . the Matamoros . . . Billy held his levee in the
cabin of the steamboat and received his visitors
with royal dignity. We learn from General Blake
that Billy has entered into a solemn agreement to

emigrate next March with all the Indians he can induce to go, which he thinks will be all in the country. We feel disposed to believe that at last we may succeed in getting rid of our unwelcome neighbors, but shall not feel *certain* till *they are gone.*" If he ever so agreed, he did not carry out his promise, for it was not until several years later, and after a third Seminole war, that Billy was finally transported to the Indian Territory.[74]

After this brief flare of publicity Abraham sank into an obscurity from which he did not again emerge. He returned to his home on Little river, in the region to which the Seminoles had removed according to the provisions of the treaty of 1845, where his name is still remembered by the older generation. Ed Payne, an intelligent and prosperous Seminole Negro of the Little River (Seminole county) settlement, has heard much of him as a resident of that vicinity. Mr. Payne knew two of his sons, including Washington, whose freedom his father had purchased in 1841. Washington used to mention that he and his father had both been slaves, but had been freed. Washington described his father as an able and successful cattle-raiser, and remembered that he used to come back from the sale of a herd of cattle with a sack full of gold and silver—no paper-money in those days. He would then pry up a plank in the cabin floor and

74. Jacksonville Public Library, Jacksonville, Fla., Long, Elizabeth V., comp., "Florida Indians, 1836-1865: a collection of clippings from contemporary newspapers," clipping, 1852, from unidentified newspaper; clipping, Sept. 12, 1852, from unidentified New York City newspaper; *New York Daily Tribune,* Sept. 17, 1852, p. 6, quoting from *Savannah Georgian; ibid.,* Sept. 25, 1852, p. 3; " 'Billy Bowlegs' and Suite," *The Illustrated London News,* May 21, 1853, pp. 395-396, illustration; National Archives, Department of the Interior, Indian Office, Seminole File 1852-J121, T. S. Jesup, Washington, Oct. 5, 1852, to Luke Lea, Commissioner of Indian Affairs.

drop the sack into the space beneath—this was his bank.[75]

The Civil War, which so convulsed the Indian Territory as well as the United States in general, probably did not greatly affect Abraham. He was in his seventies at its outbreak, and all the serious fighting was to the east, in the vicinity of Ft. Gibson. He probably did not therefore flee to Kansas with the loyal Seminoles, under Halleck Tustenuggree and the Creek chief Opothla Yahola, and as a Negro he could hardly have been a partisan of the Seminole head-chief John Jumper, who served as a colonel in the Confederate army. Doubtless he continued to live quietly on his Little River farm while the storm of war rolled by.

He seems to have been still living late in 1870, for a newspaper item notes: "The old interpreter for General Jackson [sic], the Negro Abraham, is still alive on Little River at the advanced age of one hundred and twenty years. A gentleman saw him the other day."[76]

The date of Abraham's death is unknown to me, but presumably it took place not long after 1870.

---

75. Ed Payne, Aug. 11, 1942.
76. *Report of the Board of Indian Commissioners to the Secretary of the Interior*, 1870, Washington, 1871, quoting from a newspaper account dated from Ft. Gibson, Dec. 16, 1870. No evidence exists elsewhere that Abraham ever interpreted "for" Gen. Jackson or at any conference to which Old Hickory was a party—but probably the reporter had the First Seminole War, in which Jackson participated, confused with the more important Second Seminole War, which began during his presidency and in which Abraham did ultimately serve as interpreter to the general in command. The age ascribed to Abraham is absurd, since it would put him in his late eighties at the time of the Seminole War, 1835-1842, and it would have been impossible for a man of that age to pass, as he did, for 45 or 50—but it would not be difficult for an aged weather-beaten Negro in his eighties to pass for well over a century if it tickled his own vanity and sense of humor thus to play upon the credulity of a white questioner. Already in 1852 Abraham was being estimated as a decade or two older than his actual age.

According to Mr. Payne, he is buried at Bruner-town, west of the Little River settlement, near Hazel. Mr. Payne has seen a stone shaped into a marker, with his name on it, over the grave, but cannot recall whether or not it bears a date. Some young Oklahoma historian could profitably spend a few days in the vicinity of Wewoka, Sasakwa, Noble Town, Little River, and Brunertown, visiting the grave and searching for further traditional information on the later life of this remarkable personality.[77]

* * *

Abraham's record, considering his opportunities, stands out as extraordinary by any standard. Born in slavery among an alien race, he took refuge among another strange but more hospitable people and raised himself by his own exertions to a position of prominence and authority. He clearly recognized the issues and reasonable objectives of the Florida War, fought bravely and skilfully until that latter had, as it seemed, been secured, and then successfully directed his energies toward the termination of hostilities. His activities in the Indian Territory were hardly comparable to those in Florida, but it is probable that he did much, in a conservative fashion, to benefit the Seminole Indians and Negroes with whom he was associated by assisting them in adjustment to their new environment. Interpreter, counsellor, war-leader, diplomat, he deserves a niche in American history.

* * *

77. Mr. Payne gives the name and address of a great-grandson: John Fay, 1211 N.E. 7th St., Oklahoma City, Okla. Letters, however, have brought no response.

APPENDIX

[*Negro Abraham to Gen. T. S. Jesup, commanding at Tampa Bay.**]

Fort Deynaud, Florida
General,   25th April, 1838.

I have the honour to present my best respects to you. Myself and 'Tony Barnet have done every thing promised by us, and expect the General will do by us as he said at the beginning of this Campaign. I send 'Tony to see you, and he can afterwards come and join me wherever I may be. We wish to get in writing from the General, the agreement made with us. We will go with the Indians to our new home, and wish to know how we are to be protected, and who is to have the care of us on the road. We do not live for ourselves only, but for our wives & children who are as dear to us as those of any other men. When we reach our new home we hope we shall be permitted to remain while the woods remain green, and the water runs.

I have charge of all the red people coming on to Pease's Creek, and all are satisfied to go to Arkansaw. They all wish to see you, and hope you will wait until they come to Tampa. Whoever is to be chief Interpreter we would wish to Know. I cannot do any more than I have. I have done all I can, my heart has been true since I came in at TohopoKilka I wish 'Tony to come to Pease's Creek immediately. I hope Toskeegee is satisfied. All his Seminole Bretheren are coming in. Hotatoochee has done well. All the black people are contented I hope.   Your Servant
                                        X his
                                   ABRAM
                                        mark

———

*Original in P. K. Yonge Library of Florida History, University of Florida.

P.S. John Cavallo is in and contented. Glad to hear of the peace.
[on cover:]
Abraham
25th April 1838

> Genl. Jesup
> Comdg Army
> Tampa

Recd. 30th Apl. '38

[*Negro Abraham to Cae Hajo**]

> Tampa Bay
> 11th Sept. 1837

Abram sends this talk
    to Cäe Hajo.—,

When I heard that you had gone in to Fort King —I longed to have a talk with you but we are too far apart for that and I have asked our Agent to write to you what I would say.

I wish you to remember that you and I went to Arkansas together and now recollect that one rainy evening after passing a hill we sat down together on a bee tree which we had found & felled. The country was a good one and while sitting there a deer came down close to us—We had no arms and could not shoot it.—You said—"Abram, I used to think that all the whites hated us, but I now believe they wish us to live. This is a rich country and we will return home & tell the truth. That talk remains on my memory and my tongue and heart remain the same. I have one tongue & one heart only.

Now remember that during the late Treaty you and I sat down one day on a pine tree near this post —The country around was pine barren and we were hungry & had nothing to eat.—You spoke of the

---

*National Archives, War Dept., Gen. Jesup papers, no. 2.

same subject as when we sat together on the bee
tree in the rich soil of Arkansas.

Cäe Hajo—You have since talked to the General
as you then talked to me. You did not know who
would Kill you first—the whites or yr own people.

If you can believe me listen to me—and I have
been known to you so long that I think I have a
right to expect credit for my talk.

Come in with as many of yr people as you can
& if you can bring none come alone.

Do not sacrifice yourself to the advice of crazy
men.

My heart is heavy. for you and Micconope &
Jumper. If my advice was ever friendly to you—
believe it to be so now.

The Miccosucos threaten me and you and others
—Why fear them? Are the Seminoles conquered
by the Miccosucos—*I* am not, for one, & I expect
yet to see some of them by a want of bread at my
door as they have done heretofore.

You have passed yr word and let that prevail
over the advice of crazy people.—Think in a minute
as much as in a day and act.

Your friend

SOUANAFFE TUSTENUKKE
[busk-name of Abraham]

Fort Gibson July 27, 1845*

General:—

The day you left, I heard that *"Miconopy"* and
some of his principal men had arrived on the opposite bank of the river, and were much disappoint-
ed to learn that you had already gone to Fort Smith
—I thought no more of it—but, yesterday afternoon,
I was honoured with a call from *Miconopy,* his

---

*Original in P. K. Yonge Library of Florida History, University
of Florida.

chiefs, attendants, interpreters, &c—You know my partiality for Indians—

After listening to *talks,* and congratulations:—in order to get rid of my red brethren. I promised to write to-day, and relate to you, so minutely, all they desired you to know, that it would be almost as well for them as if they had had a personal interview—Whereupon, they concluded to go into *Council* until this morning, and then favour me with their presence, and, at the same time, dictate and have written under their own supervision, the *"talk"* to be sent to you—You have the result of their meditations, together with *"Wild-Cat's"* personal notions and recollections, herewith enclosed—

"Abram" says his conduct in Florida in favour of the whites, has procured him many enemies, and that he leads an uncertain and unhappy life—Knowing "Abram", you will be able to judge how much of this is true—I am. General,

Maj. Genl Jesup	Your most obedient Servant
Q. Master General	Chas O. Collins
Fort Smith	
Arks	

———————

Fort Gibson July 27, 1845*

Miconopy (*"The Governor"*):—*"WildCat"*, *"Alligator," "Tiger," "old-bear," "The broom,"* and *"George Cloud"* (nephew of old *"Cloud"*). Chiefs and sub-chiefs of the Seminoles, send by the mouth of *"Wild-Cat"* this *"talk,"* to the War-Chief *General Jesup*—

"General

"We have scarcely come in time to see your foot-"print"—

"The moment we heard You were here, we start-

———————

*Original in P. K. Yonge Library of Florida History, University of Florida.

"ed to meet "You face to face- We are too late"—
"You were a great way from home, and were *lonely*
"—You have gone to see your wife "and little ones
"—"It is right"—

"When you come again towards the setting sun,
"send word "*beforehand,* to our First Chief and
"Governor, *Miconopy,* and we will all come and
"shake hands with you"—"You are a friend"

"May the Great Spirit spare us to meet once
"more, face to face, and have a straight talk"—The
"before-written "talk" was delivered by "*Wild-*
"*Cat*" in presence of all the named Chiefs, and in-
"terpreted by "*Abram*" and "*Cudjoe*"—It was
"written, paragraph by paragraph, as delivered:—
"when finished; was read by *sentences,* and inter-
"preted to the Chiefs by the negroes, and each sen-
"tence received the full sanction of all assembled—

"*Wild-Cat*" then said, in presence of all the
"Chiefs—"I wish to send a "short talk" of my
"own"—Permission was granted and "Wild-Cat"
"spoke as follows—all present, *Abram-* interpreter—

"Now speak to the General for *Wild Cat*"—

"After seeing you in Washington, I started for
"home And arrived safely"— "I have not yet fin-
"ished my *cabin* and have, therefore, much to do,
"and am very busy"—"The Seminoles were scat-
"tered all about when I returned"—"The Presi-
"dent promised to feed them *nine* months—whereas
"the *treaty* says but *six* months"—

"We are *very hungry,* and do not expect to make
"much corn"

"I hope you will see that "the promise for *nine*
"months is not "forgotten"—

"All the promises made "to us, have not been
"fulfilled"—

"When I see you, I shall "tell you all that has "happened and all that you said to me "in Florida "and in Washington"—

"I send my respects to "Your Wife—She gave me "a *good dinner!* I remember your "children—they "can sing—

"If the Great Spirit will "allow me, I shall visit "your Wife and children again, "and shall sing to "them"—

"This *Coacoochee* says"

Corrections and Additions

p. 304, l. 14; note 20: More careful examination indicates that Abraham's Indian or busk name was "Souanakke Tustenukke." He is elsewhere referred to as "Sohanac." "Letters of Samuel Forry, Surgeon U.S. Army, 1837-1838," *FHQ*, VI (April, 1928), p. 214.

p. 305, l. 13: The Seminole Negro who was married to "the widow of the former chief of the nation," King Bowlegs, was not Abraham but Toney Barnett, whose wife's name was Polly. See similar correction on p. 92 for "Relations between Negroes and Indians," p. 61-62.

p. 312, l. 29: The Holato Micco (chief governor) here mentioned was probably not the chief bearing that title whose white-man's nickname was "Billy Bowlegs" and who was not known as Holata Micco until *ca.* 1839. See Porter, "Billy Bowlegs (Holata Micco) and the Seminole Wars," *FHQ*, XLV (January, 1967), pp. 220, 224-25.

p. 314, top of page: The characterization as "a good soldier and an intrepid leader" was intended to apply not to Abraham but to Toney Barnett. See correction above for p. 305, l. 13.

p. 321, l. 14: Although Alligator was Mikonopi's (or Micanopy's) principal warchief, that he was also his nephew cannot be substantiated.

The last article in this section, "John Caesar: Seminole Negro Partisan," originally appeared in *JNH*, April, 1946 (Vol. XXXI, No. 2).

JOHN CAESAR: SEMINOLE NEGRO PARTISAN[1]

The importance of Negro participation in the Seminole War, though well known at the time, particularly to army officers who found themselves pitted, frequently to their discomfiture, against Negro chiefs and warriors, was, during the subsequent century, largely lost to the knowledge even of students and writers of American history, though during the last few years it has been in process of again being brought to the notice of the interested public.[2]

The principal Negro leader was undoubtedly Abraham, interpreter, counsellor, and "sense-bearer" to Mikonopi, Seminole head-chief, but the important part he played over a period of several years (1835-1839), has tended unfairly to obscure the lesser, but still great, significance of another Negro chief, whose activities, though very brief in duration, nevertheless proved a decisive factor in making possible Abraham's success as a peace-maker.

John Caesar's life is obscure, save for a period of little over a year (Dec., 1835-Jan. 18, 1837), during which he is mentioned in only four connections: as an inciter of plantation-slaves in December, 1835; as a raider of plantations at the very beginning of the war, late in the same month; as an interpreter and would-be diplomat in March, 1836; and as a partisan leader, January, 1837, in which role he met

[1] An article by me, entitled "John Caesar: a forgotten hero of the Seminole War," appeared in *The Journal of Negro History*, XXVIII (Jan., 1943), 53-65. It was based entirely on printed sources—consisting, however, of contemporary newspapers and narratives, government documents, and personal reminiscences—but in my opinion its fundamental conclusions still stand. Research in the War Department records has, however, added so many details to his story that an expanded narrative seems to be called for, which, obviously, must, in the interests of completeness, repeat portions of the earlier article.

[2] The author's principal contributions to this end, in addition to that mentioned in note 1, have been: "Abraham," *Phylon*, II (1941), 107-116 (an expanded article, using manuscript sources, is shortly to appear in *The Florida Historical Quarterly*), and "Florida Slaves and Free Negroes in the Seminole War, 1835-1842," *The Journal of Negro History*, XXVIII (Oct., 1943), 390-421.

his end—but in June, 1837, a reference to his death by the general commanding in Florida is coupled with a reflection which reveals in a vivid flash the disproportionate importance of his brief military career.

John Caesar is reputed to have been a rather old man at the outbreak of the Seminole War; perhaps he was in or approaching the sixties. He was an "Indian Negro," that is, a Negro who had either been born among the Seminole or had lived among them so long that he had become thoroughly identified with them in tastes and interests, though without losing some of the capacities which he or his ancestors had acquired among the whites, such as a knowledge of the English language. He was evidently a dependent, a so-called "slave," of King Philip, as the whites called Emathla, the principal chief of the St. John's River Seminole, who was married to a sister of Mikonopi, and was regarded as next only to his brother-in-law in authority. John Caesar was probably Philip's "chief Negro," occupying the same relation to him as Abraham to Mikonopi—interpreter, counsellor, and commander of his Negro retainers. He was regarded even by the whites as "very intelligent," "an active smart negro,"[3] and either because of his master's importance, or his own abilities, or both, he was considered "next to the negro Abraham in influence & importance among the Indian negroes and Indians."[4] When one considers the overpowering influence ascribed to Abraham, it is evident that even to be "next" to him in importance was to occupy a position of great distinction.

When the United States decided upon the compulsory removal of the Seminole to the West, and they determined to resist, the Negroes took a leading part in the preparation

---

[3] *Douglas, Thomas, Autobiography of,* N. Y., 1856, pp. 120-123; A Lieutenant of the Left Wing, *Sketch of the Seminole War,* Charleston, 1836, pp. 19-20.

[4] National Archives, Washington, D. C., War Department, General Jesup's Papers, Box 5, Brig. Gen. Joseph M. Hernandez, St. Augustine, Feb. 2, 1837, to Maj. Gen. Thos. S. Jesup.

for warfare. They stood to lose more than the Indians, and they had everything to gain. Though looked upon by whites as "slaves" to the Indians, they were actually as free as their supposed masters, save for a slight annual tribute, and were even more prosperous; and their influence upon the Indians was so great that qualified observers declared them to be the real rulers of the tribe. Most of them, however, were either runaways or the descendants of runaways, and they were convinced, with reason, that their surrender to United States troops for transportation to the Indian Territory would be merely a preliminary to their enslavement by the whites.

Many of the slave-men on the sugar plantations "had wives among the Indian negroes, and the Indian negroes had wives among them."[5] John Caesar himself "had a wife on one of the plantations" and because of this close connection between plantation-slaves and Seminole Negroes it was easy for Abraham and Caesar to visit the plantations and confer with the principal slaves with a view to inciting them to insurrection in co-operation with the Seminole; not until it was too late did the owners realize that they were "engaged in effecting a junction with the negroes now under arms," that "Caesar, . . . it was supposed . . . had been commissioned by the chiefs to hold out inducements to the negroes to join them," and that as a result he had "an understanding with all the slaves before the war, that they were to unite with the Seminoles."[6]

Late in December, 1835, hostilities broke out on a large scale, beginning with attacks by the St. John's River Seminole under King Philip and John Caesar upon the plantations of that region. David Dunham's house at "New Smyrna south of Mosquito inlet" was plundered and burned

[5] Douglas, 120-123.

[6] National Archives, War Department, General Jesup's Papers, No. 2, John C. Casey, Tampa Bay, Aug. 25, 1837, to Lieut. F. Searle; *The Charleston Courier*, Apr. 30, 1836; Douglas, *loc. cit.*; Cohen, M. M., *Notices of Florida*, Charleston, 1836, pp. 81, 86-89.

by Philip, at the head of his band of Seminole and Euchee Indians, and by "a number of Indian negroes," under John Caesar, and Dummett's house was ransacked. "Indian John *Casar* [sic], (a great scoundrel)," also visited Mr. Hunter's house, probably earlier, and attempted to "decoy him off into the woods on the pretence of selling him cattle and Horses"—the offer being intended to indicate that Caesar was a "friendly," who was disposing of his live-stock preparatory to emigration, but this clever device did not succeed.[7]

John Caesar's "tampering" with the plantation Negroes proved highly effective; on several plantations the slaves rallied to the Seminole with enthusiasm. "Depeyster's negroes were . . . in league with the Indians; they assisted them with a boat to cross over to Dummett's . . . the whole of Major Heriot's and Depeyster's negroes . . . moved off with the Indians." "Upwards of two hundred and fifty negroes . . . have joined the Indians and are more desperate than the Indians." Some of the Depeyster Negroes even "painted their faces" in symbol of their new allegiance, although "Anderson's negroes behaved with the utmost prudence and fidelity," and Dummett and Hunter succeeded in bringing off most, at least, of their slaves. Caesar had been particularly active among the Depeyster and Cruger slaves, and while he had probably succeeded beyond all expectations with the former, what, if anything, he accomplished with the latter is not on record. The extent to which the plantation Negroes were joining the Indians, Gen. Hernandez understandably declared, "is the very worst feature of the whole of this war."[8] For this result, John Caesar evidently deserved principal crédit.

---

[7] National Archives, War Department, AGO, Maj. Benjamin A. Putnam, Cantonment Rosetta, Dec. 29, 1835, to Brig. Gen. J. M. Hernandez, St. Augustine (316); Cohen, *loc. cit.; Niles Register*, XLIX (Jan. 30, 1836), 369; A Lieutenant of the Left Wing, *loc. cit.*

[8] *The Charleston Courier*, Jan. 12, 21, 22, 1836; National Archives, War Department, AGO, Putnam, Dec. 29, 1836, to Hernandez (316), Putnam,

John Caesar, after he had "caused so much destruction at Mosquito,"[9] dropped out of public notice for a couple of months. The St. John's River Seminole devoted themselves in this period to desultory action in the region below St. Augustine and seem to have taken little if any part in the really heavy fighting which the Alachua Seminole and Osceola's Mikasuki were doing in the Withlacoochee area. John Caesar, however, either with a force from the St. John's, or alone, as an observer or liaison officer, appeared at the siege of Fort Izard, when, after the Second Battle of the Withlacoochee, Feb. 27, 1836, Gen. Gaines and his troops were for over a week blockaded, under attack, and reduced nearly to a starving condition. At this point, on the night of Mar. 5, a Negro called to them and declared that the Indians were tired of fighting and wanted an armistice. This Negro, it is said, was Caesar. Gen. Gaines agreed to a conference to be held the following morning, whereupon Caesar expressed the desire that, the next day being the Sabbath, the soldiers should not do any work or cut down trees, called a courteous "Good night," and vanished.

The principal authority on the Seminole War says: "Intelligent Indians and negroes who were upon the ground at the time, state that the conduct of John Caesar was without the authority or knowledge of the chiefs. With the Indians he was a privileged character, and from his age and long residence among them, he felt at liberty to do that which he conceived for the general good. . . . Unknown to anyone, he crossed the Withlacoochee river, hailed the camp, and said the Indians wished to make peace." The author goes on to

Bulowville, Jan. 4, 1836, to Hernandez (25), Hernandez, Dec. 30, 1835, to Lewis Cass (H129/316); Cohen, 86-89. Two slaves, surnamed Anderson and Hunter, respectively, were among a band of hostile Negroes subsequently led by John Caesar, which indicates that not all of "Anderson's negroes" behaved in the fashion asserted by the quotation and that at least one of the Hunter Negroes was not "brought off."

[9] National Archives, War Department, General Jesup's Papers, Box 6, Brig. Gen. Joseph M. Hernandez, St. Augustine, Feb. 2, 1837, to Maj. Gen. Thos. S. Jesup.

say that when it was learned what he had done, some of the chiefs wanted to kill him, his life being saved only by the strenuous personal intervention of Osceola, who urged that since the offer of a conference had been made and accepted, the meeting should take place.[10]

Accordingly, on the next day, two conferences were held at which "Osceola, Jumper, Albeti Hajo (Crazy Alligator), all Indians, with Abram, principal adviser of Micanopy, and Caesar, both Indian negroes, were present." They had just come to an agreement that the Seminole should retire south of the Withlacoochee, that the troops should not attempt at the time to cross, and that a general peace-conference be held, when a relief-force under Gen. Clinch arrived, the advance-guard of which, not knowing the situation, fired on the Seminole, who disappeared into the underbrush, delegates and all. Had it not been for this untoward event, an agreement might have been achieved, which, like the subsequent ones of 1837, 1838, and 1839, would have brought the war appreciably nearer a termination.[11]

In view of the presence of Caesar at the negotiations, it hardly seems he was as much out of favor with the chiefs as Sprague's account would indicate. Perhaps he had been deputed, though at his own request, by at least one band of Seminole, to open a discussion with Gen. Gaines. Certainly this was the psychological moment for the Seminole to attempt an agreement. The overwhelming and annihilation of Gen. Gaines' forces, following upon the destruction of Maj. Dade's detachment of over a hundred men, would have accomplished nothing save to arouse the determination of the United States government to destroy the Seminole root and branch. The Seminole, furthermore, knew that relief for the besieged soldiers was at hand and that the siege could not ultimately be successful. To negotiate with the commander of a weak, sick, and half-starving company, who

10 Sprague, John T., The Florida War, N. Y., 1848, pp. 111-113.
11 Niles Register, 1, 85; Army and Navy Chronicle, II, 214.

was not sure when, if ever, relief would arrive, might well, on the other hand, result in an agreement which would give the Seminole Indians and Negroes all or most of what they could reasonably expect—at the least delay. Caesar, whether acting for the St. John's River Seminole, or purely on his own initiative, was displaying statesmanlike qualities, even though his efforts bore no immediate fruit.[12]

John Caesar again drops out of sight, this time for over ten months. Presumably he returned to the St. John's and took part, later in the month, in the desultory action conducted by Philip's people against the South Carolina volunteers constituting the Left Wing of Gen. Scott's futile campaign. Until nearly the end of 1836 the Seminole rather more than held their own, but in December a new commander-in-chief for Florida, Maj. Gen. Thomas Sidney Jesup, went into action and proceeded to scour the Wahoo Swamp and the Cove of the Withlacoochee so vigorously

---

[12] According to some authorities, not Caesar but Abraham was the Negro who "hailed the camp, and said that they were tired of fighting and wished to make peace." (25th Cong., 2d Sess., 1837-1838, Ex. Doc. 78, Vol. II, pp. 173, 487, 801.) It is probable that any Negro, seemingly in authority, and seen or heard from a distance, would be assumed to be head-chief Mikonopi's principal Negro, and this impression would be strengthened by his appearance as interpreter at the subsequent conferences. One writer, in fact, in recounting the initial dialogue, writes: "Presuming the voice was Abraham's, his name will be used." ([Potter, Woodburne], *The War in Florida*, Baltimore, 1836, pp. 154-162). Still another authority says that "the interpreter, who was also the herald of the preceding night, [was] a very tall negro, rejoicing in the name of Dr. Johnston." (Barr, Capt. James, *Correct and Authentic Narrative of the Indian War in Florida*, N. Y., 1836.) This description would seem applicable to Abraham, who was at least tall, if not "very tall," and had a fluency of speech which might have resulted in his being briefly nicknamed "Dr. Johnston [sic]." Sprague, however, says that negotiations were opened by Caesar and, in view of Abraham's importance, it is unlikely that the credit would have been given to Caesar without good reason; it should be noted, however, that Sprague himself is somewhat confused as between Abraham and Caesar when he says that the latter, "belonging to Micanopy, . . . thought himself of as much importance as his master." All available evidence indicates that Caesar "belonged" to King Philip, whereas Abraham had been Mikonopi's "slave" but had been freed some years earlier. Caesar was at least present at the negotiations, whatever his part in their initiation.

that the Alachua Seminole and Osceola's Mikasuki, who had
been hitherto bearing the brunt of the war, were driven eastward toward the Kissimee and incidentally in the direction
of Philip's territory.

John Caesar again went into action—as it turned out,
for the last time. His master, King Philip, had been active
only spasmodically, preferring, it was said, to avoid the
white man rather than to fight him. Satisfied with his
achievement of devastating the plantations of the St. John's
River valley and driving their owners to take refuge in, or
in the vicinity of, St. Augustine, he had lapsed into apathy.
John Caesar, either out of temperamental restlessness and
recklessness, or because he had enough of a military mind
to detect the danger of allowing the Alachua Seminole and
Osceola to be defeated and driven east without the St.
John's River bands intervening, determined to inaugurate
a guerrilla campaign on his own initiative, utilizing primarily the runaway slaves who had left their plantations at his
instigation at the beginning of the war. He was assisted by
what Gen. Jesup accurately or otherwise referred to as "six
or seven vagabond Indians, who had no character among
their people as warriors," but who, whatever their deficien-
cies, were probably of considerable use in furnishing leadership, and training in warfare, to the inexperienced runaway
Negroes, whose knowledge of the terrain of their own plantations and of St. Augustine was, however of great importance.

Probably at least two or three bands were operating
under the general leadership, or at the instigation, of John
Caesar; if the gang under his personal command was representative, each consisted of a dozen or so men, mostly plantation slaves, but with a "stiffening" of one or two each of
Indians and Indian Negroes. John Caesar, at the time of
his last raid, headed a band of probably fourteen, made up,
in addition to himself, of eight runaway slaves, a free Negro, a couple of Indians, and two Indian Negroes.

Andrew Gué, or Gay, the most prominent of the runaways, was "a young negro, not exceeding 21 years of age, and active and enterprising. He went off, joined the Indians, and after being with them for some weeks, he returned clandestinely to town and held a meeting with some of his friends, and enticed some of them off. At this meeting he stated that he had become high in the confidence of the Indians and he only wanted a white man's scalp to make him a great man." On one such occasion, two out of three emissaries from the Seminole Negroes to St. Augustine were captured, but Andrew escaped and "on several occasions since made his appearance in the vicinity."[13]

Another runaway was Stephen Hernandez, slave to no less a person than Brig. Gen. Joseph M. Hernandez, commanding the Florida militia in the St. Augustine area. "Stephen," the general remarked apologetically when the activities of his slave were called to his attention, "is quite a young and inexperienced lad, who has always been kept up on the plantation, and I have no doubt, he has been misled, by his Indian asociates."[14] Other runaways in the John Caesar band—Phillip Hunter, John Bicente, Toney Weightman, Hector Anderson, Benet Depeyster, Ormond Depeyster—revealed by the surnames ascribed to them the probable identity of their masters.

The free Negro, young Joe Merritt, son of Stephen Merritt *alias* Wright, of Anastasia Island, had joined the hostiles sometime between mid-September and early December, 1836.[15] One of the Indian Negroes, Phillip's John or John Phillip, subsequently went over to the whites; the other's

[13]*Charleston Courier*, Mar. 21, 1837; St. Augustine Historical Society, Letter Book of Benjamin A. Putnam, Putnam, July 26, 1836, to Gov. R. K. Call.

[14] National Archives, War Department, General Jesup's Papers, Box 5, Brig. Gen. Joseph M. Hernandez, St. Augustine, Mar. 16, 1837, to Maj. Gen. Thomas S. Jesup.

[15] *Charleston Courier*, Jan. 21, 1837; National Archives, War Department, General Jesup Papers, Box 4. "The United States *vs.* Randal Irving & Stephen Merritt, Free persons of Color."

identity is unknown. Uchee Indian Sam was in the band, and probably another Indian, name unknown.[16]

John Caesar's band or bands moved up into the vicinity of St. Augustine, established contact with sympathizers, particularly free Negroes, arranged for the purchase of supplies through them, and prepared for a guerrilla campaign against the plantations which were so near St. Augustine that they had not been laid waste a year before. "John Bicenty, Joe Merritt, and Andrew Gué" visited the free Negro Randal Irving, living on Anastasia Island, "Saturday night [January] (the 14th) when"—as Irving later testified at his trial for "treason against the United States, in supplying the Seminole Indians with provisions and ammunition"—"he was sick and could not defend himself and took tobacco and calico he had bought." They said, according to his testimony, that "there were 10 or 12 more at the little bar, amongst whom was John Caesar. . . . An Indian chief was with the waiting party."

For an effective campaign horses were needed, and on the night of Jan. 17, 1837,[17] John Caesar's hostiles attempted a raid on John M. Hanson's plantation, only two miles west of St. Augustine. They had pried a plank off the stable and carried out a saddle, but before they could enlarge the opening sufficiently to bring out the animals, they were discovered by a sentinel, and fired on. Two of them returned the fire, the shots being clearly heard by the night watch in St. Augustine. The raiders then withdrew. Capt. Hanson took up the trail and followed it for a while, but, becoming aware that their number was too large for the force at his disposal, he returned, raised a larger company, trailed them all that day, and at about 10 p.m. discovered their camp, which was on the Williams plantation about thirty miles

[16]National Archives, War Department, General Jesup's Papers, Box 5, "List of Negroes Composing the Party of John Caesar, on the Night of the Attack by Captain Hanson, Furnished by the Negro Fellow Andrew Gué."

[17] The newspaper account says this was Sunday, but that would have been the 15th; an official report says that the next day was the 18th.

from St. Augustine. The St. Augustine troop crept up close to the camp fire—the raiders must have been extraordinarily bold or careless—discovered about a dozen sitting around it, and poured in such a well-aimed volley at close range that they killed three, badly wounding at least one other. The rest fled, in such confusion that they left not only their packs and blankets, but also two rifles and six muskets. Two of the dead were found to be Indian Negroes, one of them the notorious John Caesar—they had perhaps been singled out by their costume as more formidable than the others—and the third was the free Negro, Joe Merritt. In a trial of free Negroes charged with assisting the hostiles, it was testified that, two years earlier, John Caesar and Stephen Merritt or Wright, father of the slain Joe Merritt, had quarrelled over ten dollars owed by Merritt to the Indian Negro, and that "Caesar . . . said he would take one of Stephen Merritt's children." That hasty threat had been fulfilled—John Caesar had taken young Joe into his band and death had taken them both.[18]

One would have expected that such a *coup* would have produced general congratulations and unmixed satisfaction among the whites, but it seems to have resulted in at least as much alarm as relief. That a band composed almost entirely of Negroes—and plantation slaves at that—should have had the temerity to attempt a raid in the immediate vicinity of St. Augustine, even with results so lamentable to themselves, and that their abandoned packs should have been found to contain calico, needles, thread, buckshot, tobacco, and other articles which could be identified as having been purchased in St. Augustine shops only a few days earlier, indicating close relations with St. Augustine Negroes, revived something of the panic of the earlier days

---

[18] *Charleston Courier*, Jan. 21, 1837; National Archives, War Department, General Jesup's Papers, Box 5, "List of Negroes Composing the Party of John Caesar . . ."; *loc. cit.*, Box 3, Capt. J. M. Hanson, St. Augustine, Jan. 19, 1837, to Col. Jos. S. Sanchez; Hanson, John M., *To the Public*, 1841 (Library of Congress), p. 5.

of the war when "strong apprehensions were felt . . . that they [the slaves and free Negroes] would fire the town, and . . . during the confusion resulting therefrom, the Indians might rush in.''[19] The city council declared that "we know not how soon firebrands may be thrown amongst us'' and demanded that Capt. Hanson's militia company be kept near home and "employed to scour the country in the neighborhood.''[20]

The greatest effect of John Caesar's abortive raid was, however, probably not upon the citizens of St. Augustine but upon the commanding general. A few days later, Jan. 27, 1837, he met and defeated the Seminole Indians and Negroes in the Battle of Hatcheelustee, in the Great Cypress Swamp, but instead of following up his immediate advantage by an attempt utterly to crush the Seminole by military means, he instead offered, through the Indian Negroes Ben and Abraham, favorable terms of peace. On Mar. 6, 1837, an agreement was signed providing that "the Seminoles and their allies, who come in and emigrate West, shall be secure in their lives and property; [and] that their negroes, their bona fide property, shall also accompany them West.'' This was understood by the Seminole as protecting not only the Negroes to whom some of the Indians might have a more or less valid title, but also "their allies,'' the other Negroes who were then living among them and fighting with them. Gen. Jesup himself insisted on that interpretation—at first. "The negroes,'' that is, the Indian Negroes, "rule the Indians,'' he wrote on Mar. 26, 1837, "and it is important that they should feel themselves secure; if they should become alarmed and hold out, the war will be renewed.''[21] From what source had Gen. Jesup derived this conviction of the importance of the Indian Negroes? No

[19] Douglas, 123.
[20] City Building, St. Augustine, Fla., "Minutes of the City of St. Augustine, Nov. 18, 1836-Nov. 15, 1854,'' pp. 8, 11, 13.
[21] *American State Papers: Military Affairs*, vii, 825-828, 835.

doubt in large part from his conferences with the able Negro chief Abraham, but he must have already known of John Caesar's activities, and they were to assume greater and greater importance in his mind.

Gen. Jesup's decision that the runaway Negroes among the Seminole were "their allies" and protected by the terms of the capitulation, was inevitably greeted with violent protest by planters who had lost slaves during the war, and finally, unwisely yielding to their pressure, he was induced to make a clandestine arrangement on Apr. 8 with certain Indian chiefs, "to surrender the negroes taken during the war,"[22] thus endeavoring to introduce a division, based on the time of their escape, into the ranks of the Negroes among the Seminole. Slavehunters began to enter the emigration camp at Tampa Bay in search of Negroes whom they might claim or seize without claim, and as a result both Negroes and Indians took the alarm and most of them fled the camp, at the beginning of June, taking with them the principal hostages whom they had given for the fulfillment of the treaty. The war was revived.

Too late Gen. Jesup recognized his error. He was so badly upset that later in the month he was almost or entirely ready to make terms with the Seminole Indians for their continuance in Florida. His reasons were bound up with the situation which had prevented the carrying out of the treaty he had negotiated earlier in the year. "The two races, the negro and the Indian, are rapidly approximating; they are identified in interests and feelings; and I have ascertained that at the battle of the Wahoo, a negro, the property of a Florida planter, was one of the most distinguished leaders." By "negro" Gen. Jesup evidently meant not the Indian Negro, whose identity "in interests and feelings" with the Indian was self evident, but the "plantation negro." He feared, in other words, lest this Indian war—which he admitted was more properly a Negro war—should,

22 *Niles Register*, Apr. 29, 1837, p. 133.

if allowed to continue, be turned into a general slave insurrection which would spread from Florida to neighboring states and endanger the whole slavery-system. In pursuance of this thought, the general unconsciously wrote John Caesar's epitaph: "I have learn that the depredations committed on the plantations east of the St. John's were perpetrated by the plantation negroes, headed by an Indian negro, John Caesar, since killed, and aided by some six or seven vagabond Indians, who had no character among their people as warriors. Should the Indians remain in this territory, the negroes among them will form a rallying point for runaway negroes from the adjacent states; and if they remove, the fastnesses of the country would be immediately occupied by negroes. I am very sure they could be confined to a small district near Florida Point, and would accept peace and the small district referred to as the condition for the surrender of all runaway negroes."[23]

Gen. Jesup was learning that no arrangement with the Indians could be effective which did not also satisfy at least the Indian Negroes. His exact plan at this point, if he had one, is not entirely clear. He was willing to allow the Indians to remain in "a small district near Florida Point" if they would "surrender . . . all runaway negroes," but unless the Seminole Negroes were removed from the territory, they would inevitably, he felt, "form a rallying point for runaway negroes from the adjacent states." But, as he had written on Mar. 26 and must now have realized even more clearly, "The negroes rule the Indians, and . . . if they should become alarmed and hold out, the war will be renewed." They now *had* been thoroughly alarmed and the war *was* renewed.

The problem, as Gen. Jesup saw it, was, apparently, to get the Seminole Negroes to leave Florida willingly, in which case the Indians who refused to leave might be permitted to remain on condition of pledging themselves in the

[23] *American State Papers: Military Affairs*, VII, 835, 871, 876.

future to give up runaways. Gen. Jesup consequently in the following year, addressed himself directly to the Seminole Negroes, endeavoring to drive a wedge between them and the Indians, as he had previously striven to separate the Seminole, both Indian and Negro, from the recently escaped slaves. He issued an order "that all the property [sic] of the Seminole Indians in Florida at war with the United States who separated themselves from the Indians, and delivered themselves up to the Commanding officer of the troops, should be free." Gen. Jesup's idea was now to send the Seminole Negroes to the Indian Territory with those who had already been transported, and put the Indians on a reservation in a remote part of the peninsula, trusting that its inaccessibility to the plantation region, and the absence of Negroes, would prevent its becoming a haven for runaways. "Separating the negroes from the Indians," he explained, "weaken [sic] the latter more than they would be weakened by the loss of the same number of their own people."[24]

Since this offer followed a serious weakening of the Seminole forces by the treacherous seizure at a conference of about a hundred Indians and Negroes, and the consequent surrender of over a hundred more, and was accompanied by a tentative offer to the Indians to permit them to remain on a reservation in Florida, it drew in nearly 700 Seminole, who were also treacherously seized, 450 more surrendering in consequence. But Gen. Jesup, in so far as he could, lived up to his promise of freedom to the Negroes who came in—which amounted, practically, to saying that the United States government would protect the freedom which the Negroes had actually enjoyed with the Indians but which the Indians could no longer assure.

---

[24] National Archives, Seminole files W244-1848, T. S. Jesup, Washington, Apr. 3, July 1, 1848, to William L. Marcy, Secretary of War; *loc. cit.*, War Department, General Jesup's Papers, Box 15, Thomas S. Jesup, Washington, Apr. 3, 1848, to Wm. L. Marcy, Secretary of War.

Eventually the policy of sending captured or surrendered Negroes to the Indian Territory was extended to all Negroes, regardless of how long or how short their period of residence with the Indians had been, including the plantation slaves escaped to or "captured" by the Seminole during the war. Runaways who had enjoyed a taste of comparative freedom with the Seminole, who had perhaps wielded axe or leveled musket in raids on plantations or skirmishes with the United States troops, would be no Christmas package for a Georgia or Florida plantation owner. The general belief was that they would promptly run away again, seek refuge in the swamps with which they had become familiar, and then, as one officer commented, "Ten resolute negroes, with a knowledge of the country, are sufficient to desolate the frontier, from one extent to the other."[25]

The practice consequently developed of regarding captured Negroes as the "property" of the chief with whom they were found. If they were claimed by a white man, a board of officers would receive his evidence and, if it seemed adequate, admit his claim and recommend that he receive compensation for the slave—who, in the meantime, would have been shipped to the Territory. Col. Worth, commanding in the last stages of the war, officially formulated this policy, which had already long been accepted in practice, in a letter of Aug. 19, 1841: "Indians have been solemnly guaranteed retention of slaves indifferently . . . to the mode or time . . . they obtained possession . . . If . . . the swamps of Florida . . . become the resort of runaways"—and this, it is evident, is what the colonel thought would result if the runaways already there were not given every encouragement to come in for shipment to the west—"their intelligence [sic], so superior to the Indian, might impose upon the general government a contest, quadruplicate in time and

[25] Sprague, 309.

treasure than that now being waged.''²⁶ (The war had already been going on between five and six years and would, within another year, attain the cost of 20 million dollars.) By these tactics, practically all the Negroes were induced to surrender for shipment to the west, and the few Indians who held out until the summer of 1842 were permitted to remain, as Gen. Jesup had suggested five years earlier.

For this result—that the war was ultimately ended on terms at all favorable to the Negroes involved—John Caesar, dead over five years, bones mouldering in an unmarked grave either on the Williams plantation or in some potter's field of St. Augustine to which his body may have been brought for identification, was in a large measure responsible. He was the chief agent in bringing into the movement that unforeseen element, the plantation slaves, not merely arousing them to revolt at the beginning of the war, but also keeping up agitation among slaves not yet openly hostile, and organizing partisan warfare as the struggle entered its second year and the Seminole began to lose ground—in this last operation losing his life.

The plantation slaves in their turn not only took a principal part in winning control of the St. John's River valley up to the gates of St. Augustine in the early days of the war, but subsequently kept that region terrorized—and various commanding officers alarmed—both through the menace of those actually in the field and by the threat of revolt on the part of those still nominally under white control, thus tying up militia companies which otherwise would have been used against those openly hostile, convincing Gen. Jesup that the war must be speedily terminated lest it result in widespread slave insurrection, inducing him to grant favorable terms to the Seminole Negroes in the capitulation of Ft. Dade, Mar. 6, 1837, causing him early in 1838 to offer freedom to

²⁶ National Archives, War Department, AGO, ''Headquarters 9th M Department. Letters. June 2d, 1841, to February 1st, 1842, Vol. I,'' pp. 192-194, Col. W. J. Worth, Ft. Brooke, Aug. 19, 1841, to Maj. Gen. Scott.

Seminole Negroes who would surrender, and ultimately leading to the establishment of the double policy of sending *all* captured Negroes to the west—thus saving them from slavery—and of permitting the Indian residue to remain in Florida. This policy, not fully carried out until the last year or two of the war, was the one which ultimately proved successful—the only one, actually, which could have succeeded. If applied in 1837-1838, when first tentatively formulated by Gen. Jesup, it would have saved hundreds of lives and millions of dollars. It is obvious from Gen. Jesup's own words that it was John Caesar's operations with the plantation slaves which stood out in his mind as the incentive to, and justification for, this policy in its earliest stages.

The comparatively brief period—slightly over a year—between John Caesar's entering the field and his death has prevented his receiving proper attention, but a careful examination of the record will reveal that during that crucial first year or so of the war he was easily one of the half dozen most daring and effective leaders, inferior only to Osceola, Alligator, Jumper, and Abraham, and, for that period, ranking above even such better-known figures as his superior, King Philip, and the latter's subsequently famous son, Wild Cat, not to mention head-chief Mikonopi himself. His chief weakness seems to have been the recklessness which resulted in his death, but he should nevertheless be remembered as a brave, independent, far-seeing old warrior whose untutored mind recognized that success for the Seminole struggle depended on bringing together Indians, Indian Negroes, plantation slaves, and free Negroes for a united effort, and who risked, and lost, his life in endeavoring to make his understanding of the situation effective.

Corrections and Additions

I am mildly disturbed that, nearly a quarter-century after publication, I can detect neither errors nor omissions in this article.

Further Reading

The East Florida annexation plot is comprehensively dealt with, so far as the importance of the Negroes, and particularly the Seminole Negroes, of Florida is concerned, on pp. 183-203, with additional details on pp. 205-36. For still other details, however, see the book-length history of the plot and invasion by Rembert W. Patrick, *Florida Fiasco: Rampant Rebels on the Georgia-Florida Border, 1810-1815* (Athens, Georgia, 1954). See also the fascinating narrative, from the viewpoint of English-speaking settlers hostile to the invasion, by James Ormond, *Reminiscences . . . Concerning the Early Days of the Halifax Country* (Ormond Village Improvement Association, 1941), pp. 5-7.

The Red Stick War, the destruction of the Negro Fort, and the First Seminole War — so far as the role of the Creek and Seminole Negroes are concerned — are adequately treated on pp. 205-36. However, a few further details concerning Andrew Jackson's attack on the Negro villages of Suwanee can be found in *House Reports, 27th Congress, 2d sess.,* no. 722, Vol. III, pp. 1-6.

Far more important than the preceding four conflicts — which might be regarded as curtain raisers to the main events — was the great Seminole War, 1835-1842, which began as an attempt to remove the Seminole Indians from Florida and simultaneously enslave or reenslave the Negroes living among them. "Negroes and the Seminole War, 1835-1842" (pp. 238-61) is a concise but comprehensive account of Negro participation in this war; it utilizes and synopsizes — as its footnotes reveal — much of the material included in "Florida Slaves and Free Negroes in the Seminole War," "The Negro Abraham," and "John Caesar," which deal with particular aspects of the Negro role in this conflict. These other articles, however, present many details which could not be included in the more comprehensive account.

For the controversial figure of a Negro involved in the Dade disaster at the beginning of the war, see Porter, "The Early Life of Luis Pacheco ne Fatio," *NHB* (December, 1943), pp. 52, 54, 62, 64.

These articles all emphasize the Negro militants — Seminole Negroes, plantation slaves, free Negroes — who fought for the freedom of themselves and their families. Not reprinted here — partly because newly discovered material makes it too far out-of-date — is Porter, "Negro Guides and Interpreters in the Early Stages of the Seminole War, Dec. 28, 1835-Mar. 6, 1837," *JNH*, XXV (April, 1950), pp. 174-82, which deals with the slaves, Seminole Negroes, and free Negroes who assisted their masters and/or the United States government, and considers their possible motivation. Supplementary material on this subject can be found in John Lee Williams, *The Territory of Florida* (New York, 1837), pp. 250 (Polidore), 257, 275 (Cudjo. Nero, Billy); *House Reports, 27th Congress, 2d sess.*, no. 722, Vol. III, pp. 1-6, (Nero); Ormond, *Reminiscences*, pp. 8-10, and *House Executive Documents, War Department, 27th Cong., 2d sess.* (1842), no. 283, Vol. V, pp. 33, 55-57, 85, 87, 118-20 (Ben Wiggins).

Negroes were involved as allies of their Indian masters, protectors, or associates in two other border wars of this general period: the Creek War of 1836 and the Third Seminole War, 1855-1858. Their roles, however, were obscure and comparatively insignificant. What little I have been able to discover about Negro participation in the Third Seminole War is presented in "Billy Bowlegs (Holata Micco) in the Seminole Wars," *FHQ*, XLV (January, 1967), p. 238, note 30.

WHALING AND COMMERCE
1784-1860

Most westerly of all American frontiers was the Pacific Ocean, where, shortly after the end of the Revolutionary War, the crews of American vessels, both white and Negro, were pioneering as whalers and traders. The first Negro known to have set foot on the shores of the Pacific Northwest was a Cape Verde Islander, a servant of the famous Captain Robert Gray, maritime fur-trader and ultimately discoverer of the Columbia River, who was killed by Tillamook Indians on August 16, 1788, in a scuffle over a cutlass.

A comprehensive study, or studies, of the Negro in the maritime fur-trade, in whaling, and on the maritime frontier of the Pacific in general, would be well worthwhile. However, except for a brief treatment of the Negro in whaling — Lawrence C. Howard, "A Note on New England Whaling and Africa before 1860," *NHB* (October, 1958), pp. 13-16 — no such study has to my knowledge been published. Much material for this purpose can be found in published histories and personal narratives of whaling and commerce. Examples of the sort of published material available for a study of the Negro on the whaling frontier are Clifford W. Ashley, *The Yankee Whaler* (Boston and N.Y., 1926), pp. 5, 15, 18-19, 100, 108, 209; and Harold Williams, editor, *One Whaling Family* (Boston, 1964), pp. 83-84, 205-206, 267. Negroes — mostly, probably, deserters from whaling and trading vessels — were an important element in early Hawaii; cf. Porter, "Notes on Negroes in Early Hawaii," *JNH*, XIX (April, 1934), pp. 193-97. Most of the necessary material, however, remains in newspapers and in such unpublished sources as logbooks, journals, and letters.

THE TRANS-MISSISSIPPI WEST
1803-1860: General

The articles that appear in this volume about Negroes on the southern frontier (pp. 155-80), the East Florida Annexation Plot (pp. 183-203), the Fur Trade (pp. 139-57), and on their relations with Indians in the United States (pp. 8-88 and 96-135), deal to a considerable extent with regions east of the Mississippi River.

After the Louisiana Purchase of 1803, Anglo-Americans and civilized or semi-civilized Indians with their Negro slaves or dependents, together with a few free Negroes, began to cross the Mississippi. By the middle of the century, not only were Louisiana, Missouri, and Arkansas, with their substantial Negro populations, members of the Union of the States, but Texas had gone through the transformation from part of a state of Mexico to an independent republic to a state of the United States; Oregon had become a United States territory; and California, as a result of the Mexican War and the discovery of gold, had been admitted to the Union. Negroes — Indian Negroes, runaway slaves, free black people — had also begun to seek refuge from slavery and discrimination in the free republic of Mexico. Even before the Louisiana Purchase — or only a few years later — some Negroes had reached the Pacific. Well over half the forty-six men, women and children from Mexico who, in 1781, founded Los Angeles, were to a greater or lesser degree of Negro ancestry, although nearly all of these also had Spanish and/or Indian blood. (See Hubert Howe Bancroft, *History of California*, I, *1542-1800* [San Francisco, 1884], p. 345, note 24.) Negroes, shortly after the achievement of American independence, had skirted, and even made landfalls on Pacific shores as crewmen on whaling and trading vessels. Other Negroes reached the Coast overland in the early years of the nineteenth century as members of exploring and fur-trading expeditions.

These movements, west of the Mississippi and even to the

shores of the Pacific, overlapped chronologically with the break-up of the Indian and Negro settlements on the southeastern frontier, from 1813 to 1842, and the death or removal of their inhabitants. Anglo-American settlers with their Negroes, and civilized Indians with their own Negroes, were moving into Texas (then a part of Mexico) at approximately the same time, the former voluntarily, the latter under the compulsion or strong persuasion of federal and state governments. Other civilized Indians, with their Negroes, were simultaneously being moved into the Indian Territory — the ultimate home of most of the Seminole Indians and Negroes who survived the Seven Years' War (1835-1842). The first permanent Negro settler of the Oregon Country, a former trapper, arrived in 1834, just a year before the outbreak of the Second Seminole War.

All the above-mentioned states, territories, and regions included in their populations Negro elements that were sometimes substantial or, if not, then at least significant. The frontier regions in which, prior to or immediately after the Civil War, the Negroes were of greatest significance — because of their numbers or their unusual character or both — were the Indian Territory, Texas, northern Mexico, the Pacific Northwest, and the mining regions of California, Colorado, the Dakotas and elsewhere. However, chronological and other factors suggest that it would be more expedient to consider these frontiers in an order unrelated to the numbers of importance of their Negro inhabitants.

We have, thus far, been emphasizing those frontier Negroes who, because of their association with powerful Indian tribes, were important far beyond the extent that their numbers would seem to justify. But most Negroes, even on the frontiers, were not "Indian Negroes." Consequently, I shall turn not from the experiences of the Seminole and Creek Negroes on the southeast frontier to their subsequent activities on the southwestern frontier, as might seem most logical, but rather to an examination of Negroes on frontiers most remote from those identified with these Indian Negroes. Subsequently, however, we shall of course consider the problems of Negroes, both Indian Negroes and others, on the important southwest frontier.

MISSOURI, ARKANSAS, LOUISIANA
1803-1860

The frontier of the Old Oregon Country, the California gold-rush frontier, the maritime frontier of commerce and whaling, required leaps across half a continent or more to the shores of the Pacific, or a long voyage around Cape Horn or the Cape of Good Hope. Other frontiers, however, lay immediately west of the Mississippi River. The Negro in these territories and states has received little attention. For the barest knowledge of the Negro in the frontier periods of Louisiana, Missouri, and Arkansas we must turn to state and local histories, particularly histories emphasizing slavery. Our lack of knowledge concerning the Negro on the Missouri frontier is particularly unfortunate, for Missouri, as territory and state, gave birth to or influenced many of the Negroes who were prominent on other frontiers, such as the mountain-man, James P. Beckwourth; Fremont's companion, Jacob Dodsworth; the Washington pioneers, George Bush and George Washington; and the runaway slaves who served so splendidly in Kansas regiments during the Civil War on the frontier.

THE PACIFIC NORTHWEST
1834-1893

Negroes were probably fewer on the frontier of the Pacific Northwest — the region west of the Continental Divide, north of the 42nd parallel, and south of the line of 54-40 — than on any other frontier of the nineteenth century United States, both because of its distance from regions of Negro concentration and the avowed hostility of its white settlers to Negro immigration. Nevertheless, some of the few Negroes who reached the region during the period of early settlement played a positive role — probably more important in proportion to their numbers than on any other comparable frontier.

No adequate published treatment of Negroes on this frontier has yet appeared, but a number of brief general articles are available, *viz.*, W. Sherman Savage, "The Negro in the History of the Pacific Northwest," *JNH*, XIII (July, 1928), pp. 255-64, dealing with the period prior to 1850; Savage, "The Negro in the Westward Movement," *JNH*, XXV (October, 1940), pp. 533-34; Savage, "The Negro Pioneers in the State of Washington," *NHB* (January, 1958), p. 93; Robert W. O'Brien and Bernard E. Squires, "The Negro in the Northwest before the Civil War," *NHB* (June, 1942), pp. 195-97.

Two remarkable mulattoes — George Bush, a leader in the first significant American settlement north of the Columbia, and George Washington, the founder of Centralia — settled in the present-day state of Washington prior to the Civil War. The history of the Negro in early Washington, and indeed in the early Pacific Northwest, is very largely the story of these two Negroes. The life of George Bush, prior to his settlement in the Oregon Country in 1845, is obscure and controversial. The principal basic published accounts for his career are Francis Henry, "George Bush," *Transactions of the Oregon Pioneer Association for 1887* (Portland, 1887), pp. 68-69, the author of which knew Bush personally; Hubert Howe Bancroft, *History of Washington, Idaho, and Montana, 1845-1889* (San Francisco, 1890), p. 4, note 8; The Rev. H. K. Hines, *An Illustrated History of the State of Washington* (Chicago, 1893), pp. 378-79; John Edwin Ayer, "George Bush, the Voyageur," *Washington Historical Quarterly*, VII (January, 1916), pp. 40-45, which, in regard to Bush's early life, completely disagrees with Henry's pioneer account; Harvey W. and Leslie Scott, *History of the Oregon Country*, 6 vols. (Cambridge, Mass., 1924), II, pp. 31, 250, note 7. Detailed secondary works on the Pacific Northwest usually mention Bush and he has been the subject of any number of popular articles. A particularly good example is Ruby El Hult, "The Saga of George Bush," *Negro Digest* (September, 1962).

A scholarly biography of Bush, including an accurate treatment of his early life, is badly needed.

George Bush's sons, particularly William Owen Bush, carried on the family tradition. See "A Negro Pioneer in the West," *JNH*, VIII (July, 1923), pp. 333-35, from the *Advertiser-Journal* (Kent, Washington), December 23, 1920. A scholarly treatment of the Bush family would also be a worthwhile project.

Articles and books dealing with the mulatto pioneer and town founder, George Washington, include Colonel William Farrand Prosser, *A History of the Puget Sound Country* . . ., 2 vols. (New York and Chicago, 1903), pp. 325-26; Robert W. O'Brien, "George Washington, Founder of Centralia," *NHB* (June, 1942), pp. 194, 197, 215 (portraits of George Washington and wife) and Herndon Smith, *Centralia: The First Fifty Years, 1845-1900* (1942) — both apparently derived principally from a series of stories by Dorothy Mae Riggs, *Centralia Chronicle*, September, 1941; W. Sherman Savage, "The Negro Pioneers in the State of Washington," *NHB*, (January, 1958), pp. 93-95 (utilizes some primary material) and, Savage, "George Washington of Centralia, Washington," *NHB* (November, 1963), pp. 44-47.

A consideration of the Negro on the frontier of the Pacific Northwest would not be complete without reference to those Negroes who — fleeing discrimination in the "democratic" United States — settled north of the 49th parallel in the region which, by the Treaty of 1846, became a British possession. O'Brien and Squires, "The Negro in the Northwest before the Civil War," *NHB* (June, 1942), pp. 196-97, gives a general account of this migration.

Although Negroes were few in Oregon and Washington, they were even fewer in Idaho and western Montana, and no Negro in these latter territories approached George Bush and George Washington in significance. The only study of the Negro in Montana known to me — J. W. Smurr, "Jim Crow Out West," *Historical Essays on Montana and the Northwest*, J. W. Smurr and K. Ross Toole, editors (Helena, Montana, 1957), esp. pp. 157-60, 163-97 — is concerned almost exclusively with anti-Negro discrimination. Any study of the Negro in Idaho and Montana would have to begin at the grass roots.

MINING, 1849-1879

The great United States gold rushes, from the California rush which began in 1849 through the rush to the Black Hills in the late 1870's, occurred in regions remote from those with the heaviest concentration of Negro population. Moreover, for over half the period, the overwhelming majority of Negroes in the United States were slaves, who could not participate except at the permission, and normally under the supervision, of their masters. Even after Emancipation, Negroes on the average were less mobile than whites. Consequently, comparatively few Negroes were to be found in the mining camps. Nevertheless, the attractions of an opportunity to acquire, over a short period of time, prosperity and prestige, were so great that Negroes in the mining regions were few only in comparison to whites and, in the Far West, with Chinese. For example, while Negroes in the Old Oregon Country in 1850 probably numbered only about sixty, there were in the same year nearly a thousand Negroes in gold-rich California. Negroes were also to be found on every subsequent United States mining frontier. From California to the Dakotas they acquired in mining-field folklore the reputation of being particularly successful as gold-finders, as betokened by such names on the land as Negro Bar, Negro Gulch, Negro Hill, etc.

The presence of Negroes in old California has attracted the most attention from historians, even as the California gold rush has received more attention than any other. Delilah L. Beasley, *The Negro Trail Blazers of California* (Los Angeles, 1919), is a pioneer work. W. Sherman Savage, "The Negro on the Mining Frontier," *JNH*, XXX (January, 1945), pp. 30-39, although emphasizing California, also gives some attention to Colorado. A recent brief scholarly treatment is Rudolph M. Lapp, "The Negro in Gold Rush California," *JNH*, XLIX (April, 1964), pp. 81-98.

Mention of the Negro on other mining frontiers, such as those of Oregon, Washington, Idaho, Montana, Colorado, Arizona, and the Dakotas, is scattered through regional, state, and local histories, personal reminiscences, census reports, newspapers, etc. The Negro in the mining regions of Colorado and the Dakotas has probably received more, if scattered, attention than those in other regions.

Many — probably most — of the Negroes on the mining frontier were not themselves prospectors or miners. An example is the remarkable Barney Ford of Colorado and Wyoming, who, frustrated by racial discrimination in gaining a fortune as a prospector, won — and also lost — several small fortunes as restaurateur and hotel-keeper. The only full-length biography is Forbes Parkhill, *Mister Barney Ford: A Portrait in Bistre* (Denver, 1963), which is without footnotes and admittedly supplies "the workings of Barney's mind, his thoughts and feelings," as well as all the dialogue, although it allegedly does not "in any way distort or exaggerate his record of accomplishment." There are also some highly sensational popular articles that vary widely from the Parkhill volume. A sober, scholarly, documented treatment of Barney Ford's career would be a worthwhile project, as would similar studies of other important Negroes on the California and Colorado mining frontiers.

Except for California, the story of the Negro on the mining frontier is virtually untouched, and even in California there is abundant opportunity for fuller treatment.

THE SOUTHWEST
ca. 1825-1860: General

The southwestern frontiers, particularly of the generation preceding the Civil War, can, so far as Negroes are concerned, conveniently be divided into three major regions: the Indian Territory, occupied largely by immigrant Indians from east of the Mississippi and, in the case of the so-called Civilized Tribes of the South, their Negro slaves or dependents; Texas, settled primarily from the southern states, and thus including among its population considerable numbers of slaves and some free Negroes; and northern Mexico, which was a haven of refuge for runaway Negroes from Texas, Arkansas, and the Indian Territory and for free colored settlers from the United States.

The following article, "Negroes and Indians on the Texas Frontier," was originally published in two issues of *JNH*, July, 1956 (Vol. XLI, No. 3), and October, 1956 (Vol. XLI, No. 4).

NEGROES AND INDIANS ON THE TEXAS FRONTIER, 1831-1876[1]

A STUDY IN RACE AND CULTURE

No state is richer than Texas in opportunities for observing the varied relations of Negroes and Indians under frontier conditions. It included almost every variety of frontier settlement from the good-sized cotton plantation to the small farm and the large cattle ranch. Its Indians ranged from semi-civilized and sedentary agricultural tribes to wandering and predatory hunters. Their attitude toward the whites varied according to tribe and time: some were usually friendly; some consistently hostile; others were at first more or less friendly but subsequently became hostile; still others were friends or enemies according to immediate circumstances. Indians were eliminated as an important factor in Texas history by the mid-1870's but

[1] A brief, preliminary article on this subject, entitled "Negroes and Indians on the Texas Frontier, 1834-1874," appeared in the *Southwestern Historical Quarterly*, LIII (Oct., 1949), 151-163. My thanks are due to the editors of that publication for permission to use it as basis for this revised, reorganized, and greatly enlarged treatment.

during the period of their significance Texas was a part of Mexico, an independent republic, a State of the United States, a State of the Confederacy, and a State of the Union again, was at peace and at war—at war not merely against Indians but also against Mexico and against the United States. At the beginning of the period most Texas Negroes were slaves; at its end they had for several years been freemen—a change which for our purpose is particularly important. The relations between Negroes enlisted in the United States Army after the Civil War and the Indians against whom they frequently served is, however, a story in itself.[2]

Relations between Negroes and Indians have received considerable scattered attention from Texas writers, but their statements are frequently contradictory and confusing and probably often inaccurate. S. H. Blalack is quoted as saying: "The Indians weren't afraid of a Negro at all. They were afraid of a white man but they seemed to hate a Negro and would kill him any chance they got."[3] Anyone acquainted with Texas frontier history is aware that Indians frequently seemed to hate white men as well, as indicated by this same readiness to kill them. T. A. Babb asserts that the Comanche did not scalp Negroes, who, according to them, had no souls. "However, they would kill negroes so as to get them out of the way and also to prevent them from killing any of the Indian tribe."[4] Here again one might wonder whether it was actually such an advanced theological concept as the alleged lack of a soul, or rather the texture of the scalp-hair, so different from that of In-

[2] The author has told part of the story in "The Seminole Negro-Indian Scouts, 1870-1881," *SWHQ*, LV (Jan., 1952).

[3] Florence Fenley, *Oldtimers* (Uvalde, 1939), 119.

[4] T. A. Babb, *In the Bosom of the Comanche* (Amarillo, 1912), 44. "Kiowa and Comanche . . . positively assert that no Indian was ever known to scalp a negro": "Annual Report of the Commissioner of Indian Affairs, 1867-1868," in "Report of the Secretary of the Interior," *House Executive Documents*, 40th Cong., 3rd sess., II (1366), No. 1, p. 499.

dian or white, which often exempted Negroes from this characteristic mutilation. And Indians, including Comanche, certainly did sometimes scalp Negroes.[5] James T. De Shields is in general disagreement with both the foregoing authorities. "Usually," he says, "Indians did not kill negro slaves, but held them for large ransom. . . . When circumstances were such as to preclude . . . holding negroes to ransom, the darkies were killed, and generally scalped, like other victims." De Shields thus contradicts Blalack's assertion of the Indians' special antipathy for Negroes and Babb's statement that they were never scalped; he is probably correct on both these points but is entirely too extreme as to the infrequency with which Negroes were killed.[6] Wilbarger broadens the picture somewhat when he writes: "Very frequently runaway negroes would join the Indians and render valuable assistance in fighting and stealing, but their dead bodies were never moved, nor was a negro ever scalped by them.'"[7] This contradicts, in agreement with De Shields, Blalack's assertion of the Indian's general antipathy for the Negro, and agrees, in contradiction to De Shields, with Babb's statement that Negroes were never scalped. Some more careful examination is obviously called for.

The contradictions in the above statements probably derive at least partly from the failure to distinguish between Indians and Indians. The Texas Indians, before the Civil War and particularly prior to the Republic's admission to the Union as a State, were divided culturally into two large main groups, each, however, with various divisions and sub-divisions.

In East, East Central, Northeast, and North Central Texas were numerous tribes which, although varying widely

[5] Ernest Wallace and E. Adamson Hoebel, *The Comanches* (Norman, 1952), 189.

[6] James T. De Shields, *Border Wars of Texas* (Tioga, Texas, 1912), p. 337.

[7] J. W. Wilbarger, *Indian Depredations in Texas* (1st ed.: Austin, 1889), 412.

in language, characteristic dwellings, the extent and character of their previous associations with whites, and their assimilation of European culture, were fundamentally similar in certain important characteristics: they were sedentary or semi-sedentary, living in more or less permanent habitations; they cultivated the soil, raising considerable quantities of corn, beans, and squash; and they manufactured and used pottery. These semi-civilized Indians can be divided in turn into two main groups, according to their locations at the proclamation of the Texas Republic, although each group can also be variously subdivided.

One of these main groups lived on the wooded banks of the East Texas rivers. The first of their two principal subdivisions were the tribes of Caddo stock—Caddo proper, Hainai or Ioni, Adai, Anadarko, Kichai, and Bidai. From time immemorial their characteristic conical straw houses had stood on the banks of the Lower Red River in Louisiana and on those of the Red, Sabine, Neches, Trinity, Brazos, and Colorado Rivers in East Texas, but by 1835 pressure from settlers in the United States had concentrated them within the Republic of Mexico, in what is now Texas.

The second principal subdivision of semi-civilized, sedentary, agricultural East Texas Indians were migrants from east of the Mississippi, some even from north of the Ohio, who had also sought refuge on Mexican soil from the relentless advance of the American frontier. The Cherokee, of Iroquoian stock, who about 1824 had moved from East Tennessee to a tract along the Angelina, Neches, and Trinity rivers, were the most important. Associated with them were not only their Caddoan predecessors but also other tribesmen from the United States: Creeks or Muscogee, Seminole, Choctaw, Coushatta, and Alabama (Muskhogeans); the Biloxi and Quapaw (Siouan); and from north of the Ohio such Algonquin immigrants as Kickapoo, Delawares, and Shawnee. The East Texas Indians from long intercourse with the whites were expert in the use of the rifle, although they retained the bow and arrow for hunting purposes and as subsidiary weapons.[8]

The other large body of sedentary, semi-civilized, agricultural Indians inhabiting Texas or its borders during the early days of Anglo-American settlement were the members of the Wichita confederacy, of Caddoan stock, who ranged from the Arkansas River in Kansas south into Texas. The confederacy was composed of the Wichita proper, who lived north of the Red River beyond the Texas borders; the Tawéhash, also known from their custom of tattooing their faces as the Pawnee Picts, upon the Upper Red River; the Tawakoni in Texas, on the middle Brazos and Trinity rivers, principally east of the Brazos and north of the San Antonio Road; and the Waco, a division of the Tawakoni, whose principal village until after 1830 was on the site of the present-day city of Waco and who ranged with the Tawakoni in the Trinity and Brazos valleys. Although primarily sedentary and agricultural, the Tawéhash even to the extent of raising a surplus of corn for trading purposes, the Wichitans were also buffalo hunters. Toward the whites they tended to be "dangerous and troublesome," although they usually confined themselves to "small-scale theft and murder."[9]

The other large main division of Texas Indians, as opposed to the sedentary and agricultural native sons and intruders, were the wild, uncivilized, non-agricultural tribes. The ferocious and cannibalistic Coast-dwelling Karankawa, who lived in the vicinity of Matagorda Bay, were the earliest Texas Indians encountered by white settlers; they were, however, too few to constitute a serious problem and

[8] Walter P. Webb, *The Texas Rangers* (Boston, 1935), 5-7, 54, 132. William Ransom Hogan, *The Texas Republic* (Norman, 1946), 14-15. Rex W. Strickland, "History of Fannin County," *SWHQ,* XXXIII (Apr., 1930), 286, quoting from William Kennedy, *Texas,* 336-337. F. W. Hodge, editor, *Handbook of North American Indians,* 2 vols. (Washington, 1907-1910): See under tribal designations.

[9] Hodge: See under names of individual tribes. Webb, 5-7. Hogan, 14-15.

soon disappeared. The Tonkawa, a tribe of cannibalistic hunters who ranged the interior of Texas between the San Antonio and the Brazos Rivers, were cordially disliked by other tribes because of their anthropophagy and were in consequence usually friendly to the whites. The Lipan Apache occupied an area to the west and northwest of San Antonio and were originally friendly to the white settlers, whom they regarded as potential allies against their enemies the Comanche; eventually, however, as the frontier moved west, the Lipanes too were numbered among the foes of the whites. The fierce and nomadic Comanche were of all Texas tribes the most dangerous; they were consistently hostile from their first encounter with European settlers to their complete elimination from the Texas scene. Of Shoshonean stock, their range was the Great Plains from Kansas to southern Texas; in the early days of the Republic they were located west and northwest of the partially settled areas. They were allied with the Kiowa, a small tribe of even more ferocious and hostile disposition, whose range, though overlapping with the Comanche's, usually lay somewhat farther to the north.[10]

A logical tentative judgment would be that both Negroes and whites would have somewhat different relations with the agricultural and sedentary Indians of Eastern Texas than with the wild predatory marauders of the Southern Plains. The East Texas Indians were familiar with white civilization. They had no particular fondness for the whites, but recognized their power and were dependent on them for such necessities as firearms, ammunition, metal tools and utensils, and even to a considerable extent for clothing and blankets. They were willing to live and let live if given the opportunity. Those from the Southern United States, particularly the Cherokee, Creeks, and Seminole, were acquainted with Negroes, their characteristic and normal role in white society, and the extent to which at least some Ne-

[10] Webb, 5-7. Hogan, 14-15.

groes wished to escape from their subordinate position. Culturally, these corn-planting, house-dwelling Indians were not far removed from white and Negro frontiersmen. Life among them would not have appeared impossible even to an adult white man or Negro; it might even seem attractive. Slaveholding whites moving into East Texas in the 1830's probably selected the Negroes they intended to take with them with some care and, if possible, disposed of any whose trustworthiness was doubtful; the danger of their running away to the Indians, or to Mexican settlements, was too great a hazard.

To test the accuracy of this hypothesis concerning Negro-Indian relations in Texas and to determine how they differed, if at all, from those between whites and Indians, the relations of Negroes with the sedentary, agricultural tribes will be considered first. Since these Indians, except for obscure remnants, were expelled from Texas by 1859, such relations lie entirely within the pre-Civil War period of slavery.

Relations with the Tawéhash of the Red River: The Martin Affair, 1834

The earliest important episode in Texas or on its borders in which Indians and Negroes were involved[11] was the murderous attack on the Judge Martin party in 1834 and the consequent dispatch of a military force into the Indian

---

[11] A still earlier episode of Indian-Negro relations on the Texas-Louisiana border might be inserted here for the record: "Natchitoches Nov. 30th. 1810. . . . This Side of the Mississippi River is very much Invested with Vagabond parties of Choctaw Indians. . . . About a Month Ago a Party of seven or eight . . . Came to the rancheria of a Mr. Lamber a French gentleman about ten Miles from this place, where they Murdered a Mulatto Man a slave of Mr. Lamber & an Indian Woman of the Aiche (Aliche, Ais) Tribe, who had been raised from a Child Amongst the white People. . . ." Julia Kathryn Garrett, editor, "Dr. John Sibley and the Louisiana-Texas Frontier, 1803-1814," *SWHQ*, XLVIII (July, 1944), pp. 67-68. Obviously, this episode does not significantly involve either race or culture, but is a manifestation of frontier lawlessness in which the parties involved could equally well have all been whites.

country; the relations between Negroes and Indians displayed in the course of this affair were remarkably varied. The Indians who were most conspicuously concerned were the Tawéhash of the Red River, who, although agricultural and sedentary, were more ferocious than their Caddo kinsmen of the Texas-Louisiana border.

In June, 1834, Judge Gabriel N. Martin was hunting on the False Washita in the southeastern part of the Indian Territory "with a small party composed of himself, his little son, Matthew W., a negro playmate of the latter, Daniel Davis, James and Robert Gamble, Zack Bottom (a negro servant who had been partly raised among the Indians), and a few other companions," possibly including still another Negro servant. The Tawéhash or "Pawnee Picts" attacked the camp "when none but the elder Martin, the little negro, . . . Bottom, the servant," and perhaps another Negro were present, "killed the Judge and negro boy—'because he fought so desperately and screamed so loud,'" and captured the Martin boy. "Zack Bottom, the old servant," according to this account, "escaped, barefooted, and eventually, after much suffering and almost famished, reached the settlements." Or perhaps, since one account states that a Negro servant was captured and escaped, he escaped *after* capture rather than *from* capture? George W. Wright, Mrs. Martin's brother, with a party of thirty men, guided by " 'Hardy,' the brave old Indian-trained negro"—who perhaps had been a member of the Martin party, else how could he have guided the expedition to the scene of the tragedy?—and, according to one account, accompanied by Zack Bottom, "repaired to the camp" and buried the horribly mangled bodies of the Judge and of "the little colored boy." They were, however, unable to locate the Martin boy.[12]

12 The story of the Martin affair, thus far, is based primarily upon James T. De Shields, *Border Wars*, 111-118, who gives by far the fullest and also the most critical account of an almost hopelessly confused episode. ''Radical dis-

A dragoon expedition was dispatched to recover the captive boy, but when it arrived at the Tawéhash village at the mouth of Devil Canyon, northeast of the junction of Elk Creek and the North Fork of the Red River, the Indians at first denied that the boy was in their possession. The expedition had, however, earlier encountered Comanche, who assured Colonel Dodge that the boy was indeed a prisoner of the Tawéhash. Furthermore, on July 21, 1834, "a negro man who had been taken by the Comanches on the Arkansas river" the previous spring came into camp and informed the dragoons that a white boy was living among the Indians. With the aid of this information the Martin boy was found hidden in a corn patch, entirely naked, and his captors were forced to give him up.

The nameless Negro informant "had ran away from his master on the Arkansas & had wandered on the Prairies until taken up by a hunting party"—either of Comanche or Tawéhash; in the former case the Comanche had given or sold him to their Tawéhash allies. The Negro said that

---

crepancies," he very correctly writes, "exist in regard to the circumstances attending the killing of Judge Martin, and whether a negro was captured with the boy. One version is that . . . the Judge was killed, and the boy and negro man were made prisoners. Others give a wholly different recital—one saying . . . that Judge Martin and a negro man were killed in camp. . . ." See also: J. W. Wilbarger, *Indian Depredations in Texas* (1st ed., Austin, 1889), 295-296 (says judge and Negro servant were killed and boy captured). George Catlin, *Illustrations of the Manners, Customs, & Conditions of the North American Indians* (London, 1876), II, 47 (ditto). Philip St. George Cooke, *Scenes and Adventures in the Army* (Philadelphia, 1865; 1st ed., 1859), 227 (no mention of Negro servant or servants). Wilbur Sturtevant Nye, *Carbine and Lance* (Norman, 1942), 11-12. Grant Foreman, *Pioneer Days in the Early Southwest* (Cleveland, 1926), 120-121 (follows Catlin and Wilbarger). Louis Pelzer, editor, "A Journal of Marches by the First United States Dragoons, 1834-1835," *Iowa Journal of History and Politics*, VII (July, 1909), 357 (says that the Negro servant escaped). "The Autobiography of Andrew Davis," *SWHQ*, XLIII (Oct., 1939), 162-163 (says judge was killed and boy and Negro servant captured). The story, so far as it involves Negoes, must be pieced together from several sources, since, except for De Shields, no single authority, primary or secondary, mentions even *two* Negroes—one killed and one escaped or captured—still less three.

"after he was taken he came ten days with those Indians without anything to eat save some plumbs, berries &c but since he had been living among them they had treated him well and had given him corn mellons Buffaloe meat &c to eat—he appeared very well satisfied with his situation [they] requireing of him nothing but to graze their horses." Another source says that his captors "found him of considerable service in learning [sic] them many of the customs of civilized life"—although just what civilized customs a solitary Negro captive could have taught or would have been permitted to teach the sedentary and prosperous Tawéhash is never specified.

Why a Negro who admitted that his captors had "treated him in a friendly manner at least the best manner that they could" and that he "had his own horse & Indian equipment & was much better contented there than at home," should have endangered—indeed sacrificed—his position by assisting in the recovery of the Martin boy is a mystery. Perhaps he had become acquainted with the little fellow and, moved by the fondness for children which is so much a part of Negro culture, had become sorry for him and wished to help restore him to his mother. Certainly he gained nothing by his kindly or treacherous act. When Colonel Dodge, having recovered the Martin boy, was preparing to depart, he thus questioned the "Wichita" chief: "How came you by the negro who is with you here?" The chief thereupon replied: "This Comanche brought him; he found him on the Red River; you can take him and do as you please with him." Colonel Dodge therefore took the Negro with him, though an observer says that "he was loth to leave there & we were obliged to bring him home in the Capacity of a Prisoner." The colonel really had no other alternative. Had the Negro been left behind, his captors or hosts would probably have killed him for betraying their possession of the Martin boy; moreover, an American army officer could not consistently with his duty have neglected to recover a runaway slave. So when Dodge's command marched from the Indian village it was with both "the white boy and the negro in company."[13] Presumably the Negro was returned to his master; it is to be hoped that he did not long or often regret the freedom he had enjoyed on the prairies and the foolish or generous impulse which had caused him to exchange it for a life of slavery and whatever satisfaction he may have derived from his part in restoring a captive white boy to his home and relatives.

Judge Martin had at least two Negro servants with him on the fatal expedition. One of these, a boy, was killed with his master, while another, Zack Bottom, is said to have escaped, but, according to the son of one of the judge's white companions, one of his Negro men, "an old servant," was captured and taken to an Indian village "at the foot of the [Wichita] mountains and near to Red River," although apparently not the one in which the Martin boy was held. The Negro was not badly treated or kept a close prisoner and although not allowed a gun was permitted to use a bow and arrows. He decided to escape. At first he followed the river downstream, hiding during the day and traveling at night. Then, after his feet became sore, he used a cottonwood log for a raft. He lived on berries and crawfish until he succeeded in making fire by rubbing sticks together; then he killed and cooked birds, rabbits, and squirrels. Eventually he got home to his children and grandchildren.[14]

[13] "The Journal of Hugh Evans covering the First and Second Campaigns of the United States Dragoon Regiment in 1834 and 1835," Fred S. Perrine and Grant Foreman, editors, *Chronicles of Oklahoma*, III (Sept., 1925), 189, 192-194. Pelzer, ed., *loc. cit.*, VII, 358. American State Papers, Military Affairs, V, 377-378. Catlin, II, 71. (James Hildreth) *Dragoon Campaigns to the Rocky Mountains* (New York, 1836), 165, 176. Wilbarger, 296-297. Ralph Smith, "The Tawéhash in French, Spanish, English, and American Imperial Affairs," *West Texas Historical Association Year Book*, XXVIII (Oct., 1952), 47-48.

[14] "The Autobiography of Andrew Davis," *SWHQ*, XLIII (Oct., 1939), 162-163. Very probably this Negro was Zack Bottom, the Indian-raised Negro who is elsewhere said to have escaped when Judge Martin was killed.

The Martin story is revelatory of the attitude of the sedentary and semi-civilized Tawéhash toward Negroes. When they encountered a party of white men and Negroes encroaching on their buffalo-hunting preserves they killed one white and one Negro and took prisoner a white boy and perhaps an old Negro. A little earlier they had picked up on the prairie, or received from the Comanche, a runaway Negro slave. Both the white boy and the Negro or Negroes were treated well. The Indians were probably well enough acquainted with the ways of white men to realize that in their economy Negroes occupied a peculiar status which would justify giving them special treatment if their conduct seemed to warrant it. The little Negro boy who was killed with Judge Martin is said to have screamed and struggled, whereas the old man who is said to have been captured probably did not show fight or otherwise give trouble. Toward the runaway Negro—who, by running away had voluntarily disassociated himself from the whites—the Tawéhash were particularly friendly—at least until he turned traitor to his new allegiance.

It is also worthy of note that two out of three or four Negroes involved in this affair are described as "Indian raised" or "Indian trained"; evidently such Negroes constituted a special and recognized class on the Southwestern frontier.

Toward neither white man nor Negro did the Tawéhash display the violent antipathy which, as we shall see, was characteristic of the Comanche. Those nomads of the prairie would probably have killed not only Judge Martin but also both his Negro servants and perhaps even the boy as well, although the latter's fate would have been much less certain. But, according to one account, it was Comanche who found the runaway Negro on the prairie and brought him in; if so, even the Comanche were capable on occasion of distinguishing between a Negro and a white man if the Negro were not associated with whites in activities which identified him as a member of a hostile culture. A lone white man, or a Negro traveling with a white man, would probably have immediately been made a pincushion for Comanche arrows.

Relations in East Texas, 1835-1839

Some of the Indians from the United States who were settled in East Texas belonged to tribes in which the possession of Negro slaves or vassals was a part of the tribal culture. The most important of such tribes was the Cherokee, who must have had Negroes among them — either brought from the United States or runaways from Texas plantations or both—although little definite information on this subject is available. There is, however, evidence that discontented Negroes in East Texas looked upon the Cherokee as potential allies. The Texas Revolution, which broke out in October, 1835, seems to have inspired some Texas Negroes to seek their own rights through rebellion; perhaps Mexican agents were even then at work among them. "The negroes on the Brazos," it was reported on October 17, 1835, "made an attempt to rise . . . near 100 had been taken up many whipd nearly to death some hung etc. divided all the cotton farms and they intended to ship the cotton to New Orleans and make the white men serve them in turn." On December 12 Sam Houston charged that Santa Ana was "departing from chivalric principles of warfare" by ordering arms to be distributed to the Negroes. A slave rebellion at this time—prior to a Mexican invasion of Texas in force—would, however, have been premature. The best time for such a rising would have been during the "Runaway Scrape" of March-April, 1836, when Santa Ana's army, after storming the Alamo, was moving rapidly across eastern Texas. Some Negroes, apparently, recognized this. On March 24 "Colonel James Morgan reported . . . that overtures were being made to the Indians by Texas Negroes who wished to join the Mexicans." But if such advances were made, the Indians were at this time insufficiently receptive, and the defeat and capture of Santa Ana the following month terminated such negotiations, at least for the time being.[15]

Relations between the Texans and the Cherokee and other allied tribes of East Texas for a couple of years more remained peaceful, although uneasy and uncertain. An episode of about 1838 exemplifies the situation, and also gives us a glimpse at the Negro's role among the Texas Cherokee. A four-man surveying party commanded by the famous Jack Hays was camped on Comal Creek in the Bexar District when a band of Cherokee invested their camp and surrounded the Texans so closely as in effect to make them prisoners, although they retained their guns. The Cherokee had with them "a Negro who did a fair job of translating. ... The Negro said that the Cherokee had been fighting the Comanche"—they were in Comanche country—and "had taken many scalps." The Indians agreed, through the Negro, to liberate the whites if Hays would write a statement that they were friendly, which he did.[16] Their friendship, however, was obviously wearing thin and soon broke down completely.

When in 1838 intermittent warfare broke out between the Anglo-Americans and the allied tribes living in East Texas which in the following year led to their expulsion, one would expect to find Negroes fighting with the hostile Indians. When on October 16, 1838, "a motley gang" attacked General Rusk at the Kickapoo Town, his assailants included "Mexicans, negroes, Coshattees, Caddoes, & some thought Keechies."[17] In March, 1839, another "motley crowd" of Mexicans, runaway Negroes from the eastern

15 Elgin Williams, *The Animating Pursuits of Speculation: Land Traffic in the Annexation of Texas* (New York, 1949), pp. 64-65.

16 James Kimmins Greer, *Colonel Jack Hays: Texas Frontier Leader and California Builder* (New York, 1952), 26-27.

17 *The Papers of Mirabeau Buonaparte Lamar*, 6 vols. (Austin, 1920-1927), II, 265-266.

Texas plantations, and Biloxi Indians, commanded by the Mexican General Vicente Cordova, encountered Edward Burleson's rangers "near Mill Creek, five miles east of Seguin, in the Guadalupe valley." Cordova's force suffered defeat and in the battle at least two Negroes were killed and two captured. One of the captives is variously described as an old man and as "a big French negro, weighing about two hundred pounds. . . . This Negro claimed to have always been free, but would not acknowledge any allegiance to the Texas government; on the contrary, claimed to have always maintained a hostile attitude toward the Texans, and . . . was accordingly court-martialed and sentenced to be shot the next day," which was done. His less defiant companion was sold into slavery.[18]

The Red River Frontier, 1837-1843

Indians pushed or driven out of East Texas—Cherokee, Delawares, Shawnee, Kickapoo, Caddo, Ioni, Andarcos or Unataqua, Tohooktoni (Tawakoni?), Quapaw, etc.—moved west, and from 1837 to 1843 gave a great deal of trouble to the settlers in Fannin County on the Red River across from the Indian Territory.[19]

The Negroes on the Red River frontier displayed a remarkable loyalty to their masters, particularly for Negroes on a frontier where the Indians were sedentary agriculturists. When in 1837 Daniel Davis moved his family and slaves to North Sulphur, eight miles south of Honey Grove in Fannin County, he was accustomed each night to hide the women and children in the woods and then "return and, with the colored people, guard the house through the night."[20] In 1839 a Fannin County Negro boy named Smith, equipped with a pistol and butcher knife for his protection

---

[18] Sowell, *Rangers and Pioneers*, 187-189. Sowell, *Early Settlers*, 15, 117. Wilbarger, *Indian Depredations*, 151-157.

[19] Strickland, "Fannin Co." *SWHQ*, XXXIII, 286-298, XXXIV, 38-60. Webb, 54.

[20] "The Autobiography of Andrew Davis," *SWHQ*, XLIII (Oct., 1939).

while pulling corn, was attacked by three Indians but shot one and made his escape.[21]

About March 14, 1841, when Captain John Yeary, his little son, and a Negro slave named Bob Anderson, were working in a field near present-day Bagby, a party of fifteen Indians approached the cabin. A daughter saw them coming and bolted the door, which the Indians endeavored to break down. Her father and the Negro, armed only with their heavy hoes—although according to one authority the Negro had an axe—rushed to the relief of the cabin and the Indians met them about thirty feet from the door. They attempted to shoot the captain with arrows, but the two parties were mixed up so closely and Yeary and the Negro laid about them so furiously that the Indians could not take aim and resorted to beating the captain over the head with their bows. When Mrs. Yeary and the daughter sallied out with loaded rifles and the captain jumped the fence and seized a weapon, the Indians fled. The captain then sent the Negro for help. The Indians in the fight seem to have concentrated their attack on the captain, though the Negro was apparently little if any behind the master in wielding his hoe.[22]

But although the Davises and Captain Yeary and the

[21] Wilbarger, *Indian Depredations*, 431.

[22] *Lamar Papers*, IV, pt. 1, pp. 235-236 (the principal contemporary source). Strickland, "Fannin Co.," *SWHQ*, XXXIV, pp. 39-40 (based on above account). John Henry Brown, *Indian Wars and Pioneers of Texas*, 85. *Lamar Papers*, IV, Pt. 1, pp. 219-220 (similar to first account but less direct). *Ibid.*, IV, pt. 1, 276 (exaggerated and confused; nothing about Negro). J. K. B. Yeary, "Troublesome Times in Texas," *Frontier Times*, XXI (April, 1944), pp. 289-291, from *The Dallas News*, Dec. 12, 1926 (by son of Captain Yeary who was, however, only two years old in 1841; he tells of *two* Indian attacks, one in 1841 which his father and an eighteen-year-old Negro boy beat off by limbering up their guns and firing as fast as they could load, and the other in 1848 in eastern Collin County. Probably the narrator made two episodes out of one). J. Marvin Hunter, Sr., "A Desperate Hand to Hand Fight," *FT*, XXVII (April, 1950), pp. 229-231 (puts the fight with hoes in Collin County in 1848). W. S. Adair, "Redhaired Aunt Object of Indian Attack," *Dallas Morning News*, July 24, 1927 (not consulted).

master of the trigger-quick Smith boy treated their Negroes as trusted allies, they also were of the opinion that the Indians on the Red River frontier were generally less hostile toward Negroes than toward whites. "It was believed that Indians never killed Negroes—that the worst they did to them was to take them prisoner. It was not often that they did that."[23] But, despite this belief, the Indians on the Red River frontier sometimes did kill Negroes. In 1842 on Caney Creek, Indians, probably Coushatta who were then particularly active and hostile, shot Dr. William Hunter's little girl to death with arrows while she was getting water at the spring and then rushed to the house where they tomahawked, scalped, and otherwise mutilated Mrs. Hunter and a Negro woman and captured the other little Hunter girl. "The slave woman," it is said, "probably fought heroically for her life since she was found with a bloody club in her hand." The captive girl was ransomed by the Choctaw.[24] In view of what the Davis family regarded as the conventional attitude of Indians on the Red River frontier toward Negroes, the Negro woman was probably killed because she enraged the Indians by a hostile attitude, perhaps by attempting to defend her mistress. Although the Hunter slavewoman was the only Negro casualty on the Red River frontier of which I have seen specific mention, others may have suffered, for Dr. Rowlett, referring to events on this frontier during 1837-1843, states: "Several negroes have been killed [by the Indians] and it is a strange fact that not one negro has ever attempted to escape from his master in order to join the Indians."[25]

It is noteworthy that Dr. Rowlett considered it "strange" that Negroes on the Red River frontier did not attempt to escape to the Indians and probably also that the

[23] "Autobiography of Andrew Davis," *SWHQ*, XLIII (January, 1940), 329.

[24] Strickland, "Fannin Co.," *SWHQ*, XXXIV, 48-49. De Shields, p. 340, however, says the slavewoman was not scalped.

[25] *Lamar Papers*, IV, pt. 1, 220.

Indians should have killed Negroes. The Negroes on this frontier were probably, however, a particularly well selected group who demonstrated by such actions as those of the Smith boy, Bob Anderson, and the Hunter woman their loyalty to their masters and thus aroused the wrath of the hostile Indians. If as Dr. Rowlett claims, the Indians killed several Negroes, this would in turn contribute to the lack of enthusiasm about escaping to the Indians diplayed by Negroes who might otherwise have been restless enough to wish to do so.

However, despite Dr. Rowlett's assertion that no Negro on the Red River frontier attempted to join the Indians—which may mean only that they were so very few that the doctor did not personally hear of any—at least one Negro was among the hostiles; perhaps, however, he had accompanied them from East Texas or the United States. On August 1, 1841, about supper time, Indians—probably "intrusive Indians" from East Texas—attacked the Kitchens home in western Fannin County. At the first fire they killed one son and wounded another.[26] "A burly negro" made a rush for the door but Mr. Kitchens shot him down, while a young man named Stevens killed an Indian in the yard. The assailants then fled.[27]

One or more Negroes may also have participated in an attack on Daniel Dugan's house just after dark on November 15, 1841, about six weeks after the Kitchens raid. The company in the Dugan home consisted of the elder Dugans, their two daughters, three sons, and four other young men.

[26] *Lamar Papers*, IV, pt. 1, 219. Strickland, "Fannin Co.," *SWHQ*, XXXIV, 50-51, quoting Wilbarger, *Indian Depredations*, 405-411, who says that the elder Kitchens and his son Don were merely wounded in the foot.

[27] The account in the *Lamar Papers* also differs from the Wilbarger account in regard to the casualties of the attackers, stating that the leader and one other were killed as they rushed the house and that a Negro "retreated to the distance of about 30 yards and got behind a small tree . . . but the old man . . . and his wounded son . . . kept up a fire on him until he fell dead at its root. . . ." Perhaps *two* Negroes were killed—one in the rush at the house and one behind the tree.

The Indians killed Henry Green and wounded Calvin Hoover at the first fire, but, according to a tradition in the family of Judge (former Governor) James Allred, whose grandfather was one of the young men, "Old Dugan . . . shot . . . and killed . . . two Indians and a nigger. . . . Next morning they found five dead Indians and a dead nigger." The next day hogs were observed eating the bodies of the dead hostiles "in open view of the whole family who seemed to forget their own loss in the gratification thus derived."[28]

The "intrusive Indians" who troubled the Fannin County settlers did not confine their depredations to the Texas side of the border, nor were Indians the only depredators. On September 13, 1841, A. M. Upshaw informed Maj. William Armstrong, an Indian agent, that Delawares, Kickapoo, Cherokee, Caddo, Uchee, Coushatta, and others were intruding into the Chickasaw district of the Indian Territory, stealing horses from Texans and Chickasaw, trading with the Comanche, etc. He wrote that since June 15 "Indians have stolen some fine horses and some negroes; two negro men have been stolen from Blue River in the last ten days."[29] The Negroes may either have been stolen for resale or enlisted as allies. But they were not killed, which, whatever the reason, indicates that the more civilized and sophisticated "intrusive Indians" understood a Negro's value, either as a slave or as a recruit.

Mexican emissaries, operating among Indians hostile to Texas, were also reported in a letter of April 1, 1840, to have induced, by the promise of freedom, four of the "best Negro men" of Pierre Juzan, a half-breed Choctaw chief, to run away with four horses, four saddles, four bridles,

---

[28] *Lamar Papers*, IV, pt. 1, 219. Strickland, "Fannin Co.," *SWHQ*, XXXIV, 56-58. Wilbarger, *Indian Depredations*, 411-418. William David Allred, "Texas Woman Keeps Skull of Indian," *FT*, XXV (Feb., 1948), 128-130. Since other sources do not mention a Negro being killed at the Dugans' this detail may have been borrowed from the attack on the Kitchens house a few weeks earlier.

[29] Strickland, "Fannin Co.," *SWHQ*, XXXIV, 52-53.

two guns, etc.; "these negroes," the letter said, "have been
seen with the Hostile Indians, and Mexicans, on our frontier—and Mr Juzan . . . hopes per chance they may have
been captured by our valiant little Army—"[30] These Negro
runaways were evidently recruits to the Mexican and Indian cause rather than captives.

For a complete picture of life on the Red River frontier,
however, it should be added that Texans as well as Indians
and Mexicans depredated on the Civilized Indians of the
Territory.[31]

On Sept. 29, 1843, the treaty of Bird's Fort "with the
Tehuacanos, Keechis, Wacos, Caddos, Anadarcos and others . . . forever removed the menace of Indian attack from
the Fannin frontier,"[32] and also virtually terminated the
story of relations on the Texas frontier between Texas Negroes and sedentary, semi-civilized Indians. The only later
reference I have encountered appears in the report of a
Lieutenant Williams who in August, 1848, found "a fine
looking gentleman of color, somewhat inclined to be bow-
legged, also very dark . . . says his name is Abraham, and
belongs to John Ecleson on the Brazos, near Nashville" in
a camp of Waco, Keechi, Caddo, and Comanche;[33] all these
tribes except the last were sedentary and agricultural
Caddoans.

Colored Frontiersmen in Eastern Texas, 1821-1841

A small but distinctive and significant element on the
American frontier were free colored men, usually of mixed
Negro and white ancestry, sometimes with a strain of Indian blood as well, who, since they were not fully accepted
by white society, sought prestige through association of

[30] *Lamar Papers*, III, 361-362. Grant Foreman, *Advancing the Frontier,
1830-1860* (Norman, 1933), 158-159.

[31] Foreman, *Advancing the Frontier*, 160-163.

[32] Strickland, "Fannin Co.," *SWHQ*, XXXIV, 60.

[33] "Annual Report of the Commissioner of Indian Affairs, 1848" in
House Executive Documents, 30th Cong., 2d Sess., I (537), No. 1, 215.

varying degrees of intimacy and permanency with one or more Indian tribes; usually, however, even when they succeeded in attaining positions of influence, they were not entirely satisfied with life among the Indians and periodically returned to the white settlements, where they often won for themselves a better status than before through their knowledge of and skill in dealing with the aborigines. Such men included Edward Rose and James P. Beckwourth, Crow chiefs and Rocky Mountain fur traders, Ben Wiggins of Florida, guide and scout, and doubtless many others less well known or now entirely unknown. Texas also had representatives of this group.

Perhaps the most remarkable man of color in early Texas was William Goings, Goyans, or Goyens,[34] who was living in Nacogdoches as early as 1821. He owned a blacksmith shop which he operated by means of both Negro slaves, of whom he once owned as many as nine, and hired white laborers; he also speculated in land, which he made a business of buying, improving, and selling, and was regarded as a wealthy and respectable citizen. By 1832 he was married to a white woman from Georgia, whose two brothers visited them and "appeared well satisfied with their colored brother-in-law."

Goyens could write reasonably well in both English and Spanish and could speak several Indian languages, including the Cherokee. He was consequently very useful to the settlers. On Sept. 24, 1835, Thomas J. Rusk and Samuel Houston wrote from Nacogdoches to Big Mush and "Col. Bowles," principal chiefs of the Texas Cherokee: "Your

[34] His origins are unknown to me. It is, however, worthy of note, since his surname in any of its forms is not common, that among the family names of the Croatans, a people of mixed Indian, white, and Negro blood living in Robeson Co., N. C., and believed by some to be the descendants of Sir Walter Raleigh's "Lost Colony" of Roanoke, appears "Goins (D'Guin)." Stephen B. Weeks, "The Lost Colony of Roanoke," *Paps. of the Am. Hist. Assoc.*, V (Oct., 1891), 139. Goings is also a family name appearing among colored people associated with Indians on the Upper Missouri. Mari Sandoz, *Crazy Horse* (New York, 1942), p. 426.

talks have reached us by the hands of your friend William Goings. . . . We have heard that you wish Mr Goings to go with you and hear the Talk [on the Brazos] We are willing that he should go because We believe him to be a man that will not tell a lie either for the White man or the Red man.'' When Houston after the fall of Bexar went to negotiate with the Cherokee he took with him ''William Goyans'' as interpreter, ''which appointment . . . he filled with much credit to himself.'' On July 3, 1837, Houston wrote to ''Mr. William Goyens'' with a letter to The Bowl (Colonel Bowles). ''Give my compliments to your family,'' Houston concluded.

When, after the establishment of the Republic, Texas law in regard to free Negroes would have put Goyens under severe restrictions, his services were not forgotten; he was permitted to remain in Texas and his land holdings were confirmed.[35] Goyens was such a remarkably intelligent and capable business man that he was able to win for himself an almost uniquely respectable and secure position in white society, but his knowledge of Indian languages and his influence with the Cherokee obviously contributed significantly and perhaps even decisively to his prestige.

A more typical colored frontiersman was Jack Ivey, whom John Henry Brown calls ''a man of mixed Indian and African blood'' and Grant Foreman ''a half-breed mulatto''; very probably he also possessed some white blood. He had come to the west from St. Louis with the fur trader Thomas James in 1821, descending the Mississippi to the mouth of the Arkansas and proceeding overland to Santa Fé. In 1823 he had gone with John McKnight south from the North Fork of the Canadian into the Comanche country, where he was well received by the Indians and ac-

[35] Harold Schoen, ''The Free Negro in the Republic of Texas,'' *SWHQ*, XXXIX (Apr., 1936), 298-299, XL (July, 1936), 30, XLI (July, 1937), 87-89, 98, 100-101. *Lamar Papers*, I, 238-240, 559. Dorman H. Winfrey, ''Chief Bowles of the Texas Cherokee,'' *Chronicles of Oklahoma*, XXXII (Spring, 1954), p. 36.

cording to Foreman was probably among those who remained in the Indian country when James returned to St.
Louis.

Ivey was a well known figure among the Indians, frequently mentioned by early trappers and explorers, and
was obviously in a position to be very useful to the white
settlers. In 1837 he purchased from the Waco a white
woman and a two-year-old girl who had been captured in
Texas; the woman had another daughter among the Wichita
and a brother with the Waco.

In 1841 Ivey was apparently living on the Red River
frontier of Texas, for on May 14 he was "pilot" or guide
to an expedition which struck out westward along the Chihuahua trail in pursuit of Indians who had massacred the
Ripley family in Titus County. The expedition, however,
ran into a camp of Indians who were in overwhelming
numbers, lost its leaders, and had to withdraw;[36] thus
abruptly ends my knowledge of the career of this colored
frontiersman.

Relations with Plains Indians before Emancipation, *1831-1865*

Relations between Texas Negroes and the sedentary and
semi-civilized Indians of Texas were of no long duration.
They began when slaveholding settlers from the United
States began to enter Texas with their Negroes but for
several years were so slight that we have no record of them
until the middle 1830's. The expulsion of the civilized Indians from Texas began in 1839, warfare with these Indians
ended in 1843, and in 1859, except for a few strays, they
were driven from Texas into the Indian Territory. Although
opportunities for relations between Negroes and the seden-

36 Grant Foreman, *Pioneer Days in the Early Southwest* (Cleveland, 1926),
227. Thomas James, *Three Years among the Indians and Mexicans*, Walter B.
Douglas, editor (St. Louis, 1916), 98, 197, 198. Strickland, ''Fannin Co.,''
SWHQ, XXXIV, 41. John Henry Brown, *Indian Wars and Pioneers of Texas*,
85-87.

tary Texas Indians existed for a generation or so, for all practical purposes they extended over less than a decade, from the middle and late 1830's to the early 1840's.

Relations between Texas Negroes and the wild nomadic Texas Indians, particularly the Comanche, covered a much longer period. Encounters between white settlers and Comanche Indians began at least as early as 1835[37] and almost from the beginning involved Negroes; raids by Comanche and other wild Indians on the Texas frontier were frequent until the middle 1870's and did not end until the early 1880's, so that opportunities for contact between wild Indians and Texas Negroes extended over a period of forty years or more.

The first relations between Texas Negroes and wild Indians were, not surprisingly, of unalloyed mutual hostility. Negroes on the Comanche frontier were not working in gangs on cotton plantations under an overseer's lash, but were engaged in cattle-herding, carpentry, plowing, harvesting, threshing, milling, surveying, freighting—the same sort of jobs that their masters and other white men might be doing. To the wild predatory horse-riding Indians of the plains the two races were essentially the same. Both dressed in shirts and trousers, shoes and hats, used the axe, the plow, and the hoe, drove wagons, lived in houses; that their complexions differed was of little significance compared with their basic cultural similarity. The more sophisticated East Texas Indians, as well, of course, as the Mexicans, knew that the whites and the Negroes were on different social and legal levels and could recognize that, in a period of conflict with the Anglo-American whites, it might be possible to detach Negroes from their masters and make them allies. The wild predatory Comanche, however, regarded white and Negro settler alike with ferocious antipathy and even contempt; when they attacked settlements and ranches and travellers they usually killed white men and Negro men,

---

[37] Wallace and Hoebel, 292.

killed or captured white and Negro women and children, without marked racial discrimination.

The Negroes, generally speaking and before Emancipation, thoroughly reciprocated the hostility of the Comanche. A prudent slaveholder would be reluctant to bring to any Texas frontier at any time a Negro who could not be depended upon. True, a discontented Negro would probably not attempt to escape to the Comanche, since he would be aware of the danger of being put to death before he could parley, but an enterprising Negro in San Antonio or vicinity, which lay near the Comanche country, could—and over the years many did—escape to the Mexicans. A Negro on the Comanche frontier should be not only trustworthy and loyal but also cool and courageous, for on such a dangerous frontier, any man, Negro or white, who could not keep his wits in an emergency would endanger not only his own life but also the lives of others. The Negroes who were on the West Texas frontier were probably therefore an even more specially selected group than those on the Red River frontier and were about as much identified with the interests of their masters and their masters' families as if they were free men working for wages; they had nothing better to expect from the Comanche than if they were whites and they suffered from, or participated in the defense against, Indian attacks very much as if they were the same color as their masters.

A chronological list of episodes evidencing hostility between Negroes and wild Indians would speedily become monotonous, but to classify them according to the degree of such hostility, the manner in which it was manifested, and the results, should contribute to an understanding of the pattern of such relationships.

The killing by Indians of settlers going about their lawful occasions who, because unarmed, poorly armed, outnumbered, surprised, or a combination of such disadvantages, were able to make little or no effective resistance, occurred with painful regularity on all American frontiers. The West Texas frontier was no exception, and Negroes as well as whites and Mexicans were frequently among the victims who without recorded resistance fell to the Indian arrow, bullet, lance, or war club.[38]

In 1839 Hamilton White's Negro man was killed while hauling lumber from Bastrop to Austin.[39] About the same time Indians attacked a surveying party on the Brazos near Old Nashville, killing a Negro belonging to Mr. Holtzclaugh and wounding James Shaw.[40] In the great Comanche raid of August, 1840, the Indians killed seven Negroes and six whites at Victoria and four Negroes and nine whites at Linnville, as well as taking several captives, white and black.[41]

In a raid south of Austin on January 2, 1843, 15 mounted Indians, presumably Comanche, killed and scalped one white man, speared, shot, clubbed, and stripped another, but almost miraculously did not kill him, killed a white boy and a Negro boy, carried another Negro boy off, and chased, but failed to capture, a third Negro.[42] In the same year Indians in Milam County killed Peter Mercer, Captain Orr, and a Negro servant.[43]

During the 1840's and 1850's settlement moved west. Hostile manifestations by the Plains tribes toward the white and Negro carriers of an alien culture, which had declined for several years after the Comanche defeats of 1840 and had subsequently been curbed by the establishment of

[38] Accounts of Indian hostilities in Texas frequently do not identify the Indians tribally; it is possible, therefore, that some of the episodes of Indian hostility, 1838-1843, which are not specifically stated as committed by Comanche, were the work of "intrusive Indians."

[39] Wilbarger, *Indian Depredations*, 266-267.

[40] Sowell, *Early Settlers*, 299.

[41] Webb, *Texas Rangers*, 58-61. Sowell, *Early Settlers*, 418-419, 314. *Lamar Papers*, III, 428-429. The number of casualties varies with the source.

[42] *Lamar Papers*, IV, pt. 1, 236-237.

[43] L. W. Kemp, editor, "Early Days in Milam County: Reminiscences of Sarah Turnham McCown," *SWHQ*, L (Jan., 1947), 371.

State troops on the border in 1847 and the building and garrisoning of frontier forts in 1849, was resumed after the withdrawal of United States troops in 1854.[44] Indians in Comanche County in 1858 killed a Mr. Bean and a Negro;[45] in July, 1859, also in Comanche County, they killed a Negro, "a fine carpenter," worth about $2,000 belonging to Joe Hicks.[46]

The outbreak of the Civil War seems to have stimulated Indian attacks. On July 13, 1861, Indians raided the vicinity of Floresville on the San Antonio River, killed one of Captain Wayman's Negroes, shooting him with four or five arrows, and carried off another.[47] In the great raid of October, 1861, in Frio and Atascosa counties, Indians, among whom was a Mexican with "curly hair," killed three white men, wounded five, and killed two Negroes.[48] In the early 1860's Indians killed a young man named Long living on Blanco Creek west of the Frio, scalped his sister, killed other white people and a Negro, and gathered up numerous horses.[49] Also in the early 1860's Indians killed the mulatto who operated the inclined-plane oxen-powered corn mill at Palo Pinto while he was out hunting his oxen.[50]

East of the Mississippi hostile Indians not uncommonly spared white women, while killing all or most of the men, and Negroes, even when putting all whites to death, but the Comanche warrier, unlike the Shawnee or Creek, was disinclined to draw distinctions either of race or sex. When in 1834 or 1835 the Comanche raided Mill Creek in Austin County they encountered "a negro woman and her little

[44] Hogan, 15-16, 201. Wallace and Hoebel, 294, 296, 297, 300-302, 304-305.
[45] Wilbarger, *Indian Depredations*, 431-432.
[46] E. L. Deaton, *Indian Fights on the Texas Frontier* (Ft. Worth, 1927), 18.
[47] Sowell, *Early Settlers*, 840. Deaton, 18.
[48] A. J. Sowell, "The Killing of James Winters by Indians" (excerpted from *Texas Indian Fighters*), *FT*, XVIII (Oct., 1940), 24-27. *FT*, Nov., 1950, pp. 47-54.
[49] Sowell, *Early Settlers*, 996, 479.
[50] *Trail Drivers of Texas* (1925), 792.

son, two or three years old,'' whom her mistress had sent
back from a place of refuge to get some clothes. The Indians
killed the woman and carried off her little boy.[51] On July 4,
1840, on Gilleland Creek in Travis County a Negro girl belonging to Mr. Clipton was peacefully engaged in driving
home the cows when a party of Indians killed and scalped
her and threw her mutilated body down a well,[52] as ruthlessly as if she had been both white and male. When in 1855
the Indians made their last raid into Guadalupe County,
their first victim was a fourteen-year-old Negro girl carrying water to men working in the fields, whom they lanced
and left to die; they also killed Lewis McGree, a white
man.[53] About Christmas, 1864, George Todd, accompanied
by his wife, his little step-daughter Alice, who was mounted
behind him, and a Negro servant girl, were riding to the
town of Mason, when, about four miles from town, a band
of warriors surprised them, killing the Negro girl, mortally
wounding Mrs. Todd, and capturing the step-daughter. Mr.
Todd himself got away.[54]

Indian hostility toward the representatives of European
civilization on the Southern plains did not always, however,
express itself in murder. Although the Comanche or Kiowa
warrior frequently slew men, women, and children without
distinction, he also occasionally varied his treatment according to sex and, particularly, age. He normally killed
adult males, for the pleasure of the act and the prestige of
the scalp. Women, though usually killed, were more often
made prisoners than men, because they were not such
troublesome captives and could be put to sexual use. Children, whether boys or girls, were probably more often preserved, if this was convenient, than killed, with the deliberate
intention of strengthening the tribe through adoption.

[51] De Shields, 118-119.
[52] De Shields, 337. Wilbarger, *Indian Depredations,* 269-270.
[53] Sowell, *Early Settlers,* 838-839, 429.
[54] O. C. Fisher, *It Occurred in Kimble* (Houston, 1937), 132.

A good deal depended on the circumstances and the Indians' mood; when resistance was offered, particularly if an Indian life was lost, the chances of prisoners' being taken were reduced to a minimum. If prisoners gave trouble, even if only by struggles and outcries, they were likely to be promptly disposed of; the best life insurance was prompt, even smiling and cheerful, obedience and co-operation. In 1855, for example, in a raid down the Cibolo Valley, the Indians killed a Negro girl whom they had probably at first intended to take prisoner. After lassoing the water bucket which she was carrying on her head, an Indian then tossed the loop about her body, apparently at first in more or less good-humored sport, but when the frightened girl screamed and struggled their ferocity awoke and, thrusting her through with a lance, they left her to die.[55]

If about to be overtaken, the Indians made it a point to thwart their pursuers by killing all captives. In the great Comanche raid of 1840, the Indians, in addition to killing several whites and Negroes, captured a Negro woman and child and two white women; on the retreat they killed the Negro woman and one of the white women and badly wounded the other. In 1850 Indians carried away two Negro boys and a large herd of horses belonging to Mr. Ragsdale on the Frio and subsequently killed one of the Negroes.[56] In October, 1861, in a Frio and Atascosa County raid the Indians killed two adult Negroes and three whites and captured a little Negro boy; on being pursued they clubbed and stabbed him, though not fatally, and left him behind.[57]

White girls, such as Cynthia Ann Parker and Millie Durgan, sometimes became the wives of their captors. The extent to which Southern Plains Indians intermarried with captive Negro women is unknown, since cases of intermar-

---

[55] Sowell, *Early Settlers*, 838-839.

[56] Webb, 58-61. Sowell, *Early Settlers*, 418-419, 314. Col. M. L. Crimmins, "Colonel Robert E. Lee's Report on Indian Combats in Texas," *SWHQ*, XXXIX (July, 1935), 23.

[57] Sowell, *Early Settlers*, 499-502, 253. *FT*, Nov., 1950, pp. 47-54.

riage usually came to light through the efforts of relatives
to discover the fate of captives, and Negro women or girls,
particularly before Emancipation, were not normally the
objects of such a search. William Banta, however, in 1852
found in a Comanche camp a Negro woman who had been
stolen from near Dardanelle, Arkansas, and was the mother
of four part-Indian daughters.[58]

NEGROES AND INDIANS ON THE TEXAS FRONTIER, 1831-1876

The Indians of the Southern Plains occasionally permitted captives to be ransomed by relatives, friends, or
government authorities; traders with the Indians, particularly civilized Indians and half-breeds, sometimes bought
captives on speculation, trusting that their relatives would
be willing to pay a high enough reward for their return to
cover the original cost and a reasonable profit. To purchase
a white captive, however, unless specifically commissioned to
do so, might result in a loss, since the relatives might all be
dead or without funds. A Negro captive, however, was almost as good as money, since he could always be sold in
Arkansas or the Indian Territory. De Shields, however, is
exaggerating the importance of this traffic when he writes:
"Usually Indians did not kill negro slaves, but held them
for large ransom, which they seldom, or never, failed to
get."[59] We have already seen more than ample evidence
that the usual fate of the Negro was to be killed; to be "held
for ransom"—under which head De Shields probably

[59] De Shields, 337.

means to include being "held for sale"—was exceptional, although, since to purchase Negroes from the Comanche for re-sale was to deal in stolen property, it probably happened oftener than ever became a matter of record. It occurred often enough that Ethan Allen Hitchcock reported, on the basis of observations in Indian Territory in 1841-42, that Comanche sometimes stole Negroes in Texas and sold them to Cherokee and Creeks; the latter, in particular, were so anxious to obtain slaves that they would sometimes pay up to $400 and $500 per Negro.[60] In February, 1839, for example, Comanche captured two Negro boys, Abraham aged fifteen and Sambo aged ten, from Dr. Joseph W. Robertson on the Colorado River and subsequently sold them to a party of Indian and half-breed traders from the Indian Territory, who resold them to James Edwards, a white trader living on the Canadian; Dr. Robertson did not recover his property for several years. The Comanche, however, refused to sell several white children.[61]

Captain Marcy in 1850 saw at the Little River settlement in the Indian Territory two Negro girls whom a Delaware trader had brought in. They had been members of a party of Seminole Negroes whom the Comanche had attacked while crossing the plains to Mexico; all of them, except these two girls, had been massacred. The Comanche had apparently preserved the girls for scientific purposes, scraping through their skin into the flesh to find out if both were the same color and branding them with red-hot coals to see if heat caused them pain. After they had satisfied their curiosity they were willing to sell their horribly

[60] Ethan Allen Hitchcock, *A Traveler in Indian Territory* Grant Foreman, editor (Cedar Rapids, 1930), 28.

[61] Grant Foreman, *Advancing the Frontier, 1830-1860* (Norman, 1933), 218-220. Sowell, *Early Settlers*, 15, probably refers to this episode when he writes that the Comanche in 1839 captured *one* of Dr. *Robinson's* Negroes below Austin. Carl Coke Rister, *Border Captives: The Traffic in Prisoners by Southern Plains Indians, 1835-1875* (Norman, 1940), curiously enough has nothing to say about trade in captured Negroes.

scarred and disfigured victims to the Delaware. Captain
Marcy commented that the Comanche had recently "taken
an inveterate dislike" to Negroes and had massacred several small parties who were on their way from the Indian
Territory to join the Seminole chief Wild Cat and his
colony of Indians and Negroes on the Rio Grande. When
asked the reason for their massacring the Negroes, however, the Comanche replied with sardonic humor that it was
because they were slaves to the whites; "they were sorry
for them." Captain Marcy, nevertheless, shrewdly suspected that they were inspired neither by racial prejudice
nor philanthropy but rather by a desire to prevent Wild
Cat's military colony from becoming so strong that it would
interfere with Comanche raids on the Mexican border, since
they had also massacred Delaware and Shawnee Indians
who were on their way to join the Seminole chief.[62] By 1850,
some Comanche, at least, knew that Negroes were normally
slaves to the whites. They also, however, knew that these
particular Negroes, and the civilized Indians with whom
they were associated, were almost as much identified with
a hostile culture as if they had been whites; they were consequently as ruthless in putting them to death.

The relations of the Seminole Negroes of the Mexican
border with the Comanche and other wild tribes of the
Mexican border with the Comanche and other wild tribes of
the Southern Plains is, however, a story which has been told
elsewhere;[63] suffice it to say here that in the long run these

---

[62] Randolph Barnes Marchy, *Thirty Years of Army Life on the Border*
(New York, 1866), 55-56. National Archives, Washington, D. C., Dep't of the
Interior, Indian Office, Seminole File D481-605, Letter: M. Duval, Apr. 24,
1851, to Luke Lea, Commissioner of Indian Affairs. R. B. Marcy and George
B. McClellan, *Exploration of the Red River of Louisiana* (Washington, 1853),
101. Grant Foreman, *The Five Civilized Tribes* (Norman, 1934), 265.

[63] Kenneth W. Porter, "The Seminole in Mexico, 1850-1861," *Hispanic
American Historical Review*, XXXI (Feb., 1951); ditto,· "The Seminole
Negro-Indian Scouts, 1870-1881," *SWHQ*, LV (Jan., 1952).

fighting Negroes were more than capable of holding their own, even against the Comanche.

Negro as well as white captives were sometimes rescued or ransomed by United States troops. In 1850 a detachment of the 8th Infantry on the Nueces River killed one Indian, wounded another, and recovered a Negro boy and 130 horses.[64] On June 27, 1867, at Otter Creek in the Indian Territory, soldiers ransomed from the Comanche six captive children—four white and two Negro.[65]

Although some Negro captives were killed on the retreat and others were sold, rescued, ransomed, or even succeeded in escaping, the fate of others is as unknown as is that of numerous white captives. In 1834 or '35 Comanche in Austin County stole horses, killed a Negro woman, and carried off her two or three-year-old son. In 1836 in Robertson County they killed Mr. and Mrs. Harney and their ten-year-old son and captured their nine-year-old daughter and a Negro servant girl; the daughter was later ransomed.[66] In January, 1843, Comanche killed two whites and a Negro near Austin and carried a Negro boy off.[67] In 1850 they captured two Negro boys and killed one of them. On July 13, 1861, they carried off from near Floresville on the San Antonio River a Negro belonging to Captain Wayman.[68] These five Negroes, mostly children, may subsequently have been killed, sold to unknown white or civilized Indian masters, held as Indian slaves, or adopted.

Negroes, it is pleasant to relate, were not always the helpless victims of Indian hostility. By fleetness of foot,

---

[64] Sowell, *Early Settlers*, 618, 821. Crimmins, ''Robert E. Lee's Report,'' *loc. cit.* Sowell says that the troopers wounded and captured the son of Chief Yellow Wolf and that the chief offered 13 captives in exchange for his son; they were mostly Mexican but included a Negro and two or three whites.

[65] Nye, 15. I have included here this post-Emancipation episode because it presents no distinctive features.

[66] De Shields, 118-119, 195-196.

[67] *Lamar Papers*, IX, pt. 1, 236-237.

[68] Sowell, *Early Settlers*, 840.

quickness of thought, skill in concealment, or mere good
luck, they sometimes succeeded in evading death—even
when their white companions were not so fortunate. When
in 1835 Indians attacked the Mercers, living on the San
Gabriel, and killed Peter Mercer, Mrs. Mercer and a Negro
boy saved their own lives and the lives of several Mercer
children by fleeing across the swollen river. Mrs. Mercer
tied a grapevine about the waist of the Negro boy, who,
with this assistance, swam across again and again, carrying
a child to safety each time.[69] In 1839 two Maverick slaves,
Griffin and Wiley, were attacked near San Antonio while
plowing, but "ran into the river and saved themselves,"
the Indians departing with the work horses.[70] In 1843 when
Indians near Austin killed two whites and a Negro and captured a Negro boy, a third Negro boy was pursued but got
away.[71] In 1855 when Indians attacked a ranch in Kendall
County, killing two white men, a woman, and a child, a Negro woman "made her escape."[72] In July of the same year
four Indians and a white man disguised as an Indian attacked a white overseer and a Negro man in Comal County;
they killed the overseer but the Negro got away.[73] Indians
in Comanche County in January, 1858, lanced and rode over
a Negro belonging to a Mr. Barbee, who escaped by playing
'possum.[74]

In 1867, Frank Buckalew, a white boy living in Sabinal
Canyon, and a Negro boy were out looking for a lost ox-bell
and encountered an Indian who captured Frank after a
hard chase by hitting him on the head with a bow, while the

[69] De Shields, 147.

[70] Rena Maverick Green, editor, *Samuel Maverick, Texan: 1803-1870* (San
Antonio, 1952), 87. Ditto, *Memoirs of Mary A. Maverick* (San Antonio, 1921),
25.

[71] *Lamar Papers*, IV, pt. 1, 236-237.

[72] Sowell, *Early Settlers*, 754.

[73] *Ibid.*, 246.

[74] E. L. Deaton, *Indian Fights on the Texas Frontier* (Fort Worth, 1927),
114-115.

Negro escaped.[75] About 1871 Indians near the Pecos way-laid two white cowboys and a mulatto, but the mulatto escaped.[76] In 1872 Indians attacked the Wilson ranch in the Hondo country but Wilson and his Negro man both got away—Wilson on horseback and the Negro on foot into the brush.[77] In July, 1873, in Medina County Indians attacked Henry Hartman and an unarmed Negro, shooting the former's horse. Both, however, escaped—Hartman by the free and accurate use of his Winchester and the Negro by hiding in the brush.[78]

The frequency of cases in which Negroes escaped when whites were killed, although not numerous enough to establish a definite pattern, nevertheless suggests the possibility of an explanation other than mere accident. Obviously, from the long list of cases in which Negroes, or Negroes and whites, were ruthlessly put to death, the Comanche rarely if ever spared Negroes out of special affection or tolerance. One curious case, however, is worthy of record. Early in June, 1849, raiding Indians, presumably Comanche, "came upon a farm attended by two Negroes. They stripped the Negroes of their clothing, took all the food, ripped open the feather beds, and announced that they were going on to Goliad to whip the Americanos." A party of Rangers, however, struck and dispersed them.[79]. The failure of the Indians to kill these two Negroes is, however, so highly exceptional that it hardly affects the general rule. One explanation for the better fortune of Negroes in an Indian attack may be that, confronted by two potential victims, a white

[75] Sowell, *Early Settlers*, 587-588.

[76] Alma Ward Hamrick, *The Call of the San Saba* (San Antonio, 1941), 188-190.

[77] Sowell, *Early Settlers*, 550. On p. 682, however, Wilson's man is said to have been a Mexican and the date of the raid is given as 1871.

[78] Sowell, *Early Settlers*, 576-581. Here again I have included several post-Emancipation episodes because they present no features which would distinguish them from events occurring before the Civil War.

[79] Webb, *Rangers*, 142.

man and a Negro, the Indian would choose the white—not because he loved the Negro but because he preferred the white man's hair. Another may be that since a white man, particularly before Emancipation, was more likely to be armed than a Negro companion, the Indians would wish to dispose of the armed man as quickly as possible and would concentrate their attack on him, thus giving the Negro a better opportunity to escape. Sheer chance, however, may after all be the chief explanation.

A reader who assumes that frontier Texans were all dead shots, perpetually bristling with Winchester repeaters and Colt six-shooters, will be surprised, if he reads many first-hand narratives of Indian warfare, to observe how frequently the settlers were unarmed, poorly armed, or unskilled in the use of such weapons as they possessed, so that they were no match for the fierce Comanche warrior with his swift, well-trained horse, powerful, rapid-fire bow, long lance, and bullet-proof buffalo-hide shield. The Negro, particularly the slave, was even less likely than the white settler to have arms or to be skilled in their use, so that it is not surprising that when he escaped from savage attack it was usually by flight, concealment, or "playing 'possum'" rather than by armed resistance. Numerous cases can, however, be adduced in which Negro slaves assisted in repelling or resisting savage attack, usually, of course, under the orders of or in association with a white master.

Sometimes the Negro's role was a non-combatant one. About 1831, when the famous Jim Bowie was prospecting in the San Saba hills west of San Antonio, his party was attacked and besieged by Comanche. When water became scarce, Bowie's "strong young Negro man" rather unwillingly "volunteered" to bring it from a spring outside the improvised fortification. He was closely pursued by Indians on his return journey, but his master and other sharpshooters covered him so effectively with their fire that he arrived safely with the water.[80] In 1852 a thirty-five-year-old Negro named Tom, six feet six in height and weighing 240 pounds, carried his badly wounded master 30 miles to safety after an attack by Apache Indians while on a prospecting expedition in New Mexico; in reward Tom was given his freedom.[81] The first Indian fight in Brown County is said to have occurred in 1858 in the Swisden Valley. "One of W. W. Chandler's slaves discovered the Indians rounding up his horses in the valley and gave the alarm." In the ensuing encounter the whites were defeated.[82]

In other cases, however, Negroes successfully or unsuccessfully resisted by force of arms the threat or actuality of Indian attack. When James Long's widow in 1822 was en route from the San Jacinto River to San Antonio she was accompanied by her daughter Ann, who was only four or five years old, a Negro girl of twelve or thirteen named Kian, "Randle Jones & his brother James," who each had a Negro, and "a Negro man belonging to Mr. Calvert of the U. S.," named Tom. The company thus consisted of four whites—two men, a woman, and a girl-child—and four Negroes—three men and a young girls. The Negro men as well as the whites were probably armed—one of them certainly was—for it is stated that "the two Jones (sic) had each a negro; they hunted & supplied the table." At the Guadalupe, "a large body of Karankaways . . . naked & painted . . . came rushing upon the party. . . . One seized the gun in the hands of the negro Tom. The Jones (sic) and the negro Tom prepared for fight. The Indians however committed no outrage. . . ." But had not whites and Negroes been prepared for action the outcome might well have been different. On the return to the United States, it might also be noted, "The negro Tom became obstreperous. The

[80] Sowell, *Early Settlers*, 406-408.
[81] *Ibid.*, 583-585.
[82] *The Texas State Historical Association, Fifty-fifth Annual Meeting, Austin, April 27-28, 1950*, quoting from (Henry Ford) *Pocket Cotton, Cotton Seed and Cotton Picking Calculator*, 1906.

idea entered his head, that if he could keep west of the Sabine"—that is, on Mexicon soil—"he would be free; . . . he however was persuaded to move on."[83]

In 1838 the Maverick slave Griffin guarded his mistress through the night with axe and gun against the danger of attack by two Tonkawa Indians; a few years later Griffin died at the hands of Mexican soldiers in the Dawson Massacre, fighting heroically. Also in 1838 Comanche attacked two white men and two Negroes north of Austin; all "fought bravely" but were killed. In 1840, during the famous Council House Fight in San Antonio, the Negro cook Jinny Anderson stood between the battling Comanche and her own and her mistress' children with a large rock in her hand, ready to defend both alike against the imminent danger.[84]

The inexperienced Negro even when armed did not always make the most effective use of his weapons. One night in the early 1840's Shapley Ross's Negro man Armistead, who slept in the loft of his master's Milam County barn to guard the horses, detected an Indian trying to get into the building. "Forgetting the rifle with which he was armed, the negro reached down, seized the Indian by his long hair," and lifted him clear of the ground, shouting for his master, but the quick-thinking Indian drew his knife, cut his hair, and escaped.[85]

The prominence and effectiveness of Negroes in resisting Indian attacks seem, however, to have increased with the passage of time. In 1859 when Indian horse thieves approached a house at the mouth of Cherry Creek where it empties into the Guadalupe, Captain McFadin and a Negro went out to investigate, and the Negro, seeing an Indian

83 *Lamar Papers,* II, 123-132.

84 Green, *Mary Maverick,* 19, 25, 54-56. Ditto, *Samuel Maverick,* 73, 120, 108-109, 169-170.

85 L. W. Kemp, editor, "Early Days in Milan Country: Reminiscences of Susan Turnham McCown," *SWHQ,* L (Jan., 1947), 366-376, esp. pp. 370, 376.

crawling through the fence, promptly put a load of buck-shot into him.[86]

"During the Civil War," according to the aged Negro Tom Sullivan, whose master had brought him to Hondo Creek in Medina County in 1848, "most of the men went off to fight and left the slaves and young boys at home to look after the folks. . . ." Tom Sullivan was one of those slaves, and the part he played was probably similar to that of many other trusted Negroes on the Texas frontier during the Civil War. When a young neighbor invited the youths who had been left in Tom's charge to go with him to an evening function, the slave, who had noticed that the livestock had been uneasy that afternoon, dissuaded them from going; the neighbor was ambushed and fatally stabbed. After the famous Indian raid of October, 1861, about twenty men from the Hondo Creek neighborhood, including Tom, took the trail and got up to the Indian camp while the hostiles were preparing food. Tom was among those assigned to hold horses while the others slipped up and fired on the Indians. On another occasion Tom went out to bury men who had been killed by Indians, but another attack forced him to complete his work hastily and flee. He then had the privilege of cutting an iron arrowhead out of the back of a doctor who had been wounded in this attack, when no white man could be found to undertake a task calling for such coolness and skill. Tom seems to have gone armed during all these Indian troubles, but evidently served chiefly as a non-combatant.[87]

RELATIONS WITH PLAINS INDIANS AFTER EMANCIPATION, 1867-1876

After as well as before Emancipation, Negroes were killed or captured by the Indians, were rescued or ran-

---

[86] Sowell, *Early Settlers*, 538.

[87] "Tom Sullivan, Frontier Darkey," FT, Nov., 1949, pp. 48-52, from an article by Oran Warder Nolen, *San Antonio Express*, ca. 1939; J. Marvin Hunter, Sr., "Negro Slave Recalled Frontier History," *FT*, Nov.,

somed, or succeeded in escaping from the hostiles by fleetness of foot, skill at concealment, or other subterfuges.
Emancipation nevertheless is in two respects a landmark
in the history of the relations between the two races: Negroes after Emancipation were, on the one hand, more
active and aggressive in their resistance to hostile Indians
and, on the other, were more inclined to join them in their
depredations.

After the Civil War, Comanche "raids became so de-
structive and frequent that in some cases the line of settlement was driven back a hundred miles. The country west
of a line drawn from Gainesville to Fredericksburg was
abandoned, except for a hardy few who moved into stock-
ades."[88] Negroes as well as whites suffered. In March,
1867, near the line dividing Hamilton and Bosque counties,
Indians killed two Negroes, spearing one of them to death
while he begged for his life.[89] About 1868 Apache raiders
ran off cattle from the San Saba near Menard and "killed a
man and a negro woman near Fort McKavett."[90] In the
early 1870's, in Mason County, Indians raided "the Martin place," where wheat threshing was going on, stole some
horses, and shot in the back "a negro laborer" who "became frightened and ran to a haystack into . . . which he
rammed his head, his body being exposed."[91]

These episodes, however, of Negroes being killed apparently without the opportunity—or in some cases the
will—to defend themselves, were mingled with more numerous cases of Negro resistance to the hostiles. After the Civil
War the Negro as a free man could freely own arms and

1950, pp. 47-54. Tom also claimed to have hunted Indians with Bigfoot
Wallace, but without specifying time, place, or the character of his services.
    [88] Wallace and Hoebel, 308.
    [89] Deaton, *Indian Fights*, 141.
    [90] J. Marvin Hunter, Sr., "Cattle Ranching in Mason County," *FT*,
May, 1951, pp. 223-232, esp. pp. 226-227, quoting W. E. Wheeler.
    [91] Fisher, *Kimble Co.*, 89-90.

assist in defending his own and his neighbors' lives and livestock against savage attack. Settlers on the post-Civil War Texas frontier drew no color line between white and black when Indian warfare was concerned; the only line was between the representatives of a sedentary, basically European civilization, whether white, Negro, or Mexican, and the hostile nomadic culture of the Comanche, Kiowa, and Apache.

About 1867 Indians raided the Hondo settlements, stealing horses from the Rev. William Fly, Judge Harper, and various Negroes who had formerly belonged to the Harpers. A party of three whites and six Negroes organized to pursue the raiders under the command of the famous German frontiersman Xavier Wanz and followed them so closely that they were forced to abandon the stolen horses.[92] In 1869 Indians raided about 60 horses near Belton. A party went in pursuit and came up with the hostiles on Pecan Bayou where they were shoeing the horses with rawhide. A Negro named Ben, "who was very brave and a good Indian fighter," suffered a double misfortune. Although wounded in the shoulder with a bullet he ran in among the Indians and singled out the warrior who was on his own horse, but in the exchange of shots killed the horse! The Indians lost two killed and others wounded, and all the horses were re-taken—except Ben's![93]

The credit for an act of unusual quick-wittedness and heroism in 1871, in which a Negro boy was a participant, belongs to an old Mexican *remudero* at James Lowe's San José Ranch on the Nueces. When a large band of mounted Indians, who had just killed several whites within earshot, approached the ranch house, he marched out his entire force —himself, with a revolver, the only fire-arm on the ranch; Marcellus Lowe, his employer's 14-year-old son, with a crowbar; a 14-year-old Negro boy named Sam Heritage

[92] Sowell, *Early Settlers*, 547.
[93] *Ibid.*, 757-758.

with an old sabre; and a Mexican with a stick. When the Indians, despite the menacing glitter of the sun on gun barrel, sabre, and iron bar, still advanced, he withdrew into the house and began to shout orders in Spanish, whereupon the hostiles withdrew.[94]

Among a party which in 1871 gathered where Hondo City now is to pursue Indian raiders were six whites, two Negroes, and a Mexican.[95] In 1872 when Comanche stole horses near Sabinal, Uvalde County, several white men and a Negro pursued and overtook them and in the fight which ensued the Negro was killed, whereupon the whites withdrew and "the Indians, getting the best of the fight, went on with the horses."[96]

In the fall of 1875 a "mourning party" of Osages, seeking a victim to appease the spirit of a deceased friend, tried to kill a Negro cook on Pond Creek on the Salt Fork of the Arkansas in the Indian Territory but by the liberal though inaccurate use of a revolver he managed to escape from the dugout in which they had him cornered and, although on foot, outdistanced the mounted Indians for nearly four miles and reached a place of safety.[97]

In Kerr County about 1876 the Comanche killed a white man and two children and captured a little white girl and a Negro boy of twelve or thirteen named Jack Hardy, living near Comfort. Though he had never seen an Indian before, Jack behaved with such coolness and courage in the face of the ordeals to which his captors subjected him that they evidenced an intention to adopt him, giving him a bow and arrows and telling him that if the whites came up with them he must fight. After a few days, however, he succeeded in escaping; the little girl was subsequently recovered.[98]

---

[94] Sowell, *Early Settlers*, 634-635.

[95] *Ibid.*, 680.

[96] *Ibid.*, 492-493.

[97] James C. Henderson, "Reminiscences of a Range Rider," *Chronicles of Oklahoma*, III (Dec., 1925), 266-267.

[98] Sowell, *Early Settlers*, 704-709, 188-192, 263, 464.

The story of hostility between Indian and Negro on the Texas frontier is vividly epitomized in the tragic drama of Britton Johnson, "a shining jet black negro of splendid physique" belonging before Emancipation to Moses Johnson of Young County. Britton, better known as Brit, had been an orderly to officers at Fort Belknap before the Civil War and was reputedly one of the best shots on the frontier. On October 13, 1864, Comanche and Kiowa raiders swept down into Young County and ranged through the Elm Creek settlement, killing Brit's little son and several others and carrying away his wife, three children, and several white captives. Brit succeeded in establishing contact with the raiders and, according to one account, pretended that he wished to join the tribe. The predatory Indians of the Southern Plains were so subject to loss in warfare that as a matter of deliberate policy they adopted such captives, Mexicans or whites, as seemed suitable warrior material, so this band, it is said, was glad to welcome the stalwart Negro. After their initial suspicions had been lulled, Brit succeeded in escaping with his wife and children and all but one of the white captives. According to a less dramatic account, however, he merely succeeded in negotiating their release in exchange for horses.

Brit, however, had not seen the last of the hostiles. On January 24, 1871, when Brit and two or three friends were engaged in hauling supplies from Weatherford to their homes near Fort Griffin, 25 Comanche or Kiowa, or a mixture of these allied tribes, appeared on the Butterfield Trail two miles south of Flat Top Mountain and attacked the Negroes, as they would have attacked whites similarly engaged and outnumbered. Brit saw that their only chance—and that an almost hopeless one—was to hold out until a larger force of whites might by some miracle appear. He ordered his friends, following his example, to cut their horses' throats and use the dead animals for breastworks. Behind their bodies the Negroes put up a desperate defense.

His companions, less expert in firing without unduly exposing themselves than the frontier-wise Brit, were killed early in the action, and Brit took their guns, reloading them during the lulls in the action that he might pour in a particularly rapid fire whenever an attack came. Charge after charge swerved and went by, but it was inevitable that one should at last sweep over him and lay him dead by the bodies of his slain friends and their horses. Enraged at the stubbornness of his resistance, the Indians mutilated his body with peculiar ferocity, disemboweling him and thrusting into the cavity the body of a little dog which had accompanied him and shared its master's fate. On the way home the playful Indians, it is said, "amused themselves by throwing the kinky-haired scalps at one another," but finally "threw them away as the hair was too short to be of value." When Brit's body was found, 173 empty cartridge cases were counted around him.[99]

Brit Johnson's conduct is an example of heroism in conflict with the savage foe which can stand beside any tale told of the most courageous Texas Indian fighter. It is obvious from the total record that the hostile Indians of the Southern Plains drew few or no distinctions of race between whites and Negroes and that most Negroes in their turn were as hostile toward the wild Indians as were their masters or white associates. A. J. Sowell does the Negroes of the Texas frontier more justice than most historians when he writes: "They were killed, scalped, and carried away

[99] Wilbarger, *Indian Depredations*, 579-582. Nye, *Carbine and Lance*, 45-46, 158. J. Evetts Haley, *Charles Goodnight: Cowman and Plainsman* (Boston, 1936), 117. Ben C. Stuart, "The Texas Fighters and Frontier Rangers," Ms., University of Texas Library, 193-198. The wildly romantic account in *FT*, Oct., 1950, need not be taken seriously. Various Kiowa calendars state, or are interpreted as stating, that the scalps of the Negroes were not thrown away but were brought back. James Mooney, "Calendar History of the Kiowa Indians," *Seventeenth Annual Report of the Bureau of American Ethnology* (Washington, D. C., 1898), Pt. I, p. 328. Alice L. Marriott, *The Ten Grandmothers* (Norman 1945), 298-299.

into captivity the same as white men, and had to meet all the dangers of the frontier life as well as their masters, and often fought bravely around the frontier cabin in defense of white women and children"[100]—and it might be added, in defense of their own lives and their own women and children. Sowell, however, yields to a stereotyped concept when he writes elsewhere: "There were not many negroes on the frontier"—true[101]—"and most of them had a mortal terror of Indians"—as well they might, considering the savagery of the foe and the fact that the Negro slave usually, and the free Negro frequently, was without adequate arms[102]—"but," he honestly adds, "I saw one . . . in the fight at Battle Creek who stood at his post and fought when some of the white men ran in terror from the savages."[103]

The record is not, however, one of unalloyed hostility. Although most slaves on the various Texas frontiers identified their interests with those of their masters where Indians were concerned, a few Negroes ran away to the sedentary, semi-civilized Indians of East Texas and even participated with them in raids and warfare against the whites. The Comanche, Kiowa, and Apache offered no such attractive refuge to restless blacks as the Cherokee, the Biloxi, the various Caddoan tribes, etc. Discontented Negroes on the frontier of West Texas were more likely to try to escape to the Mexicans, by whom they would be welcomed and well treated, than to the wild Indians, whose way of life was not theirs and who might kill them before they could manifest

---

[100] Sowell, *Early Settlers*, 704.

[101] For example, in 1857 the whites in San Saba County in West Texas numbered 364, the Negroes, 36. Alice Gray Upchurch, "A Sketch History of San Saba County," *SWHQ*, L (July, 1946), 98.

[102] An account of a fight with Indians on June 11, 1873, on Verde Creek, Medina County, remarks of the settlers involved, "All were well armed *except the negro.*" Italics are the author's. (Mrs. George Hartman, "The Bravery of Henry Hartman," *Frontier Times*, IV (Oct., 1926), 14-15, 48. Sowell, *Early Settlers*, 576-581). A Negro slave would have been even less likely to be properly armed.

their friendly intentions. Or they could hide out in solitary independence like the armed Negro whom a Texas Ranger encountered in 1859 or 1860 on Santa Anna Peak in Coleman County and who said he had run away from Jack County and lived in the mountains several years.[104]

A few Negroes, nevertheless, joined the wild Indians and even attained to positions of leadership. The first evidence of such association does not appear until the spring of 1861, when Indians attacked the Hoover family, living along the line between Comanche and Hamilton counties, and "Mr. Hoover said there was one negro with the Indians."[105] Perhaps the outbreak of the Civil War had loosened the bonds of authority and encouraged this Negro to leave his master and join the Indians—or pehaps he was a renegade of long standing.

A Negro is said to have been a participant in 1866 in an attack on the Friend home in Llano County near Cedar Mountain when only women and children were present. The assailants left Mrs. Friend for dead and carried away two women and four children; the women and two of the children were left dead along the trail but a little boy and a little girl were later ransomed. Mrs. Friend who, after knocking down one Indian with a smoothing iron, was shot in the side with an arrow and scalped, but escaped by shamming dead, reported "one negro amongst them."[106]

Not until well after the Civil War were Negroes at all conspicuous as allies of the Texas Indian; by the late 1860's, however, they were particularly outstanding among the hostile Indians operating in Northern Texas. The Hazelwood affair is an important instance. Early in March, 1868, a Mexican wagon train, in Stephens County near Greer's ranch in the vicinity of Pickettsville, was visited by a band

103 Sowell, *Rangers and Pioneers of Texas* (San Antonio, 1884), 338.
104 James Pike, *Scout and Ranger* (Princeton, 1932), 58-62.
105 Deaton, *Indian Fights*, 98.
106 Fisher, *Kimble Co.*, 123-124.

of thirty-five hostiles, who included two Negroes and three Mexicans, under command of a big Negro. They did not molest the Mexicans, but the Negro commander threatened them with divine displeasure if they told the whites that he was fighting against them.[107] The next day George Hazelwood, a rancher, encountered the band and was killed, although according to some accounts he put up a desperate resistance, killed one Indian, and seriously wounded a Mexican and "a big negro, who was sub-chief and seemed to be the main leader."[108] Three of Hazelwood's cowboys went out to look for him and rode onto the hostiles. "A big negro . . . who appeared to be their chief"—and who had either not been incapacitated by the wound allegedly received in the earlier fight or else was not the Negro who had been wounded—exchanged shots with one of the cowboys until both revolvers were empty, but without apparent effect. He then "order a charge . . . the three men retreated to the ranch house."[109]

Soldiers and cattlemen went in pursuit, caught up with the hostiles, and according to one account killed twenty and captured a Negro and a Mexican who had been wounded in the fight with Hazelwood and who died of their wounds. According to another, all but one of a part of the band were overtaken by the soldiers and killed, "one of the dead being the big negro." Still another version lists the casualties as "five Indians and one Mexican and one mulatto (both of whom were leaders)." Yet another authority says that two wounded hostiles, one a Negro, were captured and put to death, while still another says that the Indians abandoned

[107] J. M. Franks, *Seventy Years in Texas* (Gatesville, 1924), 77-79; Captain John N. Elkins, *Indian Fighting on the Texas Frontier* (n.p., 1929), 45-47 (places the incident in 1867).

[108] Wilbarger, *Indian Depredations*, 505-506 (puts the affair in 1869); Don H. Biggers, "The Old Ledbetter Salt Works," *FT*, XXI (Mar., 1941), 241; M. L. Johnson, *The History of the Struggle with Hostile Indians on the Frontier of Texas* (Dallas, 1923), 24-26.

[109] Elkins, 45-47; Franks, 77-79.

their wounded—"three or four Indians and a negro"—
whom the settlers killed.[110]

Whatever the exact circumstances, a Negro leader of
hostile Indians evidently was killed in the aftermath of the
Hazelwood affair. Civil War and emancipation had brought
to the Texas frontier, instead of the characteristically trustworthy Negro slave of former days, free Negroes of a more
adventurous, reckless, and even lawless character,[111] sometimes resentful and hostile toward the whites and ready
to ally themselves with the wild Indians.

In the same area as the Hazelwood affair and about the
same time, a little earlier or later, a band of about 25 Comanche, commanded "by Cato, a renegade negro who was
the husband of Indian Kate, who lived on the outskirts of
Fort Griffin for a number of years," attacked the Ledbetter
Salt Works, in Shackelford County, eight miles southwest
of Albany on the Salt Prong of Hubbard Creek. The Indians, however, "after a determined attack, were compelled
to retreat, carrying off their wounded, including their leader, Cato."[112] The possibility is obvious, in view of the close
temporal and geographical proximity of these two episodes,

---

[110] Wilbarger, 505-506; Biggers, *loc. cit.;* William Harding Carter, *The Life of Lieutenant General Chaffee* (Chicago, 1917), 64-65; Johnson, 24-26; J. T. Hazelwood, "Early Days in Texas," *The Trail Drivers of Texas* (Nash-ville, 1925), 559-560. Neither Elkins nor Franks speaks of the Negro being killed, though Elkins says that the soldiers overtook a wounded Indian and a Mexican who had been left behind to take care of him and that the soldiers killed the Indian and Tonkawa scouts the Mexican.

[111] A Negro of a definitely criminal type, who in 1875 was living among the Peñateka Comanche on the Anadarko Agency, was Aaron Wilson, a dis-charged soldier, who on Sept. 21 murdered an old man and his son, travelling from Kansas to Texas, who had entertained him in their camp, and then stole their horses and other property. The Comanche, however, "did not approve of such a violation of hospitality," and reported him. He was arrested, tried before the famous Judge Parker at Fort Smith, convicted, and hanged. Nye, 243-244.

[112] Clay Chrisman, "The Story of Johnny Ledbetter," *Frontier Times,* XXIII (Nov., 1945), 25-28, from the *Baird Star; Valley Times* (Calif.), Aug. 3, 1949, 2d sec., p. 3 (interview with Mrs. H. L. Hand of Burbank, Calif.,

that the same band of Comanche under Negro leadership
was involved in both.

The attack on the Ledbetter Salt Works and the murder
of Hazelwood were not the only encounters in this general
period and area between white settlers and Indians under
Negro leadership. Near the borders of Young and Palo
Pinto counties, not far from Fort Belknap, on May 16, 1869,
a dozen entrenched cattlemen, armed only with six-shooters,
from ten in the morning until two in the afternoon fought
off a band of forty to sixty Indians from the Territory
"commanded by a large colored man, who gave his orders
from his seat on a large rock out of gun range." When the
Indians finally "blew a bugle and went away," the casualties among the cattlemen were three dead and five seriously
wounded. Help was badly needed—and it was a Negro cowboy who volunteered to go after it and successfully carried
out his mission.[113]

---

great-grand-daughter of Judge W. H. Ledbetter of Albany, Texas). Chrisman
says the attack on the saltworks occurred *some months before* the killing of
George Hazelwood, however, son of the murdered ranchman, in *Frontier Times*,
XXIV (May, 1947), 399-402, says that the Indians attacked the saltworks
immediately after his father's murder. Biggers, *loc. cit.*, says that the attack
on the saltworks took place in the early fall of 1868. "After this fight," he
says, "the Indians continued on down the Salt Prong" and in the main
valley of the Hubbard "came upon George Hazelwood, who (*sic*) they
murdered after a hard fight." The Biggers account thus puts the attack
on the saltworks *immediately before* Hazelwood's murder—which was almost
certainly in March, 1868. Biggers is the only authority giving even an approximate date for the attack on the saltworks; since the *season* of an event is
usually remembered much more accurately than the *year*, this attack was
probably either in the fall of *1867* (therefore *before* the Hazelwood murder,
as stated by Chrisman and Biggers), or in the fall of *1868* (*after it*, as stated
by Hazelwood). The weight of evidence and possibilities are somewhat, though
by no means decisively, in favor of the former sequence. The two events, in
any case, were probably not as close to one another in time as Hazelwood
and Biggers suggest.

[113] Mrs. Minnie C. Gray, "The Salt Creek Fight," *FT*, III (July, 1926),
9-10. Wilbarger, 549-551, gives an account of a fight which from the location,
numbers engaged, mention of "a negro . . . who was in command," etc.,
appears to be the same one, but dates it April 16, 1871. Mrs. Gray's account,

The indications are strong that the Indians engaged in these raids on North Texas were Comanche and Kiowa operating from the reservations in the southwestern Indian Territory on which they had been located by treaties of 1865 and 1867; the Negroes reported among them, then, very probably included "Indian Negroes" who, through long residence in the Territory among the Seminole, Creek, Cherokee, or other "Civilized Tribes," had also become friendly with the more nomadic Indians.

A Negro with Indian associations was not, however, necessarily sympathetic with the wild Indians. The more civilized Indians and their Negro associates were ordinarily as hostile to the savage Indians as any white man, or any Negro whose associations lay with the whites. The Seminole Negroes, with their military colony in Mexico on land granted by the Mexican government in return for their services against the wild Indians, are a case in point. The accusation that the Seminole Negro chief Juan Caballo (John Horse) was the leader of a band of Lipan Apache in a battle with a detachment of the Ninth Cavalry (colored) on the Pecos River in June, 1869,[114] is therefore of very doubtful validity; the official record of the action, moreover, does not mention the presence of a Negro among the Indians. The chief in actuality was probably at the time in the Laguna de Parras in southwestern Coahuila, which had been the residence of his band since 1859 and where they had distinguished themselves against the Apache. Possibly, however, a Negro, whether a Seminole or not, was a leader of the Indians in this affair, as in the three previously mentioned, and was mistaken for the famous Seminole chief.

---

however, which is much more complete and detailed, is said to be based on information from her husband, who was in command of the cattlemen. See also J. D. Fauntleroy, "Some Texas Frontier Forts," *FT* (June, 1947), 441.

114 "Depredations on the Frontiers of Texas," *House Executive Documents*, 43d Cong., 1st Sess., XVII (1615), No. 257, p. 22.

Other Negroes, as well as Mexicans and whites, were reported as merely accompanying Indians in their raids on settlements and wagon trains. The Quahada band of Comanche was said to include mulattoes and Mexicans.[115] On April 20, 1872, a band reportedly made up of Indians, Mexicans, and Negroes killed eleven Mexican teamsters near Howard Wells and badly wounded two others.[116]

The last references the writer has encountered to Negroes among hostile Indians belong to 1874. Newton C. Brown reports that in that year the Indians were defeated in a raid on the San Saba country. Shortly thereafter

My little sister . . . told me that she saw a black man . . . in the brush. . . . He was bare-headed. Had long hair . . . an old pair of ducking leggings with a belt . . . a big brass earring in his ear, and around his shoulders wore a big black skull [shawl?] with safety pins. . . . He looked very much like an Indian and could not talk or understand anything. . . . He soon learned to talk and understand. I kept him two years and took him to Concho Post and gave him five hundred dollars. . . . I told him to be honest, not to drink any whiskey or steal anything. He cried like a child and begged me to bring him back home with me. I told him to go and live with the Mexicans.[117]

If the account is to be taken at its face value—and the unusual generosity of the parting gift casts a somewhat fabulous aura over the entire episode—the circumstances suggest that the Negro, who was apparently only a boy in his teens, had been captured as a child and had forgotten

---

[115] Carter, 63.

[116] Fort Clark Medical Record, July, 1868-January, 1973, pp. 261-262 (MS.); Nye, 152-153. The report that Negroes were involved in this affair is, however, of doubtful validity. The attack on the wagon train was apparently by Kiowa under Big Bow and White Horse. Mexican captives and the half-Mexican offspring of such captives were numerous among the Kiowa, and some of them may have been present. Quitan and Tomasi were famous Mexican-Kiowa Warriors, but the latter had been killed earlier. Botalye, half-Mexican, distinguished himself in 1874. White captives were less numerous, but there were some, such as Tehan, who participated in raids on their own people. Nye, 132, 214-217. Kiowa tradition, however, preserves no record of Negro or part-Negro warriors. Letter: Miss Alice Marriott, 16 Jan. 1956, to author.

[117] Hamrick, 190.

English, at least temporarily, but had preserved a vague longing for civilization which had caused him to take advantage of his associates' repulse to put himself in the way of capture.

Much more interesting and significant is another episode of 1874. The Comanche, Kiowa, Cheyenne, and Plains Apache who, led by the half-breed Comanche chief Quanah Parker, attacked a party of buffalo-hunters at the Adobe Walls in northwestern Texas on June 27, 1874, were "directed by bugle calls until their bugler was killed late in the afternoon. . . . It has been said that their bugler was a negro soldier who had deserted." The hunters, at any rate, "found ten Indians and a negro dead" on the field.[118]

The writer has found no examples after the mid-1870's of either friendly or unfriendly relations between Southern Plains Indians and individual Texas Negroes—as distinguished from Negro regiments and troops of the United States army serving in Texas. The military campaign of 1874 against the Comanche and Kiowa was so effective that they never again engaged in a general outbreak and the opportunties for such relations were correspondingly reduced, although small-scale Comanche and Kiowa raids from the Indian Territory continued until 1879[119] and the Lipan Apache raided into Southern Texas from Mexico as late as 1881.

SUMMARY AND CONCLUSIONS

Relations between Negroes and Indians on the Texas frontiers reveal a general pattern of mutual hostility similar to that which existed between Indians and white fron-

---

[118] Rupert Norval Richardson, *The Comanche Barrier to South Plains Settlement* (Glendale, Calif., 1933), 381 n.; Robert M. Wright, *Dodge City: The Cowboy Capital* (Wichita, Kansas, n.d.), 123-124. "The Great Battle of Adobe Walls," *FT*, Mar., 1951, pp. 168-172. Cf. the mention above of a bugle being blown in 1869 among a band of Indians commanded by a Negro. *FT*, III, 9-10.

[119] Wallace and Hoebel, 327.

tiersmen; they certainly give no encouragement to the belief in a mystical bond of unity between members of the darker races. Nevertheless, examples of cooperation between Negroes and the sedentary and agricultural Indians of East Texas, and even of the attainment of leadership among the fierce Comanche Indians by Negroes after the Civil War, are sufficiently numerous to demonstrate that the pattern of relations between Negro and Indian was not absolutely identical with that between white and Indian. Few whites, except those captured in childhood, were ever associated with Texas Indians hostile to the settlers, and no case is known of a renegade white man becoming a leader among the hostiles.[120] The reckless or lawless white man was under no necessity of seeking refuge among the Indians; he could find congenial associations among other whites of similar situation and disposition, such as were all too numerous on the frontier. Negroes who chafed under bondage or were discontented with their status among the whites were, however, too few on the Texas frontier to find adequate companionship among those of their own race. For restless Negroes of unusual courage and independence, however, joining the Indians was a possibility, although flight to the Mexicans was usually more attractive. That runaway or renegade Negroes should occasionally attain leadership among their adoptive people testifies both to the advantage they derived from acquaintance with the English language and the white man's ways and to their possession of the special personal qualities of venturesomeness and initiative which had led them to dare such a drastic change in environment.

[120] The 'white man discuised as an Indian' who, in July, 1855, in company with four authentic Indians, killed an overseer in Comal County, may have been a childhood captive adopted into the tribe or a light-skinned and light-haired half-breed. If actually a renegade white his case was highly exceptional. In spring, 1859, a little girl reported a man with red hair and whiskers among the Indians who killed her father near Jacksboro, but there is doubt that any of these "indians" were authentic. *FT*, May, 1951, pp. 235-236.

According to a long-standing and familiar stereotype the Negro should always have been in "moral terror of the Indians" as a racial characteristic, an evidence of and an essential element in an inescapable "racial inferiority"; the Negro who was speared begging for his life or shot with his head buried ostrich-wise in a haystack would be typical. But, examining the evidence, we find that for one such Negro there were a dozen or more like the quick-shooting Smith boy, the hoe-wielding Bob Anderson, the heroic Hunter slavewoman, the faithful Tom, the cool and quick-thinking youngster Jack Hardy, the courageous Maverick slaves, Griffin and Jinny Anderson; like Tom Sullivan and Ben and the Harpers and the numerous other Negroes who took the trail after Indian horse-thieves; like Brit Johnson and his friends and the two nameless Negroes north of Austin who died "fighting bravely" by the side of their white companions. Nor should we forget the much smaller but still significant group who cast in their lot with the Indians in their desperate and hopeless resistance to white encroachments on their corn fields and buffalo-hunting grounds, one of whom even rode to his death with the flower of the Southern Plains warriors in the historic attack on Adobe Walls.

The over-emphasizers of race would make the Indian, on the one hand, hate and despise the Negro *as a Negro;* or, on the other hand, would insist that the Negro and Indian *must* have been drawn together by the common bond of a dark skin. But the evidence indicates that the Indian, particularly the nomadic Plains Indian, ordinarily recognized the Negro as a representative, along with the white man, of a hostile, encroaching culture, and treated him accordingly, and the average Negro, who on the frontier bore the bonds of servitude comparatively lightly, felt himself identified with the white man's sedentary culture and helped defend it and himself against the hostile Indian.

And yet the Negro, even on the frontier, was not completely integrated with the white man's culture, and the Negro of exceptional high spirit and impatience of restraint sometimes resented his position in the white man's cultural pattern to such an extent that he preferred participation in a less familiar culture, by which he nevertheless could be more completely accepted, to a subordinate and segregated status in a culture otherwise more sympathetic. The Negro's occasional acceptance by and even attainment of leadership in the Indian society further refutes the naive assumption that the Indian felt any hostility for the Negro on a racial basis, or otherwise than as a representative of an alien and hostile culture.

Corrections and Additions

Although a few details could be added to some of the episodes described in this article, I can find no serious omissions. The only errors are misprints. For example:

p. 400: Strike out third line from bottom.

p. 405, l. 21: "a young girls" should be "girl," of course.

p. 415, l. 17: " 'order a charge' " should be " 'ordered.' "

The following article originally appeared in the *Hispanic American Historical Review*, February, 1951 (Vol. XXXI, No. 1).

THE SEMINOLE IN MEXICO, 1850-1861

KENNETH W. PORTER*

Early in the summer of 1850 the Mexican authorities at Piedras Negras on the Rio Grande across from Eagle Pass were startled by the appearance of two hundred or so Seminole Indians and Negroes, whose leaders requested admission to Mexico as settlers. The chief of the band, Coacoochee or Wild Cat, was the favorite son of the late King Philip (Emathla), chief of the St. John's River Seminole and brother-in-law of Seminole head-chief Mikonopi, and had been one of the principal leaders in the recent Seminole War. He was a man of about forty, slight, active, and well-proportioned, with an attractive and intelligent appearance. He also, unfortunately, was inordinately addicted to alcoholic beverages.[1] The chief of the "Mascogos," as the Mexicans for reasons not entirely clear styled the Seminole Negroes,[2] was John Horse, better known by his nickname of Gopher John.[3] He was reputedly the son of a Negro mother with some Indian blood and of an Indian father with a trace of Spanish ancestry. A big, tall, fine-looking, "ginger-colored" man, with a proud carriage and

.*The author is research associate of the Business History Foundation.—Ed.

[1] John T. Sprague, *The Origin, Progress, and Conclusion of the Florida War* (New York, 1848), pp. 98, 324-330. A poorly reproduced photograph of a portrait in colored clays painted by Capt. John C. Casey, Seminole agent (Capt. Charles H. Coe, *Red Patriots* [Cincinnati, 1898], p. 26), gives some idea of his appearance.

[2] The Muskogee were the dominant people of the Creek Confederacy. The "original" Seminole, the Oconee, were non-Muskogee, Hitchiti-speaking people, but by the time of the Seminole War it is estimated that two-thirds of the Florida Indians were Muskogee refugees from Alabama and Georgia. Wild Cat and John Horse undoubtedly had Muskogee-speaking Negroes with them; a Mexican officer, asking one of them what he was, what language he spoke, may have been told "Muskogee," and, not being an expert in the native races of North America and their languages, may have set all the Negroes down as "Mascogos." (John R. Swanton, *Early History of the Creek Indians and Their Neighbors* [Washington, 1922], pp. 172, 181, 398, 403, 406, 414.)

[3] For a discussion of the origin of this nickname, see K. W. Porter, "Davy Crockett and John Horse," *American Literature*, XV (Mar., 1943), 10-15.

walk, renowned for his coolness and courage, his deadly accuracy with a rifle, and his tact and "management," he shared with Wild Cat a fondness for fine clothes, ornaments, and whiskey—although more successful than the Indian chief in controlling the latter taste. He was a couple of years younger than Wild Cat, with whom he had been associated, off and on, since they had met as hostages at Tampa Bay, early in 1837.[4]

The Seminole migration from the Indian Territory resulted from discontent with being forced to live in the midst of and subject to the powerful Creek Nation, from which the "original" Seminole had seceded a century before. "They look upon us as runaways, and would treat us just as they would so many dogs," was the complaint of Mikonopi's nephew Holatoochee.[5] The Seminole accused the Creeks of having occupied the best land and of discrimination in the distribution of annuities, but the chief bone of contention was the Seminole Negroes, many of whom were claimed as slaves on various pretexts by some of the Creeks.[6] The Negroes, who were mostly runaway slaves or descendants of runaways, were regarded by the Seminole rather as "vassals and allies" than as slaves. They lived in separate villages, owned property, habitually carried arms, and went into battle under their own captains. The Creek half-breeds feared the effect of this freedom on their own Negro property and insisted that the Seminole Negroes should either be expelled from the Nation or treated as slaves.[7]

[4] The best descriptions in print of John Horse (Gopher John) are in Maj. Gen. George A. McCall, *Letters from the Frontiers* (Philadelphia, 1868), pp. 399-401, and Sprague, *op. cit.*, pp. 459, 300. Alleged portraits appear in Sprague, *op. cit.*, facing p. 459, and in Joshua R. Giddings, *The Exiles of Florida* (Columbus, 1858), facing p. 64; aged Seminole Negroes find them convincing likenesses. My knowledge of his appearance and character is, however, drawn principally from the recollections of Seminole Negroes who, as children or as young men and women, knew John Horse (*ca.* 1812-1882) in his middle years or as an old man. Julia Payne (*ca.* 1862-1946), Nacimiento, Coahuila, and Molly Perryman (*ca.* 1863-), Dolly July (1870-), Rosa Fay (*ca.* 1860-), and Bill Daniels (*ca* .1868-), Brackettville, Texas, were particularly vivid in their descriptions. A good deal of miscellaneous information about John in Florida and the Indian Territory has been derived from the National Archives (War Dep't, Adjutant General's Office, and the Department of the Interior, Indian Office, Seminole Files).

[5] Grant Foreman, *Indian Removal* (Norman, 1932), chap. xxx.

[6] Grant Foreman, *The Five Civilized Tribes* (Norman, 1934), pp. 243-246; *Annual Report of the Commissioner of Indian Affairs for 1841* (hereinafter cited as *A.R.C.I.A.*) p. 77.

[7] Foreman, *Five Civilized Tribes*, pp. 259-261; "Indians—Creek and Seminole," 33 Cong., 2 sess., H. ex. doc. 15, pp. 10-11, 28-31; C. W. Dean, Ft. Smith, to George W. Monypenny, Com. of Ind. Aff., June 24, 1856, Seminole File D180, Indian Office, National Archives (hereinafter cited as I.O.N.A.); [William Hayne Simmons], *Notices of East Florida* (Charleston, 1822), pp. 41, 50, 76; *American State Papers, Military Affairs*, VI, 533, 544;

426 The Negro on The American Frontier

A kidnapping campaign, principally by whites and Creek half-breeds, with the objective of seizing Seminole Negro women and children, under a fabricated bill of sale or by sheer force, and running them into Arkansas or Louisiana for sale, was a decisive factor in deciding many Negroes and Indians to leave the Territory. The Negroes feared for the freedom of themselves and families; the Indians, some of whom were relatives or friends of the Negroes, also valued them as allies and associates, because of their superior knowledge of money, horses, agriculture, and the English language, and resented being deprived of their assistance. The more militant Seminole were by 1849 prepared to seek refuge in Mexico, which they knew to be a "land of freedom," although terribly devastated by the wild Indians—a country therefore in which such fighting-men as the Seminole might expect a welcome.[8]

Wild Cat's personal feelings and thwarted ambition were also a factor. For over a decade he had been looked on as the logical successor to head-chief Mikonopi—but when Mikonopi died early in 1849 the election fell to Jim Jumper, of the pro-Creek and kidnapping faction, probably in large measure through the influence of the Seminole sub-agent Marcellus DuVal, whose brother had induced several Seminole chiefs to make over to him an interest in Negroes they claimed to own. Wild Cat had for several years been developing a project of establishing himself as chief of a confederacy drawn from the tribes both of the Indian Territory and of the Texas plains. On three different occasions in 1846 he had visited Texas, where he had met the semi-civilized Kickapoo, skilled in the use of the long frontier rifle, the Lipan Apache, savage and predatory, the Tonkawa, hunters and reputed cannibals, and the fierce, proud, and powerful Comanche. His representatives in 1848 were circulating among all these tribes and among the sedentary and agricultural Kichai and Waco, urging them to join the Seminole in the Creek country.[9]

Wild Cat's failure to be chosen head-chief caused him to change

---

John Lee Williams, *The Territory of Florida* (New York, 1837), p. 240; William Kennedy, *Texas, Its Rise, Progress, and Prospects* (2 vols., London, 1841), I, 350; F.C.M. Boggess, *A Veteran of Four Wars* (Arcadia, Fla., 1900), p. 64; McCall, *op. cit.*, p. 160.

[8] Lt. Col. G. Loomis, Ft. Gibson, to Maj. Gen. T. S. Jesup, Washington, "Ft. Gibson #2," Q.M.G.O., Consolidated Files, War Dep't, N. A.; "Fort Gibson," Statement of John Cowaya, Rec. Mar. 26, 1846, *ibid.*

[9] Foreman, *Five Civilized Tribes*, pp. 244-245; "Journal of Elijah Hicks," Foreman, ed., *Chronicles of Oklahoma*, XIII (Mar., 1936), 68-69; Foreman, *Advancing the Frontier* (Norman, 1933), pp. 175-179; 29 Cong., 2 sess., Sen. ex. doc. 1, p. 279; Rupert Norval Richardson, *The Comanche Barrier to South Plains Settlement* (Glendale, Calif., 1933), p. 171; *A.R.C.I.A.*, 1848, p. 200.

his plans.   Instead of luring the tribes of the Southern Plains to
the Seminole country to be used in overawing the Creeks, he
would lead them south of the Rio Grande, where he would establish a military colony for oppressed and refugee Indians—as well
as for Negroes from the Civilized Tribes and from Texas and
Arkansas plantations.   Wild Cat's ambitions in some respects
exceeded those of King Philip, Pontiac, and Tecumseh, for he
envisaged a union of half a dozen linguistic groups and two races.
John Horse, when the Seminole party left the Territory late in
October, 1849, had brought away not only Seminole Negroes but
also Creek and Cherokee slaves.   Wild Cat, in his rather leisurely
nine months' passage through Texas, had not, as reported, brought
under his command "seven or eight hundred . . . Seminole, Lipan,
Wago and Tankawah," but had actually induced a band of about
a hundred Kickapoo warriors to take him as chief.[10]

The Kickapoo had presented themselves at San Fernando de
Rosas (now Zaragoza) by July 12, 1850, and two weeks later the
captains of the three tribes, numbering over 700—Gato del Monte
(Wild Cat) of the Seminole Indians, *el moreno* (colored man) John
Horse of the free Negroes or "Mascogos," and Papicua of the
Kickapoo—appeared before Col. Juan Manuel Maldonado, sub-
inspector of the colonies, to petition for land, tools, oxen, plows,
flocks, and herds, and for the repair or replacement of their firearms.   Coahuila was being over-run with unusual fury by the
wild Indians and military colonies were being established along
the border to cope with this menace.   The military skill and experience of the Seminole and Kickapoo were thus particularly
welcome; their petition was tentatively granted and arrangements
were made for their accommodation until confirmation could come
from the central government.[11]

Wild Cat immediately started back to the Territory for new
recruits.   On the way he visited the Comanche, Caddo, and Waco,
urging them to join him in Mexico, where he said they would

[10] Foreman, *Five Civilized Tribes*, p. 262; M. Duval to the Com. of Indian Aff., May 30,
1850, Seminole File D392-455, John H. Rollins, Austin, to Orlando Brown, Com. of
Indian Aff., May 6, 1850, Texas R568-596: I.O.N.A.; Walter Prescott Webb, *The Texas
Rangers* (Boston, 1935), pp. 132-136; *Fort Smith (Ark.) Herald*, July 20, 1850.

[11] Departamento Agrario, Mexico, D.F., "El Nacimiento," Informe, Primera Parte,
Anexo Num. 1; Anexo Num. 2, pp. 1-4; *Reports of the Committee of Investigation sent in
1873 by the Mexican Government to the Frontier of Texas* (hereinafter cited as *Committee
of Investigation*) (New York, 1875), pp. 407-412, 323; *Memoria de la Secretaría de Estado
y del Despacho de Guerra y Marina* (Mexico, 1851), pp. 17-18; Hubert Howe Bancroft,
History of Mexico, V (San Francisco, 1885), p. 574 n. 47, p. 575 n. 48; Joseph W. Revere,
Keel and Saddle (Boston, 1872), chap. xxvi.

fight not the "wild Indians" but the Texans, and threatening punishment to those who refused. The Comanche were not impressed and the peaceful Waco were alarmed rather than attracted, but he did succeed in recruiting another large band of Kickapoo.[12]

When Wild Cat arrived in the Seminole country in September, 1850, he was drunk and remained so for a week, thus giving the Seminole sub-agent and the Creeks opportunity to take action. He was forced to leave the Territory to avoid arrest, after recruitingly only "six or eight Seminole" and their families, all said to be his own relatives, and "about one hundred negroes." He headed for the Rio Grande with the Indians, leaving the Negroes to proceed separately. Parties of Negroes probably totalling nearly three hundred had left for Mexico before Wild Cat's return. Wild Cat's own recruits, however, were pursued by the Creeks and after a running fight were overtaken, overpowered, and most of them brought back as prisoners. The Comanche, who were not at all deceived by Wild Cat's assertion that he did not intend to fight the "wild Indians" and who had no intention of settling down as military colonists, massacred a party of sixty Negroes, except for a few women and children reserved for ransom, and also massacred several smaller parties both of Negroes and of Delaware and Shawnee Indians, suspected of being on their way to join Wild Cat. A hundred or so Negroes, however, must have succeeded in fighting their way through, judging both by the increase in the number of Wild Cat's Negro followers and by traditions among present-day Seminole Negroes that their ancestors on their way to Mexico had to fight rear-guard actions with pursuing Creeks and whites and also "had trouble once or twice wid Comanche Injuns." Wild Cat, having failed to make connection with his unfortunate Negro followers, gathered up the Kickapoo who were waiting south of the Canadian and succeeded in crossing into Mexico, despite the Comanche Indians, Texas Rangers, and United States troops who had been roused against him.[13]

[12] Webb. op. cit., p. 133.

[13] "Indians—Creek and Seminole," loc. cit. pp. 10-11; 32 Cong., 1 sess., H. ex. doc. 2, pt. 3, II, 405-410; Foreman, Five Civilized Tribes, pp. 262-266; Marcellus Duval, Van Buren, Ark., to Luke Lea, Com. of Ind. Aff. Aug. 2, 1850 (A171), Letters Rec'd, A.G.O., War Dep't, N. A.; M. Duval to Gen. George M. Brookes (sic), San Antonio, Oct. 21, 1850, Seminole File D481-605, I.O.N.A.; M. Duval to Luke Lea, Com. of Indian Aff., I.O.N.A.; Fort Smith Herald, July 6, 20, Aug. 3, Oct. 4, Nov. 8, Dec. 6, 13, 1850, Mar. 21, 1851; The San Antonio Ledger, May 22, 1851; Rodney Glisan, Journal of Army Life (San Francisco, 1874), p. 65; Randolph Barnes Marcy and George B. McClellan, Explorations of the Red River of Louisiana (Washington, 1853), p. 101; R. B. Marcy, Thirty Years of Army

Wild Cat's followers had been temporarily settled at various points on or near the Rio Grande, including Colonia de Guerrero, below Piedras Negras, and San Fernando de Rosas (Zaragoza), about twenty-five miles southwest. The Negroes were chiefly settled at Moral, several miles above Piedras Negras.[14] The three tribes, during their leader's absence, twice came to the assistance of Mexican troops and "fought well" against Indians from the United States "who were defeated with loss."[15] Their petition was favorably passed on by the president, Oct. 16, 1850, on condition that they obey the laws, preserve harmony with friendly nations, particularly the United States, and avoid intercourse with the barbarous Indians, resisting their passage through the region. On Nov. 18, 1850, at the Colony of Monclova Viejo at Moral, Col. Juan Manuel Maldonado explained through interpreters the terms of the grant, which lay at the headwaters of the rivers San Rodrigo and San Antonio about thirty miles above Piedras Negras, and on the following day the captains of the three nations took the oath of fidelity. On Feb. 4, 1851, Wild Cat subscribed to the oath and was appointed judge of the municipality and commissioned colonel in the army. Objections were raised to this original allotment and on Mar. 3, 1851, the tribes were granted land in the vicinity of the colonies of Monclova Viejo and of Guerrero, above and below Piedras Negras. The Seminole grant was called La Navaja; the Guerrero grant was probably for the Kickapoo.[16]

Life on the Border (New York, 1866), pp. 55-56; Frost Woodhull, "The Seminole Indian Scouts on the Border," *Frontier Times*, XV (Dec., 1937), 118-127, esp. 119, 123; Laurence Foster, *Negro-Indian Relationships in the Southeast* (Philadelphia, 1935), p. 46; George Deas, Ass't Adjt. Gen'l, Headquarters 8th Dep't, San Antonio, to Bvt. Lieut. Col. W. J. Hardee, Commanding Ft. Inge, Dec. 20, 1850, photostat, Col. Martin L. Crimmins Collection, U. of Tex. Library; Interviews with William (Bill) Wilson (1875-), Dolly July (1870-), and Curly Jefferson (1881-), Brackettville, 1941 and 1943.

[14] "Depredations on the Frontiers of Texas," 43 Cong., 1 sess., H. ex. doc. 257, xvii, 22; "Notes by the late Gen'l John L. Bullis, U. S. Army, Commanded the Scouts from '72 to '81 (9 Yrs.)," General Service File 1234-14308-1914, I.O.N.A.; J. Fred Rippy, "Indians of the Southwest in the Diplomacy of the United States and Mexico, 1848-1853," HISPANIC AMERICAN HISTORICAL REVIEW, II (1919), 382 n. 70; W. G. Freeman, Col. M. L. Crimmins, ed., "Report on the Eighth Military Department," *Southwestern Historical Quarterly*, LII (Apr., 1949), 444; Interview with Curly Jefferson, 1941.

[15] *Committee of Investigation*, p. 323; Bvt. Maj. Gen. George M. Brooke, San Antonio, to Gov. P. H. Bell, Austin, Nov. 12, 1850 (B707), A.G.O., War Dep't, N. A.

[16] *Committee of Investigation*, pp. 303-304, 323-407; *Derecho Internacional Mexicano*, III, 496-499; Francisco F. de la Maza, *Código de colonización y terrenos baldíos de la república mexicana* (Mexico, 1893), pp. 476-478; *Memoria de la Secretaría de Estado y del Despacho de Guerra y Marina* (Mexico, 1851), pp. 17-18; Seminoles y Mascogos, Num. 94 (1891), 44-12-60, Colonización, Archivo de la Secretaría de Relaciones Exteriores, Mexico; "El

The Indians and Negroes hardly had their first seed-corn in the ground before they were called out with other military colonists on a campaign in which they were "engaged for two months in traversing the desert, and twice gave battle to the savages." The expedition, though successful, was a costly one for Wild Cat, for most of the Kickapoo "abandoned the expedition during its return march"—and took with them the recaptured live-stock![17]

The Seminole were hardly back from this expedition before they were called on to oppose another type of invasion from Texas. Seminole Negroes were by no means the only fugitives in Mexico. It was asserted that "north of the Sierra Madre [were] three thousand colored men" belonging to Texans. Slave owners were naturally receptive to advances from Mexican revolutionists who craved assistance in setting up an independent Rio Grande republic and offered in exchange "a law for the rendition of slaves." One such revolutionist was José María Carbajal, a leader of smugglers, who invaded Mexico, Sept. 18, 1851, with a force consisting principally of three or four hundred Americans, including discharged Texas Rangers under the notorious John S. ("Rip") Ford. Revolution thus became the handmaid of slave speculation. The Seminole were called out to help resist this invasion and Wild Cat, at the head of sixty warriors, one-third of them Negroes, rendered "efficient aid in the fight at Cerralvo," northeast of Monterrey, late in November, in which Carbajal was decisively defeated.[18]

The slavers of Texas were not all prepared to hurl themselves in a wolf-pack on the North Mexican lion. Others preferred to emulate the jackal and seek out the helpless as a prey. Such was

Nacimiento," Departamento Agrario, Mexico; Rippy, *op. cit., loc. cit.*, II, 382 n. 70; Mrs. W. L. Cazneau (Cora Montgomery), *Eagle Pass* (New York, 1852), pp. 73-77, 119-120, 143-147; Interview with Penny Factor (1874-), Brackettville, 1943.

[17] *Committee of Investigation*, pp. 327, 408-409; *La Patria* (Saltillo), July 12, 1851; "Indians—Creek and Seminole," *loc. cit.*, p. 11; *Memoria de la Secretaría de Estado y del Despacho de Guerra y Marina* (Mexico, 1852), pp. 49-51; Glisan, *op. cit.*, p. 93.

[18] "Difficulties on Southwestern Frontier," 36 Cong., 1 sess., H. ex. doc. 52; 32 Cong., 2 sess., S. ex. doc. 1, II, 15-20; 32 Cong., 2 sess., H. ex. doc. 1, I, pt. 2, 16; "Indians—Creek and Seminole," *loc. cit.*, p. 4; *Committee of Investigation*, pp. 188-190; *The Texas State Times* (Austin), Oct. 6, 1855; Memoirs of John S. Ford, IV, 628, Ms. (copy), U. of Texas; F. L. Olmsted, *A Journey through Texas* (New York, 1857), pp. 323-335; Adolf Uhde, *Die Länder am untern Rio Bravo del Norte* (Heidelberg, 1861), pp. 317-328, 330-331; Cazneau, *op. cit.*, pp. 139, 144, 147; Bancroft, *op. cit.*, V, 603-605, 612; J. Fred Rippy, *The United States and Mexico* (New York, 1926), pp. 89-90, 172-176; Rippy, "Border Troubles along the Rio Grande, 1848-1860," *Southwestern Historical Quarterly*, XXIII (Oct., 1919), 91-111; Rippy, "Anglo-American Filibusters and the Gadsden Treaty," HISPANIC AMERICAN HISTORICAL REVIEW, IV (May, 1922), 159-163.

"Captain" Warren Adams, on whose behalf Gov. P. H. Bell, of
Texas, issued a proclamation the day before the Carbajal invasion,
urging all citizens to assist him in recovering runaway slaves of
the Seminole Indians and of Texans.   On the evening of Nov. 2,
when most of the Seminole warriors had marched against the
filibusters at Cerralvo, the colonel commanding Fort Duncan
"came over to Piedras Negras to advise . . . that he had heard
of a force of adventurers," numbering over a hundred, proceeding
from San Antonio to seize the free Negroes at Monclova Viejo,
and that Adams, the Negro-thief, with seventeen men, was already
encamped on the Leona, twenty leagues from the fort.   The
Mexican authorities promptly assembled 150 citizens, mounted
and armed, who marched to the Sauceda in the jurisdiction of
the Villa de Nava and repulsed the slavers, probably with little
or no fighting.   Adams and his attendant jackals did not, however, withdraw entirely empty-handed but moved southwest from
Nava, swooped down on a family of Negroes living at Santa Rosa,
and escaped to Texas with their victims.[19]

The Seminole, at the end of 1851, received high praise from the
Mexican authorities for their "faithful and useful assistance to . . .
military operations" and as "industrious workers" and hunters.[20]
They were, however, shortly to be removed from the location
where they had made such a favorable impression.   The authorities of Coahuila announced that since La Navaja did not please
the Seminole the Federal government would give then four *sitios
de ganado mayor*[21] and other *sitios* of irrigable land in the *hacienda*
of Nacimiento in the Santa Rosa Mountains northwest of Santa
Rosa (Muzquiz), which is eighty-four miles southwest of Piedras
Negras.

According to a statement of a few years earlier, "The finest
agricultural region in Coahuila is in the vicinity of Santa Rosa,"[22]

[19] *Committee of Investigation*, p. 331; Juan Manuel Maldonado, Colonia de Guerrero,
Nov. 2, 1851, to Antonio María Jáuregui, Inspector General de las Colonias de Oriente;
Emilio Langberg, Guerrero, to Ministro de Guerra y Marina, Nov. 7, 1851; "Amagos de
invación al Departamento de Río Grande por fuerzas unidas de los EEUU Año de 1851";
Rafael de la Fuente, Saltillo, to Ministro de Guerra y Marina: Archivo de la Secretaría de
la Defensa, Mexico, D. F.; Proclamation of Gov. P. H. Bell, Austin, Sept. 17, 1851 (S324),
A.G.O., War Dep't, N. A.; *La Patria*, Nov. 22, 1851.

[20] *Memoria de la Secretaría de Estado y del Despacho de Guerra y Marina* (Mexico.
1852), p. 39.

[21] A *sitio* de ganado mayor is a unit of pasture-land of about 6.6 square miles.

[22] "Colonización, Seminoles y Mascogos," *loc. cit.*; "March of Brig. Gen. John E. Wool
from San Antonio to Saltillo," 31 Cong., 1 sess., Sen. ex. doc. 32, X, 38; Interview with
Julia Payne, 1932 (courtesy of Mrs. D. S. McKellar).

but the authorities in arranging for this transfer were not primarily inspired by altruistic motives. The preservation of the peace of the border—a matter of considerable concern with the Treaty of Guadalupe Hidalgo only three years in the past—was probably a principal consideration. The settlement on such a disturbed frontier of a large band of the people who had for seven years defied the power of the United States, under a chief renowned for intelligence and daring, naturally aroused apprehension among the United States authorities. An excitable young brevet second lieutenant had even conceived the fantastic theory that the Kickapoo and Seminole were in alliance with the Comanche.[23]

The number and character of the Seminole Negroes probably constituted the principal difficulty. The presence of even one such "impudent and troublesome negro" as "Capt. Horse," who boasted that he had "made many white men bite the dust," was enough to menace the uneasy peace of the border; add forty or fifty more armed Negroes, veterans of the Florida War, and an inflammable situation became highly explosive. When John Horse called at Fort Duncan to claim a horse which had been taken up and sold, he was humiliatingly expelled—to the great glee of the border press.[24] When some of the professional slave-hunters infesting Eagle Pass kidnapped a little girl playing on the riverbank, a friendly Mexican informed the Seminole, who dispatched an expeditionary force and recovered the child. No open clash resulted, but either episode could have been the spark for an explosion.[25]

The removal of the Seminole from their border location was thus highly desirable. Their new location near Santa Rosa (Muzquiz), which the wild Indians had attacked the previous year, and on the headwaters of the Sabinas, which issued from a gap in the mountains by which the savages were accustomed to descend, was also superior strategically.

Near the end of 1851 the Seminole began to settle at Alto, just northwest of Muzquiz, so that the women and children could be in comparative safety while most of the men went on an

[23] Bvt. Maj. Gen. George M. Brooke, San Antonio, to Bvt. Maj. Gen. R. Jones, Adjt. Gen., Washington, Nov. 21, 1850 (B707); Bvt. 2d Lieut. Jos. T. Harle to Headquarters, 8th Dep't, San Antonio, May 15, 1851 (H205); Lieut. Col. T. Morris, Ft. Duncan, to Col. Juan Manuel Maldonado, Guerrero, Mar. 24, 1851 (H205); Maldonado to Morris. Mar. 29, 1851 (H205): A.G.O., War Dep't, N. A.

[24] *The Western Texan* (San Antonio), Sept. 18, 1851, Nov. 18, Dec 2, 1852.

[25] "Notes by the late Gen'l John L. Bullis . . . . ," *loc. cit.*; Interviews with Teresa C. Wilson (1866-), Penny Factor, Curly Jefferson, and Rosa Fay, Brackettville, 1941-1943.

expedition into the Laguna de Jaco in Chihuahua with Col. Emilio Langberg, military commander of the region.[26] Nacimiento was "Indian country" and the full strength of the band was needed before they attempted to go up and possess the land. Wild Cat wished to visit Mexico City immediately and obtain confirmation of the Nacimiento grant, so John Horse, who, although regarded by whites as a Negro, "was recognized as an Indian chief by adoption," and the old chief "Pasaqui" (Pasoca) were given command of the Seminole contingent.[27]

The Laguna de Jaco campaigners arrived at Nacimiento about the middle of June, 1852;[28] Wild Cat and his delegation to Mexico City got back by September. The Seminole had, on July 26, been awarded four *sitios de ganado mayor* in the hacienda of Na-

[26] The colonel was "by birth a Dane, but educated in Germany" (Julius Froebel, *Seven Years' Travel in Central America, Northern Mexico, and the Far West of the United States* [London, 1859], p. 331).

[27] The chief source for the history of the Seminole in Mexico, 1852-1861, is the Eberstadt Collection, consisting for this purpose of the Muzquiz Records and the Guajardo Notes. References to the Muzquiz Records (hereinafter cited as M.R.) and to the Guajardo Notes (hereinafter cited as G.N.) will be understood as being to the Eberstadt Collection. I wish to express at this time my gratitude to Mr. Edward Eberstadt for his generous and gracious permission to utilize this collection under conditions of unusual and possibly unprecedented freedom.

The Muzquiz Records consist principally of letters to the governing body or principal officer of government of the Municipality of Muzquiz (hereinafter cited simply as Muzquiz) and of copies of letters from said governing body or principal officer. Such copies are frequently unsigned; when the origin of a letter is not indicated it probably emanated from Muzquiz. Similarly, if the destination of a letter is not indicated, it was probably directed to Muzquiz. Writers and recipients of letters are cited on their first appearance by name in full, title or office, and address, when known; thereafter they are cited by name only. Most of the communications to Muzquiz, and some of the Muzquiz copies, are numbered; these numbers are parenthesized in the following notes.

The Guajardo Notes were collected by the late General Alberto Guajardo for the unfulfilled purpose of writing a history of Coahuila, and draw heavily on the Muzquiz Records. The general, however, also included information derived from his long and intimate acquaintance with the terrain, wild life, inhabitants, and traditions of Coahuila, as well as documents from other sources. The Guajardo Notes are cited as they are arranged by date.

"Itinerario del Coronel E. Langberg, 1851," Dec. 20-23, 1851, G.N.; "En la Villa de Musqz á primero de Julio de mil ocho sientos cincuenta y dos . . . . ," M. R.; Statement of Thomas G. Williams, Austin, Tex., June 17, 1876, Seminole File 1876-S448, I.O.N.A.; *Committee of Investigation*, p. 409; Interviews with Curly Jefferson, Brackettville, 1941, and Dindie Factor (*ca.* 1874-), Nacimiento, 1942, 1943.

[28] R. A., Muzquiz, to "S. ofic. 1º. de la Sria. del S. Gobnr. del Estado," July 5, 1852; "En la Villa de Musqz. a primero de Julio de mil ocho sientos cincuenta y dos . . . ." M.R. "—31-Apuntes, datos y noticias para la historia de Coahuila," G.N.; Froebel, *op. cit.*, p. 351.

cimiento and four, which they never occupied, in Durango.[29]

Those who had remained behind had moved up to Nacimiento early in the year despite the Indian menace; the inhabitants of Muzquiz had furnished them with seed-corn, oxen, and plows and they had put in a crop. This "voluntary offering"[30] represents the pleasant side of Seminole-Mexican relations. The Seminole were absolutely ignorant of the "Castilian language." Verbal communications between a Seminole Indian and a Mexican required the intervention both of a bi-lingual Negro and of an English-speaking Mexican. Under those circumstances understanding was difficult. To many Mexicans an Indian was an Indian—and an Indian was an enemy. Such Mexicans, here and there, began to attack the newcomers, with designs on their horses—though the Seminole proved more than capable of looking after themselves and of reclaiming their property with interest.[31] The better-informed citizens, aware that the Seminole were "civilized Indians," were often lavishly hospitable, but the Indians and Negroes did not care for the Mexican food and the *chile* at first sometimes even aroused suspicions of poison![32] Inhabitants of more remote communities, knowing only that strange Indians from the United States were settled at Nacimiento, found it convenient to blame them for all current Indian outrages, including murder. The Seminole, largely dependent on hunting, did occasionally mistake a stray beef for a deer, but the more serious accusations could easily be disproved.[33]

John Horse, whose shrewdness and tact were as notorious as his courage, is credited with a strict and watchful supervision of his people's relations with their hosts. "John Horse would never let even the little children fight with the Mexican children, because, he said, 'When we came, fleeing slavery, Mexico was a land

[29] *El Siglo Diez y Nueve*, Apr. 30, May 14, 18, July 18, 29, Aug. 31, 1852; *The National Intelligencer*, June 10, 1852; *Committee of Investigation*, p. 407; "El Nacimiento," Informe, Primera Parte, pp. 328-337, Departamento Agrario; Agreement between the Mexican Government and the Chiefs of the Seminole, Mascogos, and Kickapoo, Saltillo, Aug. 18, 1852 (copy), M.R.; Vicente E. Manero, *Documentos interesantes sobre colonizazión* (Mexico, 1878), pp. 30-31.

[30] "Musqz. Mzo. 8 de 1852," M.R.

[31] Francisco Frucino, "Presido (*sic*) del Ayuntanto de Abasolo," to Muzquiz, Feb. 4, 1852, M. R.

[32] Interviews with Rosa Fay and Bill Daniels, Brackettville, 1942, 1943, and Julia Payne, Nacimiento, 1942.

[33] R. A. to "S. oficial 1º. de la Sria. del Supmo. Gobno. del Estado," May 31, July 5, 1852; N. B., Muzquiz, to the same, Oct. 4, 1852; Alcaldía to "Sr. oficial 1º.," Nov. 20, 1852; Alcaldía to "Sr. Juez Fiscal especial Capn. D. Doroteo Nava": M.R.

of freedom and the Mexicans spread out their arms to us.' "[34] John's attitude was not only ethically sound but also wise and far-seeing, as the Seminole Negro colony of Nacimiento, now almost a century old, exists to testify.

Some Mexicans found it difficult to distinguish the Seminole military colonists from the predatory Indians; as for the *indios bárbaros* they never distinguished between Mexican and Seminole, killing their cattle and stealing their horses with absolute impartiality. Early in 1852 the savages twice stole or killed animals belonging to Mexicans, Seminole Indians, and "Mascogos"; late in June an unnamed Negro, going out at night to look after his horse, encountered four or five "Cahiguas [Kiowa] of the Comanche (*sic*) tribe," one of whom promptly whipped an arrow into him, from which he died the following day.[35] When Wild Cat and John Horse had settled their followers at Nacimiento—the Indians at the head of the Sabinas, the most attractive but the most exposed position, and the Negroes near the hill of Buenavista—they undertook a retaliatory expedition against the Comanche. The Seminole received "the thanks of the government, which, however, ordered that, in future, expeditions should be accompanied by some Mexicans."[36] The order was intended both to prevent the Seminole from depredating and to protect them against unjust accusations.

The Mexican authorities were not altogether successful in their various attempts to utilize the Seminole's unique abilities in savage warfare while simultaneously keeping them under increasingly strict control. In 1854, the district government ordered that expeditions should not be undertaken without previous license and early in the following year the Seminole were further ordered not to deviate from their prescribed route! They do not seem to have taken these well-meant but finicking restrictions very seriously. Wild Cat and other chiefs, when sent out under the official command of Mexican officers, did not hesitate to disregard orders which they considered ill-advised. The language barrier contributed to this tendency. Gen. Guajardo commented that although both the Seminole and Mascogos were "always (*sic*) triumphant" on their expeditions, they followed their own customs and were not good subjects of military discipline.[37]

[34] Interview with Rosa Fay, 1942.

[35] To "Sor. ofil. 1⁰. del Supr. Gobierno de este Estado," Feb. 16, 1852; R. A. to "Sor. ofil. 1⁰. de Gobierno," Apr. 18, 1852; R.A., "Al mismo Sr.," July 5, 1852: M.R.

[36] *Committee of Investigation*, p. 409.

[37] Manuel Ramírez, Prefectura del Distrito de Monclova, Monclova to "Sr. Como. Municipal de Muzquiz," May 16, 1854 (124), Feb. 8, 1855 (18); Muzquiz, to R.M.

During the first four or five years of the Seminole's residence in Mexico their military activities assumed something of a pattern. They assisted citizens and troops in repelling and pursuing raiders; thirteen Seminole Indians and seven inhabitants of Muzquiz, in August, 1853, cut off and killed three out of five hostiles.[38] They undertook regular expeditions into the desert, usually after corn-planting, to search for the trails and encampments of the savages and to look for water-holes, streams, and favorable camp-sites. The Seminole received high praise for their activity, perseverance, and zeal in undertaking, early in 1853, an expedition into the Laguna de Jaco with four or five Mexican observers.[39] In the spring of 1854 two parties of Indians under Captains Cat and Coyote[40] set out against the Mescaleros and Comanche of Chihuahua.[41] In cases of considerable emergency they were mustered into service by state or federal authorities. They were thrice called to arms in August and September, 1854—the Indians under Wild Cat, the Negroes under either John Horse or his second-in-command John Kibbitts—twice because of an anticipated filibustering invasion, once to resist "the invasions of the barbarous Indians," but no encounters are recorded.[42] The Seminole were also summoned, though at long intervals, to accompany Mexican troops on large-scale expeditions into the desert.

The Seminole were compensated, in addition to land, principally through "beasts, booty, and pillage"; unbranded or unclaimed animals were usually awarded to the captors, while owners of recaptured branded animals ordinarily paid a "rescue shot" of two *pesos* a head.[43] When mustered into service by the govern-

---

"Sr. Prefecto del Distrito," June 5, 1854 (70); Ygnacio Galindo, Secretaría de Guerra del Ejército del Norte, Monterrey, to "Autoridad política de Santa Rosa," Mar. 7, 1856; T.T., Muzquiz, to "Sr. Srio. de Gobierno," Mar. 10, 1856; Manuel G. Rejón, Secretaría del Gobierno del Estado Libre y Soberano de Nuevo-León y Coahuila, Monterrey, to the "Sr. Alcalde 1°. de Muzquiz, July 19, 1860: M.R.; Apr. 23, 1856; Aug. 3, 1857: G.N.

[38] Muzquiz, to R. M., May 8, 1854 (62), M.R.

[39] Juzgado, No. 9, June 2 (1853), to "Sr. Prefecto," M.R.; June, Aug. 15, 1853, G.N.; *Committee of Investigation*, p. 409.

[40] Wild Cat, ordinarily referred to as *Gato del Monte* (Catamount), is also designated simply as Capitán Gato (Captain Cat). Coyote's Indian name presumably began with Yaha (wolf).

[41] To R.M., May 1, 1854 (54), M.R.

[42] Manuel Ramírez to Muzquiz, Aug. 3, 1854 (176), Sept. 3, 1854 (204); Franco. de Casteneda (*sic*), "Ayudo. de Inspn. de Coahuila," Villa de Rosas, to "Sor. Comisario Municipal de la Villa de Santa Rosa," Aug. 15, 1854 (186); T. Serapio Fragoso, Secretaría del Gobierno, Departamento de Coahuila, Saltillo, to Muzquiz Oct. 7, 1854 (229): M.R.

[43] Juzgado to "Sr. Prefecto," June 2 (1853); Salomé de la Garza, Muzquiz, to "Sr. Srio. del Gobo. del Estado," Oct. 13, 1856; Jesús Garza González, Secretaría del Gobierno del Estado Libre y Soberano Nuevo-Leon y Coahuila, Monterrey, Sept. 8, 1857, to Muzquiz (195); Sept. 3, 1858, "Al Prefecto de Monclova:" M.R.; Aug. 21, 1857, G.N.

ment, they were apparently paid at the same rate as national troops; the men on one occasion received two *reales* per day, the commanders, four.[44] The municipality of Muzquiz was sometimes called on to furnish money for rations; once the Seminole were "assisted with loaf-sugar and tobacco."[45] It was also customary during these compulsory absences to supply their families with money or beef.[46] The Seminole were on special occasions given—or at least promised—considerable bonuses both in money and in such goods as guns and ammunition, axes, blankets, and clothing.[47]

The Seminole removal to Nacimiento neither entirely relieved the anxiety of the United States authorities nor discouraged Texas slave-hunters. When Lieut. Duff C. Green of South Carolina, commanding a detachment of troops connected with the boundary survey, approached Nacimiento on Nov. 17, 1852, he was stopped twice, by Negroes and by Wild Cat himself, and commented indignantly on Wild Cat's "insolence" and the injury which the colony was to "the slave interests of Texas as runaways will always find a safe home."[48] John Horse at the time was visiting Piedras Negras where in a brawl at a *fandango* he was shot and wounded by a visiting Texan.[49] Capt. Adams hastened to the border and succeeded, probably with the help of some of the professional slave-hunters of Eagle Pass, in capturing the wounded man and bringing him over to the Texas side, handcuffed. Wild Cat was notified and agreed to ransom John for $500 in gold and the return of a dozen or so young Seminole Negroes. John was released on payment of the money and he and Wild Cat returned to Nacimiento, supposedly to round up the young Negroes, but an examination of the gold pieces by the post physician revealed that they were carefully—probably symbolically—stained with blood and Capt. Adams did not tarry longer.[50]

[44] Manuel Ramírez to Muzquiz, Aug. 3, 1854 (176); Andrés Mena, Monclova, to Muzquiz, May 20, 1855: M.R.

[45] Muzquiz to R.M., Aug. 6, 1854 (99); T. Serapio Fragoso to Muzquiz, May 18, 1855 (219); to "Corl. Dn. E. Langberg," Oct. 25, 1855: M.R.

[46] *La Patria*, July 12, 1851; to "Corl. Dn. E. Langberg," Oct. 25, 1855, M.R.

[47] Alcaldía, Muzquiz, to "Sr. Inspector y Comandte. grl. D.J.A. Jáuregui Ayuntamto," Nov. 21, 1852, M.R.

[48] Duff C. Green, 3rd Infantry, Camp near Ft. Duncan, to Col. T. S. Cooper, Adjt. Gen., Washington, Dec. 16, 1852, Headquarters of the Army Files, A.G.O., War Dep't, N.A.; A. B. Bender, "The Texas Frontier, 1848-1861," *Southwestern Historical Quarterly*, XXXVIII (Oct., 1934), 139. It was probably this incident which Giddings romanticized in *The Exiles of Florida*, pp. 336-337.

[49] *The Western Texan*, Nov. 18, Dec. 2, 1852.

[50] A.R.C.I.A., 1852, p. 103; Seminole File 1852-D223, I.O.N.A.; "Life of Jesse Sumpter, The Oldest Citizen of Eagle Pass," p. 26, Ms. (copy), U. of Texas; Interview with Sarah Daniels (ca. 1850-1950), Nacimiento, 1942.

John Horse already had a long score against Texas, to which
Wild Cat had just added an account for $500.   They probably
determined to strike a balance.   Late in 1853 and early in the following year the Seminole were accused of aggressions on Texas.   A
terrified *vaquero* testified that the Indians who drove off a herd
in February *must* have been Seminole because he had seen a Negro
among them.

These Indians ... [reported a second lieutenant at Fort Duncan]
have a bitter hatred for many ... residents of this side of the river. ...
The Seminoles crossed to this side and stole a large number of animals
in ... March; ... they went directly to San Fernando and in the presence of the authorities, civil and military, boasted of what they had
done, and publicly announced ... that ... they did this with the
knowledge and consent of General Cordona, of Coahuila, and that
he could not sell the animals again to their former owners because. ..
half was to be delivered to his excellency the governor. ...

Wild Cat's fame caused him to be credited with every immediately subsequent act of Indian hostility on the border, such
as the attack in May on a government wagon-train in which
several men were killed, although he and Captain Coyote with
most of their warriors were then on an expedition into Chihuahua.
Maj. Gen. Persifer F. Smith, commanding in that area, issued in
August, 1854, after a careful investigation, a report which rather
surprisingly but probably correctly exonerated the Seminole from
all responsibility for depredations since March.   He announced
sweepingly that "the number of Indians under Wild Cat has been
much over-rated and the intentions of his band misstated ... the
evil comes from the ... Lipans, ... stationed ... on the Nueces."[51]   Wild Cat had probably been guilty of one or more retaliatory raids on Texas, but had then considered the score settled.
He was far from wishing to become involved in conflict with
United States troops.

The accusations against the Seminole focussed attention upon
their numbers as well as their intentions.   During the mid-1850's
four descriptions, chiefly by army officers, estimated Wild Cat's
warriors after the desertion of the Kickapoo at from forty to
seventy Indians and from fifty to eighty Negroes.   The number
and status of the Negroes, so near a slave-holding state, were of

[51]"Indians—Creek and Seminole," pp. 3-9, *loc. cit.*; *The Texas Mercury* (Seguin), Dec·
24, 1853, May 6, 1854; *The Western Texan*, Apr. 13, May 18, 1854; "Ministerio de Guerra,
Preguntando al Comandante General de Coahuila si los Indios ... ," 1854, Archivo
de la Secretaría de Relaciones Exteriores, Mexico (12-1-11-0).

particular interest. "The warriors included between 50 and 60 negroes," wrote Col. Plympton, "who are on terms of perfect equality. . . . They are armed, and almost invariably accompany them [the Indians] in their depredating excursions. . . . One company, composed entirely of Indians, is commanded by Wild Cat; the other, made up of negroes only, . . . [is] under the command of a negro known as Gopher John." A "gentleman" who had lived near the Seminole settlement described the Negroes as "well armed and good fighters" and stated that although the warriors, Indian and Negro, totalled only about 120, "there are many more capable of bearing arms . . . in an emergency . . . an attack by five hundred men on the Seminole town would be successfully resisted"—perhaps a word to the wise among the slave-hunters and filibusters of Texas. The Negroes probably somewhat outnumbered the Indians, increasingly so as they were joined by Indian Negroes from the Territory or who had earlier settled in Mexico and by runaway slaves and free colored settlers from the United States; the Indian warriors, after 1851, probably did not increase except as boys and youths developed into men.[52]

Early in 1855, Wild Cat was for the first time involved in a disagreement with Mexican authorities. The trouble was connected with his original project of uniting under his leadership both the wild tribes of the southern plains and the more sedentary peoples. In the summer of 1854 both Mexican and United States authorities believed that he was allied with the Lipanes, who were at truce with Coahuila though at enmity with Tamaulipas. The Seminole had previously been engaged principally against the Comanche and Mescaleros, but Lipan attacks against the Seminole, while working in their fields or out hunting, soon contradicted the rumors of an alliance.[53]

Four Mescaleros of the Espejo band presented themselves to Wild Cat early in April, 1855, and said that they were weary of association with the Lipanes, whom they found "stupid and impertinent," and wished to unite with the Seminole. The Mexican authorities were favorable and ordered that they should be left

[52] "Indians—Creek and Seminole," pp. 4, 6, 11, 13, 14, *loc. cit.*; *The Texas State Times* (Austin), Oct. 5, 1855. Under the circumstances no accurate census could be taken and the estimates in consequence varied considerably. Complicated calculations indicate that when the Seminole were most numerous the Indian warriors numbered about fifty-five; the Negro fighting-men were probably somewhat, though only slightly, more numerous.

[53] "Indians—Creek and Seminole," p. 5, *loc. cit.*; Santos Abilez, Monclova, to Muzquiz, July 4, 1854 (154); Muzquiz to R.M., [July] 10, 1854 (88); July 17, 1854 (92, 93); Muzquiz to "Sor. Prefecto del Distrito," Aug. 14, 1854: M.R.

in peace while awaiting the arrival of other bands. Wild Cat, one would think, would have welcomed these recruits, but near the end of the month a Lipan reported that the Seminole chief and forty-four warriors had visited the Mescalero camp near the extinct *presidio* of La Babia, under the pretense of bartering for skins, and treacherously fired on them, killing several and capturing their entire horse-herd and other property. Wild Cat's own account was that when he and a few companions in pursuit of stolen horses arrived at the camp, the Mescalero warriors surrounded them in a menacing manner while the women and children began to withdraw. Wild Cat was therefore forced in self-defense to give the word to fire, which the Seminole marksmen did with such effect that they killed seven men, seven youths, and two women; they also seized three women, two little girls, a small boy, fifty-three animals, and all the baggage, which included a new foreign portmanteau and dried human hearts.[54]

The departmental authorities, confused by the conflicting accounts, ordered the booty to be held in "strict deposit" pursuant to a thorough investigation, but Wild Cat regretfully declined to deliver the horses as they were needed for deer-hunting and corn-planting.[55] When the governor of Coahuila the following month ordered fifty Seminole Indians and Negroes to report at Saltillo, Wild Cat again expressed regrets, on the grounds that his people were engaged in corn-planting and that the Mescaleros might take advantage of the absence of so many warriors to seek vengeance.[56]

Wild Cat may also have been both irritated at the government's suspicious attitude and reluctant to respond to a call which did not specify that his warriors were to be used against either wild Indians or filibusters. The following month, indeed, it was proposed that the Seminole be employed against "*los sublevados* of Nuevo Leon."[57] John Horse's behind-the-throne influence may have been influential here. The Negro chief is still remembered for his insistence on amity with all Mexicans and strict avoidance of involvement in civil conflict. "The Seminole would never fight with one bunch of Mexicans against another. 'Here we are,'

[54] [Muzquiz, *ca.* Apr. 9, 1855] (37); [between Apr. 9-16, 1855] (40); Francisco de Castaneda, Villa de Rosas, to Ayudantía de Inspección de Coahuila, Apr. 28, 1855 (46); to "Comisario," [*ca.* Apr. 30, 1855], (47): M.R.; Froebel, *op. cit.*, pp. 352-353, 462.

[55] Manuel Ramírez to Muzquiz, May 8, 1855; [Muzquiz], May 21, 1855: M.R.

[56] T. Serapio Fragoso to Muzquiz, May 18, 1855 (219); [Muzquiz], May 23, 1855: M.R.

[57] Cornelio San Miguel, Muzquiz, "Al S. Prefto. del Disto. de Monca.," June 19, 1855 (79), M.R.

John Horse would say, 'all living as in one house. How can I take up a gun and kill you, who are my brother, or how can I take up a gun for you and kill that other man, who is also my brother?' They would only fight the wild Indians"—to which might be added—"and the Texans." The Seminole in Florida were so greatly dependent on their Negroes for advice that it was often said: "The Negroes rule the Indians." The fiery and intelligent Wild Cat could not be compared in this respect with his indolent and stupid uncle, the head-chief Mikonopi, who was almost completely under the influence of his chief Negro Abraham, but army officers in the Territory nevertheless believed that Wild Cat was "strongly influenced by Gopher John, and others of the chief negroes." Mexican authorities, though less race-conscious than those of the United States, regarded the Indians as the dominant people and dealt with both Indians and Negroes through Wild Cat, but for a complete picture John Horse must be envisaged at Wild Cat's elbow and occasionally whispering in his ear.[58]

The Seminole were able, before 1855 was over, to redeem themselves from any official opprobrium for their slaughter of the Mescaleros or their refusal to muster at Saltillo. They had been called out twice the previous year to resist filibustering invasions which did not materialize, but such reports were not always false alarms. The three thousand runaway Negroes in Northern Mexico had not been forgotten. Citizens of San Antonio, on Aug. 25, offered to compensate Col. Langberg if he would give up such runaways and threatened direct action if he refused. The colonel agreeably proposed a reciprocal exchange of runaway slaves and fugitive *peones*, but word of the negotiations leaked out and led to opposition from the citizens of Coahuila.

The San Antonio gentry—and Marcellus DuVal—now turned to J. H. Callahan, a captain of Rangers with a reputation for ruthlessness in border warfare. Presumably, he was offered a share in any Negroes he might capture. Callahan left Bandera Pass on Sept. 4, supposedly in pursuit of Lipan raiders, but did not reach the Rio Grande until nearly a month later. On the way he was joined by a band of filibusters under W. R. Henry, a man of the same stripe as Warren Adams. The combined force of 111 men crossed over at Eagle Pass on Oct. 2. Another slaving party, it is said, slipped across the river in advance and struck

[58] Interview with Rosa Fay, 1942; K. W. Porter, "The Negro Abraham," *Florida Historical Quarterly*, XXV (July, 1946), 1-43, esp. 8-9, 13-15; "Indians—Creek and Seminole," p. 10, *loc. cit.*

out for Nacimiento. Perhaps the intention was to lie in wait until the warriors had been drawn off to resist Callahan, leaving the women and children almost defenseless. But Callahan's intentions had become pretty well known on both sides of the border and the Seminole were on their guard. The first party is said to have fallen into a Seminole ambush. Word of this debacle reached the Mexican authorities before Callahan crossed over and prepared them for the invasion.

When Callahan's force, on Oct. 3, marched toward San Fernando they were consequently met in battle by a superior number of Mexicans, suffered several casualties, and retired at nightfall to Piedras Negras, whence Callahan issued an excited proclamation—asserting that he had inflicted great slaughter upon 750 Mexicans, "Seminoles, Muscaleros, and Lipans" and calling on all Texans to come to his aid. The Seminole at the time of this proclamation were, as a matter of fact, just leaving Nacimiento to join the Mexicans at San Fernando. Had Wild Cat's warriors actually been in the battle the results might have been even more unhappy for the Texans. The Seminole were, however, soon among the besiegers of Piedras Negras, where the Rangers and filibusters found themselves trapped, confronted by increasing numbers of enemies and with retreat cut off by the rising waters of the Rio Grande. The raiders, according to a Texas historian, finally escaped by setting fire to the village and crossing the river under the cover of the flames—and of the guns of Fort Duncan. The burning—after plundering—of Piedras Negras caused Callahan's dismissal from the Ranger service, but he may not have been guilty of this specific offense as the Seminole Negroes have a tradition that their ancestors burned Piedras Negras over the Texans' heads, perhaps by fire-arrows, to force them out of the town.[59]

The border continued in a disturbed state into the following month, although all the plans of Callahan and associates eventually proved abortive and were abandoned. A party of Indians under Captains Cat and Coyote, "mounted, armed, and equipped," and of "Mascogos" under John Kibbitts, marched to

[59] To "Capn. D. Mig. Patino," [Oct. 3, 1855]; to "Sor. Corl. Dn. Emilio Langberg," Oct. 4, 1855: M.R.; "Claims of the State of Texas," 45 Cong., 2 sess., Sen. ex. doc. 10, pp. 106-116; Webb, *op. cit.*, p. 146; *Committee of Investigation*, pp. 191-194; "Memoirs of John Ford," *loc. cit.*, p. 793; Sumpter, *loc. cit.*, pp. 31-36; Foster, *op. cit.*, p. 45; *San Antonio Texan*, Oct. 11, 18, 25, 1855; *The Texas State Times*, Nov. 17, 1855; Olmsted, *op. cit.*, pp. 323-335; A. J. Sowell, *Rangers and Pioneers of Texas* (San Antonio, 1884), pp. 193-194.

Nava at Langberg's orders to oppose American volunteers, but six Negroes refused to march. Possibly they were reluctant to serve under Langberg, who next year was accused by responsible Mexican citizens of having tacitly encouraged the Callahan invasion; possibly they merely did not wish to leave their families. They were threatened with expulsion but the outcome is unknown.[60]

The alacrity with which the Seminole rallied to the defense of the Republic when confronted by an actual danger apparently caused all disagreements to be forgotten. The Mexican authorities expressed great pleasure at the end of the year at the conduct of their Negro and Indian military colonists whom they described as "industrious, warlike, and desirous of education and religious instruction for their families."[61]

The Seminole had been in Mexico for five and a half years. Frequent and drastic changes in the occupancy of the presidential palace had affected them little if at all, but near the end of 1855 the powerful Santiago Vidaurri, governor of Nuevo León, a strong-willed, unscrupulous man with an orderly mind and an organizing temperament, seized and annexed Coahuila and henceforth ruled both states as a virtually independent border principality.[62] Vidaurri recognized the Seminole's effectiveness as a border-defense corps and during his regime the state government afforded them greater and more regular assistance than ever before, but he also endeavored to subject them to a much stricter control.

Vidaurri manifested his concern for the Seminole's spiritual and material welfare, late in 1855 and early in 1856, by the appointment of an instructor in religion and agriculture, a teacher of reading and writing, and an armorer—all with appropriate salaries.[63] When the secretary of war in December, 1855, ordered Wild Cat and forty-five of his warriors to accompany Capt. Diego Elguezábal on an expedition into the Bolsón de Mapimi, Vidaurri's hand probably appears in such preparations as concentrating the remainder of the tribe on the ranch of Rafael Aldape for their protection, arranging to supply eight fat beeves for their support, and distributing tools, blankets, etc., worth over a thousand

---

[60] Emilio Langberg, Villa de Allende, to Muzquiz, Oct. 22, 1855 (115); to "Corl. E. Langberg," [Oct. 25, 1855]: M.R.; *La Patria*, May 17, 1856, quoted in Olmsted, *op. cit.*, p. 506. Froebel (*op. cit.*, p. 331) found Langberg a sympathetic character but Capt. James Hobbs (*Wild Life in the Far West* [Hartford, 1875], pp. 236-237, 279, 293-297) treats him as unscrupulous and shifty.

[61] *Committee of Investigation*, p. 410.

[62] "Santiago Vidaurri," *Americana*; *do.*, *International Encyclopedia*.

[63] Ignacio Galindo to Muzquiz, Nov. 27, 1855 (138); Jesús Garza González to Muzquiz, May 11, 1856 (190), May 24, 1856 (171), Dec. 18, 1857 (290), Jan. 19, 1858 (24): M.R.

pesos.[64] The order of two years earlier that Seminole infants—and possibly adults as well—should be baptized in the parish church, probably began really to be enforced.[65] Vidaurri, however, refused to accept the recommendation that the Seminole be granted full title to Nacimiento. Perhaps *El Caudillo del Norte* felt that they would be satisfied as long as they were permitted to occupy and cultivate their lands and that their lack of a title would serve as a means of control.[66]

The return of Capt. Elguezábal from his expedition inaugurated a furious triangular controversy in which Wild Cat appeared his old unregenerate, undisciplined, arrogant, and persuasive self. Capt. Elguezábal complained that Wild Cat abandoned him "precisely in the places of greatest danger." Wild Cat replied that he had turned off to follow "a very broad trail in the direction of San Vicente" but, being unable to find the Comanche whom he was pursuing, had touched at the Presidio de San Carlos where he found "the Mescaleros . . . in great harmony with those inhabitants," protected by the commandant so that they would remain at peace with the region under his care while continuing their raids on Coahuila. José Rodríguez, the commandant, counter-attacked rather feebly by accusing Wild Cat of having entered Chihuahua without a passport. Wild Cat further informed Vidaurri that the Seminole could not accompany Elguezábal because inadequately mounted and that the charge was maliciously intended as a pretext for their expulsion from Nacimiento. He seems to have satisfied Vidaurri,[67] but the governor obviously had his work cut out if he intended to reduce Wild Cat and his followers to military discipline.

[64] Muzquiz to Juan Nepomuceno Vidaurri, Dec. 21, 1855; Muzquiz to "Sor. Sectro. de la Comda. General de N. L. y Coahuila," Jan. 7, 1856; Muzquiz to "Sor. Srio. del Gono. de Coahuila," Jan. 11, 1856: M.R.; Dec. 12, 17, 1855, Jan. 7, 11, 1856, G. N.

[65] Juan N. Gonzáles, Secretaría del Gobierno del Departamento de Coahuila, to "Como. Municipal esta Villa," Dec. 7, 1853, M.R. John Horse (Juan Caballo) is referred to from late in 1856 as Capitán Juan de Diós Vidaurri (alias Caballo); probably Juan Nepomuceno Vidaurri, instructor in religion and agriculture, was his god-father. But however widespread Catholic baptism was among the Seminole, the effects were not very permanent; of 123 Seminole Negro males in a Mexican census of 1891 ("Lista de los negroes de la tribu Mascogo agraciada per el Gobierno General con terrenos de la Colonia del Nacimiento," [Num. 94, 1891, 44-12-60, Secretaría de Relaciones Exteriores]), all but seven were listed as Baptists.

[66] Langberg, Villa de Rosas, Nov. 11, 1855, No. 22, Jan. 12, 1856, Legajo 37 (1855), Vidaurri Papers, 1847-1878, Archivo de Nuevo León, Monterrey.

[67] T. T. to "Sr. Srio. de Gobierno," Mar. 10, May 5, 1856; Ygnacio Galindo to "Autoridad política de Santa Rosa," Mar. 7, 1856; Muzquiz to "Sr. Comandante militar de la frontera," Mar. 16, 1856, with copy of a letter from José Rodríguez, San Carlos, to "Sr. Comante. militar de la frontera de Coahuila," Feb. 19, 1856: M.R.; Apr. 23, 1856, G.N.

Vidaurri's ruthlessness and energy found expression early in 1856 in further measures for reorganizing and strengthening Coahuila's frontier defense. The Lipan Apache were more or less at peace with Coahuila, though raiding neighboring states, but even toward the Coahuiltecans they were mischievous and insolent and their depredations upon Texas furnished a pretext for retaliatory invasions. Vidaurri consequently ordered that they should be exterminated; in the first onslaught his troops captured more than a hundred Lipanes, including thirty warriors who were immediately put to death. The remainder of the tribe fled into the hills. Eighty Tonkawa fugitives from a Texas reservation, who had been put under Wild Cat's command in November, 1855, but had been transferred the following month to San Vicente, deserted and joined the fleeing Lipanes; probably they feared they were next on Vidaurri's black-list. Forty Seminole Indians and twelve Negroes were among the 160 men who for ten days in March scoured the country, seeking to hunt down the fugitives like wild beasts, but they returned without success.[68]

Vidaurri, having killed or driven into the hills the unreliable Lipanes and Tonkawa, turned to the project of recruiting trustworthy Indian military colonists. On April 30, 1856, he ordered the municipal authorities of Muzquiz to collect funds for a Mexican and Seminole delegation to the United States, "with the object of drawing to the Republic the remainder of the tribe . . . , . . . since this will have the advantage of increasing the population with industrious and warlike men" who will form "a barrier which will repress in part the incursions of the barbarians." Wild Cat designated as his representative "the Kickapoo Indian José María," indicating that he intended another attempt to bring at least a part of that warlike and comparatively well-disciplined tribe under his command. But, though by June arrangements had been completed, it is doubtful that the delegates proceeded to the Territory. The summer of 1856 would have been the poorest season since the removal from Florida to arouse discontent among the Seminole, for by a treaty of Aug. 7, 1856, the Seminole were finally recognized by the United States to be entirely independent of the Creeks.[69]

[68] Langberg, Villa de Rosas, Nov. 11, 1855, Legajo 37 (1855), Vidaurri Papers, 1847-1878, Archivo de Nuevo León, Monterrey; Pablo Espinosa, "1º. Como. militar de la frontera," Morelos, to Muzquiz, Mar. 20, Apr. 21, 1856; Muzquiz to "Sr. Srio. del Gobno de Coahuila," [Mar.] 24, 1856; T.T. to "Sr. Srio de Guerra," Apr. 7, 1856; M.R.; Apr. 7, 21, 1856, G.N.; "Indians—Creek and Seminole," pp. 4-5, *loc. cit.*; Olmsted, *op. cit.*, p. 292.

[69] Jesús Garza González to Muzquiz, Apr. 30, 1856 (122); "1ª. Autoridad de Sta. Rosa," June 16, 1856: M.R.; Apr. 25, 1856, G.N.; Foreman, *Five Civilized Tribes*, pp. 270-271.

The energetic and orderly Vidaurri also endeavored to define and settle the relations between the various Seminole Indian chiefs and between the Indians and the Negroes. No evidence of dissension appears prior to this attempt; Vidaurri's intervention may indeed have stirred up difficulties which had not previously been important. He ordered, on April 25, 1856, that the Seminole captain Coyote should continue to command "the part of the Indians who have always obeyed him" and be recognized as second chief, but only as subaltern to Wild Cat. The Negroes, particularly "certain Negro slaves, fugitives from the United States," were asserted to be "abandoning work and occupying themselves with theft and other excesses." They were ordered to be "subordinated to Captain Catamount" and the runaway slaves were exhorted to live honestly and industriously. The "Mascogos," however, "displayed that it was not convenient to them to subject themselves to Captain Cat, that they had always recognized Captain Horse as their superior, that in his absence they recognize Captain Cuffee (*Cofe*), that they protest unquestioning obedience to the *alcalde* whom they will punctually obey." They had appropriately instructed and threatened the other Negroes.

Vidaurri was not accustomed to such a reply and, on May 28, reiterated: "Gov. Vidaurri approves the election by the Mascogos Negroes . . . of John Horse as captain of that tribe; but . . . imposes on them as Supreme Chief of the two tribes, Mascogos and Seminole, Captain Catamount, as being a man more competent, understanding, and energetic for managing the two tribes, among whom there has been from time to time some dissension, the Negroes being vicious and of bad customs and the Seminole much more honorable men than the Negroes." Vidaurri, however, as a conciliatory gesture toward the chief of the stubborn Negroes, stressed the necessity of their being subject to "Captain Juan de Dios Vidaurri (a) Caballo to whom they will lend blind obedience" and ordered that the Negro captain should receive a cart, plow, and oxen, described as among "other assistances" to be afforded the "subjects of Captain Catamount."[70]

The situation described by Vidaurri can hardly be accepted at face-value. The statement that the Seminole Negroes were "abandoning work" contradicts all other testimony as to their conduct in Florida, the Indian Territory, and Mexico. Aged Seminole

---

[70] T.T. "Al mismo señor" ["Sr. Srio. del Gobierno"], May 19, June 1, 1856; Jesús Garza González to Muzquiz, May 24, 1856 (172), Nov. 27, 1856 (383): M.R.; April 9, 25, May 24, 1856, G.N.

Negroes speak of Wild Cat with affection and veneration as the unquestioned head-chief; possibly, however, his increasing addiction to intoxicants—he was about this time undergoing treatment at Monterrey for an unspecified illness—was incapacitating him for leadership and had caused the Negro chiefs to adopt a more independent attitude.[71] Runaway Negroes, without traditional respect for the chief and without a secure stake in the community, had probably behaved insubordinately and stolen cattle for food. But the "honorable" Seminole Indians were certainly no freer from charges of stealing cattle and horses than the "vicious" Negroes and the attempted contrast is rather amusing.

The presumption is strong that a campaign was under way to sow dissension between Indians and Negroes with the view of detaching one or both from Nacimiento and returning it to Mexican hands, now that the efforts of the Seminole had restored to the vicinity a comparatively high order of peace and safety. Wild Cat earlier in the year had charged that accusations against his people were intended to bring about their removal. *Divide et impera* may have been the new motto.

From early May to late September, 1856, the Seminole Indians, particularly Coyote, were unusually active. In late June and early July the entire body of Seminole Indian warriors set out in three parties to comb the country for the enemy, leaving the Indian women and children entirely unprotected except for the Negroes a league-and-a-half distant. The expedition, owing to sundry lacks in discipline and supplies, was without immediate results, but Coyote, returning from San Vicente to La Babia, observed trails and smokes which indicated the presence of Tonkawa cattle-thieves. He set out again with ten men, picked up the trails of horses and cattle, and followed them for twenty days, but an Indian spy they had captured escaped and warned the village so that only the twenty-five or thirty warriors were left to greet the Seminole. Despite the disparity in numbers, Coyote's party invested the village, which was on the Mexican bank of the Rio Grande, and kept up a fire from 10 A.M. until 5 P.M. Their ammunition was running low and they had killed four enemies, so they retired, taking with them eleven horses and other "pillage." The Muzquiz authorities gave Coyote high praise and the governor awarded him five of the unbranded horses.[72]

---

[71] Wild Cat's inordinate addiction to alcohol is only too thoroughly attested by contemporary sources. Uhde, *op. cit.*, pp. 330-331, presents merely one of the more detailed and startling accounts of his tastes.

[72] T.T. to the "Sr. Srio. de Gobierno," May 26, 1856; Jesús Garza González to Muzquiz,

The indefatigable Coyote almost immediately set out again with twenty men in pursuit of Comanche and "Caigua" raiders. Three of his company took ill and returned with ten whose horses had given out, but Coyote and his six remaining warriors kept to the trail. On the morning of Oct. 9 they caught sight of the enemy, got up to them while they were breakfasting, and poured in such a volley that out of thirteen only seven escaped, four of them badly wounded, one mortally. Coyote and company returned with six scalps, eight horses, and two mules, and, in addition to the usual reward, were given a contribution by the inhabitants of Muzquiz.[73]

These brilliant exploits were Coyote's last. Vidaurri, who was in rebellion against a central government which had refused to recognize his annexation of Coahuila, late in October ordered twenty Seminole Indians and fourteen Mascogo Negroes to march to Monterrey to join his Army of the North. Wild Cat was absent and the Negroes, true to John Horse's principle of amity with all Mexicans, refused to obey, "pretending that they had no wish to fight in political wars." "Capn. Juan de Dios Vidaurri (a) Caballo" and four other Negroes nevertheless set out for Monterrey in company with Coyote and twenty-one Indians, probably to explain his people's position. He apparently did so convincingly. The secretary of war, it is true, ordered that the "subjects of Captain Horse" should be reproved for their disobedience, "making them understand that our land being their adoptive country they are obliged like Mexicans to render profound respect to the public authorities and to obey their orders," but it was, nevertheless, sensibly decided that, "it not appearing convenient that this class of men take part in our political dissensions," they should instead be employed against the barbarians. This exemption also applied to the Indians and Coyote was, accordingly, ordered to scour the entrances and lurking-places of the enemy in the region of Parras while John Horse returned to Muzquiz.[74]

At the beginning of 1857 an enemy grimmer than Comanche raider or Texas slaver swooped down on the Seminole—*la viruela negra* or smallpox. First, it struck the bands of Coyote and Wild

June 2, 1856; T.T. "al Mismo Senor," July 7, 1856; [Muzquiz, between July 21 and 28, 1856]; S.G., Muzquiz, to "Sr. Srio. del Gobierno," Aug. 4, 1856; Salomé de Garza to "Sr Srio. Grra. del Ejército del Norte," Sept. 8, 1856: M.R.; May 5, 1856, G.N.

[73] Salomé de la Garza to "Sr. Srio. del Gobo. del Estado," Oct. 13, 27, 1856, M.R

[74] Bancroft, *Mexico*, V, 698-699; Teodocio Elizondo, Muzquiz, to "Sr. Tesorero Gral. del Estado," Nov. 5, 1856; the same to "Sr. Srio. del Gobierno," Nov. 5, 1856; Jesús Garza González to Muzquiz, Nov. 25, 1856: M.R.; Interview with Rosa Fay, 1942.

Cat, recently returned from expeditions and camped at Alto.
The plague then spread to Nacimiento and late in January the
panic-stricken Indians were fleeing into the hills in a vain search
for safety. By March the disease had spent itself among the
Indians, but twenty-eight women and twenty-five men had perished, including nineteen warriors and both Wild Cat and Coyote.
The Negroes were assailed next, "although," according to the
physician in charge, "they suffered less, being more regular in the
observance of curative methods and of the diet which the disease
demands"; hereditary resistance was in actuality probably more
significant. By the middle of March the pestilence was over and
the fugitives had returned to Nacimiento.[75] Its effects, however,
were far-reaching and permanent.

Nokosimala (Bear Leader), Wild Cat's kinsman and sometime
second-in-command, was passed over for succession to the chieftaincy because allegedly a better hunter than a war-chief. The
choice fell on "an honorable, brave, and active young man," named
León, or Lion, not previously known to fame. He remained, indeed, entirely undistinguished, particularly in comparison with
several Mexican-named sub-chiefs, Susano, Felipe, and Juan
Flores—or even with Nokosimala himself.[76]

The Seminole despite—or perhaps because of—their losses
undertook more expeditions than usual in 1857. A retaliatory
expedition early in the spring under Captain Horse and Juan
Flores against hostiles who had mortally wounded a traveler, resulted only in the capture of seven horses. During July and
August, however, the Seminole Indians under Susano and Felipe,
particularly the former, engaged in three actions against the
Lipanes, of whom they killed six, including a chief, and once
encountered the Comanche, wounding one; they captured over a
hundred horses and sixteen mules and received the usual reward,
as well as contributions in money and goods. Nokosimala and
thirty Seminole Indians, with seventeen Mexicans, retaliated in
December for the murder of four shepherds by a successful expedition against Lipan and Tonkawa *rancherías*. But the Mascogos,
it was complained, did not coöperate.[77]

[75] José María Jiménez, Rosas, to Muzquiz, Feb. 22, 1857 (55); Jesús Garza González
to Muzquiz, Feb 23, 1857 (54), Mar. 24, 1857 (77): M.R.; Jan. 20, Feb. 17, Sept. 6, 1857,
G.N.; *San Antonio Texan*, June 18, 1857; Interviews with Sarah Daniels and Rosa Fay,
1942; K. W. Porter, "Wild Cat's Death and Burial," *Chronicles of Oklahoma*, XXI (Mar.
1943), 41-43.
[76] Jesús Garza González to Muzquiz, Apr. 21, 1857 (149), M.R.; May 28, June 20,
1857, G.N.
[77] Jesús Garza González to Muzquiz, Mar. 25, 1857 (81), Apr. 21, 1857 (102), Sept.
8, 1857 (195), Dec. 27, 1857; Miguel Muzquiz Dávila, Muzquiz, Apr. 7, 1857: M.R.; July
8, Aug. 3, 8, 21, Sept. 8, Dec. 14, 1857, G.N.

The complaint concerning the Mascogos' noncoöperation was merely one charge in a controversy, centering in the Negroes and involving the Indians, the authorities of Muzquiz, and the state government, which had gotten under way in April, 1856, and continued at intervals until January, 1859.   The Seminole Indian chiefs complained that the Negroes had more horses and property than the Indians because they planted land and stayed at home to tend it instead of going out against the savages and that being "superior in number" they used more water than they were entitled to.   They requested that "the Negroes subject themselves to the care and command of the Seminole chiefs as they were previously under the command of the Cat."   The *alcalde* of Muzquiz charged that the Negroes, particularly runaways from the United States, did not respect private property and were accused of cattle-stealing.   The Indians were discontented and wanted to go to Mazatlán but if either tribe went it should be the Negroes, who were not so helpful, who stole, and who were the object of attack by Texans.   John Horse, on his part, complained that the authorities of Muzquiz did not supply his people with proper assistance for their campaigns.   The governor warned the Mascogo captain and his followers to respect property, avoid vice, devote themselves to labor and warfare against the savages, and to separate themselves from the ill-behaved Negro and quadroon runaways.   If, despite all warnings, the "Negros Mascogos" continued "their customary excesses," the guilty should be sent to Monterrey for condign punishment by labor on public works. He ordered that the tribes on their expeditions should be commanded by Mexicans, authorized the appointment of a Mexican police-judge to regulate land and water rights—and salved his reproofs somewhat by presenting Capt. Horse with forty-two *pesos* and a twenty-five-pound keg of gunpowder.[78]

The complaints against the Negroes—except possibly the accusation of cattle theft—turn out, upon analysis, to be largely baseless, trivial, or contradictory.   The Seminole Negroes, accused in 1856 of "abandoning work," were now blamed for their greater industry and prosperity; the latter "accusation" fits in with what we know of their character and conduct in Florida and

[78] Jesús Garza González to Muzquiz, Aug. 27, 1857 (183), Sept. 20, 1857 (225), Feb. 24, 1858 (93); "Al Prefecto de Monclova," Apr. 11, 1858; J. Felipe Ramón, Monclova, Sept. 3, 1858, with a copy of the complaint of the Seminole chiefs, Monterrey,,Aug. 29, 1858 (172); Ramón, Muzquiz, Prefectura del Distrito de Monclova, to Muzquiz, Sept. 13, 1858 (170), Mar. 14, 1859 (50), June 27, 1859: M.R.; July·20, Sept. 6, 28, 1857, Sept. 3, 1858, G.N.; *Committee of Investigation*, p. 409.

the Indian Territory. They were primarily farmers and stock-raisers and naturally objected to leaving their crops at inconvenient times in order to go on expeditions—as Wild Cat himself had objected; these objections would be strengthened if, as their captain claimed, Muzquiz did not supply sufficient ammunition and rations. The Indians, however, would rather fight than work; they were primarily hunters and warriors and strictly as mercenary troops were probably more useful than the Negroes. Sarah Daniels, the oldest Seminole Negro living in 1943, states that at the time of Wild Cat's death about half the Indians camped permanently at Alto, awaiting the call to go on an expedition and conveniently near the grog-shops. The Negroes, more numerous than the Indians and cultivating more land proportionately, probably used more water than previously and went on fewer expeditions, but the Indians' complaints sound as if put into their mouths by Mexicans. Disorderly runaways probably continued to be a problem so that the misconduct of a few strays was charged to the Negroes in general. Muzquiz did not always have such a low opinion of the "Mascogos"; early in 1859 the local authorities stated that "although among this tribe are some badly inclined young men, the majority are industrious, upright, and dedicated to labor." The Negroes had their roots much more deeply in the soil of the hacienda than the Indians and their removal was particularly important to those who sought to have Nacimiento returned to private hands. Vidaurri was, by 1857, involved in the War of the Reform on the liberal and constitutional side[79] and had little time for investigating the case of the Seminole; probably he was under the influence of interested parties whose views he accepted with little question.[80]

The Seminole had been proud that during the six years they had occupied Nacimiento, its immediate vicinity had been so safe that their families had been able to travel the ten or eleven leagues between it and Muzquiz unescorted, without the slightest accident from savages. This long period of immunity was broken at midnight, March 2, 1858, when savages, believed to be Mescaleros, carried off thirty horses belonging to the Negroes and six of the Indians'. Difficulties about water-rights were forgotten and the Indian and Negro warriors, good comrades again, vowed to follow the raiders even to the frontiers of Chihuahua. Twenty warriors of each tribe set out, under the promise of provisions for their families and supplied by the authorities of Muzquiz with ammuni-

[79] Bancroft, *Mexico*, V, 705, 746-747.   [80] Aug. 3, 1857, G.N.

tion and official documents.   They were under the nominal command of Ensign Jesús Castillo Morado and were accompanied by a sergeant and a soldier to avoid the confusion which might result from their ignorance of "the Castilian language."   For three weeks there was silence.   Then the Muzquiz authorities were able to announce "with unspeakable enthusiasm and satisfaction" that on the 18th the party had encountered the enemy on the bank of the Rio Grande and put them to utter rout, killing a warrior and a youth and capturing a prize greater than ever before in their history—not merely their own animals but also 70 horses and two mules, 71 Apache saddles, two carbines, three *chamales* [shields of buffalo-bull hide],[81] and seven quivers.   The only casualty suffered was an arrow-wound to "the valiant Seminole Juan Flores."   The governor highly praised this deed of arms by "warriors as valorous as expert" and ceded to them the captured animals.[82]

The triumphant Seminole expedition of March, 1858, was, however, the last of importance of which we have clear record. Their diminished numbers, lack of adequate general leadership, and the civil war then in progress, increasingly hampered their effectiveness.   A party of Indians and Negroes, who went out in September to scout the entrances of the savages, discovered a camp of about 140 enemies and offered, if reinforced by fifty additional men, to go out and attack them, but Muzquiz was completely out of ammunition.   The state government eventually dispatched fifty pounds of powder, authorized Muzquiz to purchase lead, and promised to furnish thirty horses, but, after nearly two months, the Seminole Indian, Juan Flores, appeared at the *alcaldía* with the "Mascogo" captain Felipe Sánchez and stated that the Indians were nearly all out hunting and only five of his warriors were available.[83]   The campaign was presumably abandoned.

The Seminole in Mexico had never lost touch with the Territory.   The achievement of Seminole independence of the Creeks in 1856 made the United States seem more attractive to the Indians, while the failure to receive full title to Nacimiento, the

[81] J. Frank Dobie, *Tongues of the Monte* (New York, 1935), pp. 243-246.

[82] To the "Prefecto de Monca" [Mar. 3 or 4, 1858], Mar. 6, 1858, [*ca.* Apr. 3, 1858]; Muzquiz to the "Prefecto de Rio Grande," Mar. 5, 1858; to the "Alférez Dn. Jesús Castillo," [Mar. 6 or 7, 1858]; Pablo Espinosa, Prefectura del Partido de Río Grande, Morelos, to Muzquiz, Mar. 9, 1858 (25); Ramón, Muzquiz, to Muzquiz, Apr. 8, 1858 (125): M.R.; *Committee of Investigation,* p. 327.

[83] Ramón, Muzquiz, to Muzquiz, Sept. 13, 1858 (171), Nov. 3, 1858 (220); to the "Prefecto de Monclova," Oct. 17, Nov. 7, 1858: M.R.

disputes over water-rights, and the civil war caused Mexico to appear less so. In the fall of 1858, a party of Seminole Indians, including "Kotza-fexico-chopko, or Long Tiger," "Parsakee," and "young Coacoochee, or Wild Cat," went on a visit to the United States and returned in January, 1859, with a son of "Parsakee," called "Pasaqui chico," and "an order from the chief of the Seminoles to bring the remnant of the tribe back to Arkansas."

The inhabitants of Muzquiz, anxious to retain these daring warriors, eagerly accepted an offer of the younger "Pasaqui" to go on an expedition if supplied with munitions, hoping that the Seminole might capture so much booty that they would decide to stay. The state government stressed the superior advantages of Mexico. But a charge of horse-stealing, which proved only too true, an investigation of a report that the Indians were planning an uprising, and the urgings of two foreigners that they should return to "Arkansas," combined to estrange the Seminole. The expedition was abandoned and preparations for departure were speeded. In February, 1859, "the Indians Tiger and Pasaqui" and their families, joined by "ten warriors, among them the captain of the tribe (Lion) and the valiant Juan Flores, with their families," fifty-one men, women, and children in all, set out for the Territory. They left behind twenty-two Indian fighting-men and sixty women and children, over whom Nokosimala at long last was recognized as chief.[84]

The departure of so many warriors seemed to serve as a signal for another period of filibustering alarms. Lieut. F. A. Washington, adjutant of the First Infantry, Fort Duncan, informed the *alcalde* of Piedras Negras in March, 1859, that filibusters were mustering near San Antonio intending to cross the Rio Grande and carry off the Negroes at Muzquiz. Merchants at Eagle Pass three months later notified the prefect of the Rio Grande district that another band of filibusters "under the command of Jemré," probably W. R. Henry, was preparing in San Antonio for a march on the frontier. State and local governments promptly rushed men and munitions to the border and the threatened invasions did not materialize.

[84] "Depredations on the Frontiers of Texas," p. 22, *loc. cit.*; *Committee of Investigation*, p. 410; *A.R.C.I.A.*, 1859, p. 328; Zenas R. Bliss, "Reminiscences," (Ms. copy) II, 50-51, U. of Texas; Maj. Gen. D. E. Twiggs, San Antonio, to Com. of Ind. Aff., Texas File T359, I.O.N.A., Twiggs to Col. S. Cooper, Washington, Texas File W726, *ibid.*; "Al Prefecto de Monclova," Jan. 29, 1859 (Feb. 12, 1859); Ramón, Muzquiz, to Muzquiz, Feb. 17, 1859 (27), Mar. 19, 1859 (54), Feb. 9, 1859 (2, 15), Feb. 24, 26, 1858 (1859): M.R.; Feb, 9, 17, 1859, G.N.

The former rumored invasion, however, drastically affected the position of the Seminole, particularly the Negroes. The foreigners who had been trying to get the Indians to leave Mexico had already been warned to desist. Only the general government, which had gone to great expense in furnishing them land, equipment, and instruction in reading, writing, and the Catholic religion, was entitled to permit their removal. One foreigner was ordered expelled on suspicion of communication with the filibusters. Even the Seminole Indians were suspected of complicity, although such suspicion proved to be based on nothing more substantial than accusations against three of the tribe by a notorious Seminole trouble-maker appropriately known as "Conepe" (Konip), or Skunk! (Complicity with filibusters was one accusation which the Negroes managed to escape!) A commission, sent to ascertain whether the Indians had any cause for discontent, gained the significant information that Doña Guadalupe Echaiz had been "indiscreet" in asserting a claim to part of Nacimiento. But the Indians, it was asserted, had been assured that they would never be removed without the consent of the supreme government and were again content and tranquil.[85]

The filibustering alarm's most important result was to furnish a pretext for the removal of the Seminole Negroes. The order from the Secretariat of Government of the state of Nuevo León and Coahuila, March 23, 1859, was couched in the most discreet and humane terms. Since the Negroes were the principal objective of filibustering invasions, they should be removed to Parras where, in safety, they would be supplied with lands, water, and other assistance and could aid "to repel the aggressions of the barbarians." The officials of Muzquiz were urged to recognize that this would be a means of saving "these unfortunates from becoming the prey of . . . certain soulless men . . . , . . . who, contrary to natural law, wish to traffic in their fellows, solely because of the difference in color"—and that the citizens of this and other frontier communities would be freed thereby from "the fatal

[85] Gregorio Galindo, Prefectura del Distrito de Rio Grande, Morelos, to Muzquiz, Mar. 6, 1859 (39), Mar. 8, 1859 (41); "Al Prefecto de Monclova," [ca. Mar. 8, 1859], June 4, 1859; J. Felipe Ramón, Mar. 9, 1859 (42); Prefectura del Distrito de Monclova [ca. Mar. 11, 1859] (45); J. Felipe Ramón to the "Sor. Srio. del Supmo. Gobn. del Estado de Nuevo León y Coahuila," Mar. 1, 1859 (46); Gregorio Galindo to "Sor. Srio. del Supmo. Gobno. del Estado," Mar. 13, 1859 (49); Miguel Blanco, Coronel en Gefe, Sección de Río Grande, Ejército del Norte, Piedras Negras, to "Sor. Srio. de Guerra del Ejército del Norte," Monterrey, Mar. 13, 1859; Ramón, Muzquiz, to Muzquiz, Mar. 7, 1859 (40), Mar. 15, 1859 (53), Mar. 17, 19, 31, 1859, Apr. 28, May 17, June 6, 1859 (115); S. de la Garza to the "Prefecto de Monclova," May 7, 1859: M.R.; Mar. 6, Apr. 28, 1859, G.N.

consequences of an invasion in which the laws of war would not be observed." They were further informed that "the citizens . . . know very well that the Negroes have not been beneficial to the country, that they have evil propensities which . . . they have not been able to correct"—a verdict as to their inutility which oddly conflicts with their intended use in resisting the wild Indians. The removal of the Negroes was apparently something which it was felt necessary to "sell" to Muzquiz, whose authorities the previous year had referred to "the very important services" which both the Indians and the Negroes "have lent and are lending to all the frontier, pursuing and skirmishing with the savages." Despite the primary reason alleged for the removal, it was probably a part of the campaign for clearing Nacimiento of both Indians and Negroes in order to make it available for private exploitation.[86]

The Negroes attempted no resistance, which would in any case have been futile. Although the Federal government alone was legally entitled to order their removal, the War of the Reform was raging, the reactionaries controlled Mexico City, and Vidaurri, who was supporting the Liberal president, Juárez, was too powerful to be offended. Perhaps John Horse accepted Vidaurri's explanations and promises at face-value and was glad to withdraw his people from a situation in which they were exposed not merely to the Texas menace but also to the hostility, however artifically provoked, of their Mexican neighbors and erstwhile Indian comrades. The first contingent of "Mascogos," numbering eighty or more persons, including two recent runaways, equipped with carts for their possessions, a scanty supply of ammunition, and a single beef for provisions, set out from Nacimiento on May 21, 1859, under the command of the Negro Felipe Alvarez.[87] The remainder probably departed by the end of the summer, leaving at Nacimiento only the diminished Indians.

Nokosimala early in April had marched with nine warriors as escort to a caravan proceeding to Chihuahua; in the following month they are said to have assisted in destroying a Comanche

[86] Ramón, Muzquiz, to Muzquiz, Mar. 31, 1859 (66), M.R.; Aug. 3, 1857, G.N.; *Committee of Investigation*, p. 410.

[87] Prefectura del Distrito de Monclova to Muzquiz (*ca.* Apr. 14. 1859) (78); Jesús Garza González to Muzquiz, [*ca.* Apr. 28, 1859] (92); "Al Prefecto de Monclova," May 21, 25, July 6. 7, 1859; "Al Alcalde de San Buenva," June 18, 1859; "Al Alca. 1°. de Rosas," June 13, 1859: M.R.; Mar. 4, Apr. 14, 1859, G.N.; "Notes by the late Gen'l John L. Bullis . . . ," *loc. cit.*; Foster, *op. cit.*, p. 43; Interviews with Dindie Factor, 1943, and Julia Payne, 1942, 1943.

camp and capturing more than a hundred horses.   On their return they reported having discovered in the desert "two villages of Mescaleros and Comanche in harmony, who had a great number of horses and much money and gold," but though Nokosimala in July, and again in August, requested and received "munitions and other necessaries" and scoured the country toward Chihuahua with as many as eighteen warriors, his expeditions had no known results—unless, perhaps, to arouse the savages against their pursuers.[88]

The pretext for the removal of the Negroes had been the danger of an attack by marauding Texans.   The absence of the Negroes so weakened the colony that the wild Indians seem to have felt the time was ripe for vengeance.   Early in 1860 a large body of savages was twice reported moving on Nacimiento; the usual defense-measures were organized but on the first occasion the attack did not materialize and on the second, though the enemy actually appeared and was pursued, results were not favorable, allegedly due to the Seminole's disobedience of orders.[89] The Negroes gone, the Indians had to bear the full brunt of Mexican criticism.

Dissension between Negroes and Indians and complaints by Mexicans against the Seminole were followed by dissension within the Indian community and Seminole complaints against Mexicans. Konip the Skunk complained to the governor that Chief Nokosimala had not been properly elected and that ten colored families were encroaching on the Seminole and taking their water and killing their hogs—much the same accusations that had been brought against the Seminole Negroes.   But the Indians "unanimously" denied these charges; they gladly acknowledged Nokosimala's authority, Wild Cat's son considering himself too little experienced for the chieftaincy, and the quadroons—worthy men who were a protection to the Seminole families when the men were on a campaign or out hunting—"lived in that hacienda by their full consent."   They declared the complainant to be a drunken brawler, liar, and fugitive from justice.[90]   One wonders

[88] "A la Prefectura de Monclova," [ca. May 25, 1859], June 4, July 7, Aug. 13, 1859; Jesús Elguezábal, Muzquiz, "Al Prefecto de Monclova," July 30, 1859: M.R.; July, Aug. 13, 1859, G.N.; Capt. George F. Price, Across the Continent with the Fifth Cavalry (New York, 1883).

[89] Muzquiz, "Al Juez Auxiliar de Policía del Buena Vista," Jan. 29, 1860; Muzquiz, "Al Capitancillo de los Seminoles," Jan. 29, 1860; "Al Srio. del Gobo. del Estado," Feb. 5, 19, 1860; "Al Alce. 1°. de Rosas," July 24, 1860; Manuel G. Rejón to Muzquiz, July 19, 1860: M.R.

[90] Manuel G. Rejón to Muzquiz, Oct. 15, 1860 (160); Muzquiz, "Al Srio.," Nov. 4, 1860: M.R.

how much of the dissension between the Indians and Negroes was the work of Konip and others of his stripe—and who and what lay behind it.

Not all the occupants of Nacimiento resided there by the "full consent" of the Seminole. Early in 1860 they complained that both strangers and residents of Muzquiz were using their land without consent or payment. Late in the year, several Indians appeared before the governor to state that they had been informed that Don Jacobo Sánchez Navarro claimed that he had never been compensated for Nacimiento and intended to sell it. The Seminole were assured: first, that they would *not* be deprived of their lands; and second, that if they *were*, "they would be given others as good or better." Then the Indians, who could hardly have been greatly satisfied by this highly equivocal reassurance, were promised valuable presents: two horses with saddles, fire arms, gunpowder, axes, spits, blankets—and an investigation of their request for oxen and plows.[91] It was pretty evident, despite official reassurances, that Sánchez Navarro was preparing to reclaim Nacimiento and that the Indians were being softened up for removal by presents and promises.

Vidaurri had no intention of forcing the Seminole entirely out of Coahuila. His plan, apparently, was to induce the Indians to transfer to some other part of Coahuila, such as the Apache-devastated Laguna where the Negroes were proving "very successful" as Indian fighters.[92] But he failed to realize that, whereas the Negroes could not return to the United States because of slavery, the Indians, if they left Nacimiento, would probably leave Mexico entirely.

By the end of March, 1861, twenty-two of the remaining Seminole, under pressure of invitations from kinsfolk in the Territory, or discouraged by the increasing menace of removal, had decided to leave Mexico; eight had decided to remain and had been rewarded with six yoke of oxen, three bushels of seed-corn, and a beef. But in July it was announced that since most if not all of Nacimiento belonged to Doña Guadalupe Echaiz—to whom presumably Sánchez Navarro had sold it—the few Indians remaining should either be removed or have their holdings correspondingly reduced. This sufficed to dislodge the remnant, though there is a tradition that the decisive factor was a message from

[91] To "El Srio. del Gobo. del Esto.," Feb. 25, 1860; Manuel G. Rejón to Muzquiz, Nov. 24, 1860 (184): M.R.

[92] James Pearson Newcomb, *History of Secession Times in Texas and Journal of Travel from Texas through Mexico to California* (San Francisco, 1863), pp. 14-15.

the Seminole chief John Jumper that they should return to take part in the Civil War, in which the Seminole were officially allied with the Confederacy.   In August, 1861, "the rest of the Seminoles went to Texas."   Confederate captain "Buck" Barry was ordered early in October to furnish an escort and rations to a hundred Seminole en route to Red River.[93] The history of the Seminole in Mexico was henceforth to be exclusively that of the Seminole Negroes— and that is another and less well-documented story, which, moreover, extends to the present time.

The value and importance of the Seminole Indians and Negroes to Coahuila, 1850-1861, are difficult to assess.   A statistical approach, though highly inadequate, is at least suggestive.   During about a decade on the border they participated in over forty campaigns, expeditions, mobilizations, and encounters of varying importance—eight against filibusters, the others against *los indios bárbaros*.   They clashed with the enemy about twenty times, twice with filibusters.   They are recorded as having captured at least 432 horses and mules and killed at least thirty-eight of the enemy without themselves losing a single warrior in battle.   They are frequently described merely as "giving battle," defeating the enemy—sometimes, it is added, with loss—or destroying their camps, or an expedition is referred to merely as "successful," so these casualties and damages represented the barest minimum.

These figures may appear insignificant, but the Indians who devastated Northern Mexico were not great warrior-nations, on the war-path primarily for adventure and prestige, but comparatively small tribes of but a few hundred warriors, raiding for horses and mules and captives in parties of a dozen or so or a few score at most, and yet terrorizing vast regions because of their mobility, savagery, and skill in arms, and the unarmed, disorganized, and unaggressive character of the population.[94] The Seminole—skilled horsemen, expert marksmen, seasoned warriors, excellent trailers, loyal to their engagements, ready to attack an enemy far superior

[93] Manuel G. Rejón to Muzquiz, Apr. 7, 21, 1861 (106); Galván, "Ofl. Myor," Secretaría de Gobierno, to Muzquiz, July 11, 1861: M.R.; Wm. C. Yeas, Adjt., Camp Colorado, Texas, to Capt. James B. Barry, Comdg., Camp Cooper, Folder 2, 1860-1862, James Buckner Barry, C.O., Ms. University of Texas; *Committee of Investigation*, p. 412; *A.R.C.-I.A.*, 1870, p. 328; Buck Barry, *A Texas Ranger and Frontiersman*, James K. Greer, ed. (Dallas, 1932), p. 142; Interview with C. C. Patten, Wewoka, Okla., 1942.

[94] A German traveler (Froebel, *op. cit.*, pp. 346-354) who spent some time in Northern Mexico in the early 1850's, gives examples of great individual courage on the part of Mexicans, particularly of the lower class, but emphasizes the lack of organization, arms, and leadership which laid the region in general open to and almost helpless before the attacks of the savages.

in numbers—were probably the most dangerous opponents who could have been mustered against these gangsters of the desert. When the Seminole appeared on the scene, the savages discovered that an initially successful raid might mean that they would be trailed relentlessly for weeks, over hundreds of miles, and at the end of the trail, when in apparent safety, lose both plunder and scalps in a surprise attack. Gen. Alberto Guajardo of course exaggerated when he referred to the Seminole, Indians and Negroes, as "always triumphant," but his exaggeration nevertheless indicates the impressiveness of their record, traditions of which still survive in the region of their principal activity. Thus, through the operations of no more than a hundred or so Seminole, raiding temporarily ceased to be such a safe, pleasurable, and attractive occupation and a large area of the frontier began to know a measure of peace and security. Unfortunately, however, the selfish interests of the Mexican claimants to Nacimiento weighed more heavily in the balance than the Seminole's value to the region and cost Coahuila their future service—except in the Laguna, where the Negroes continued to operate effectively for several years.

A decade after the last of the Seminole left Nacimiento—and a few years before a part of the Negroes returned—a Mexican author wrote: "Coahuila has been almost entirely abandoned to the hordes of savages that swarm over the plains and valleys of that distant territory."[95] The statement, of course, is exaggerated and a long period of civil war rather than the departure of the Seminole was doubtless the principal reason for the unfortunate condition which, whatever the exaggeration, certainly prevailed. Nevertheless, the contrast between the situation of Muzquiz in 1850, when the town was actually attacked by the savages, and the comparative freedom of its vicinity from depredations after the Seminole settlement is striking and suggests the considerable difference which the continued presence of the Seminole military colonists might have meant to the Coahuila frontier.

[95] Enrique Parmes, "Among the Mexican Mines," *The Southern Magazine*, X (Apr., 1872), 416-426.

Corrections and Additions

p. 437, bottom of page: Recently discovered documents indicate that Captain Adams captured John Horse in September, 1851, not in 1852, as stated in Jesse Sumpter's reminiscences (note 50). The circumstances of his capture must therefore be revised accordingly.

THE INDIAN TERRITORY
ca. 1825-1860

Scholars have given little special attention to the Negroes of the Indian Territory, although histories of the Territory and of Oklahoma and of the various Civilized Tribes, particularly the Seminole, Creek, and Cherokee Nations, usually deal to some extent with the Negro slaves, associates, or dependents of these tribes. "Relations Between Negroes and Indians" (pp. 42-44, 69-70, and 72) includes a few references to these Negroes. Grant Foreman, *The Five Civilized Tribes* (Norman, Oklahoma, 1934), is the best general account of these slaveholding Indians from their removal from east of the Mississippi to the Civil War, while Annie Heloise Abel stresses the Civil War period in *The Slaveholding Indians*, 3 vols. (Cleveland, 1915-1925). Angie Debo, *The Road to Disappearance* (Norman, Oklahoma, 1941), a history of the Creek Nation, gives more attention to the Creek Negroes than most historians of a Civilized Tribe have given to this element. Although a current work-in-progress, which I have tentatively entitled *O Freedom Over Me!: The Saga of John Horse and the Seminole Negroes in Florida, the Indian Territory, Coahuila, and Texas*, will deal with the Seminole Negroes from their removal from Florida to the Indian Territory, *ca.* 1838-1842, to the departure of the Wild Cat-John Horse band for Mexico in 1849-1850, this narrative will cover a period of only about a decade within the Indian Territory.

Interested scholars have almost a clear field before them so far as the history of the Negro in the Indian Territory — and, indeed, in the territory and state of Oklahoma — is concerned.

TEXAS, ca. 1825-1876

As part of a Mexican state, as an independent republic, and as a state of the United States again, Texas was — with the possible exception of the Indian Territory — the frontier region in which Negroes were relatively most numerous and important. Although no comprehensive account of Negroes on the various Texas frontiers is available, a number of scholarly articles treat particular major or minor aspects of Negro frontier activity in Texas.

"Negroes and Indians on the Texas Frontier," pp. 369-423, is a much more mature and better organized study, in detail and on a limited number of related frontiers, of the relations between Negroes and Indians, than that which the author attempted in more general terms in the articles on pp. 8-88 and 96-135. This analysis of the cultural factors conditioning the relations under frontier conditions between Negroes, both slave and free, on the one hand, and the various Texas Indian groups, on the other, also reveals the varied roles essayed by slaves and free Negroes in this important frontier region and their status in the larger white-dominated society. George R. Woolfolk, "Turner's Safety Valve and Free Negro Westward Migration," *Pacific Northwest Quarterly*, LVI (July, 1965), pp. 125-30, and *JNH*, L (July, 1965), pp. 185-97 (these simultaneous publications are essentially the same although with minor variations in language), applies the safety-valve theory to the movement of free Negroes into the Spanish borderlands, particularly of Texas, utilizing manuscript material in the Texas Archives. Harold Schoen, "The Free Negro in the Republic of Texas," *SWHQ*, XXXIX (April, 1936), pp. 292-308; XL (July, 1936), pp. 26-34; (October, 1936), pp. 85-113; (January, 1937), pp. 169-99; (April, 1937), pp. 267-89; XLI (July, 1937), pp. 83-108, a book-length monograph, should long since have been made more generally available through separate publication. Although limited in its coverage, as its title indicates, it effectively brings out the fashion in which, during the early days on almost any frontier (in this case that of Texas), Negroes tended to occupy a higher position than they did later on. Although subject to racial discrimination, free Negroes fought for the Republic of Texas, sometimes enjoyed considerable prosperity, and engaged in friendly conversation and correspondence with Sam Houston. There was a surprising amount of interracial marriage. Andrew Forest Muir, "The Free Negro in Jefferson and Orange Counties, Texas," *JNH*, XXV (April, 1950), pp. 183-206, supplements the Schoen study by examining in depth a particular family group of prosperous free Negro cattle-raisers in early Texas.

The extent of slave discontent and restlessness, whether on the frontier or in more settled regions, is a topic of persistent interest and controversy. Although, supposedly, only the most trustworthy Negroes were brought to the Texas frontier — exposed as it was both to Indian and to Mexican raids — nevertheless, from the beginning, Texas slaves manifested discontent which sometimes took the form of plotting the accumulation of arms in order to seize horses and escape to Mexico, in a fashion that had a precedent in South Carolina, a century earlier — substituting Spanish Florida for Mexico (see pp. 155-80). On the other hand, the proximity of Mexico also made it possible to attain freedom through flight by small groups, without the necessity of a previous mass uprising. Wendell G. Addington, "Slave Insurrections in Texas," *JNH*, XXXV (October, 1950), pp. 408-34, is the principal attempt to study this problem. It should, however, be used with caution. It is questionable that more than one or two of the episodes with which the author deals reached the point even of "an assemblage of three or more [slaves] with arms, with intent to obtain their liberty by force," which, the author states, was the legal definition of "insurrection" according to the Texas statutes; nearly all were no more, at most, than

plots or conspiracies. The supposed "insurrection," or plot, of
1860, would, in fact, seem to have had about as much validity as
the "Negro Plot" of 1741 in New York City; it was probably
concocted by pro-slavery extremists with the aim of whipping to
frenzy the existing anti-Republican, pro-secessionist sentiments.

The attempts of slaves to escape from, and across, Texas to
Mexico, regardless of the methods used, call loudly for comprehensive, scholarly treatment, material for which is abundantly
available in Texas newspapers and the Texas State Archives.

NORTHERN MEXICO, 1850-1861

The history of Negroes in Mexico, since they entered the country in 1519 with Cortez, is an important subject in itself. Negroes were a significant element in the northward-advancing Mexican frontier from the sixteenth century on. However, our primary interest is in the Negroes from the United States, who, in antebellum days, sought refuge from slavery and discrimination in northern Mexico. A possibly exaggerated estimate by a Texan is that in 1855 there were in northern Mexico 3,000 runaways from the United States. Certainly, at any rate, their numbers were substantial.

The only study, however, of any of these Negro frontiersmen is "The Seminole in Mexico," pp. 424-59; which concentrates on the Seminole Negro and Indian military colonists of the border during the short, although highly significant, period of 1850-1861. This article entirely supersedes the brief and superficial account on pp. 69-71. These Seminole Negroes, never numbering more than a few hundred, were far more important than the much more numerous runaways without Indian associations because they constituted a well-organized band of seasoned fighting men and during most of the period were allied with Wild Cat's formidable Seminole Indians.

"The Seminole in Mexico," however, leaves out of consideration the subsequent history in Mexico as frontiersmen and Indian-fighters of the Seminole Negroes — some of whose descendants are still living in Nacimiento, Coahuila — although I plan to deal with this subject at least up to 1882 in the projected "life and times" of the Seminole Negro chief John Horse, *O Freedom Over Me!*

The history of the Negroes of northern Mexico who were not

465

associated with the Seminole military colony is a wide-open subject, best undertaken in connection with the earlier-suggested
study of the movement of runaway slaves from Texas to Mexico.

THE CIVIL WAR, 1861-1865

The Civil War was the most important turning point in American Negro history. On its eve, slavery appeared a permanent institution of United States society; at its end, slavery was dead or dying. Thereafter, American Negroes, however handicapped by social discrimination and, in the declining years of the century, increasingly by state and municipal legislation, were at least legally free to move about, own property, establish families, and acquire an education.

An important but frequently disregarded contribution to the defeat of the Confederacy, with its avowed basis in human slavery and racial inequality, was what may properly be regarded as an uprising of southern Negro slaves, in support of the increasingly anti-slavery government of the United States. Before the war was won, over 200,000 Negroes — principally ex-slaves — in the armed forces of the Union had contributed to that result. This uprising was the culmination of similar movements of Negro slaves, going back well over a century, in support of whatever nation or people offered them an opportunity for freedom: the Spaniards in Florida (see pp. 155-80 and 183-203); the British during the Revolution and the War of 1812 (see pp. 205-236); various Indian tribes at enmity with the British colonies or, later, with the United States, particularly the Seminole Nation (pp. 183-356, *passim*); and, most recently, the free republic of Mexico (pp. 381-83, 387-88, and 425-59).

Negroes on the frontier were the first of their race to take up arms during the Civil War on behalf of the Union and their own freedom. The Negroes who were active on the frontier of the Civil War — that is, primarily in the Indian Territory, Missouri, Kansas, and Arkansas — belonged to two principal categories:

Negroes who were slaves of or associated with the Creek, Seminole, and Cherokee Indians; and runaway slaves from Missouri
and Arkansas who were enlisted in Kansas Negro regiments.

The first Negroes to participate in the Civil War were the two
or three hundred Indian Negroes among the Creek, Seminole,
and Cherokee Unionists who, during the last weeks of 1861,
fought their way north to Union territory, suffering terrible
hardships from cold, hunger, and Confederate harassment. In
Kansas these refugees were organized into Union regiments. A
few references to the activities of these Indian Negroes can be
found on pp. 73-75 and 121-22. A very brief account of the
Union Seminole and Creek participation in the Civil War appears
in Porter, "Billy Bowlegs (Holata Micco) in the Civil War," *FHQ*,
XLV (April, 1967), pp. 391-401; however, it should be noted
that, through careless editing of the author's manuscript, paragraph 2, p. 395, is grossly erroneous; it is corrected on p. 148
of the October, 1967 issue (Vol. XLVI) of *FHQ*. Wiley Britton,
The Union Indian Brigade in the Civil War (Kansas City, Missouri, 1922), is the fullest — and probably, indeed, the only extended — treatment of this special topic; since Creek, Seminole,
and Cherokee Negroes served in the Union Indian regiments on
equal terms with the Indians; when one reads of an action in
which Union Indians were involved one should envisage black
as well as brown faces in the ranks. Moreover, Indian and Kansas Negro units frequently served together, so that this volume
also has a good deal to say about Negro regiments.

Although what is officially recognized as the first regiment of
freed slaves in the Union Army — the First South Carolina Volunteers — was mustered into service in November, 1862, Kansas
Negro troops during the previous month were actually engaged
against Confederate irregulars on the Missouri border. A brief
account of the Kansas Negro troops appears in Dudley Taylor
Cornish, "Kansas Negro Regiments in the Civil War," *KHQ*, XX
(May, 1953), pp. 417-29. See also Albert Castel, "Civil War
Kansas and the Negro," *JNH*, LI (April, 1966), pp. 125-38. For

a brief, clear account of one of the most important — and disastrous — actions in which Kansas Negro troops were involved, see Ira Don Richards, "The Battle of Poison Spring," *Arkansas Historical Quarterly*, XVIII (Winter, 1959), pp. 338-49.

Other works with information about Negroes on the Civil War frontier fall into two main categories: general histories of Negro participation in the Civil War; and general histories of border warfare.

The best and most recent full-length accounts of Negro troops in the Civil War are Benjamin Quarles, *The Negro in the Civil War* (Boston, 1953); and Dudley Taylor Cornish, *The Sable Arm* (New York, 1956), both of which have a good deal to say about Negro troops in the West — Cornish a great deal.

Wiley Britton, *The Civil War on the Border*, 2 vols. (New York and London, 1904), is a general treatment, as is his *Memoirs of the Rebellion on the Border, 1863* (Chicago, 1882), although the latter is, of course, limited in its time span. Jay Monaghan, *Civil War on the Western Border, 1854-1863* (Boston, 1955), is the most recent general account from the Union viewpoint. Albert E. Castel, *A Frontier State at War: Kansas, 1861-1865* (Cornell, 1958), is also useful in its more limited way. Richard S. Brownlee, *Gray Ghosts of the Confederacy; Guerrilla Warfare in the West, 1861-1865* (Baton Rouge, 1958), treats the subject from a Confederate viewpoint.

THE INDIAN-FIGHTING ARMY
1866-1890

After the Civil War, the army of the United States was reduced to a permanent peacetime establishment of ten cavalry and twenty-five infantry regiments, primarily for service against the hostile Indians of the Western plains, deserts, and mountains. Of these, the Ninth and Tenth Cavalry and the Twenty-fourth and Twenty-fifth Infantry consisted of Negro privates and non-coms under white officers. For a quarter-century these regiments served without intermission against hostile Cheyenne, Comanche, Kiowa, Apache and Utes, and against Mexican outlaws and border desperadoes, taking part in nearly 200 engagements, major and minor. More than once detachments from these regiments came to the aid of white troops in desperate straits. For months and years at a time the garrisons of many frontier posts consisted of detachments from Negro regiments and their white officers. The campaigns against the Apache chiefs Victorio and Nana — more important actually than those against the more publicized Geronimo — were conducted almost entirely by Negro troopers. The quality of their service is indicated by the fact that during 1870-1890 fourteen Negro soldiers won the prestigious Medal of Honor, while several others received Certificates of Merit.

A principal problem in coping with the hostile Indians, particularly those in the southwest, who often operated in small bands of hit-and-run raiders, was in following their trails and locating their camps so as to bring them to action. Expert scouts — Indian, white, and Negro — were indispensable. The most effective scouting organization in the United States army was enlisted from the Seminole Negro military colonists of northern Mexico (see pp. 425-59). Operating both independently and in connection

470

with detachments from Negro and white regiments, they are given major credit for having finally freed West Texas from Indian raids. Although they never at any one time numbered more than fifty, no less than four won the coveted Medal of Honor. Their operations during the dozen years of their greatest activity are dealt with in the article that follows. Before being disbanded in 1914, however, they had another generation of more routine activity on the Texas-Mexican border, principally against bandits and horse thieves, which might be worth investigation. "The Seminole Negro-Indian Scouts, 1870-1881" originally appeared in the *Southwestern Historical Quarterly* January, 1952 (Vol. LVI, No. 3).

THE SEMINOLE NEGRO-INDIAN SCOUTS
1870-1881

THE Seminole Negro-Indian Scouts never at any time mustered more than fifty men but, operating on both sides of the Rio Grande during the Indian fighting period of the 1870's and early 1880's, were effective far out of proportion to their numbers. Although frequently referred to merely as "Indian scouts" and "Seminole scouts," their official designation was a more accurate, if somewhat cumbrous, description.

Although a good many were undoubtedly of part-Indian ancestry, the scouts were hardly distinguishable racially from the soldiers of the colored infantry and cavalry regiments with whom they frequently served[1] and with whom they shared some of the distinctive cultural traits of the southern Negro. The older men, at least, spoke a broken plantation English, sometimes with a Gullah twang. Despite twenty years' residence in Catholic Mexico, young as well as old were mostly staunch Baptists. The older Seminole who had been brought up in the United States wore their native garb by preference and spoke Hitchiti or Muskogee. Some had achieved such a blending of the two principal elements of their culture that in their Baptist praisehouses they even prayed in "Injun."[2] What was most important as frontier scouts, whether born in Florida, Alabama, the Indian Territory, or Mexico, all were Indian in their trailing, hunting, and fighting skills. Their Indianism, however, was not that of the wild, nomadic, predatory Comanche and Apache but rather that of the sedentary, semi-civilized Seminole and Creek, with whom hunt-

---

[1]Melville J. Herskovits has pointed out that Negroes have "mingled with the American Indians on a scale hitherto unrealized." Approximately one-third of the general Negro population in the United States, according to samplings, are of partial Indian ancestry.—*The American Negro* (New York, 1928), 3, 9, 16.

[2]Dindie Factor (*ca* 1874-   ), personal interview, Nacimiento, Coahuila, 1943. Factor is the son of Scout Pompey Factor and the grandson of Scout Hardy Factor; his grandmother was a Biloxi.

ing was subordinate to stock raising and farming and who usually took the warpath only in self-defense.

How the Seminole Negroes came to be available for service as United States scouts is a long story. Their ancestors were for the most part runaway slaves who had taken refuge among the Florida Seminole. Though referred to by some white observers as slaves to the Indians, General Edmund P. Gaines described them more accurately as "vassals and allies." They lived in separate villages; had their own fields, flocks, and herds; habitually carried arms; went into battle under their own captains; and, except for an annual tribute in corn to the chiefs who were their protectors, were as free as the Indians themselves. In fact, their knowledge of the English language and of the white man's ways and their superior industry and prosperity gave them such influence that some observers styled them the real rulers of the Seminole nation.[3] They took a leading part in the resistance to the annexation of Florida and to the Seminole removal[4] but were finally transported, along with the Indians, to the Indian Territory,[5] where they were exposed to the danger of kidnapping by whites and Creeks.[6]

[3]For discussions of relations between Seminole Indians and Negroes in Florida, see [William Hayne Simmons], *Notices of East Florida* (Charleston, 1822), 44-45, 50, 76; George A. McCall, *Letters from the Frontiers* (Philadelphia, 1868), 160; Jedidiah Morse, *A Report to the Secretary of War on Indian Affairs* (New Haven, 1822), 149-150, 309-311; John Lee Williams, *The Territory of Florida* (New York, 1837), 214; William Kennedy, *Texas, Its Rise, Progress and Prospects* (2 vols.; London, 1841), I, 350; *American State Papers: Documents, Legislative and Executive, of the Congress of the United States, from the First Session of the Fourteenth to the Second Session of the Nineteenth Congress, Inclusive, Commencing December 4, 1815, and Ending March 3, 1827; Class II, Indian Affairs, Volume II* (Washington, 1834), 412; *American State Papers: Documents, Legislative and Executive, of the Congress of the United States, from the First and Second Sessions of the Twenty-fourth Congress, Commencing January 12, 1836, and Ending February 25, 1837; Military Affairs, Volume VI* (Washington, 1861), 465, 533-534.

[4]John T. Sprague, *The Origin, Progress, and Conclusion of the Florida War* (New York, 1848), 81, 100, 166, 309; *Army and Navy Chronicle*, IV, 12, 80, quoting from New Orleans *Bulletin*, January 7, 1837; Lieutenant Colonel W. S. Harney, Fort Mellon, East Florida, to Major General T. S. Jessup, dated May 4, 1837 (photostat in possession of Florida Historical Society, St. Augustine); journal of Captain J. Rhett Motte (MS. in possession of Florida Historical Society), 255.

[5]See appropriate sections in Grant Foreman, *Indian Removal* (Norman, 1932) and *The Five Civilized Tribes* (Norman, 1934).

[6]Documentary material on the kidnapping of Seminole Negroes is to be found in the Seminole Files, Indian Office, Department of the Interior, National Archives, Washington, D. C., and in the Quartermaster General's Office, War Department

Many Seminole Indians were also disgusted with the Creek domination to which they were subjected, and in 1849 and 1850 several hundred Seminole Indians and Negroes, under the command of the Indian chief Wild Cat and the Negro chief John Horse, crossed to Mexico and were settled on the border as military colonists, where they did good service against Indians and Texas filibusters.[7]

The Indians returned to the United States following Wild Cat's death in 1857; because of slavery, the Negroes stayed in Mexico and were joined by other Seminole, Creek, and Cherokee Negroes and also by runaway slaves, free Negro settlers, and refugee Biloxi Indians. The need for their services against hostile Indians, the disturbed situation of Mexico, and the abolition of slavery in the United States resulted in the Seminole Negroes becoming scattered. By 1870 head chief John Horse and the main body of 150 Negroes were in Laguna de Parras in southwestern Coahuila; John Kibbitts, the second-in-command, and one hundred others were at Nacimiento, Coahuila, not far from Eagle Pass, Texas; several families were at Matamoros across from Brownsville, Texas; and a band of Creek Negroes under Elijah Daniel were on the Nueces River in Uvalde County, Texas.[8]

The Comanche and Apache Indians, who had long been making raids into the United States from bases in Mexico and vice versa, had been emboldened in their expeditions into Texas by the

National Archives. See also Grant Foreman, *Pioneer Days in the Early Southwest* (Cleveland, 1926), 174, and Grant Foreman, *Advancing the Frontier* (Norman, 1933), 69.

[7]The history of the Seminole Indians and Negroes in Mexico is treated in the author's "The Seminole in Mexico, 1850-1861," *Hispanic-American Historical Review*, XXXI, 1-36. The chief printed sources on the flight of the Seminole from the United States and their Indian-fighting activities in Mexico are: "Indians—Creek and Seminole," *House Executive Documents*, 33d Cong., 2d Sess., No. 15; *Reports of the Committee of Investigation Sent in 1873 by the Mexican Government to the Frontier of Texas* (New York, 1875), 188-194, 303-304, 327, 331, 407-412.

[8]*Annual Report of the Commissioner of Indian Affairs to the Secretary of the Interior for the Year 1870* (Washington, 1870), 328-329; Ninth United States Census (1870), Population Schedule, Texas, Uvalde County (microfilm, Archives Collection, University of Texas Library); Rosa Fay (ca 1860-   ), widow of Scout Adam Fay and sister of Scout Joe Dixey (Dixon), personal interview, Brackettville, Texas, 1942; John Jefferson (1879-   ), former scout and also former sergeant in the 10th Cavalry, son of Scout Joe Coon and grandson of Chief John Horse, personal interview, Del Rio, Texas, 1941; Bill Daniels (ca 1868-1950), son of Sergeant Elijah Daniel, Creek Negro band chieftain, and brother of Scout John Daniels, personal interview, 1942.

abandonment of many of the frontier posts during the Civil War. Even after the re-occupation of these forts the raids continued. Parties of Indians would stealthily cross the Rio Grande on foot, conceal themselves, and wait for the full moon to give them light enough for their operations, which consisted principally of rounding up horses and cattle and driving them across the river but which readily included murder and arson if the opportunity presented itself. The officers commanding posts on the border were rarely able to detect or intercept these thieves and murderers either in their comings or goings, so skillful were they in concealing their tracks.[9] Scouts were desperately needed, but a few Tonkawa and renegade Lipans were the only ones available.

The Seminole Negroes at Nacimiento in the meantime were becoming discontented with Mexico and wanted to return to the Indian Territory. Major Zenas R. Bliss of the 25th United States Cavalry (colored), commanding at Fort Duncan, authorized Captain Frank W. Perry to visit Nacimiento and invite the Seminole Negroes to return to the United States to serve as scouts. The Seminole's understanding of the agreement finally arrived at between Captain Perry and John Kibbitts, which the Negroes call "de treaty" or sometimes "de treatment," was that it provided that the government would pay the able-bodied men's expenses to the United States and would furnish them pay, provisions for their families, and grants of land in return for their services as scouts.[10] If the agreement was ever reduced to writing, it has long since disappeared.

---

[9]Numerous similarly-named government documents of this general period, as well as of the pre-Civil War period, deal with Indian depredations on the Texas frontier. One of the most informative is "Texas Frontier Troubles," *House Report*, 45th Cong., 2d Sess., III, No. 701, especially pp. 31-35. Others are: "Depredations on the Frontiers of Texas," *House Executive Documents*, 42d Cong., 3d Sess., VII No. 39; *ibid.*, 43d Cong., 1st Sess., XVII, No. 257. Still others will be cited in connection with activities of the Seminole scouts in thwarting or punishing these raids. J. Frank Dobie, *Tongues of the Monte* (New York, 1935), pp. 243-246 graphically epitomizes the Comanche raids.
[10]Deposition No. 545, John Kibbets, in "Depredations on the Frontiers of Texas," *House Executive Documents*, 43d Cong., 1st Sess., XVII, No. 257, p. 22; "Texa Frontier Troubles," *House Report*, 45th Cong., 2d Sess., III, No. 701, p. 224; Captain J. D. De Gress, Fort Duncan, to Brevet Brigadier General H. Clay Wood assistant adjutant general, dated March 17, 1870 (MS., Adjutant General's Office 488M, War Department, National Archives, Washington, D. C.); F. H. French second lieutenant, 19th Infantry, Fort Clark, to Adjutant General, Department o Texas, San Antonio, dated May 23, 1883 (MS., Seminole File 1882-11398, India)

The Kibbitts band crossed over to Fort Duncan on July 4, 1870.[11] A month later, on August 16, the first contingent of scouts —Sergeant John Kibbitts, also known by the Seminole name of Sit-tee-tas-to-nachy (Snake Warrior),[12] and ten privates—were enlisted for six months at the pay of cavalry soldiers.[13] The duties of the Seminole Negro-Indian scouts during their first two or three years were largely of a routine nature. Recruiting was a principal activity. During the summer and fall of 1871, twenty scouts were enlisted from Elijah Daniel's band and the Matamoros families; most of these were transferred to Fort Clark, near Brackettville, Texas, the following summer and were soon joined by several others.[14] During the latter part of 1872 and the spring of 1873, a dozen or so recruits, mostly Seminole from John Horse's Laguna band, were enlisted at Fort Duncan.[15] Half

Office, Department of the Interior, National Archives); Lieutenant Colonel Z. R. Bliss, Fort Clark, to Adjutant General, Department of Texas, dated August 26, 1884 (MS., Seminole File 1884-18287, Indian Office, Department of the Interior, National Archives); *Report of Commissioner of Indian Affairs, 1870*, 328-329; *Report of Committee of Investigation*, 415; Notes by the late General John L. Bullis, U. S. Army, Commanded the Scouts from '72 to '81 (MS., General Service Files 123-14308-1914, Indian Affairs, National Archives); J. H. Bliss, assistant secretary, Committee on Indian Affairs, Public Lands, to the Commissioner of Indian Affairs, dated August 18, 1932 (MS., Indian Affairs Office, Department of the Interior, National Archives); Laurence Foster, *Negro-Indian Relationships in the Southeast* (Philadelphia, 1930), 46; Julia Payne (*ca* 1862-1946), step-granddaughter of Sergeant John Kibbitts and widow of Scout Isaac Payne, personal interview, Nacimiento, Coahuila, 1944; Curley Jefferson (1881-   ), former scout, personal interview, Del Rio, Texas, 1941; John Jefferson, personal interview, 1941.

11Dolly July (1870-   ), daughter of Sergeant John Ward (Warrior) and widow of Scout Billy July, personal interview, Brackettville, Texas, 1941; John Jefferson to K. W. P., 1948 (letter in possession of author).

12Useful sources of information on the Seminole scouts are the Monthly Reports, 1870-1881, and the Enlistment Records, Seminole Negro-Indian Scouts (MSS., Adjutant General's Office, War Department, National Archives). See also Ninth United States Census (1870), Population Schedule, Texas, Maverick and Uvalde counties (microfilm); Tenth United States Census (1880), Population Schedule, Texas, Kinney County (National Archives).

13*Report of Commissioner of Indian Affairs*, 328-329; Notes by General Bullis (MS.).

14Major Henry C. Merriam, Fort Duncan, to the Commanding Officer, Fort Clark, dated July 8, 1872, and August 5, 1872; Special Orders No. 96, 2d Lieutenant H. F. Leggett, 24th Infantry, post adjutant, Fort Duncan, dated August 3, 1872, in Memoranda relative to Seminole Negro Indians, Military Division of Missouri, dated August 5, 1872 (MSS., War Department, National Archives). Rebecca Wilson, daughter of Sergeant Sampson July, niece of Chief John Horse, and wife of Scout Bill Wilson, Brackettville, Texas, 1941.

15Major Henry C. Merriam, Fort Duncan, to Assistant Adjutant General, Department of Texas, dated August 5, 1872, in Memoranda relative to Seminole Negro Indians (MS.).

a dozen of the recruits, however, were apparently either Texas Negroes who had intermarried with Seminole and Creek women or were time-expired soldiers from colored regiments.[16]

The Seminole scouts were supplied by the government with arms, ammunition, and rations. They were equipped at first with Spencer carbines, for which Sharps carbines were soon substituted[17]—a welcome exchange for the old muzzle-loaders of their Mexican days.[18] The scouts furnished their own horses, for which they received compensation, and seem to have dressed in a modified Indian style. Their appearance and manner were probably a source of exasperation to young officers brought up in the spit-and-polish West Point tradition. One report reads: "Discipline, Fair; Instruction, Progressive; Military Appearance, Very Poor; Arms, Spencer Carbines—Good; Accoutrements, Good; Clothing, Fair." Another report concludes: "Clothing, Good enough for Indians." Some, indeed, were so Indian that they sported buffalo-horn war-bonnets.[19]

The scouts had not, however, been employed as military fashion plates. Major Bliss described them as "excellent hunters, and trailers, and brave scouts ... splendid fighters."[20] Their trailing skill in particular was almost uncanny.[21] Conspicuous among their other useful qualities were the lack of any language barrier between their officers and themselves, their ability to speak the "Mexican" which was the *lingua franca* of the border,[22]

---

[16]Ninth United States Census (1870), Population Schedule, Texas, Maverick and Uvalde counties (microfilm).

[17]Frank D. Reeve (ed.), "Frederick E. Phelps: A Soldier's Memoirs," *New Mexico Historical Review*, XXV, 113; W. C. Parker, first lieutenant and adjutant, 4th Cavalry, Fort Clark, to Lieutenant J. L. Bullis, dated July 10, 1873 (MS., in possession of General Bullis' daughter, Mrs. W. S. Halcomb of San Antonio, Texas).

[18]Bill Daniels, personal interview, Brackettville, Texas, 1943; Adam McClain (?-1950), former scout, personal interview, Brackettville, 1943.

[19]Henry W. Strong, *My Frontier Days and Indian Fights on the Plains of Texas* (n. p., n. d.), 51-53; Curley Jefferson, personal interview, 1941; Penny Factor (1874-   ), daughter of Scout Ben Wilson, Sr., personal interview, Brackettville, Texas, 1943.

[20]Zenas R. Bliss, Reminiscences (typescript, University of Texas Library), V, 106-109.

[21]*Ibid.*, 126-127; Mrs. Orsemus Bronson Boyd, *Cavalry Life in Tent and Field* (New York, 1894), 336-337.

[22]This statement concerning the scouts' linguistic ability is contradicted, so far as English is concerned, from two quarters. A former Negro cavalryman, Jacob Wilks

their knowledge of the country and of the ways of the Indians against whom they were operating, and their thorough dependability.

The Seminole scouts in the spring of 1873 were about to begin nearly a decade of fierce border warfare under an officer exceptionally well-qualified for such a command. Lieutenant John Lapham Bullis had entered the service in 1862 at the age of twenty-one as a corporal of the 126th New York Volunteer Infantry and in 1864 had been commissioned a captain in a Negro infantry regiment. He had been mustered out in 1866 but had re-enlisted the following year as a second lieutenant; two years later he had been transferred to the 24th Infantry (colored), serving on the Texas frontier. On September 1, 1871, with four privates of the 9th Cavalry (colored), he had attacked a party of twenty-eight Indians, maintained the fight for over half an hour, and had taken with him a herd of stolen cattle when he finally had been forced to retire.[23] A fellow officer describes Bullis as "thin and spare, . . . a small, wiry man with a black mustache, . . . his face burned red as an Indian."[24] Commander and men

("A Negro Trooper of the Ninth Cavalry," *Frontier Times,* IV, 9-11) says of Bullis' scouts: "They all spoke Spanish; only a few of them, the Texas ex-slaves, spoke any English." Lieutenant Frederick E. Phelps (Reeve, ed., "Phelps: A Soldier's Memoirs," *New Mexico Historical Review,* XXV, 216) says that "Mexican . . . was the language the Seminoles used" and tells a story based on the fact that a particular Seminole "could talk very little English and perhaps understand less." These, however, are the only suggestions encountered that the Seminole Negroes could not speak English, and both the Negro cavalryman and the lieutenant make statements about their origins which indicate that, although they undoubtedly served with the scouts, their knowledge of them was not particularly intimate. Some of the young scouts, in their twenties or less, who had been born and reared in Mexico may have been deficient in English, but it seems unlikely that those in their thirties or older who had been brought up entirely in the United States and whose prestige with both Indians and whites had depended to a large extent on their ability as interpreters would have completely forgotten the English language. All the writer's conversations with widows and children of scouts, themselves contemporary with the Indian-fighting days, indicate that the Seminole at that time were basically an English-speaking people. Those in Brackettville, Texas, today are entirely bilingual, and although the Seminole in Nacimiento have now been living in Mexico for sixty or seventy years, all but the young children speak both English and Spanish fluently.

[23]Martin L. Crimmins, "The Border Command: Camp Bullis," *The Army and Navy Courier,* II, 20-21; *Who Was Who in America, 1897-1942* (Chicago, 1943), 164; Francis B. Heitman, *Historical Register and Dictionary of the United States Army* (2 vols.; Washington, 1903), I, 261.

[24]Reeve (ed.), "Phelps: A Soldier's Memoirs," *New Mexico Historical Review,* XXV, 203.

were to participate in the nine-year period from 1873 to 1881 in twenty-six expeditions, ranging in duration from a few days to several months;[25] they were to prove well worthy of one another in hard-fought combat, sometimes with foes outnumbering them six or eight to one.

Elijah Daniel's band at Fort Clark was the first to see important action. Sixteen scouts under Lieutenant Bullis accompanied six troops of the 4th Cavalry on Colonel R. S. Mackenzie's expedition against the Lipan and Kickapoo camps at Remolino, Mexico, on May 18, 1873, an encounter which resulted in the destruction of three villages, the killing of nineteen warriors, and the capture of forty prisoners. Among the Lipan captives was the aged Chief Costillitto, who was lassoed by Scout Renty Grayson,[26] and his daughter Teresita, who later married Scout James Perryman, the ceremony being performed "with a Bible" by Lieutenant Bullis himself.[27]

Twenty-one Seminole scouts accompanied Colonel Mackenzie on his 1874 expedition against the stronghold of the Cheyenne, Comanche, and Kiowa Indians in Palo Duro Canyon in the Panhandle of Texas, the principal result of which was the capture and slaughter on September 30 of fourteen hundred Indian ponies. One of the scouts distinguished himself in a skirmish on the way to the canyon by the nonchalance with which he swung from his saddle to shoot the horse of a charging Comanche.[28]

25"Record of Engagements with Hostile Indians in Texas, 1868 to 1882," *West Texas Historical Association Year Book*, IX, 101-118, abstracted from *Record of Engagements with Hostile Indians within the Military Division of the Missouri from 1868 to 1882, Lieutenant-General P. H. Sheridan, Commanding* (Washington, 1882); Heitman, *Historical Register of the Army*, II, 439-446; "Mexican Border Troubles," *House Executive Documents*, 45th Cong., 1st Sess., No. 13, especially pp. 187-196; "Texas Border Troubles," *House Miscellaneous Documents*, 45th Cong., 2d Sess., VI, No. 64.

26Carl Coke Rister, *The Southwestern Frontier* (Cleveland, 1928), 153-154; Robert G. Carter, "Raid Into Mexico," *Outing*, XII, 2ff; Martin L. Crimmins, "General Mackenzie and Fort Concho," *West Texas Historical Association Year Book*, X, 16-31; Frost Woodhull, "The Seminole Indian Scouts on the Border," *Frontier Times*, XV, 120-121; Crimmins, "Border Command," *Army and Navy Courier*, II, 20-21; San Antonio *Daily Express*, May 29, 1873, p. 3, col. 1.

27Deacon Warren (Juan) Perryman, son of Scout James Perryman and Teresita, personal interview, Brackettville, 1941; Penny Factor, personal interview, 1943; John Jefferson, Del Rio, to K. W. P., letters dated November 4, 1948, and December 28, 1948 (in possession of writer).

28Robert G. Carter, *The Old Sergeant's Story* (New York, 1926), 102-111; W. S. Nye, *Carbine and Lance* (Norman, 1937), 284-289; J. Evetts Haley, *Charles Good-*

The expeditions to Remolino and to Palo Duro had given the scouts comparatively little opportunity to display their trailing skill and their capacity for daring, quick-thinking action. These qualities were, however, conspicuously manifested on April 25, 1875. Lieutenant Bullis, with Sergeant John Ward, Trumpeter Isaac Payne, and Trooper Pompey Factor, struck the trail of about seventy-five stolen horses, followed it to the Eagle's Nest Crossing of the Pecos, and came upon the Indians as they were attempting to cross to the western side. Tethering their mounts and creeping up to within seventy-five yards, the members of the little party opened fire and kept it up for about three-quarters of an hour with such effect that they killed three warriors, wounded a fourth, and twice forced the raiders to retire from the horse herd. Eventually, however, the Indians—twenty-five or thirty Comanches mostly armed with Winchesters—discovered the small numbers of their attackers and worked around until they nearly succeeded in cutting the scouts off from their horses. Bullis and his men had to run for it.

The scouts had reached their horses, mounted, and were getting away when the sergeant, glancing back, saw that Bullis' mount, a wild, badly-trained young animal, had broken loose, leaving him dismounted among the Indians who were rapidly closing in with yells of triumph. "We can't leave the lieutenant, boys," Sergeant Ward cried. Wheeling his mount, he dashed back, closely followed by his comrades. The Indians opened a tremendous fire on the rescue party, particularly on the sergeant. A bullet cut John Ward's carbine sling; as he reached the lieutenant and helped him to mount behind, a ball shattered the stock. Factor and Payne meanwhile had been fighting off the swarming savages; now, firing right and left, the three scouts and the rescued officer rode again through the hostiles and, as Bullis wrote, "saved my hair." It was an episode which should have

night: *Cowman and Plainsman* (Boston, 1936), 196-197; J. Marvin Hunter (ed.), "The Battle of Palo Duro Canyon," from Captain George E. Albee's account in the New York *Herald* of October 16, 1874, *Frontier Times*, XXI, 177-181; Strong, *Frontier Days and Indian Fights*, 51-53; One Who Was There, "Scouting on the 'Staked Plains' (Llano Estacado) with Mackenzie in 1874," *United Service*, XIII, 400-412, 532-543; Woodhull, "Seminole Indian Scouts on Border," *Frontier Times*, XV, 124-125.

been immortalized by Frederic Remington; it did win the three scouts the Congressional Medal of Honor.[29]

The two hundred or more Seminole Negroes at Forts Duncan and Clark[30] had in the meantime become impatient for the land grants which had been a principal inducement in causing them to return to the United States. After three years they were still squatting with their families on the military reservations. It now developed that the War Department possessed no land for their permanent occupancy, and the Indian Office declared that the rolls of the Seminole tribe had been closed in 1866, shutting out those who were in Mexico. The Indian commissioner added that they should not have left the United States in the first place or should have stayed in Mexico. To add to their difficulties, the rations previously issued were cut off from those who were not regularly enlisted scouts. The whole community was thus forced to live on the wages of about fifty scouts, most of whom were married men with from three to six children, supplemented by what little work the women could find in the border communities of Eagle Pass and Brackettville and such scant crops as could be raised on the military reservations. In their destitute condition some had to forage for stray cattle for food.[31]

John Kibbitts and John Horse appealed to Brigadier General C. C. Augur, commander of the Department of Texas, in San Antonio, but the general, although convinced of the justice of

[29]Lieutenant John L. Bullis, 24th Infantry, Fort Clark, to Lieutenant G. W. Smith, 9th Cavalry, post adjutant, April 27, 1875, in General Orders No. 10, Headquarters Department of Texas, San Antonio, Texas, dated May 12, 1875 (photostat of orders in possession of Colonel Martin L. Crimmins of San Antonio, Texas) ; Mrs. O. L. Shipman, *Taming the Big Bend* (n. p., 1926) , 58-63; Woodhull, "Seminole Indian Scouts on Border," *Frontier Times*, XV, 121-122; Crimmins, "Border Command," *Army and Navy Courier*, II, 20-21. The Medal of Honor awarded to Pompey Factor was in the possession of his son, Dindie Factor, in 1943.

[30]Colonel Commanding, Fort Clark, to Assistant Adjutant General, Department of Texas, dated July 10, 1873, in Memoranda relative to Seminole Negro Indians (MSS.) .

[31]Petition of Eligah [*sic*] Daniel, Fort Clark, dated June 28, 1873; order for termination of issuance of rations to other than enlisted men, dated December 22, 1873; Bullis to Assistant Adjutant General, Department of Texas, dated May 28, 1875; and Sergeant John Kibbetts, Fort Duncan, to Assistant Adjutant General, Department of Texas, dated February 8, 1874, endorsed by Lieutenant Bullis on February 9, 1874, in Memoranda relative to Seminole Negro Indians (MSS.) ; Bullis to Lieutenant George W. Smith, post adjutant, dated May 1, 1875 (MS., Seminole File 1875-B791, Indian Office, Department of the Interior, National Archives) .

their case, could do nothing for them.[32] Ironically enough, on December 10, 1873, the day that Seminole chiefs were vainly pleading for their people, nine Seminole scouts participated with forty-one men of the 4th Cavalry in an action near Kickapoo Springs, in which nine hostile Kiowa and Comanche were killed and sixty-one horses were captured.[33]

A special Indian commissioner reported about a year later, however, that the Indian Bureau was under obligation to remove the Seminole Negroes to the Indian Territory and to provide for them.[34] Lieutenant Bullis emphasized in their favor that they were "fine trailers and good marksmen"; Colonel Edward Hatch of the 9th Cavalry characterized them as "brave and daring, superior to the Indians of this region in fighting qualities"; and both Colonel Mackenzie and Lieutenant General Philip H. Sheridan endorsed their claims to land but to no avail.[35]

A few discouraged Seminole families returned to Mexico[36] and a couple of scouts deserted, but most remained stubbornly confident that somehow, some time, justice would be done. New scouts enlisted during the latter part of 1873, in 1874, and in 1875; some of them were direct from Mexico,[37] some were from families already represented on the muster roll, while others were American Negroes, many of whom had intermarried with the Seminole, or were discharged soldiers, or both. One was a Mexican. Of German and mulatto parentage, William Miller,

---

[32]Transcript of talk, John Horse, San Antonio, to Brigadier General C. C. Augur, on December 10, 1873; transcript of talk, John Kiveth [sic], San Antonio, to Brigadier General Augur, on December 10, 1873; Augur to Adjutant General of the Army, dated February 21, 1874, in Memoranda relative to Seminole Negro Indians (MSS.).

[33]"Record of Engagements with Hostile Indians," *West Texas Historical Association Year Book*, IX, 101-118.

[34]H. M. Atkinson, Special Indian Commissioner, Fort Duncan, to Edward P. Smith, commissioner of Indian affairs, Washington, November 16, 1874 (MS., Seminole File 1874-A1085, Indian Office, Department of the Interior, National Archives, Washington, D. C.); *Annual Report of the Commissioner of Indian Affairs to the Secretary of the Interior for the Year 1875* (Washington, 1875).

[35]Bullis to Assistant Adjutant General, Department of Texas, dated May 28, 1875; Hatch to Assistant Adjutant General, Department of Texas, dated August 9, 1875; "Elizey Danuel," Fort Clark, to "Genuel," dated March 7, 1876, endorsed by Colonel R. S. Mackenzie, Fort Sill, I. T., on April 20, 1876, and Lieutenant General P. H. Sheridan, Headquarters, Military Division of the Missouri, Chicago, on April 29, 1876, in Memoranda relative to Seminole Negro Indians (MSS.).

[36]John Jefferson, personal interview, 1941.

[37]Rebecca Wilson, personal interview, 1943.

who "looked like a white man and acted like an Indian,"[38] was a non-Seminole recruit who proved well worthy of his new title.

In 1875[39] and again in 1876 and 1877, Lieutenant Bullis and the Seminole scouts were principally engaged in accompanying Colonel W. R. Shafter on various large-scale expeditions into the Indian country. When Indian signs were encountered, the scouts would be detached to follow up the trails and inflict such damage as they could on the hostiles. They were sometimes accompanied by detachments of the 8th Cavalry and of the 10th Cavalry (colored) but generally operated independently.

The Seminole scouts' method of campaigning was such that it was a severe ordeal for soldiers from other commands to keep up with them. Their effectiveness, aside from their unrivalled trailing skill, was due in large measure to their rapidity of movement and their ability to stay on the trail for months at a time, both of which qualities were derived from their lack of dependence on the commissariat. They could subsist indefinitely on half-rations and, when necessary, live off the country—eating rattlesnakes if no other game was available. Bullis, "a tireless marcher" whom the hostile Indians for obvious reasons called the Whirlwind and the Thunderbolt, could endure the same hardships and eat the same food as his men; it is said that if he wished to be really luxurious on a march, he would put a single can of corn into his haversack. According to another story, when he did have rations, he made it a rule to live on one can of food a day, whether it was corned beef or peaches.[40]

Bullis and his scouts were quite close personally. They were more like a large patriarchal family than an ordinary cavalry troop, and Bullis' relationship to the scouts was more that of a war chief to his braves than the conventional officer-man rela-

---

[38]John Jefferson, personal interview, 1941; Elsa Payne (ca 1860-1949), daughter of Scout Caesar Payne and widow of Scouts Sandy Fay and Bill Williams, personal interview, Nacimiento, Mexico, 1943.

[39]Martin L. Crimmins, "Shafter's Explorations in Western Texas, 1875," *West Texas Historical Association Year Book*, IX, 82-96.

[40]Reeve (ed.), "Phelps: A Soldier's Memoirs," *New Mexico Historical Review*, XXV, 203, 214; Frederic Remington, "On the Indian Reservations," *Century Magazine*, XXVIII, 395-396; testimony of Scout Joe Phillips in Foster, *Negro-Indian Relationships*, 47-48, and Woodhull, "Seminole Indian Scouts on Border," *Frontier Times*, XV, 120; Crimmins, "Border Command," *Army and Navy Courier*, II, 20-21.

tionship. Within two or three days of the birth of a child to any of his scouts, Bullis would appear at the Seminole camp on Las Moras Creek to inspect the infant; if the baby was a male, the lieutenant would lift him up and remark that he would make a "mighty fine scout some day."[41] This relationship of mutual affection and confidence was inestimably important to the scouts' effectiveness as a fighting organization.

Only a few of the more interesting or more important of the scouts' expeditions and actions during the years 1875-1877 can even be mentioned. On the night of October 16, 1875, for example, Lieutenant Bullis and Sergeant Miller, the white-appearing, Indian-acting mulatto, crept into an Indian camp at Laguna Sabinas and stole upwards of thirty horses and mules. Sergeant Miller also started off the military season of 1876 for the scouts by boldly entering an Indian camp in Mexico, presumably in disguise, and remaining five days.

During the summer of 1876, Bullis and his scouts were almost constantly on the march or in action and several times entered Mexico. On July 29, Bullis, with twenty Seminole scouts, twenty Negro cavalrymen, and one other officer, was sent south on the trail of Lipan Indians; the men covered 110 miles in twenty-five hours and reached the San Antonio River, near Saragossa, Mexico, at 3 A.M. At daybreak they succeeded in locating the enemy village of twenty-three lodges, mounted under cover of the trees, and charged into the sleeping camp. After the first volley, Bullis' men were involved in a wild, confused melee in which the two parties were so intermingled that the fighting was chiefly hand-to-hand—clubbed carbines against long Lipan lances. The struggle raged for a quarter of an hour; when it ended, fourteen Indians lay dead, and four squaws were prisoners. Three of Bullis' men had been cut, but none was killed or badly wounded.[42]

It is worthy of comment that in a dozen actions with hostile Indians, occurring over a period of eight years, not a single Seminole scout was killed or even seriously wounded. The older

41Retired Sergeant John Jefferson states that, according to his mother, he was visited shortly after his birth by Lieutenant Bullis.

42Woodhull, "Seminole Indian Scouts on Border," *Frontier Times,* XV, 122; Theodore F. Rodenbough and William L. Haskins (eds.) , *The Army of the United States* (New York, 1896) , 295.

generation of Seminole today confidently ascribe this immunity to divine protection. "The old people in those days were so loving with one another," says Penny Factor. "That's why things went the way they did in the fighting; the old people were doing some powerful praying." Bill Daniels adds: "When you are fighting for the right and have your trust in God, he will spread his hand over you." The Seminole, however, were not so fortunate in their encounters with the Texas citizenry.

While the scouts had been fighting to defend the frontier, their personal situation had on the whole been deteriorating rather than improving. Despite their services against the hostiles and their generally orderly, law-abiding, and industrious character,[43] they had incurred the enmity of some of the Texas borderers. One of their enemies was the notorious "King" Fisher, who liked to boast that he had killed a man for every year in his life, "not counting Mexicans," and whose outlaw band dominated the Eagle Pass area.[44] About Christmas, 1874, King Fisher and his gang and some of the scouts had engaged in a barroom gun battle in which the outlaw leader had narrowly escaped death from a bullet that creased his scalp and in which Corporal George Washington, Chief Horse's nephew, had received a stomach wound. Corporal Washington had died after lingering several months.[45]

This episode may have contributed to the decision to remove the rest of the scouts to Fort Clark on the wooded banks of the

---

[43]Colonel Mackenzie, Fort Sill, I. T., to the Secretary of War, dated April 20, 1876, in Memoranda relative to Seminole Negro Indians (MS.); Statement by P. H. Sheridan (MS., Seminole File 1883-20047, Indian Office, Department of the Interior, National Archives); Reeves (ed.), "Phelps: A Soldier's Memoirs," *New Mexico Historical Review*, XXV, 203.

[44]Dora Neill Raymond, *Captain Lee Hall of Texas* (Norman, 1940), 54-56; Mrs. Albert Maverick, "Ranch Life in Bandera County in 1878," *Frontier Times*, XVIII, 141-146; Frank H. Bushick, *Glamorous Days* (San Antonio, 1934), 174-181; Herman Lehman (1888-   ), sheriff, Maverick County, personal interview, Eagle Pass, Texas, August 22, 1950; Julia Payne, personal interview, 1942. See also murder indictments against John King Fisher, Maverick County courthouse, Eagle Pass, Texas.

[45]W. A. Bonnet, "King Fisher," *Frontier Times*, III, 36-37; Adolfo Sierra (1864-   ), former sheriff of Maverick County, personal interview, Eagle Pass, Texas, August 22, 1950; Julia Payne, personal interview, 1944; John Jefferson to K. W. P., dated May 27, 1949 (letter in author's possession). Scout Dan Johnson may also have been wounded in the fight, as he was noted as suffering from a wound at the same time as George Washington.

cool-flowing Las Moras, which had been carried out by 1876. The Fort Clark reservation was a much pleasanter location than Fort Duncan,[46] but the Seminole were no nearer than before to obtaining a permanent land grant. Here, too, the scouts encountered hostility. Certain residents of Kinney County accused them of "constantly preying on the property of citizens" and giving shelter to horse-thieves. The heart of the difficulty seems to have been that some of the Seminole who were trying to raise crops on the reservation came into conflict with local citizens who were interested in the same land. On the evening of May 19, 1876, Chief John Horse and Titus Payne were fired on near the post hospital. Payne was killed instantly, and the chief was badly wounded, but the strength and courage of his horse American, which was also wounded, and the chief's own horsemanship enabled him to escape from the ambush and reach the Seminole camp. Members of King Fisher's band were credited with being the hired triggermen. This assassination produced another spasmodic effort to find a permanent home for the Seminole. Brigadier General E. O. C. Ord suggested that the scouts be sent to a reservation occupied by recently hostile tribes, where he believed "their simple manners and religious tendency" would be a God-sent good influence.[47] But nothing came of this suggestion.

The culmination of these difficulties came on New Year's morning of 1877, just after midnight. A former scout named Adam Payne, who was wanted in Brownsville for knifing a Negro soldier, was at a dance in the Seminole camp when a sheriff blasted him from behind with a double-barrelled shotgun at such close range that his clothes were set on fire. Five scouts and former scouts, including Pompey Factor, were so exasperated by

[46]"Journal of William H. C. Whiting," *Exploring Southwestern Trails, 1846-1854* ("Southwest Historical Series," Vol. VII; Glendale, 1938), 347-348; Maria Brace Kimball, *A Soldier-Doctor of Our Army* (Boston, 1917), 119-121; John C. Reid, "Reid's Tramp," *Frontier Times*, XX, 198-199; Julia Payne, personal interview, 1942.

[47]Petition of thirty-five citizens of Kinney County, Fort Clark, dated April 24, 1876, for removal of Seminole Negroes; and Colonel Gregg, Fort Clark, to Assistant Adjutant General, Department of Texas, dated May 23 and 25, 1876, endorsed by General E. O. C. Ord, in Memoranda relative to Seminole Negro Indians (MSS.); Rebecca Wilson, personal interview, 1941; Curly Jefferson, personal interview, 1941; John Jefferson, personal interview, 1941; Julia Paye, personal interview, 1942; Rosa Fay, personal interview, 1942.

this second killing within a year—the third in less than two years—that they washed the dust of Texas from their horses' hooves in the waters of the Rio Grande. In Mexico they again fought Indians, under Colonel Pedro Avincular Valdéz, known as "Colonel Winker,"[48] whom Major Bliss characterized as "one of the bravest men I ever knew."[49]

The majority of the scouts, however, remained loyal—if not to the United States, at least to Lieutenant Bullis. Other scouts were found to replace the deserters, but of the scouts enlisted for the first time during the five years following the shooting of John Horse and Titus Payne, only four were of the original Seminole-Creek-Cherokee Negro stock from Mexico;[50] two were Indians, and no less than a dozen were Mexican.

Among the Mexicans was a former *comanchero*, or trader with the Comanche, named José Pieda Tafoya, whom General Mackenzie had induced to guide the 1874 expedition to Palo Duro Canyon by threatening to hang him to the tongue of a wagon.[51]

48Curley Jefferson, personal interview, 1941; John Jefferson, personal interview, 1941; Penny Factor, personal interview, 1943; Julia Payne, personal interview, 1942.

49Bliss, *Reminiscences* (MS.), VI, 160; Charles Judson Crane, *The Experiences of a Colonel of Infantry* (New York, 1923), 74.

50Of the hundred or so men whose names at one time or another appeared on the roster of the Seminole scouts during the Indian fighting period of 1870-1881, about one-third were discharged Negro soldiers, Texas Negroes, Mexicans, and Indians, some of whom intermarried with the Seminole. The backbone of the organization, however, both in numbers and in length and quality of service, was the Indian Negro element from Mexico which made up two-thirds of the total personnel.

The surnames, which, according to the best information obtainable, were borne by Indian Negro scouts from Mexico, in the order of their numbers, were: Wilson, 9; Payne, 8; Bruner, 6; Factor, 5; Bowlegs, July, and Thompson, 4; Daniel, Perryman, Phillips, and Warrior (Ward), 3; Fay, Gordon, Johns[t]on, Kibbitt[s], and Washington, 2; Coon, Dixie or Dixey (Dixon), Grayson, Kennard, McCallip, Williams, Wood, 1. Most Indian Negroes derived their surnames from the Indian chiefs who were their ancestors' masters or patrons—Payne, Bowlegs, Factor, Perryman, Thompson, etc. Others adopted parental personal names as surnames—July, Fay (Felipe), perhaps Daniel. John Horse's nephews assumed the surname of Washington, and his son Joe's surname of Coon was originally a nickname.

The Wilsons, Warriors, and Daniels, as also Grayson, Kennard, and McCallip, were Creek; the Thompsons were Cherokee. The Gordons are traditionally said to have become "Seminole"—runaways or secessionists—by running away to Mexico from slavery in Georgia. Those named Payne, Bruner, Factor, Bowlegs, July, Perryman, Phillips, Fay, Kibbitts, Johns[t]on, Washington, Coon, Dixie, Wood, and Williams (?) were of Florida Seminole origin. Since Seminole Indians were essentially Creeks who had moved to Florida, the line between Creek names and Seminole ones is rather uncertain.

51Haley, *Charles Goodnight*, 196-197; Crane, *Experiences of a Colonel*, 106.

Another Mexican scout was Julian Longorio, who had been brought up among the Indians and who, to obtain a $500 reward offered by Colonel W. R. Shafter for the capture of a Mescalero Indian, went into Mexico, lassoed one, and brought him back. Unfortunately Longorio broke the captive's neck in the process.[52]

During 1877 the scouts were again almost constantly on the trail and several times crossed into Mexico. The enemy was growing wary, and it was hard to bring him to bay. The scouts trailed Apache horse-thieves for two weeks deep into Mexico without other success than the incidental recovery of two or three hundred head of cattle. They trailed another large party into Mexico, crossing the Rio Grande on a raft of logs, surprising the Indian camp, and killing one Indian, wounding three, and capturing twenty-three of their horses.[53] In a running fight with Lipans, also in Mexico, the scouts captured three women, two children, fifteen horses, and two mules.[54]

Near the end of the year on an expedition which lasted two months, Bullis and his scouts were caught on a narrow ledge in a deep canyon of the Big Bend by Mescaleros; greatly outnumbered, the scouts were "severely handled," but by their "skill and courage" succeeded in extricating themselves without loss. They sent for reinforcements, picked up the trail again, although it was twenty-three days old, and followed it for several days. By leaving their horses and walking over a mountain nearly a mile high, the scouts and cavalrymen succeeded in surprising the enemy camp but were unsuccessful in trapping the Indians, although they killed two warriors, including the chief, wounded three, and captured thirty horses and mules, with all camp equipment.[55]

---

[52]John Jefferson, personal interview, 1941; "Texas Border Troubles," *House Miscellaneous Documents*, 45th Cong., 2d Sess., VI, No. 64, pp. 267-268. The Bullis Papers (MSS. in possession of General Bullis' daughter, Mrs. W. S. Halcomb of San Antonio, Texas) contain mention of one Julian, in all probability Longorio, who evidently operated as a spy in Mexico and as such was frequently sought by Mexican police.

[53]Carlysle Graham Raht, *The Romance of Davis Mountains and Big Bend Country* (El Paso, 1919), 205; "Mexican Border Troubles," *House Executive Documents*, 45th Cong., 1st Sess., No. 13, pp. 171-189.

[54]*Ibid.*, 240; Rodenbough and Haskin (eds.), *Army of the United States*, 275.

[55]Reeve (ed.), "Phelps: A Soldier's Memoirs," *New Mexico Historical Review*, XXV, 206ff; Rister, *Southwestern Frontier*, 187-189.

The campaigns of 1876 and 1877 so put the fear of God—or of Bullis and the scouts—into the Lipan and Mescalero raiders that although the scouts went out on expeditions as before and at least once entered Mexico,[56] they encountered no Indians. They did, however, perform one of their greatest feats of trailing and endurance. On January 31, 1879, Bullis, thirty-nine Seminole, fifteen cavalrymen, three friendly Lipans, and the former *comanchero* José Tafoya set out in pursuit of Mescalero raiders, whom they trailed across the desert for thirty-four days. At one time the Bullis party was nearly perishing from thirst, when Sergeant David Bowlegs displayed uncanny desert craft by discovering a "sleeping spring" which the hostiles had stopped up and hidden; by the greatest care and skill, he made the spring flow freely again. Although they trailed the raiders to within two miles of the Fort Stanton, New Mexico, reservation, the agent refused to give them up, and the scouts had to return empty-handed. They had been gone eighty days and had covered 1,266 miles.[57]

The scouts' last Indian battle[58] followed the last important Indian raid on Texas soil. A small band of Lipans killed a Mrs. McLauren and a boy named Allen Reiss on April 14, 1881, at the head of the Rio Frio. Lieutenant Bullis, two weeks later, was ordered to take thirty scouts and to pursue the raiders. The Indians had "killed a horse and made shoes out of the rawhide so they wouldn't make tracks,"[59] but despite this device and the elapsed time, the scouts picked up the trail and pursued the raiders "over the rugged, precipitous mountains and canyons of Devil's River, where the marauders killed thirty of their horses." The scouts followed them across the Rio Grande and trailed them into the Sierra del Burro, where on May 2 the Seminole discovered the hostile camp. They surrounded it and attacked at daybreak, killing four warriors and capturing a squaw, a child,

[56]James Parker, *The Old Army: Memories, 1872-1918* (Philadelphia, 1929), 99.

[57]Alexander E. Sweet and J. J. Amory Knox, *On a Mexican Mustang Through Texas* (St. Louis, 1884), 520-521; Rister, *Southwestern Frontier*, 189-190; Woodhull, "Seminole Indian Scouts on Border," *Frontier Times*, XV, 124-125; Grace Lowe Butler, "General Bullis: Friend of the Frontier," *Frontier Times*, XII, 358-362.

[58]On October 20, 1881, Sergeant Bobby Kibbitts and nine men recovered thirteen horses from seven Indians near the Rio Grande, but this encounter is not listed in Heitman's *Historical Register* as an engagement.

[59]Julia Payne, personal interviews, 1942, 1944.

and twenty-one animals. Only the chief, San Da Ve, escaped, and he was mortally wounded.[60]

In the following year twelve expeditions from Texas posts covered 3,662 miles, but not the slightest trace of Indian raiders was found.[61]

The Seminole scouts and their leader were not, of course, by any means wholly responsible for achieving permanent cessation of Indian raids on the Texas frontier. Regular United States troops had played an important part, but without the scouts the work of the regular troops would to a large degree have been futile. The scouts alone could follow a weeks-old trail across hundreds of miles of desert and mountains and could so locate and surround a hostile camp that the enemy could be overwhelmed and terrorized by a surprise attack when it was feeling most secure. Indian campaigns along the Texas-Mexican border would otherwise have been a series of games of hide-and-seek on a large scale, in which the hostiles, except by rare accident, probably would have been the winners. It was to the trailing skill, the endurance, the desert craft of those hard riders, dead shots, and fierce hand-to-hand fighters, the Seminole scouts,[62] that Texas in large measure owed her final exemption from such Indian raids as had plagued her borders from her earliest history.

J. L. Bullis, in recognition of services which would have been impossible except as commander of the Seminole scouts, was most deservedly dubbed "The Friend of the Frontier," presented with two handsome swords,[63] breveted as captain and major, promoted to captain and, eventually, to brigadier general;[64] he was even acclaimed as "the greatest Indian fighter in the history

---

[60]Woodhull, "Seminole Indian Scouts on Border," *Frontier Times*, XV, 122-123; Rister, *Southwestern Frontier*, 267-268; A. J. Sowell, "Last Indian Raid in Frio Canyon," *Frontier Times*, XXIV; Crimmins, "Border Command," *Army and Navy Courier*, II, 20-21.

[61]Rister, *Southwestern Frontier*, 268-269.

[62]For additional comments of contemporaries on the Seminole scouts' trailing and fighting skill, see Parker, *Old Army*, 99; Vinton Lee James, *Frontier and Pioneer* (San Antonio, 1938), 26; Florence Fenley, *Oldtimers* (Uvalde, 1939), 185-187, quoting David W. Barnhill.

[63]The swords are on exhibition in the Witte Museum, San Antonio.

[64]*Who Was Who in America*, 164; Crimmins, "Border Command," *Army and Navy Courier*, II, 20-21.

of the United States Army."[65] The scouts themselves, however, were rewarded by the gradual reduction and ultimate disbandment of the organization,[66] followed by the eviction of the survivors and their successors and kinsmen from their homes on the Fort Clark reservation.[67]

---

[65]Raht, *Romance of Davis Mountains*, 198.

[66]The older generation of Seminole Negroes at Brackettville are firmly convinced that if General Bullis had lived, this disbandment would not have taken place. John Jefferson tells the story that Bullis was ill in his home in San Antonio when news of the intended disbandment reached him. He immediately called for his clothes and began to dress. "General, what are you doing out of bed? Don't you realize that you are a sick man?" the nurse protested. "Colonel ————— says he's going to disband my old scouts," the general replied. "I'm going to Fort Clark and stop him." According to the story, the general then collapsed and died. As a matter of fact, the general died of a heart attack at a boxing match on May 26, 1911, and the final order for the disbanding of the scouts was not issued until July 10, 1914. The story, however, is indicative of the feeling between Bullis and the scouts even though the details do not jibe with the actualities.

[67]Memoranda relative to Seminole Negro Indians (MSS.); Woodhull, "Seminole Indian Scouts on Border," *Frontier Times*, XV, 126-127.

Corrections and Additions

p. 475, last line, note 10:   The interview with Curley Jefferson was at Brackettville.

p. 477, l. 7:   The Seminole Negroes in Mexico were armed with Indian spears and Mexican *machetes* as well as with muzzle-loading firearms.

Further Reading

William H. Leckie, *The Buffalo Soldiers: A Narrative of the Negro Cavalry in the West* (Norman, Okla., 1967), is an excellent detailed account of the two Negro cavalry regiments — known to the Plains Indians as "buffalo soldiers" because of the texture of their hair. See *American Historical Review*, LXXIII (February, 1968), pp. 930-31. The less glamorous, but nonetheless indispensable Negro footsloggers are promised attention in Arlen Fowler, *The Negro Infantry in the West, 1869-1891*, scheduled for publication in October, 1970, by Negro Universities Press.

A few individual scouts, guides, and interpreters to the "Indian-fighting army" were of Negro, or part-Negro, ancestry. Of these the best-known, although hardly the most important, was Isaiah Dorman, who was killed, fighting desperately, in the Battle of the Little Big Horn, as a member of Major Reno's detachment. He is dealt with briefly on pp. 86-87 and 130-31. The most nearly adequate of several studies of this Negro guide and interpreter is Roland C. McConnell, "Isaiah Dorman and the Custer Expedition," *JNH*, XXXIII (July, 1948), pp. 344-52; however, his career would repay still further investigation, as would the lives of the Indian and Negro mixed-breed scouts, Frank Grouard and Sam Bowman.

THE CATTLE COUNTRY
1866-ca. 1900

Negroes were an important element in the cattle country in all ranks from wrangler to trail boss and rancher. An authoritatively estimated one-fourth of the trail hands who drove cattle from southern Texas to the northern railheads, Indian reservations, and grazing grounds, were Negroes. They were particularly conspicuous as chuck-wagon and ranch-house cooks — the most important men in cattle outfits save for the trail bosses and foremen — and as horsebreakers and ropers.

The following article is a digest of several important chapters from my forthcoming book, *Black Riders: The Negro on the Frontier of the Cattle Country,* scheduled for publication by Quadrangle Press (Chicago). It originally appeared in *Labor History,* Summer, 1969 (Vol. 10, No. 3).

NEGRO LABOR IN THE WESTERN CATTLE INDUSTRY, 1866-1900

Introduction

The range-cattle industry in its various aspects, and in its importance to the United States and particularly to the Great Plains for the post-Civil War generation, has been the subject of numerous studies. This industry was rendered possible by such factors as vast expanses of grazing land, projected railroad lines across the Missouri and onto the Great Plains, the rise of heavy industry and the consequent demand for beef of less-than-high quality by the meat-hungry industrial population. But like the steel, mining, packing, and other industries, it also needed a labor force—workers with special abilities and qualities—for although the cowhand or cowboy possibly was no more than a "hired man on horseback,"[1] he was a hired man with skills in riding, roping, and branding which could not be easily acquired. Most of his working hours were spent in such routine tasks as riding the range and turning back drifting steers; rounding up, branding, and castrating calves; selecting beeves for the market; and, even on the "long drive," jogging along and daily "eating dirt" on the flanks or in the rear of a few

Research for this paper and for the larger project of which it is a part was facilitated by grants from the American Philosophical Society and the Graduate School of the University of Oregon. This article is extracted from seven chapters of a nearly-completed book-length manuscript tentatively entitled *Black Riders: The Negro on the Frontier of the Cattle Country*, which is a functional and interpretative study. Therefore, it would hardly be an exaggeration to state that complete documentation of every statement might occupy almost as much space as the text. Consequently, I have frequently restricted my references to the more important and particularly controversial statements. The most nearly complete published account of the Negro in the cattle country is Philip Durham and Everett L. Jones, *The Negro Cowboys* (N. Y., 1965), which is to a large extent regionally organized. My deepest gratitude goes to the late J. Frank Dobie, for his kindness in turning over to me his files on Negro cowboys.

[1] May Davison Rhodes, *The Hired Man on Horseback: A Biography of Eugene Manlove Rhodes* (Boston, 1938), ix-xiii.

thousand "cow critters." But he also needed the inborn courage and quick thinking to use these skills effectively while confronting an enraged bull, swimming a milling herd across a flooded river, or trying to turn a stampede of fear-crazed steers.

But the general public, under the influence of decades of "Western" movies and, more recently, television shows has come to regard the cowboy's workaday activities as altogether secondary to fighting off hostile Indians, pursuing rustlers and holding "necktie parties" for them, saving the rancher's daughter from Mexican raiders, and engaging in quick-draw gunfights in dusty streets. From similar sources this same public has also learned that cowboys, with the exception of an occasional low-browed villain or exotic and comic-accented *vaquero,* were all of the purest and noblest Anglo-Saxon type, as in Owen Wister's *The Virginian.*

In reality, as George W. Saunders of the Texas Trail Drivers Association has authoritatively estimated, of the fully 35,000 men who went up the trail from Texas with herds during the heroic age of the cattle industry, 1866-1895, "about one-third were Negroes and Mexicans."[2] This estimate is closely confirmed by extant lists of trail-herd outfits which identify their members racially. These lists also demonstrate that Negroes out-numbered Mexicans by more than two to one—slightly more than 63 percent whites, 25 percent Negroes, and slightly under 12 percent Mexicans.

The racial breakdown of individual outfits, of course, varied widely. Some were nearly all of one race, such as the 1874 outfit which was all-Negro, except for a white boss, or the 1872 outfit which consisted of a white trail-boss, eight Mexicans, and a Negro; but more typical were the two 1877 outfits composed, respectively, of seven whites and two Negro cowboys, and a Negro cook; and seven whites, two Negroes, and a Mexican hostler. Many outfits had no Mexicans at all, but it was an exceptional outfit that did not have at least one Negro and enough outfits were nearly all Negro, or a third or more Negro, to bring the number up to the estimated twenty-five percent of the total.[3] A trail-herd outfit of about a dozen men would on the average consist of seven or eight whites, including the trail boss, three Negroes—one of whom was probably the cook, while another might be the horse wrangler,

[2] John Marvin Hunter (ed.), *The Trail Drivers of Texas* (Nashville, 1925), 453.
[3] *Ibid.,* 987, 255, 717, 157, 505, 472, 817, 138-139, 805, 718-719; R. J. (Bob) Lauderdale and John M. Doak, *Life on the Range and on the Trail,* Lela Neal Pirtle, editor (San Antonio, 1936), 169.

and the third would simply be a trail hand—and one or two Mexicans; if a Negro was not the wrangler, then a Mexican often was. Needless to say, this is not the typical trail outfit of popular literature and drama.

The racial make-up of ranch outfits, with their seasonal and day-by-day fluctuations, was not so well recorded as that of the trail-herd outfits, but available information indicates that ranch hands, in Texas at least, were white, Negro, and Mexican in proportions varying according to locality and to ranchowner tastes; probably the overall proportions differed little from those of trail outfits. A ranch in the Indian Territory during the late 1890s, for example, was staffed by eight cowhands, two of whom were Negroes.[4] Negro cowhands were particularly numerous on the Texas Gulf Coast, in the coastal brush east of the Nueces and at the mouth of the Brazos and south of Houston, and parts of the Indian Territory; in some sections they were in the majority, and some ranches worked Negroes almost exclusively.[5]

Negro trail drivers swarmed west and north with herds from the Texas "hive" and, though most returned, a few remained as ranch hands as far north as Wyoming, the Dakotas, and even Canada and as far west as New Mexico, Arizona, and even California and Oregon.[6]

Wranglers

Negroes occupied all the positions among cattle-industry employees, from the usually lowly wrangler through ordinary hand to top hand and lofty cook. But they were almost never, except in the highly infrequent case of an all-Negro outfit, to be found as ranch or trail boss.

Negroes and also Mexicans were frequently wranglers, or *remuderos*[7] —in charge of the saddle horses not immediately in use—usually regarded as the lowliest job in the cattle industry, except for the boy who sometimes served as wrangler's assistant.[8] There were exceptions, how-

---

[4] John Hendrix, *If I Can Do It Horseback* (Austin, 1963), 205.
[5] John M. Hendrix, "Tribute Paid to Negro Cowmen," *The Cattleman,* XXII (Feb., 1936), 24. See also J. Frank Dobie to KWP, Jan. 30, 1953, J. Frank Dobie, *The Longhorns* (Boston, 1941), 309.
[6] William A. Keleher, *The Fabulous Frontier: Twelve New Mexico Items* (Albuquerque, 1962), 162-163, 245, 271; Theodore Roosevelt, *Ranch Life and the Hunting Trail* (N. Y., 1920; 1st ed., 1888), 10-11. See also Floyd C. Bard as told to Agnes Wright Spring, in *Horse Wrangler: Sixty Years in the Saddle in Wyoming and Montana* (Norman, 1960), 12-13; Sir Cecil E. Denny, *The Law Marches West* (Toronto, 1939), 187.
[7] J. Frank Dobie, *A Vaquero of the Brush Country* (Dallas, 1929), 12-13; Lauderdale and Doak, *op. cit.,* 11; Hunter, *op. cit.,* 679, 204.
[8] Douglas Branch, *The Cowboy and His Interpreters* (N. Y., 1926), 42-43; Ross Santee, *Men and Horses* (N. Y., 1926); Agnes Morley Cleaveland, *No Life for a Lady* (Boston, 1941), 111; William T. Hornaday, "The Cowboys of the Northwest," *Cosmo-*

ever, including some Negro wranglers who became "second in authority to the foreman" in a few camps.[9] Such wranglers were "horse men"
in the highest sense: capable of detecting and treating illness and injury, selecting the proper horse for each job, and taking the ginger out
of unruly animals. Among these wranglers-extraordinary were Nigger
Jim Kelly, the horsebreaker, horsetrainer, handyman, and gunman of
the notorious Print Olive; and the famous John Chisum's "Nigger
Frank," "who spent a lifetime wrangling Long I horses" and whom a
white cattleman declared "the best line rider and horsewrangler I ever
saw."[10]

Cowboys

The majority of Negroes on the ranch or "long drive" were neither
wranglers nor yet authoritative cooks (of whom more later). They
were top hands or ordinary hands who, on the long drive, rode the
point, the swing, the flank, or the drag, according to their experience
and ability. The point—the position of honor—was at the front of
the herd where the steers were strongest, most restless, and most likely
to try to break away. There the most experienced top hands rode. Farther back, the cattle were somewhat less troublesome, while in the rear,
where the tired beasts were comparatively easy to manage, could be
found the fledgling cowboys of the drag, "eating the dust" of the entire
herd. Negroes rode in all these positions.[11]

These Negro cowboys, whether on ranch or trail, were generally
regarded as good workers, who got along well with others and who
took pride in their work. A white Texan, a former cowboy and rancher,
went so far as to write that "there was no better cowman on earth than
the Negro."[12]

---

politan, II (Dec., 1886), 226; Edward Everett Dale, *Cow Country* (Norman, 1942),
46-47.
[9] Branch, *op. cit.*, 42-43. "For my money he [the wrangler] was one of the most capable
  fellows around an outfit." Hendrix, *If I Can Do It Horseback*, 185-186.
[10] Harry E. Chrisman, *The Ladder of Rivers: The Story of I. P. (Print) Olive* (Denver,
  1962), 34-35, 77, 102, 147, 217, 378; Dane Coolidge, *Fighting Men of the West*
  (Bantam Books, 1952; 1st ed., 1932), 14, 32, 41; Frank Collinson, *Life in the
  Saddle*, Mary Whatley Clarke, editor, (Norman, 1963), 145.
[11] Charles A. Siringo, *Riata and Spurs: The Story of a Lifetime Spent in the Saddle as
  Cowboy and Ranger* (Boston, 1931; 1st ed., 1927), 27.
[12] Ramon F. Adams to KWP, Feb. 6, 1953; Roosevelt, *op. cit.*, 10-11; Ellsworth Collings,
  "The Hook Nine Ranch in the Indian Territory," *Chronicles of Oklahoma*, XXXIII
  (Winter, 1955-56), 462; Angie Debo, editor, *The Cowman's Southwest, being the
  Reminiscences of Oliver Nelson, Freighter, Camp Cook, Frontiersman, in Kansas,
  Indian Territory, Texas, and Oklahoma, 1876-1893* (Glendale, 1963), 98-99, 107-
  108; Hendrix, *If I Can Do It Horseback*, 161, 205.

Old, experienced Negro cowhands frequently served as unofficial, one-man apprentice systems to white greenhorns. This was particularly true, of course, when the fledgling was the employer's son or relative. Will Rogers, for example, got his first lessons in riding and roping from a Cherokee Negro employee of his father.[13] Almost any young would-be cowboy who showed the proper spirit, however, might have the good fortune to be "adopted" and "showed the ropes" by one of these black veterans, who would sometimes take on the inexperienced boy as partner when white cowboys were unwilling to do so.[14] Charles Siringo, later famous as a cowboy-detective-author, recalled that Negro cowboys again and again came to his rescue when, in his reckless cowboy youth, his life was threatened by a mad steer, a wild bronc, and even a hired assassin.[15]

Negro cowhands confronted all the dangers and met all the tests of the long trail. One poorly clad cowboy froze to death in his saddle during a "Norther" rather than give up and go in to the chuckwagon.[16] Stampedes were an ever-present danger, and experienced Negroes were frequently prominent in attempting to prevent or control them. Indeed they were also often among the few cowboys who stayed with the herd when others threw in their hands.[17]

Crossing the wide, deep, frequently flooded rivers was even more dangerous than stampedes. According to a white ex-cowboy, "it was the Negro hand who usually tried out the swimming water when a trailing herd came to a swollen stream"[18]—either because of his superior ability or because he was regarded as expendable. But whether or not this statement is valid, it probably would not have been made had not Negroes frequently demonstrated their ability to cope with the problems of river crossings. Numerous anecdotes about such crossings tell of Negro cowhands saving themselves by their own efforts, being assisted

---

[13] Homer Croy, *Our Will Rogers* (N. Y. and Boston, 1953), 19-20, 250, 334; Donald Day, *Will Rogers: A Biography* (N. Y., 1962), 11-16, Chrisman, 77; John Rolfe Burroughs, *Where the West Stayed Young: The Remarkable History of Brown's Park* . . . (N. Y., 1962), 109.

[14] Collinson, *op. cit.*, 25-26; James Emmit McCauley, *A Stove-Up Cowboy's Story*, with an introduction by John A. Lomax (Dallas, 1956; 1st ed., 1943), 12.

[15] Siringo, *A Texas Cowboy* (Signet Books, 1955; 1st ed., 1886), 38; Siringo, *Riata and Spurs*, 17, 18.

[16] Dobie, *Vaquero*, 100-101.

[17] Hunter, *op. cit.*, 112, 417-418; James C. Shaw, *North from Texas: Incidents in the Early Life of a Range Cowman in Texas, Dakota, and Wyoming 1852-1882*, Herbert O. Brayer, editor (Eavnston, 1952), 46-47.

[18] Hendrix, "Negro Cowmen," 24.

to dry land by white cattlemen[19] and, on more than one occasion, saving their lives.

Negroes not only often showed courage and quick thinking in extricating themselves and others from the danger of swollen rivers, but in at least one case also displayed ingenuity superior to that of a great trail boss. In 1877 Ab Blocker, "the fastest driver on the trail," had reached the Platte River, which was spanned by a bridge of sorts, but the wild longhorns had never seen a bridge and refused to cross it. It looked as if, after all, they would have to swim the herd when a Negro hand suggested—and his suggestion was adopted—that they should drive the chuckwagon slowly across, followed by old Bully, an ox; the lead steers would follow Bully and the rest of the herd would trail them.[20]

Riders and Ropers

Although every top hand had to be a skillful rider and roper, some were so outstanding as to be considered "bronco busters" and/or ropers *par excellence* rather than as merely uncommonly able cowboys. Numerous references suggest that Negroes and Mexicans were widely regarded as particularly expert in both these capacities—the Mexicans especially noted for their prowess with the *reata* (or lasso). Mexicans were also, correctly or not, blamed for cruelty toward animals and consequently fell into disrepute as horsebreakers,[21] whereas the Negroes maintained and even advanced a reputation which went back to antebellum days.

A white ex-cowpuncher-writer states that Negroes were hired largely for their ability to cope with bad horses which the white cowhands did not want to tackle. "The Negro cow hands of the middle 1880s . . . were usually called on to do the hardest work around an outfit. . . . This most often took the form of 'topping' or taking the first pitch out of the rough horses of the outfit. . . . It was not unusual for one young

---

[19] Hunter, *op. cit.,* 47-48, 987-988; A. J. Sowell, *Early Settlers and Indian Fighters of Southwest Texas* (Austin, 1900), 757-758; J. Frank Dobie, interview with Joe McCloud, Beeville, Texas, *ca.* 1928, in letter to KWP, Feb. 16, 1953.

[20] Dobie, *Longhorns,* 246-247; E. C. Abbott ("Teddy Blue") and Helena Huntington Smith, *We Pointed Them North: Recollections of a Cowpuncher* (N. Y., 1939), 263.

[21] Emerson Hough, *The Story of the Cowboy* (N. Y., 1934; 1st ed., 1897), 91; James W. Freeman (ed.), *Poetry and Prose of the Live Stock Industry* (Denver and Kansas City, 1905), I, 13; Louis Pelzer, *The Cattleman's Frontier . . . 1850-1890* (Glendale, 1936), 48; Roosevelt, *op. cit.,* 10-11; Stanley Walker, "Decline and Fall of the Hired Man," *The New Yorker,* Sept. 12, 1953, p. 110; Clifford P. Westermeier, *Man, Beast, Dust: The Story of Rodeo* (n.p., 1947), 173.

Negro to 'top' a half dozen hard-pitching horses before breakfast."
Andy Adams, the cowboy-author and a man who was far from being
a Negrophile, declared that the "greatest bit of bad horse riding" he
ever saw was performed by a dozen Negro cowboys who were assigned
to ride a dozen horses which the white cowpunchers of their outfit were
afraid to tackle. But each of the Negroes stayed on his horse till the
animal was conquered.[22]

The list of Negro bronc riders—the comparatively few whose names
have survived—is still a long one. A few of the better known, partly
because they attracted the attention of published writers, were the
following: Isam, Isom, or Isham Dart of Brown's Hole, "where Colorado, Wyoming, and Utah cornered," who, although now remembered
principally as a reputed rustler, was also "numbered among the top
bronc stompers of the Old West";[23] Nigger Jim Kelly, whom oldtime
cowboys considered the peer of any rider they had seen in the United
States, Canada, or the Argentine;[24] a mulatto named Williams in the
Badlands of South Dakota, who was a horse-trainer rather than a
horsebreaker and whose methods won the admiration of Theodore
Roosevelt;[25] and Jim Perry, the famous XIT cook, who was even better
known as "one of the best riders and roper ever to hit the West."[26]

While most of the famous riders were bronco busters only as one
aspect of their work as cowhands, some, including a number of Negroes,
were officially recognized as ranch horsebreakers, and a few were full-
time or nearly full-time professionals. Perhaps the most famous of the
professionals was Matthew (Bones) Hooks of the Panhandle—remembered, after his retirement from horsebreaking to Pullman-porter-
ing, for having once taken off his jacket and cap and laid aside his
clothes brush, to mount and break an outlaw which no one had been
able to ride, while his train stood in the station.[27]

[22] Hendrix, "Negro Cowmen," 24; Elmo S. Watson, "Tales of the Trail," probably in a
  Colorado Springs newspaper in 1916, and Arthur Chapman, interview with Andy
  Adams, *Denver Times*, Aug. 18, 1915, p. 2. See also Wilson M. Hudson, *Andy
  Adams: His Life and Writings* (Dallas, 1964), 184, 251. To Professor Hudson's
  kindness I owe copies of the two newspaper items, *supra*.

[23] Burroughs, *op. cit.*, 192-195; Coolidge, *op. cit.*, 79; Dean Krakel, *The Saga of Tom
  Horn: The Story of a Cattlemen's War* (Laramie, 1954), 9-12.

[24] Chrisman, *op. cit.*, 34-35, 77, 217, 378; Harry E. Chrisman, Denver, to KWP, Oct. 23,
  1965.

[25] Lincoln A. Lang, *Ranching with Roosevelt* (Philadelphia, 1926), 286.

[26] Lewis Nordyke, *Cattle Empire: The Fabulous Story of the 3,000,000 Acre XIT* (N. Y.,
  1949), 138.

[27] Jean Ehly, " 'Bones' Hooks of the Panhandle," *Frontier Times*, XXXVI (June-July,
  1963), 20-22, 54-55 (illustrated).

Other Negro cowhands were particularly renowned as ropers, such as Ab Blocker's Frank, who was, according to a white cowboy, "the best hand with a rope I ever saw," and whose roping skill once saved his employer from an angry steer;[28] Ike Word, according to Charles Siringo, "the best roper" at a roundup near Beeville, Texas;[29] Jim Simpson, "about the best roper" on his part of the Wyoming range;[30] and, more recently, the Negro rancher Jess Pickett who, according to a white neighbor, was "the world's best roper."[31]

Naturally enough, many of the famous Negro riders, such as Isom Dart and Jim Perry, were almost or quite as renowned as ropers. One of the most spectacular at both riding and roping was "Nigger Add," "one of the best hands on the Pecos," who would as a matter of course "top off" several bad horses of a morning. Walking into a corral full of tough broncs, he would seize any one he chose by the ear and nose, lead him out of the bunch, and then show him who was boss. As a roper he was even more sensational, and had the unusual technique of roping on foot, a practice which would have killed an ordinary man. He would tie a rope around his hips, work up to a horse in the corral or in the open pasture, rope him around the neck as he dashed by at full speed, and then, by sheer strength and skill, flatten the horse out on the ground where a lesser man would have been dragged to death.[32] Indeed, the prowess of such Negro riders, horsebreakers, and horse-trainers was so outstanding as to contribute to the commonly held belief of the time that there was some natural affinity between Negroes and horses.[33]

Singing to the Cattle

Riding, roping, and branding were not the only skills required of a top cowhand. Singing to the cattle, particularly on night herd but sometimes during the day's march, was not only a practical necessity for calming the animals and reducing the danger of a stampede, it also had recreational and esthetic values for the drivers. Negro trail hands were conspicuous in this practice, although Negro chuckwagon cooks were the most noted cow-country musicians, singers, and composers.

---

[28] Edward Seymour Nichols, *Ed Nichols Rode a Horse,* as told to Ruby Nichols Cutbirth (Dallas, 1943), 8-9.
[29] Siringo, *Texas Cowboy,* 82-83.
[30] Bard, *op. cit.,* 67.
[31] Fred Herring, Lometa, Texas, to KWP, July 20, 1965.
[32] J. Evetts Haley, *George W. Littlefield, Texan* (Norman, 1943), 181-186.
[33] Frederic Remington, "Vagabonding with the Tenth Horse," *The Cosmopolitan,* **XXII** (Feb., 1897), 352.

"Nigger" Jim Kelly, the Olives' versatile horsebreaker and gunman, is also credited with composing a humorous song, "Willie the Cook," which he sang to accordion accompaniment furnished by a white trail hand. "Teddy Blue," a white cowhand whose autobiography is a cow-country classic, tells movingly of his first memory of the "Ogallaly song," which had a verse for every river on the trail, beginning with the Nueces and ending in 1881, when he first heard it, with Ogallala.

> There were [he recalled] thirteen herds camped on the Cimarron that night and you could count their fires. A Blocker herd was bedded close to ours; it was bright starlight, and John Henry was riding around the herd singing the Ogallaly song. John Henry was the Blocker's [sic] top nigger. . . .
>
> 'We left Nueces River in April eighty-one
>
> With three thousand horned cattle and all they knowed was run
>
> O-o-o-o-oh!'
> and so on.[34]

The special quality which these Negro cowhands gave to the cattle country is epitomized in an episode at Doan's store on the Red River, which was the last place where a trail herd hand could receive mail and purchase supplies before reaching the Kansas cattle towns. One night a crowd sitting around the little adobe store heard the strains of "a lively air on a French harp." The door opened and in sailed a hat, closely followed by a big Negro who began to dance to his own accompaniment. "It was one of Ab Blocker's niggers"—perhaps John Henry himself—"who had been sent up for the mail, giving first notice of the herd's arrival."[35] The ranch or cattle trail, without its many Negroes, would not only have suffered from a lack of expert riders, ropers, and cooks, but would also have lacked much of its vitality and vivacity and spontaneous gaiety, and ranching and trail-driving would have been duller occupations.

Cowboy Cooks — Men of Parts

High in the hierarchy of cow-country employees was the ranch or trail cook,[36] who ranked next to the foreman or trail boss and, in camp,

---

[34] Abbott and Smith, *op. cit.,* 261-264.
[35] Hunter, *op. cit.,* 778.
[36] The standard work on the cow-country cook is, of course, Ramon F. Adams, *Come an' Get It: The Story of the Old Cowboy Cook* (Norman, 1952)'. Almost every general work on the cowboy or the cattle country, and many reminiscences and special studies, also contain useful information.

ruled supreme over an area of sixty feet around the chuckwagon. In addition to culinary skill—including the ability to prepare a meal in a blizzard, cloudburst, or high wind—the cook also had to be an expert muleskinner or bullwhacker, capable of driving two or three yoke of oxen or a four-mule team attached to the chuckwagon over the most difficult terrain, including flooded rivers. He could do more than anyone else to make life pleasant and many a cowboy selected an outfit because of the reputation of its cook. In compensation for duties which few men could satisfactorily perform, the cook normally was paid from $5 per month more than the ordinary cowhand up to even twice as much.

The cowboy cook was also commonly credited with other qualities less essential and certainly less endearing than the ability to cook and drive the chuckwagon. He was frequently something of a despot; bad-tempered, hard-featured, and unlovely. "As tetchy as a cook" is still a ranch byword. He was often an old "stove-up" cowpuncher who resented having to "wait on" cowboys still in their prime, "just kids" in his opinion. He often was also a "hard character," and frequently had a drinking problem. Finally, as one authority has stated, cooks were seldom good riders.

The above description of the cowboy-cook is synthesized from the reports of numerous observers on cooks of all races and backgrounds in all parts of the cow-country. Some of these qualities doubtless applied to most of them, and all to some of them. But numerous accounts of Negro cow-country cooks suggest that the traditional "hard character" pattern fitted them much less than it did whites. The cow-country cook of the Texas and Texas-influenced range, if not typically a Negro, was at least very frequently one.[37] To be sure, the historian of the cowboy-cook writes: "Most bosses preferred a native white cook. . . . Some Negroes were good cooks, but were usually lazy, and, too, white cowboys refused to take orders from them." This statement, however, is not confirmed by the literature of the cattle country, which strongly suggests that many if not most cattlemen were in agreement with the trail boss who wrote: "For cooks I always preferred darkies."[38]

[37] Rufus Rockwell Wilson, *Out of the West* (N. Y., 1933), 377; Hough, *op. cit.*, 138-139; J. Frank Dobie, *Cow People* (Boston, 1964), 132; Hunter, *op. cit.*, 485, 43, 307, 535, 295-303, 416-417, 981, 688, 231, 606-607, 81, 679.
[38] R. F. Adams, *op. cit.*, 21-22; Lauderdale and Doak, *op. cit.*, 183-185.

The primary reason for this preference is probably that Negroes simply were on the average better workers than the available whites. They could, of course, occasionally be lazy, stupid, careless, dishonest, and many whites were excellent cooks, but the cow-camp menus on record seem to have been disproportionately the work of Negro cooks. Good cooks occasionally supplemented the filling but somewhat monotonous diet of biscuits, "sowbelly," beef, molasses, and coffee by carrying a gun in the wagon and, between dishwashing and starting the next meal, hunted deer, turkey, and other game. An extraordinary cook who took full advantage of such opportunities was a thirty-year-old Negro named Sam who, in 1878, prepared for an outfit on Pease River what one of its members years later described as "about the most luscious eating. . . . I have ever enjoyed . . . an oven of buffalo steaks, another . . . of roast bear meat, better than pork, a frying pan full of the breast of wild turkey in gravy of flour, water, and grease, . . . antelope ribs barbecued on a stick over the coals." Sometimes he would roast a turkey in its feathers in a pit. He also cooked wild plums, stewing them or making them into a cobbler. Small wonder that the cowboys of his outfit always saw to it that he had plenty of wood.[39] Sam was merely one of a galaxy of Negro cow-country cooks, each with his specialty— Dutch oven-baked peach pies, "cathead biscuits," son-of-a-gun stew," etc.

The cook was frequently in sole charge not merely of the kitchen but of the ranch house itself, and on the long drive was of course frequently left alone to protect the chuckwagon and its contents in any emergency, whether crossing a river or encountering Indians. A Negro cook distinguished himself in an episode of 1877 in which the other members of his outfit played no very heroic roles. Four white men and three Negroes were working cattle in Coleman County, Texas, when Indians suddenly swooped down upon them. All took refuge in a cave except "old Negro Andy, the cook," who stayed by the wagon, fought off the Indians, and saved the supplies.[40]

By and large, Negro cooks managed their kitchens or chuckwagon, dealt with Indians, and accomplished their culinary feats without the "crankiness" which was almost as much standard equipment for cow-country cooks as was their "starter" for salt-rising bread. Some white

---

[39] Dobie, *Vaquero*, 137-139; Dobie, *Cow People*, 140.
[40] J. S. Hart, "Jesse Hart, Callahan County Pioneer," *Frontier Times* (Jan., 1953), 86.

cooks manifested such behavior to an almost psychopathic extent, and some Negro cooks lived up to the tradition, to be sure, but more typical were those remembered for opposite qualities.[41] Jim Perry was not only a fine cook but also "the best Negro who ever lived"; Sam "always had a cheerful word or a cheerful song"; etc. Frank Dobie believes that Negro and Mexican cooks were notably above average in their tendency to be "providers by nature" and in their readiness to go out of their way to furnish extra services, from medicinal supplies to home-made remedies. When, for example, a young cowboy drank alkali water, and "wasn't feeling too good," Jim Simpson, the Negro cook, told him to roll a can of tomatoes in his slicker for both food and drink; the acid from the tomatoes would help neutralize the alkali.[42]

The Negro cook often possessed other skills beyond the culinary. So many Negro cooks, in fact, were noted riders and ropers that something of a pattern emerges. The wild-game cook extraordinary, Black Sam, was such a good rider that "frequently one of the boys would get him to 'top' a bad horse." Jim Perry of the XIT was not only the best cook that ever lived, according to a white hand, but he was also the best rider as well. Jim Simpson, roundup cook and fiddler, who had come up from Texas in the 1880s with a herd of longhorns, was at one time also "about the best roper" in that part of the Wyoming range.[43] When an associate of one of the famous Blockers expressed some doubt about his roping ability, Blocker told his Negro cook, "Goat," to wipe the the dough off his hands and get a rope and a horse. Blocker swung a regular "Blocker loop" on the first cow, which picked up her front feet, and the cow pony did the rest. "Goat" similarly roped and threw the next cow, Blocker the third, and so on, until they had roped about twenty, never missing.[44]

Negro cooks often left the chuckwagon for the saddle in an emergency. "Doc" Little, who had risen from cowboy to volunteer cook's assistant to full-time cook, "always remained the good cowboy" and in the event of a stampede was usually the first on a horse. The same was said of the Slaughter cook, "Old Bat." When a drove of 500 horses

[41] Cordia Sloan Duke and Joe B. Frantz, *6,000 Miles of Fence: Life on the XIT Ranch of Texas* (Austin, 1961), 172n.; Dobie, *Vaquero*, 137-139; Frazier Hunt, *The Long Trail from Texas: The Story of Ad Spaugh, Cattleman* (N. Y., 1940), 141-145; Bard, *op. cit.*, 145-146.

[42] Dobie, *Cow People*, 139-140; Bard, *op. cit.*, 82.

[43] Dobie, *Vaquero*, 137-139; Duke and Frantz, *op. cit.*, 172n, 84; Bard, *op. cit.*, 67.

[44] J. Evetts Haley, *The XIT Ranch of Texas and the Early Days of the Llano Estacado* (Norman, 1953), 77-78.

stampeded, taking the *remuda* with them, including the *remudero's* own picketed horse, the Negro cook threw himself on the trailing rope and "went bumping along for about a hundred yards" before he could stop the animal. He then mounted and took the lead in rounding up the herd.[45]

All cowboys, we have noted, were expected to be able to "sing" in order to soothe the restless cattle. Just as they were expert riders and ropers, Negro cooks were frequently singers, musicians, and even composers. Although hard-worked, they were about the only men in an outfit with the opportunity to carry and play a musical instrument. "The Zebra Dun," a song about a supposed greenhorn who surprised everyone by riding an outlaw horse, is said to have been composed by Jake, who worked for a Pecos River ranch.[46] One chuckwagon cook who supplemented his menu with deer and turkey which he shot himself, also sang and played the guitar.[47] Another, Old Bat, the Slaughter cook, played both the fiddle and the fife. Jim Perry, the XIT cook, was not only the best cook, the best rider, and the best Negro in the world, but also the best fiddler. Jim Simpson, Negro cook and roper of the Wyoming range, was also the regular fiddler for the Saturday night dances. Big Sam, cook and rider, played the banjo and sang until someone stepped on the instrument, whereupon the bunch bought him a fiddle on which he would play such songs as "Green corn, green corn, bring along the demijohn."[48] But the Negro cook-musician who made the most spectacular appearance on the cow-country stage was Gordon Davis, who led Ab Blocker's trail herd through Dodge City while mounted on his left wheel ox, fiddle in hand, playing "Buffalo Gals."[49]

Negro cooks, in addition to riding and roping, singing and playing, sometimes possessed skills so various as to be unclassifiable. The Negro cook, "Old Lee," was "handy as a pocket shirt, ready to do anything, and with the 'know-how' for almost anything that showed up, from cooking to horsewrangling to mending saddle leathers and boots." One of the most versatile of Negro cooks was John Battavia Hinnaut ("Old Bat"), probably the most useful man on the Slaughter spread. Although

[45] Lauderdale and Doak, 183-185; Allen A. Erwin, *The Southwest of John H. Slaughter* (Glendale, 1965), 147-149; Hunter, *op. cit.*, 272.

[46] John A. and Alan Lomax, *Cowboy Songs* (N. Y., 1938), 78-81, xvii-xix.

[47] Max Krueger, *Pioneer Life in Texas* (San Antonio, 1930), 58-71.

[48] Erwin, *op. cit.*, 147-149, 159; Dobie and Frantz, bet. 102 and 103; Bard, *op. cit.*, 102; Dobie, *Vaquero*, 137-139.

[49] Colonel Jack Potter, *Cattle Trails of the Old West* (Clayton, N. M., 1939), 75.

primarily and officially a roundup cook, he was a first-class ranch-hand, a musician, an expert teamster and coachman, an Indian fighter, a mighty hunter, and also served as the boss's valet, practical nurse, and bodyguard.[50]

That the Negro cow-country cook frequently possessed unusual abilities was due in part to limitations imposed because of racial discrimination. He was much more likely than the average white man to have been brought up about the kitchen and stables of a plantation or ranch and there, at an early age, to have become acquainted with cooking and horses. He was less likely to regard kitchen chores as somehow beneath him. The unusually able and ambitious white cowboy could look forward to possible promotion to foreman or trail boss; the Negro of equal ability knew he had little chance of attaining such a position. To become a ranch or roundup cook was about as much as could be expected. Age, inexperience, or physical handicap might preclude a white man from any ranch job outside of the kitchen; but for the superior Negro cowboy to preside over a chuckwagon or ranch kitchen meant an increase in pay and prestige.

Foremen and Trail Bosses

The Negro cowhand, however able, could, as we have seen, rarely rise to a position higher than chuckwagon or ranch-house cook. The principal obstacle to his becoming a ranch foreman or trail boss was a general belief that a Negro simply did not possess the qualities necessary for such a position. But even if a ranch owner or group of cattlemen were confident that a Negro had the necessary intelligence, initiative, and general capacity, there was always the practical consideration that such a man, even if in charge of an all-Negro outfit, would on occasion have to deal with white foremen and trail bosses who might refuse to recognize his authority, and that expensive trouble might ensue. A Negro, however great his ability, thus had difficulty in attaining greater authority than could be exercised over a chuckwagon or kitchen. The phenomenal success of Ora Haley, who for three decades was the dominant figure in the range-cattle business of Northwestern Colorado, is said to have been partly due to his Negro top hand Thornton Biggs, who although he "taught a whole generation of future range managers, wagon bosses, and all-round cowpunchers the finer points of the range-

---

[50] Potter, *op. cit.*, 79-80; Erwin, *op. cit.*, 102, 147, 150, 159, 307-308, 317, 323.

cattle business," himself "never became a range manager or even a foreman." The fairer-minded recognized the handicaps under which their Negro cowhands labored. Jim Perry, redoubtable cook, rider, and fiddler of the XIT ranch, once wryly remarked: "If it weren't for my damned old black face I'd have been boss of one of these divisions long ago."[51] "And no doubt he would have," a white employee commented.

And yet a very few Negroes of exceptional ability, and sometimes under unusal circumstances, did make the grade. There was the master West Texas rider and roper, "Nigger Add" or "Old Add" who, by 1889 if not earlier, was the LFD's range boss, working "South Texas colored hands almost entirely." One of his qualifications was that he was a "dictionary of earmarks and brands" but probably more important was his universal popularity among cattlemen from Toyah, Texas, to Las Vegas, New Mexico.[52] Nigger Add's outfit consisted "almost entirely" of Negroes—and one wonders who the exceptions were. Probably they were Mexicans.

But did any Negro break through the color line to direct outfits including at least some whites? A leading authority on the cow country doubts that it could have happened.[53] Nevertheless at least one Negro, it seems, through sheer ability and force of character was able to defy the tradition that the white man always gives the orders and the black man obeys. Al Jones was a six-footer with a proud carriage and finely chiseled features of a somewhat "Indian" type. He went up the trail no less than thirteen times, and four times—once was in 1885—he was trail boss, directing Negroes, Mexicans, and sometimes white men. As a trail boss he was resourceful and decisive, but probably needed an abundance of tact to get the job done.[54]

Paradoxically, the race prejudice which prevented more than a very few Negro cowhands from rising to the status of foreman or trail boss may have spurred able and ambitious Negroes into taking up land, acquiring cattle, and setting up as independent small ranchers, whereas, lacking the incentive such an obstacle provided, they might have re-

---

[51] Burroughs, *op. cit.*, 71; Duke and Frantz, *op. cit.*, 171-172.
[52] N. Howard (Jack) Thorp, *Songs of the Cowboys* (Boston, 1921), 166-168; Thorp, "Banjo in the Cow Camps," *Atlantic*, CLXVI (Aug., 1940), 195-196; Thorp, *Pardner of the Wind* (Caldwell, Ida., 1945), 22, 285.
[53] Ramon F. Adams, Dallas, to KWP, Feb. 6, 1953.
[54] Frank Dobie, "Notes on Meeting of Trail Drivers of Texas, San Antonio, *ca.* October 1924"; Dobie, "The Old Trail Drivers," *Country Gentleman*, XC (Feb., 14, 1925), 8, 28 (photograph); Dobie to KWP, Feb. 16, 1953; Dobie, *Cow People*, 222-223 (photograph); Hunter, *op. cit.*, 378.

mained satisfied with a position as ranch foreman. But the story of the Negro rancher belongs to the history of petty capitalism rather than to labor history.

Henchmen, Bodyguards, "Bankers," and Factotums

Some especially able and trustworthy cow-country Negroes fulfilled roles for which there was no equivalent among white cowhands; as confidential assistants, factotums and, when it was necessary to transport large sums of money, bodyguards and "bankers."

Colonel Charles Goodnight wrote of Bose Ikard, his right hand man: "I have trusted him farther than any living man. He was my detective, banker, and everything else." Bose would sometimes have on his person proceeds from his employer's cattle sales amounting to as much as $20,000, since it was reasoned that a thief would be unlikely to search a Negro's belongings.[55]

John Slaughter's "Old Bat" played a similar role. Officially a roundup cook, he could also do almost any ranch work, but his major importance was as a general factotum in anything connected with Slaughter's personal needs—valet, practical nurse, and, above all, bodyguard. When Slaughter was on a cattle-buying trip, Bat always went along to guard the approximately $10,000 in gold which Slaughter usually carried in his money belt, watching while his employer slept. When Slaughter went into Mexico, where silver was preferable, Bat had charge of a mule loaded with "dobe" dollars. His fitness as bodyguard was demonstrated in action against the Apache and when, with another Negro, he stood at Slaughter's side and helped beat off an attack by Mexican bandits.[56]

Print Olive's handyman and bodyguard was Nigger Jim Kelly—wrangler, horsebreaker, gunman—who in the fall of 1869 accompanied his boss back from Fort Kearney, Nebraska, their saddlebags stuffed with currency and gold, and who in 1872, with a quick well-aimed bullet, saved Print's life after he had been shot three times and was about to be killed.[57]

Still another formidable Negro henchman was Zeke, a giant "two-knife" Negro, who in 1879 accompanied Colonel Draper to

[55] J. Evetts Haley, *Charles Goodnight: Cowman & Plainsman* (Boston and N. Y., 1936), 166-167, 207, 215, 242-243; *The West Texas Historical Association Year Book* (Oct., 1942), 127.
[56] Erwin, *op. cit.*, 102, 147-150, 159, 307-308, 317, 323.
[57] Chrisman, *op. cit.*, 93, 124, 321, 358-359, 401.

Dodge City on a cattle-buying trip with a paper-wrapped bundle of
$5,000 in currency.[58] Finally, there was "Old Nep." The famous
"Shanghai" Pierce may have thought more of him, according to Frank
Dobie, than of anyone else; for thirty five years Neptune Holmes used
to accompany Shanghai on his cattle-buying expeditions, leading a mule
loaded with saddlebags which bulged with gold and silver and on which
he would pillow his head at night.[59]

Where large sums of money were involved, and courage and loyalty
in protecting and defending it was needed, prominent cattlemen such
as Goodnight, Slaughter, Olive, and Pierce, characteristically preferred
to depend on Negro bodyguards.

Wages

For a generation and more, cow-country Negroes distinguished themselves as riders and ropers, cooks and bodyguards, as well as in the
more common and still highly necessary positions of wranglers, ordinary cowboys, and top hands. What compensation, financial and psychological, did they receive for their services? And how did their wages,
working, and living conditions, and opportunities for advancement and
a "good life," compare with those of white hands of corresponding
abilities and of Negroes outside the cattle country?

In view of the racial situation which then prevailed throughout the
United States, particularly in the South and West, it can be assumed that
Negro cowmen encountered discrimination and segregation. The question therefore is not: Did discrimination and segregation exist? But
rather: What was their extent and character? And how uniform were
they? For although racism was general, it did vary from region to region, from state to state, and even from community to community. It
also varied from period to period, probably increasing rather than di-
minishing during the years in question.

Racial discrimination in the cattle country falls into several categories: wages and working conditions on the job; personal and social
relations on the ranch or on cattle trails; and in town or at the end of
the cattle trail.

Discrimination was probably least evident on the job. As to wages,

---

[58] George Bolds, *Across the Cimarron: The Adventures of "Cimarron" George Bolds, Last
of the Frontiersmen,* as he related his life story to James D. Horan (N. Y., 1956),
48-49.
[59] Dobie, *Cow People,* 47; Chris Emmett, *Shanghai Pierce: A Fair Likeness (Norman,*
1953), viii, 4, 10, 47, 51-52, 101, 127, 130, 133, 265-266.

cow-punching was, of course, by no means a highly paid occupation, regardless of race. Wages of various categories of cowhands varied widely not only from year to year and from region to region, but even within the same year and region and sometimes within the same outfit as well. Wages were generally low, but increased somewhat from the 1860s into the 1890s and were higher on the Northern Range than in Texas and Kansas. An ordinary hand in the South received from a minimum $15 per month immediately after the Civil War, to $20-$30 through the late 1860s, 1870s, and into the 1880s, to as much as $45 in the 1890s. An experienced top hand would receive $5 or $10 per month more than a less experienced man, and trail hands were paid somewhat more than ordinary ranch hands. Especially experienced trail hands, below the rank of trail boss, occasionaly drew double wages of as much as $60 or even $75; but a "green" boy would receive half-wages of $10-$15. The wages of trail bosses and foreman normally ranged during this period from $100 to $150. Cooks' salaries, as we have seen, might be as little as that of a top hand or as much as double an ordinary cowhand's, but customarily were $5 or $10 more than those of the best-paid cowhand in the outfit. In the North, cowhands usually got about $10 a month more than those in the South. In all cases compensation included food and, in the case of ranch hands, sleeping accommodations, such as they were.[60]

Strange though it may seem, there is no clear-cut evidence that Negro cowhands were generally or seriously discriminated against in the matter of wages, though this was obviously so with Mexicans, who sometimes received one half to one third that of white cowboys earning $20-25.[61] "Teddy Blue," to be sure, says of the Olive outfit, for which he worked in 1879, that they hated Mexicans and "niggers" but "hired them because they worked cheaper than white men." He gives no details, however, and the notoriously violent Olives may have been no more typical in their wage policy than in their conduct generally. On the other hand, one trail boss stated: "I have worked white Americans, Mexicans, and Negroes and they all got just the same salary."[62] Wages were so much under the control of the individual employer that no doubt Negroes

[60] All the general works on the cattle industry and most of the personal reminiscences give more or less attention to wages. Perhaps most generally useful is Louis Pelzer, *op. cit.*, 166, 246.
[61] Freeman, I. *op. cit.*, 559; James Henry Cook, *Fifty Years on the Old Frontier as Cowboy, Hunter, Guide, Scout, and Ranchman* (New Haven, 1925; 1st ed., 1923), 8-9.
[62] Abbott and Smith, *op. cit.*, 39; Lauderdale and Doak, *op. cit.*, 183-185.

were sometimes discriminated against; but such discrimination seems not to have been characteristic and, when it occurred, was never nearly as serious as that to which Mexicans were subjected.

Cowboy Strikes

The question of wages naturally brings up the further question: Did cowboys, through united action, ever endeavor to raise their low wages? The general impression is that the happy, carefree, independent-spirited cowboy could not have cared less about wages, so long as they were sufficient to keep him in smoking tobacco and to finance a spree on pay day at the trail's end. The late Stanley Vestal—a better authority on the Northern Plains Indians than on the cattle industry—was writing in this spirit when he enquired, rhetorically and contemptuously, "What cowboy ever wished to join a union?"[63] The answer could have been supplied by anyone acquainted with the cattle industry of the Texas Panhandle and of the Powder River region of Wyoming during the 1880s.

In 1883, just before the spring roundup, cowboys on a number of big Panhandle ranches issued an ultimatum to their bosses demanding higher wages—$50 per month instead of the $25-35 they were then receiving. Better food, particularly more vegetables, is said to have been another objective, but there was apparently no demand for shorter hours than the usual 105 for a seven-day week—15 hours a day! According to the official record of the Federal Bureau of Labor Statistics, the strike was a prompt and unequivocal success, but all other evidence indicates that, though from five to seven large ranches and over 300 cowboys were involved, the strike dragged on for over a year and finally "petered out." Texas Rangers, hired gunmen, and dancehall girls, who soon consumed the strikers' savings, are all credited with responsibility for the failure of this first cowboy strike.[64]

The Panhandle cowboy strike, though the first, was not the last. The Wyoming cattle industry was largely in the hands of absentee ranch owners from Great Britain and the Eastern states, and early in 1886

---

[63] Stanley Vestal, *The Missouri* (N. Y., 1945), 163.
[64] The only treatment of this strike in any detail is by Ruth Allen, *Chapters in the History of Organized Labor in Texas* (Austin, 1941), 33-42. Excellent as is this pioneer study, the "cowboy strike" deserves still further attention. Other accounts of, or references to, this strike—not mentioned in the Allen article—are in Charles A. Siringo, *A Lone Star Cowboy* (Santa Fe, 1919), 268-269; and Lewis Nordyke, *Great Roundup: The Story of Texas and Southwestern Cowmen* (N. Y., 1955), 109-111.

they ordered a general cut of at least $5 in the prevailing monthly wage of $35-40. Just before the spring roundup the cowboys on the south fork of Powder River struck for $40 a month all around; the strike was led by men who were themselves getting $40, but who objected to working beside men who were getting only $35 and even $30. The strike, which spread to the Sweetwater-Platte area, was generally successful, though its leader was later blackballed.[65]

Negro cowboys could hardly have played any important part in these strikes, as there were not many in the Panhandle and very few in Wyoming. The only Negro cow-country employee in the Panhandle strike about whom we have clear-cut evidence was loyal to his employer rather than to his fellow workers. When it was rumored that a delegation of strikers was descending on the T-Anchor ranch, its owner planted a black-powder mine in an outbuilding—in case strikers should attempt to use the structure as cover for an attack on the ranch house. He commissioned "Gus Lee, the faithful and later famous Negro cook," in the event of such an attack, to crawl out and light the fuse. But the strikers, after a few bullets had kicked up dirt about their horses, advanced no farther and thus relieved Lee of this responsibility.[66]

A Negro or two may, however, have been among the Panhandle strikers. Both in the Panhandle and on Powder River the cowboy strike against the big ranches was followed within a few years by a bloody feud between the big ranchers and the "nester ranchers and little men," with the big ranchers hiring cowboy-gunmen and their opponents drawing support from disgruntled and sometimes blackballed cowboys. The little town of Tascosa in the Panhandle was headquarters for both the striking cowboys in 1883, and for the "nester ranchers" and their supporters in 1886. Among the cowboy partisans of the "little men" was "Nigger Bob" who, when cowboy-gunmen about 2 a.m. on March 21 invaded Tascosa, was "sleepin' on a hot roll" between a woodpile and a small adobe. As the gunmen advanced, firing, rifle shots apparently from the woodpile, drilled one of them through the chest. "Nigger Bob" claimed that, when the bullets got too close, he prudently left

---

[65] Helena Huntington Smith, *The War on Powder River* (N. Y., 1966), 31-33, 289; John Clay, *My Life on the Range* (Chicago, 1924), 123, 125 (Clay mistakenly places this strike in 1884 rather than 1886; he also mentions another strike in the fall).

[66] John L. McCarty, *Maverick Town: The Story of Old Tascosa* (Norman, 1946), 112-113; Boone McClure, "A Review of the T Anchor Ranch," *Panhandle Plains Historical Review*, III (1930), 68-69.

the scene, but his "tough hombre" reputation raised the suspicion that he might have done more shooting than he was willing to admit. If "Nigger Bob" and others like him were around during the strike, they probably supported it.[67]

Working Conditions

Negroes were not discriminated against in the work permitted them—below the rank of foreman and trail boss. An experienced Negro would not be told to help the wrangler or to "eat dust" on the drag while a white greenhorn rode at point. On the other hand, Negroes may have been worked harder and longer than whites. John M. Hendrix, a white former cowpuncher and rancher, writing in the middle 1930s, approvingly presented the most extreme picture of discrimination. Negroes, he says, "were usually called on to do the hardest work around an outfit," such as "taking the first pitch out of the rough horses," while the whites were eating breakfast. "It was the Negro hand who usually tried out the swimming water when a trailing herd came to a swollen stream, or if a fighting bull or steer was to be handled, he knew without being told that it was his job." On cold rainy nights, moreover, Negroes would stand "a double guard rather than call the white folks" and would even launder everyone's clothes when the opportunity offered. "These Negroes knew their place, and were careful to stay in it."[68]

Their "place," according to this white Texan, was to do the most dangerous and difficult work, and more of it than any white hand, and in addition to serve as *valets de chambre* to the white hands..

But such a picture cannot be accepted as generally valid. There may have been some outfits to which this description applied and some Negro hands who endeavored to win favor by such works of superogation, but firsthand accounts of the cattle industry in its heyday—Hendrix's own experiences belonged entirely to the twentieth century—hardly seem to confirm this picture. Negroes were frequently expert riders and did "top" horses for less able wranglers, but contemporaries indicate that such work was regarded as a favor, not as a duty, and its beneficiaries were grateful for it. That Negroes were usually sent to test a swollen stream or handle a dangerous animal cannot be confirmed. There is a similar lack of information about Negroes gratuitously acting

---

[67] McCarty, *op. cit.*, 141-149, esp. 144 and 149.
[68] Hendrix, "Negro Cowmen," 24.

as valets. The only Negro trail hand so described did it exclusively for the trail boss and even this was regarded as unprecedented.[69]

The Negro, to be sure, was occasionally given unpleasant chores, but due to individual unfairness rather than to accepted custom. They might be given jobs which no one else would do—such as killing the calves dropped during the night on a cattle drive.[70] They were sometimes tricked or bullied into doing more than their share of work.[71] But there is no evidence that Negroes were normally expected to do double night-herding duty or guard the cattle while the whites went on a spree—merely that some cowboys were cheats or bullies who were ready to take advantage of Negroes or, for that matter, of inexperienced white cowhands.

Living Conditions

Discrimination and segregation off the job, whether on the ranch or the cattle trail, would have been difficult. Hendrix insists on at least partially segregated eating facilities when he describes the Negroes as "topping" the white hands' horses while the whites ate breakfast—presumably the Negroes ate at the "second table"—and he also states that the Negroes "had their own dishes"! But one can hardly imagine the independent and even cranky chuckwagon cook actually taking the trouble to segregate the dishes! Hendrix may have been reading back into the 1870s and 1880s the pattern of race relationships which he considered proper in his own times.[72]

Actually, firsthand accounts of ranch and cattle-trail life indicate about as much segregation as prevailed on Huckleberry Finn's and the "Nigger Jim's" raft before the appearance of "The King" and "The Duke." The sleeping arrangements were usually such as to defy any idea of racial segregation. Ranchowner, trail boss, Negro and white cowhands—particularly in bad weather—frequently not only slept in the same shack or tent but also shared the same blankets.[73] The one case of such segregation I have encountered occurred on a Wyoming ranch in 1885 when an Irish cook (sex not specified) refused to allow a Negro

---

[69] Dobie, *Cow People*, 233.
[70] Haley, *Goodnight*, 136.
[71] Dobie, *Vaquero*, 97, 34-36, 46-47; Shaw, *op. cit.*, 34-36, 46-47.
[72] C. Vann Woodward, *The Strange Career of Jim Crow* (N. Y., 1955), presents the thesis that segregation in the extreme form which it had assumed by the early 1900s was a comparatively recent development.
[73] Siringo, *Riata and Spurs*, 27; Haley, *Littlefield*, 55, 90, 93, 100-101, 114, 134; J. Evetts Haley, *Jeff Milton: A Good Man with a Gun* (Norman, 1948), 19.

bronc buster to sleep in the bunkhouse.[74] But when white women began to appear, those extreme manifestations of racial 'integration" belonging to the womanless world of the cattle trail and the wintering camp yielded to a more formal and conventional pattern of conduct. When a highly respected Negro cowboy, in the midst of a blizzard, was permitted to sleep on the kitchen floor of a shack in which a camp manager was living with his wife it was regarded by the Negro as an example of extreme condescension or of humanity or both.[75]

Hazing and Ill Treatment

A good deal of hazing and practical joking is inevitable in a community made up largely of rough and uneducated men. Negro hands, particularly those who were young, inexperienced, or timid, probably were subjected to more than their share of such horseplay. But no one in the cattle country—Negro or white, tenderfoot or old timer—was entirely immune to such treatment.[76] In the case of rough treatment which went beyond hazing and became grossly insulting or physically injurious, the Negro cowhand—nearly always a minority member of an outfit composed principally of whites—was in a difficult position. He was almost never a gunslinger. If he were, and if he succeeded in shooting a white opponent in a quarrel, it might have had very serious consequences for him. Negro cowhands rarely used, or attempted to use, a gun in a quarrel within their own outfit. One exception occurred in 1872, when Jim Kelly got the drop on a white cowboy with whom he had had words; but the boss, Print Olive, finally intervened on behalf of the threatened man.[77] Kelly, however, was not only a gunman; he was Print Olive's gunman as well, so nothing happened to him. In 1880 a Negro cowhand, who also served as the trail boss's flunky, attempted to draw on a recently-hired white cowboy who had "cussed him out" for taking his horse's hobbles after repeated warnings, but fell dead with three bullets through the heart.[78] In both these cases the Negro had a special relationship with his employer which encouraged him to brook no nonsense from a white man.

---

[74] Amanda Wardin Brown, "A Pioneer in Colorado and Wyoming," *The Colorado Magazine*, XXXV (Oct., 1958), 274.

[75] Duke and Frantz, *op. cit.*, 163-164.

[76] Debo, *op. cit.*, 108; Dobie, *Longhorns*, 107-108; Hunter, *op. cit.*, 205; Ray M. Beauchamp, "The Town That Died Laughing," *Frontier Times* (Summer, 1960), 30-31, 50-52; Westermeier, *Trailing the Cowboy*, 202-203.

[77] Chrisman, *op. cit.*, 104, 201; Harry E. Chrisman, Denver, to KWP, Oct. 23, 1965.

[78] Dobie, *Cow People*, 233-237.

Cowboys seldom engaged in fisticuffs and I have found only one case of a fist fight between a Negro cowhand and a white: this involved the later famous "80 John" Wallace, then a youthful wrangler, and a white boy from another outfit, during a roundup. Wallace claimed the victory. But both participants were mere boys, who were encouraged by the older cowhands;[79] an inter-racial fight between adults probably would not have been so favorably regarded.

Negro cowhands normally depended for protection against insult or injury—whether from members of their own outfits or outsiders—not on fists or weapons but on good conduct, tactful behavior, and their standing among the better element of whites. Negro cooks, though supported by their traditional prestige and real power, were always in danger of encountering violently prejudiced white cowhands who would challenge their authority. For the most part, Negro cooks avoided such a challenge (or insured that, should it materialize, they would have the support of other white cowhands) by a policy of tact and good management—by means of their excellent cookery and, when they were exceptionally good riders, as they often were, by occasionally "topping" a difficult horse. Black Sam of Pease River was particularly skillful in maintaining his prestige without causing ill-feelings. He was an exceptional cook and rider and a popular musician, as well as the biggest and most powerful man in camp. One day when a cowboy jokingly said that he was "too big for a man but not big enough for a horse," he promptly replied that he *was* a horse and would give a dollar to any man who could ride him without spurs. Sam then stripped, with only a bandanna around his neck to hold on by, and one by one he hurled his would-be riders to the ground—thereby demonstrating, but in a friendly and tactful fashion, his ability to take care of himself. He never had any trouble.[80]

White cowhands repeatedly came to the support of Negro members of their outfits. When a drunken cowpuncher in Dodge City began to abuse a Negro cook, for no reason except that he was colored, a sixteen-year-old boy belonging to the Negro's outfit promptly sailed in—carrying guns was banned in Dodge at this time—and soon had the best of the fight. Potentially, a much more serious occasion arose in 1879. It involved the Olive brothers' trail boss, Ira Olive, who had killed a

---

[79] Hettye Wallace Branch, *The Story of "80 John": A Biography of the Most Respected Negro Ranchmen in the Old West* (N. Y., 1960), 17-18.
[80] Dobie, *Vaquero*, 137-139.

Mexican cowhand a year or so before and who for some reason now began to abuse Jim Kelly—with the aim, E. C. Abbott believed, of getting Kelly to go for his gun so that he could kill him. Kelly, himself a gunman, later claimed that he would have drawn and killed Ira except for the knowledge that he would have to reckon with his brother Print if he did; this he wished to avoid, since Print was his friend. So he took the abuse until Ira struck him in the mouth with his gun, knocking out two teeth. What might have happened next will never be known for at this point the nineteen-year-old Abbott brashly intervened. "If you hit that boy again," he warned ("that boy" was forty years old) "I'll shoot your damn eyes out."[81]

But such protection was not always available. In 1878 a Negro was hired to work on the 22 Ranch, but a member of the outfit—a "nigger killer" type—set out to run him off and one morning began shooting at him. In desperation, the Negro scrambled onto a horse and fled, with the white man in pursuit. Only the white man returned to camp and the Negro's horse showed up the next day with the saddle still on; a few years later a human skeleton, believed to be the Negro's, was found in the neighborhood. The Negro, during this fracas, apparently never attempted to defend himself nor did any member of the outfit lift a finger or even his voice on behalf of the man, or venture to question the white man's conduct. Possibly, had the Negro been with the outfit long enough to establish himself, someone would have intervened, but this is speculation: the outfit stands condemned, with not a single man of the calibre of young Abbott or the sixteen-year-old boy in Dodge City.[82]

Recreation and Social Life

The Negro cowboy engaged in the same amusements as the white—on a basis ranging from apparently complete integration to rigid separation. The extent of this segregation depended upon how well the parties knew one another and, more important, upon whether or not the whites included women.

To understand the character and degree of this segregation, and the way in which it was regarded by both whites and blacks, one must remember that the white men and women of the cow country were largely

---

[81] Hendrix, "Negro Cowmen," 24; Ross Santee, *Lost Pony Tracks* (Bantam Books, 1956; 1st ed., 1953), 202-203; Abbott and Smith, *op. cit.,* 38-40; Chrisman, 201.
[82] William Joseph Alexander Elliot, *The Spurs* (Spur, Texas, 1939), 209-210.

Southerners, or Westerners with a Southern exposure, while the Negroes, if not former slaves, were usually the children of ex-slaves. Both whites and Negroes were thus acquainted, by personal experience or recent tradition, with racial *discrimination* far more severe than anything practiced in the post-bellum cow country, even though racial *segregation* under slavery was less rigid than it became during the late nineteenth century.

When ranch work was slack, particularly in the winter, the hands sometimes held a dance, either a "bunkhouse 'shindig'" in which the participants were all males or a "regular dance" with girls from neighboring ranches or from town if one was close enough. On these occasions the Negro hands had the opportunity to shine, as musicians or dancers or both. Although serving as musicians at either type of dance, they were more conspicuous as dancers in the womanless bunkhouse affairs. Indeed, they might not appear on the dance floor with white women, though, singly or in groups, they might present dancing exhibitions as part of the entertainment.[83]

Segregation in a cattle town, where the Negro cowhand was more of a stranger and white women were present, was much more clearcut than on the familiar ranch. But even here the restrictions were not always as rigid as one might perhaps expect. On the town's streets and among members of the same outfit, segregation might be non-existent. A French baron, returning in 1883 from a visit to the Black Hills, was astonished to see a group of cowboys throwing the lasso and wrestling in front of the door to the hotel bar, with a Negro participating "on a footing of perfect equality." Consequently, he naively assumed that race prejudice had disappeared,"[84] but had the cowboys *entered* the bar this illusion would probably have vanished, even though the region was the Northern Range, not Gulf Coast Texas.

Even in Texas, however, segregation in the saloons was apparently informal. Whites, it seems, were served at one end of the bar, Negroes at the other. But should a white man and a Negro choose to drink and converse together in the "neutral zone" between the two sections probably no objection would be raised. The gunman and gambler Ben Thompson once undertook to "integrate" a San Antonio saloon at the

---

[83] Duke and Frantz, *op. cit.*, 102-103, 189-190; Santee, *op. cit.*, 158-159.
[84] Edmond Mandat-Gracey, *Cow-Boys and Colonels: Narrative of a Journey across the Prairie and over the Black Hills of Dakota,* translated by William Conn (Philadelphia and N. Y., 1963), 325-326.

point of a revolver, forcing the bartender to permit the Negroes to "spread out" from their crowded corner into the vacant space at the "white" end of the bar. His friends charitably assumed that he was suffering from a nervous breakdown, but since, upon an earlier occasion, Thompson had shot a white bully who was trying to force a Cherokee-Negro cowboy to down a beer mug full of whiskey, he may actually have been in part influenced by a fleeting impulse to defend the underdog.[85]

If the Negro, however, moved from the saloon to a restaurant, he would encounter a completely segregated situation, partly because of the symbolic value attached to sitting down and eating together—as opposed to standing up at the same bar[86]—but principally because women might be guests in the dining room or cafe. In a town without a colored restaurant, the Negro might have food handed to him at the back door of a cafe—perhaps he might even be permitted to eat in the kitchen—but more probably would, like many white cowboys, prefer to purchase groceries and eat sitting on a hitching rail.[87]

Negroes, of course, were not lodged in "white" hotels—unless they were in attendance on prominent white cattlemen—but cowboys, black and white, usually felt that they had better use for their money than to spend it on hotel rooms. They preferred to spread their "hot rolls" in a livery stable or some other sheltered spot.[88]

The most rigorously segregated cow-town establishments, at least so far as Negro cowhands were concerned, were brothels staffed with white prostitutes. However, the larger cow-towns at least, such as Dodge City, were also equipped with *bagnios* occupied by "soiled doves of color," while smaller communities usually had a few "public women" of color who operated independently. The rule that Negroes must not patronize white prostitutes did not of course bar relations between white cowhands and colored women.[89]

---

[85] J. H. Plenn, *Texas Hellion: The True Story of Ben Thompson* (N. Y., 1955), 60, 142; Hendrix, "Negro Cowmen," 24; O. C. Fisher with J. C. Dykes, *King Fisher: His Life and Times* (Norman, 1966), 124-126.

[86] Harry Golden, *Only in America* (Permabooks, 1959; 1st ed., 1958), 105-107, presenting his "Vertical Negro Plan" for abolishing segregation, advances the theory that no Southerner objected to mingling with Negroes so long as neither party sat down!

[87] See Rhodes, *op. cit.*, 86-88, for the attempt of a Negro to eat in a white restaurant in a New Mexico cowtown.

[88] Bolds, *op. cit.*, 48-49; McCarty, *op. cit.*, 149.

[89] Nyle E. Miller and Joseph W. Snell, *Why the West Was Wild* (Topeka, 1963), 614-615, 127, 453; Burroughs, *op. cit.*, 71; William R. Cox, *Luke Short and His Era*

The cow-town gambling-house, on the other hand, was apparently entirely unsegregated. A gambler who intended to separate a Negro trail hand from his wages through the more than expert use of cards and dice could hardly do so without sitting down with him at the same card or crap table.[90]

The Negro cowhand was accustomed to a degree of segregation and apparently did not resent it—at least not to the extent of risking his life in defiance of the practice. Clashes between Negro cowhands and whites were exceedingly rare. When racial encounters occurred in cattle towns, the Negroes involved were almost always colord soldiers.

Conclusion

Without the services of the eight or nine thousand Negroes—a quarter of the total number of trail drivers—who during the generation after the Civil War helped to move herds up the cattle trails to shipping points, Indian reservations, and fattening grounds and who, between drives, worked on the ranches of Texas and the Indian Territory, the cattle industry would have been seriously handicapped. For apart from their considerable numbers, many of them were especially well-qualified top hands, riders, ropers, and cooks. Of the comparatively few Negroes on the Northern Range, a good many were also men of conspicuous abilities who notably contributed to the industry in that region. These cowhands, in their turn, benefitted from their participation in the industry, even if not to the extent that they deserved. That a degree of discrimination and segregation existed in the cattle country should not obscure the fact that, during the halcyon days of the cattle range, Negroes there frequently enjoyed greater opportunities for a dignified life than anywhere else in the United States. They worked, ate, slept, played, and on occasion fought, side by side with their white comrades, and their ability and courage won respect, even admiration. They were often paid the same wages as white cowboys and, in the case of certain horsebreakers, ropers, and cooks, occupied positions of considerable prestige. In a region and period characterized by violence, their lives were probably safer than they would have been in the Southern cotton regions where between 1,500 and 1,600 Negroes were lynched in the

---

(Garden City, N. Y., 1961), 54-55; Westermeier, *Trailing the Cowboy*, 209, 213; Walker D. Wyman and Bruce Sibert, *Nothing But Prairie and Sky: Life on the Dakota Range in the Early Days* (Norman, 1954), 142-143.
[90] Lauderdale and Doak, *op. cit.*, 161; Haley, *Jeff Milton*, 95; Rhodes, *op. cit.*, 86-88; W. M. Hutchinson, editor, *A Bar Cross Man: The Life & Personal Writings of Eugene Manlove Rhodes* (Norman, 1956), 3-5.

two decades after 1882.[91] The skilled and handy Negro probably had a more enjoyable, if a rougher, existence as a cowhand then he would have had as a sharecropper or laborer. Bose Ikard, for example, had a rich, full, and dignified life on the West Texas frontier—as trail driver, as Indian fighter, and as Colonel Goodnight's right-hand man—more so undoubtedly than he could ever have known on a plantation in his native Mississippi.

Negro cowhands, to be sure, were not treated as "equals," except in the rude quasi-equality of the round-up, roping-pen, stampede, and river-crossing—where they were sometimes tacitly recognized even as superiors—but where else in post-Civil War America, at a time of the Negro's nadir, did so many adult Negroes and whites attain even this degree of fraternity? The cow country was no utopia for Negroes, but it did demonstrate that under some circumstances and for at least brief periods white and black in significant numbers could live and work together on more nearly equal terms than had been possible in the United States for two hundred years or would be possible again for nearly another century.

[91] Walter White, *Rope & Faggot: A Biography of Judge Lynch* (N. Y., 1929), *passim;* Jessie Parkhurst Guzman, editor, *Negro Year Book, 1941-1946* (Tuskegee, Ala., 1947), 306-307.

Corrections and Additions

p. 497, top line: "... some Negro wranglers." Strike out "Negro."

p. 498, note 17: Place of publication of Shaw volume should be "Evanston."

p. 512, l. 27-28: "works of superogation." Should be "supererogation."

p. 514, last line: "... which encouraged him to brook no nonsense from a white man." Better: "try issues with" or "stand-up to."

p. 518, l. 10-18: The sweeping generalizations that a Negro in a cow-country restaurant "would encounter a completely segregated situation" and that "Negroes, of course, were not lodged in 'white' hotels" illustrate the dangers of being too positive. A Texas trail-herd outfit that arrived at Cheyenne, Wyoming, in 1879, was horrified to discover that "not a hotel in the city would turn away a Negro if he had the money to pay for his room and meals." (Baylis John Fletcher, *Up the Trail in '79*, Wayne Gard, editor (Norman, Okla., 1967), p. 63.) How typical or otherwise the Cheyenne situation was and how long this lack of discrimination continued, even in Cheyenne, I do not know. We badly need a careful and comprehensive study of racial discrimination and segregation in the postbellum Western states and territories.

Further Reading

A pioneer study, utilizing a regional framework, is Philip Durham's and Everett L. Jones's, *The Negro Cowboys* (New York, 1965), which, however, is somewhat given to exaggeration.

THE SODHOUSE FRONTIER
ca. 1875-1913

The sodhouse frontier — so-called because the early dwellings were usually built from blocks of prairie sod — was the Central Plains region, settled under the impetus of the Homestead Act of 1862 and the postbellum construction of transcontinental railroads. Negroes rarely settled on this frontier, probably for much the same reasons that the antebellum Irish immigrants seldom sought the frontier of their day. Both were oppressed, poverty-stricken peasant peoples, and neither people, from their experiences on the land, regarded its cultivation as a pleasant pursuit, nor did they have either the funds or the experience for its purchase and successful development. If they mustered the determination to leave their tenant farms in Ireland or the South, they usually preferred to seek urban employment. Nevertheless, Negroes with a desire for independence and the willingness to undergo extreme hardship to attain it, did seek — and even achieve — such independence on the sodhouse frontier, principally of Kansas.

Shortly after the fall of Reconstruction governments in the South, thousands of Negro "Exodusters," as they called themselves, sought refuge from political, social, and economic discrimination by settling in Kansas — the state that they associated with Old John Brown, antebellum martyr to Negro freedom. The Moses of their exodus was Benjamin (Pap) Singleton. Although most of the Exodusters drifted into Kansas towns and cities, or even back to the South, some of them settled and doggedly stuck it out on the land.

John G. Van Deusen, "The Exodus of 1879," *JNH*, XXI (April, 1936), pp. 111-29, is concerned principally with the causes of the exodus. Roy Garvin, "Benjamin, or 'Pap' Singleton and His Followers," *JNH*, XXXIII (January, 1948), pp. 7-23, is the fullest account of the whole movement. Glen Schwendemann, "Nicodemus: Negro Haven on the Solomon," *KHQ*, XXXIV (Spring, 1968), pp. 10-31, treats the most important and the only permanent Exoduster community, located in Graham County, northwest Kansas. "Negro Community Shrinks in West," *The New York Times*, October 18, 1964, p. 74, deals with Nicodemus in recent years.

Other early Negro farming communities in Kansas, Oklahoma, Colorado, etc., should also receive special treatment.

THE CRAZY SNAKE UPRISING, 1909:
THE LAST FRONTIER FIGHT FOR FREEDOM

Negroes and Indians of the Creek and Seminole tribes had been allied in resistance to white encroachment on their freedom and independence since at least as early as the East Florida annexation plot of 1812 (pp. 183-203) and the Red Stick War of 1814 (pp. 213-15), and extending through the struggles incident to Indian removal (pp. 238-357, passim). When a cleavage developed in these and other Civilized Tribes between the full-bloods, who mostly wished to adhere as closely as possible to the old ways, and the half-breeds, or full-bloods under white and half-breed influence, who sought acceptance from the whites by attempting to bring the tribes fully into the orbit of white culture — including Christianity, slavery, and discrimination against Negroes — the Negroes, naturally, to the best of their ability supported the full-bloods, who, without being at all Negrophiles, at least had a more tolerant and relaxed attitude toward Negroes than the "progressive" half-breeds. In the Civil War, for example, with full-bloods more than half-breeds tending to support the Union and half-breeds more than full-bloods the Confederacy, Negroes almost to a man were defenders of the Union. See references for "Civil War on the Frontier, 1861-1865," pp. 467-69.

Negroes and full-bloods were also united in the factional struggles that took place, particularly in the Creek Nation, after the Civil War, and which sometimes developed into small-scale civil wars, such as "The Green Peach War," in which the full-blood leader was Isparhecher. Negroes, particularly in the Creek and Seminole nations, enjoyed political and a large degree of social equality and were jealous of any trend that might debase them to the position of Negroes in the white-man's civilization. For a brief description of the postbellum position of Negroes in the Civilized Tribes, see pp. 74-79. Studies of Negroes in the various Civilized Tribes from the Civil War to the admission of Oklahoma into the Union as a state in 1907 — and, indeed, subsequently — are badly needed. The role of Negroes in the maintenance of law and order as federal marshals and tribal lighthorsemen would be a particularly significant subject for investigation.

The admission of Indian Territory and Oklahoma Territory to the Union as the single state of Oklahoma was disastrous for the conservative Indian full-bloods and their Negro allies. Tribal independence was conclusively ended and the Indians were subjected to the white-dominated state government, the Negroes to southern-type segregation and discrimination.

The last flare, or flicker, of the old spirit of Indian and Negro freedom and independence was the so-called Crazy Snake Uprising, after the full-blood Creek, Chitto Hajo (Crazy — i.e., recklessly brave — Snake), a Union veteran and Isparhecher supporter, who was credited with being its leader. Crazy Snake had no particular fondness for Negroes, but he knew that they were indispensable allies in his movement for the restoration of tribal government. Although sometimes incorrectly referred to as "the last Indian war" in the United States, the Crazy Snake Uprising — less romantically known as "The Smoked Meat Rebellion" because the alleged theft of bacon from a smokehouse was the spark that set it off — was in actuality very largely a movement of disgruntled Creek and Seminole Negroes, with some full-blood support. In this movement, the Negro-Indian alliance against racist white domination, which had manifested itself in resistance to the annexation of East Florida, in the Red Stick and Seminole Wars, and in the Civil War, was making its final, futile stand. Thus, during a week or so late in March, 1909, in a few sputters of rifle fire, ended the last attempt of allied frontier Negroes and Indians to defend by force of arms their rights to self-government and equality against the advance of a dominating white racist civilization.

The principal publications dealing with this last Negro-Indian frontier uprising are Eleanor Patricia Atwood, "The Crazy Snake Rebellion: A Study in the Breakdown of Tribal Government," *Vassar Journal of Undergraduate Studies* (Poughkeepsie, N.Y., May, 1942), pp. 44-60, devoted primarily to the background of the principal "rebellion"; and Mel H. Bolster, "The Smoked Meat Rebellion," *CO*, XXXI (Spring, 1953), pp. 37-55, which treats the 1909 "uprising" in greater detail. The Bolster article, although it does not recognize openly the basic reasons for Negro participation, and is not at all sympathetic to the Negro rebels, or outlaws, nevertheless, almost unconsciously, makes it clear that the uprising was principally a Negro affair. A study that would both utilize a wider range of sources and concentrate on the Negro aspects of the uprising would be useful.

THE END OF THE OLD FRONTIER
AND THE BEGINNING OF THE NEW

The month before the Crazy Snake Rebellion, on Lincoln's Birthday, 1909, Negroes and whites issued a call for the founding of an organization, the National Association for the Advancement of Colored People, to fight in the courts and legislatures against the racial discrimination that the Creek and Seminole Negroes on Oklahoma's Hickory Ground were preparing to protest, ineffectually, through the muzzles of their Winchesters. One of the first triumphs of the new organization was a Supreme Court decision invalidating Oklahoma's discriminatory "Grandfather Clause."

The Western frontier, on which whites, and at least some Negroes, had sought and sometimes obtained a measure of freedom and an approach to equality, had vanished. Henceforth the frontier, for both whites and Negroes, was the entire United States, and the weapons for its conquest were no longer the rifle, axe, and plow, but political and economic organization for the common benefit.

BLACK HISTORY

Other Books of Interest

Individual titles in Series I, II, and III of the Arno Press collection THE AMERICAN NEGRO: HIS HISTORY AND LITERATURE are listed on the following pages. These reprints are, in many instances, the actual records of those who were part of the Negro experience; they encompass the economic, political, and cultural history of the Negro from colonial time to the present. The 139 clothbound books in the collection are listed alphabetically by author/editor; immediately following is a list of the titles which are also available in paperback.

The books in THE AMERICAN NEGRO collection were selected by an Editorial Advisory Board made up of the following members:

William Loren Katz, General Editor, and author of **Eyewitness: The Negro in American History** and **Teacher's Guide to American Negro History**

Arthur P. Davis, Professor of English, Howard University

Jean Blackwell Hutson, Curator, The Schomburg Collection, New York Public Library

Sara D. Jackson, National Archives, Washington, D.C.

Ernest Kaiser, The Schomburg Collection, New York Public Library

Ulysses Lee (deceased), Professor of English, Morgan State College

James M. McPherson, Professor of History, Princeton University

Dorothy B. Porter, Curator, Negro Collection, Howard University

Benjamin Quarles, Professor of History, Morgan State College

Darwin T. Turner, Dean of the Graduate School, North Carolina A & T College

Doxey A. Wilkerson, Professor of Education, Yeshiva University

To order, or for an annotated brochure, please write to:
ARNO PRESS, 330 Madison Avenue, New York, N.Y. 10017.

The American Negro Academy Occasional Papers, Numbers 1-22. . . . .
. . . . ISBN 0-405-01913-0 $21.50

Andrews, Sydney **The South Since the War:** As Shown by Fourteen Weeks of Travel and Observation in Georgia and the Carolinas. . . . . ISBN 0-405-01847-9 $12.00

The Anglo-African Magazine, Volume 1, 1859. . . . . ISBN 0-405-01803-7 $12.50

Anti-Negro Riots in the North, 1863. . . . . ISBN 0-405-01848-7 $ 3.50

Atlanta University **Atlanta University Publications, Numbers 1, 2, 4, 8, 9, 11, 13, 14, 15, 16, 17, 18** . . . . ISBN 0-405-01804-5 $30.00

Atlanta University **Atlanta University Publications, Numbers 3, 5, 6, 7, 10, 12, 19, 20** . . . . ISBN 0-405-01914-9 $33.00

Bell, Howard H. (editor) **Minutes of the Proceedings of the National Negro Conventions, 1830-1864** . . . . ISBN 0-405-01916-5 $17.00

Bell, Howard H. **A Survey of the Negro Convention Movement, 1830-1861**. . . . .
. . . . ISBN 0-405-01915-7 $12.00

Bonner, T. D. **The Life and Adventures of James P. Beckworth, Mountaineer, Scout, and Pioneer, and Chief of the Crow Nation of Indians**. . . . . . ISBN 0-405-01850-9 $16.00

Botume, Elizabeth Hyde **First Days Amongst the Contrabands**. . . . .
. . . . ISBN 0-405-01805-3 $10.50

Brown, Sterling **The Negro in American Fiction** and **Negro Poetry and Drama**. . . . .
. . . . ISBN 0-405-01851-7 $10.50

Brown, Sterling; Davis, Arthur P. and Lee, Ulysses (editors) **The Negro Caravan**. . . . . . .
. . . . ISBN 0-405-01852-5 $35.00

Brown, William Wells **Clotel, or, the President's Daughter**. . ISBN 0-405-01853-3 $ 8.00

Carleton, George W. (editor) **The Suppressed Book About Slavery!**. . . . .
. . . . ISBN 0-405-01806-1 $13.50

Cashin, Herschel V., et al. **Under Fire With the Tenth U.S. Cavalry**. . . . .
. . . . ISBN 0-405-01854-1 $12.00

Chestnutt, Charles W. **The Marrow of Tradition**. . . . . ISBN 0-405-01855-X $10.00

The Chicago Commission on Race Relations **The Negro in Chicago:** A Study of Race Relations and a Race Riot. ISBN 0-405-01807-X $15.00

Child, Lydia Maria **An Appeal in Favor of That Class of Americans Called Africans**. . . . . .
. . . . ISBN 0-405-01808-8 $ 7.00

Child, Lydia Maria **The Freedmen's Book**. . . . . ISBN 0-405-01809-6 $ 8.50

Clark, Peter **The Black Brigade of Cincinnati:** Being a Report of Its Labors and a Muster-roll of Its Members; Together With Various Orders, Speeches, etc. Relating to It. . . .
. . . . ISBN 0-405-01917-3 $ 4.50

Coffin, Levi **Reminiscences of Levi Coffin, the Reputed President of the Underground Railroad:** Being a Brief History of the Labors of a Lifetime in Behalf of the Slave, With the Stories of Numerous Fugitives, Who Gained Their Freedom Through His Instrumentality, and Many Other Incidents. . . . . ISBN 0-405-01810-X $16.50

Commissioner of Education in the District of Columbia **History of Schools for the Colored Population:** Part I: In the District of Columbia; Part II: In the United States. . . . .
. . . . ISBN 0-405-01918-1 $ 7.50

Craft, William and Ellen **Running a Thousand Miles for Freedom:** Or, the Escape of William and Ellen Craft From Slavery. . . . . ISBN 0-405-01923-8 $ 5.00

Cullen, Countee **Color** . . . . ISBN 0-405-01919-X $ 4.50

Culp, D. W. (editor) **Twentieth Century Negro Literature:** Or, a Cyclopedia of Thought on the Vital Topics Relating to the American Negro by One Hundred of America's Greatest Negroes . . . . ISBN 0-405-01856-8 $20.00

Cummings, John **Negro Population in the United States, 1790-1915**. . . . .
. . . . ISBN 0-405-01811-8 $23.50

Daniels, John **In Freedom's Birthplace:** A Study of Boston Negroes................. .... ISBN 0-405-01857-6 **$12.50**

Delany, Martin Robinson **The Condition, Elevation, Emigration, and Destiny of the Colored People of the United States:** Politically Considered. ISBN 0-405-01812-6 $ 6.50

Donnelly, Ignatius **Dr. Huguet.**........................ISBN 0-405-01920-3 $11.00

Douglass, Frederick **My Bondage and My Freedom**........ISBN 0-405-01813-4 $14.50

Du Bois, W. E. B. **The Black North in 1901:** A Social Study. . ISBN 0-405-01921-1 $ 4.00

Du Bois, W. E. B. **The Quest of the Silver Fleece**........ISBN 0-405-01922-X $13.00

Dunbar, Paul Laurence **Lyrics of Lowly Life**.............ISBN 0-405-01858-4 $ 7.00

Dunbar, Paul Laurence **The Sport of the Gods**............ISBN 0-405-01859-2 $ 8.00

Dunbar, Paul Laurence **The Strength of Gideon and Other Stories**................... .... ISBN 0-405-01860-6 $11.50

Emilio, Luis F. **History of the Fifty-Fourth Regiment of Massachusetts Volunteer Infantry, 1863-1865** .... ISBN 0-405-01861-4 $14.50

Epstein, Abraham **The Negro Migrant in Pittsburgh:** A Study in Social Economics...... .... ISBN 0-405-01924-6 $ 4.50

Fisher, Rudolph **The Walls of Jericho**...................ISBN 0-405-01862-2 $ 9.50

Flipper, Henry Ossian **The Colored Cadet at West Point**....ISBN 0-405-01863-0 $ 8.00

Foley, Albert S. **Bishop Healy:** Beloved Outcaste.........ISBN 0-405-01925-4 $10.00

Foley, Albert S. **God's Men of Color:** The Colored Catholic Priests of the United States, 1854-1954 .... ISBN 0-405-01864-9 $10.00

Fortune, Timothy Thomas **Black and White:** Land, Labor, and Politics in the South..... .... ISBN 0-405-01814-2 $ 9.00

Frazier, E. Franklin **The Free Negro Family:** A Study of Family Origins Before the Civil War .... ISBN 0-405-01815-0 $ 2.50

Garrison, William Lloyd **Thoughts on African Colonization:** Or, an Impartial Exhibition of the Doctrines, Principles, and Purposes of the American Colonization Society Together With the Resolutions, Addresses, and Remonstrances of the Free People of Color .... ISBN 0-405-01816-9 $ 9.00

Gibbs, Mifflin Wister **Shadow and Light:** An Autobiography With Reminiscences of the Last and Present Century.........................ISBN 0-405-01817-7 $12.00

Griggs, Sutton E. **Imperium In Imperio**.................ISBN 0-405-01865-7 $ 8.00

Hall, Charles **Negroes in the United States 1920-32**......ISBN 0-405-01866-5 $25.00

Haynes, George Edmund **The Negro at Work in New York City:** A Study in Economic Progress .... ISBN 0-405-01818-5 $ 4.50

Haynes, George Edmund and Brown, Sterling **The Negro Newcomers in Detroit** and **The Negro in Washington** ....ISBN 0-405-01926-2 $ 4.50

Heard, William H. **From Slavery to the Bishopric in the A.M.E. Church:** An Autobiography .... ISBN 0-405-01867-3 $ 3.50

Henson, Matthew A. **A Negro Explorer at the North Pole**...ISBN 0-405-01868-1 $ 6.00

Herndon, Angelo **Let Me Live**.........................ISBN 0-405-01869-X $12.50

Higginson, Thomas Wentworth **Black Rebellion**..........ISBN 0-405-01870-3 $ 7.00

Higginson, Thomas Wentworth **Cheerful Yesterdays**.......ISBN 0-405-01819-3 $11.50

Hinton, Richard J. **John Brown and His Men:** With Some Account of the Roads They Traveled to Reach Harper's Ferry...................ISBN 0-405-01820-7 $23.00

Holmes, Dwight Oliver Wendell **The Evolution of the Negro College**................. .... ISBN 0-405-01871-1 $ 7.50

Howe, Samuel Gridley **The Refugees from Slavery in Canada West:** Report to the Freedmen's Inquiry Commission, 1864 .... ISBN 0-405-01872-X $ 3.50

Hurston, Zora Neale **Dust Tracks On A Road:** An Autobiography....................
.... ISBN 0-405-01927-0 $12.00

Jacques-Garvey, Amy (editor) **Philosophy and Opinions of Marcus Garvey, Volume I**....
.... ISBN 0-405-01821-5 $ 3.50

Jacques-Garvey, Amy (editor) **Philosophy and Opinions of Marcus Garvey, Volume II**....
.... ISBN 0-405-01873-8 $10.00

Jay, William, and Clarke, James Freeman **The Free People of Color:** On the Condition of
the Free People of Color in the United States; Present Condition of the Free Colored
People of the United States.......................ISBN 0-405-01928-9 $ 4.50

Johnson, James Weldon **Black Manhattan**...............ISBN 0-405-01822-3 $13.00

Jones, Thomas Jesse (editor) **Negro Education:** A Study of the Private and Higher Schools
for Colored People in the United States..............ISBN 0-405-01874-6 $35.00

Katz, Bernard (editor) **The Social Implications of Early Negro Music in the United
States** ....ISBN 0-405-01875-4 $ 7.50

Katz, William Loren (editor) **Five Slave Narratives:** A Compendium.................
.... ISBN 0-405-01823-1 $15.00

Keckley, Elizabeth H. **Behind the Scenes:** Or, Thirty Years a Slave, and Four Years in the
White House .... ISBN 0-405-01824-X $ 9.00

Kerlin, Robert T. **The Voice of the Negro 1919**...........ISBN 0-405-01825-8 $ 7.50

Kester, Howard **Revolt Among the Sharecroppers**.........ISBN 0-405-01876-2 $ 3.50

King, Edward **The Great South:** A Record of Journeys in Louisiana, Texas, the Indian
Territory, Missouri, Arkansas, Mississippi, Alabama, Georgia, Florida, South Carolina,
North Carolina, Kentucky, Tennessee, Virginia, West Virginia, and Maryland........
.... ISBN 0-405-01929-7 $28.50

Langston, John Mercer **From the Virginia Plantation to the National Capitol:** Or, the First
and Only Negro Representative in Congress From the Old Dominion...............
.... ISBN 0-405-01877-0 $18.00

Larsen, Nella **Passing** ....ISBN 0-405-01930-0 $ 8.00

Livermore, George **An Historical Research Respecting the Opinions of the Founders of
the Republic on Negroes as Slaves, as Citizens, and as Soldiers**...................
.... ISBN 0-405-01878-9 $ 6.50

Locke, Alain **The Negro and His Music** and **Negro Art, Past and Present**..............
.... ISBN 0-405-01879-7 $ 8.00

Locke, Alain (editor) **The New Negro:** An Interpretation...ISBN 0-405-01826-6 $ 9.00

Lockwood, Lewis C. J., and Forten, Charlotte **Two Black Teachers During the Civil War:**
Mary S. Peake, the Colored Teacher at Fortress Monroe; Life on the Sea Islands....
.... ISBN 0-405-01931-9 $ 5.00

Love, Nat **The Life and Adventures of Nat Love, Better Known in the Cattle Country as
"Deadwood Dick"** .... ISBN 0-405-01827-4 $ 6.00

Lynch, John R. **The Facts of Reconstruction**.............ISBN 0-405-01828-2 $10.00

McKay, Claude **A Long Way From Home**..................ISBN 0-405-01880-0 $12.00

May, Samuel J. **Some Recollections of Our Anti-Slavery Conflict**....................
.... ISBN 0-405-01829-0 $10.50

Mayer, Brantz **Captain Canot, or Twenty Years of An African Slaver:** Being an Account of
His Career and Adventures On the Coast, In the Interior, On Shipboard, and In the
West Indies ....ISBN 0-405-01830-4 $14.50

Miller, Kelly **An Appeal To Conscience:** America's Code of Caste, a Disgrace to Democracy
.... ISBN 0-405-01881-9 $ 3.50

Miller, Kelly **Out of the House of Bondage**..............ISBN 0-405-01882-7 $ 7.50

Miller, Kelly **Race Adjustment:** Essays on the Negro in America, and The Everlasting Stain
.... ISBN 0-405-01831-2 $20.50

National Association for the Advancement of Colored People **Thirty Years of Lynching
in the United States, 1889-1918** ....ISBN 0-405-01932-7 $ 4.50

National Negro Conference **Proceedings of the National Negro Conference, 1909**......
.... ISBN 0-405-01890-8 $ 7.00

Nell, William C. **The Colored Patriots of the American Revolution, With Sketches of Several Distinguished Colored Persons:** To Which Is Added a Brief Survey of the Condition and Prospects of Colored Americans........ISBN 0-405-01832-0 $12.00

Nesbit, William, and Williams, Samuel **Two Black Views of Liberia:** Four Months In Liberia, or African Colonization Exposed; Four Years In Liberia, a Sketch of the Life of Rev. Samuel Williams ....ISBN 0-405-01936-X $ 5.50

Nichols, J. L., and Crogman, William H. **Progress of a Race:** Or, the Remarkable Advancement of the American Negro From the Bondage of Slavery, Ignorance, and Poverty To the Freedom of Citizenship, Intelligence, Affluence, Honor, and Trust............
.... ISBN 0-405-01883-5 $16.50

O'Connor, Ellen M., and Miner, Myrtilla **Myrtilla Miner: A Memoir** and **The School for Colored Girls in Washington, D.C.**....................ISBN 0-405-01933-5 $ 5.50

Ottley, Roi **New World A-Coming:** Inside Black America....ISBN 0-405-01833-9 $11.50

Ovington, Mary White **The Walls Came Tumbling Down**....ISBN 0-405-01884-3 $ 9.50

Payne, Daniel A. **History of the African Methodist Episcopal Church**................
.... ISBN 0-405-01885-1 $15.00

Payne, Daniel A. **Recollections of Seventy Years**.........ISBN 0-405-01834-7 $10.00

Pearson, Elizabeth Ware (editor) **Letters From Port Royal, Written at the Time of the Civil War** ....ISBN 0-405-01886-X $10.50

Penn, I. Garland **The Afro-American Press and Its Editors**..ISBN 0-405-01887-8 $18.00

Porter, Dorothy (editor) **Negro Protest Pamphlets:** A Compendium.................
.... ISBN 0-405-01888-6 $ 7.00

Porter, James A. **Modern Negro Art**....................ISBN 0-405-01889-4 $10.00

Rollin, Frank A. **Life and Public Services of Martin R. Delany:** Sub-Assistant Commissioner, Bureau Relief of Refugees, Freedmen, and of Abandoned Lands, and Late Major 104th U.S. Colored Troops ....ISBN 0-405-01934-3 $13.00

Schurz, Carl **Report on the Condition of the South**.......ISBN 0-405-01938-6 $ 5.00

Scott, Emmett J. **Negro Migration During the War**........ISBN 0-405-01891-6 $ 6.00

Scott, Emmett J. **Scott's Official History of the American Negro in the World War**......
.... ISBN 0-405-01892-4 $18.00

Siebert, Wilbur H. **The Underground Railroad from Slavery to Freedom**..............
.... ISBN 0-405-01835-5 $14.50

Silvera, John D. **The Negro in World War II**..............ISBN 0-405-01893-2 $14.00

Simmons, William J. **Men of Mark:** Eminent, Progressive, and Rising..............
.... ISBN 0-405-01836-3 $39.50

Sinclair, William A. **The Aftermath of Slavery:** A Study of the Condition and Environment of the American Negro ....ISBN 0-405-01894-0 $11.00

Smedley, R. C. **History of the Underground Railroad:** In Chester and the Neighboring Counties of Pennsylvania ....ISBN 0-405-01895-9 $14.00

South Carolina Constitutional Convention **Proceedings of the Constitutional Convention of South Carolina:** Held at Charleston, S. C., Beginning January 14th and Ending March 17th, 1868 ....ISBN 0-405-01837-1 $28.00

Spiller, G. (editor) **Papers on Inter-Racial Problems:** Communicated to the First Universal Race Congress Held at the University of London, July 26-29, 1911..............
.... ISBN 0-405-01935-1 $17.50

Steward, T. G. **The Colored Regulars in the United States Army:** With a Sketch of the History of the Colored American and an Account of His Services in the Wars of the Country, From the Period of the Revolutionary War to 1899....................
.... ISBN 0-405-01896-7 $10.50

Still, William **The Underground Railroad:** A Record of Facts, Authentic Narratives, Letters, etc., Narrating the Hardships, Hair-Breadth Escapes and Death Struggles of the Slaves in Their Efforts for Freedom, as Related by Themselves and Others, or Witnessed by the Author ....ISBN 0-405-01838-X $25.00

Stowe, Harriet Beecher **The Key to Uncle Tom's Cabin:** Presenting the Original Facts and Documents Upon Which the Story is Founded Together With Corroborative Statements Verifying the Truth of the Work..............ISBN 0-405-01839-8 $15.50

Taylor, Susie King **Reminiscences of My Life in Camp With the 33rd United States Colored Troops Late 1st S. C. Volunteers.....................ISBN 0-405-01840-1 $ 4.00

Thorne, Jack (David Bryant Fulton) **Hanover, Or the Persecution of the Lowly, A Story of the Wilmington Massacre.........................ISBN 0-405-01937-8 $ 5.50

Thurman, Wallace **The Blacker the Berry**................ISBN 0-405-01897-5 $ 8.00

Torrence, Ridgely **The Story of John Hope**..............ISBN 0-405-01939-4 $16.50

Trowbridge, J. T. **The South:** A Tour of Its Battle-Fields and Ruined Cities, A Journey Through the Desolated States, and Talks With the People.ISBN 0-405-01898-3 $18.00

Truth, Sojourner **Narrative of Sojourner Truth:** A Bondswoman of Olden Time, Emancipated by the New York Legislature in the Early Part of the Present Century, With a History of Her Labors and Correspondence Drawn From Her "Book of Life"......
.... ISBN 0-405-01841-X $11.50

Turner, Edward Raymond **The Negro in Pennsylvania:** Slavery — Servitude — Freedom, 1639-1861 .... ISBN 0-405-01899-1 $10.00

Turner, Lorenzo Dow **Africanisms in the Gullah Dialect**....ISBN 0-405-01900-9 $12.50

Walker, David and Garnet, Henry Highland **Walker's Appeal in Four Articles** and **An Address to the Slaves of the United States of America**..ISBN 0-405-01901-7 $ 4.50

Walker, Margaret **For My People**.......................ISBN 0-405-01902-5 $ 5.00

Ward, Samuel Ringgold **Autobiography of a Fugitive Negro:** His Anti-Slavery Labours in the United States, Canada and England..............ISBN 0-405-01842-8 $12.50

Warner, Robert Austin **New Haven Negroes, A Social History**.ISBN 0-405-01940-8 $14.00

Washington, Booker T. **Working with the Hands:** Being a Sequel to "Up from Slavery" Covering the Authors Experiences in Industrial Training at Tuskegee..............
.... ISBN 0-405-01941-6 $11.00

Washington, Booker T; Du Bois, W. E. B; Dunbar, Paul Laurence, et al. **The Negro Problem:** A Series of Articles by Representative American Negroes of Today............
.... ISBN 0-405-01903-3 $ 7.00

Washington, Booker T; Wood, N. B., and Williams, Fannie Barrier **A New Negro for a New Century** .... ISBN 0-405-01904-1 $13.50

Webb, Frank J. **The Garies and Their Friends** ....ISBN 0-405-01905-X $12.00

Weld, Theodore Dwight **American Slavery As It Is:** Testimony of a Thousand Witnesses
.... ISBN 0-405-01843-6 $ 7.00

Wells-Barnett, Ida **On Lynchings** ....ISBN 0-405-01849-5 $ 7.50

West, Dorothy **The Living Is Easy** ....•..........ISBN 0-405-01942-4 $14.00

White, Walter **A Man Called White**......................ISBN 0-405-01906-8 $12.00

White, Walter **Rope and Faggot:** A Biography of Judge Lynch.......................
.... ISBN 0-405-01907-6 $ 9.00

Williams, George W. **History of the Negro Race in America from 1619 to 1880:** Negroes as Slaves, as Soldiers, and as Citizens; Together With a Preliminary Consideration of the Unity of the Human Family, an Historical Sketch of Africa, and an Account of the Negro Governments of Sierra Leone and Liberia......ISBN 0-405-01844-4 $34.50

Wilson, Joseph T. **The Black Phalanx:** A History of the Negro Soldiers of the United States in the Wars of 1775-1812, 1861-65............ISBN 0-405-01845-2 $15.50

Woodson, Carter G. **The Education of the Negro Prior to 1861:** A History of the Education of the Colored People of the United States From the Beginning of Slavery to the Civil War .... ISBN 0-405-01846-0 $14.00

W. P. A. Writer's Project **The Negro in Virginia**..........ISBN 0-405-01910-6 $12.00

W. P. A. Writer's Project **These Are Our Lives**............ISBN 0-405-01911-4 $13.50

Wright, Richard R., Jr. **The Negro in Pennsylvania:** A Study in Economic History......
.... ISBN 0-405-01908-4 $ 7.00

Wright, Richard **Twelve Million Black Voices:** A Folk History of the Negro in the United
States .... ISBN 0-405-01909-2 $10.00

Paperbacks

Baker, Henry E. **The Colored Inventor:** A Record of Fifty Years.....................
.... ISBN 0-405-01943-2 $ 1.00

Brown, William Wells **Clotel, or, the President's Daughter**..ISBN 0-405-01951-3 $ 2.45

Delany, Martin Robinson **The Condition, Elevation, Emigration, and Destiny of the Colored People of the United States:** Politically Considered..ISBN 0-405-01952-1 $ 2.45

Douglass, Frederick **My Bondage And My Freedom**........ISBN 0-405-01967-X $ 3.95

Dunbar, Paul Laurence **The Strength of Gideon and Other Stories**...................
.... ISBN 0-405-01953-X $ 3.45

Fisher, Rudolph **The Walls of Jericho**....................ISBN 0-405-01954-8 $ 3.25

Fortune, Timothy Thomas **Black and White:** Land, Labor, and Politics in the South....
.... ISBN 0-405-01955-6 $ 3.25

Garrison, William Lloyd **Thoughts on African Colonization:** Or an Impartial Exhibition of
the Doctrines, Principles, and Purposes of the American Colonization Society Together
With the Resolutions, Addresses, and Remonstrances of the Free People of Color....
.... ISBN 0-405-01956-4 $ 3.25

Griggs, Sutton E. **Imperium in Imperio**.................ISBN 0-405-01957-2 $ 2.45

Herndon, Angelo **Let Me Live**........................ ISBN 0-405-01958-0 $ 3.75

Higginson, Thomas Wentworth **Black Rebellion**........ ISBN 0-405-01959-9 $ 2.45

Jacques-Garvey, Amy (editor) **Philosophy and Opinions of Marcus Garvey** 2 volumes in 1
.... ISBN 0-405-01960-2 $ 4.50

Katz, Bernard (editor) **The Social Implications of Early Negro Music in the United States**
.... ISBN 0-405-01961-0 $ 2.45

Katz, William Loren (editor) **Five Slave Narratives:** A Compendium.................
.... ISBN 0-405-01962-9 $ 3.75

Locke, Alain **The Negro and His Music** and **Negro Art, Past and Present**...........
.... ISBN 0-405-01964-5 $ 2.95

Lynch, John R. **The Facts of Reconstruction** ....ISBN 0-405-01965-3 $ 3.25

McKay, Claude **A Long Way From Home** .... ISBN 0-405-01986-6 $ 3.45

Ottley, Roi **New World A-Coming:** Inside Black America....ISBN 0-405-01966-1 $ 3.45

Payne, Daniel A. **Recollections of Seventy Years**........ISBN 0-405-01968-8 $ 3.45

Pearson, Elizabeth Ware (editor) **Letters from Port Royal, Written at the Time of the
Civil War** .... ISBN 0-405-01969-6 $ 3.45

Porter, Dorothy (editor) **Negro Protest Pamphlets:** A Compendium.................
.... ISBN 0-405-01963-7 $ 1.95

Porter, James A. **Modern Negro Art** . . . . ISBN 0-405-01970-X $ 2.95

Scott, Emmett J. **Negro Migration During the War** . . . . . . ISBN 0-405-01971-8 $ 1.95

Sinclair, William A. **The Aftermath of Slavery:** A Study of the Condition and Environment of the American Negro . . . . ISBN 0-405-01972-6 $ 3.45

Stowe, Harriet Beecher **The Key to Uncle Tom's Cabin:** Presenting the Original Facts and Documents Upon Which the Story is Founded, Togther With Corroborative Statements Verifying the Truth of the Work . . . . ISBN 0-405-01973-4 $ 3.95

Walker, David, and Garnet, Henry Highland **Walker's Appeal in Four Articles** and **An Address to the Slaves of the United States of America** . . ISBN 0-405-01901-7 $ 1.75

Washington, Booker T; DuBois, W. E. B; Dunbar, Paul Laurence, et al. **The Negro Problem:** A Series of Articles by Representative American Negroes of Today . . . . ISBN 0-405-01975-0 $ 2.45

Webb, Frank J. **The Garies and Their Friends** . . . . ISBN 0-405-01976-9 $ 3.45

Weld, Theodore Dwight **American Slavery As It Is:** Testimony of a Thousand Witnesses . . . . ISBN 0-405-01977-7 $ 2.45

Wells-Barnett, Ida **On Lynchings** . . . . ISBN 0-405-01978-5 $ 1.95

White, Walter **Rope and Faggot:** A Biography of Judge Lynch . . . . ISBN 0-405-01979-3 $ 3.25

Four New Compilations

Gilbert, Peter (ed.) **The Selected Writings of John Edward Bruce: Militant Black Journalist** . . . . ISBN 0-405-01982-3 $ 9.00

Marks, George P. III (ed.) **The Black Press Views American Imperialism, 1898-1900** . . . . ISBN 0-405-01985-8 $11.00

Porter, Kenneth W. **The Negro on the American Frontier** . . ISBN 0-405-01983-1 $15.00

Redkey, Edwin S. (ed.) **Respect Black: The Writings and Speeches of Henry McNeal Turner** . . . . ISBN 0-405-01984-X $ 9.00

To Be Published Fall 1971

Fisher, Rudolph **The Conjure-Man Dies: A Mystery Tale of Dark Harlem** . . . . ISBN 0-405-02800-8 $ 5.95

McKinney, Richard I. **Religion in Higher Education Among Negroes** . . . . ISBN 0-405-02804-0 $ 7.00